TREASURY OF
GARDENING

Contributing Writers

Wayne Ambler
Carol Landa Christensen
Larry Hodgson
Peter Loewer
Ted Marston

Project Consultant

C. Colston Burrell

Contributing Consultants

Dr. Darrel Apps
Judy Glattstein
Kathi Keville
Dr. Steven Still

Illustrators

Mike Muir:
Annuals; Perennials

Roberta Simonds:
Herbs

Mike Wanke/Steven Edsey & Sons:
Landscape Design; Trees, Shrubs & Vines;
Specialty Gardens; Vegetables & Herbs

PUBLICATIONS INTERNATIONAL, LTD.

Louis Weber, C.E.O.
Publications International, Ltd.
7373 North Cicero Avenue
Lincolnwood, Illinois 60646

Permission is never granted for commercial purposes.

Manufactured in China.

8 7 6 5 4 3 2 1

ISBN: 0-7853-1914-X

Contributors:

Wayne Ambler is an active horticulturist, teacher of horticulture, and has completed a master's degree thesis in horticulture education. He has provided gardening consultation for books and periodicals.

Carol Landa Christensen graduated cum laude from the Pennsylvania School of Horticulture for Women, and went on to work at Longwood Gardens as a horticultural information specialist and as a floral designer. Her articles have appeared regularly in many newspapers and magazines, including *Plants Alive* and *Gurney's Gardening News*.

Larry Hodgson is a gardening specialist whose articles have appeared in numerous publications, including *Horticulture, Fine Gardening,* and *Harrowsmith*. He is editor-in-chief of *Houseplant Magazine,* appears frequently on radio and in newspapers, and has hosted 30 garden tours on five continents.

Peter Loewer is a member of the Garden Writers Association of America and has written a number of books on gardening, including *Growing and Decorating with Grasses, American Gardens, The Annual Garden, Gardens by Design,* and *A Year of Flowers*.

Ted Marston has been writing about gardens and gardening for more than 20 years. His articles have appeared in such national publications as *The New York Times, Family Circle,* and *Flower and Garden*.

C. Colston Burrell has an M.S. in horticulture; is a garden designer, writer, consultant; and is horticulture editor of *Landscape Architecture Magazine.* He coauthored the *Illustrated Encyclopedia of Perennials*, contributed to both the *New Encyclopedia of Organic Gardening* and *Landscaping with Nature,* and has served as a consultant to many other gardening books. He is a member of the American Association of Botanic Gardens and Arboreta and the Perennial Plant Association; he is also proprietor of Native Landscapes Design and Restoration Ltd.

Dr. Darrel Apps was the departmental head of education at Longwood Gardens for 12 years before he began his own consulting and training business, Garden Adventures. He is a frequent lecturer on horticultural topics and teaches courses on perennials.

Judy Glattstein has been a landscape consultant since 1976. She is a frequent contributor to such national horticultural publications as *Horticulture, Garden Designs, Flower and Garden,* and the Brooklyn Botanic Garden Handbook, *Plants for Problem Places.* Ms. Glattstein is also a workshop instructor and lecturer.

Kathi Keville is the author of *American Country Living: Herbs* and *An Illustrated Encyclopedia of Herbs* and has served as the editor of the *American Herb Association's Quarterly Newsletter.* She has also written numerous articles on herbs for national magazines.

Dr. Steven Still is a professor of horticulture at Ohio State University and author of the widely used textbook, *Manual of Herbaceous Ornamental Plants.* Photographs from Dr. Still's extensive picture library appear frequently in many horticultural publications.

CONTENTS

LANDSCAPE DESIGN 10

CHAPTER 1: **Planning Your Landscape** 12
Assessing Your Landscaping Needs 14
Growth & Overgrowth 16
The Magic of Movement 18
Paving, Patios, & Privacy 20
Garden Accents & Special Needs 22

CHAPTER 2: **Planting Lawns & Ornamental Grasses** 24
Planting Techniques 26
Turfgrass Hardiness Zone Map 28
Using Ornamental Grasses 30

CHAPTER 3: **Pests & the Rest** 32
Safety with Pesticides 34
Pests & Other Problems 35

CHAPTER 4: **Encyclopedia of Grasses and Ground Covers** 40
Turf Grasses 42
Ground Covers 46
Ornamental Grasses 50

ANNUALS 52

CHAPTER 1: **Planning a Seasonal Kaleidoscope of Color** 54
Soil & Light 56
Color/Form/Texture/Scale 58
Massing Colors 60
Mingling Annuals with Other Plantings 63
Selecting Annuals for Color & Characteristics 65

CHAPTER 2: Secrets to Successful Annuals Gardening   70

Tools for Gardening Projects   72
Preparing the Soil   74
Bedding Plants by the Boxful   76
Selecting Quality Plants & Seeds   82
Sowing Seeds   84
Propagating Stem Cuttings   86
Collecting Seeds from Your Garden   89

CHAPTER 3: Caring for Annuals   92

Quenching a Plant's Thirst   94
Keeping Weeds at Bay   97
Feeding Alternatives   100
Ways to Increase/Control Growth   102
Staking Garden Plants   104
Pests & Other Problems   106
Preparing for Winter & Another Year   110
Zone Map: When's the Last Frost in Your Area   112
Maintaining Annuals Month by Month   114
Ease of Care   116

CHAPTER 4: Gardening with Annuals   118

Laying Out an Annuals Garden   120
Mixed Gardens   123
Container Gardening   126
Cutting Garden   130
Drying & Pressing Annuals   132

CHAPTER 5:   Encyclopedia of Annual Delights   136

PERENNIALS   190

CHAPTER 1:   How To Plan for Lasting Color   192
             Color   194
             Form & Texture   196
             Selecting Perennials for Color &
                 Characteristics   200
             Sequence of Bloom   204
             Selecting Perennials by Bloom Date   206

CHAPTER 2:   Getting Your Garden Off to a Good Start   208
             Transplanting from Pots   210
             Setting Bare-Root Plants   213
             Buying Healthy Plants   215
             Watering, Weeding, & Feeding   217
             Starting from Seed   222
             Starting Stem & Root Cuttings   227
             Dividing Perennials   233

CHAPTER 3:   Landscaping with Perennials   236
             Putting a Garden on Paper   238
             Entrance Gardens, Borders, & Island Beds   242
             Perennials in Containers   246

CHAPTER 4:   Encyclopedia of Perennial Favorites   248

TREES, SHRUBS, & VINES   296

CHAPTER 1: Getting Cozy with Woody Plants   298
    Woody Plants in the Landscape   300
    Defining Woody Plants   301

CHAPTER 2: Checking Out the Options   304
    Designing with Trees, Shrubs, & Vines   306
    Putting Woody Plants to Use   308
    The Size & Shape of Woody Plants   309
    Selecting for Hardiness   315
    Shopping: The Nursery Versus Buying
      Mail-Order   317

CHAPTER 3: The Cultural Needs of Your Plants   318
    Soil, Water, & Drainage   320
    Sun, Shade, & Wind   324

CHAPTER 4: Caring for Your Woody Plants   326
    Planting & Transplanting   328
    Fertilizing & Mulching   333
    Maintaining Your Trees, Shrubs, & Vines   335
    Pruning   337

CHAPTER 5: Keeping Ahead of the Challenges   342
    Environmental Hazards   344
    Mechanical & Other Types of Damage   347
    Pests & Diseases   349

CHAPTER 6: Encyclopedia of Trees, Shrubs, & Vines   352
    Trees   354
    Shrubs   374
    Vines   392

SPECIALTY GARDENS   398

CHAPTER 1: The Rose Garden: Roses Are for Everyone   400
    Starting Your Rose Garden   402
    Maintaining Your Rose Garden   406

CHAPTER 2:	The Rock Garden: An Alpine Meadow in Your Yard	410
	Planning a Rock Garden	412
	Building a Rock Garden	413
	Maintaining a Rock Garden	416

CHAPTER 3:	The Bulb Garden: Nature's Season Extenders	418
	Planning the Bulb Garden	420
	Bulb Maintenance	424

CHAPTER 4:	The Shade Garden: A Haven of Serenity	426
	Coping with Shade	428
	Color, Texture, & Naturalizing	430

CHAPTER 5:	The Water Garden: Water Adds Life	432
	Planning a Water Garden	434
	Installing Your Own Pool	435
	Movement in the Water Garden	439
	Planting the Water Garden	442
	Maintaining the Water Garden	445

CHAPTER 6:	Encyclopedia of Specialty Garden Plants	446
	Rose Garden Plants	448
	Rock Garden Plants	451
	Bulb Garden Plants	458
	Shade Garden Plants	462
	Water Garden Plants	466

VEGETABLES & HERBS 470

CHAPTER 1:	Planning Your Garden	473
	Climate	474
	Getting Your Garden Started	476
	Getting Your Garden on Paper	478
	Gardening Tools	480

CHAPTER 2:	Preparing the Soil	484
	Improving Your Garden Soil	486
	Fertilizing: How & Why To Do It	488
	The Gardener's Recycling Plan	490

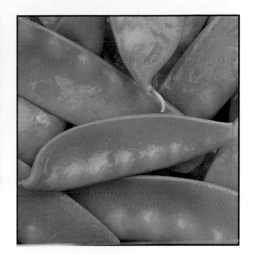

CHAPTER 3: **Planting Your Garden**   492
            Starting Transplants Indoors   494
            Caring for Seedlings   496
            Direct-seeding in the Garden   498
            Starting New Plants from Parts   502

CHAPTER 4: **Caring for Your Garden**   506
            Staking & Plant Support   508
            Weeding: Keep Out Intruders   510
            Mulches   511
            Water for Your Garden   514
            Preparing for Winter   516

CHAPTER 5: **Garden Health**   518
            Controlling Insect Pests   520
            Nonchemical Pest Control   521
            Pests & Other Problems   523

CHAPTER 6: **Herbs in Your Garden**   528
            Growing Your Own Herbs   530

CHAPTER 7: **Encyclopedia of Vegetables & Herbs**   534
            Vegetables   536
            Herbs   558

INDEX   568

LANDSCAPE DESIGN

Every landscape is made up of a variety of plants: from trees to perennials and annuals to grass. A truly beautiful yard needs a design that fits these elements together. So turn the page and begin a gardening adventure.

This landscape mixes a combination of lawn, perennials, shrubs, and a variety of trees, resulting in a pleasant setting for strolling, picnicking, or sitting and thinking.

CHAPTER 1

PLANNING YOUR LANDSCAPE

Thoughts of a quiet, private space in which to relax on a warm summer evening lead you right to your own backyard. You'll want your outdoor space to be as comfortable as a cozy room with a glowing fire on a cold winter night. The terrace may lead to a swath of lush green grass bordered by beds of rich ground covers, evergreens, and budding flowers. A canopy of trees overhead can provide dappled shade that moves with the breeze. Your landscape is a place of peace and beauty because of thoughtful planning, hard work, and patience.

Whether you're looking to screen an eyesore or frame a beautiful vista, you'll become personally involved in developing a landscape that suits your needs and desires. You may like to dabble in the yard after a hard day's work, or you may prefer to spend weekends in the garden working on routine chores. Any way you look at landscaping, you can choose the style that fits your needs.

Start with an assessment of your personal needs. Make a list of what you want to incorporate in your design. Take notes of special functions or service areas your landscape will need to provide. Then, consider the tips on the following pages as you build your landscape. You'll discover ideas that you'll enjoy for a lifetime.

Assessing Your Landscaping Needs

These trees and flowering plants make a nice setting against the backyard wall.

Any beautifully designed landscape may be attractive to view, but if it doesn't accommodate the needs of the people who use the property, the design is not practical. Before making a plan for your space, discuss with the members of your household the needs and plans for use of the landscape. Make a list of desired functions before making the actual plan. The following functions are some that you may want to consider: sitting/dining area, clothesline, barbecue, dog pen, wind protection, vegetable garden, compost, lawn recreation, children's play area, and firewood storage. Draw a simple sketch showing the general location of the elements needed in relation to the house and one another. For instance, if an outdoor eating area is needed, sketch it near the kitchen, and firewood storage should be convenient to the door nearest the fireplace. The relationship diagram will help you in the beginning steps of putting a plan together. In addition, decide the level of maintenance you are willing to meet. Your plan should reflect the amount of maintenance time you're interested in spending in the yard.

If your house is visible from a road, you have a public view area. Think of your house, or front door, as the focal point of a picture. You'll want to frame the view, to draw attention to your house. Typically, foundation plantings are set at the base of the house to create a transition between the house and the landscape. Foundation plantings can be a simple mix of small evergreens and flowering shrubs, ornamental trees, ground covers, and herbaceous plants. Consider shade when choosing trees; deciduous trees will shade the house in the summer while allowing sunlight in during the winter. Be sure to screen service areas—trash cans, laundry lines, and the like—from the public area.

You'll want to develop other sections of your landscape for outdoor living. You may decide to incorporate a service area—toolshed, doghouse, clothesline, potting area. It should be convenient to the house yet tucked away from public view and private entertaining. If children will be using the landscape, plan for a children's play area: A swing set and sand box may be in your plans. You'll want this area set aside but in full view for easy supervision. Separate the children's area from the eating and entertaining area with a low border, and you'll get a feeling of separate outdoor rooms.

A private entertaining and eating area is among the most common functions of a well-planned landscape. Design it as you would a comfortable room in your house. The size of the area should be determined by the number of people who will be accommodated. A patio or terrace with adjacent lawn for occasional spillover works well. Privacy from neighbors as well as shade can be achieved through the proper selection and placement of screening materials and a canopy of trees.

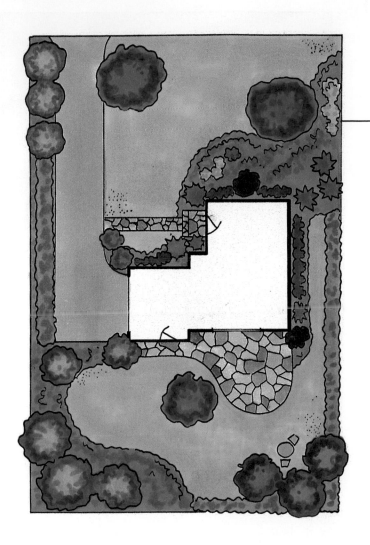

Create a Functional Sketch

When you plan for outdoor activities and traffic patterns, related functions should be grouped together. For example, parking and entrance to the house go together. With a sketch pad, carefully plot the relationship between the indoor space—windows and doors—with the outdoor space—public, private, and service. From the list of functional areas you need, designate space to accommodate each function.

Traffic Flow Design

The purpose of paths, walks, and driveways is to direct and safely move traffic from place to place. The heavier the traffic, the sturdier, wider, and more permanent the path should be. Make entrance walks comfortable enough for at least two people to walk abreast (a minimum of four feet, five is better). Service and rear-entry paths should be three to four feet wide. Garden paths should be designed so visitors will feel comfortable on a stroll through the garden. Stepping-stone or mulch-covered paths allow easy access to corners of the garden during maintenance. All paths should be flush with the ground for safety. Make sure steps and grade changes are stable, safe, and well-lighted.

Growth & Overgrowth

I t's always difficult to visualize how large a plant will grow once it becomes part of your landscape. For instance, an eight-inch high Chinese juniper will grow to eight feet tall and eight feet wide in a few short years. Plants mature at varying rates: Some establish themselves very slowly, others very quickly. You'll need to determine the size you want the plant within a particular time frame. If you're planning a patio and need a quick source of shade, a fast-growing tree may be just what you need. Foundation plantings need a different solution: Slow-growing dwarf shrubs and ground covers are often the answer for a foundation around a home where space is limited. You may want to plan on planting some fast-growing materials, which are sometimes short-lived, along with some slower-growing species, which are often long-lived plants. When the slow-growing species become established, remove some of the faster-growing species that have outlived their position in the landscape.

Choose plants according to their position in the landscape. Consider the natural shape, height, and width of plants before you install them. Improper plant selection often disappoints the homeowner when drastic renovation measures are required. As you plan your design, think about the plant characteristics you need before you decide the plant to install. Think about the shape of the plant: Would a round or vase-shaped shrub suit the area best? Think about the size: Do you need a tall shade tree, or a short, round ornamental? Consider the growth habits that fit into the design best: Is a ground cover with an extensive root system needed to hold together a bank, or would low, arching shrubs work as well? Existing soil conditions, wind, sun exposure, and hardiness are also serious considerations: Do you need a plant that can tolerate wet soils, or one that will thrive in dense shade? Once you've answered these questions, find a plant that is suited to all of the requirements and your success will be almost guaranteed.

Pruning to keep plants in bounds is an integral part of landscape upkeep. Some plants, such as formal hedges, are sheared to maintain a formal appeal. Most plants require thinning to maintain their natural shape while reducing their size. The season of flowering is a good guide to direct your pruning shears. Flowering shrubs are best pruned when flowering ends; the plant can then generate new stems to produce next year's blossoms. Evergreens are best pruned in early spring. Pruning initiates new stem and leaf growth. If you prune too late in the season, new growth will be damaged by winter before it can fully develop.

A good landscape design takes the house into account, as this entrance makes clear, without allowing overgrowth.

Landscape plants may be kept under control by implementing a "special effects" pruning plan. Multistem shrubs, such as holly, bayberry, and lilac, can be pruned into a "standard," or single-stemmed small tree. When the plant is young, remove all but the strongest, straightest trunk. Stake the single trunk and remove all side branches to the point where you want the tree to branch out. Annual pruning is necessary to remove suckers from the base and side-branch shoots. An espalier is a tree or shrub that has been drastically pruned to grow flat along a fence or wall. Whether a formal or informal shape is desired, regular pruning and bending of the main stems is practiced. This produces interesting character in a plant species that might not otherwise fit in an allotted space.

Out-of-bounds Ground Cover

Once ground covers become established, they seem to creep up on you. If your ground cover needs to be contained, it's best to prune annually. If too much of the plant is removed, an unsightly effect will be the result. Shrubs are best pruned by following their natural growth habit.

A Formal Sheared Hedge

You may choose to renovate an existing hedge. With lopping shears (scissors-type shears with long handles for leverage), cut out stems and trunks that have been damaged or show little top growth. As new growth appears from the base of the hedge, use a hedge shear to uniformly cut the ends of the branches. Keep the bottom of the plants wider than the top, allowing plenty of sun to reach all sides of the row. As the hedge matures, a concentration of small branches will develop among the outer shell. Renovate the hedge again by cutting the top and side lower so sunlight can increase branching from the inside of the plants.

Renovation by Thinning

Flowering shrubs look their best when maintained by thinning. Thinning allows the plant to keep its natural shape. After the plant has matured and the size of the plant needs reduction, remove up to one-third of its oldest stems by lopping at ground level. Select shoots to remove that will not destroy the shape of the shrub. This will promote new growth from the base of the plant. Newer growth generally flowers heavier than mature growth.

The Magic of Movement

These decorative grasses will gently sway in the breeze.

When designing your garden, the position of sunlight and shade at different times of the day and different times of the year is an important piece of information. You'll need a basic knowledge of the movement of the sun in relation to the garden's features. Understanding this movement will help in deciding the placement and choice of plants. The sun rises north of the east-west line in the summer, exposing all sides of a house to a certain amount of sunlight. It's high in the sky, producing short shadows from buildings and plants. In the winter, the sun rises south of the east-west line, producing long shadows from structures and plants.

Choose plants that will best suit the natural effects of exposure. The sun can have different effects throughout the day. The introduction of shade provides relief for plants and daily movement of color and mood. A plant needing full sun may do well even if it is shaded for a few hours in the late afternoon, but a shade-loving plant might burn if it receives a few hours of sun during the afternoon. A garden in the morning has characteristics that may not be evident during the later, shady hours. During a summer day when the sun is rising, parts of a shady garden may light up with sunlight and then give way to dappled shade as the sun rises higher in the sky. Plant and construction materials appear to take on different textures as the angle of the sun changes. Sun and shade are constantly changing patterns, changing the feel of the garden from hour to hour and season to season.

People are attracted to natural movement in the garden. Water cascading into a pool, for instance, always attracts attention. Grow plants that will attract visitors: Butterflies and hummingbirds are among the easiest and prettiest guests to entice. You'll have to allow some natural food for the caterpillars and plenty of flowers that provide nectar for hummingbirds, but the activity in the garden is wonderful.

Use plants to accentuate the movement of the wind as it blows through the garden. Plants with paper-thin leaves flutter like birds, creating interest through movement. Many plants—particularly ornamental grasses with flowers and seed heads high atop tall, slender stalks—produce a quiet rustle with seed against seed creating a natural wind chime. Summer breezes add romance to a garden, carrying the fragrance of honeysuckle or moonvine through the air. Scent is one of the garden's most subtle delights. As fragrance drifts through the garden, the garden visitor will feel inspired and refreshed.

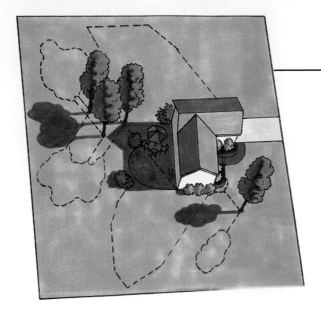

Tree Placement for Afternoon Shade

Carefully consider the placement of shade trees for your outdoor living space; it is difficult to remedy a poorly placed tree after it has matured. Each variety of tree has its own growth habit: Some are tall, broad, and slow-growing; others grow quickly into vase-shaped or rounded crowns. Allow at least 15 feet from foundations for large trees and at least eight feet for small, ornamental trees. To create afternoon shade, plant medium trees 15 feet south and 20 feet west of your living area; increase the distance for large trees.

Knowing Your Garden Soil

The most important element of successfully growing plants is a working knowledge of your garden's soil. The ideal garden soil is deep, fertile, well-drained, and contains high amounts of organic matter. Most new gardens aren't blessed with such soil, but each deficiency can be solved (see page 74 for more information). Soil testing can tell you much about your soil, and you can improve it through soil amendments. The addition of organic matter (such as peat moss) can solve many problems. When your soil is dry enough to crumble, cultivate organic matter, fertilizer, and other amendments deeply into the soil.

A Raised Bed for Improved Drainage

Plant roots need air as well as water. The best soil offers a balance between water-holding capacity and drainage. Clay soils hold a lot of water, while sandy soils don't hold enough. To test your soil's drainage, dig a hole about 20 inches deep and fill it with water. If the water remains 24 hours later, you have poor drainage. One solution is to build a bed higher than the surrounding area and then mix sand and organic matter into your soil.

Paving, Patios, & Privacy

This patio provides a private setting for entertaining guests.

One economical way to expand your living space is to go outdoors—patios and decks are functional and are significant design elements in the landscape. If you decide to add a patio, terrace, or deck, calculate how large it needs to be to accommodate all the people who will use it on a regular basis. Also think about the type of furniture you'll be using; outdoor furniture takes up a lot of space. Study potential locations throughout the seasons and at different times of the day; you'll have to decide whether you want the deck, patio, or terrace in sun, shade, or both. If a shady site is not available, the planting of a single tree or the construction of an overhead canopy are possible solutions. It's best to place the deck or patio in relation to the house; entrances, traffic flow, and food preparation are considerations. A patio needs a fairly flat area; decks and terraces lend themselves more easily to sloped land.

If an existing patio is in poor repair or too small, renovation may be in order. Loose and disjointed bricks or stones set in sand are easily repaired by removing disjointed pavers and regrading the sand surface. Matching brick or stone can usually be purchased for expansion. If an old concrete patio is cracked and deteriorating, either remove the old patio—usually a massive chore—or build a deck over it. The shape of your patio depends on your creativity. Complement the shape and style of the surrounding garden and the style of the house. Squares and right angles tend to look formal and traditional; wide sweeping curves can soften the lines of a small yard. Integrate plantings to help soften lines, increase privacy, and add interest. Most of all, be creative; grid patterns and paving combinations are unlimited.

The choice of paving materials is the most important element in the design. Choose a material that complements your landscape and home. Wood decks add a modern yet often informal appeal to the landscape. They are easy to build but should be considered major construction. Concrete is strong and durable and should be done by a professional. Brick and stone are the easiest to construct.

Screening, whether by plants or fencing, is sometimes necessary for wind and noise reduction or for privacy. Patios and decks at high levels tend to be exposed to excess wind. To reduce wind, plant open trees or shrubs that will reduce a gust to a gentle breeze. Vine-covered lattice or fence sections work well for protecting the seating area from wind. Where noise is a problem, as in urban areas, you'll need a dense planting of shrubs to significantly absorb sound. Thick-leaved, dense conifers work best.

An important concern for an outdoor entertainment area is privacy. Even if your home is an estate in the country, a patio or deck is most comfortable when it feels like an outdoor room, with some feeling of enclosure. Small trees and shrubs are effective in building the "walls," and a canopy of trees gives the feeling of a ceiling. Plants should be placed to achieve all these effects as well as providing screening for privacy. Keep part of the patio or deck open for easy traffic flow into the lawn space and other surrounding areas. Fencing can be effective in providing privacy as well as adding elements of texture, color, and interest to the garden. A simple eight-foot section of fence can screen an unpleasant view and provide privacy.

Edgings are used to permanently outline and separate garden beds and borders from lawns. They help define and organize space and make mowing easier; they keep garden maintenance low by preventing creeping grasses from invading the bed; and they restrain mulch from washing into the lawn. Use a string line to mark straight edgings. Lay a garden hose for long sweeping curves; keep curves wide for easy mowing. Before digging, view the hose line from all angles to make certain it is a shape you like.

Paving with Brick

To build a brick-surfaced patio, choose a paving brick from the wide assortment of sizes, shapes, and colors available. Mark the area to be paved with string and remove six inches of soil. To carry off rainwater, grade the slope of the patio two inches for every six feet of distance. Tamp the soil as flat as possible. Build a lumber or brick edging frame along the perimeter of the patio. Spread a two-inch layer of gravel, then a sheet of landscape fabric. Next, lay two inches of sand. Use a screed to flatten the sand layer; firmly tamp the sand. If the sand is not tight, the bricks will settle, making an uneven surface. Following a pattern you've selected, lay the bricks flat and tap each one lightly into place. Sweep sand into the joints.

Using Fences for Privacy

Fences and screens can be constructed from ready-made panels or created by the builder. Decide the function of the fence, and determine the style needed to fit that purpose and position. Fence panels need not be completely solid to provide privacy. Long sections of solid-board fencing can be monotonous. Integrate lattice or patterns into panels and use plants to soften the space.

Garden Accents & Special Needs

A simple bench can serve as an accent to take advantage of shade or fragrance.

Garden accents lead the viewer's eye to something special. Strategically placed, specimen plants and accents provide points of interest in the garden. Trellises, arbors, and gates, in addition to becoming the focal point of a view, can create a transition from one part of your garden to another. Individual plant specimens, or plant groupings with contrasting texture, color, or form, can serve as points of interest. As the seasons change, consider how different plants become the focal point of a garden. The white bark of birch trees in front of a dark evergreen backdrop is dramatic in winter. A golden-rain tree might go unnoticed without the brilliant yellow flowers in early summer. The constant trickling sound of water spilling into a small garden pool is soothing as well as creating a focal point for a small, walled garden. A garden pond, planted with ever-changing water lilies, grasses, and irises can add a new dimension to your landscape as form and color are reflected in the water.

You can incorporate smaller accents as the garden becomes established and you've assessed the area after the major construction and planting has been completed. The assortment of garden accents is almost endless. Statuary provides points of interest when worked into the overall garden design. A simple birdbath or bird-feeding station can be used to lead the eye to individual points of interest. Use planters to add interest to an unused corner of a patio or to serve as a focal point at the end of a garden path. Planters with bright-colored foliage, light flowers, or interesting shapes can brighten up dark spaces. Two planters can frame a point of interest. A bench with a style that fits the fashion of your landscape can serve as a focal point in addition to being functional.

Among the many ways to deal with grade changes in your landscape, one method is to construct a retaining wall. Use materials that will not decay; once the garden is planted it's almost impossible to replace a wall without destroying the planting. The best walls are made of stone or brick. Railroad ties and treated lumber are also good, but they eventually deteriorate and need repair.

Outdoor lighting is mainly used for safety (to illuminate steps or a path). But it can also extend the hours you'll enjoy your garden. Ordinary spotlights and floodlights can be too obtrusive and annoying in the garden. Easy-to-assemble, low-voltage lighting kits are available in many styles. Use low-voltage lighting to highlight special features and add a dramatic effect in your landscape. Uplight a tree or shrub that has interesting bark or structure to create a statuary appearance. Direct lights downward from the branches of a tree to create a moonlight effect. Wash a wall or fence with soft lighting to silhouette plants against the wall. Mushroom-type, low-level lighting along a garden path invites visitors to enjoy the quiet of the garden at night.

Specimen Plants

Shrubs are usually used in mass—to provide a backdrop or screen—but a single shrub can be used effectively as a specimen or accent. Although the plant need not be evergreen, it should be attractive and interesting throughout the seasons. Colorful autumn leaves, interesting trunk or bark patterns, and summer flowers are some characteristics to consider. A single flowering tree or shrub set against a backdrop of dark evergreens provides an all-season point of interest.

Moving Water

The sight and sound of moving water can be a fascinating feature in a garden. Even the smallest garden can have a water feature; a lined half whiskey barrel is ideal for your first water garden. Garden pools of any shape, size, or design can be incorporated into your plan. The use of a fountain or waterfall in your pool creates movement in the garden and improves the oxygen content of the water. Use a submersible recirculating pump, which operates off normal household electric current.

Vine-Covered Arbor

An arbor is an open framework designed to support vines and provide shade underneath. It can be as simple as a freestanding trellis or large enough to provide an entire patio with shade. If you'll be passing through or if you plan on taking advantage of the shade, make the arbor high enough for comfort. Also give plenty of consideration to the types of vines you want to grow on the arbor. Arbors are an ideal way to display such vines as wisteria and clematis. Train young vines by tying them with loose string or plastic ties to the structure.

The ground covers and ornamental grasses in this tropical garden help tie all its elements together. Grasses can be much more than just the well-manicured lawns of a typical home.

CHAPTER 2

PLANTING LAWNS & ORNAMENTAL GRASSES

Grasses of many kinds cover all corners of the earth. Some grow tall with wispy flowers that turn to seed. Some hug the ground, spreading by creeping stems. Some species of grass tolerate wear and regular mowing: These are the grasses that are used for lawns. When most people think of grass, visions of neat, well-manicured, deep green lawns come to mind. When a gardener thinks of grass, the response is a bit different.

There are many varieties of grasses to choose. Turf grasses are the most durable and commonly grown ground cover. Other species of grasses, while not durable enough to serve as a lawn, are wonderful garden plants. Some grasses are at home tucked in a border, waving gracefully with the slightest breeze. Ornamental grasses can serve as long-lived ground covers with year-round interest and low maintenance requirements.

In this chapter, you'll learn how to choose grasses to fit each function. You'll avoid the mistakes of the first-time gardener and learn how to plant a successful lawn from sod or seed. We'll also discuss how ornamental grasses can fit into your landscape and enhance your garden's year-round appeal. Discover just how versatile grasses can be.

Planting Techniques

Whether you're starting a new lawn or renovating an old one, some important elements should be considered before just throwing some grass seed around. Decide what type of grass you'll want to grow. There are many options. (The plant directory starting on page 40 can help you decide.) There are basically two types of lawn grasses; those that bunch, and those that creep. Many cool-season grasses are the bunching type. They continue to grow from new shoots at the base of the plant. Creeping grasses, as most Southern varieties are, spread by sending out rhizomes or stolons—stems that creep along or just below ground level, forming a new plant at the tip. Both grasses form thick mats if they're properly cared for. Creeping grasses form a better turf for high-traffic areas. You'll also have to consider the climatic zone you live in. Not all varieties will grow under all conditions. See the turf map on pages 28 and 29.

Have your soil tested. Inform the soil test lab which type of grass you intend to grow, and they will recommend what soil amendments may be needed. Add lime and fertilizer if called for by the soil test report. (See pages 56 and 486 for more information on soil testing.) Grade the soil; level hills and add top soil to low spots. Don't use subsoil on the top surface; turf grasses need a well-drained soil for roots to grow. Construction debris under the surface prevents roots from growing deeply, creating dead spots in the lawn. Cultivate the soil thoroughly, and remove rocks, roots, clods, and debris. Use a garden rake to fine-grade the area and roll the soil lightly to prevent uneven sinking. If you're renovating small patches of an old lawn, follow the same steps on a lesser scale.

Once the soil is graded, you're ready to sow seed. Sow cool-season grass in the early fall so the grass will have four to six weeks to establish before frost. Spread the seed with a hand spreader at the recommended rate found on the package. Use a garden rake to gently work the seed into the top ⅛ inch of soil; seed that is planted too deeply will not germinate. Roll the area with a lawn roller to ensure good contact between the soil and the seed. Using clean, weed-seed-free straw, lightly mulch the seedbed, light enough that half the soil is left exposed. The straw will help shade the soil and your seedlings, preventing them from drying too quickly. Keep the top layer of soil evenly and constantly moist. Heavy watering with a sprinkler is not useful because seed will easily wash away. Water with a fine spray several times a day until the seedlings become strong enough to withstand regular irrigation.

Whether planting grasses, vines, or other plants, site selection (such as the placement of this trellis) is vital.

Sod is commercially produced turf. It is available in cool-season and warm-season varieties. Sod is harvested and sold to be planted as an immediate lawn. Prepare the soil as you would for seeding, but make the final grade one inch lower than the grade for seeding. Without stretching or overlapping the rolls of sod, piece them together like a puzzle. Cut irregular pieces with a spade or knife. Roll the new lawn to ensure close contact between the roots and the soil. New sod needs regular watering until the roots are so well established that you can no longer pick up the pieces of sod. Cool-season sod can be installed any time of the year that the ground isn't frozen. Warm-season sod should be installed in spring or summer.

The best varieties of most warm-season, spreading grasses are available only in vegetative form: sod, plugs, or sprigs. A plug is a two-inch by two-inch piece of sod of a spreading grass variety. Plugs are planted individually 12 inches apart during the warm season. With proper care, the plugs take root and rapidly spread by rhizomes or stolons. Sprigs are pieces of sod that have been shredded into one- to three-inch pieces of rhizomes. Sprigs are planted either by hand or by spreading them onto the bed and gently cultivating them into the top inch of soil. Each piece of rhizome will root into the soil and send up new leaves and rhizomes in a short time.

Starting a Lawn From Seed

To start a new lawn from seed, proper soil preparation is critical. Start by removing rocks, lumps, and grass clods after the ground has been graded and the pH adjusted. Choose a turf variety that suits your climate and sun exposure. Use a hand spreader to apply the seed at the recommended rate. If you plan to mix seed varieties, make two applications with the spreader: It's difficult to evenly mix two sizes of seed. Scratch the seed into the soil with a garden rake and tamp with a lawn roller; the close contact between the seed and the soil will aid in sprouting. Apply a light mulch of clean straw, covering about half the soil surface. Water regularly without allowing the soil to dry out.

Installing Sod

The quickest way to establish a new lawn is by installing sod. Proper soil preparation is important. Remove all lumps and be certain the soil is perfectly smooth. Bumps and holes are difficult to repair after the sod is established. Purchase high-quality, certified turf from a reputable source. Unroll strips of sod and tuck them into place. Don't overlap or stretch the strips. Fill in any visible joints with topsoil. Roll with a lawn roller so the roots come in contact with the soil. Keep a newly sodded lawn well watered until it becomes established.

Plugging a Lawn

Rapidly spreading lawn grasses—such as Zoysia and Bermudagrass—are easily established by planting pieces of sod, or plugs. Prepare the soil as you would for seeding a new lawn. Purchase high-quality plugs of a variety of turf that suits your climate. Use a 1-inch by 12-inch board to space plants 12 inches apart. Using the board as a guide, plant a row of plugs flush with the soil level; tamp each plug tightly into the soil. Start the second row 12 inches away from the first row. Keep the lawn watered until it becomes well established.

Turfgrass Hardiness Zone Map

A different hardiness zone map is usually followed to determine turfgrass hardiness. The continental United States is divided into three sections. Cool-season grasses grow best in zone A. Zone B is a transition zone, where both cool-season and warm-season grasses grow. Warm-season grasses grow in zone C.

The hardiness of plants used for your landscape will determine the success of a species in a particular zone, or climate. Generally, the hardiness of a particular plant refers to its ability to survive certain minimum low temperatures. Other factors, however, play important roles: soil-moisture availability, wind conditions, and length of growing season are factored in for recommended hardiness zones. Keep in mind that a plant species hardy to zone 3a may not be hardy in a much warmer zone, such as zone 9b. Some plants do not tolerate excessive heat, especially high night-time temperatures. See pages 112 and 113 for more information on the USDA Plant Hardiness Zone Map.

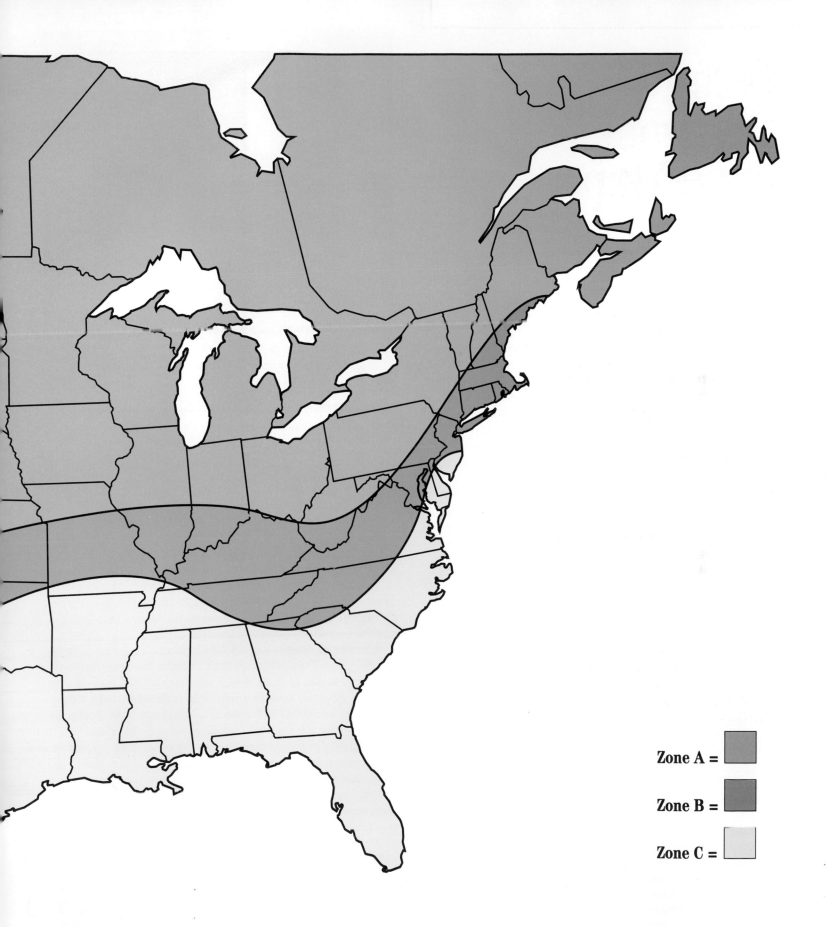

Zone A =

Zone B =

Zone C =

Using Ornamental Grasses

Ornamental grasses, shrubs, and border plants can be mixed together effectively.

Ornamental grasses add grace to any garden. With their array of colors, textures, and sizes, ornamental grasses add year-round interest to a garden. They even become animated when wind weaves in and out of their leaves. Only your imagination limits their use in your garden. Whether as a specimen or a massed planting, grasses can be used for screening, accent, focal point, or to frame a view. Since grasses are found over the entire earth, you're certain to find a variety to suit your decorative and cultural needs.

As with turf grasses, ornamental grasses are categorized as cool-season grasses and warm-season grasses. Many ornamental grasses are perennials, but some are so tender they're treated as annuals. Cool-season grasses actively grow during the cool parts of the year; some even stay green throughout the winter. Before the warm-season grasses begin to show much life after dormancy, cool-season grasses burst into quick, lush growth. They bloom early in the season. When frost comes, the foliage and seed heads turn a bright golden tan and continue to offer a fine display through winter.

Warm-season grasses remain dormant through the winter. When the weather and soil has warmed up sufficiently, they grow rapidly. Warm-season grasses are best left alone except for an annual cutting back at the end of winter. They thrive on hot, long days and, once established, are tolerant of drought conditions. Most require a long growing season to flower in late summer and autumn, when many garden perennials have ceased blooming.

Ornamental grasses are also grouped as to how they grow. Some grasses form dense clumps, others spread by stolons or rhizomes. Clump grasses are easiest to use unless you have unlimited space to allow the grass to roam. Clump grasses will stay where you plant them, but give them ample space to grow. Determine each variety's space needs and expect a properly tended grass to mature in three years. Grasses that spread will quickly invade the space of other nearby plantings unless they are planted in an area where you can contain their growth.

Ornamental grasses require little maintenance. Most varieties prefer well-drained soil in full sun; some varieties tolerate partial shade. Fertilizer needs are low; over-fertilization results in tall, lush growth that may require staking. Enjoy the grasses throughout the winter season; they add interest when nearly everything else is dormant. In late winter, cut the grasses down to allow for new growth, but be careful not to cut too low since damage to the growing shoots may occur. Two to six inches, depending on the size of the grass, should be sufficient.

Designing with grasses is easy. Use small grasses as edging plants; they're often hardier than many commonly used edging plants. Try planting a bank with two or three varieties of grasses; use taller varieties behind shorter ones to create a feeling of depth. Grasses mixed with perennials tie materials together during interim periods when one season's blooms have finished and the next season's blooms have yet to begin.

Ornamental grasses are an excellent choice for an unusual ground cover. They have appeal throughout the year, and there are many varieties to choose from. Ornamental grasses also serve as effective screens from early summer through winter. Choose varieties that will grow to at least eye level. Space the plants so they will form an impenetrable mass at maturity. Mix in evergreens to form a deep screen for all seasons. Any single, large ornamental grass can be used as a specimen plant. Use grass as a focal point in an open garden, or use a giant variety to break up expansive spaces. A single, fine-textured upright specimen breaks the monotony of a flat, coarse-textured planting. Grasses are also well suited to container growing, as long as they receive the moisture and nutrients necessary for continual growth.

Winter—Possibly the best season of all is winter for enjoying ornamental grasses. After the colorful leaves have fallen and the last of the fall flowers are gone to frost, grasses reach their peak with their bold masses of tans, golds, and buff colors. They'll hold their seed stalks and heads until the snow becomes quite heavy. This is the time of the year when the garden's grasses predominate. Plant for your winter garden with the same elements of design as any season's garden.

Spring—Just when spring bulbs are coming to a close, cool-season grasses come into their own. The basal leaves of many cool-season grasses remain green through the winter, ready to jump at the first sign of spring. Spring is the time of year when they grow the fastest, providing your garden with a transitional period between early flowering bulbs and later arriving perennials and annuals. Cool-season grasses begin to bloom in spring. Warm-season grasses grow slower until the soil has warmed considerably.

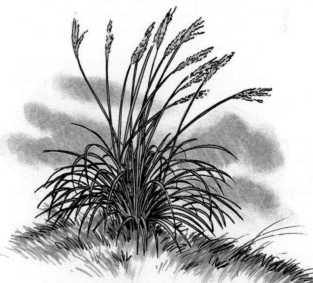

Summer—Warm-season grasses grow with a sudden burst of energy. Their textures are still soft and the colors of variegated varieties add interest to your garden. Green varieties serve as a filler among shrub borders, tying together elements as they soften contrasting colors. Near the end of the summer, the large varieties of warm-season grasses rapidly grow to massive proportion. Cool-season grasses often go dormant, turning gold and brown from the summer heat.

Autumn—Most garden plants begin to look ragged by now, but warm-season grasses are at their peak. They begin to bloom, sending up long, arching stems of pink and white feathery blossoms. The flowers turn to seeds, taking on many forms and shades of beige and gold. On some varieties, the leaves turn brilliant yellow, red, or purple. Tall seed stalks and drying foliage sway in the breeze, creating a quiet rustling sound as autumn begins to turn into winter.

This yard contains many pieces of a well-designed landscape: fencing, border plants and shrubs, lawn, and a pathway for traffic. A well-maintained landscape will help keep pests at bay.

CHAPTER 3

PESTS & THE REST

Some kind of pest is sure to arrive when it's least expected, no matter how much effort you put into the landscape design, planting, and care. Stunted plant growth, yellow patches in the lawn, or tiny holes in the leaves of a new planting of ground cover may seem mysterious, but the next few pages will show you how to identify the cause and determine a control method. You may discover that the more you fertilize and water, the more you play host to pests. In other instances, diseases and insects are making an already neglected area worse. Don't despair; once the problem is identified, the cure is sometimes as simple as changing the height on your lawn mower. The presence of pests doesn't always indicate a need for a spray. A small insect population may be easily picked off the plant. If you decide to use chemicals, some safety tips are included. You'll also find an illustrated section for easy identification of the most common weeds, diseases, and other pests of lawns and ground covers. Included are recommendations for dealing with each problem. Finally, plan for a trouble-free landscape. Select plants wisely, lay out beds and plantings that require minimal maintenance, and keep your plants healthy by supplying them with all of their cultural needs.

Safety with Pesticides

Take special care when using pesticides on plants around the house.

When maintaining a landscape, whether lawns or ground covers, there is no doubt you'll use some sort of pesticide. It's wise to understand some basics about pesticides, as well as using common sense for safety when around pesticides.

Pesticides are chemicals that are used to control pests. They include insecticides, herbicides, fungicides, and others. For a pesticide to be effective, it must interfere with the normal development of the pest without doing harm to the host. This does not mean all pests will be eliminated. In fact, your pest problem might not be severe enough to warrant the use of a chemical. For instance, a few dandelions in the lawn can easily be removed by hand.

Safety when handling, mixing, applying, and storing pesticides is critical. Most poisoning occurs during the mixing process. Splashing concentrated chemical on the skin or in the eyes, for instance, can be prevented by wearing long sleeves and trousers, rubber gloves, and safety goggles. Pesticides must be stored in their original containers; never store a diluted solution in a bottle or jar. And, of course, keep all pesticides out of reach of children. Read the pesticide label and follow the directions each time the pesticide is used. Follow the directions precisely; the proper dose and calibrations have already been scientifically calculated for the most effective use.

Insecticides are pesticides that are used to control insect pests. You'll first need to accurately identify the pest because not all insects can be controlled with one insecticide. Insect damage is done by insects that chew leaves and roots and by insects that pierce the plant and suck sap from the plant. Insecticides that control root-feeding insects may be applied as granules with a lawn spreader or with a sprayer in liquid form. Either way, it is important to wash the chemical into the soil and prevent children and pets playing on the lawn according to the label's recommendation. Top-feeding insects, which feed on the leaves of ground covers and turf, are best controlled by spraying the pesticide and allowing it to dry on the foliage. The pesticide's effectiveness is lost if it is washed off by rain or irrigation.

Herbicides—pesticides that control weeds—are chemicals you'll potentially use on your lawn and, to a lesser degree, in beds of newly planted ground covers. Weeds are divided into two main categories. Perennials, which may be broad-leaf or grassy, live for many years. Annuals, either broad-leaf or grassy, live for only one season and reseed.

Preemergent herbicides are used to prevent the germination of many weed species, mostly annuals. They are often used early in the spring to prevent weeds, such as crabgrass, from germinating in late spring. Postemergent herbicides are directly applied to newly germinated or established weeds. Broad-leaf weeds and perennial grasses are most often treated with a postemergent herbicide. Postemergent herbicides are classified as either a contact herbicide, which kills the part of the plant that it comes in contact with, or a systemic herbicide, which translocates throughout the entire plant. Systemic herbicides are most effective for perennial weeds.

Herbicides are also grouped as selective or nonselective. A selective herbicide controls one category of plants (for instance, broad-leaf weeds but not grasses). Nonselective herbicides kill any green plant the chemical comes in contact with. Nonselective herbicides are useful for controlling weeds in paths, driveways, and patios. Be aware, however, that the slightest breeze may cause the chemical to drift to nearby ornamental plants, causing damage or death to those plants. When using a nonselective herbicide, keep the spray nozzle close to the weeds and never apply during breezy or windy weather. The goal is to control the weeds while minimizing damage to non-target ornamentals and turf.

Pests & Other Problems

I f you've ever maintained a lawn, you know that weeds, insect pests, and other problems are inevitable. Insects and diseases thrive on plants, which have all the essentials: water and nutrients. If you're taking care of your plants, you're liable to see a few pests. Luckily, a well-maintained lawn develops less weed growth than a poor lawn. Weeds have difficulty establishing themselves where the soil is covered with a dense mat of turf.

The list below is designed to help you identify the most common pests of lawns and ground covers. If you feel uncertain about what is causing symptoms of damage, take a sample to your local garden center or your county Cooperative Extension office to have it identified.

Once you've identified the cause of the problem, you'll need to know how to control it. A change in cultural maintenance—less water for instance—may be the best control, or the use of chemicals may be necessary. If chemical control is required, choose a chemical that is recommended for use on your plant variety. Read the label at least twice and follow the directions for use. It is illegal to use a pesticide on something for which it is not labeled.

Dandelions are a common problem throughout the United States.

LAWN AND GROUND COVER WEEDS

WEED	DESCRIPTION	CONTROL
Black Medic. *Medicago lupulina.*	Annual. Spreading plants form a dense mat of dark green foliage that resembles clover. Small yellow flowers appear in spring, forming black seeds. It is a particular problem during dry periods.	Use a postemergent systemic herbicide when turf is not water stressed.
Common Chickweed. *Stellaria media.*	Cool-season annual. It is low-growing with branching stems and small, pointed yellow-green leaves with small starlike white flowers. It actively grows from autumn through spring. Grows in thin turf and bare soil.	Use a preemergent herbicide in fall or early spring.

LAWN AND GROUND COVER WEEDS

WEED	DESCRIPTION	CONTROL
Crabgrass, Smooth and Hairy. *Digitaria ischaemem and D. sanguinalis.*	Both are summer annuals. Thick clumps of smooth or hairy leaves with a spreading habit crowd out turf grass.	Use preemergent herbicide in spring when forsythia is in bloom.
Dandelion. *Taraxacum officinale.*	Perennial. Leaves are broad with deep notches, forming a rosette. Flowers are yellow and develop into fluffy white seed heads.	Use a postemergent systemic herbicide when plants appear; or dig by hand taking care to remove the entire taproot.
Ground Ivy. *Glechoma hederacea.*	Perennial. A creeping plant with round, scalloped edges; stems are squared. Bright purple flowers appear in spring.	Easily removed by hand; or use a postemergent systemic herbicide when plants appear.
Knotweed. *Polygonum aviculare.*	Summer annual. Stems spread across the ground, forming dense mats of small blue-green leaves. Small white flowers appear in late summer.	Use a postemergent systemic herbicide when plants appear.
Purslane. *Portulaca oleracea.*	Summer annual. Small yellow flowers appear on thick mats of small, succulent, green leaves with reddish stems. It grows vigorously in the heat of summer where lawns are thin or soil is bare.	Easily pulled and edible. Use a preemergent herbicide in spring or a postemergent contact herbicide when plants appear. It is especially troublesome in new plantings.
Red Sorrel. *Rumex acetosella.*	Perennial. Green leaves are arrow-shaped; reddish brown flowers appear in late spring. Spreads rapidly by rhizomes. Evergreen in mild climates.	Use a postemergent systemic herbicide when plants appear.
Oxalis. *Oxalis stricta.*	Annual or perennial. Yellow-green leaves resemble clover. Flowers are yellow and develop seedpods that eject mature seed throughout the lawn or garden.	Use a postemergent systemic herbicide when plants appear; some control is gained from preemergent herbicide in spring.

LAWN AND GROUND COVER WEEDS

WEED	DESCRIPTION	CONTROL
 Plantain, Broadleaf and Buckhorn. *Plantago major; P. Lanceolata.*	Perennial. Both plantains form a rosette of leaves, either wide or lancelike; they produce slender stalks on which the seed heads develop. Both species develop long taproots.	Dig plants to remove entire taproot; or use a postemergent systemic herbicide when plants appear.
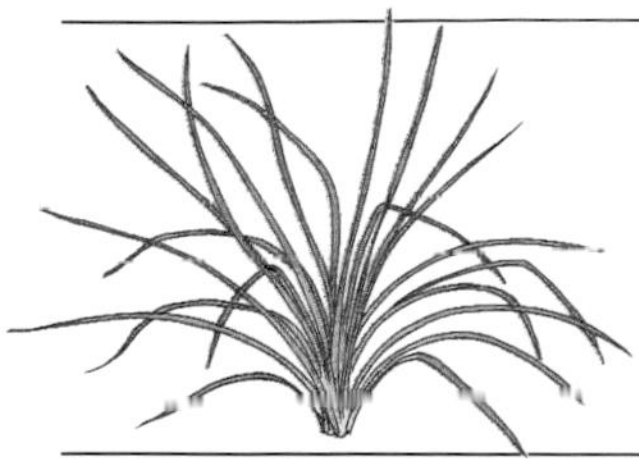 Wild Garlic, Wild Onion. *Allium species.*	Perennial. Narrow, tall, green hollow stems appear in early spring. Plant forms clumps and multiplies by underground bulblets.	Use a postemergent systemic herbicide.

PESTS THAT ATTACK GROUND TURF

SYMPTOM	CAUSE	CONTROL
Lawn becomes spotted with yellow or brown patches in late spring or summer. The patches become large if left untreated.	*Black insects, ¾ inch long*	Apply insecticide in spring and when larvae are feeding on stems. Water lawn to wash insecticide into the soil.
Round or irregular yellow patches in turf during hot, dry summer weather. Dead patches rapidly become quite large.	*Chinch bugs.* 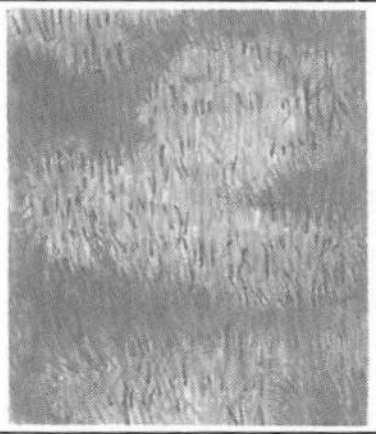	Apply an insecticide labeled for chinch bugs as soon as symptoms appear. Re-treat lawn at three-week intervals until control is obtained.
Stunted clumps of yellow grass appear throughout the lawn.	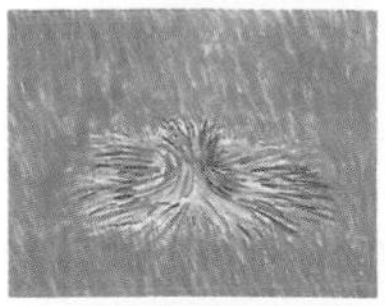 *Downy mildew.*	Apply fungicide labeled for downy mildew in early spring or when symptoms appear. Mow lawn when grass is dry.

PESTS THAT ATTACK GROUND TURF

SYMPTOM	CAUSE	CONTROL
Patches of dead turf appear in early spring and again in late summer.	*Grubs.*	Apply soil insecticide labeled for use for grubs in turf in early spring and late summer. Control adult beetle population in trees, shrubs, and flowers by hand-picking or with recommended insecticide when they appear in late spring and early summer.
Hollow, long, trailing ridges of soil across the lawn, followed by decline of turf. Holes that lead to underground tunnels are visible.	*Moles and voles.*	Control soil insect population to deplete food source of moles. Use spike-traps when pests are active.
Large patches of St. Augustine grass decline and turn yellow; individual leaves become mottled with yellow. Turf becomes thin.	*St. Augustine Decline (SAD).*	Plant SAD-resistant varieties of St. Augustine grass. Control aphids, which transmit the virus. Keep lawn cutting equipment clean.
Patches of yellow or brown turf appear as winter snows melt. Deteriorating grass mats together, turning pink or gray, while white, cottony growth develops.	*Snow mold.*	Apply a fungicide in early spring to prevent spread. Reduce water and fertilizer in the fall to prevent recurrence.
Small patches of dead grass in spring, enlarging throughout the summer. Grass blades appear to have been cut off in affected areas. Small tunnel holes are visible in affected areas.	 *Sod webworm.*	Spray with insecticide in the evening, when feeding larvae are out of their tunnels. Repeat applications until adult moths, larvae, and symptoms disappear.

PESTS THAT ATTACK GROUND COVERS

SYMPTOM	CAUSE	CONTROL	PLANTS
Growing tips become distorted. Leaves curl and begin to wither. A clear, sticky substance appears on leaves that may attract ants.	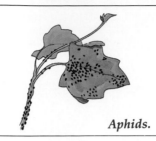 *Aphids.*	Wash insects from plants with a strong jet of water; or apply insecticidal soap or insecticide labeled for control.	Ajuga, English Ivy, Turfgrass.
Leaves turn yellow, and tiny, elongated white bumps appear along stems and leaves. Small, round, brown bumps also appear. The plant becomes stunted and loses its leaves.	 *Euonymus scale.*	Use a dormant oil spray in early spring for prevention. Cut out severely infected parts, and spray with recommended insecticide until signs of insects are gone.	*Euonymus* sp.
Plants show decreased vigor, and leaves become speckled from loss of color. The undersides of leaves are covered with small black specks.	 *Lace bugs.*	Spray the undersides of foliage when symptoms appear. Use an insecticide recommended for lace bugs. Apply three times at seven- to ten-day intervals.	Azaleas, Cotoneaster.
New growth is distorted, and foliage is covered with white, powdery substance.	 *Powdery mildew.*	Spray with a lime-sulfur fungicide at 10- to 14-day intervals.	Ajuga, Candytuft, Euonymus, Periwinkle.
Foliage has irregular-shaped holes, especially near base of plant.	 *Snails and slugs.*	Pick pests when visible; lay a board near the infested areas for slugs and snails to hide and collect them during the day. Shallow pans of beer will lure the pests and drown them.	Ajuga, Daylily, Hosta.
Leaves lose their green color, speckled with white. A fine white webbing appears between leaves and stem, especially on young tips.	 *Spider mites.*	Spray with an insecticidal soap; or apply a miticide three times at three-day intervals.	Cotoneaster, English Ivy, Juniper.

Use your imagination when planning your landscape. A variety of grasses, climbing vines, and blooming perennials will make your yard a joy in every season.

40

CHAPTER 4

ENCYCLOPEDIA OF GRASSES & GROUND COVERS

Lawns have been cultivated in America since colonial times. Since then, great strides have been made in developing varieties of grass that will withstand adverse conditions. Turf grasses today can tolerate heavier wear, colder weather, and drier conditions. This plant directory will help you select the right plant varieties for your landscape. It is divided into three sections: turf grasses, ground covers, and ornamental grasses.

A listing of all plants suitable for ground cover use would be almost infinite. Ground covers are plants—shrubs, vines, or herbaceous plants—that are planted in mass to add interest to the landscape's floor. This list of easy-to-grow ground covers is a start toward choosing a variety to meet your design needs.

Ornamental grasses are unlike turf grasses. They won't tolerate foot traffic and can't be mowed. They can be used as specimens, accents, or quiet transitions between contrasting plantings. Some are planted as ground cover. Several ornamental grasses that merit attention are included in this directory.

TURF GRASSES

Bahia Grass

Paspalum notatum

Bahia grass is a medium green, coarse-textured lawn grass of the Southeast and South coastal areas. It spreads by creeping rhizomes. It is not cold hardy.

How to grow: Bahia grass grows best in the humid Southern coastal areas, in a light, sandy, infertile soil. Grow Bahia grass from seed in full sun to partial shade. Fertilize in the spring with four to six pounds of nitrogen per 1,000 square feet. It is an aggressively spreading grass that has an extensive root system. It is good for erosion control and low-maintenance lawns. Bahia grass has good wear tolerance. Seed stalks are tall and fast-growing, requiring frequent mowing. Mow to 3 inches.

Related varieties: 'Argentine,' the most commonly grown variety, is less coarse-textured and forms a thicker mat. 'Pensacola' is medium-textured and establishes quickly.

Bermudagrass

Cynodon dactylon

Bermudagrass, a warm-season grass that forms a dense mat, spreads by rhizomes. This turf grass is grown in the South and the Southwest. It likes heat and is easy to grow in most soils. Bermudagrass tolerates wear and can withstand drought conditions. Bermudagrass is a high-maintenance turf that grows vigorously in warm weather but turns brown in the winter if temperatures drop below 50 degrees Fahrenheit.

How to grow: Bermudagrass grows well in most soils but must have full sun. Plant sprigs or plugs of named varieties purchased from a reputable nursery or sod producer in your area. Bermudagrass from seed is unreliable and will produce an inferior lawn. Bermudagrass must be planted during the warm growing season for it to become established before winter dormancy begins. Fertilize during the growing season when growth is active; it's a heavy feeder. Fertilize in early spring with one pound of nitrogen per 1,000 square feet, followed by late spring and midsummer applications each of one pound per 1,000 square feet. Bermudagrass is susceptible to insects and diseases. Mow from ½ to 1 inch.

Related varieties: 'Midiron' is medium-textured, dark green, and cold-tolerant. 'Ormond' is medium-fine-textured, with bluish green tint; thatch buildup is slower. 'Tiflawn' is medium-fine-textured, bright green, and with a high tolerance to foot traffic. It is often used on playing fields.

Buffalograss

Buchloe dactyloides

Buffalograss is a warm-season turf grass grown mostly in the Great Plains and the southern Rockies. It's a fine-textured, low-growing grass with curly leaf blades that grows into dense sod by spreading stolons. It is used for lawns and banks in dry areas.

How to grow: Plant buffalograss in full sun where soils are dry. It will thrive in the alkaline soils of the West. Buffalograss resists wear from foot traffic and is commonly used for non-irrigated lawns. Fertilize in spring with 1½ to 2½ pounds of nitrogen per 1,000 square feet; repeat the application in summer. It grows slowly and should be mown to a height of ½ to 1½ inches. Plant buffalograss from seeds, sprigs, or plugs.

Related varieties or species: There are no related varieties or species.

Centipedegrass

Eremochloa ophiuroides

Centipedegrass is a spreading, warm-season turf grass grown in the Deep South and Florida. It is medium-coarse and slow-growing, forming a dense mat. It is light green in color.

How to grow: Centipedegrass grows in full sun but is tolerant of partial shade. Use it for a low-maintenance lawn where foot traffic is limited; it cannot tolerant wear. This grass is adapted to soil with low fertility and an acid pH. Plant centipedegrass from sprigs for rapid establishment. It can also be grown from seed but is slow to develop and may take two years to form a dense mat. Fertilize in the spring with two pounds of nitrogen per 1,000 square feet. Water centipedegrass regularly; its shallow root system makes centipedegrass sensitive to drought conditions. Mow to 2 inches.

Related varieties: 'Oaklawn' is a named variety available from sprigs.

Creeping Bentgrass

Agrostis stolonifera palustris

Creeping bentgrass is a cool-season and transition zone turf that grows best from the Midwest to the Pacific Northwest and in the Northeast. It's a fine-textured, high-maintenance turf that is used for golf putting greens. The plant spreads by creeping stolons. Creeping bentgrass will not generally survive heavy foot traffic.

How to grow: Plant creeping bentgrass in climates that are cool and humid. It does best in full sun but will tolerate partial shade. Creeping bentgrass may be propagated by seed, but named varieties are propagated by plugs. Sow seeds or plant plugs in well-drained, fertile, acid soil. Fertilize in spring and again in summer with two pounds of nitrogen per 1,000 square feet. Keep the soil well watered during dry conditions. Creeping bentgrass needs a low mowing height, from $\frac{1}{4}$ inch to 1 inch; otherwise, thatch will build up quickly. Creeping bentgrass is susceptible to several turf diseases.

Related varieties: 'Emerald' is dark green and heat-tolerant. 'Arlington,' a fine-textured medium green, is tolerant of drought conditions and foot traffic. 'Pencross' is medium green, heavier textured than other varieties, and adapts to foot traffic.

Creeping Red Fescue

Festuca rubra rubra

Creeping red fescue, also called fine fescue, is a densely clustered, fine-textured, medium to dark green turf grass that spreads by creeping. It grows well in shaded areas and is tolerant of drought. It is often mixed with bluegrass or turf-type fescue blends. Grow creeping red fescue in the North and transition zone.

How to grow: Grow creeping red fescue in shaded areas where drought conditions are expected. Plant creeping red fescue from seed. When it becomes established, it tolerates drought but does not tolerate heavy wear. It grows best in cool-season and high-altitude areas. Fertilize in the fall with two to four pounds of nitrogen per 1,000 square feet. Mow to 2 inches.

Related varieties: 'Pennlawn' is medium dark green with fine texture and disease resistance. 'Illahee' is dark green, medium-textured, and vigorous. Chewing fescue, *Festuca rubra commutata*, is similar to creeping red fescue, although it tends to form clumps. 'Jamestown' is dark green, fine-textured, and tolerant of low mowing. 'Wintergreen' keeps good winter color.

Tall Fescue

Festuca arundinacea

Tall fescue is a cool-season grass that grows in the North and is especially suited to the transition zone. It is a coarse-textured, clumping turf that remains medium-green all year. Since it is tolerant of wear and drought, tall fescue is used for play areas.

How to grow: Tall fescue prefers fertile, moist, slightly acid soil and a location in full sun or partial shade. Soil should be moderately well drained, but tall fescue can tolerate wet soils. Plant seed in the fall or early spring so turf becomes established before hot weather. Sow seed heavily; tall fescue has wide blades and tends to clump. It is one of the most drought-tolerant and wear-resistant turf varieties for cool-seasons. Use tall fescue from the transition zone and north for playing fields and lawns with heavy traffic. Fertilize in the fall with four to six pounds of nitrogen per 1,000 square feet. Mow from 2 to 2½ inches.

Related varieties: 'Alta' is medium-green and coarse-textured. 'Kentucky 31' is the standard tall fescue variety. It is coarse, medium-green, and tolerant of drought and wear. 'Kentucky 31' is rapidly being replaced by turf-type fescues. Turf-type fescues have a finer texture and display better wear-resistance and drought-tolerance than tall fescue. Turf-type fescues are dense, dark green, and resistant to many turf diseases. Good varieties include: 'Falcon,' which is medium-textured, slow- and low-growing, and shade tolerant, and 'Jaguar,' which is dark green and shade tolerant.

Kentucky Bluegrass

Poa pratensis

Kentucky bluegrass is a cool-season turf grass that grows in the Northern regions. It spreads by rhizomes and forms a dense, medium-textured, medium green turf. A Kentucky bluegrass lawn is the standard other grasses are compared with.

How to grow: Kentucky bluegrass grows best in full sun in moist, fertile soil with a pH between 6.0 and 7.0. Some varieties are more tolerant of partial shade conditions. Plant Kentucky bluegrass from seed. Fertilize annually with two to four pounds of nitrogen per 1,000 square feet. Mow from 1 to 2 inches.

Related varieties: 'Aldelphi' is dark green, dense, medium-textured, and resistant to disease. 'Baron,' a heavy feeder, is dark green, medium-textured, and disease-resistant. 'Fylking' is dark green with a finer texture; it can be mown to 1½ inches. 'Merion,' disease-resistant and tolerant of heat, forms a dense mat of medium-textured dark green turf. 'Touchdown' is dense, medium dark green, with a fine texture. It tolerates low mowing and is resistant to disease. Rough bluegrass, *Poa trivialis*, is fine-textured, light green, tolerates shade, and spreads by rhizomes.

Japanese Lawngrass

Zoysia japonica

Japanese lawngrass is a fine-textured warm-season grass that spreads by rhizomes and stolons. It grows best in the transition zone and the South. It forms a dense, low-growing, lawn of high quality. It's relatively pest free and, when established, is resistant to weeds.

How to grow: Grow Zoysia grass in full sun to partial shade where summers are long and hot. The soil should be well-drained and fertile. Zoysia grass is slow to become established. Plant plugs or sod in spring to allow for development before the onset of winter. It is a heavy feeder during the warm season. Fertilize with one pound of nitrogen per 1,000 square feet in spring, midsummer, and early fall. Since the leaves of Zoysia are wiry, mow regularly; remove grass clippings from the lawn since thatch builds up quickly. Mow from ½ to 1½ inches. Zoysia is tolerant of wear during the growing season but less so in winter when the grass goes dormant. When temperatures drop below 50 degrees Fahrenheit in winter, the grass turns brown. Overseed with annual rye to provide green winter color.

Related varieties: 'Meyer' is fine-textured and dark-green. *Zoysia tenuifolia* is light green and the finest-textured of the Zoysias. 'Emerald,' a hybrid, is fine-textured and medium dark green.

Annual Ryegrass

Lolium multiflorum

This annual ryegrass is a cool-season grass that grows in the North where winter temperature are above −20 degrees Fahrenheit. It is a light green clumping grass with a medium texture. Because it is an annual, it is often used to over-seed warm-season grasses that turn brown in winter.

How to grow: Annual rye germinates quickly; it is robust and is used where a quick cover is needed. It is best grown in sun or partial shade in soil that is fertile and moist. Mix annual rye-grass at a rate of less than 25 percent with Kentucky bluegrass or fine fescue. Since it is not tolerant of extreme heat or extreme cold, it is generally used as a temporary cover to prevent erosion while permanent grass seed is becoming established. When using annual rye-grass as an overseed crop, mow warm-season turf to one inch after it has turned brown for the winter, then sow annual rye. Sow annual ryegrass for green winter color. When perma-nent turf begins to actively grow, the ryegrass will die. Annual ryegrass does not mow cleanly; mow from 1½ to 2 inches.

Related varieties: There are no named vari-eties of annual ryegrass. Perennial ryegrass, *Lolium perenne*, is a short-lived perennial used in mixtures with Kentucky bluegrass and fine fescue. 'Citation II' is dark green and more tolerant of heat than others. 'NK-200' has good density, is medium dark green, and tolerant of cold. 'Omega II' is dark green, tolerant of heat and cold, and mows clean.

St. Augustine Grass

Stenotaphrum secundatum

St. Augustine grass is a warm-season, coarse-textured grass, best suited to the Southeast Coast and Florida. It is aggressive and spreads by branching stolons. St. Augustine grass devel-ops into a thick spongy mat as stolons grow on top of one another. It is blue green in color.

How to grow: Grow St. Augustine grass in full sun to full shade in humid climates. It is the most shade-tolerant of all the warm-season grasses. It prefers fertile, well-drained, sandy soil and is tolerant of salty conditions. It is moderately tolerant of wear. St. Augustine grass requires frequent watering to keep its vigor. Fertilize annually with three to six pounds of nitrogen per 1,000 square feet. Mow from 1½ to 2½ inches. The grass turns brown in winter if temperatures drop to 55 degrees Fahrenheit. St. Augustine grass is started by cuttings; plant sprigs, plugs, or sod in spring or early fall.

Related varieties: 'Bitter Blue' is medium-tex-tured and holds better color in cool weather. 'Floratine' is fine-textured and holds good win-ter color. 'Seville' is the most shade-tolerant variety.

Western Wheatgrass

Agropyron smithii

Western wheatgrass is a clumping cool-season turf grass that grows in the cooler regions of the Rocky Mountains, the western Great Plains, and the high altitudes of the Southwest. It is native from the Great Plains to California.

How to grow: Wheatgrass is tolerant of drought conditions and does not like a heavy, wet soil. It is more tolerant of alkaline soils than other grasses. Wheatgrass will develop creeping rhizomes, but it is planted from seed, which is slow to germinate. Use wheatgrass for lawns and play areas in full sun; it's a tough variety that can withstand foot traffic. Fertilize in fall or spring with two pounds of nitrogen per 1,000 square feet. Mow to 2 inches. Wheatgrass may turn brown during hot, dry summers.

Related varieties: *A. cristatum*, crested, or fairway, wheatgrass, has a finer texture than western wheatgrass. It is also used for pasture in cold- and drought-susceptible areas.

GROUND COVERS

Bugleweed

Ajuga reptans
Zone: USDA 3b to 9a

A member of the mint family, this perennial herb is commonly grown as a ground cover because of its low-growing, spreading habit. Varieties of bugleweed produce a carpet of blue, pink, or white blooms in spring and early summer.

Description: Dense mats of green, bronze, or variegated oval-shaped leaves form close to the ground. The plants spread rapidly by stolons. An abundance of blue flower spikes are produced on 3- to 6-inch stalks for several weeks in spring. Grow bugleweed in mixed borders or on an embankment as an effective, low-maintenance erosion control ground cover.

How to grow: Bugleweed grows well in any ordinary, moist, garden soil with adequate drainage. It is easy to grow in sun or shade, but prefers shade where summers are hot. Bronze-leaf forms hold their leaf color best in sunny locations.

Propagation: Start new plants in spring or fall by division or by separating new plants from stolons; plant them directly into the garden on 12- to 18-inch centers to form a dense carpet.

Related varieties: 'Alba' has white flowers. 'Bronze Beauty' has bronze foliage and blue flowers. 'Burgundy Glow' has blue flowers and variegated foliage of white, pink, purple, or light green; it is less aggressive than the straight species.

Cranberry Cotoneaster

Cotoneaster apiculatus
Zone: USDA 3b to 7a

Due to their shiny foliage, red berries, and diversity of size and form, many species of cotoneaster grow in the North American landscapes. Cotoneasters are woody shrubs, with stiff, arching branches. Pink or white flowers cover the plant in mid to late spring. Many species develop showy red or orange berries that persist deep into winter.

Description: Cranberry cotoneaster is a semi-evergreen or deciduous, low-branching, wide-spreading shrub, growing to three feet in height. The leaves are small, oval, and a glossy dark green. Pale pink flowers in spring produce ³⁄₈-inch round, scarlet fruit that holds through winter. Use cotoneaster where the long, sweeping branches are allowed to spill over embankments and retaining walls. It's a plant for large areas.

How to grow: Cranberry cotoneaster prefers full sun or partial shade in well-drained, neutral or slightly alkaline soil. Established plants are tolerant of drought conditions. Annual pruning is necessary to keep the plants in a confined area.

Propagation: Take softwood cuttings in late spring or layer stems in autumn. Grow rooted cuttings in containers or beds until they're large enough to plant in the landscape. Plant on three- to five-foot centers for mass plantings.

Related species: *Cotoneaster dammeri* is an evergreen shrub that grows to 12 inches high with long trailing branches that often root in the soil. The white flowers appear as a dusting of snow in midspring. *C. horizontalis* spreads close to the ground; its flowers are pink, and the fruit is red.

Dichondra

Dichondra micrantha
Zone: USDA 9 to 10

Grown as a warm-season lawn substitute, dichondra has round- to kidney-shaped leaves and spreads by runners.

Description: The light green, round leaves of dichondra are ½ to 1 inch across on stems less than 1½ inches long. Its pale green flowers are small and inconspicuous. It spreads by underground runners, forming a dense mat. Use dichondra as a lawn grass substitute in areas of low foot traffic where winter temperatures do not drop below 25 degrees Fahrenheit.

How to grow: Dichondra can be grown in full sun to full shade, in rich, fine-textured soils of slight acidity. Dichondra demands high moisture, and it requires regular watering. Fertilize in early spring with one pound of nitrogen per 1,000 square feet; repeat applications in late spring, summer, and fall. Dichondra requires little mowing; mow to a height of ½ to 1 inch when the lawn becomes uneven in appearance.

Propagation: Start new lawns by seed or from plugs. Seed germinates easily; sow seed in spring or fall to allow seedlings to establish during cool weather. Plant plugs on 6- to 12-inch centers. Water seed and plugs frequently to encourage rapid establishment.

Related varieties or species: There are no related varieties or species.

English Ivy

Hedera helix
Zone: USDA 6a to 9a

English ivy has long been used to cover walls, climb tree trunks, and blanket embankments. A woody vine that creeps along the ground or over supports while attaching itself with little roots, English ivy may be trained to grow upright or as a ground cover.

Description: English ivy is an evergreen, woody vine that develops long trailing stems. The leaves of juvenile English ivy are five-lobed, dark green, and glossy; mature plants develop oval or triangular leaves. Adult plants produce inconspicuous green flowers that mature into clusters of black fruit. Ivies grown as ground covers will grow 6 to 12 inches high and seldom produce adult foliage or flowers. Use English ivy to cover large areas in sun or shade. Regular pruning allows ivy to be used in small spaces.

How to grow: Grow English ivy in rich, well-drained soil in sun or shade. Once established, English ivy will tolerate drought. To prevent leaf burn, grow yellow and white variegated forms in partial shade. Fertilize annually with a complete fertilizer in the spring. Prune trailing stems any time of year to confine the planting to small spaces. English ivy can easily become invasive, so it should be trimmed and regulated in order to keep it under control.

Propagation: Start new plants by stem cuttings from immature plants in late spring. Plant rooted cuttings on 12- to 18-inch centers for a fast-growing, dense ground cover.

Related varieties: 'Baltica' is a well-branched variety, with two-inch, white-veined leaves that turn purple in winter. There are many ivy varieties, some of which have green and white or green and yellow variegations.

Variegated Goutweed

Aegopodium podagaria **'Variegatum'**
Zone: USDA 3b to 10

Goutweed, or Bishop's-weed, is a fast-growing European native that has become naturalized in North America. The variegated form, which is not as fast-spreading, is a popular ground cover for shady areas. The plant is grown for its easy care and white-edged leaves.

Description: Goutweed is a deciduous, perennial, foliage ground cover used for edging and massing. The variegated form produces divided green leaves that are edged in white. Small, white flowers bloom in early summer atop 14-inch stems, above the 6-inch leaf stalks. Brightening dark, shady beds, this aggressive herb spreads from underground rootstocks. It is a good choice for dry, shady areas, where it is less invasive.

How to grow: Grow goutweed in ordinary soil; goutweed spreads rapidly if the soil is rich and moist. It does best in shade to partial shade but is tolerant of sun. Goutweed can become invasive if it is not controlled; it can be mowed to slow its growth.

Propagation: Start new plants by digging the plants in spring or fall and dividing their slender rootstocks. Replant directly in the garden on 12-inch centers for a solid ground cover mass.

Related species: Although other species exist, none are appropriate for gardening

Trailing Ice Plant

Lampranthus spectabilis
Zone: USDA 9 to 10

Ice plant is a trailing perennial with succulent, curved, three-sided gray-green foliage. Flowers bloom during late winter and spring.

Description: Trailing ice plant sprawls across the ground, rooting into the soil as it spreads. It reaches 8 inches in height, and the 3-inch, gray-green leaves are thick and succulent. In winter and early spring the daisylike flowers reach 2 to 3 inches in diameter in shades of pink and purple. Use ice plant in a rock garden or in dry beds and slopes.

How to grow: Ice plant prefers well-drained, dry soil in full sun. Once established, it tolerates drought conditions; do not overwater.

Propagation: New plants start easily by cuttings any time of year, or by seeds in spring. Plant on 18-inch centers to quickly produce a covering mat.

Related species: *Lampranthus aureus* produces orange flowers on 15- to 18-inch plants.

Creeping Juniper

Juniperus horizontalis
Zone: USDA 2 to 9a

The *Juniperus* genus includes many species of evergreen trees and shrubs. Some are low-growing and used as ground covers. Leaves are scalelike and may be dark green, yellow-green, or blue-green.

Description: Creeping juniper is a prostrate shrub with wide-spreading branches and grows to 24 inches high. The leaves are scalelike and bluish green, turning purple in winter. The flowers are inconspicuous, and female plants produce small, round, blue-green berries. Use junipers in full sun where low maintenance is desired. Junipers withstand hot, dry situations in the landscape.

How to grow: Plant junipers in full sun in well-drained, dry soil. They are tolerant of heavy and slightly alkaline soil. Fertilize in early spring with a well-balanced, complete fertilizer.

Propagation: Start plants from stem cuttings in late spring. Grow rooted plants in containers or propagation beds until they're big enough to place in the landscape. Plant on four- to five-foot centers for a massed ground cover.

Related varieties: 'Bar Harbor' grows to 12 inches high with a 6- to 8-foot spread. Leaves are bluish green, turning purple in winter. 'Blue Chip' grows 8 to 10 inches high and holds an excellent blue color throughout the year. 'Plumosa' grows 18 to 24 inches high, spreading up to 10 feet; its gray-green leaves turn purple in winter. 'Wiltoni' (Blue Rug) grows to 6 inches high with silver-blue foliage.

Lily-of-the-Valley

Convallaria majalis
Zone: USDA 3 to 8

A member of the lily family, and native to Europe and North America, lily-of-the-valley spreads by rhizomes, from which grow buds, called pips. Each pip develops two or three leaves and a flower stalk.

Description: This deciduous perennial produces 8-inch long, lance-shaped leaves in clusters of two or three. Each cluster sends up an 8- to 12-inch flower stem from which nodding, fragrant, bell-shaped flowers grow. The white, or sometimes pale pink, flowers grow on one side of the stalk. Lily-of-the-valley is a long-lived perennial and a good ground cover for moist, shady sites where low maintenance is required. Use lily-of-the-valley as ground cover under shrubs on the north side of a house or in naturalized plantings in the shade of a woodland garden. The cut flowers last long and offer a nice fragrance.

How to grow: Plant lily-of-the-valley in rich, moist, well-drained soil that is high in organic matter. It prefers a slightly acidic soil in partial or full shade. Being herbaceous, the plant will die to the ground during winter. In early spring, before the pips have emerged from the soil, apply a complete fertilizer and a light dressing of mulch.

Propagation: Divide plants in fall or early spring so that each division has at least one pip. Transplant divisions directly to their new location.

Related varieties or species: There are no related varieties or species.

Periwinkle

Vinca minor
Zone: USDA 4 to 10

Periwinkle forms a fine, dense carpet of shiny, dark, evergreen leaves with early flowering. Fine, wiry stems trail across the soil, rooting at the nodes.

Description: Periwinkle has glossy dark green, ½- to ¾-inch, oval-shaped leaves on long, thin trailing stems. The 1- to 1½-inch flowers bloom in spring in blue, white, or lavender. Plants spread rapidly and grow to 6 inches high.

How to grow: Grow periwinkle in full or partial shade. It will tolerate full sun in cool climates. Soil should be moderately fertile and enriched with organic matter. Once established, it tolerates drought. Fertilize with a complete fertilizer in early spring before new growth appears; water generously to work nutrients into the root zone. Shear long stems to keep the plant compact and confined to small spaces. Use periwinkle to carpet slopes or flat ground in full or partial shade. It can be used effectively as an underplanting for spring-flowering bulbs.

Propagation: Periwinkle easily develops roots from stem cuttings in spring and early summer. In fall, plant rooted cuttings in the garden on 12- to 18-inch centers six to eight weeks before the ground freezes. Plants can be divided any time of year: Remove rooted stems from the original plant and replant in new location.

Related species: *Vinca major* is similar to *V. minor*; it has larger leaves and flowers and is hardy in USDA zones 7 to 10. *V. major* 'Variegata' has variegated green and cream leaves.

Moss Pink

Phlox subulata
Zone: USDA 3 to 9

The Phlox family includes many diverse species of garden plants. Some grow several feet in height, while others grow close to the ground. Spreading species grow several inches high and produce flowers in shades of red, pink, blue, and white. Moss pink is an effective ground cover where low maintenance is desired.

Description: *Phlox subulata* is an evergreen ground cover that develops woody stems that creep along the ground and reach 6 inches in height. Its small, needlelike leaves are deep green to reddish green. The ¾-inch flowers cover the plant for several weeks in the spring. Use moss pink in full sun on dry banks. It is also attractive when allowed to spill over walls or blanket the ground.

How to grow: Grow moss pink in ordinary garden soil in full sun. Once established, it can withstand drought conditions. After the blooms have faded, shear plants to 4 inches to keep the plants compact.

Propagation: Start new plants by division at any time of the year, or from stem cuttings in early summer. Spreading stems that have rooted in the soil can be cut from the plant and moved to the new location. Plant on 18-inch centers to create a dense mat.

Related varieties: 'Appleblossom' has an extended bloom period with pale pink flowers with a deep pink eye. The foliage of 'Scarlet Flame' turns reddish in winter; the flowers are deep pinkish red. 'White Delight' has pale green foliage and pure white flowers.

Rock Cress

Arabis procurrens
Zone: USDA 5 to 8

Rock cress is a perennial member of the mustard family. It is used as a long-flowering ground cover. Varieties of rock cress grow in many parts of the world, producing white, pink, or purple flowers.

Description: Rock cress is an evergreen, flowering ground cover that spreads through creeping stolons. The oblong, green leaves are rounded at the base of the 12-inch plant. Heavy clusters of small, white, showy flowers bloom from late winter through spring.

How to grow: Rock cress grows best in well-drained sandy soil; it prefers dry soils with low fertility. Grow rock cress in full sun or, for an extended bloom period, in partial shade. Rock cress does best in climates with low humidity and cool summers.

Propagation: Propagate by division or by runners in spring or fall. Set new plants directly in the garden on 12- to 20-inch centers to establish a ground cover. Water new plants well and allow soil to dry once roots are established.

Related varieties: 'Variegata' is a form of rock cress that has green and white variegated foliage.

Japanese Spurge

Pachysandra terminalis
Zone: USDA 4 to 8

Pachysandra has become a popular ground cover in the North. Originating in Japan, pachysandra forms a dense covering in shaded areas with whorls of evergreen foliage and small clusters of white flowers. Use Japanese spurge under trees and in the shade of buildings where there is ample moisture.

Description: Pachysandra is an evergreen ground cover that spreads by underground stems. It forms a dense mat up to 12 inches high. As the terminal stems grow, stems mat down and root in the soil. The 4-inch leaves are dark green and glossy and formed in whorled clusters. Small, insignificant white flowers bloom in spring.

How to grow: Japanese spurge prefers partial to full shade. Leaves will turn yellow and burn in sunny sites. Grow pachysandra in rich, fertile, well-drained soil. In cool climates, it tolerates drought. Fertilize with a complete fertilizer in early spring.

Propagation: Stem cuttings root easily in spring or fall, or divide plants in spring or early summer. Plant on 12-inch centers.

Related varieties: 'Variegata' has green leaves with white markings. It is especially effective in small, dark areas of the landscape.

Fountain Grass

Pennisetum alopecuroides
Zone: USDA 6 to 10

A few of the many species of *Pennisetum* are grown ornamentally. The genus includes annuals and perennials with narrow, flat leaves that have a graceful arching habit. The nodding, bottlebrush seed heads are spiked and slightly plumed.

Description: Fountain grass is a perennial, warm-season grass growing to 3 feet tall. Its leaves are bright green with a fine to medium texture growing into a mounded form. Buff-colored flower heads, 6 to 8 inches long, appear in summer; they later take on a pinkish cast. The seed heads remain attractive through winter. Fountain grass is an excellent ornamental grass for long-season interest. Use as a border or in mixed perennial beds. Fountain grass is an effective ground cover when planted in mass.

How to grow: Plant fountain grass in full sun; it will tolerate partial shade in the South. It prefers fertile, well-drained soil. Fertilize in spring with a complete fertilizer. In late winter, cut plants to the ground.

Propagation: Start plants from seed indoors or in a coldframe six to eight weeks before setting plants outdoors. Don't set plants until the danger of frost has passed; young seedlings are not hardy. Or, divide plants in spring and replant divisions in a new location.

Related species: Crimson fountain grass, *P. setaceum*, grows to 3 feet tall with gracefully arching, fine-textured 6- to 10-inch-high foliage. Seed heads are pink. Feathertop, *P. villosum*, grows to 3 feet tall with 4-inch-long, creamy white seed heads. Grow as a perennial in zone 9 or higher, as an annual elsewhere.

Related varieties: 'Hameln' is more compact than the species.

Pampas Grass

Cortaderia selloana
Zone: USDA 8 to 10 (7 with winter protection)

Pampas grass is native to South America. A perennial grass, it has dense, upright clumps of long, narrow, sharp-edged leaves. Large, showy, plumed panicles bloom in late summer and fall.

Description: Pampas grass is a warm-season grass. Heavy clumps of long, rough, blue-green, cascading leaves grow to 5 feet high and 5 feet wide. Flower stalks shoot up in late summer to 12 feet. Female plants produce showy, plume-like blossoms of pink or silver-white. Use pampas grass as a windbreak; it contributes to the landscape as a year-round accent. It can serve as a specimen in spacious gardens.

How to grow: Plant pampas grass in full sun or light shade in fertile, well-drained, moist soil. It is tolerant of drought conditions if well established. Fertilize in spring when new growth begins. Cut the plant back to the ground in late winter to keep a tidy appearance.

Propagation: Divide plants in spring. Use a sharp spade or saw to make divisions through tough roots.

Related varieties: 'Rosea' has pink plumes. 'Sonningdale' has silver plumes. 'Pumila' is a dwarf variety, hardy to zone 7.

Quaking Grass

Briza media
Zone: USDA 4 to 8

Native to Europe and Asia, *Briza* includes annual and perennial grasses with slender, gracefully arching foliage. They're grown ornamentally for their showy, drooping seed heads.

Description: Quaking grass is a perennial that grows 10 to 18 inches high with slender foliage. The 5- to 10-inch-long flower panicles develop thin, flat seed heads that hang on threadlike stems. The seed heads and panicles turn purple and fade to gray. The flower stalks are stiff, and nodding seed heads tremble with the slightest breeze. Quaking grass is a cool-season grass and blooms in early summer. Use quaking grass as an accent or in a mixed border for movement in the landscape.

How to grow: Grow quaking grass in full sun in dry, poor soil. Fertilize in fall or early spring with a complete fertilizer.

Propagation: Quaking grass grows easily from seed, or divide plants in early fall.

Related species: Large quaking grass, *Briza maxima*, is an annual that grows to 24 inches tall. Its 4- to 6-inch coarse leaves are medium green.

Feather Reed Grass

Calamagrostis acutiflora stricta
Zone: USDA 4 to 9

The genus *Calamagrostis* includes perennial and annual grasses from Africa and Europe. A few species are used ornamentally. They form upright clumps and bloom in spring and early summer.

Description: Feather reed grass grows into a strong, upright clump reaching 5 feet in height. The dull green leaves are 2 feet long and arch slightly. In late spring, flower stalks rise 2 to 3 feet above the foliage. The 12-inch-long flower head is purplish in spring, turning to buff-colored seed heads in fall. Use feather reed grass as a screen or as a vertical accent. The plant is well suited to wet soils around pools and streams. It is a cool-season grass that keeps its interest from spring into fall.

How to grow: Grow feather reed grass in full sun with moist, fertile soil. It tolerates poorly drained wet soils (such as at the edge of a pond) and, once established, it will tolerate drought.

Propagation: Feather reed grass is a hybrid that is propagated by division in early fall or early spring.

Related species: Foxtail grass, *Calamagrostis arundinacea abrachytricha*, grows to 3 feet tall and produces 12-inch-long, lavender, fluffy, foxtail-shaped flowers.

Ribbon Grass

Phalaris arundinaceae picta
Zone: USDA 3 to 10

Grown for its spreading habit and variegated leaves, ribbon grass is a perennial with flat leaf blades and narrow spikes of flattened seed heads.

Description: Ribbon grass grows to 3 feet tall. Its pointed leaves are 12 inches long and striped in green, white, and sometimes pink. It forms a dense mound that spreads by rhizomes. In summer, 4- to 6-inch-long inconspicuous white flowers develop into pale pink seed heads on 3-foot stems. Ribbon grass makes an excellent, semievergreen ground cover, but it must be restrained.

How to grow: Grow ribbon grass in poor, dry or wet soil. If the soil is rich, its spreading habit becomes extremely invasive. To keep the sun from fading its variegated color, plant ribbon grass in partial shade. It's a cool-season grass, producing most of its growth in spring.

Propagation: Start new plants by division in early spring or fall.

Related varieties or species: There are no related varieties or species.

Zebra Grass

Miscanthus sinensis 'Zebrinus'
Zone: USDA 4 to 9

Several species of *Miscanthus* are grown ornamentally. Most species are clump-forming; some have gracefully arching foliage. Feathery flowers are either flat or fan-shaped, with soft hairs.

Description: Zebra grass grows 6 to 8 feet high. The medium green leaves are banded horizontally with yellow stripes. The flower stalks produce pinkish flowers that turn beige or orange-brown in the fall. The upright, stiff form holds well into winter. Use zebra grass as an accent in mixed borders or as a screen.

How to grow: Zebra grass grows best in full sun or light shade. Increased shade weakens the flower stalks, which may require staking. Soil should be moist and moderately fertile. This warm-season grass begins its growth after the soil has thoroughly warmed up in the spring. Fertilize with a complete fertilizer in spring.

Propagation: Start new plants in spring by division.

Related varieties: Maiden grass, *M. sinensis* 'Gracillimus,' is fine-textured and has a graceful arching habit that reaches 5 feet in height. *M. sinensis* 'Variegatus' reaches 5 feet in height; the narrow green foliage is variegated with white and yellow vertical stripes.

ANNUALS

Every garden can be changed from year to year simply
by changing the annual plants placed there.
You may have large, bright red flowers one year and
then decide to plant clumps of tiny blue flowers the next.
For easy, quick, and satisfying results, annuals
can't be beat. Pep up your border and add color to each
season for little effort and even less cost.

This lovely annuals garden is awash with the many colors of lobelias, verbenas, zinnias, petunias, and plumed cockscomb. Note the various shades—whites, pinks, lavenders, purples, and reds—that blend so harmoniously to create this garden.

CHAPTER 1

PLANNING A SEASONAL KALEIDOSCOPE OF COLOR

Annuals are those plants that go through an entire life cycle germinate, grow, flower, produce seed, and die—all in a single growing season. Generally, they reach the point of flower production within six to eight weeks after sprouting and continue in abundant bloom until they're killed by frost. In some parts of the United States, perennials that would not survive a severe winter are used as annuals for seasonal color as well.

No wonder, then, that annuals are such a boon to gardeners! Most grow quickly and easily, provide a long season of color, and require minimal special care at very low cost. They also offer a wondrous variety of sizes, flower forms, and leaf types from which to choose. A gardener's problem is not whether to grow annuals— it's how to narrow the choice to those few that space allows.

In this first chapter, we'll discuss some of the important factors to be considered when planning the planting of annuals. Subjects such as soil and light conditions and how they affect plant choices; the palette of colors, forms, and textures available from different annuals; and the attractive ways in which various plantings of annuals can beautify your yard will all be dealt with. These basics will get you started properly toward successful use of annuals in your garden.

Soil & Light

Crested cockscomb, sweet alyssum, and dusty miller combine beautifully in a well-designed garden.

Soil and light are especially important factors to consider when planning the use of annuals (as well as perennials; see the "Perennials" section, page 190, for more information on perennials). Let's talk about soil first.

Soil types vary from the extremes of constantly dry, nutrient-poor sand to 90 percent rocks held together with 10 percent soil to rich, heavy clay (which forms a slick, sticky, shoe-grabbing mass when wet, then dries to brick hardness). Fortunately, most soil conditions fall somewhere between these extremes. Still, very few homeowners find they have that ideal "rich garden loam" to work with!

Therefore, the first order of business is to learn just what kind of soil you *do* have. The way to do this is to have your soil tested. In some states, the county Cooperative Extension office will do soil tests; in others, it's necessary to use the services of a private testing lab.

To obtain a representative sample of the soil in your flower bed, take a tablespoonful from each end of the bed and another from somewhere in the middle. Dig 4 to 6 inches down before taking each sample. Mix all of the samples together thoroughly in a single container. Then hand carry or mail the mixture to those doing the testing.

You'll want a complete soil test. One part will be a pH test that reads for acidity or alkalinity. A pH test result between 6.0 and 7.0 is ideal and requires no adjustment. A result below 6.0 indicates the soil is too acid. Ground limestone should be added to correct this problem. If the reading is over 7.2, the soil is too alkaline. To solve this problem, add powdered sulphur or, for quicker results, iron sulfate.

In addition to pH, you'll receive information about the nutrients in your soil. If there is a deficiency in any of these, you'll need to add the missing elements as recommended in the report. A third result will tell you the percentage of organic materials contained in your soil; this information will help you decide whether or not you need to supplement your soil with additional organic matter. (Further details on fertilizing and improving garden soil can be found in "Preparing the Soil," page 74.)

Some homesites have so little soil or the soil is so poor that it cannot—or should not—be used at all. One solution in these situations is to build raised beds and fill them with high-quality soil brought in from elsewhere. Such beds should be at least 6 inches deep to allow good root penetration. This may seem a costly solution in the short term, but the beds will last for years and prove well worth your initial investment.

Another solution, especially in a small area, is to garden entirely in containers. An imaginative approach, such as installing a deck or patio over the useless ground and then decorating it with container-grown plants, can transform a sad eyesore into an oasis. (You'll find more details on pages 126 to 129.)

Light is another important factor in gardening. How much is there and for how many hours each day? In other words, does the area where you want to grow your flowers have full sun, partial shade, or full shade?

At least to some extent, the amount of light the flower bed receives will dictate the plant species you'll be able to grow. Those plants that love full sun may become leggy and produce very few flowers if they're planted in a shady spot. By the same token, some plants are sensitive to too much light and will burn when placed in bright sunlight. Fortunately, there are annuals for all lighting conditions. Therefore, except for those places of deepest shade, there are many different annuals from which to choose.

Obtaining a Soil Sample

To obtain a good representative sample of garden soil for testing, dig down 4 to 6 inches below the surface in several different locations in the planting bed. Take a tablespoonful from each hole. Mix all of the samples together thoroughly to make one single large sample. Then hand carry or mail this single sample to the testing lab for analysis. Soil samples can be taken in the fall if you want to add slow-acting pH adjusters during the fall or winter months.

Gardening with Raised Beds

Raised beds are a good choice where soil is either of particularly poor quality or nonexistent. Constructed of pressure-treated wood, reinforced concrete, or mortared brick, stone, or blocks, these beds can be of any length, but should have a soil depth of at least 6 inches. For easy maintenance, beds should be no wider than 4 feet. By filling some beds with a rich loam mixture and others with a more sandy, well-drained mix, it's possible to provide the ideal soil requirements for a wide range of plants.

Color/Form/ Texture/Scale

A very dramatic effect can be created by combining different-colored flowers in various forms with foliage of varied texture.

Annual plantings will have more impact if, as part of the planning process, you consider *all* that each variety has to offer. Frequently, we only think about the color of the flowers annuals produce: Will a pale pink petunia look best beside blue ageratum, or would a bright pink be better?

Color *is* an important factor, but many plants have even more to offer. They may have both colorful blooms *and* foliage of an unusual texture or color: bold-leaved geraniums and nasturtiums; heart-shaped morning glory and moon vine foliage; purple-red cockscomb leaves; feathery cosmos and baby's breath.

Or they may be grown primarily, or even exclusively, for their foliage. Outstanding examples are silvery gray dusty miller, rich purple basil and perilla, and the myriad colors of coleus. Finally, there are those annuals primarily treasured for their seedpods. This group includes decorative peppers, ornamental eggplants, and purple-beaned dolichos.

We see, then, that color comes not only from bloom. It can come from foliage and seedpods as well. The same is true of texture, or surface. Most often we think of foliage as the sole textural source, when in fact texture can be added equally often by flowers themselves.

Besides color and texture, form of both flowers and of the overall growth habit of the plant needs to be considered. Flower forms include tall spikes, round globes, sprays, and clusters. Plant forms range from tall and skinny to low and spreading.

In addition, scale (the size of the plant) also must be kept in mind. Miniature plants are great to use in small spaces and where people are close enough to see them, but in a large area, they can become completely lost. On the other hand, large growing plants such as cleomes, cosmos, and nasturtiums may dominate and even smother out smaller neighbors when space is limited.

When selecting plants to be combined in a garden, all of these factors should be taken into consideration at the time of planning. The design will be more effective if a pleasing mixture of contrasting textures, colors, and plant and flower forms is used.

Learn to look for the bonus a plant may offer. Try to discover the best plant for a given location, rather than settling for one that happens to be readily available. Above all, don't worry about making a bad choice. The beauty of annuals is that you get another chance every growing season!

58

The Varied Characteristics of Annuals

Flowers are not the sole source of color in annual gardens. Many plants such as this dramatic purple perilla and more muted silver-gray dusty miller are treasured for their foliage alone. Others such as cockscombs have both colorful foliage *and* flowers. Still others—ornamental peppers, corn, and castor beans, for instance—provide garden color with their attractive fruits.

Variety of scale can be provided by both flowers and plants. Here, a large, wide-spreading cosmos and compact calliopsis provide similar flowers on very different-sized plants. Other species, zinnias, for example, offer a wide range of flower sizes and forms on plants that are all very much alike in form and size. Make use of this full range of flower and plant size to provide interest in your garden.

The broad, velvety leaves of this nicotiana, as well as its tall spikes of trumpet-shaped flowers, are a complete contrast in form to the low-spreading impatiens. A garden is more visually stimulating when a variety of forms are used.

This cloud of baby's breath illustrates the role that texture can play in a garden. A flower bed planted exclusively with such open, airy plants would appear to be a floating mist. By contrast, a bed planted entirely with bold, massive plants such as these marigolds would be heavy and solid-looking. Mixing plants of differing textures provides a pleasant variety and balance.

Massing Colors

Plumed cockscomb in bold colors of red and yellow give this massed garden a dramatic tone.

The easiest, most straightforward way to use annuals is to select one favorite and flood the entire planting area with it. This approach eliminates deciding where to plant a particular variety, selecting colors and textures that blend together effectively, or learning the cultural requirements for more than one kind of plant. It can be a money-saving solution as well: You only need to purchase one or two packets of seed to obtain enough plants to fill an entire planting area.

Certainly, the impact of all one kind and color of bloom can be very dramatic. Imagine an entire garden awash with fiery red geraniums or bold, yellow marigolds; fluorescent-pink fibrous begonias, or cooling white petunias!

Variations of this approach are also possible. For those who prefer variety of color, but all the same kind of plant, a checkerboard design would allow the use of large clumps of several different colors in a single species. The lipstick shades of impatiens work well in this kind of massing. Geraniums would, too.

Alternatively, some species come in an abundant variety of flower and plant sizes. A bed filled with zinnias, for example, could include everything from dwarf 10- to 12-inch mounds in front to giant 3- to 4-foot tall background clumps, with a wide range of flower colors and sizes in double, single, and spider forms. Marigolds are another species that grow in great variety, all of which are extremely vigorous and foolproof.

Another way to mass annuals is to keep to a single color but use several different plant varieties. The resulting garden would contain plants of different forms and heights with a variety of different flower shapes, all in varying shades of one color. A unique option for this style of massing would be a silver-gray garden!

Whichever design option is selected, massed plantings are generally rather formal looking—bold and dramatic rather than homey or quaint. They're the perfect complement to a large or formal house. Massing can also provide a clean, uncluttered look where garden space is severely limited.

For something simple, something easy, something different, consider the massed approach. Using annuals for this purpose allows the added option of changing the entire look of your yard every growing season simply by selecting a different plant or color. However, if that's too much bother, you can always repeat the same theme year after year.

GOOD CHOICES FOR MASSED PLANTINGS

Globe Amaranth	Marigold
Fibrous Begonia	Ornamental Kale
Canna	Ornamental Pepper
Chrysanthemum	Petunia
Cleome	Pocketbook Plant
Cockscomb	Red Salvia
Coleus	Snapdragon
Dusty Miller	Zinnia
Geranium	

Simple Massed Layout

This simple massed garden layout uses bedding geraniums in several varieties. All of the bed sections are the same size. Note that white varieties have been used as buffers between flower shades that might possibly clash. This garden is full of color all at one height.

	15'					
Orbit Apple Blossom	Orbit Violet	Sprinter White	Orbit Cherry	Hollywood Star	Orbit White	Elite Salmon

3'

Elaborate Massed Layout

Here is a more elaborate massed layout for the same garden bed, using the same geranium varieties. Two standard or tree geraniums have been added as focal points that will stand above the rest of the flowers in the bed. Potted plants on pedestals could be substituted for the tree geraniums. Other possible substitutes include a pair of dwarf columnar evergreens, small boxwood bushes, or clumps of tall, decorative grasses.

Tree Geranium   15'   Tree Geranium

Sprinter White	Elite Salmon	Orbit Cherry	Elite Salmon	Sprinter White
Orbit Violet	Orbit Apple Blossom	Orbit White	Orbit Apple Blossom	Orbit Violet

3'

Gardening in a Single Color

This all-yellow garden plan utilizes many different annuals. A variety of plant and flower forms, as well as different plant heights, adds interest to this planting. As the color-coding shows, the tallest varieties are located in the center back of the bed and the low-growing varieties at the front, with intermediate heights filling in between. As a result, none of the plants will be hidden from view.

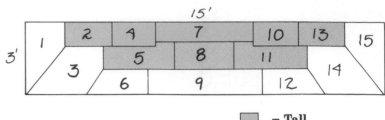

☐ = Tall

☐ = Intermediate

☐ = Low

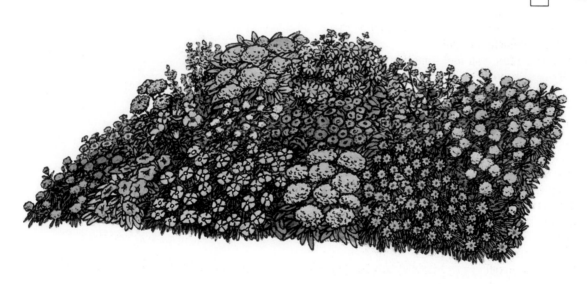

All Yellow Garden:

1 Pot Marigold
Yellow

2 Zinnia
Yellow Zenith

3 Marigold
Gold Lady

4 Snapdragon
Golden Rocket

5 California Poppy
Sunlite

6 Petunia
California Girl

7 Crested Cockscomb
Yellow

8 Marigold
Yellow Fireworks

9 Marigold
Signet Lemon Gem

10 Dahlia
Sunny Yellow

11 Feverfew
Gold Ball

12 Crested Cockscomb
Yellow

13 Nasturtium
Golden

14 Cosmos
Sunny Yellow

15 Marigold
Yellow Nugget

Mingling Annuals with Other Plantings

Just take a look at this glorious garden of candytuft, cosmos, China pinks, and perennials.

Although annuals make a splendid display on their own, they also combine effectively with other plants. Any dull spot can be brightened almost immediately with the addition of a few colorful annuals.

If, as you look at your garden, you feel something is lacking, see if you can identify one or more areas where accents of color would improve it. For example, although shrub borders are flower-filled in spring and early summer, they often provide only a few blooms the rest of the season. In many gardens, shrub plantings provide no summer color at all. It's amazing how much more attractive such an area becomes when just a few groupings of annuals are inserted. It's not necessary to plant a large bed in front of the entire length of the shrub border. Several strategically located accent clumps are usually all that is needed.

Annuals can also provide the perfect midsummer boost a perennial border may need. Plant them in the spaces where spring bulbs and some perennials are dying back, or where early flowering biennials such as foxgloves and English daisies have been removed—anyplace an empty spot occurs.

If a perennial bed is so packed that there is no free space in which to plant annuals, consider another approach: Place pots or boxes of annuals on small outdoor tables or stools. Tuck these display stands here and there in the border. Or, if there is a fence or wall behind the border, use it as a support from which to hang half-baskets or window boxes full of flowering annuals.

Another good place to add annuals is in the vegetable patch. Not only will they enliven an area not normally expected to be colorful, they'll also provide an excellent source of cut flowers to bring indoors. Because the vegetable garden is not usually a display area, every flower can be picked if desired.

Plantings combining annuals with vegetables can be laid out in various ways. One approach would be to plant annuals around the outer edges of the garden, hiding or disguising the vegetable patch. Another alternative would be to plant rows of annuals here and there among the vegetables. Finally, a handsome combination design, especially where the total garden space is limited, would be a very formal geometric garden, laid out with some of the beds planted with annuals and others with vegetables. The final choice, of course, depends on your personal preferences as well as on the dictates of your garden site.

HANDSOME FOLIAGE AND FRUIT	
Globe Amaranth	Dusty Miller
Alternanthera	Moses-in-a-Boat
Asparagus Fern	Nasturtium
Basil	Ornamental Corn
Rex Begonia	Ornamental Kale
Blood Leaf	Ornamental Pepper
Burning Bush	Perilla
Caladium	Polka-Dot Plant
Castor Bean	Purple Heart
Cockscomb	Scarlet Runner Bean
Coleus	Snow-in-Summer
Dracaena	

Livening up a Shrub Border

Most shrub borders have few blooms, if any, during the summer months. To liven up what is normally a dull area, add a few sweeps of colorful annuals, using the shrub border as a backdrop. This plan shows the way informal groupings can be inserted. Either plants of one kind and color or several different kinds of plants can be used. In the latter case, taller varieties should be located as indicated by the red-shaded areas.

▨ = Low-growing annuals

▨ = Tall annual varieties

Annuals in a Perennials Border

This plan shows part of a perennial border, indicating where each grouping of perennials, biennials (plants that have a two-year life cycle, blooming and dying their second year), and bulbs is planted. Areas shaded in gray indicate sections that will be in bloom in spring months.

1" = 2'

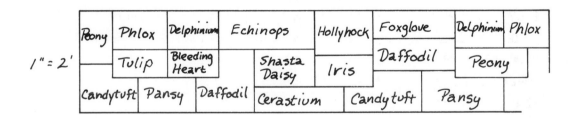

This overlay of the above plan shows how annuals can add color in those sections of the perennial border where bulbs and early spring flowering biennials have died back or have been removed (shaded in gray). Red-shaded areas indicate where perennials will provide summer bloom. Note: When bedding plants are planted in bulb areas, care must be taken to place them between—rather than directly on top of—the bulbs in order to avoid damaging the bulbs while digging.

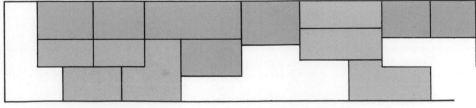

Selecting Annuals for Color & Characteristics

An eye-catching garden can be achieved by combining annuals of different colors and sizes.

Planting annuals can be as simple as selecting one favorite flower and flooding an entire planting area with it. When using this approach, you don't need to decide where to plant a particular variety; you don't need to be concerned about selecting colors and textures that blend well together; and there's no need to learn the cultural requirements for more than one kind of plant.

Most people, however, prefer to mix different annuals varieties in their gardens, even though it requires a bit more work and planning. Available colors, height of plants, shade or sun preference, soil requirements—all of these factors have to be taken into consideration.

Planning an annuals garden in advance is the only way to make sure that an annuals bed is color balanced and that the plants work well together in terms of sun or shade, height, and soil.

If you list your favorite plants on paper first, noting their available colors and cultural requirements, you're off to a good start. As you narrow down those that work well together, you can actually see a workable garden emerge in front of you. By taking this extra bit of time, you can save yourself from being disappointed later.

The charts that follow are a quick reference for selecting plants for your garden. However, it should be kept in mind that they give only a simplistic first screening. When scanning these lists, you may find many plants that seem appropriate for your garden. However, on further investigation, you'll find that some of them aren't appropriate after all. Use the charts to narrow down the choices; then refer to the more detailed description in the "Encyclopedia of Annual Delights" starting on page 136, to identify those best-suited to your climate, soil, and light conditions.

These charts are very easy to use since they identify plants by color range (in most instances by flower color). However, those marked with an asterisk (*) and the "Grasses and Foliage" category have colorful foliage, fruits, or seedpods instead.

It's important to remember that the "Multicolor" category lists those plants that come in nearly every color range (any annual that comes in more than three color ranges has been put into this category). Because it contains the most universal and versatile annuals, be sure to use it often when making your selections.

Whether you are a novice or a gardener with many years of planting experience, using a chart with information on color, light, soil, and height can be the difference between a picture-perfect garden and one that just doesn't quite work.

MULTICOLOR

	Dry Soil	Average Soil	Moist Soil	Full Sun	Part Shade	Full Shade	Under 12 Inches	12–24 Inches	Over 24 Inches	Vining
Alternanthera	•	•		•		•				
Amaranth, Globe	•	•		•			•			
Begonia, Fibrous		•		•	•	•	•			
Begonia, Tuberous*		•	•		•	•	•			
Candytuft	•	•		•		•				
Chrysanthemum		•		•			•	•	•	
Coleus			•		•	•	•			
Cosmos		•		•				•	•	
Dahlia		•	•	•				•	•	
Daisy, African (Arctotis)	•			•			•			
Daisy, Livingstone	•	•		•		•				
Daisy, Swan River		•		•			•	•		
Daisy, Transvaal		•	•	•			•	•		
Everlastings	•	•		•		•				
Four O'Clock	•	•		•	•			•	•	
Foxglove			•	•	•	•			•	
Gazania	•			•			•	•		
Geranium, Ivy-Leaf		•		•		•	•	•	•	
Geranium, Other			•	•			•			
Geranium, Zonal			•	•			•			
Gladiolus		•		•			•	•	•	
Godetia (Clarkia)	•			•	•		•	•	•	
Hollyhock		•	•	•					•	
Impatiens		•	•		•	•	•	•		
Impatiens, New Guinea		•	•	•			•			
Lupine			•	•					•	
Marigold, Cape	•			•		•				
Nemesia		•		•	•		•			
Nicotiana		•	•	•	•			•	•	
Pansy		•	•	•	•		•			
Petunia		•		•				•		
Phlox		•		•		•	•			
Portulaca	•			•		•				
Primrose		•	•		•		•			
Salpiglossis		•	•	•				•		
Schizanthus		•	•	•				•		
Snapdragon		•		•			•	•	•	
Sweet Pea		•					•	•		•
Toadflax	•			•		•				
Verbena	•	•		•		•				
Zinnia		•		•			•	•	•	

BLUE TO PURPLE

	Dry Soil	Average Soil	Moist Soil	Full Sun	Part Shade	Full Shade	Under 12 Inches	12–24 Inches	Over 24 Inches	Vining
Alyssum, Sweet	•	•		•		•				
Aster		•		•		•	•	•		
Baby Blue Eyes	•	•		•	•		•			
Bachelor's Button		•	•	•				•	•	
Beard Tongue		•		•			•			
Blue Bells, California	•			•		•				
Blue Lace Flower		•		•					•	
Blue Marguerite		•	•	•	•		•			
Canterbury Bells		•		•	•			•		
Chilean Bell Flower	•			•		•				
Cup and Saucer Vine			•	•						•
Echium		•	•	•			•	•		
Floss Flower		•		•		•				
Forget-Me-Not		•	•	•	•					
Forget-Me-Not, Chinese		•		•	•		•			
Forget-Me-Not, Summer		•		•	•		•			
Fuchsia		•	•		•		•			
Heliotrope		•		•			•			
Lantana	•	•		•		•	•			
Larkspur		•		•				•	•	
Lisianthus		•	•	•				•	•	
Lobelia		•	•	•		•	•			
Love-in-a-Mist		•	•	•			•			
Morning Glory Vine	•	•		•						•
Moses-in-a-Boat*		•		•	•		•			
Nierembergia			•	•			•			
None So Pretty		•		•			•			
Perilla*	•	•		•					•	
Purple Heart		•		•	•		•			
Salvia		•		•	•	•	•	•		
Sapphire Flower		•		•	•		•			
Scabiosa		•		•			•	•		
Scarlet Flax	•	•		•		•				
Scarlet Pimpernel	•	•		•		•				
Southern Star		•		•			•			
Stock		•	•	•			•	•		
Torenia		•	•		•	•	•			
Violet, Persian			•		•		•			

* = foliage or fruits/pods this color
** = bulb

RED

Plant	Dry Soil	Average Soil	Moist Soil	Full Sun	Part Shade	Full Shade	Under 12 Inches	12–24 Inches	Over 24 Inches	Vining
Abelmoschus		•	•	•				•		
Blanket Flower	•			•				•		
Blood Leaf*		•	•	•	•		•	•		
Calliopsis	•	•		•				•		
Canna**		•	•	•					•	
China Pink	•	•		•			•			
Cockscomb		•		•			•	•	•	
Daisy, English		•	•	•	•		•			
Firecracker Plant		•		•			•			
Hibiscus, Chinese			•	•					•	
Joseph's Coat*	•	•		•					•	
Lantana	•	•		•			•	•	•	
Lotus Vine		•		•					•	
Flowering Maple			•	•	•		•			
Marigold, Pot		•		•			•	•		
Monkey Flower			•		•	•				
Nasturtium	•	•		•			•			•
Ornamental Pepper*		•		•			•	•	•	
Poppy, Iceland		•		•			•			
Salvia		•		•	•		•	•	•	
Scarlet Flax	•	•		•			•			
Scarlet Pimpernel	•	•		•			•			
Scarlet Runner Bean		•		•						•
Stock		•		•				•	•	
Vinca		•	•	•				•	•	
Wallflower, English	•	•		•	•			•	•	

PINK TO FUCHSIA

Plant	Dry Soil	Average Soil	Moist Soil	Full Sun	Part Shade	Full Shade	Under 12 Inches	12–24 Inches	Over 24 Inches	Vining
Abelmoschus		•	•	•				•		
Alyssum, Sweet	•	•		•		•				
Aster		•	•	•			•	•	•	
Baby's Breath		•		•			•			
Bachelor's Button		•	•	•			•	•		
Beard Tongue		•		•	•		•			
Caladium* **			•		•	•	•			
Calla**		•	•	•			•	•		
Canna**		•	•	•					•	
Canterbury Bells		•		•	•				•	
China Pink	•	•				•				
Cleome		•		•					•	
Cockscomb		•		•			•	•	•	
Corn Cockle		•		•					•	
Daisy, English		•	•	•	•		•			
Echium		•	•	•			•	•		
Forget-Me-Not		•	•	•	•		•			
Forget-Me-Not, Chinese		•		•	•		•			
Forget-Me-Not, Summer		•		•	•		•			
Fuchsia		•	•		•		•			
Hibiscus, Chinese			•	•					•	
Lantana	•	•		•			•	•	•	
Larkspur		•		•				•	•	
Lisianthus		•	•	•				•	•	
Lobelia		•	•	•	•		•			
Love-in-a-Mist		•	•	•			•			
Magic Carpet Plant		•		•	•		•			
Mallow		•		•					•	
Monkey Flower			•		•		•			
Morning Glory Vine	•	•		•						•
None So Pretty		•		•			•			
Ornamental Cabbage, Kale*		•		•			•			
Poppy, Iceland		•		•			•	•		
Rose Mallow	•	•		•					•	
Scarlet Flax	•	•		•			•			
Scotch Thistle		•		•					•	
Stock		•	•	•				•	•	
Torenia		•	•		•	•	•			
Vinca		•	•	•		•	•			
Violet, Persian			•		•	•	•			

These cultural recommendations are intended to suggest the average conditions over a wide geographical area. It is important to be aware of local requirements.

YELLOW TO ORANGE

	Dry Soil	Average Soil	Moist Soil	Full Sun	Part Shade	Full Shade	Under 12 Inches	12–24 Inches	Over 24 Inches	Vining
Black-Eyed Susan	●	●		●				●	●	
Blanket Flower	●			●				●		
Calla**			●	●	●			●	●	
Calliopsis	●	●		●				●		
Canna**		●	●	●					●	
Cockscomb		●		●			●	●	●	
Daisy, African (Golden Ageratum)	●			●				●		
Daisy, Dahlberg	●			●				●		
Hibiscus, Chinese			●	●					●	
Joseph's Coat*	●	●		●					●	
Lantana	●	●		●			●	●	●	
Flowering Maple			●	●	●			●		
Marigold, American			●	●				●	●	
Marigold, French			●	●				●		
Marigold, Pot		●		●			●	●		
Meadow Foam			●	●				●		
Melampodium		●		●				●		
Monkey Flower			●	●		●		●		
Nasturtium	●	●		●				●		●
Ornamental Pepper*		●		●			●	●	●	
Pocketbook Plant			●		●			●		
Poppy, California	●			●				●		
Poppy, Horned	●			●				●		
Poppy, Mexican Tulip	●			●				●		
Sanvitalia	●	●		●	●			●		
Scarlet Pimpernel	●	●		●				●		
Sundrop		●		●				●	●	
Sunflower		●		●					●	
Thunbergia		●		●						●
Tidy Tips	●			●			●	●		
Tithonia	●	●		●					●	
Venidium	●			●				●		
Wallflower, English	●	●		●	●		●	●		

GRASSES & FOLIAGE

	Dry Soil	Average Soil	Moist Soil	Full Sun	Part Shade	Full Shade	Under 12 Inches	12–24 Inches	Over 24 Inches	Vining
Alternanthera	●	●		●		●				
Amaranth, Globe	●	●		●					●	
Asparagus Fern		●		●	●			●		
Basil	●			●				●		
Begonia, Tuberous		●	●		●	●		●		
Burning Bush	●	●		●				●		
Caladium**			●		●	●		●		
Castor Bean		●	●	●					●	
Cloud Grass	●	●		●			●			
Coleus		●	●		●	●		●		
Dracaena		●		●	●			●		
Dusty Miller	●	●		●			●	●		
Geranium, Ivy-Leaf		●		●	●				●	
Geranium, Other			●	●				●		
Geranium, Zonal			●	●				●		
Golden Top	●	●		●			●			
Impatiens, New Guinea		●	●	●				●		
Job's Tears	●	●		●					●	
Gourds		●		●						●
Love-in-a-Mist		●	●	●				●	●	
Moses-in-a-Boat		●		●	●		●			
Ornamental Cabbage, Kale		●		●				●		
Ornamental Corn		●	●	●					●	
Ornamental Peppers		●		●			●	●		
Perilla	●	●		●				●		
Polka Dot Plant		●			●			●	●	
Quaking Grass	●	●		●			●			
Snow-in-Summer	●	●	●	●				●		
Wheat Grass	●	●		●					●	
Wild Oats		●		●				●		

* = foliage or fruits/pods this color
** = bulb

WHITE TO GREEN

	Dry Soil	Average Soil	Moist Soil	Full Sun	Part Shade	Full Shade	Under 12 Inches	12–24 Inches	Over 24 Inches	Vining
Alyssum, Sweet	●	●		●		●	●			
Angel's Trumpet		●	●	●					●	
Aster		●		●		●	●	●		
Baby's Breath		●		●			●			
Bachelor's Button		●	●	●			●	●		
Beard Tongue		●		●	●		●			
Bells of Ireland*		●	●	●	●		●			
Caladium* **			●		●	●	●			
Calla**			●	●	●			●	●	
Canterbury Bells		●		●	●		●			
Sweet False Chamomile		●		●			●			
China Pink	●	●		●		●				
Cleome		●		●			●			
Cup and Saucer Vine			●	●						●
Daisy, English		●	●	●	●		●			
Floss Flower		●		●	●		●			
Forget-Me-Not		●	●	●	●		●			
Forget-Me-Not, Chinese		●		●	●		●			
Forget-Me-Not, Summer		●		●			●			
Hibiscus, Chinese			●	●					●	
Larkspur		●		●				●	●	
Lisianthus		●	●	●				●	●	
Lobelia		●	●	●	●		●			
Love-in-a-Mist		●	●	●			●			
Flowering Maple			●	●	●		●			
Marigold, American			●	●			●	●		
Marigold, Pot		●		●			●	●		
Mignonette		●	●	●	●		●			
Morning Glory Vine	●	●		●						●
Ornamental Cabbage, Kale*		●		●			●			
Poppy, Iceland		●		●			●			
Rose Mallow	●	●		●					●	
Salvia		●		●	●		●	●	●	
Sapphire Flower		●		●	●		●			
Scabiosa		●		●				●	●	

WHITE TO GREEN

	Dry Soil	Average Soil	Moist Soil	Full Sun	Part Shade	Full Shade	Under 12 Inches	12–24 Inches	Over 24 Inches	Vining
Snow-in-Summer*	●	●	●	●				●		
Stock		●	●	●				●	●	
Torenia		●	●		●	●	●			
Tuberose		●		●					●	
Venidium	●			●					●	
Vinca		●	●	●				●	●	
Violet, Persian			●		●				●	
Wallflower, English	●	●		●	●		●	●		

These cultural recommendations are intended to suggest the average conditions over a wide geographical area. It is important to be aware of local requirements.

This waterside annuals border is filled with flowers in various shades of red and pink. Interspersed with foliage and surrounded by trees, this is truly an annuals oasis. Surprisingly little work is needed to create such beauty.

CHAPTER 2

SECRETS TO SUCCESSFUL ANNUALS GARDENING

Many annuals are easy to start from seed, either indoors or directly in the garden. However, if they're given the extra boost of the best possible growing conditions, they're bound to thrive and bloom more abundantly than they would under less ideal circumstances. This chapter focuses on proper soil preparation, the supplies and tools needed to achieve good results, and selection and care of boxed bedding plants. Also included is information on starting seeds indoors and their planting in outdoor beds.

Included are tips on collecting seeds from your own plants for use the following season, along with information about why propagation from seeds works for some varieties and not for others. A list of those plants for which home seed collection is appropriate is an added feature. Similarly, you'll learn which annuals can readily be propagated from cuttings, as well as how to take cuttings, root them, and plant them out (transplant them outdoors).

For those who have the time and interest, starting your own plants from seeds and cuttings can be fun. For those who need quicker results, or don't have time to start their own plants, buying boxed plants is the perfect solution. Whatever your needs, there's much information here to help you grow annuals successfully.

Tools for Gardening Projects

I n any enterprise, the proper tools make the work much easier to accomplish. You don't necessarily need a large array of tools to garden successfully. The basic hand tools needed for annuals (as well as perennials; see the "Perennials" section, page 190, for more information on perennials) are: a hand trowel, a cultivator, a spading fork, a square-ended spade, an iron bow rake, a narrow-bladed hoe, a pair of small pruning shears, and a narrow-bladed paring knife or jackknife. Several additional tools worth considering are a hoe with a small blade that will fit into narrow spaces, a scuffle hoe, and a sprayer. Another piece of equipment that's handy, but not essential, is a large-wheeled garden cart for hauling. When selecting tools, it's worthwhile to invest in good quality at the outset. Buying cheap tools is false economy. Not only do they make the work harder to do, they're very likely to break as soon as stress is exerted on them. Thus, you save money by paying a higher price for one shovel every ten years than buying two or three at a slightly lower price over that same period.

At the same time, remember that higher price does not automatically *guarantee* higher quality. Check to see if the manufacturer provides a long-term or lifetime guarantee on the product. Willingness to stand behind a product is a good indication that the producer is conscientiously trying to make a well-made tool.

Carefully study the construction of several different brands of each tool you're buying to see which are most solidly built. Details to look for include wooden handles made of hickory or ash with the grain running straight along the full length of the handle; the metal portion fitted and securely attached to the wood portion—avoid those where a single rivet holds the entire tool together; a rolled edge along the top of the blade to allow more pushing surface for your foot; blade shanks that are reinforced rather than of a single thickness; and blade shanks extended along the wooden handle for added strength.

Consult garden center employees. Ask them to point out the comparative advantages and disadvantages of each brand they carry. Confer with experienced gardening friends about which features they've found to be important.

In addition to the basic tools listed here, many other garden tools and gadgets are available. Invest in them only after you own the basics and gain quite a bit of hands-on gardening expe-

Few tools are needed to successfully grow garden plants.

rience. Over time, you may conclude that some of these specialty tools would make your work easier; more often than not, you'll find that the basic tools you have already do the job satisfactorily. Buy others only as you experience a need for them.

Keep tools in top condition by storing them carefully in an area protected from the weather. Remove dirt and mud after each use, wiping the metal parts with a lightly oiled cloth. Periodically sharpen the blades on shovels and hoes, as well as on knives and shears. Hanging tools for storage helps keep blades sharp longer, while also cutting down on storage area clutter.

Treat your tools well, and they'll give you many years of fine service.

Necessary Garden Tools

Illustrated here are the basic tools and gardening equipment. Start with these, adding others only if you find you need them. Items such as a garden cart, for example, may prove useful, but certainly are not essential.

Trowel

Rake   **Spade**   **Fork**   **Hoe**   **Cultivator**

Preparing the Soil

The fruit of your labors—a tiny hibiscus seedling grows.

As was mentioned in the section on soil and light on page 56, characteristics vary widely. Naturally, then, there's also wide variation in the ways to amend and improve soil to achieve the best possible growing conditions.

If the results of your soil test indicate a lack of certain nutrients, you should follow the recommendations made by the testing company for supplementing the soil. If the imbalance is slight, organic fertilizers can be used. Because they generally contain a low percentage of nutrients that are slowly released into the soil, organic fertilizers are inadequate when fast results are needed, or if the imbalance of nutrients is great. In these situations, inorganic fertilizers are the better choice. A combination of both kinds may be a good compromise solution, using the quick-to-feed commercial plant foods first, then following up in subsequent years with the slow-feeding organic fertilizers.

Chemical fertilizer is commonly formulated in some combination of the three major nutrients: nitrogen, phosphorous, and potassium—N, P, K. The numbers featured on each bag represent the percentage of each of these nutrients in the mix. For example, 5-10-5 contains 5 percent nitrogen (N), 10 percent phosphorous (P), and 5 percent potassium (K). 10-10-10 contains 10 percent of each. The NPK formula is also listed on each container of organic fertilizer. The percentages of each nutrient are lower in organic fertilizers than in inorganic fertilizers. Therefore, larger amounts of organic plant food are required to achieve the same results.

It's also possible to purchase fertilizers separately rather than in a three-nutrient mix. These are useful when there's a deficiency in a single nutrient. Consult with your Cooperative Extension office or garden center staff if you feel uncertain about solving nutrient deficiency problems.

Adjusting the nutrient and pH levels in your soil will not make any difference in its *consistency*. To improve soil texture will require the addition of one or several "soil conditioners." The most commonly used conditioners are leaf mold, compost, well-rotted cow manure, and peat moss. Vermiculite, perlite, and sand (coarse builder's sand, *never* use beach sand) can also be added, especially when the basic soil is heavy.

To properly prepare a planting bed, first remove any sod from the area, then rototill or hand dig the soil, turning it over thoroughly. (Rototillers can be rented by the day, and it's often possible to hire someone to come and till by the hour, if you don't have a tiller of your own.)

If the area is rocky, remove as many stones as possible as you till. Next, spread the necessary fertilizer, soil conditioners, and pH-adjusting chemicals over the area. Till again. You should be able to till more deeply the second time; ideally, you want to loosen and improve the soil to a depth of more than 6 inches. Turn and loosen soil by hand with a spade where the area is too small to require a rototiller. After this inital treatment, fertilizers, soil conditioners, and pH-adjusting chemicals will be added at different times of the year for best results.

If possible, allow the soil to stand unplanted for a week or more. Stir the surface inch or two every three to four days with a scuffle hoe or cultivator to eradicate fast-germinating weed seeds. This will make your weeding chores lighter during the rest of the season.

Now is the perfect time to install some kind of mowing strip around the garden bed. Patio squares or slate pieces laid end-to-end at ground level will keep grass and flowers from intermixing. Other options include landscape logs, poured concrete strips, or bricks laid side-by-side on a sand or concrete base. The mowing strip must be deep and wide enough so grass roots cannot tunnel underneath or travel across the top to reach the flower bed, and the top of the strip must not extend above the level of the adjacent lawn.

Planting Preparations

1 Mark the flower bed boundaries with pegs and string for straight edges and with a garden hose for curved lines. Cut through the sod along laid-out lines with a spade. Remove the sod from the entire bed. Till the area, removing rocks as you proceed. For a small planting area, dig and break up the soil by hand or with a spade.

2 Spread well-rotted manure, compost, or leaf mold onto the bed to provide organic matter and improve soil quality. If other soil conditioners are needed, perlite, sand, and moistened peat moss should be added at this time.

3 Rototill or hand dig the bed deeply a second time to thoroughly incorporate these additions. This second digging will allow the tiller to loosen soil to a greater depth than could be achieved by tilling only once.

4 To keep the grass out of the flower bed and the annuals from overflowing onto the lawn, install an edging strip around the bed. This strip should be at least 2 inches deep and 6 inches wide. The top of the strip should be at ground level to allow the wheel of the lawnmower to run along it. Installation of an edging strip will save many hours of maintenance effort each year.

Bedding Plants by the Boxful

Boxed bedding impatiens are ready for your garden.

For those who want to have an almost instant show of annual bloom, boxed bedding plants are the answer. Every garden center and nursery, many roadside stands, and quite a few grocery and discount stores offer a selection of prestarted annuals. The main drawback to purchasing boxed bedding plants is the limited selection. There are many annuals that are unavailable from any commercial sources. A gardener who wants them will have to start them at home. Also, if large numbers of plants are needed, the cost of boxed plants can be prohibitive.

In these instances, or just for the pleasure of it, you may want to start your own bedding plants. It's quite possible for any gardener to succeed with only a small initial investment in equipment and supplies.

Light—The most essential ingredient for successful seed starting is adequate light. It's possible to start seeds on the sill of a sun-filled window, but plants often stretch out toward the light source and become leggy. A three-sided white or silver reflector shield set up behind the plant trays will reflect light back onto the plants to help combat this problem.

Where there is not enough light available naturally, an easy alternative is to raise seedlings under fluorescent growlamps. To provide maximum light from all sides, surround the area under the lights with a white or silver-painted reflector.

Heat—Along with light, another need is adequate heat. The bottom heat that warms the soil in which the seedlings are grown is very important. If the air temperature in the chosen growing area is colder than 70° F, bottom heat can be supplied by a heating cable installed under the growing medium.

Water—Water is a third requirement for plant growth. A rimmed watering tray will allow the seed trays and young plants to be watered from the bottom. Top watering can batter plants down, as well as increase the possibility of fungus problems.

The primary concern with bottom watering is overwatering. Water shouldn't continuously stand in the watering tray. Pour lukewarm water to a ¼ inch depth into the tray. Leave it for five to ten minutes. At the end of that time, observe how much water is left in the tray. Also, roll a small pinch of the planting soil between thumb and finger to test for moisture. What you want is soil that feels wet with very little or no water remaining in the tray.

Test the soil moisture once each day by rolling a small amount between your fingers. Water again when the soil feels more dry than wet. It's impossible to predict how many days will be needed between waterings. You'll be able to make a fairly accurate "guesstimate" of your own circumstances after a few weeks.

Soil—Planting soil for starting and growing young seedlings should be free of weeds and disease. This can be accomplished by sterilizing the planting mix. First, spread it in a thin layer on cookie sheets and bake at a low temperature (150 to 200° F) until it is completely dried out. Next, cool the soil and mix the water back into it until it's moist. Finally, pour the soil into sterile containers, allowing it to settle for a day before planting the seeds. A simpler approach is to purchase a specially formulated plant starter mix made up of inert materials. Fill the sterile containers with this mix, firm or tamp it lightly with your fingers, then sow the seeds.

Containers—Seeds can be started in a variety of containers: milk or egg cartons with holes punched in their bottoms or low on their sides, plastic or wooden boxes, clay or plastic pots, peat pots, or special seed starter cubes and trays are all equally acceptable. Virtually anything that will hold soil and allow easy passage of water through drainage holes in the bottom will work.

Containers designed to hold a single plant are the best choice for large plants, which tend to crowd each other out in six-packs; for plants that don't like to have their roots disturbed by transplanting; and for climbing vines. Most annuals do well in any container.

Equipment and Supplies for Starting Plants Indoors

1

The equipment needed for starting plants indoors includes:

1. A fluorescent light fixture with full-spectrum growlamp bulbs. Ideally, you should be able to easily raise and lower the fixture in order to maintain about 3 inches between the light bulbs and the plant tops at all times.

2. An automatic timer to turn the light fixture on and off each day is optional. However, it does take the worry out of trying to remember this twice-a-day chore. Since plants require between 16 to 18 hours of light daily, don't leave the lights on all of the time; darkness is also essential.

3. White or silver-colored reflectors placed around three, or all four, sides will bounce light onto plants from all angles. It will help keep them from leaning and stretching toward a single light source. A homemade reflector can be made of cardboard covered with aluminum foil.

4. If the seed starting setup is in a cool room, a thermostatically controlled heating cable should be laid under the seed boxes and pots. Bottom heat is more important than air temperature to encourage strong growth.

5. A drip tray allows watering of seedlings from the bottom. Water poured into the tray is absorbed upward into the soil.

Seed Sowing—Seeds can be sown individually in single pots. Plant two seeds in each, removing the weaker of the two seedlings when they grow their first real leaves (the very first leaves to unfold from a new seedling are called the seed leaves; the second set of leaves is its first real leaves).

When sowing a packet of seeds in a box or larger pot, they can either be broadcast over the surface in a scatter pattern or be planted in rows. If only a few plants of each kind are wanted, rows make more sense; when larger numbers of plants are desired, broadcasting is faster. If the seeds are very small, don't cover them with additional planting mix after sowing; medium to large seeds should have a layer of planting mix sprinkled on top. Lightly press the surface of the planting mix after sowing.

Label—Be sure to label each planting in some way. The system doesn't matter as long as you have one.

Once the seeds are sown, water the seed trays from the bottom until the mix feels moist. Allow excess water to drip out of the container bottom before placing the container in your growing setup.

Lay two sheets of newspaper over each seed tray. For the first few days, this provides the semi-darkness some seeds prefer for germination. Inspect each seed tray closely every day. As soon as you see seedlings pushing through, remove the newspaper layer. Germination time varies widely. Ideally, you should start the slower growers earlier than those that germinate rapidly in order to have them all at the same stage when planting time arrives. Study the descriptions of each plant to know when to get each of them started.

Damping Off—Probably the worst enemy of successful seed starting is a problem known as "damping off." It strikes within two weeks of germination when seedlings are very young. When it hits, the plants simply lay down and die, usually in less than a day's time. Damping off is a fungus infection that can best be avoided by making certain that both the soil and containers in which seeds are planted are sterile. The seeds themselves can be lightly dusted with fungicide powder prior to planting as an additional precaution. Young seedlings should be looked at morning and evening to check for any sign of a problem. Even if only two or three plants have lain down, take the precaution of immediately spraying the plants with a fungicide or, if none is available, try a mild vinegar solution.

Food—Prepared starter mixes usually have plant nutrients in them that feed the seedlings. If you make your own homemade starter from milled sphagnum, vermiculite, or sterilized sand, you'll need to fertilize in some way. The easiest method is to add a soluble fertilizer at a very weak rate to the regular waterings. (For details on various organic and inorganic fertilizers, see "Feeding Alternatives," pages 100 to 101.)

Pricking Off—Other than those that were planted individually, all seedlings should be transplanted from the seed trays when the first true leaves appear. This first transplanting is usually referred to as "pricking off." At this stage, seedlings should be planted into small individual peat pots, planting cubes, or partitioned growing boxes. They will remain in these containers until planting time.

Fill the boxes with a good potting soil or commercial growing mix. To make your own soil, mix equal amounts of garden soil or sterilized potting soil, moistened peat moss, and perlite or coarse builder's sand. Gently lift out and separate the young plants, holding them by their seed leaves.

Place the seedling in the new container so the soil line will be at the same level on the stem as it was in the seed tray. Gently firm the soil around the plant roots, bringing it to within ¼ inch of the container rim. Water from the top with a weak fertilizer solution. Place these pricked-off plants back by the window or under growlamps to continue their growth.

Hardening Off—By this time, plants should be stocky and strong, but they will need some toughening up. This process is referred to as "hardening off." It'll keep the plants from suffering shock, or trauma, when they are planted outside.

Carry the plants outdoors each day for a few hours, bringing them back inside overnight. Shade them with an old window screen to protect them from strong light and wind. Start with two or three hours, then increase the length of time they're outside by an additional hour each day. After a week, they can be outdoors all day, and only need to be brought in at night.

Planting Out—At this point, the plants are ready to plant out into the garden bed. Those in individual peat pots can be dropped into planting holes, the soil firmed around the pot, an earth dam formed around the stem to form a water-holding area, and a weak fertilizer solution poured in.

Plants in multi-plant containers will need to be turned out of the container and separated before planting. Water the plants well before removing them. If the soil is moist, they'll slide out easily, subjecting the plants to less shock. Some roots are bound to be broken off in this process; pinching out the top growth on the plant will help keep the top and root areas in balance. This pinching will also encourage side shoots to push out, helping to form a fuller flowering plant.

Shading—If possible, do your transplanting on an overcast and still day to cut down on wilting. If you must plant on a sunny and/or windy day, cover the transplants with a protective shield for a day or two. There are commercial blankets made of a nonwoven material that will do this and can also be used at night to protect against light frosts. A do-it-yourself way to provide shading is to form newspaper sheets into cones and place one over each plant, anchoring the edges with soil.

Although starting your own boxed plants takes a bit of time and effort, it can be a very enjoyable activity. Best of all, you can have as many plants as you want of exactly the species and varieties you prefer.

2 Sowing Seeds

For a small number of seeds, plant two seeds per starting cube, then remove the weaker seedling when they grow their second true leaves. Or plant seeds in rows—one or two rows per variety—in a seed tray. For larger quantities, sprinkle a packet of seeds over the entire seed tray. *Be sure to label* each row or tray; otherwise, seedlings can be difficult to identify by sight.

3 Transplanting Seedlings

Except when planted in individual cubes, seedlings should be transplanted from seed starter trays when they grow their first set of true leaves. Hold a seed leaf (*never* hold by the stem at this stage) and lift the soil from underneath it with a fork or similar tool, gently removing the seedling. Insert it in a hole already poked in the soil of a six-pack or peat pot. The soil level on the plant stem should be the same in the new planter as it was in the seed tray. Firm the soil around the roots with your fingers. Water to firm the soil more. Plants remain in these containers until they're planted outdoors or into planters for the summer.

PLANTS TO START INDOORS

Globe Amaranth	Lisianthus
Asparagus Fern	Lobelia
Aster	Nicotiana
Fibrous Begonia	Ornamental Pepper
Tuberous Begonia	Pansy
Candytuft	Petunia
Cleome	Polka-Dot Plant
Coleus	Salpiglossis
Dahlia	Salvia
African Daisy	Sapphire Flower
Dahlberg Daisy	Snapdragon
Dracaena	Stock
Dusty Miller	Verbena
Floss Flower	Vinca
Geranium	Persian Violet
Impatiens	

(Note: Some plants will be found on both this list and the list of plants to sow directly in the garden. Either option will work; you may want to start those with short growing seasons indoors in order to enjoy the longest possible period of bloom.)

Water bedding plants just before transplanting them into garden beds or planters to ensure that they slip out and separate easily. Pinch out the center growth bud to encourage bushiness. Turn the plants out of the pack and divide by pulling gently apart. Avoid excess damage to tender roots. Place the plant in a hole at the same depth or slightly deeper than it was in the pack. Firm the soil around the root with your fingers. Form a shallow dam around the plant to hold water—this is especially helpful if a flower bed is on a slope. Fill each dam with water that contains a weak fertilizer solution. This will get rid of air pockets around the roots and provide food to encourage quick growth.

Selecting Quality Plants & Seeds

Healthy flats of colorful impatiens are available at most nurseries and garden centers.

Seeds and boxed bedding plants available in the United States are generally of high quality. Whether you make your purchases through a local greenhouse or nursery, a chain store, or a roadside stand, you'll usually find fresh, high-quality seeds and vigorous, insect- and disease-free plants. What's more, with very rare exceptions, these offerings can be relied upon to be correctly labeled.

Because of this consistently good quality, it's possible to buy plants wherever you find the best price on the variety you want. However, before buying, be sure that it really *is* the lowest price. That is, one retailer may sell a "box" for $1.25 and another sell a "box" of the same variety for only $1.00. But if the first box contains eight plants and the second contains six, the higher-priced box is the better buy.

When possible, purchase boxed plants early in the season, especially if the store you buy them from is not a nursery or garden shop. Too often, the plants arrive at the store in vigorous condition, but then are tended by personnel who know nothing about plants. As a result, watering is frequently haphazard and inadequate. Added to the problem is the fact that boxed plants are usually displayed in a hot and brightly sunlit outdoor location where the sun and wind dry them out. Unfortunately, each time the plants wilt down some of their strength is lost. Bedding plants that suffer from these conditions will be slow to recover when they're put in the garden.

If the last frost date isn't yet passed, or your planting bed isn't fully prepared, it still makes sense to buy plants when they first arrive at the retailer's. Bring them home where you can care for them properly until you can plant them out.

When purchasing packets of seeds, there are two things to check on. First, be sure the seeds are fresh. Somewhere on the label it should read "Packed for sale in 19☐☐." Make sure it's the current year. Second, when deciding between several sources for the same kind of seed, look at the number of seeds each company offers in its packet. As with the boxed plants, the lower-priced packet is not always the best buy.

All of the large seed houses supply reliable, fresh, high-quality seed. In addition, you'll find there are many small specialty seed companies sending out catalogs. Little is known about these suppliers; they may or may not be reputable. When dealing with a seed company you haven't ordered from before, it's a good idea to buy only two or three packets the first season. How well those seeds perform will determine whether or not you want to order more from that company in the future.

Over time, you'll develop your own list of reliable garden supply sources. The list below is intended to introduce a few well-known, reputable mail-order seed companies that offer a large selection of annual seeds. Start with these, then add others after trying them personally or receiving recommendations from experienced gardeners in your area.

Park Seed Company
P.O. Box 31
Greenwood, SC 29648

Comstock, Ferre & Co.
Box 125
Wethersfield, CT 06109

W. Atlee Burpee & Co.
300 Park Ave.
Warminster, PA 18974

Stokes Seeds Inc.
Box 548
Buffalo, NY 14240

CONTAINER-GROWN PLANT

What to Look for In Container-Grown Plants

Look for these signals when selecting plants grown in containers. They'll go a long way toward indicating how long the plant has been in the container and how it's been cared for during that time. Strong, vital plants that have been given good care have a far better chance of surviving when transplanted into the garden.

GOOD SIGNS

BAD SIGNS

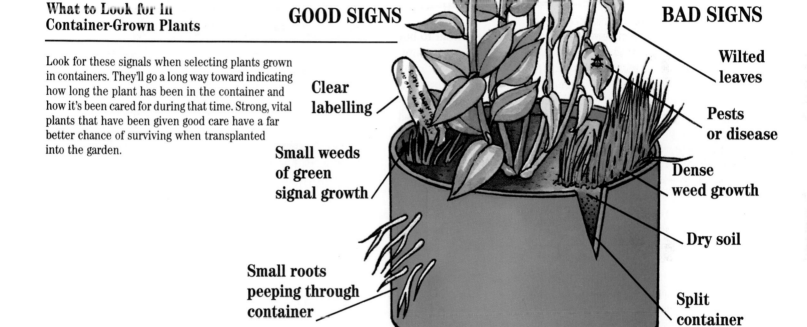

Clear labelling

Small weeds of green signal growth

Small roots peeping through container

Wilted leaves

Pests or disease

Dense weed growth

Dry soil

Split container

Thick root growing through base

Sowing Seeds

Seeds sown in the garden can reward you with these stunning marigolds.

Sowing seeds directly into the garden is the simplest method of growing annuals. For those who have neither the extra money nor the inclination to buy boxed plants, sowing directly into the garden in springtime is the answer. Once the ground is warm and the planting bed properly prepared, it's amazing how quickly most annuals sprout and grow to the flowering stage!

There are some plants that grow better when planted directly in the garden rather than started ahead as boxed plants. For example, both Shirley poppies and zinnias experience difficulty surviving transplanting. You'll also find that trailing and vining plants can't be started very much ahead of planting out time or they become hopelessly entangled. As a result, most vines don't gain enough of a head start to make the extra effort worthwhile.

There are several ways to approach direct seeding. For a somewhat structured but still informal cottage garden look, use a stick to mark out flowing sweeps on the prepared bed. Plant each sweep with a different kind of seed. If the garden is large enough to allow it, repeat the same variety in several sections. Place taller varieties toward the rear of the bed and the lower ones at the front. There is really no reason to precisely plan in advance where each kind will go.

Broadcast the seeds in each section and rake lightly, then briefly sprinkle a fine spray of water over the bed to settle the soil a bit. When the young seedlings sprout, they'll need to be thinned to prevent overcrowding. When thinning, adjust the space you leave between the plants according to their growth characteristics: Tall upright-growing plants such as plumed cockscomb, bachelor's buttons, and larkspur can be left much closer together than wide-spreading plants such as sweet alyssum, petunias, cosmos, and baby's breath. Surplus seedlings can be discarded, passed on to friends, or moved to grow in planters or other garden areas.

For a more formal garden design, make a precise plan on paper beforehand. Then carefully copy the layout onto the prepared seedbed. With this approach, each preselected variety is planted in rows or clumps in the appointed order—two or three seeds to a cluster, spaced 4 to 12 inches apart depending on their growth habits. When the plants are 1 to 2 inches tall, thin out all but the strongest one from each cluster. The resulting beds will have a neat, organized, well-planned look that will enhance any formally laid-out garden design.

Another approach to flower bed layout is simply to mark off rows the length of the bed and plant each one with a different annual favorite. By planting the tallest kind in the back row and increasingly shorter ones in each row in front of it, it's possible to effectively display all varieties. Take into account the width to which each type grows when spacing the rows. Maintenance of this garden is easy because you always work along straight rows.

To decide which design style to use, consider what is best suited to your own tastes and talents, as well as to the style of your house and the already existing garden.

PLANTS TO START OUTDOORS

Sweet Alyssum*	Morning Glory
Baby's Breath	Nasturtium
Blanket Flower	Nierembergia*
Castor Bean*	Ornamental Corn, Kale
Coleus*	Petunia
Cosmos*	Phlox*
Cup and Saucer Vine	California Poppy
Dahlia*	Horned Poppy
Forget-Me-Not	Portulaca
Four O'Clock	Scabiosa
Gazania	Sunflower
Ornamental Grasses	Zinnia*
Marigold*	

*Those plants that might be started ahead indoors or bought as boxed bedding plants in Zone 5 and colder.
(Note: Some plants on this list also appear on the list of those that can be started ahead as boxed plants. Either option is acceptable.)

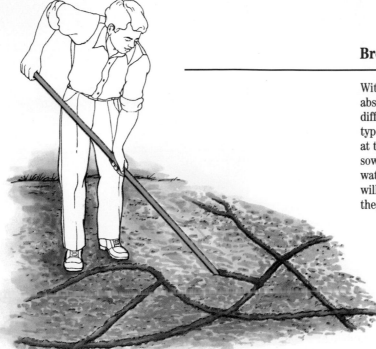

Broadcasting Seeds

With a stick or rake handle, mark out flowing abstract sweeps on the prepared bed. Broadcast a different variety of plant in each section, with taller types located toward the back and low-growing ones at the front. Rake the soil surface lightly after sowing, then briefly sprinkle with a fine spray of water after the entire bed is seeded. Seedlings will need to be thinned to appropriate spacing when they're 2 to 3 inches tall.

Planting Seeds over Mulch

For large plants that need to be spaced a foot or more apart, it's easiest to lay mulch over the bed prior to planting. Cut 3-inch holes at proper intervals in the mulch sheet. (If an organic mulch is used, push mulching aside for appropriate spacing.) Plant three seeds in a triangular pattern in each hole. Pat soil gently over each group. When seedlings grow their second set of true leaves, thin out the weaker plants, leaving just the strongest one to continue growing.

Planting Seeds in Rows

Flower seeds planted in rows are easily cared for. If varieties are arranged so the tallest is in the back row with each row forward planted with a shorter variety, all of them will be visible from the front of the bed. Mulch can be laid in place before or after seed rows are sown. Thinning of seedlings for proper spacing should be done when plants are 2 to 3 inches high.

Propagating Stem Cuttings

Certain annuals such as these New Guinea impatiens can be propagated by stem cuttings.

Most annuals are grown from seeds. However, impatiens, fibrous begonias, coleus, and geraniums can be grown from stem cuttings.

Select a mature plant that is in a stage of active midsummer growth. Prepare a container filled with rooting medium. It should be at least 3 to 4 inches deep, filled with 2½ inches or more of rooting medium. Clean, coarse builder's sand, a mixture of half perlite and half peat moss, or half perlite and half vermiculite are good choices. Fill the container with the moistened medium, then let it settle and drain for a half hour.

Take cuttings in the morning. Using a sharp knife, cut off growth tips just above the node, or the point where a leaf or side shoot attaches to the main stem. Each of the cuttings should be between 3 and 6 inches in length and have 4 to 6 nodes. The stem tissue should be easy to cut through.

Don't spend more than five minutes taking cuttings from the parent plants. To prepare a cutting for rooting, remove the leafless piece of stem at the bottom. Cut it off about ⅛ inch below the first node with a clean knife or razor cut, leaving no torn or dangling pieces of tissue hanging from the stem. Remove *all* of the leaves from the lower half of the cutting. These can be cut off with a knife or manually snapped off.

If there are any flower buds on the cutting, cut these off as well. Cut back the tips of any large leaves remaining on the cutting so that one-third to one-half of their surface remains. To help stimulate root formation, it's helpful to coat the lower one-third of each stem cutting with rooting hormone powder. Just dip each stem in the rooting powder and shake off any excess. Poke a hole in the dampened rooting medium, insert the cutting in the hole to one-third of its length, and press the medium firmly around the stem with your fingers. When all of the cuttings are set in the medium, water the surface.

Place a plastic bag over the cuttings to form a tent, using bamboo stakes or wooden dowels as supports. This will serve as a mini-greenhouse, which should be kept out of direct sunlight. If the bottom edge of the plastic tent is left a bit loose, some fresh outside air will be able to circulate up inside. This will help reduce the possibility of mildew and mold problems. Some growers prefer to hold the plastic tightly against the container with an elastic band. In this case, it's necessary to remove the elastic and lift up the tent sides for a short period each day or else to poke holes in the plastic bag in order to supply the cutting with necessary fresh air. With a plastic tent there will be little need for watering the cuttings.

Annual cuttings will root quickly. They should be checked in a week to ten days. Insert a narrow knife blade or a fork beneath one of the cuttings and gently lift it out. When the longest roots are ¼ inch long, remove cuttings from the rooting medium and transfer each to a 1–1½-inch pot filled with planting mix.

Propagating Healthy Plants from Stem Cuttings

1 Cut 3- to 6-inch growth tips from the parent plant with a small, sharp paring knife. Make a clean, slanted cut just above a leaf node, side shoot, or growth bud. The plant should be in a stage of active growth with young and succulent stems. If stems are woody and difficult to cut, try recutting closer to the tip.

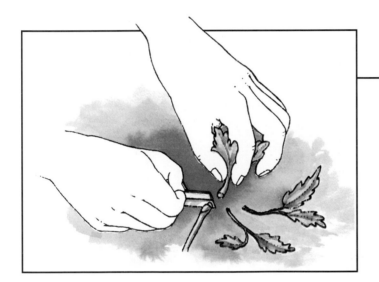

2 Bring the cutting indoors immediately. Recut the stems just below the bottom node. Use a single-edged razor blade or a sharp paring knife to give the cleanest possible cut. Crushed stem cells and hanging strands of tissue cause problems that you want to avoid.

3 A cutting is ready to plant after the side shoots and leaves have been removed from the lower half of the stem. Any flowers or flower buds should also be removed, and large leaves trimmed back to about half their original size. Dip the lower one-third to one-half of the stem in rooting powder. Tap off any excess powder.

4 Poke a hole in the rooting medium and insert a cutting to between one-third and one-half of its length. Firm the rooting medium around the stem with your fingers. When all the cuttings are inserted, water them in place. A large, clear plastic bag forms a mini-greenhouse over the cuttings. The bag is held several inches above the tops of the cutting by sticks or stakes inserted around the edge of the container.

5 Annual cuttings root quickly. After seven to ten days, check for roots by gently lifting one of the cuttings out. When the longest roots are ¼ inch long, transplant them into 1½-inch pots. After several weeks, replant them into larger pots when a good strong root system has formed.

Collecting Seeds from Your Garden

How legitimate is the impulse to collect your own seeds? Will these seeds germinate? If they do, will the resulting plants look exactly like or differ greatly from the parent plant? How much and what kind of care do collected seeds require?

The results from collecting your own seeds will vary widely. Seeds from pure species, or nonhybrid plants, produce plants very similar to the parent plant. Flower color may vary more if there was cross-pollination between the parent plant and other nearby plants of the same kind but of different colors. For example, if you pick a seedpod from a deep purple foxglove but there are white foxgloves nearby, some of the resulting seedlings will have white flowers and some will have purple ones.

Least successful are seeds collected from hybrid plants. These are varieties developed by seedsmen who deliberately cross-pollinate specific parents. Seedlings from these plants will revert back; they'll look like their respective "grandparents" rather than the hybrid parent plant.

Annuals generally produce seeds abundantly—one or two seed heads are likely to provide enough plants for the average home garden. And the germination rate is usually very high if the seeds are planted within a year. So there is a good chance of success with collecting your own seeds.

Here's what you need to know before you start. Seedpods vary in design. Some are challenging to collect because they fling or spill the seeds out when they're ripe. To avoid losing these seeds, attach paper bags or squares of panty hose over the seed heads after pollination but before maturity. *Never* use plastic bags for this purpose, as destructive molds will develop.

Other pod types hold the seeds or sprinkle or spill them out a few at a time. Some retain their seeds tenaciously. These seed heads can be allowed to mature undisturbed, then harvested when ready. Label each kind as you collect it, or you may easily lose track of which is which.

After harvesting, separate the seeds from the pods and spread them out in a dry place away from the sun. Allow them to dry out for a couple of weeks. Then store in airtight containers in a cool, dry place until planting time. Seeds stored in the refrigerator may retain a high germination rate even when planted several years later.

Picking and planting seeds you collect from sunflowers can result in this beautiful flower.

Collecting and growing your own seeds can be fun, especially if you like an informal mixed garden. But when you want a particular plant of a certain color in a specific location, the only sure way to get it is by buying seeds or bedding plants of the proper variety from a reputable dealer.

Catapulting Seedpods

Some seedpods catapult or spray seeds when they're ripe. After they've been pollinated, but before they dry out, a small paper bag or squares of panty hose (*never* plastic) should be secured over the seed head in order to catch the seeds. Examples: pansy, impatiens, cleome, geranium, sweet pea, and lupine.

Seed Heads That Drop Seeds

Other seedpods hold the seeds until they dry completely; then their tops open and allow seeds to drop out. To harvest, shake the newly ripe seed heads over a bowl. Examples: larkspur, poppy, sweet William, petunia, nicotiana, calliopsis, and pot marigold.

Seed Heads to be
Torn Apart by Hand

This group of seed heads remains tightly packed to maturity, often well into winter. These can be torn apart by hand when they're well-dried to release the seeds. Examples: marigold, zinnia, morning glory, scabiosa, and hollyhock.

Seedpods Requiring Protection

Some seed heads are especially appealing to birds and animals. The trick is to harvest them before the competition! Protect these seed heads by covering them with brown paper bags as they near maturity and then pick promptly. Examples: sunflower, cosmos, and sweet pea.

This well-maintained annuals border features zinnias and marigolds against an evergreen hedge. Basic care techniques are not difficult for these flowers and certainly result in beautiful seasonal color.

CHAPTER 3

CARING FOR ANNUALS

Most gardeners ramble around their yard regularly, stopping to admire a healthy plant here, snapping off a few dead flower heads there, then pulling out some weeds in another area.

At the same time, they're noticing clues that signal possible problems. If some of the plants have limp-hanging leaves, the gardener will check how dry the soil is and turn on the soaker hose if needed. If some leaves or flowers are peppered with holes or totally eaten away, a closer inspection will be made to discover whether a caterpillar or bug has invaded. This, in turn, will lead to spraying or powdering with the appropriate insecticide or hand removal of the insect.

There are tips included that will help make your summer's work easier: ways to minimize weeding and watering chores, feeding and plant staking alternatives, followed by suggestions on how to prepare for winter and the next growing season.

An illustrated section that allows easy identification of garden pests and diseases contains recommendations for dealing with each problem. Also included are two handy charts. One outlines the proper time of year to perform specific activities, the other indicates how easy or difficult various annuals are to grow.

By selecting those plants that are easiest to grow and are best-suited to your garden site, then following gardening techniques that reduce the need for maintenance, your summer can be both carefree and color-filled.

Quenching a Plant's Thirst

Dew supplies this blossom with necessary water.

Along with soil and light, water is an essential ingredient for plant growth. The soil and light requirements of annuals have been dealt with on page 56; ways to take care of water needs will now be considered.

It's not easy, especially at first, to gauge exactly when plants require water—so much depends upon current weather and soil conditions. For example, if good soaking rains fall frequently, it's obvious additional watering is unnecessary. However, when there's a light rainfall every few days, it's possible that only the soil surface has been dampened without much water actually reaching plant roots, necessitating the addition of water. Plants subjected to bright sun and wind also lose a lot of water that needs to be replenished. Similarly, because trees continually pull large quantities of moisture from the surrounding soil, annuals planted near or under them need more frequent watering than those in the open. All of these factors affect the rate at which soil dries out.

So how do you judge when to water and how much water to give? The one sure way to test is by poking your finger 2 to 3 inches into the soil and feeling how moist or dry it is. Taking a pinch from the surface isn't good enough; you need to know what it's like down in the root zone. Inexperienced gardeners should check soil moisture any day that there is little or no rainfall. Over time, you'll develop a feel for the overall conditions and check only when you suspect the soil may be turning dry. Remember, it's always better to check too often rather than not often enough. Don't wait until drooping plants indicate that the soil is parched.

When you do water, water deeply. Many people briefly spray a thirsty flower bed with a hand-held hose. When they tire of holding it, become bored, or think they have watered enough because the water has stopped soaking into the soil as rapidly as it did at first, the watering session is ended. Always pause to check how deeply the water has penetrated. Guessing usually results in reaching only the top ½ inch leaving the soil beneath it still dry.

A better approach is to use an automatic sprinkler, letting it gently "rain" for an extended period of time. Check at half-hour intervals to see how deeply the water has penetrated. Turn the water off when the soil is moistened to a 2-inch depth. Don't water again until your testing indicates the need.

One problem with sprinkler water is that the foliage becomes very wet, creating an ideal environment for the spread of fungus diseases. In addition, flower clusters heavy with water are more likely to bend and break or to become mildewed.

The best way to water is with a soaker hose. The water slowly oozes from the hose's many tiny holes for several hours—even overnight. All of the water soaks directly on the soil and down to the plant roots without any waste or damage.

Drip irrigation is another excellent slow-soaking system, but it's more expensive than a soaker hose. Thus it's probably a sensible alternative for those who have large plant beds or who garden in climates where irrigation is constantly needed in order for cultivated plants to survive. Once the system is laid out, it can remain in place year after year; in areas that freeze, however, it must be drained for the winter.

There are two additional factors that will help conserve moisture and thus reduce the frequency of need for watering. One is the incorporation of peat moss into the planting area; this causes the soil to be able to soak up and hold water longer. (This is true when peat is added to light and sandy soils; conversely, when it's added to heavy soils, it helps to lighten and aerate them.)

The second technique that helps retain moisture is the use of mulch. Laid on the soil surface between the plants, a mulch protects the soil from sun and wind drying. (More on the benefits of mulch, as well as descriptions of mulch alternatives, can be found in the following section, "Keeping Weeds at Bay," page 97.)

By using these two ideas, you can cut down on the time needed to care for your garden, and even more importantly, help conserve water, nature's precious resource.

Soaker Hose Watering

An easy way to handle deep watering of an annual bed is to lay a soaker hose in place when plants are small and leave it there for the season. Mulch can be laid on top of the soaker hose without disruption. A quick connector on the soaker hose allows speedy attachment to the regular garden hose whenever watering is needed. When the soil is well-soaked, the garden hose can easily be disconnected and stored out of the way until it's needed again.

Plants with Water Dams

A dam of soil ringed around each plant when it's transplanted into the garden helps to keep the water from settling in and early rains from running off immediately. This gives the water time to soak in around the plant's roots. Where flower beds are level, this isn't essential, but when planting on a slope, a dam is a great help. The dam disappears after a week or two and is no longer needed.

The Benefits of Deep Watering

When plants are watered infrequently but heavily, they'll develop large and deep root networks. Frequent light waterings cause plants to develop shallow root systems just below the soil surface. This causes plants to be poorly anchored and therefore subject to toppling in heavy wind or rain, as well as liable to wilting unless they're watered daily. Therefore, slow, deep-soak watering produces stronger and hardier plants. Whenever possible, water in the evening or overnight rather than in the morning or the heat of the day.

Watering with a Drip Irrigation System

For very large planting beds or in very dry or sandy conditions, a drip irrigation system may be the best watering solution. It allows slow, deep watering directly into each plant's roots. This helps keep foliage dry, thus reducing the possibility of the spread of diseases. Use this system in conjunction with a mulch for greatest water conservation. An on-off timer and a soluble fertilizer feeder are optional parts of a drip-irrigation system for those wanting additional ease of maintenance.

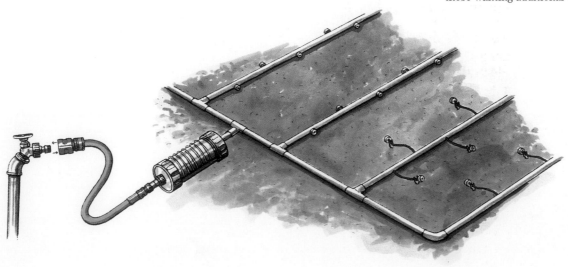

Keeping Weeds at Bay

The mulch on this conifer garden helps prevent weeds and gives the landscape a neat, defined appearance.

Weed seeds are quick to germinate and grow rapidly. As soon as they're brought to within an inch of the soil surface (through digging), they'll begin to sprout. After digging deeply in early spring to ready the bed for planting, wait a week or more before doing any planting or seed sowing. Every three days, stir up the top 1 inch of soil with a scuffle hoe or cultivator, leaving the lower soil undisturbed. This will expose several cycles of young sprouted weeds to dry out and die in the sun and air.

This approach can be used when seeds are going to be planted either in addition to, or instead of, bedding plants. But in places where *only* bedding plants will be used, the use of a pre-emergent chemical is recommended. This is sprinkled on the soil around the already planted annuals. It's important that the annuals be at least 3 to 4 inches tall before the chemical, triluralin, is applied. In the case of seedlings, this same chemical can be applied once the young plants have grown to this 3- to 4-inch size.

Finally, the most popular way of dramatically reducing weed problems is by using some kind of mulch. Mulch is a layer of organic or inorganic material laid on the soil surface to shade out weeds, retain soil moisture, and have a moderating effect on soil temperature.

Many materials can achieve these results, but some are more practical, less expensive, easier to handle, and more attractive than others. The list of organic mulches includes: pine needles, leaves, straw, dried seaweed, tree bark strips, bark chunks, peat moss, old newspapers, sawdust, wood chips, cocoa bean hulls, and cotton seed hulls. Inorganic mulches include "blankets" made from solid sheets of black plastic (**Caution:** These can become very slippery when wet); black plastic made porous with thousands of small holes; porous, nonwoven fiberglass landscape fabric; and pieces of new or used carpets.

Perhaps the choice of which kind of mulch to use isn't as important as the decision to use *some* kind of mulch. Mulching cuts down dramatically on weed problems, conserves soil moisture, keeps soil warmer in cool weather and cooler on hot days, and, if it's an organic mulch, will improve the quality of the soil as it breaks down and adds to what gardeners call "soil tilth."

Some mulches are not very attractive-looking. Other organic mulches may alter the soil chemistry as they break down (annual soil tests will detect these changes so you can adjust fertilizer applications to compensate). Still other types have an odor when they're fresh or may prove too expensive for use in large quantities.

Still, there must be at least one among all of the alternatives that will satisfy your needs. The use of a mulch will dramatically reduce weed problems in any garden.

Using a Pre-Emergent Chemical

Granules of a pre-emergent chemical can be scattered on the soil between the already planted bedding plants. It will prevent weed seeds from sprouting in these open areas. Because it kills *all* seeds—weeds, annuals, and perennials—do *not* use a pre-emergent in any area where you have recently planted, or plan to plant, flower seeds. A pre-emergent can be used once seedlings have germinated and grown to bedding plant size or larger.

Boxed Plants and Mulching

Mulch, whether organic or inorganic, can be laid before planting of boxed plants. Holes can be cut through sheeting or dug through organic mulches at proper spacing for the plants.

Seedlings and Mulch

Where seeds are to be planted instead of bedding plants, wait to lay in organic mulches until seeds have germinated and the seedlings are 3 inches or taller. This reduces possible smothering of vulnerable, young seedlings by mulch that the wind may blow over them. Watering down of organic mulches after they're laid helps settle and hold them in place.

Cultivation of Nonmulched Areas

In beds where no mulch is used, frequent cultivation of the top 1 to 2 inches of soil is the best way to control weeds. Newly germinated weed seedlings die quickly when stirred up this way. Larger weeds should be hand-pulled and removed from the bed, since they can easily reroot if left in the garden.

Feeding Alternatives

Healthy marigolds and floss flowers provide color enjoyment.

As mentioned on page 56, the best course to follow is to have your garden soil tested each year, then follow the recommendations given with your test results. Knowing what nutrients are needed helps cut down on the number of choices, but still leaves the decision of whether to use an organic or inorganic source up to you. If you're able to obtain the nutrients you need from organic fertilizers, you reduce the risk of possibly harming the environment. However, if the nutrients you require cannot realistically be obtained from such sources, there's little danger in using inorganic fertilizers as long as you apply only as much as is needed.

As you study the NPK formula on each plant food, you'll notice that organic fertilizers contain much lower percentages of nutrients per pound than do inorganic fertilizers. For the most part, this doesn't matter when feeding annuals. Where this *can* become a problem is when you're trying to adjust a large garden bed's nutrient content at the beginning of the growing season. You may find that, in order to raise the nutrients to the recommended level, you'll have to add 4 inches of the organic material. This can be done if the area to be covered is small, but for large areas, it could become unwieldy. In these cases it's more practical to make major adjustments with inorganics, then proceed with organics for minor adjustments in future years.

Fertilizers are applied in a dry granular or powder form, or mixed with water for a liquid application. The granular or powder foods should be broadcast over the soil surface and dug in; liquid applications can be made with a hand sprayer or a special mixing attachment for your garden hose.

To supply food for immediate use by bedding annuals that are newly planted out, a weak solution of water soluble fertilizer—either fish emulsion or an inorganic type—can be poured from a watering can directly around each plant. Thereafter, a couple of side dressings of granular plant food sprinkled around each plant at two-week intervals should carry them through the rest of the summer.

For best absorption, fertilize when the soil is moist. Take care to apply it on the soil rather than on the plant leaves. The plants, your hands, and the fertilizer should be dry when you fertilize. **Caution:** Always wash your hands after handling fertilizer.

A final word regarding two homemade soil amenders: compost and liquid manure. Compost is made by combining plant wastes with soil and fertilizer, allowing them to decompose for several months, then mixing them back into the garden. Liquid manure is made by combining animal wastes and water, allowing them to decompose, then watering the garden with the resultant liquid. Both are good organic nutrient sources even though their level of nutrients is low. However, neither is especially practical for the average, small home garden.

Making Organic Fertilizer

Gardeners preferring organic fertilizers can make their own liquid manure by fermenting animal and vegetable wastes in water for several weeks. An easy and reliable source of soluble organic fertilizer is fish emulsion, which can be purchased at any garden center. When adding this concentrate to water, there is a strong fish odor. Therefore, it's best to do this job outdoors or in a well-ventilated area. Fortunately, the odor is very short-lived.

Composting

Making your own compost from plant wastes, soil, and nutrients takes several months. Many gardeners find it easier to purchase bagged compost instead. Either way, compost is a good additive for soils low in organic materials.

Sidedressing

Granular and powdered commercial fertilizers release nutrients more quickly than organic fertilizers. Sprinkling a small handful of 5-10-5 or 10-10-10 around each plant (known as sidedressing) in late spring and again in midsummer will give annuals a feeding boost that will keep them in top growing and flowering condition through the summer.

Liquid Fertilizer Solution

Another fast source of nutrients is a liquid fertilizer solution. This comes in a concentrated form that is diluted by mixing it with water according to the manufacturer's directions. Use a mild solution in water on newly planted bedding plants or recently thinned seedlings to help them quickly recover from the shock. Liquid fertilizer can also be applied in place of powdered or granular sidedressings, if preferred.

101

Ways to Increase/Control Growth

Zinnias and vincas benefit from proper growth care.

Annuals (as well as perennials; see the "Perennials" section, page 190, for more information on perennials) will flourish when provided with the best possible growing conditions. However, there are a few simple care techniques that will help increase and control their growth.

Pinching Back—To encourage plants to fill out, remove the growth bud at the end of the main stem when the plant is in its rapid growth stage that precedes first flower bud formation. For bedding plants, the best time to do this is when you're planting them out in the garden. They're at a good stage of growth and, in addition, the removal of some of their foliage will help balance any root damage they may suffer in the transplanting process. Plants grown from seeds sown directly in the garden should be pinched back when they're 3 to 4 inches tall.

Simply pinch out or snap off the last inch or so of the main growing tip. This will redirect the plant's energy from this single shoot to numerous latent side buds—there is a latent growth bud located at the point on the stem where each leaf is attached. Several days after pinching, you'll see several small shoots pushing from the remaining stem. These will grow into a cluster of stems to replace the original single stem. The plant will be shorter, stockier, and fuller than if no pinching had been done. It will also be neater-looking, more compact, and have many more branches on which to produce flowers. A second pinching can be done two weeks after the first one if an even fuller plant is desired.

Deadheading—Once annuals (or perennials) begin to bloom, it's important to remove spent flowers promptly for several reasons. First, once the flower dies, it detracts from the good looks of the garden. Second, even though we say it's dead, it's actually very much alive and continues with its growth toward seed production. This process pulls plant energy that would otherwise be available for new foliage and flower production into the seed head. Third, removal of spent flowers helps to quickly redirect plant energy to side shoots for smooth and speedy transfer to new growth.

To make this rerouting most efficient, always cut back to just above the first side bud that is already beginning to grow. If there is no active side bud below the bloom, cut back either to a side branch or immediately above a leaf node where a latent bud will be likely to push out new growth. Make a clean cut with a sharp-bladed knife, since ragged cuts take much longer to heal and are likely sites for entry of rot and disease. These rules for cutting apply to the removal of cutting flowers as well.

Occasionally it becomes necessary to cut back growth in order to keep a plant from becoming leggy or from drowning out neighboring plants. Cutting back should be approached in the same way as removing dead flower heads. Always cut back to a side growth shoot or branch that is headed in the direction you want future growth to go. This way you can steer and control growth as you see fit.

Pinching out Growth Tips

Pinching out the plant growth tip helps encourage multiple branching. This, in turn, causes production of more flower buds along these additional branches. At the same time, pinching produces a more sturdy, compact plant that not only looks nice but is also less subject to breakage due to wind, rain, or heavy bloom weight.

Deadheading Flower Heads

Deadheading, or removing dead flower heads, should be done soon after the flower dies, so no plant energy is wasted on seed formation. Cluster flowers will look fresh and attractive longer if the individual florets are snapped out of the group as they die. Single flowers should be cut back to the place on the stem where a side shoot is already pushing out. If none is evident, then cut back to above a leaf, a node, or a side branch. Cut on a slant to allow water to run off of the wound.

Staking Garden Plants

Larkspur grow better if staked properly.

Most healthy annuals (as well as perennials; see the "Perennials" section, page 190, for more information on perennials) are sturdy and self-supporting. They often don't require any special staking to keep them looking good. However, plants with heavy flower clusters, especially those on tall, slender stems such as snapdragons and dahlias (or perennials such as lilies), may flop over when exposed to strong winds or heavy rains. Another group that sometimes requires support to keep their flower heads visible are those with stems that will either bend over or break off when the weight of their leaves and blooms becomes too great. Asters, baby's breath, salpiglossis, and some zinnias (and such perennials as carnations and peonies) are known to have these problems.

Often plants gain enough support when a kind of corral is placed around them. The plant stems lean out against the metal or string sides of the corral instead of flopping down to the ground. Another simple type of support consists of poking many-branched pieces of brush into the ground beside the plants. These form a network of twigs through which the plants can grow and against which they can lean for support. The tops of these branches can be bent over to form an even more inter-laced network if needed.

These two support systems work well with plants that have a spreading growth habit. For those that produce tall, single spikes, a third staking method is more suitable. Poke a wooden or bamboo stake into the ground 2 to 3 inches from the plant stem. It should be pushed deeply enough into the soil to be solidly secure. Loosely tie each plant stem to this central stake every 6 inches along the stem's height. A final tie should be made just below the flower bud cluster. To keep the ties from sliding downward, first form a half-granny knot around the stake, then a full granny knot around the plant stem.

Although tying plants seems a nuisance, it really only takes a few minutes to do and is only necessary for a few varieties. If those that need it aren't tied, however, they'll either bend over, becoming impossible to see, become mud covered, or snap off and die. Either way, there's little sense in growing these kinds of plants if you aren't willing to stake them. Select easier care annuals (or perennials) instead. Or, if they happen to be your favorites, make up your mind to give them this little extra care that will make it possible for them to look their best.

Single Staking

Tie stems to a stake that is firmly anchored in the soil. First tie the string around the stake with a half-granny knot, allowing an inch or more of slack between the stake and the plant stem. Then tie a full-granny knot around the stem. As the plant grows taller, add ties further up on the stake 6 to 8 inches apart. The topmost tie should be located at the base of the flower spike. All of the branches can be tied to a single stake in the center of the plant.

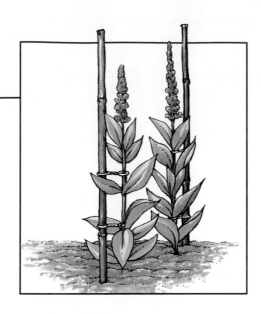

Stake Corrals

A better way to hold clumps of fine stems upright is by inserting four or more stakes around the plant. Tie a string to the first stake, then wrap it one turn around each of the other stakes along the perimeter and back to the starter stake. For a large clump, run string diagonally across within this corral for more support. Several tiers of string may be needed for tall plants—space tiers 4 to 6 inches apart. Flower heads should float 4 to 6 inches above the top tier of string.

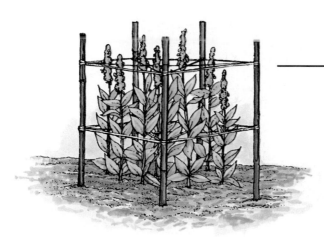

"L" Shaped Metal Stakes

A more expensive, but easier to install, corral can be made from "L" shaped metal stakes specially designed and sold for this purpose. They hook together quickly to make whatever size is needed. These can be used year after year once the initial investment is made. String can be diagonally cross-woven between these stakes if more support is needed.

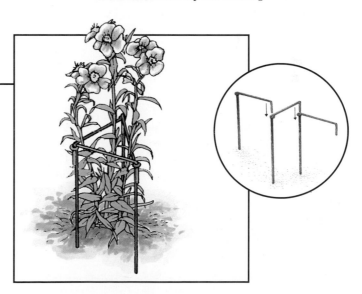

Brush Thicket Staking

A simple no-cost plant support for fine-stemmed plants can be made by poking the stems of well-branched brush into the ground next to the young plants. The plants' stems simply lean against the twigs for support without any tying. This brush thicket will give even more support if the tops are bent over and interwoven. Plant stems will grow up through the resulting tangle and hide it from view.

Pests & Other Problems

The following lists are designed to help you identify the most common garden pests and diseases for annuals or perennials. If you feel uncertain about what is causing damage to your plants, take a specimen to your local garden shop or your county Cooperative Extension office.

Once you know what your problem is, you'll need to decide how to control it. When an infestation is slight, it's often possible to simply remove the sick plants or individual insects. For a heavy infestation, you'll probably need to turn to chemical insecticides or fungicides.

Follow manufacturer's instructions precisely and read and follow any cautions on the package label. Apply these chemicals as directed and only when they're absolutely necessary. One final note: New biological and chemical controls are continually being developed. Those listed here are current at the time of this writing, but more effective new ones may well be discovered in the future.

Healthy flowers and foliage make this all-white garden especially attractive.

INSECTS AND ANIMALS

SYMPTOM	CAUSE	CURE	PLANTS	
			Annuals	**Perennials**
Cluster of small, soft-bodied insects on buds and growth tips; sticky secretions may be evident	*Aphids*	Spray with rotenone or malathion[1] in evening.	Pot Marigold Nasturtium Primrose Sweet Pea	Chrysanthemum Delphinium Lupine
Leaves chewed away; hard-shelled beetles on plant and burrowed into flowers	*Beetles of various kinds*	Spray with rotenone or Sevin*[1]; pick by hand and destroy.	Gourds Hollyhock American/ French Marigold Zinnia	Chrysanthemum Mallow

[1] = Inorganic treatment
* = Copyrighted brand name.

SYMPTOM	CAUSE	CURE	PLANTS	
			Annuals	**Perennials**
Growth tips wilted; small hole in plant stem at point where wilting begins	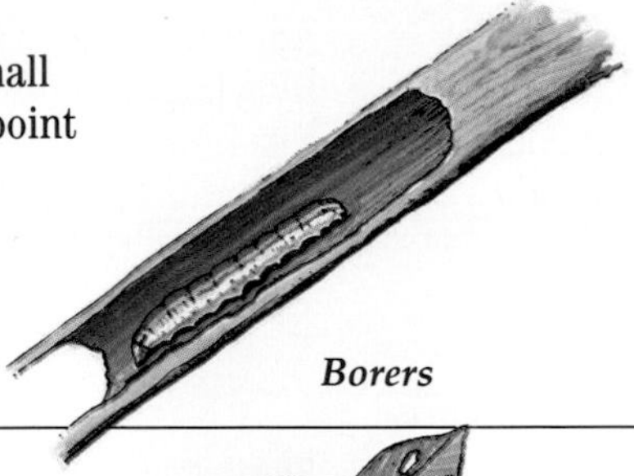 *Borers*	Snap off at level of hole; spray with endosulfan[1], pyrethrum, or rotenone.	Gourds American/ French Marigold Ornamental Corn Zinnia	Dahlia Delphinium Iris
Leaves and flowers chewed away; caterpillars on plant	 *Caterpillars of various kinds & sizes*	Pick off by hand and destroy; spray with pyrethrum, malathion[1], or *Bacillus thuringiensis*.	Nicotiana Ornamental or Flowering Cabbage Petunia	Butterfly Weed Chrysanthemum Mallow Yarrow
Entire young plants wilted; partially or entirely chewed through at ground level	 *Cutworms*	Dig in soil around plant base; find rolled up caterpillars and destroy; circle plant with cardboard collar on edge (1″ below ground and 1″ above ground).	China Pink Nicotiana Ornamental or Flowering Cabbage Petunia	
Leaves peppered with small round holes; small triangular-shaped bugs seen when disturbed	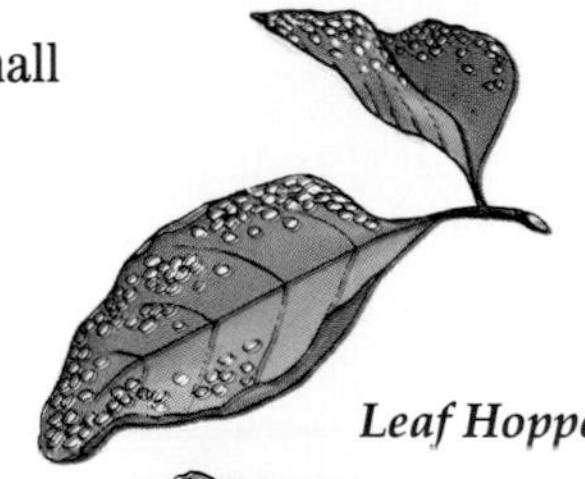 *Leaf Hoppers*	Spray with malathion1 or methoxychlor[1]; dust with diatomaceous earth.	Aster Dahlia Pot Marigold	Aster Chrysanthemum Coreopsis Pincushion Flower
Leaves "painted" with whitish, curling trails	 *Leaf Miners*	Spray with malathion[1]; remove badly infested leaves.	China Pink Hollyhock	Columbine Pink
White or pinkish fuzzy clumps on stems and at base of leaves; sticky to the touch	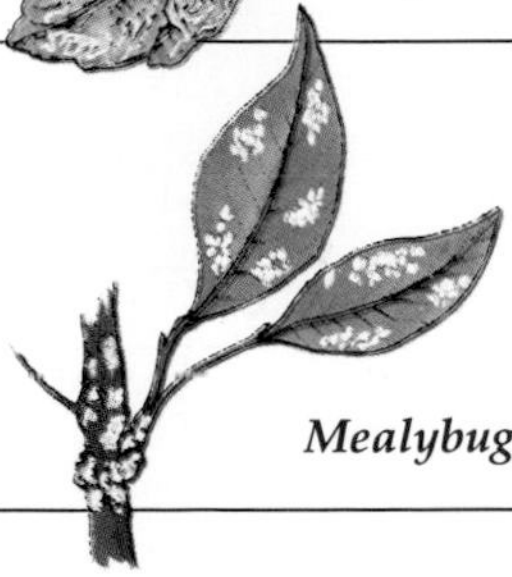 *Mealybugs*	Spray with malathion[1] or pyrethrum; hand kill by painting each bug with alcohol.	Asparagus Fern Moses-in-a-Boat Transvaal Daisy	

[1] = Inorganic treatment
* = Copyrighted brand name

SYMPTOM	CAUSE	CURE	PLANTS	
			Annuals	**Perennials**
Slime trails on plants; soft sticky slugs on plants after dark; holes eaten in leaves	 *Slugs and Snails*	Set out shallow containers of beer; set out metaldehyde slug bait[1]; pick by hand.	Hollyhock Nicotiana Petunia Primrose	Daylily Hosta Phlox
Leaves yellowing with speckled look; fine spider webs on plant; tiny bugs on backs of leaves	 *Spider Mites*	Spray with a miticide[1] on backs of leaves; wash or spray with soapy water.	Flowering Maple Impatiens Primrose	Bush Clematis Yellow Coneflower Daylily
Small glob of white bubbles on plant stem or leaves; small insect hidden inside	 *Spittlebugs*	Ignore unless very pervasive; spray with malathion[1]; wash off repeatedly with hose	Bachelor's Button Four O'Clock	Chrysanthemum
Brown or white flecks on plant leaves	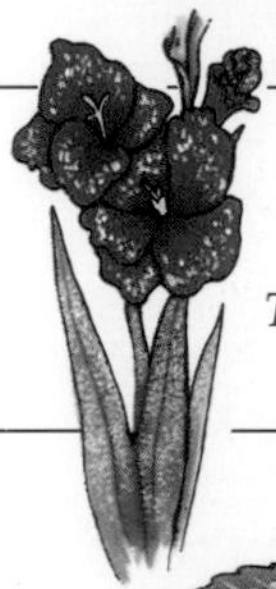 *Thrips*	Spray with malathion[1] or dust with sulphur.	Gladiolus	Daylily
Cloud of tiny white flies fluttering around plant	 *White Flies*	Spray with malathion[1] or diazinon[1]; use yellow sticky traps.	Heliotrope Lantana Morning Glory Vine	Aster Mallow

[1] = Inorganic treatment
* = Copyrighted brand name

DISEASES

SYMPTOM	CAUSE	CURE	PLANTS	
			Annuals	**Perennials**
Leaves become mottled, curl, and shrivel; plants become deformed	 *Blights and Viruses*	Remove and destroy plants; buy blight-resistant strains; do not smoke; wash hands before handling plants.	Aster Snapdragon	Japanese Anemone Lupine Peony
Newly sprouted seedlings fall over and die	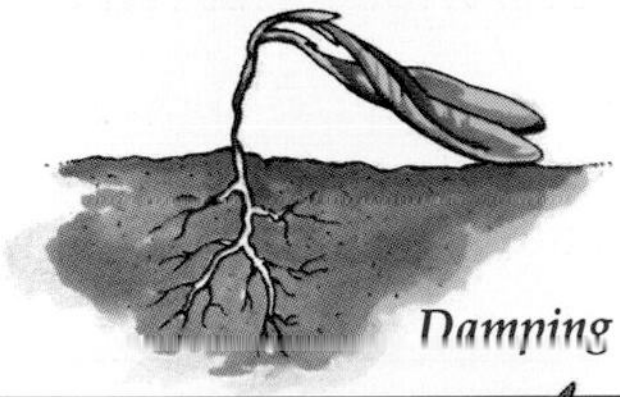 *Damping Off*	Start seeds in sterile soil mix. Dust seeds with Captan*[1] before planting.	All plants	All plants
Round, dusty brown or black spots on leaves; leaves drop from plant	 *Leaf Spot*	Remove badly diseased leaves; spray with benomyl[1] or zineb[1].	Aster Chrysanthemum Foxglove Phlox	Garden Phlox Iris
Lower leaves and stems turn grayish and look slightly wilted	 *Powdery Mildew*	Increase air circulation; spray with benomyl[1] or sulfur.	Bachelor's Button Floss Flower Phlox Sweet Pea Zinnia	Boltonia Delphinium Garden Phlox
Orange or reddish-brown raised dots form on backs of leaves; leaves look wilted	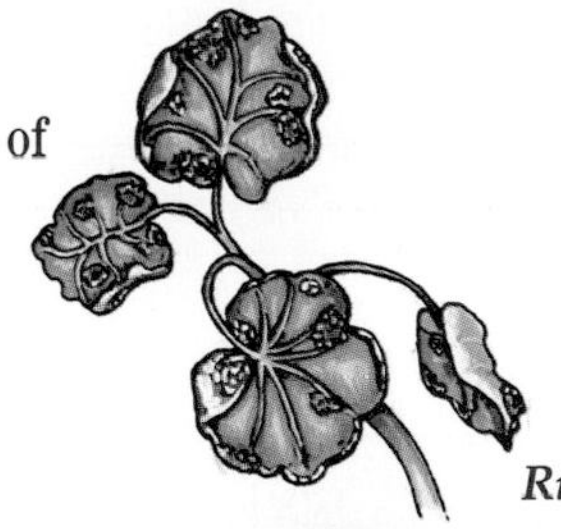 *Rust*	Increase air circulation; keep foliage dry; buy rust-resistant varieties; spray with ferbam[1] or zineb[1]; spray flowers with sulfur or benomyl[1].	Cleome Hollyhock Snapdragon	
Leaves wilt and turn yellow; entire plant shuts down and dies	 *Wilt*	Remove infected plants and destroy; buy wilt-resistant varieties.	Aster Dahlia Snapdragon	

[1] = Inorganic treatment
* = Copyrighted brand name

Preparing for Winter & Another Year

Sowing seeds indoors in the winter can be an enjoyable experience.

Most gardeners find they begin preparing for another growing season while still in the midst of the present one. Certainly, this is the best time to study your yard and to plan for next spring. It's also the best time to note down your conclusions.

In addition to making future plans, there are also some basic gardening preparations you'll want to consider. For instance, if you wish to carry some annuals indoors over winter—many people bring in geraniums, impatiens, and fibrous begonias as potted plants to use as the source of rooted cuttings for the following summer—late summer is when you'll transplant them into pots, cut them back, and move them inside.

An even better approach for carrying such plants over winter is to take cuttings from them in midsummer when they're still in a very active growing phase, then root and pot them up to grow through the winter. By late winter, they'll be mature plants from which to take cuttings for next summer's garden.

Dahlias, tuberous begonias, cannas, callas, caladiums, and gladiolas are treated as annuals in colder climates. Many people simply discard them each fall and buy new ones each spring. However, it's possible to dig and store them for replanting the following season after the first frost when the tops die back. Remove the dead tops along with any loose soil and feeder roots from the swollen tubers (or corms) and store them loosely in brown paper sacks or open-weave bags in a dark, cool area. Packing material around them will help keep them from drying out.

Later in the fall, there are other chores to do. Soaker hoses should be rolled up and stored, drip irrigation systems should be drained, and the dead plants should be removed and disposed of. Where an organic mulch has been used, an additional layer should be laid over the existing mulch. The new layer added in the fall will replenish any soil that has been lost, cover bare areas, protect the soil from wind or water erosion over winter, and help discourage weed growth during late fall and early spring.

Inorganic mulch sheeting should be rolled up and stored for the winter. In its place, either spread an organic mulch or seed in annual ryegrass or buckwheat to provide a winter cover crop that will need to be turned under in early spring as a source of organic nutrients (referred to as a "green manure").

Autumn is a good time to take soil samples and have them tested. If slow-working nutrients such as lime are needed, they can be spread over the area during the fall or winter. The faster-releasing fertilizers should be applied when the beds are readied for planting the following spring.

Some annual enthusiasts like to sow seeds in containers each autumn for winter display indoors. Select those annuals that require only a short-day length for blooming. Otherwise, grow those that have attractive foliage and enjoy them as houseplants all winter. You can even add a few annual herbs to spice up your winter cooking!

ANNUALS SUITED TO OVERWINTERING	
Asparagus Fern	Geranium*
Fibrous Begonia*	Impatiens*
Tuberous Begonia	Ornamental Pepper
Coleus*	Polka-Dot Plant
Dracaena	Vinca
Flowering Maple	Persian Violet
Fuchsia*	

* = Those that can be propagated from stem cuttings.

Preparing Garden Plants for Winter

Bringing full grown garden plants inside for the winter should be done several weeks before frost. Dig them up with a large ball of soil so that as few roots as possible are lost. Set in the ground so that the plant is at the same level in the pot as it was in the garden. Fill in around the plant roots with good soil mix and firm with fingers to eliminate air pockets. Cut back plant tops by 40 to 50 percent to reduce wilting. Water with a mild liquid fertilizer solution. Keep in a cool location out of direct sunlight for at least a day before moving indoors.

Raising Cuttings over Winter

An alternative to bringing large garden plants inside for the winter is to take cuttings from them and raise the resulting plants instead. Cuttings should be made in midsummer while plants are still in an active stage of growth, since plant growth slows down when night temperatures cool.

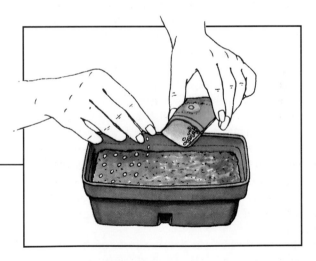

Starting Annuals from Seed

A third alternative for raising annuals in the winter is to start them from seed. Coleus and annual herbs such as parsley and basil do well treated this way, as do flowering annuals that bloom with short day lengths.

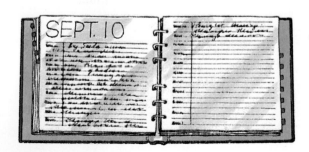

Keeping Notes

A helpful end-of-season task is to jot down thoughts for use in future years: which plants did well and which poorly, where to add plants to brighten dull spots, how many plants it took to fill a particular area, and names of plants you've admired in other people's gardens. Also make a note of where you've planted bulbs this fall so you don't dig into them next spring.

Zone Map: The Last Frost in Your Area

The United States Department of Agriculture Plant Hardiness Zone Map is a guide designed to link frost dates with regions. It divides the United States into 10 zones based on average minimum winter temperatures, with Zone 1 being the coldest in North America and Zone 10 the warmest. Each zone is further divided into sections that represent 5 degree differences within the 10-degree zone.

This map should only be used as a general guideline, since the lines of separation between zones are not as clear-cut as they appear. Plants recommended for one zone might do well in the southern part of the adjoining colder zone, as well as in the neighboring warmer zone. Factors such as altitude, exposure to wind, and amount of available sunlight also contribute to a plant's winter hardiness. Also note that the indicated temperatures are average minimums—some winters will be colder and others warmer than this figure.

Even though the USDA Plant Hardiness Zone Map is not perfect, it is *the* most useful single guide for determining which plants are likely to survive in your garden and which ones are not.

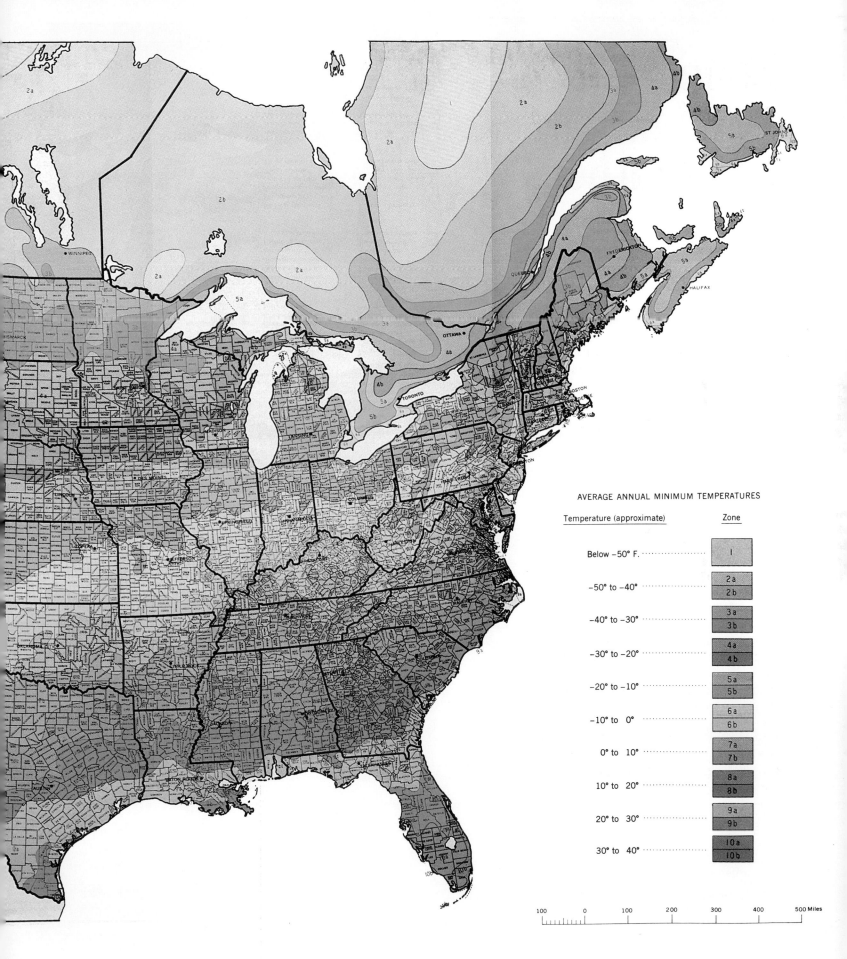

AVERAGE ANNUAL MINIMUM TEMPERATURES

Temperature (approximate)	Zone
Below −50° F.	1
−50° to −40°	2a
	2b
−40° to −30°	3a
	3b
−30° to −20°	4a
	4b
−20° to −10°	5a
	5b
−10° to 0°	6a
	6b
0° to 10°	7a
	7b
10° to 20°	8a
	8b
20° to 30°	9a
	9b
30° to 40°	10a
	10b

100   0   100   200   300   400   500 Miles

Maintaining Annuals Month by Month

Careful preparation rewards a gardener with colorful blooms.

T
he following list includes the various gardening tasks to be done each year. *When* they should be done depends on the climate in your area. Our month-by-month chart indicates when each task should be performed in the different hardiness zones in North America. Because conditions can differ within a zone and dates of first and last freezes of the season vary each year, these are only approximate guides. But they will provide you with a general outline for your garden year. One additional task—that of making notes for future years—should actually be carried out throughout the season. Be sure not to forget it just because it isn't on the list!

Tasks to be Done	Zones 1–3	Zones 4–5	Zones 6–7	Zones 8–10
1—Plan garden for coming season*	NOV/DEC/JAN	DEC/JAN	JAN	JAN/AUG
2—Order seeds*	FEB	FEB	JAN	JAN/AUG
3—Buy seed starting supplies*	FEB	FEB	JAN	JAN
4—Take cuttings*	MAR	MAR	FEB	JAN
5—Start slower-growing seeds indoors*	APR	MAR	MAR	
6—Prick off seedlings*	APR	APR	MAR	
7—Start faster-growing seeds indoors*	MAY	APR	APR	
8—Prick off later seedlings*	MAY	APR	APR	
9—Lay out new beds	APR	APR	APR	FEB
10—Take soil samples if not done in the fall	APR/MAY	MAR/APR	MAR	JAN
11—Adjust pH if not done during the winter	MAY	APR	APR	FEB
12—Add conditioners to soil	MAY	APR	APR	FEB
13—Add fertilizers to soil as recommended by testing lab	MAY	APR	APR	FEB
14—Till soil	MAY	APR	APR	FEB/SEPT
15—Purchase and plant nontender bedding plants	MAY	APR/MAY	APR	FEB
16—Harden off home-grown bedding plants*	MAY	MAY	APR	
17—Lay mulch on beds for bedding plants. (See step 24 for direct seed sowing.)	MAY	MAY	APR	MAR/SEPT

Tasks to be Done	Zones 1–3	Zones 4–5	Zones 6–7	Zones 8–10
18—Sow seeds directly in outdoor beds. Feed as needed until seeds sprout. (Do not allow them to become dry.)*	JUNE	MAY	APR	MAR/SEPT/OCT
19—Purchase tender bedding plants	JUNE	MAY	ARP	MAR
20—Pinch and plant tender bedding plants	JUNE	MAY	APR	MAR
21—Plant out tender bulbs	JUNE	JUNE	MAY	APR
22—Sprinkle pre-emergent weed killer on soil between bedding plants (**Caution:** Do not use with direct-sown seeds or young plants.)	JUNE	JUNE	MAY	APR
23—Thin seedlings from direct-sown seeds*	JUNE	JUNE	MAY	APR/OCT
24—Lay mulch when seedlings reach 4 to 6 inches*	JUNE	JUNE	MAY	APR/OCT
25—Put in plant supports	JUNE	JUNE	MAY	APR/OCT
26—Deep water as needed	JULY	JULY/AUG	JUNE/JULY/AUG	MAY/JUNE/JULY/OCT/NOV/DEC
27—Fertilize with general plant food (sidedress or water on)	JULY	JULY/AUG	JUNE/JULY/AUG	MAY/JUNE/JULY/OCT/NOV/DEC
28—Weed as needed	JULY	JULY/AUG	JUNE/JULY/AUG	MAY/JUNE/JULY/OCT/NOV/DEC
29—Remove dead flowers, as needed	JULY	JULY/AUG	JUNE/JULY/AUG	MAY/JUNE/JULY/OCT/NOV/DEC
30—Control pests and diseases, as needed	JULY	JULY/AUG	JUNE/JULY/AUG	MAY/JUNE/JULY/OCT/NOV/DEC
31—Plant biennial seeds for next year*	JULY	AUG	AUG	JULY
32—Take cuttings	JULY	AUG	AUG	JULY
33—Pick flowers for drying	AUG	SEPT	SEPT	JULY
34—Harvest mature seeds	AUG	SEPT	SEPT	JULY
35—Pot plants to bring indoors for the winter	AUG	SEPT	SEPT	
36—Protect beds from early frosts	AUG	SEPT	SEPT	
37—Dig and store tender bulbs	SEPT	SEPT	OCT	JAN
38—Pull out dead plants; destroy or compost	SEPT	OCT	OCT	
39—Make notes for next year's garden	SEPT	OCT	OCT	
40—Apply mulch to depleted and bare spots for winter	SEPT	OCT	NOV	
41—Take soil samples	SEPT	OCT	NOV	
42—Clean and sharpen tools; store for winter	OCT	NOV	DEC	DEC
43—Adjust pH according to soil test recommendations	OCT	NOV	DEC	

* Applies only to those plants that are started from seed. Does *not* apply to purchased bedding plants.

Ease of Care

	Ease	Comments
Abelmoschus moschatus	E	Needs abundant water
Alternanthera species	E	Frost-tender
Alyssum, Sweet	E	Survives light frosts
Amaranth, Globe	E	
Angel's Trumpet; Trumpet Flower; Horn of Plenty	E	Frost-tender
Asparagus Fern	E	Gross feeder
Aster; China Aster	MD	Prone to disease carried by insects
Baby Blue Eyes	E	Reseeds vigorously
Baby's Breath	E	Lime-loving
Bachelor's Button; Cornflower	E	
Basil	E	Poor soil makes leaves more pungent
Beard Tongue	E	Needs acid soil
Begonia, Fibrous, Wax, Everblooming	E	
Begonia, Tuberous	MD	Prone to mildew, brittleness
Bells of Ireland; Shell Flower; Molucca Balm	E	Reseeds vigorously
Black-Eyed Susan; Gloriosa Daisy	E	
Blanket Flower	E	May need fungicide
Blood Leaf	E	Frost-tender
Blue Bells, California	E	Heat-sensitive
Blue Lace Flower	E	Heat-sensitive
Blue Marguerite	E	Heat-sensitive
Burning Bush; Summer Cypress; Belvedere	E	Reseeds vigorously
Caladium hortulanum	E	
Calla; Calla Lily	E	
Calliopsis; Tickseed	E	Reseeds vigorously

	Ease	Comments
Candytuft	E	Lime-loving
Canna	E	
Canterbury Bells	E	Shade makes stems weak
Castor Bean	E	
Sweet False Chamomile	E	Reseeds vigorously
Chilean Bell Flower	E	
China Pink	E	Needs alkaline soil
Chrysanthemum	E	
Cleome; Spider Flower	E	Reseeds vigorously
Cockscomb, Plumed	E	
Coleus	E	
Corn Cockle	E	Reseeds vigorously
Cosmos	E	Reseeds vigorously
Cup and Saucer Vine; Cathedral Bells	E	Frost-tender
Dahlia	E	Needs air circulation
Daisy, African (Arctotis)	E	
Daisy, African (Golden Ageratum)	E	
Daisy, Dahlberg; Golden Fleece	E	Reseeds vigorously
Daisy, English	E	
Daisy, Livingstone	E	Resistant to salt spray
Daisy, Swan River	E	
Daisy, Transvaal; Barberton Daisy	E	
Dusty Miller	E	
Echium	E	Avoid too much fertility
Everlasting; Strawflower	E	
Firecracker Plant	E	Frost-tender
Floss Flower	E	
Foliage Plants	E	
Forget-Me-Not	E	Reseeds vigorously
Forget-Me-Not, Chinese; Hound's Tongue	E	
Forget-Me-Not, Summer; Cape Forget-Me-Not	E	Do not fertilize
Four O'Clock; Marvel of Peru	E	Reseeds vigorously
Foxglove	E	Reseeds vigorously
Fuchsia; Lady's Ear Drops	E	Gross feeder
Gazania; Treasure Flower	E	Heat-sensitive
Geranium, Ivy Leaf	E	Heat-sensitive
Geranium, Regal	E	
Geranium, Zonal	E	Frost-tender
Gladiolus; Glad	E	
Godetia; Farewell-to-Spring; Clarkia	E	

	Ease	Comments
Gourds, Ornamental	E	Frost-tender
Grasses, Ornamental	E	
Heliotrope; Cherry Pie	E	Tolerates high humidity
Hibiscus, Chinese; Hawaiian Hibiscus; Rose of China	E	
Hollyhock	MD	Prone to rust
Impatiens; Busy Lizzie; Patience	E	
Impatiens, New Guinea	E	
Variegated Ground Ivy	E	
Joseph's Coat; Love Lies Bleeding; Prince's Feather	E	Avoid root rot
Lantana	E	Frost-sensitive
Larkspur; Annual Delphinium	E	
Lisianthus; Prairie Gentian	E	
Lobelia	E	May need fungicide
Lotus Vine; Parrot's Beak	E	
Love-in-a-Mist; Devil in a Bush	E	
Lupine	E	
Magic Carpet Plant	E	
Mallow; Cheese	E	
Flowering Maple	E	
Marigold, Cape; African Daisy; Star-of-the-Veldt	E	Heat-sensitive
Marigold, American; Marigold, French	E	
Marigold, Pot; Field Marigold	E	
Meadow Foam; Fried Eggs	E	Reseeds vigorously
Melampodium	E	
Mignonette	E	Reseeds vigorously
Monkey Flower	E	Tolerates wet soil
Morning Glory Vine	E	
Nasturtium	E	Reseeds vigorously
Nemesia	E	
Nicotiana; Flowering Tobacco	E	
Nierembergia; Cup Flower	E	
None So Pretty	E	
Ornamental Corn	E	Frost-tender
Ornamental Cabbage; Ornamental Kale	E	
Ornamental Peppers	E	Drought-tolerant
Pansy	E	
Perilla; Beefsteak Plant	E	Frost-tender
Petunia	E	
Phlox, Annual; Texas Pride	MD	Prone to mildew
Pocketbook Plant	E	

	Ease	Comments
Poppy, California	E	Hard to transplant
Poppy, Horned; Sea Poppy	E	
Poppy, Iceland	E	
Poppy, Mexican Tulip	E	Drought-tolerant
Portulaca; Moss Rose	E	Reseeds vigorously
Primrose	E	
Rock Purslane	E	
Rose Mallow	E	
Rose-of-Heaven	E	
Salpiglossis; Painted Tongue	E	Frost-tender
Salvia; Scarlet Sage	E	
Sanvitalia; Creeping Zinnia	E	
Sapphire Flower	E	
Scabiosa; Pincushion Flower; Mourning Bride	E	Sensitive to water
Scarlet Flax	E	
Scarlet Pimpernel; Poor-Man's Weather Glass	E	
Scarlet Runner Bean	E	
Schizanthus; Butterfly Flower; Poor Man's Orchid	E	Blooms best with root restriction
Scotch Thistle	E	Reseeds vigorously
Snapdragon	E	
Snow-In-Summer; Ghost Weed	E	Reseeds vigorously
Southern Star; Star of the Argentine	E	
Stock	E	Survives light frost
Sundrop	E	
Sunflower	E	
Sweet Pea	E	
Thunbergia; Black-Eyed Susan Vine; Clock Vine	E	
Tidy Tips	E	Drought-resistant
Tithonia; Mexican Sunflower	E	
Toadflax	E	
Torenia; Wishbone Flower	E	Tolerates high humidity
Tuberose	E	Frost-tender
Venidium; Monarch of the Veldt; Cape Daisy	E	Heat-sensitive
Verbena	MD	Prone to mildew
Vinca; Madagascar Periwinkle	E	Needs air circulation
Violet, Persian	E	
Wallflower, English	E	
Zinnia	MD	Prone to mildew

E = Easy   MD = Moderately Difficult

This beautiful border of marigolds, cosmos, zinnias, dusty miller, and snapdragons illustrates the versatility of annuals. They brighten up this porch splendidly, adding seasonal color to an otherwise stark location.

CHAPTER 4

GARDENING WITH ANNUALS

Any visitor to commercial public gardens such as Disney World or Busch Gardens can tell you just what a fantastic display annuals provide. Bare walls are decorated with half-baskets full of flowers; large massed plantings line sidewalks and fill sitting areas; huge planters are jammed with color; baskets of blooms hang from tree limbs and archways; and window boxes decorate balconies.

The versatility of annuals makes them the perfect choice in many planting situations. After all, they bloom for a long time and come in a wonderful variety of colors, sizes, and forms—all producing an abundance of blossoms or decorative leaves. Most of them thrive with minimal care. And they're inexpensive to grow.

Whether you plan to tuck annuals into a few blank spots to brighten the summer yard or to plant them in containers for use both indoors and outside, there is information in this chapter to help you. Likewise, if you feature them in large planting beds, use them to mask an ugly wall, or grow them as a source of blooms to cut and bring inside as decorations, the following pages will show you how to do so with ease and success.

Whether you have a large yard, a small one, or just a balcony, you'll find ideas here for ways to appreciate the beauty of annuals. Above all, you can enjoy the experience of planning your own garden, keeping in mind that there is no "right way" or "wrong way," there's just *your way*. If you're happy with the garden you create, that's what's important.

Laying Out an Annuals Garden

Colorful marigolds bring added life to this Japanese-style bridge.

It is seldom possible to create an attractive annuals garden simply by planting out boxed plants or flower seeds without any plan. More often than not, this approach will produce unsatisfactory results. You need advance planning. Without it, it's easy to slip up and be disappointed.

The best way to plan is with a simple sketch. Draw a quick outline of your garden bed, noting down its approximate dimensions and the amount of sun the area receives each day. Also list the names of your favorite annuals so you'll be sure to include most, if not all, of them in your plan.

The next step is to look up your favorites and to note the colors they come in and their growth habits. Mark down whether they prefer full sun, partial shade, or full shade. Also specify how tall they grow (T=tall, I=intermediate, L=low, V=vining). Check to see if any of your favorites prefer a different amount of sun than your site has available; cross out those that aren't suitable. In other words, if you love impatiens, but your bed is in full sun, only New Guinea impatiens will succeed there. (Since other varieties of impatiens do not tolerate full sun, you may want to see if there's a shady location elsewhere in the yard or on a covered porch where you can enjoy a few instead.)

If you have very few favorites and a large space to fill, add a second list of annuals that you find attractive and that fit the light and color limitations of your site. Use seed catalogs to help choose the variety of petunia, marigold, snapdragon, or whatever, with the color and height you want. Be sure to note down several variety names and sources if a plant comes in more than one desirable color.

Use colored pencils to color in planting sections within your bed outline. A more informal and interesting design will result if you vary the size and shape of these sections. Then decide which plants should go into what sections of your plan. Remember to keep tall plants in the back and low plants up front, filling in with intermediate heights. That way none of the plants will be blocked from view. If a bed is going to be in an area where it will be seen from all sides, the tallest plants should be in the center of the bed with low ones around the outer edges.

As you plan, be sure flower colors in adjacent sections vary but don't clash. Maintain a balance of color in the bed—avoid placing all the same-colored flowered plants on one side. In large beds, repeat the same variety in several sections, making the sections much larger than you would in smaller beds. Once you've decided what will go in each section, double-check to be sure you haven't inadvertently made a mistake—such as putting a tall plant up front or all the marigolds in one area. If you have, it's easy to change on paper.

Once the plan is in its final form, you can then figure out approximately how many plants you'll need of each kind to fill the allotted space. This will help in ordering seeds for sowing or starting ahead and in buying boxed bedding plants. **Caution:** If you plan to buy bedding plants rather than grow your own, remember that the variety of plants available will be limited. It might be best to visit suppliers and make a list of what colors and kinds of plants they have available *before* making your garden plan. That way you won't have to settle for substitutions or totally redo your garden plan.

Annuals Garden Against a Wall or Fence

This plan shows how to lay out a garden bed so all of the plants will be well displayed against the backdrop of a wall, fence, or building. Note that space has been left between the wall and the rear of the flower bed so gardening work—weeding, watering, spraying, etc.—can be done from both sides of the bed.

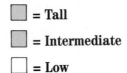

☐ = Tall

☐ = Intermediate

☐ = Low

Wall or fence

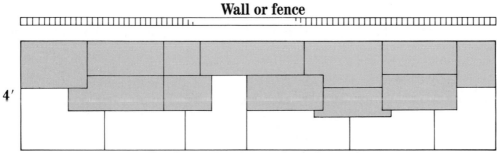

4′

Garden to be viewed from front side

Annuals Garden Displayed From All Sides

☐ = Tall

☐ = Intermediate

☐ = Low

When planting a flower bed that is to be on display from all sides, the plants should be placed as illustrated in this plan. A pathway through the middle of the bed allows easy access for plant care if a bed is wider than 3 to 4 feet.

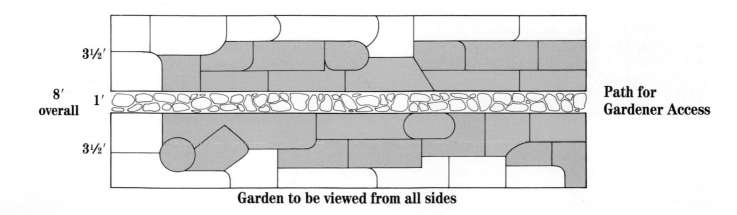

8′ overall

3½′

1′

3½′

Path for Gardener Access

Garden to be viewed from all sides

Planning an Annuals Garden

3 To plan a flower bed, sketch its shape, noting its dimensions and the amount of sun available to it (full sun, partial shade, or full shade). Make a list of your personal plant favorites with notes about their height and colors. Cross off any that are inappropriate for the amount of light available beforehand. Once you've found niches for all of your favorites, make a second list of other plants you'd like to try—use some of these to fill any empty slots in your plan.

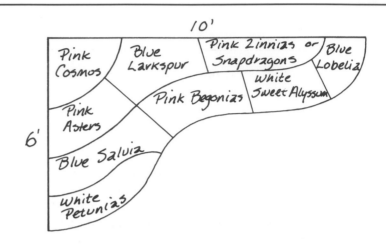

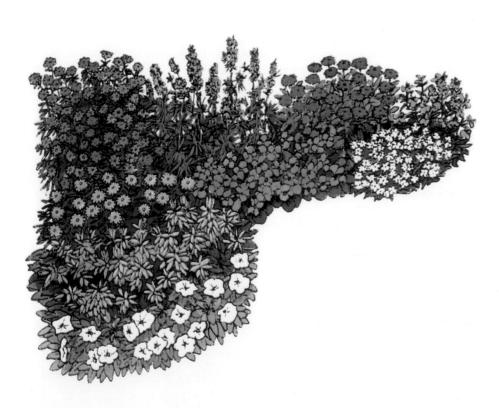

Scale
    1″ = 2′

Colors
    blue = B
    pink = P
    white = W

Height
    Low = L
    Intermediate = I
    Tall = T

Favorites - *must* have:
√ Sweet Alyssum W; L
√ Asters   B, P, W; I
√ Larkspur   B, P, W; I
√ Lobelia   B, W; L
√ Petunia   B, P, W; L
√ Salvia   B, P, W; I

Other possibilities:
√ Begonia   B, W; L
√ Cosmos   P, W; T
√ Geranium   P, W; I
   Lantana   P, W, B; L
√ Snapdragon   P, W; L, I, T
√ Zinnia   W, P; L, I, T

√ = Those actually used in plan.

Mixed Gardens

Many of us recall the old-fashioned gardens of our grandparents or other elderly relatives and neighbors. These were usually a hodge-podge of annuals, perennials, and shrubs. Frequently, there were also trees, vegetables, and small fruits—strawberries, raspberries, or currants—mixed in.

It seemed that gardens, rather than being planned, more or less "happened." More likely, they evolved. As the gardener fancied something new or was given a plant by a friend, it was inserted into an available blank spot. Where yards were small and space was limited, these mixed gardens combined whatever was at hand. The end result often had an individual charm that was undeniable and delightful.

There's no reason, of course, why we can't create a similarly informal effect in a modern garden. For those with limited garden space, a mixed garden makes especially good sense. It allows us to have some of our personal favorites, rather than limiting us to only a few kinds of plants—as is the case of massed garden designs.

A mixed garden is a very personal one that truly reflects the individual taste of the homeowners. Rather than being a garden for show, it's a garden designed for the pleasure of those who own it. If others who visit it also find it enjoyable, so much the better.

Some uniquely charming mixed gardens are possible. Fruit trees, such as peach, pear, or apple, can supply partial shade to flower beds filled with combinations of different-colored annuals and perennials. Clumps of favorite vegetables can also be placed among these flowering plants. The casual visitor might never notice these, since so many vegetables have attractive foliage to add to the garden scene. Feathery carrot tops; purplish beet greens; the bold and interesting foliage of parsnips; smooth, blue-green onion spikes; and large rhubarb leaves all make attractive additions to any flower bed.

If you don't want to be limited to only a few kinds and colors of flowers in your garden, consider planting a mixed garden. With the wonderful array of annuals at your disposal, it's even possible to have an entirely different and unique garden every growing season.

Multicolored snapdragons and petunias give this garden an informal look.

ANNUALS FOR MIXED GARDENS

Sweet Alyssum	Nasturtium
Aster	Nicotiana
Baby's Breath	Pansy
Bachelor's Button	Petunia
Cockscomb	Phlox
Coleus	Shirley Poppy
Cosmos	Portulaca
Dahlia	Blue Salvia
Forget-Me-Not	Scabiosa
Heliotrope	Snapdragon
Hollyhock	Sweet Pea
Impatiens	Torenia
Larkspur	Verbena
Lisianthus	Vinca
American/French	Xeranthemum
Marigold	Zinnia

Combining Annuals, Fruits, and Vegetables

This small garden contains a mixture of annuals, fruits, and vegetables. This plan could easily be modified to include your own food favorites.

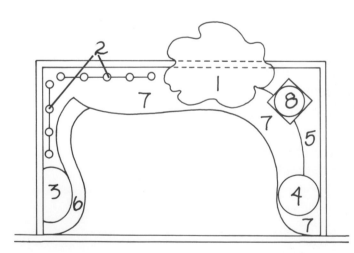

1. Favorite flowering tree
2. Pole beans, snap peas, or raspberries on trellis
3. Rhubarb
4. Blueberry (2 different varieties for cross-pollination)
5. Beets or Swiss chard
6. Herbs and other vegetable favorites
7. Flowering annuals
8. Fountain, statue, or other garden feature

The same small space is packed full of color while providing a private, vine-covered sitting area. The birdbath might be replaced with a piece of garden sculpture or an unusual accent plant—perhaps a tree lantana, topiary evergreen, or rosemary.

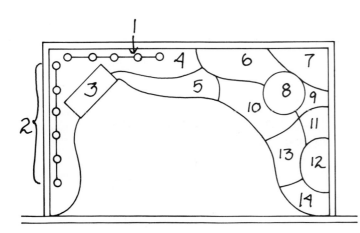

1. Morning Glory ⎱ over trellis
2. Moon Vine ⎰
3. Garden seat or other garden feature with impatiens planted around and behind it.
4. Marigold
5. Lobelia – blue
6. Cosmos – mixed
7. Hollyhock – mixed
8. Birdbath
9. Marigold
10. Red salvia or red peppers
11. Perilla
12. Pot Marigold – yellow
13. Sweet alyssum – white
14. Swan River daisy

Container Gardening

Geraniums are excellent choices for all sorts of containers.

Probably no form of gardening allows more versatility than container gardening. Growing plants in containers makes it possible to garden in situations where there is no yard or soil available: on a rooftop, a high-rise balcony, a deck, a fire escape, or even in an area that's covered with concrete.

The containers themselves can be as plain or elaborate as you wish. Clay or plastic pots; wood, plastic, or metal window boxes; decorator pots of ceramic, terra cotta, alabaster, or wrought iron; recycled plastic or metal pails; wire frames lined with sphagnum moss; a child's cast-off metal wagon; hanging planters; a plastic-lined bushel basket—any of these can be used. Here's a chance to give your imagination free rein!

All that's essential is that the container be capable of holding soil as well as allowing excess water to drain away. Keep in mind that plants thrive more readily in larger amounts of soil, because the soil temperature and moisture level fluctuate less as soil volume increases. Unless the gardener is extremely vigilant, plants are more likely to suffer frequent drying out and overheating when planted in small pots.

Annuals are particularly well-suited for use in container plantings. They quickly fill and overflow the planters. You can also plant them in masses of a single species or in a mixture of different kinds and colors.

Another advantage to growing plants in containers is their portability. You can move them from one area to another at will, as long as you remember that shade-loving plants can quickly burn if shifted into brilliant sun. Conversely, sun lovers won't flourish if shaded for more than a few days.

Planters full of annuals can be used singly or in groups. They can be mixed with houseplants brought outdoors for summer or inserted here and there in between shrubbery. Container plants can be hung from a garden fence, a low-hanging tree limb, or a porch rail. Even a small apartment balcony can be turned into a colorful garden by filling it with annuals.

Care of container plantings takes little total time, but it does require daily attention. Soil moisture needs to be checked every evening. When the weather is dry and windy, you may even need to check soil moisture morning and evening. Rub a small amount of the surface soil from each pot between your thumb and finger to test the moisture level. Ideally, you want to rewater each planter *before* the soil becomes bone dry. On the other hand, the soil should not be constantly soaking wet or the plants will drown. Therefore, it's necessary to keep track of the moisture level very conscientiously.

To be sure that water reaches all of the soil in the container, fill the planter to the rim with water, allowing it to soak in completely. If no water comes out of the drainage holes, fill again. Repeat this process until water starts to drip from the bottom of the container.

To keep the plantings looking full and to encourage abundant blooming, remove dead flower heads promptly. At the same time, check for any signs of insect or disease problems. Once every ten days to two weeks, water with a mild fertilizer solution. That's all it takes to keep container gardens in peak condition.

Container gardening can be an ideal solution for people with physical limitations that prevent them from working down at ground level. It can also be the answer for those with soil problems. For anyone, growing annuals in containers can provide an extra dimension of gardening pleasure, both outdoors in summer and indoors in winter.

Drainage in Container Gardening

To grow plants successfully in containers, good drainage is essential. Drainage holes need to be covered to keep soil in place: Pieces of broken pottery, fine screening, or a coffee filter are all good choices. You can also add a layer of small stones, perlite, or coarse sand in the bottom of the container. Indoors, or on a porch where dripping water would do damage, place a drip tray under the container to catch excess water.

Gardening in Decorative Containers

When using a decorative container with no drainage holes, place a well-drained pot inside of it in which to actually grow plants. Raise the inner pot on a layer of pebbles to keep it above water level. Peat moss in the space between the inner and outer pots would provide insulation to help stabilize soil temperatures.

ANNUALS THAT DO WELL IN CONTAINERS	
Fibrous Begonia	Nasturtium
Coleus	Pansy
Dracaena	Ornamental Pepper
Geranium	Perilla
Impatiens	Petunia
Lobelia	Phlox
American/French Marigold	Sweet Pea
	Verbena
Pot Marigold	Vinca
Morning Glory Vine	

The Versatility of Window Boxes

Window boxes are versatile planters that are not just useful on window ledges. They can also hang from porch rails or fences, perch along the tops of walls, mark the edge of a deck, or line a walk or driveway. Add them wherever you want color without creating a flower bed.

The Many Uses of Hanging Baskets

Hanging baskets provide another almost endless source of color. You can group them at different levels on a porch; hang them from tree limbs; or add half-baskets to brighten a blank wall or bare fence. You can even create tall pillars of color by hanging baskets from an old coat rack or other suitable recycled stand.

Cutting Garden

If you'd like to have containers full of flowers brightening your home, a perfect source is a cutting garden filled with annuals. Most gardeners are unwilling to cut many blooms from their regular flower beds because they want as full and colorful a display as possible. Therefore, a garden specially set aside to supply flowers for cutting is a good solution. This can be a separate flower bed, or you can devote a row or two of your vegetable patch to a flower crop.

Most seed companies offer packets of "Cutting Flower Mix" that contain a variety of flowering annuals. The mixture varies, but it will always include seeds that are easy to grow and produce nice, bouquet-type flowers. Mixes usually include some, but not all, of the following plants: marigolds, zinnias, plumed cockscomb, baby's breath, bachelor's buttons, pot marigolds, cosmos, asters, blanket flowers, and seedling dahlias.

The major disadvantage to buying such a mix is that you don't know in advance what colors the flowers will be. If you want to key the flower colors to the colors in your home or if you only want specific kinds of cut flowers, then you'll need to purchase those varieties separately.

When cutting for indoor use, select flowers that are in bud or in early stages of bloom. Those in later stages of bloom should be cut from the plant and discarded. If they're left, plant strength will be wasted on the formation of seeds. To obtain the longest period of enjoyment possible from cut flowers, pick them in the early morning. Use a sharp knife and make a slanted cut. Cut just above the point where another flower bud or a side shoot is beginning to grow. This way, plant energy will quickly shift to production of additional blooms.

As you cut, place the flowers in a container of water and bring them indoors promptly. Remove the leaves from the lower portion of each stem, immediately putting the flowers back into a tall container of fresh water. You can either arrange bouquets right away or keep cut flowers in a cool location to arrange later.

Each time you recut a stem, always use a sharp knife and cut on a slant. This keeps all available stem cells open to the transfer of water up into the cut flower. Scissors and shears can pinch some of these water channels closed. Also, remember to remove all leaves that will be under water once the flower is in a container. If left on, they'll rot, which not only causes a terrible odor, but also shortens flower life by clogging stem cells needed for water transfer.

Annuals are lovely in both elaborate formal arrangements and in simple, informal bouquets. It's easy to quickly make

A cutting garden full of marigolds, zinnias, daisies, and baby's breath can bring annual color into a home.

attractive bouquets if you keep these hints in mind as you pick and arrange flowers:

- Select flowers in bud as well as in early bloom.
- Select colors that blend well.
- Separate clashing colors with gray foliage or white flowers.
- Cut flowers at different lengths. Leave longer stems on smaller flowers; shorter stems on larger ones.
- Mix flowers of varying sizes and forms.
- Use containers that are narrower at the top than at the bottom for an easy, informal bouquet. If a different effect is desired, use cylindrical vases or containers with flared mouths.
- Match container size to bouquet size.

ANNUALS FOR THE CUTTING GARDEN	
Canna	Pansy
Chrysanthemum	Poppy (sear stems)
Coleus	Salpiglossis
African Daisy	Blue Salvia
Transvaal Daisy	Scabiosa
Ornamental Grasses	Snapdragon
Larkspur	Stock
Pot Marigold	Sweet Pea
Nasturtium	Vinca
Nicotiana	Zinnia

Elements of Attractive Bouquets

1. Stems of different lengths make bouquets more interesting.

2. Flowers in different stages of bloom provide more variety of form than when they're all at the same stage.

3. Matching vase size to bouquet size keeps a good balance between flowers and container.

4. Daisy-type flowers are fresh when all of the buds in the flower center are closed or when only the outermost ring is blooming. When the entire center shows pollen, the flower is finished blooming and ready to die.

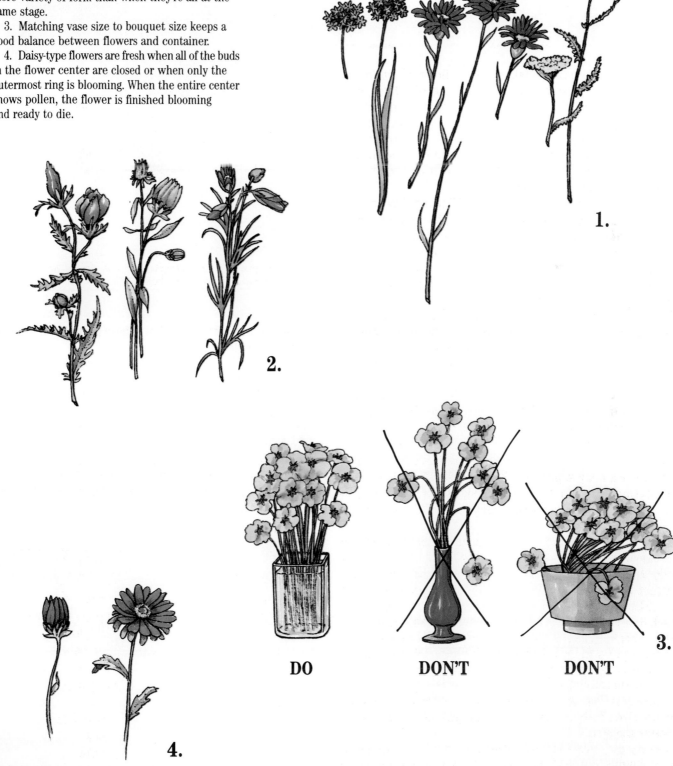

1.

2.

DO   DON'T   DON'T

3.

4.

Drying & Pressing Annuals

A basket of dried annuals is a year-round treat.

There are several different drying techniques for annuals. The easiest is hang drying. After picking, all leaves should be removed, and flowers grouped in bunches of 6 to 8 stems. Wind an elastic band tightly around the stems.

Hang bundles upside-down out of the light in a well-ventilated, dry area. Leave enough space between bundles to allow for good air circulation and protect the bundles by enclosing them in large paper bags. The flowers will dry in two to three weeks. They can then be laid in covered boxes or left hanging.

Some flowers are too thick and others too delicate to successfully hang dry. Instead they can be dried with a desiccant—a material that will draw moisture into itself. Floral desiccant is sold commercially. Or you can make it yourself by mixing equal parts of fine, dry sand and borax powder.

To use, pour an inch or more of desiccant in the bottom of a box, then lay the flowers on top. Very carefully spoon more desiccant up and around each flower head. Once all of the flowers are mounded over, an additional inch or two of desiccant should be gently poured on top. Use a large, shallow box for long spikes of bloom such as larkspur. For single, dense blooms, like roses and marigolds, remove the flower stem first and replace it with a stiff wire stem. Lay the flowers flat on the surface of the desiccant, then mound more dessicant around and over them.

Drying will take several weeks, depending on the density of the flowers. When they're dry, carefully unbury them, gently brush away any adhering desiccant with a soft artist's brush, and store them in covered boxes in a dry place until ready to use.

A third drying method is to press flowers and leaves between layers of absorbent blotting paper or paper towels. The drawback to this method is that everything comes out flat. But for use in pictures, notepaper, or as a frame around a motto or wedding announcement, flowers dried this way can be very effective.

This technique works best with small flowers that are not very thick, such as pansies, petunias, and baby's breath. It is also suited for parts of flowers, such as single petals of sweet peas, poppies, and cosmos. To dry, start with a piece of heavy cardboard at the base; then lay a sheet of drying paper on top. Carefully arrange flowers and leaves, making sure that there is space between them. Lay one or two more layers of drying paper on top. Arrange another layer of leaves and flowers. Keep alternating until there are a half dozen layers of plant materials. Top these with more drying paper and a final piece of cardboard. Finally, place a heavy weight on top of the stack. Moisture will be squeezed out of the flowers into the paper. Check after a week to see how drying is progressing. If any mold has formed, remove and replace the drying paper. After several weeks, the plant materials will be ready to use or store.

FLOWERS TO AIR DRY	
Globe Amaranth	Ornamental Grasses
Baby's Breath*	Love-in-a-Mist pods
Bells of Ireland	Pansy*
Cockscomb	Single Pink*
Dusty Miller foliage*	Strawflower
Forget-Me-Not*	Zinnia

*=Press

Air Drying Flowers

Hang small bunches of flowers upside-down in a dry, well-ventilated area away from direct sun. Brown bags protect them against dust.

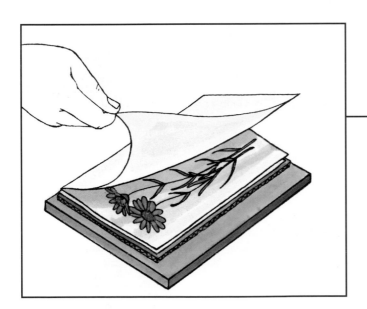

Drying Flowers with Weights

Alternate layers of absorbent paper and flowers, applying steady pressure on the stack to flatten and dry them.

FLOWERS TO DRY IN DESICCANT	
Dahlia*	Nasturtium
Gladiolus	Petunia
Hollyhock	Double Pink
Lantana	Snapdragon
Larkspur	Verbena
Marigold*	Zinnia*

*=Use wire stem

Drying Flowers in Desiccant

1

Replace natural stems with wire ones before laying large, individual flowers (such as marigolds, zinnias, asters, pot marigolds, and dahlias) in desiccant.

2 Lay tall flowers (such as larkspur, Canterbury bells, salvia, and gladiolus) horizontally on a layer of desiccant and gently sprinkle more desiccant around and over them.

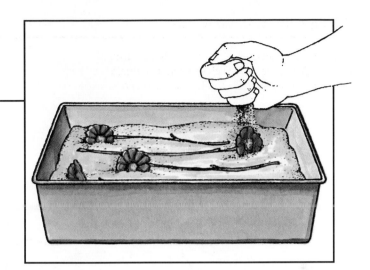

When flowers are dry, carefully remove them from the desiccant. Use a soft artist's brush to gently brush away any desiccant adhering to the blooms. **3**

This colorful garden uses only a few of the hundreds of annual species and varieties that are available. Even this simple planting of marigolds, salvia, and floss flowers is visual proof of the versatility of these lovely flowers.

CHAPTER 5

ENCYCLOPEDIA OF ANNUAL DELIGHTS

The plants selected for this directory cover a wide base—some are annuals, others are biennials, still others are perennials in some parts of the world. A few can even be recognized as houseplants. But they can all be used successfully to provide seasonal color outdoors as annuals. Names, descriptions, how-to-grow techniques, propagation, uses, and related species and varieties are all dealt with in depth. Photos are included for each entry.

Whether you live in a suburban home with a large yard or in a condominium 14 stories above the ground with only a windy balcony to plant in, you will find annuals here that will work for you. Given their extensive variety, there are types that can be used to beautify your particular living space, allowing you the opportunity to make entirely different planting choices each year.

Many of the plants listed in the directory are everywhere—a relatively reliable guide to their success rate. Some can be found as started plants at garden centers. Others you will have to start yourself from seed, either from seed packets found on racks locally or from mail order catalogs that offer the greatest selection available. You will be able to familiarize yourself with enough annuals so that you can decide for yourself what will work best for you, depending on your location and the amount of time and effort you want to put into starting and maintaining an annuals garden.

Abelmoschus moschatus

Abelmoschus moschatus

Newly introduced to ornamental gardens in the United States, this brightly colored flower is the same genus as the vegetable okra. Hibiscus is also a close relative and their resemblance is striking. Three- to 4-inch flowers appear in July from an early start indoors. Each flower lasts only a day, but the profusion of buds provides a continuous show of color.

Description: Plants grow 15 to 20 inches high and wide. Flowers are pink or red with white centers appearing above the arrowhead-shaped leaves.

How to grow: As with other members of the genus, it thrives in heat in full sun. Abundant water and a rich soil are also important for its best performance.

Propagation: By seed. Seeds take at least 15 days to germinate at 70° F. For husky plants, start at least 8 weeks prior to planting in the garden. First bloom is approximately 100 days after sowing. Plant 1 foot apart when the soil has warmed and nights remain above 50° F.

Uses: This bright plant can be used for a sunny garden ground cover. Plant it mid-border or as an edging for borders in front of taller plants. Use it as a container plant where its mounding, flowing habit combines well with taller plants. Its tropical appearance looks attractive with cannas, caladiums (in shade only), callas, and other exotic-appearing plants. Abelmoschus can also be grown on sunny windowsills indoors.

Related varieties: New varieties include *A. moschatus* 'Mischief,' bearing cherry-red flowers with white centers; 'Oriental Red,' similar in appearance; and 'Pink,' a bright pink. The Pacific series includes 'Pacific Pink' and 'Pacific Scarlet,' an orange-scarlet variety.

Alternanthera species

Alternanthera species

Alternantheras, of which there are possibly 200 species, are brilliantly colored foliage plants used for their leaves. Different species and varieties are strongly marked with yellow, pink, red, and coppery red.

Description: *A. ficoidea* forms a bushy plant up to 1 foot tall with leaves veined with brownish-red, carmine, and orange. Varieties include *A. f. amoena*, a compact form with red-splashed leaves and *A. f. rosea-nana*, with rosy pink leaves. *A. f. bettzickiana* is taller with olive-green to red leaves; *A. f. aurea-nana* has yellow leaves; and *A. f. brilliantissima* bears bright red leaves. *A. f. versicolor* has dark green or red leaves with pink veins and leaf margins of white and pink.

How to grow: High temperatures in full sun bring out the brightest coloring in alternantheras. They do best in well-drained soil that is not excessively moist. They are very frost-tender and should not be planted out until all danger of frost has passed and the soil is warm. They are usually kept sheared to induce uniformity in formal bedding situations. Plant small varieties 8 inches apart and tall ones every 12 inches.

Propagation: By cuttings or by division. Cuttings root easily and quickly.

Uses: Alternantheras are at their best combined in patterns of color in formal bedding situations, but they also make handsome container and hanging basket specimens. They can also be planted in design combinations with flowering annuals, the brightly colored leaves being especially effective with light-colored flowers. In areas without frost, they are often used for bed and walkway edgings.

Related species: *A. dentata rubinginosa* is a red- or purple-leaved form of a species that is normally green-leaved. It will normally grow from 1 to 2 feet tall.

Sweet Alyssum

Lobularia maritima

Alyssum is covered with thimblelike flowers for months on end, even through the winter in milder climates. A member of the mustard family, alyssum has a pervasive fragrance.

Description: Alyssum grows only a few inches high but spreads as much as 1 foot in diameter. The tiny flowers are closely packed around the small racemes that grow upward as the lower flowers fade. Although white is the most planted color, pink, lavender, and darker shades of violet are also available.

How to grow: Alyssum grows best in full sun in cool weather, but it will tolerate partial shade. Plants will survive light frosts. Space 6 to 8 inches apart. Alyssum will reseed vigorously.

Propagation: By seed. In mildest climates, it can be planted in the fall for cool season display. Otherwise, sow seeds outdoors as soon as the ground can be worked. For earliest bloom, sow seeds indoors 4 to 6 weeks earlier and transplant to the garden while plants are still small. Seeds germinate in 7 to 14 days at 65 to 70° F.

Uses: Alyssum is traditionally used for edging beds and borders. However, it can also tumble over the rocks in a rock garden or be planted in niches between paving stones. Place it where the scent can perfume the air for passersby. It makes a good, sunny ground cover for large or small areas. It is good in containers.

Related varieties: 'New Carpet of Snow' is the most planted, but the newer 'Wonderland' series has three distinctive colors: 'White,' 'Rosy-Red,' and 'Deep Purple,' the darkest alyssum color so far. Medal-winning 'Rosie O'Day' is a rose color. 'Snow Crystal' is a new, award-winning white variety.

Globe Amaranth

Gomphrena globosa

Here's a weather- and soil-tolerant plant. This tropical native has small, cloverlike flowers that continue coming through the whole summer season. It's a member of the amaranth family.

Description: Globe amaranth can grow up to 2 feet with newer, smaller varieties that are bushy dwarfs. The flowers are about 1 inch in diameter and have a papery texture. The flowers nestle in two large, modified leaves called bracts. The basic color is violet, but varieties have red, orange, pink, and creamy white flowers. The flowers are small, but there are many of them.

How to grow: The only demand for good performance is sun. Plant in the garden after the last frost and, depending on variety, space from 10 to 15 inches apart.

Propagation: By seed. Soak seeds in water for 3 to 4 days before sowing. Sow seeds in place in the garden after last frost. For earlier bloom, start transplants 6 to 8 weeks earlier. Seeds germinate in 14 to 21 days at 65 to 75° F.

Uses: The tall varieties are ideal for mid-border. Use dwarf varieties for edging beds, borders, or for a colorful ground cover. Combine them with other plants for container plantings. The tall varieties are especially good for cutting and drying.

Related species: *Gomphrena haageana* has yellow to orange, pinecone-shaped flowers, each about 1 inch in diameter. It also dries well.

Related varieties: 'Buddy' is a compact variety, growing only 9 to 12 inches tall. Flowers are deep purple in color. 'Strawberry Fields' is bright red and grows to 2 feet with long stems. It is splendid for cutting. Several mixtures are offered including white, pink, rose, and reddish-purple flowers.

Angel's Trumpet, Trumpet Flower, Horn of Plenty

Datura metel

A tropical native, the angel's trumpet has long flowers (up to 10 inches and 4 inches across the face). It is related to Jimson weed, and, like its cousin, contains a poisonous alkaloid called hyoscyamine.

Description: Angel's trumpet will grow 3 to 5 feet tall and has oval leaves up to 8 inches long with toothed margins. The flowers have 5 large lobes with pointed tips. Flowers are mostly white; but there are yellow, blue, and red forms too. Double-flowered varieties that contain duplicates of the flowers inside the spreading face are also available.

How to grow: Angel's trumpet grows well in any good, moist garden soil in full sun. They're very tender—so plant them out after all danger of frost has passed and the ground is warm. Prune freely to shape plants. To prolong bloom, remove the flowers as soon as they finish blooming to prevent seed formation. In frost-free areas of Zones 9 and 10, they can be overwintered outdoors. For overwintering indoors, move container plants to a cool but frost-free location and keep barely moist until spring. In late spring, cut back the plant and resume feeding and watering.

Propagation: By seed. Start seeds indoors 8 to 12 weeks before planting out. They germinate in 8 to 15 days at 70 to 85° F. Seeds may be saved from blooming plants for replanting the following season.

Uses: Because the trumpets hang down, it is of great advantage to plant them where they can be seen at eye level—on slopes, beside upward-leading paths, or as raised container plants.

Related species: *Datura sauveolens* has richly scented, white, lilylike trumpets that hang down. *Datura sanguinea* produces the same type of flowers in orange-red. It is perennial, sometimes producing flowers the first year.

Asparagus Fern

Asparagus densiflorus

Asparagus fern, of which there are many kinds, is related to the favorite springtime vegetable, and you'll notice that new shoots look like skinny asparagus spears. The most frequently used ornamental one is called *A. sprengeri.*

Description: New asparagus growth expands to form feathery, branched shoots 1 to 2 feet long. From a small plant in spring with 3 to 4 stems, at summer's end up to 10 or more billowing stalks emerge from pots or containers.

How to grow: Key factors to good growth include moderate water, a rich, well-drained soil, and full sunlight. Asparagus fern will tolerate low light (even existing satisfactorily as a houseplant), but growth will be diminished. Asparagus fern is a gross feeder; at planting use a slow-release fertilizer lasting summer long or feed weekly with a water-soluble fertilizer mixed at half the recommended strength.

Propagation: By seed (must be fresh) or by division. It's most readily available as started plants.

Uses: Asparagus fern is primarily used as a filler plant in containers of mixed flowers growing during the summer. It works in wall boxes, hanging baskets, window boxes, and planters of all kinds. Asparagus fern also grows well in partially shaded ground beds, alone, or intermixed with larger, shade-tolerant flowers such as tuberous begonias. Because asparagus fern is a vigorous plant, combine with plants of some stature so they are not overpowered.

Related varieties: Several other asparagus relatives are also used as ornamentals. *A. densiflorus* 'Myers' is a selection with stiff, upright growth like foxtails. *A. asparagoides,* the florist's smilax, is sometimes planted in flowering containers. Leaves are coarser, and it is a definite trailer.

Aster, China Aster

Callistephus chinensis

From one highly variable species has come a whole range of China asters—singles, semi-doubles, and doubles as well as tall, medium, and dwarf—all in a wide range of colors that includes white, pink, yellow, blue, and red.

Description: China asters are available from petite varieties that form compact mounds at 1 foot all the way to tall ones that grow to 2½ feet tall. Bloom times differ too, with early summer, midsummer, and late summer varieties. For a continuous show, you'll need to pick different varieties and/or stagger sowing dates.

How to grow: China asters grow best in full sun in rich soil. Two disease problems have plagued them in the past: aster yellows, carried by leafhoppers, and fusarium wilt, a soil-borne disease. Select disease-resistant varieties when you buy seeds or plants. Spray to control insects. Don't plant them in the same ground two years in a row. Sow seeds indoors 6 to 7 weeks before planting outside. They germinate in 10 to 20 days at 70° F. Otherwise, sow them into the ground outside after the last frost. Each variety blooms only 3 to 4 weeks, so for a continuous show, successive plantings must be two weeks apart.

Propagation: By seed.

Uses: Use China asters in beds and borders. Alternate a space and a plant, then fill the spaces with young plants that bloom later. Tall varieties make superb cut flowers.

Related varieties: 'Pinocchio' is a dwarf strain of mixed colors with a garden mum flower form and garden habit. 'Perfection Mixed' plants grow to 2 feet with 4-inch fully double flowers. 'Super Giants Mixture' grows to 2½ feet with 5-inch double spidery flowers.

Baby Blue Eyes

Nemophila menziesii

Baby blue eyes is a California native found in woodland sites. It blooms well all summer in full sun as long as it is kept well watered and night temperatures drop below 65° F.

Description: Baby blue eyes is a small plant, rarely growing over 10 inches high. The mounding plants are covered with flowers that are up to 1½ inches in diameter. Most commonly, the flowers are sky-blue centered with white; some forms are spotted or veined with deeper colors.

How to grow: Nemophila does best in cool, dry climates where it will grow well in full sun as long as it is kept moist. In warmer regions, it will benefit from partial or dappled shade. In the warmest areas, it should be planted for a spring display. Baby blue eyes must have good drainage; a light, sandy loam is best. Transplant plants into the garden after the last frost. Space 6 to 9 inches apart. Nemophila readily reseeds itself in the garden.

Propagation: By seed. To get a jump on warm weather in hot summer areas, sow seeds indoors 4 to 6 weeks prior to planting out. Seeds germinate in 7 to 12 days at 55° F. In cool summer areas, seeds can be sown in place outdoors in the spring as soon as the ground can be worked. Thin seedlings to a 6- to 9-inch spacing.

Uses: This low-growing plant is wonderful in front of borders and as an edging for beds, walkways, and paths. Try it tucked between the paving stones in a patio. Plant it in rock gardens. It's a natural for containers.

Related species: *Nemophila maculata* is commonly called "Five Spot." Very similar in growth habit, it's so named because the white, open-faced flowers have a purple spot at the tip of each petal.

Related varieties: Most seed houses offer their own selection of the species. Sometimes available is 'Insignis Blue.'

Baby's Breath

Gypsophila elegans

Their light, airy texture and petite white or pink flowers make baby's breath a wonderful addition to the garden. This annual is native to the Caucasus and is related to carnations. Because they bloom for only 6 weeks, new seedlings should be started to replace those that have finished blooming.

Description: Annual baby's breath grows to 1½ feet tall, forming an airy bush with many forked branches covered with flowers. Although the flowers, up to ½ inch in diameter, are usually white, there are pink, rose, and carmine forms.

How to grow: Grow in full sun in average, lime-rich garden soil. They grow rapidly and will come into bloom about 8 weeks after germination. Sow new baby's breath every 2 to 4 weeks to assure continuous bloom for the summer.

Propagation: By seed. Sow seeds outdoors in place after the danger of frost has passed. For earlier bloom, sow indoors in peat pots 2 to 3 weeks before planting out, then plant—pot and all. (They grow so rapidly, it is difficult to separate the seedlings, so plant them in a clump.) Germination takes 10 to 15 days at 70° F.

Uses: Baby's breath is effective in borders or cottage gardens. Baby's breath also makes a superb cut flower. It is used primarily as a filler to give unity to arrangements with strong vertical or horizontal lines.

Related species: *Gypsophila paniculata* is a perennial and widely planted. Both single- and double-flowers are found, with 'Bristol Fairy' the most popular species.

Related varieties: The favorite white is 'Covent Garden,' which is also the favorite cut flower strain. 'Kermesina' is a deep rose. 'Red Cloud' has shades ranging from pink to carmine. Mixtures of rose, white, and red are also available.

Bachelor's Button, Cornflower

Centaurea cyanus

The boutonniere flower is reputedly where this favorite got its name. And "cornflower blue" has frequently been used in the fashion trade to merchandise that particular shade. The flowers also come in soft shades of pink, lavender, maroon, red, and white.

Description: Bachelor's buttons grow 1 to 3 feet tall with innumerable round flowers held above the rather sparse, long and narrow gray-green leaves. The habit of growth is relatively loose.

How to grow: Full sun in average soil is good. For earliest bloom, sow seeds outdoors in the fall so they will start to grow before the first frost and bloom the next spring. They may also be started indoors and transplanted. Otherwise, sow seeds outdoors as early in the spring as the soil can be worked. Thin to 8 to 12 inches apart. Early bloom is heavy and prolific; it tapers off later. Repeat sowings will maintain a lush bloom.

Propagation: By seed. To grow seedlings indoors, germinate at 65° F four weeks before planting out. Germination time is 7 to 14 days.

Uses: Bachelor's buttons lend themselves to informal planting, especially with other annuals and perennials in beds and borders. When planting in containers, the gardener should take into consideration their informal growth habit. The flowers dry well, but stems are weak and must be wired for arrangements.

Related species: *C. moschata*, commonly called "sweet sultan," bears sweetly scented, fuzzy, 3- to 4-inch yellow, pink, lavender, or white blossoms. Growing to 2 feet, sweet sultans are good for cutting.

Related varieties: 'Blue Boy' grows to 2½ feet. Award-winning 'Jubilee Gem' is shorter at 12 inches. 'Polka Dot Mixed' and 'Frosty Mixed' have white or pastel contrasts at petal tips.

Basil

Ocimum basilicum

Basil is one of the world's favorite flavorings, used in all kinds of meat, fish, and vegetable dishes. The purple-leaved varieties can stand on their own in any ornamental garden, a feast for both the eye and the stomach.

Description: Basil is an herb that grows rapidly to form a bright green (or purple) bush. Standard varieties will grow 12 to 18 inches high with a 12-inch spread. Dwarf varieties may only grow 6 inches high and as wide. The arrow-shaped leaves are used for flavoring. The inconsequential flowers are best cut off when they appear, for they diminish foliage production. Plants should be sheared back hard to 6 inches to force young, new growth.

How to grow: Full sun and hot weather suit basil perfectly. Grown in poor soil, the flavoring oils will intensify, making the leaves more pungent. However, for ornamental use, moderate water and fertility (feed once a month) will increase basil's succulence and good looks.

Propagation: Sow seeds indoors 4 weeks prior to the last frost date. They'll germinate in 5 to 7 days at 70° F. Or sow seeds outdoors when the soil is warm and danger of frost has passed. Depending on the variety, plant 8 to 12 inches apart for ornamental use.

Uses: Compact, mounding varieties such as 'Spicy Globe' make ideal edging plants, while tall plants such as 'Green Ruffles' add a bright chartreuse note to borders. 'Purple Ruffles,' the best dark-leaved variety, is an admirable contrast to whites, pinks, and shades of green. Any of these also grow well in containers on decks and patios. For crisp overtones of extra flavor, look for other basils reminiscent of cinnamon or camphor.

Related varieties: 'Spicy Globe' (small, compact), 'Dark Opal,' and 'Purple Ruffles' (purple).

Beard Tongue

Penstemon heterophyllis

All but one of the 250 species of penstemon are American natives, although they vary greatly. Virtually all of them are perennial, but some are grown as summer annuals. The name "beard tongue" alludes to the fuzzy, insect-attracting stamens protruding from the open-faced flowers.

Description: *P. heterophyllis* is a shrub that grows up to 2 feet tall. A native of California, it has many flowers of dark blue, purple, or lilac. The long, narrow flowers are slightly over 1 inch long.

How to grow: Penstemons will grow in full sun or light shade in hot summer areas, needing slightly acid soil enriched with compost or leaf mold. They grow best in cool, mild winter climates. Set plants 12 to 18 inches apart. In Zones 8, 9, and 10, plants may be started in summer to bloom the next season. Elsewhere, seeds should be sown in mid-winter 12 to 14 weeks before flowering the same season.

Propagation: By seeds, cuttings, or division. Seed germination takes 10 to 15 days at a temperature of 55° F. Cuttings or division are often used for choice, named varieties. Cuttings may be taken in the spring and root readily.

Uses: Penstemons can be used at mid-border and are beautiful in mixed plantings or cottage gardens. They can be planted in beds combined with other flowers. Use them at the transition point between garden and woodlands. They make attractive cut flowers.

Related species: *Penstemon gloxinioides* is a cross between *P. gentianoides* and *P. Hartwegii*, with large flowers resembling gloxinias. 'Skyline' is a mix of large-flowered penstemons on bushy, compact plants. Colors are scarlet, rose, pink, violet, and deep gentian blue.

Related variety: 'True Blue' has deep blue, tubular flowers that contrast nicely with the gray-green leaves.

141

Fibrous Begonia, Wax Begonia, Everblooming Begonia

Begonia semperflorens

The brightly colored bedding begonias are equally at home in full sun (except where temperatures stay above 90° F for days on end) or dappled shade and will even bloom moderately well in full but bright shade (where trees are pruned high). From first setting them out until laid low by frost, they'll be packed with white, pink, rose, or red blossoms (some even have white petals edged in red), each flower centered by a cheery yellow eye. Virtually untouched by bugs or blight, their only shortcoming is a relatively narrow color range.

Description: Uniformity is the trademark of most tight mounds of closely packed leaves covered with blossoms. All four flower colors are available with your choice of leaf color: chocolaty-red or shades of green. The deeper-colored or bronze-leaved varieties offer especially eye-catching contrast with flowers. Though not as well known, there are also varieties with double flowers that resemble fat, little rosebuds and others with variegated foliage.

How to grow: Begonias perform well in rich, well-drained soil, but the soil must be allowed to dry between waterings. They'll form tight, compact plants in full sun, with increasingly looser form and fewer flowers as you move them deeper into the shade. Most hybrids will grow 6 to 9 inches high and spread as wide.

Propagation: By seed or cuttings. Most hybrids are grown from seed, but great patience is required. Dustlike seeds (2 million per ounce) must be sown in December or January for large, husky plants by May. Seeds need light to germinate. The seeds should be covered with glass in starting containers to maintain high humidity during germination. Germination temperature is 70 to 85° F and requires 14 to 21 days. Cuttings also root readily. A good way to start plants is on a sunny windowsill during winter.

Uses: Wax begonias lend themselves to large, formal plantings because of their uniform size and shapeliness. They're also suitable in front of summer annual borders and combine well with other cool-colored (blue and green) flowers in mixed plantings and containers. (They tend to be overwhelmed by hot colors.) Even a small planting of begonias in a small pot by a window or door will bloom lustily all summer.

Related varieties: The most popular, dark-leaved kinds are the 'Cocktail' series: 'Brandy,' 'Vodka,' 'Whiskey,' and 'Gin.' Good green-leaved varieties are found in the 'Olympia' and 'Prelude' series. 'Avalanche' begonias in pink or white are rangier, suited for containers and hanging baskets where their arching growth habit is handsome. 'Charm' begonias, grown only from cuttings, have green foliage marked with white. Calla lily begonias, which can be grown from seed, have green and white variegated foliage and pink flowers. 'Lady Frances' is one of the several double-flowered varieties you'll be able to find at garden centers.

Tuberous Begonia

Begonia tuberhybrida

A triumph of the breeder's art, tuberous begonias at their biggest have flowers of salad-plate size in fanciful forms and bright colors, even with petal edges tipped in a contrasting color (picotee). These beautiful flowers that grow well in morning sun and light shade have been joined in recent years by new varieties with altogether more modest flowers but many more of them.

Description: The large-flowered tuberous begonias come with many flower types, both upright and pendulous, single or double-flowered, and with frilled or plain petals. Unlike their *semperflorens* cousins, tuberous begonias offer wide color choices: white, pink, rose, red, orange, and yellow. They grow upright with large, arrow-shaped leaves. Both the large- and small-flowered tuberous begonias alternately bear male (ravishingly beautiful) and female (single and smaller) flowers. The smaller-flowered tuberous begonias bear many flowers up to 3 inches in diameter.

How to grow: Tuberous begonias grow best in midday and afternoon shade; otherwise the foliage will scorch. They need rich, well-drained soil with high organic matter. Allow soil to dry between waterings. The large-flowered varieties easily become top-heavy and require judicious staking, while the smaller-flowered ones can usually support their own growth. Powdery mildew is frequently a problem with tuberous begonias, especially if they are grown where the air around leaves and stems is stagnant. At the first signs of a white powder on leaves, spray with a fungicide.

Bells of Ireland, Shell Flower, Molucca Balm

Molucella laevis

Propagation: By seed, tubers, or cuttings. Most of the big-flowered tuberous begonias are sold as named-variety tubers. When tiny, pink growth appears on the upper side (with a depression where last year's stem was attached), place the tuber with the hollow side up at soil level in a pot filled with packaged soil mix. Water well once to firm the tuber in the pot and provide a temperature of 65° F. As the top swells and grows, roots will be forming below the surface. Do not allow the soil to dry out, but avoid drenching until the leaves expand. Provide high light until time for planting outside (after all danger of frost has passed, the weather has settled, and the soil has warmed). Carefully plant at the same level as the begonia was growing in the pot.

Uses: Grow the large-flowered kinds as specimen plants in semi-shady locations. Pendulous varieties make good container plants. The new, small-flowered kinds (varieties include 'Memory,' 'Non Stop,' and 'Clips,' all with separate colors) can be used for larger beds, in containers, and in hanging baskets. Watch container plantings to prevent drying out.

Related species: The iron cross begonia (*Begonia masoniana*), a widely grown indoor plant, makes a handsome foliage specimen for shade in summer planted directly into the ground or plunged in its own pot. The chartreuse leaves strongly marked with a chocolate-brown iron cross make a bold statement. Be sure to take this plant inside before cool weather starts because it is very frost-sensitive. *Begonia richmondensis* exhibits a graceful, flowing habit, vigorous growth, handsome, glossy leaves, and copious flowers, making it a very popular hanging basket plant in many parts of the country. Flower buds are cherry-red opening to a bright pink. It is easily rooted from cuttings. Morning sun and afternoon shade are ideal. Rex begonias (*Begonia rex*) are foliage plants colored in every conceivable combination: steel-gray, red, pink, green, and with splashes of white. They do well outdoors in the summer in shady spots. Elatior begonia (*Begonia hiemalis*) are hybrid begonias produced by crossing several species. One series is upright, good for planters, while the other has a flowing character and is ideal for hanging baskets and other containers to be viewed at eye level or above. Because much of the early development work was done by the Rieger firm in Germany, they are frequently known by this name. Flowers are 1 to 1½ inches in diameter, single, semi-double, and double. Colors are red, orange, pink, and a luscious white that looks green when the light shines through it.

Related varieties: Tubers of large-flowered varieties in separate colors and flower forms are usually available at garden centers and from specialists as named varieties. Smaller-flowered types are available as seed or started plants in garden centers.

Bells of Ireland form dramatic spires of green in the garden, the tiny white or pinkish flowers being almost hidden within the large, green bells (or calyxes). Native to western Asia, the name "Molucca balm" and "Molucella" were applied mistakenly, for at one time they were thought to be natives of the Molucca Islands.

Description: Bells of Ireland at their best grow in spires to 3 feet, surrounded by the netted, green, bell-like calyxes. The flowers are fragrant.

How to grow: Grow bells of Ireland in full sun or partial shade in an average garden loam with good drainage. They can be sown outdoors in spring as soon as the ground can be worked. Space them 12 inches apart. To prevent their toppling, plant them in areas protected from high wind; they may also be staked. They mature fairly rapidly and do not rebloom. For a longer show, start plants at different intervals. They reseed themselves readily. After maturity, plants are not especially attractive, so they should be planted where the residual foliage is out of sight.

Propagation: By seed. Sow in place. For earlier flowers, start 8 to 10 weeks prior to planting out. Seeds germinate in 25 to 35 days at 55° F. Don't cover the seeds; they need light to germinate.

Uses: Plant at the rear of the border for a vertical thrust. The chartreuse color of the bells combines nicely with lemon-yellows, sky-blues, and pinks. Especially revered by flower arrangers, the light green flowers hold unfaded for a long time in arrangements. For drying, hang them upside down in a dark place. They'll mute to a warm tan when dry and will last well in winter arrangements. They are especially attractive with other warm-toned components such as ornamental grasses and seedpods.

Related varieties: Seed companies offer their own selections.

Black-Eyed Susan, Gloriosa Daisy

Rudbeckia hirta

This widespread native of the prairie states has been turned into a horticultural delight. The name "gloriosa daisy" has been applied to the multitude of varieties that have grown out of this prairie weed. Although they're short-lived perennials, they'll bloom the first year and are often grown as annuals.

Description: Varieties of black-eyed Susan grow from 1 to 3 feet tall and are relatively erect. The flowers are available in many warm-toned colors: yellow, gold, orange, russet, and mahogany. Many of them have bands of color intermixed. The single varieties all have a large black or brown center, contrasting with the color surrounding it. Double flowers may reach 6 inches in diameter.

How to grow: Bright sun is the gloriosa daisy's main requirement. It will tolerate poor soil and erratic watering, although it does flourish with better care. Transplant it into the garden in the spring after the last frost. Space plants 10 to 15 inches apart. The taller varieties may need protection from strong winds or staking to keep them from toppling. Cutting the flowers encourages increased blooming.

Propagation: By seed. Treated as biennials or perennials, the seeds can be sown in the garden the preceding summer or fall. For bloom the same season, start seeds indoors 8 to 10 weeks prior to transplanting. Seeds germinate in 5 to 10 days at 70 to 75° F.

Uses: Any sunny location is ideal. Beds, borders, and planting strips will benefit from them. Plant them with ornamental grasses. They'll do well in large containers and are good cut flowers.

Related varieties: 'Goldsturm' has black-centered, single yellow flowers up to 5 inches in diameter. 'Rustic Colors' is composed of many gold, bronze, and mahogany shades. 'Irish Eyes' has golden flowers with green eyes.

Blanket Flower

Gaillardia pulchella

The annual gaillardia is a native of the Plains states to the East Coast. The name "blanket flower" comes from its resemblance to Indian blankets, blooming in yellow, orange, red, and their combinations.

Description: The annual gaillardia grows erect, 1 to 2 feet tall, with narrow leaves 2 inches long and flowers on long stems. In addition to single-flowered varieties, there are doubles with numerous quilled petals. In these, the original orange, red, and yellow colors have been extended to bronze and cream colors.

How to grow: The annual gaillardia will grow well in full sun in any well-drained soil. It does not like clay, excess water, or fertilizer. A fungicide may be needed in areas with high humidity. It continues to perform admirably under dry conditions. Space it from 9 to 15 inches apart.

Propagation: By seed. Barely cover, since gaillardia needs light to germinate. Sow seeds outdoors after the danger of frost has passed. For earlier bloom, sow indoors 4 to 6 weeks prior to planting out. Seeds germinate in 4 to 10 days at 75 to 85° F.

Uses: Plant gaillardias in groups. Grow them in meadows, in the cottage garden, at the edge of lawns, or near woodlands. The flowers are good for cutting.

Related species: Hybrids under the name *G. grandiflora* behave as perennials. Two dwarf forms are 'Goblin,' with flowers of deep red edged in yellow, and 'Yellow Goblin,' a pure yellow. 'Portola Giants,' growing 2½ feet tall, have bronze-colored flowers with yellow tips. The long flower stems are good for cutting.

Related varieties: 'Gaiety' is a mixture of heavily quilled, double flowers in bright yellow, orange, rose, maroon, and bicolors, many tipped with yellow. 'Double Mixed' flowers are 3 inches in diameter in cream, gold, crimson, and bicolors.

Blood Leaf

Iresine herbstii

These plants are grown for their colorful foliage, especially the purple-red color that brings the name "blood leaf." Originally from tropical South America, blood leaves are very easy to grow. They're from the amaranth family.

Description: Although in the tropics they can reach 5 to 6 feet, summer planting here tops out at 1 foot, usually less. The leaves are round, somewhat puckered, and colored red—except for yellowish midribs and veins. There are variants with green leaves, yellow veining, and bright red stalks and veins. Their white or yellow flowers are tiny and insignificant.

How to grow: Blood leaf tolerates no frost, so plant outside after all danger has passed and the soil is warm. They thrive in any well-drained, moist soil. Full sun is most desirable to develop the strongest foliage color, but they will grow in partial shade or shade. Pinch out the tips of shoots to promote bushiness. Space 6 to 9 inches apart. They can be sheared periodically for a neater appearance.

Propagation: By cuttings. Keep them misted during rooting to prevent wilting. Take cuttings 4 to 6 weeks in advance for husky plants to be set out after frost.

Uses: They're favorites for edging beds, borders, and for formal plantings. Blood leaf is also good in containers, especially mixed with other flowering plants. Given a sunny window sill, they are nice indoor plants, especially if they are trimmed.

Related species: *Iresine lindenii* has narrow, sharp-pointed leaves of deep red. Another variant, *I. l. formosa,* has green leaves with yellow veining. The leaf stalks and stems of both are red.

California Blue Bells

Phacelia campanularia

This native of southern California adapts to gardens or wildflower plantings with equal ease. The name *Phacelia* comes from the Greek word *phakelos* for "cluster," referring to the groups of flowers the plants bear.

Description: California blue bells grow about 8 inches tall with a branched, open form. They have triangular-shaped leaves and blue, bell-like flowers. The stamens stick out beyond the flower, resembling the clapper of a bell.

How to grow: Phacelias grow best in full sun in dryish, sandy soil, although they will tolerate other conditions if they have good drainage. They bloom best given cool, dry, sunny weather in the spring and diminish in the hot, humid weather of summer. Space plants 6 to 8 inches apart. Plant in areas protected from high winds or stake them. Brushwood stakes inserted in the ground when plants are small will be concealed when foliage grows around them.

Propagation: By seed. In mild winter climates, seeds can be sown outdoors in the fall for earliest bloom. Elsewhere, sow as early in the spring as the ground can be worked. Thin them to the proper spacing shortly after they emerge. For earliest bloom, start plants indoors 6 to 8 weeks prior to planting outside as soon as the danger of frost has passed. Seeds germinate in 8 to 15 days at 60 to 70° F. Growing them in peat pots will facilitate transplanting.

Uses: California blue bells are good in informal situations. Plant them in masses for the dominant blue tones they provide. Grow phacelias in natural gardens and wildflower meadows.

Related species: *Phacelia viscida* has deep blue flowers with white- and blue-speckled throats. It grows up to 2 feet tall. *P. tanacetifolia,* sometimes called "wild heliotrope," bears clusters of purple-to-violet flowers with lighter centers.

Blue Lace Flower

Trachymene coerulea

You might think of this as a glorified version of Queen Anne's lace in sky blue. Although a relative, this one is from Australia. The plant has the same, flat-headed flower form with tiny flowers. It's also fragrant—an extra bonus for discerning gardeners.

Description: The grayish, feathery leaves cover tall stems that grow 24 to 30 inches in height. They bloom in July and August with quantities of light blue flowers in large flower heads. Tiny, white stamens stick up above the flowers adding to their charm.

How to grow: Blue lace flowers need full sun in light, sandy, well-drained soil. They're best under cool-to-moderate temperatures. They do not tolerate heat well. Plant in the garden after the last frost. Space 12 inches apart. Protect them from high winds. As a precaution, brushwood stakes can be pushed into the ground among them when they are young. The foliage will cover the stakes as they grow.

Propagation: By seed. Sow in the garden outdoors after all danger of frost has passed. For earlier plants, sow seeds indoors 6 to 8 weeks prior to planting out. Cover seeds thoroughly; they need darkness to germinate. Seeds germinate in 20 to 25 days at 70° F.

Uses: Blue lace flower shines in the mixed border where its cool color tones down hot shades and mixes well with pastels. It's also recommended for cottage gardens where the old-fashioned look and informality blend together. Mix it with yarrows and other flowers for meadow plantings. Blue lace flower is good for arrangements where its airiness lightens up heavier flowers.

Blue Marguerite

Felicia amelloides

The blue marguerite's sky-blue color contrasts nicely with each flower's bright yellow center. Although perennial, this is a tender plant, so except for Zones 9, 10, and occasionally 8, it will not live over winter. It is a native of South Africa.

Description: Blue marguerite is normally an erect subshrub growing from 1 to 2 feet tall. It has glossy, deep green leaves with flowers on relatively short stems in sky-blue to darker shades, centered with a yellow eye.

How to grow: Felicias thrive in moist but well-drained soil, in full sun to partial shade. Truly hot weather causes their decline, making them best as a summer plant for maritime or mountain climates, as a spring and autumn plant elsewhere, and as a year-round plant for mild winter regions. At the young stage, pinching out tips will induce bushiness. Plant outside after all danger of frost has passed, spacing them 9 to 12 inches apart.

Propagation: By seed or by cuttings. Trailing forms are available only by cuttings; seed-grown plants are mostly upright. Sow seeds 6 to 8 weeks prior to planting out after all danger of frost has passed. Germination rate and speed is improved by refrigerating seeds in a moistened medium for 3 weeks prior to sowing. Germination takes up to 30 days at 70° F. Cuttings root quickly and easily.

Uses: Group them in beds and borders or use them in moist rock gardens. They combine well in containers with other flowers.

Related species: *Felicia bergerana* is called the "kingfisher daisy." It is smaller than *F. amelloides* and leaves are longer and narrower. The kingfisher daisy grows to about 8 inches tall with bright blue flowers with yellow centers.

Related varieties: Selections that trail will be found at garden centers.

Burning Bush, Summer Cypress, Belvedere

Kochia scoparia trichophylla

A native of Europe and Asia, kochia is named for a German botanist, Wilhelm Koch. "Summer cypress" refers to its mimicry of the true cypress in form and shape. "Burning bush," of course, refers to its brilliant autumn color.

Description: Kochia develops into an egg-shaped bush, reaching about 2 feet tall. Best in hot climates, it develops slowly in cooler regions. Foliage is finely textured, bright green, and dense. This becomes purplish by the end of summer, finally turning a brilliant red. The tiny, green flowers are inconspicuous.

How to grow: Give kochia full sun and avoid overwatering; otherwise it tolerates virtually all other conditions. Early season growth in cool weather is slow, but it rapidly develops when heat arrives. For individual specimens, plant 15 to 24 inches apart. For use as a summer hedge, space 12 inches apart. Kochia can be sheared easily for a more formal shape. It reseeds prolifically.

Propagation: By seed. Sow outdoors after all danger of frost has passed. For earlier development, plant indoors 4 to 6 weeks before outdoor planting. Do not cover the seeds, since they need light to germinate; keep them moist. Seeds germinate in 10 to 15 days at 70 to 75° F.

Uses: Kochia is a good hedge or background for summer flowers. In formal beds, individual plants can be used to define corners. Kochia is good for defining paths or walkways. It can also be used as a planting around other garden features. Tolerant of wind, kochia is often used in containers in balconies and other high-rise plantings.

Related variety: The only readily available selection is 'Childsii.'

Caladium hortulanum

Caladium hortulanum

Tropical caladiums are grown entirely for their brightly colored and wildly patterned foliage. Gardeners can choose from many combinations of green, pink, red, white, and creamy yellow.

Description: Large, spear- or arrowhead-shaped leaves on long stems rise directly from the tuber buried in the ground below. Depending on weather and soil, each leaf can grow up to 12 inches in length on 1-foot stems.

How to grow: In hot sections of Zones 9 and 10, caladium tubers are planted directly in the ground 1 inch deep, but in the rest of the country, it's usual to start them in pots indoors and plant them outside when the weather is warm. Plant tubers in pots 1 inch deep in soil high in organic matter. Kept moist, they grow at 70 to 85° F. Caladiums thrive in high temperature and humidity. Outdoors, grow in moist, rich soil, and protect them from intense sun. High, overhead shade or eastern exposures will provide maximum growth and color development of the leaves. Feed weekly with a diluted water-soluble fertilizer to assure continued growth of new leaves. A slow-release fertilizer may also be mixed into the soil before planting. In the fall, dig tubers before frost, allowing them to gradually dry off. Store in a frost-free location.

Propagation: By cutting tubers in pieces similar to potatoes, being sure each piece retains growing "eyes."

Uses: Caladiums are unexcelled for foliage color in bright, shady beds or borders, window boxes or containers. Grow in moist areas to reduce water needs.

Related varieties: 'Candidum' is primarily white with green ribs and leaves. 'Pink Beauty' has patterns of pink overlaid on a green background. Leaves of 'Frieda Hemple' are solid red with a green border.

Calla, Calla Lily

Zantesdeschia aethiopica

The great, white, waxy flowers so often seen at florists are nearly weeds in their native South Africa. They're actually perennials in Zones 8, 9, and 10, but since they are not tolerant of frost, they are grown as annuals in other parts of the United States. Gardeners throughout the country can enjoy their lush, green leaves and bright flowers in summer by planting the tuber each spring.

Description: Glistening, white flowers grow to 2½ feet above the arrowhead-shaped leaves that arise from the rhizome planted below ground. By summer's end, a large clump of leaves displays a more or less continuous succession of flowers.

How to grow: For maximum enjoyment, start rhizomes indoors 8 weeks prior to warm weather. Plant the large tubers in a soil mix high in peat or other organic matter and grow at 70° F. Keep uniformly moist and fertilize weekly with a water-soluble fertilizer. Plant outside in a rich soil high in organic matter that retains moisture. Incorporate a slow-release fertilizer before planting. Grow in full sun for maximum growth. In the fall, lift before frost, drying off foliage and rhizomes. Store in a frost-free place until spring.

Propagation: Buy rhizomes at garden centers in the spring. Check to make sure they are firm and moist.

Uses: Plant callas anywhere you want to achieve a tropical look. They also make dramatic container plants and superb cut flowers.

Related species: *Z. rehmannii* is the pink calla, although it shows much variation in spathe color from wine-red to nearly white. It is smaller, growing to 18 inches. *Z. elliotiana* is a species with white, spotted foliage, and a golden-yellow spathe.

Calliopsis, Tickseed

Coreopsis tinctoria

Native to many parts of the United States, calliopsis have bright, daisylike flowers. The name "tickseed" comes from the resemblance to an insect, as does the name *coreopsis*, which is derived from the Greek.

Description: Growing 1 to 3 feet tall, coreopsis plants are sparsely branched with bright, toothed, daisy flowers. Some have extra layers of petals and include double varieties. Colors range from yellow through orange and cinnamon-red to burnished mahogany. Many varieties are bicolored with sharply contrasting colors in the petals.

How to grow: Any sunny site with good drainage will grow coreopsis. They will even tolerate poor or dry soils after seedlings are well established. They will reseed year after year if not deadheaded.

Propagation: By seed. Seedlings grow quickly; sow them outdoors after final frost, covering them with ¼ inch of soil. Seeds may also be sown indoors 6 to 8 weeks prior to planting out. Germination takes 5 to 7 days at 70° F.

Uses: The dwarf forms make good bed edgings, while the taller varieties are effective at mid-border. Coreopsis also makes good cut flowers and can be dried for arrangements.

Related species: Some perennial coreopsis can be grown as summer annuals. Medal-winning varieties of *Coreopsis grandiflora* are: 'Sunray,' with bright, double-yellow flowers and 'Early Sunrise,' with glowing, yellow, semi-double flowers.

Related varieties: Most annual coreopsis is found in mixed colors, separated into dwarf and taller varieties. 'Tiger Flower Improved' is a dwarf mixture with bicolored flowers. 'Finest Mixed' is a taller selection with a full range of colors.

Annual Candytuft

Iberis hybridus

Candytufts have flowers in white, pink, lilac, red, and purple. Where *Iberis amara* "blood" predominates, they're called rocket candytufts, since their growth is upright. Globe candytufts, with a more mounding form, emphasize the *I. umbellata* parentage.

Description: Rocket candytufts have compact clusters of flowers on top of short, erect stems. In globe candytufts, the flower clusters are flat with a more bushlike appearance. Neither will grow more than 1 foot tall and usually remains compact.

How to grow: Candytuft needs full sun and good drainage. The addition of lime to acid soils will improve the growth of candytufts. Plant as soon as the danger of frost is over. Space 6 inches apart.

Propagation: By seed. In mild climates, seeds can be sown in the ground in the fall for earlier bloom. Elsewhere, sow in the spring after the last frost. For earlier bloom, start candytuft indoors 6 to 8 weeks before planting out. Germination takes 15 to 20 days at 68 to 85° F.

Uses: Candytuft naturally grows as an informal plant. However, with shearing, it can be tamed to a more formal appearance. Plant candytuft in the front of borders or as edging of beds and borders. Grow it along sidewalks and pathways; tuck it into pockets in rock gardens; and display it in containers. The rocket kinds will have an erect growth habit, while the globe candytuft will drape over the edges. They combine effectively with other flowers in mixed plantings. The rocket candytuft can be used for cut flowers. Seed heads can be used for everlasting arrangements.

Related varieties: 'Dwarf Fairy Mixed' mixes lilac, pink, maroon, red, and white. 'Flash' is a mixture that includes several shades of pink, bright red, maroon, purple, lilac, and white. 'Hyacinth Mixed' is a rocket type with large, white, fragrant blooms.

Canna

Canna species

The name *canna* comes from the Greek word for "reed," referring to the stems. The parentage of garden hybrids is very mixed, but breeders have provided many sturdy and colorful kinds.

Description: Cannas grow from fleshy roots with erect stalks from which broad, long leaves emerge. Flower stalks rising in the center bear large flowers. Foliage may be green, bronze, or purplish in hue.

How to grow: Cannas need full sun and grow best in a deep, rich, moist but well-drained soil. Incorporate extra organic matter and a slow-release fertilizer in the soil before planting. For earliest bloom, start in pots indoors. Otherwise plant roots directly into the ground after soil is warm and all danger of frost has passed. Use pieces of rootstock with 2 or 3 large eyes and plant 2 inches deep. Space 1½ to 2 feet apart. Remove spent flower heads for more prolific bloom. In fall after the first light frost, cut back stems to 6 inches, dig roots with soil attached, and store in a cool, frost-free place. While in storage, water sparingly.

Propagation: By seed or by division of roots. Seed propagation is slow; cut roots into pieces, each with 2 to 3 eyes, in the spring just prior to planting.

Uses: Use cannas in the center of island beds, at the sides or back of brightly colored borders, or near pools and ponds. They also dominate large containers.

Related varieties: Tall ones that grow up to 4 feet include: 'Yellow King Humbert,' yellow with scarlet flecks; 'The President,' bright crimson; and 'City of Portland,' a deep pink. Dwarf kinds growing to 2½ feet tall are known as "Pfitzers" for their German breeder: 'Chinese Coral,' a soft coral-pink; 'Primrose Yellow,' a sunny yellow; and 'Salmon-Pink.'

Canterbury Bells

Campanula medium

The name comes from *campanula* meaning "little bells," an accurate term, since the flowers are bell-shaped. Although biennials, they can be grown to bloom the first year by sowing seeds indoors early.

Description: Plants grow 2½ feet to 4 feet tall, with roughly the top two-thirds covered with pink, rose, lavender, blue, or white flowers. The plant shape is pyramidal and leaves are long and narrow.

How to grow: Canterbury bells need rich, moist, well-drained soil and full sun. Although partial shade is tolerated, stems may grow weak under these conditions. Planting a group together will help plants support each other without staking, although in windy locations stakes may be needed. Plant 8 to 12 inches apart.

Propagation: By seed. To grow for first year bloom, sow seeds 10 weeks prior to the last frost. Do not cover the seeds, since they require light to germinate. Germination time is 6 to 12 days at 70° F. To grow as a biennial, sow seeds outdoors in July or August. The small plants will bloom late the next spring.

Uses: Canterbury bells are ideal for the informal, cottage garden look, where they can be intermixed with a variety of other plants. They're also useful for planting at the center of island beds, where they're viewed from all sides.

Related species: *Campanula isophylla,* a tender perennial, is a species with a many-branched trailing habit, smothered in powder-blue or white flowers. 'Stella' is available both in blue and white. *Campanula ramosissima* grows 6 inches to 1 foot high. Its most prevalent form has violet-blue flowers, but also appears in pink, rose, and lavender.

Related varieties: *Campanula medium calycanthema,* called "cup and saucer," has double bells, one inside the other.

Castor Bean

Ricinus communis

This plant brings great distinction to the garden quickly, growing to a large shrub of treelike proportions in a single season. The seeds yield an oil that is used commercially. The coats of the seeds contain ricin, a deadly poison. If there is any chance of their being eaten, break off the flowers. This native of Africa is naturalized in tropical parts of the world.

Description: In the tropics, castor bean becomes a small tree. In areas with long growing seasons in the United States, it will reach 10 feet. The distinctive tropical character comes from the large, hand-shaped leaves that are up to 3 feet wide. Each one has from 5 to 12 deeply cut lobes.

How to grow: Castor beans are indifferent to soil if they receive full sun, adequate heat, and plenty of moisture. In areas with long growing seasons, plant them directly in the ground after all danger of frost has passed and the ground is warm enough to germinate the seeds. In frost-free areas of Zones 9 and 10, they will live through the winter. Plant them at least 3 feet apart.

Propagation: By seed. Before sowing the seeds, soak them for 24 hours in water or nick the seed coat with a file. Start seeds indoors 6 to 8 weeks prior to planting in the garden. Start them in individual pots for transplanting.

Uses: Castor beans are one of the most useful plants for shielding eyesores or providing temporary screens in the garden. They need lots of room; this plant is not modest in size. Side branches with flowers are cut to make attractive floral arrangements; the spiny seedpods are used in dried arrangements. Some people have a skin reaction to the foliage and seedpods.

Related varieties: 'Impala' has maroon-to-carmine young growth and sulfur-yellow blooms. 'Carmencita' has deep brown leaves.

Sweet False Chamomile

Matricaria recutita

White, daisy flowers with bright yellow button centers make this annual a pleasant sight in the garden. Originally from Europe and Western Asia, it is naturalized now in parts of the United States. The foliage is scented, releasing a pleasant, sweet fragrance when leaves are crushed.

Description: Sweet false chamomile grows up to 2½ feet tall. It's a many-branched plant, with numerous small flower heads. Flowers are up to 1 inch in diameter, with about 25 white petals surrounding a golden-yellow disc. Finely cut leaves are 2 to 3 inches long.

How to grow: Sweet false chamomile will grow easily in any average garden soil. It needs full sun to flower its best. Continuous moisture will ensure larger, more vigorous plants. Apply a balanced fertilizer at planting to develop good plants. Plant in the spring when frost danger has passed. Space 6 to 10 inches apart. It is a prolific reseeder.

Propagation: By seed. Sow in the ground in the spring as soon as the ground can be worked. For an earlier start, sow seeds indoors 6 to 8 weeks prior to planting out. Seeds germinate in 20 to 25 days at 70° F. Do not cover seeds; they need light to germinate.

Uses: Grow them in the front of beds and borders, grouping a number of plants together for a mass effect. Because they grow informally, sweet false chamomile also look good in cottage garden plantings and in containers. Grow them in herb gardens for their scent. Plants and foliage are often dried for sachets.

Related species: Four species from South Africa are sometimes grown: *M. globifera, M. grandiflora, M. suffruticosa,* and *M. africana,* although it is suspected that plants cultivated under these names may really be *Chrysanthemum parthenium.*

Chilean Bell Flower

Nolana paradoxa

Natives of South America, they're tender perennials that are grown like annuals in the garden. The name *Nolana* comes from the Latin *nola* or "little bell," an apt description of the flower shape.

Description: The Chilean bell flower is a prostrate, spreading plant growing 6 to 8 inches tall and spreading a foot or more by summer's end. The leaves and stems are somewhat succulent. Flowers resemble morning glories, a twilight-sky-blue with white centers, shading to yellow in the throats. There are also forms with white- or violet-colored flowers. Bloom is continuous over a long season.

How to grow: Chilean bell flowers thrive in light, poor soils and tolerate drought, although they will grow under a wide range of conditions, including high humidity. They must have good drainage and full sun. With adequate moisture, the plants grow more vigorously. Plant them in the garden as soon as all danger of frost has passed. Space them 10 to 15 inches apart for full coverage. In frost-free areas, nolana will be perennial, but should be cut back halfway in the spring to induce new growth and tidiness.

Propagation: By seed. Start seeds indoors 6 to 8 weeks prior to planting in the garden after the last frost date and when the soil is warm. Seeds germinate in 10 to 20 days at 70° F.

Uses: This is a versatile plant. Use it for trailing over rock walls or rock gardens. Try it as a sunny ground cover for difficult sites. It's a good edging plant for hot pockets by houses and fences. Plant nolana in containers, too.

Related varieties: 'Blue Bird' has dark sky-blue flowers with white and yellow throats. The bell-shaped flowers are slightly ruffled, enhancing the light and shadow patterns. 'Sky Blue' is similar.

China Pink

Dianthus chinensis

These compact plants have a clove scent as well as colorful flowers. They produce blooms in pink, white, rose, scarlet, and crimson; many are bicolored. The original species comes from Eastern Asia.

Description: China pinks grow 6 to 12 inches high—clumps of blue-gray foliage surmounted continuously with the single, semi-double, or fringed flowers. In Zones 8 to 10, they will live in the garden for 2 or 3 years as short-lived perennials.

How to grow: Dianthus grows and blooms best during cool temperatures of spring and fall and in cool summer locations. In Zones 9 and 10, they're widely used as winter flowering annuals. Plant them in full sun, in well-drained soil on the alkaline side. (Acid soils can be amended by incorporating lime into the soil before planting.) Plant in the garden after danger of frost has passed. Space 6 to 10 inches apart.

Propagation: By seed. Seeds germinate in 8 to 10 days at 70° F. They may be sown outdoors as soon as the soil is workable. Starting indoors 8 to 10 weeks ahead of planting out will bring an earlier display.

Uses: Use China pinks in rock gardens, in rock walls, or planted in cracks in paving stones. Mass them in at the front of beds or borders. Grow them in containers, alone, or combined with other flowers. They're good cut flowers for small arrangements.

Related species: Sweet William (*Dianthus barbatus*) has a cluster of flower tops in pink, white, and red.

Related varieties: The 'Telstar' series has a mixture of scarlet, salmon, rose, pink, and white fringed flowers. Separate colors are available, with 'Telstar Picotee' outstanding. It has crimson flowers edged in white. 'Magic Charms' series is similar, including some speckled flowers. 'Snowfire' has white fringed flowers centered in cherry-red. 'Princess' series is heat-resistant.

Chrysanthemum

Chrysanthemum paludosum, multicaule

Two species of the multitudinous chrysanthemum family are especially popular with gardeners as flowering summer annuals. One bears small, perky, yellow blossoms and the other has white, daisylike flowers.

Description: *C. paludosum* grows about 10 inches in height and has a mounding, trailing habit that spreads to 15 inches. The single, small, white flowers are borne profusely all over the plant. *C. multicaule* is slightly more vigorous, growing to 12 inches with a 20-inch spread. Flowers are single yellow daisies and are visible from a distance. Both will bloom all summer, but if bloom diminishes, shear back by half to encourage new growth and flowering.

How to grow: Grow in rich, well-drained soil in full sun if roots can be kept cool and shaded by other plants; otherwise, in partial sun. An eastern exposure would be ideal for both. Incorporate a slow-release fertilizer in the soil before planting. Plant after the last frost date when the soil has warmed. Space 8 to 12 inches apart for solid coverage.

Propagation: By seed or by cuttings. Germination is 14 to 21 days at 60 to 65° F. Sow 6 to 8 weeks prior to transplanting to the garden. Plants will bloom approximately 10 weeks after sowing. Cuttings root quickly and easily.

Uses: Plant in rock gardens, on slopes, and in the front of beds or borders. Use at gates, along pathways, and at doorsteps where a colorful ground cover is desired. The trailing quality adds grace to hanging baskets, window boxes, and other containers. The white of *C. paludosum* is a good choice in mixed plantings, cooling down hot colors and intensifying dark ones.

Related varieties: 'White Buttons' is the most commonly grown selection of *C. paludosum*. 'Yellow Buttons' is the most popular selection of *C. multicaule*.

Cleome, Spider Flower

Cleome hasslerana

Cleome starts blooming early and flowers continue opening at the top of 6-foot stems. Exceedingly long stamens that extend well beyond the orchidlike flowers—somewhat like a daddy longlegs spider—are what give spider flower its name.

Description: Cleome flowers, with many opening at once, grow in airy racemes 6 to 8 inches in diameter. Flowers are white, pink, or lavender in color. When flowers fade, they are followed by long pods that extend outward from the stem below the terminal raceme. Leaves grow on long stalks from a single stem.

How to grow: Cleome grows well in average soil in full sun or minimal shade. It is very drought-tolerant, although it will look and grow better if it is watered well. Space plants 1 to 3 feet apart.

Propagation: By seed. Sow after the last frost when the ground is warm, later thinning to final spacing. Cleomes may also be started indoors 4 to 6 weeks earlier at a temperature of at least 70° F. Germination time is 10 to 14 days. In the garden, it reseeds prolifically.

Uses: Plant cleome for its height, to back up borders, in the center of island beds, or for statuesque beauty where its dramatic quality stands out. It can also be used as a space-defining hedge, although other plants should hide its bare stems later in the season. Cleome can be used for tall container plantings. It also makes a good cut flower for use in large bouquets.

Related varieties: 'Helen Campbell' is the most popular white variety. 'Rose Queen' is salmon-pink, and 'Ruby Queen' bears rose-colored flowers. Additional color variations including lilac and purple are found in seed mixtures.

Plumed Cockscomb

Celosia cristata v. plumosa

The name *celosia* comes from the Greek word for "burned." These airy, feather duster look-alikes bear the vibrant colors that aptly fit the name. The exotic plumes make superb dried specimens, retaining their color long after harvest.

Description: Shades ranging from electric reds, yellows, pinks, and oranges to more subtle, sand tones are available. Height ranges from 8 to 30 inches. Bloom lasts from June to October.

How to grow: Full sun in average soil is recommended for celosias. Seeds may be sown in the garden after danger of frost has passed and soil has warmed. Initial flowers may last as long as 8 weeks after opening, but removing them will encourage development of side branches and new bloom.

Propagation: By seed. For earlier bloom, celosias may be planted indoors 4 to 5 weeks in advance of planting out. Germination is at 70 to 75° F and takes 10 to 15 days. Plants should not dry out.

Uses: Tall varieties add complementary textures to the center and sides of beds and borders, while the short kinds are good edging plants. They're good container plants, too.

Related species: *Celosia cristata* bears the contorted flowers known as cockscomb. Varieties include: dwarf 'Jewel Box Mixture' and 'Toreador,' a 20-inch variety with large red combs.

Related varieties: The tall 2½-foot celosias include 'Forest Fire,' with orange-scarlet plumes and 'Golden Triumph,' a golden-yellow. Just shorter is the award-winning 'Century Series,' with separate colors of scarlet, red (with bronze foliage), rose, yellow, and cream, as well as a mixture of all colors. Miniatures up to 10 inches are found in the 'Geisha Series' and are especially fluorescent in carmine red, orange, scarlet, and yellow.

Coleus x hybridus

Coleus x hybridus

Coleus is one of the few plants where late blooming is an asset, for the insignificant flowers detract from the beautiful foliage. Tender perennials, they're very frost-sensitive and are used as annuals except in frost-free areas.

Description: Coleus forms a well-branched, spreading plant up to 2 feet tall and as wide. The leaves vary tremendously, from intricately dissected and lobed forms to broad solids. Colors, too, are varied from solid colors of red, bronze, chartreuse, white, pink, yellow, or green, to variations that combine two or more colors.

How to grow: Coleus is ideal in shade and will excel in northern exposures. It will grow in any well-drained, moist soil. As to light, the deeper the shade, the taller the plant. Leaves are less colorful in deep shade.

Propagation: By seed or by cuttings. Sow seeds 6 to 8 weeks before setting outside. Wait until the ground is warm and all danger of frost has passed. Seeds need light to germinate, so do not cover. Seeds germinate in 10 to 15 days at temperatures of above 75° F; lower temperatures inhibit germination. Cuttings root quickly and easily—even in water.

Uses: Coleus are unparalleled shade plants. They are useful as ground covers, massed in the front of borders, or grouped in clusters. Coleus grow well in containers. Indoors, they make good foliage plants.

Related varieties: The 'Wizards' have heart-shaped leaves with contrasting colors. 'Rose Wizard' has patches of rose in leaf centers and is edged with green and white to the margins. 'Saber' varieties have narrow, tapered leaves in many colors. The 'Fiji' series features heavily fringed leaves with contrasting color combinations. Small, deeply lobed leaves distinguish the 'Carefree' series.

Corn Cockle

Agrostemma githago

The name "corn cockle" comes from its appearance in the corn fields of England, where it has been unwelcome for years. However, its 3- to 4-foot height with rosy pink flowers rippling in the wind make it a welcome addition to the garden, where it will bloom from June on.

Description: Plants grow up to 3½ feet tall, with thin, narrow foliage and slender, wiry flower stems. Flower color is a rich, plummy pink. Flowers are often more than 2 inches in diameter, each petal marked with dots or lines to guide insects to the flower center for pollination.

How to grow: Grow in full sun in average soil. Growing in partial shade will cause them to grow taller with weak stems (that may require staking) and reduce flower production. Space plants about 12 inches apart. Deadheading prevents seed formation and encourages bloom throughout the summer.

Uses: Because the foliage is light, it can be planted as a see-through plant surrounded and backed by other flowers. Their delicate grace makes them a good foil for more substantial plants. The flowers can be readily seen if grown at the back of borders or beds. Use them, too, for height in island beds. The informal character lends distinction to cottage gardens with a variety of plantings. They also make good cut flowers.

Propagation: Seeds are large, germination is fast (10 to 12 days outdoors), and growth is rapid. Corn cockle is best direct-seeded into the garden. Plants readily reseed, so they can have their own space in the garden year after year. Currently, seed companies offer many separate selections.

Related varieties: 'Milas' is a somewhat shorter selection, and 'Milas Cerise' is offered for its cherry-red color.

Cosmos

Cosmos bipinnatus

Cosmos is one of the fastest-growing annuals. Some varieties reach up to 6 feet by summer's end. They're natives of Mexico.

Description: Cosmos forms a lacy, open plant with flowers 3 to 4 inches in diameter. These daisies are in pink, red, white, and lavender with a contrasting yellow center. Foliage is feathery.

How to grow: Cosmos grows best in full sun, but it will bloom acceptably in partial shade. Grow in well-drained soil. It does not need fertilizing. Space at least 12 inches apart. Cosmos needs space and is not easily staked. It reseeds vigorously.

Propagation: By seed. Because it grows so fast, sow outdoors after frost danger has passed. Barely cover seeds, since they need light to germinate. For very early bloom, sow indoors 4 weeks prior to planting out. Germination takes 3 to 7 days at 70 to 75° F.

Uses: Because of its height, cosmos should be planted at the back of borders and grouped against fences or other places as a covering. Its informal habit works best in mixed plantings. Cosmos also can provide height for the center of an island bed. The flowers are good for cutting, especially for informal arrangements.

Related species: *Cosmos sulphureus* is the source of the hot red and yellow colors of cosmos. They're also more compact, growing up to 2 feet in the garden. Bloom is heavy from start until frost. A medal winner, 'Sunny Red' has 2½-inch, semi-double flowers of vermilion red. Its companion is 'Sunny Gold.'

Related varieties: Most popular is the 'Sensation' series that comes in mixed colors. Separate colors of this series are also available. 'Candy Stripe' has white petals stippled with crimson. 'Sea Shells' has a unique form with rolled, quilled petals. 'Psyche Mixed' bears semi-double flowers.

Cup and Saucer Vine, Cathedral Bells

Cobaea scandens

The flowers of cup and saucer vine come in white, green, violet, and purple. The name refers to its flowers, which appear to sit within a saucer of foliage. The prominent stamens resemble the clapper of a bell—hence its other common name.

Description: A perennial, cup and saucer vine is grown as an annual in most parts of the country. Rapid-growing, it can reach 25 feet by summer's end. It has leaves composed of 2 to 3 sets of leaflets. The saucer of the flower is a prominent calyx within which the cup, or flower, sits. The hooked tendrils will move within a few minutes after being rubbed on one side—which is why they climb so successfully without support.

How to grow: Cup and saucer vine needs full sun and an average-to-rich soil for best growth. It must have a continuous supply of moisture to grow well. Plant outdoors after all danger of frost has passed, spacing 1 foot apart.

Propagation: By seed. The seeds can be planted in the ground outdoors but, because they germinate somewhat irregularly, earlier and more dependable results can be gained by starting them indoors 8 to 10 weeks prior to outdoor planting. The seeds will germinate in 30 to 60 days at a temperature of 70 to 75° F. They grow rapidly once germinated. Transplant to the garden when all danger of frost has passed and the soil is warm.

Uses: Cup and saucer vine is ideal for screening large areas or covering eyesores. Plant it to cover fences; grow it up and over arches, pergolas, trellises, and porches. It also grows well in a cool greenhouse.

Related varieties: *Cobaea scandens* with flowers that open green and turn deep blue is available; *C. s. alba* is the white form. In addition, a mixture of blue and white forms can be found.

Dahlia

Dahlia hybrids

From huge, dinner plate-sized blooms down to midget pompoms only 2 inches in diameter, dahlias show as much diversity as any summer flowering plant. Once they start blooming in the summer, there is a continuous flood of flowers until frost. They're tender perennials, forming tuberous roots that may be dug and stored in the fall and replanted the following spring. Where the ground does not freeze, they may be left in the ground over winter.

Description: Dahlias grow from 1 to 5 feet tall. Flowers come in every color except blue, and the form is varied: singles; anemone-flowered; peonylike; round, shaggy mops; formal, ball-shaped; and twisted, curled petals. The flowers are carried on long stems above the erect plants. The American Dahlia Society has classified dahlias by both type and size. There are 12 different flower types: single, anemone-flowered, collarette, peony-flowered, formal decorative, informal decorative, ball, pompom, incurved cactus, straight cactus, semi-cactus, and orchid-flowered. Flower size designations are A (large, over 8 inches); B (medium, 6 to 8 inches); BB (4 to 6 inches); M (miniature, not over 4 inches in diameter); Ball (over 3 inches); Miniature Ball (2 to 3½ inches); and Pompom (not over 2 inches in diameter).

How to grow: Dahlias are sun lovers and need air circulation around them. Soil should be fertile, high in organic matter, and moist but well-drained. Incorporate a slow-release fertilizer into the soil before planting. Plant outdoors when the soil is warm and danger of frost has passed. To plant, dig a hole 10 inches deep and as wide. Place the tubers so that the eye is 2 to 3 inches below ground level. Plants growing in pots can be planted at the same level as they were growing in the pot. Space tall varieties 12 to 18 inches apart, reducing the spacing for dwarf plants to as little as 8 inches. Tall varieties, and particularly those with large flowers, must be staked to prevent toppling. Drive the stakes before planting to avoid damaging the plant underground.

Propagation: By seed, division, or cuttings. Most of the large-flowered varieties are grown from tuberous roots available at garden centers or specialist growers. Each fleshy portion must have a piece of old stem with an eye attached in order to grow (unlike potatoes, which can be sliced into pieces so long as there is an eye in the cut piece). At the end of a summer's growing season, a roughly circular mass of tuberous roots will form a clump. These clumps should be stored in a cool but frost-free location until spring. Where the ground does not freeze, tubers can be left to winter in place. In the spring, divide these pieces (an eye attached to a portion of the stem) just before planting. Sow dahlia seeds at 70° F 4 to 6 weeks prior to planting out. Germination will take 5 to 14 days. Cuttings root in 10 to 15 days.

Uses: Taller varieties can be planted as a hedge with shorter flowers growing in front. Groups of three plants can be effective at the back of a border or in the center of large island beds. Compact varieties can be used in the front of beds and borders or planted in containers. For exhibition, disbudding the side buds will result in substantially larger flowers. Dahlias make good cut flowers, especially those with long stems. They may also be floated in a bowl of water.

Related varieties: There are hundreds of varieties; consult your garden center or a specialist grower. A few tuberous, rooted varieties are: 'Los Angeles,' a semi-cactus variety with deep red flowers and petals tipped in white; and 'Canby Charm,' an informal decorative type with pink flowers that can reach a diameter of 12 inches. 'Clown' is golden-yellow with streaks of red in the petals. 'Lavender Chiffon' has lavender-shaded blooms up to 7 inches across. Seed-grown varieties will be available as started plants or can be grown from seeds at home. From seeds, tall varieties include 'Cactus Flowered,' growing to 4 feet with many different flower colors and curved petals. 'Large Flowered, Double, Mixed' will grow to 5 feet and bears large, double and semi-double flowers. Compact varieties include: 'Redskin,' growing up to 15 inches with bronze foliage—a remarkable contrast to the many different flower colors. 'Figaro' grows to 12 inches with semi-double and double flowers.

African Daisy

Arctotis stoechadifolia

In its native South Africa, arctotis bursts into bloom when the spring rains come, although in gardens plants bloom copiously all summer. A tender perennial, it is grown most commonly as an annual. Like many of the plants in the daisy family from South Africa, it's tough enough to live in hot, dry conditions, but a modicum of moisture will bring out stellar blooms. On dull days and at night, arctotis closes its flowers.

Description: The native species has pearly white flowers centered with steel-blue and encircled with a narrow, yellow band. The flowers are held well above the plant, which forms a compact mound. The leaves are handsome grayish-green that combines well with other colors in the garden. Hybrids with flowers up to 4 inches in diameter have brought other colors—yellow, cream, white, purple, orange, and red.

How to grow: Bright sunny days and cool nights are ideal. Arctotis also thrives in mild winter areas with high winter light. The plant needs full sun and will tolerate lots of abuse. With richer soil and moderate moisture, there are larger flowers and lusher foliage. Fertilize only lightly. Where summers are very hot, arctotis may cease flowering but will resume again when cooler weather prevails.

Propagation: By seed primarily, although cuttings of choice kinds will root quickly. Sow indoors 6 to 8 weeks prior to last frost at 65° F. Seeds germinate in 15 to 20 days. Plant 8 to 10 inches apart at the same depth they were growing in the flat or pot. For later flowers, sow outdoors after danger of frost has passed and the soil has warmed somewhat. Thin garden seedlings to 8 to 10 inches apart.

Uses: Plant arctotis in beds or borders where full sun is available. They will tolerate growing in dry rock gardens for early season bloom. They will also bloom indoors in cool sunrooms or greenhouses.

African Daisy, Golden Ageratum

Lonas inodora

The name "African daisy" comes from a portion of its native territory—this plant is found surrounding the Mediterranean Sea, including northern Africa. Because it somewhat resembles the more common ageratum—but with yellow flowers—the name "golden ageratum" is sometimes used. However, the flower clusters are a bit more formal-looking than ageratum.

Description: Although lonas is a member of the daisy family, it does not have the long-ray flowers that give the daisy look. Instead, the small flowers are grouped together in clusters up to 5 inches across. The branched plants grow up to 1 foot tall, and leaves are finely divided into long, narrow segments.

How to grow: Lonas grows best in full sun. It's not particular as to garden soil as long as it is well-drained. It should be planted outside after frost danger has passed. The plant grows best if spaced 6 inches apart; it does not need staking.

Propagation: By seed. Seeds may be sown outdoors in early spring where plants are to grow, thinning to a 6-inch spacing. They may also be started indoors 6 to 8 weeks prior to outdoor planting for earlier bloom. Germination will take 5 to 7 days at 60 to 70° F.

Uses: Plant lonas in flower borders, combined with other flowers in complementary shapes and colors. They blend beautifully in informal mixed plantings and add a bright, golden note to wildflower gardens. For best effect, plant them in groupings, rather than as single plants. They are effective if used to make a bright, golden ribbon through a border. They can also be planted in rows in the cutting garden and used fresh or for dried arrangements. Lonas flowers last a long time on the plant.

Dahlberg Daisy, Golden Fleece

Dyssodia tenuiloba

A charming little plant with sunny flowers, the Dahlberg daisy is now becoming widely available in the spring as a started plant at garden centers. Native to the southern United States down through Central America, it has become naturalized in warmer parts of the world. The plants have pleasantly scented foliage.

Description: The Dahlberg daisy bears many upright, golden-yellow flowers about ½ inch in diameter. The prominent yellow eye is surrounded by ray flowers. The long, narrow leaves are divided, giving a very feathery appearance. Plants grow from 6 to 12 inches high, spreading as much as 18 inches by the end of the growing season.

How to grow: Dahlberg daisies grow well in full sun and well-drained, moderately fertile soil. However, they will also grow and bloom abundantly in poor soil. Unlike many annuals, they thrive in hot weather. For plants started indoors, plant outdoors when the soil is warm and the danger of frost has passed. Space 6 to 12 inches apart. Dahlberg daisies will reseed and appear in the same place the following year. They may winter over in relatively frost-free areas of Zones 9 and 10.

Propagation: By seed. Sow seeds in place when the ground is warm, thinning plants to the proper spacing. For earlier bloom, start seeds indoors 6 to 8 weeks prior to planting out. Germination takes 8 to 12 days at 60 to 80° F.

Uses: Dahlberg daisy can be planted in rock gardens or in pockets among paving stones or patio blocks. It makes a superb edging for beds and borders and can be used as a ground cover plant for sunny areas. Use it also to edge paths and walks. Its habit of reseeding makes it ideal for naturalized gardens. It is also suited for container gardens.

English Daisy

Bellis perennis

In nature, the English daisy, immortalized by poets, bears single flowers. However, breeding and selection have added semi-doubles and doubles to the array of varieties available to gardeners. Particularly in the Northeast, the English daisy has become naturalized. In order to enjoy the improved forms, the gardener must start with named-variety seeds.

Description: Flowers of white, pink, or red rise on 6-inch stems from a rosette of basal leaves. Single and semi-double flowers are centered in yellow, but in fully double varieties this distinguishing feature is covered. Normally, flowers are 1 to 2 inches in diameter; in newer varieties they are larger. Most flowers appear in spring and early summer repeating again in the fall, but in cool and coastal climates they may bloom all year.

How to grow: Grow in full sun or light shade in moist soil, well-enriched with organic matter. When used as an annual, set out as early as the ground can be worked or plant in the fall for earliest bloom when weather warms (except in Zones 3 to 5 where they are not hardy except in well-protected cold frames). Plant 6 to 9 inches apart. Frequently, they are replaced with warm season annuals in late June.

Propagation: By seed or by division. Seeds germinate in 10 to 15 days at 70° F.

Uses: English daisies will liven up small beds and are good for edgings and small containers during the cool spring period.

Related species: *B. rotundifolia* has white flowers; *B. r. caerulescens* bears blue flowers.

Related varieties: The largest-flowered variety is the fully double 'Goliath Mixed,' with flowers up to 3 inches in diameter in shades of white, red, pink, and salmon. Others are 'Pompanette Mixed,' with 1½-inch flowers, and the petite 'Bright Carpet Mixed,' with 1-inch flowers.

Livingstone Daisy

Dorotheanthus bellidiformis (many seed catalogs still list it under *Mesembryanthemum criniflorum*)

Formerly grouped under the name *mesembryanthemum*, Livingstone daisies are now widely dispersed under other names. Frost-tender succulents, they thrive in sunny, dry conditions and locations. Livingstone daisies bloom for weeks in the spring and summer.

Description: Livingstone daisies have flat, succulent leaves up to 3 inches long, with the plants hugging the ground. Flowers have dark centers and are colored pink, white, purple, lavender, crimson, or orange. Plants grow up to 8 inches high and spread to 12 inches wide. The flowers close at night and on cloudy days.

How to grow: Livingstone daisies need full sun and sandy, well-drained soil. They tolerate drought and are resistant to salt spray, making them good for seaside plantings. Livingstone daisies tend to sunburn in hot, humid weather. Space plants 6 inches apart for full coverage.

Propagation: By seed. Sow seeds indoors 10 weeks prior to last frost date. Seeds germinate in 7 to 14 days at 60° F. In frost-free locations, they can be seeded directly into the garden and thinned to the proper spacing. They will reseed, although the colors will not be the same in following years.

Uses: These are ideal plants for mass plantings. They're wonderful sunny ground covers. Plant them in rock gardens; they are especially beautiful on slopes and hillsides. They're among the best plants for seaside locations.

Related species: The primary variety of *Mesembryanthemum occulatum* is 'Lunette,' bearing lemon-yellow flowers with cherry-red centers.

Related varieties: 'Magic Carpet Mixed' combines all colors of Livingstone daisies. 'Livingstone Daisy Mixed' is another blend of all colors. Other available mixes may include a variety of Livingstone daisy varieties as well as similar species.

Swan River Daisy

Brachycome iberidifolia

The Swan River in Western Australia is home to this daisy-flowered charmer. Quite variable in nature, flowers are blue, pink, white, and purple, each one centered with either yellow or black.

Description: The Swan River daisy forms a loose mound up to 18 inches tall with equal spread. Much branched, it holds its many 1½-inch flowers upright on slender stems. The flowers are mostly single with contrasting centers.

How to grow: Brachycome needs full sun and a rich but well-drained soil. Water when soil appears dry, but avoid overwatering. It also grows and blooms better where temperatures of more than 90° F accompanied by high humidity do not continue for long periods of time. To encourage bushiness, young plants can be pinched once. For solid plantings, space plants 9 inches apart in the garden. To reinvigorate bloom if it diminishes, shear plants back to 6 inches.

Propagation: By seed or by cuttings. For early bloom, sow seeds indoors at 70° F 6 weeks prior to planting out after frost danger has passed. Germination will take 10 to 18 days. Seeds may also be sown outdoors after the frost-free date. Thin seedlings to 9 inches. Cuttings will root in 15 days and are very useful for multiplying good forms of brachycome. Adjust humidity to keep leaves firm during rooting, but watch the plants carefully to avoid rot.

Uses: It is the blue brachycome that is so scarce in summer gardens. Because of its mounding habit, brachycome is an ideal hanging basket or container plant. It also accents rock gardens and is useful for edging tall borders. Given bright sunlight, it can be grown in pots indoors.

Related varieties: One selection is 'Blue Splendor.' 'Purple Splendor' will give shades of blue to purple. For a range of all colors, plant 'Mixed Colors.'

Transvaal Daisy, Barberton Daisy

Gerbera jamesonii

Both common names of this South African native spell out its geographical origin, Transvaal being a province and Barberton a city there. A perennial, it is too tender to live through winter except in parts of Zones 9 and 10, but it will bloom the first year from seed.

Description: Gerbera forms a nice rosette of notched, glossy leaves, from which the flowers grow 12 to 18 inches high, depending on the variety. Flowers are single, semi-double, or double in shades of pink, orange, red, yellow, and white and are up to 4 inches or more in diameter.

How to grow: They grow best in full sun but will tolerate partial shade. They need moist, well-drained soil high in organic matter and high humidity. Use started plants and plant out after last frost and when the ground has warmed. Make sure to plant at ground level. Depending on the variety, space 12 to 15 inches apart.

Propagation: By seed. Be sure to use fresh seeds. Press seeds into the soil but do not cover; they need light to germinate. Sow 14 to 18 weeks before setting out. Seeds will germinate in 10 days at 70 to 75° F.

Uses: Cluster them at the front or side of a bed, or in a border. Mix them with other plants. Individual flowers last a long time on the plant, but when they're done, you need to deadhead to keep new flowers coming. Gerberas are good container plants. As cut flowers, they last up to two weeks.

Related varieties: 'Happipot' is a compact variety with a 10- to 15-inch height. The flowers are single red, rose, pink, salmon, orange, yellow, and cream. 'Parade' is a dwarf series with double flowers in many colors. A taller, cut flower type is 'Gigi,' with 18- to 24-inch stems and 4- to 4½-inch flowers. Many of the flowers are crested.

Dusty Miller

Senecio cineraria, Chrysanthemum cinerariaefolium

The term "dusty miller" originated from the effect of shimmering gray foliage rather than as a name for a particular plant. The name has been commonly applied to a variety of similar plants including *Artemisias, Centaureas,* and *Lychnis.*

Description: *Chrysanthemum cinerariaefolium* grows 1 to 2½ feet tall with finely divided leaflets. It has decorative white daisy flowers about 1½ inches in diameter. *Senecio cineraria* is a bushy subshrub that grows up to 2½ feet tall. The ornamental value is in the finely divided gray foliage.

How to grow: Preference for both plants is full sun and a rather ordinary, well-drained soil, although they will brighten lightly shaded areas, too. Plant in the garden when the soil has warmed and after danger of frost has passed. Space 8 to 10 inches apart. Pinch the tips of plants to induce shapely branching.

Propagation: By seed or by cuttings. Germinate seeds of *Senecio cineraria* at 75 to 80° F and those of *Chrysanthemum cinerariaefolium* at 65 to 75° F. Germination will take 10 to 15 days. Sow seeds 12 to 14 weeks before planting out.

Uses: These are the classic plants to use in urns with bright summer flowers. They are effective in all kinds of planters. However, they also make great ribbons of light in flower beds and borders. They're especially good to use as a bridge between two clashing colors; to intensify cool colors like blue; or to tone down hot colors.

Related varieties: The most commonly available selection of *C. cinerariaefolium* is 'Silver Lace,' with very dissected, feathery leaves. It is not as vigorous a grower as *S. cineraria.* Two varieties of the latter are commonly found: 'Diamond' and 'Silver Dust,' with more silvery and finely divided leaves.

Echium

Echium vulgare

A native of western Europe, including England, echium is really a biennial, producing flowers the year after planting. Its striking flower form of tall racemes is attractive in the garden. The most common form bears blue flowers, but selections are available with rose, pink, mauve, lilac, lavender, and purple flowers.

Description: Long, hairy leaves support a tall spike of flowers. Buds are purple, with flowers opening to a violet-blue. In other forms, the flowers open pink, then fade to blue. Plants are 12 to 24 inches tall and need about 10 to 15 inches of growing space.

How to grow: Echiums thrive in full sun in average soil. Too much fertility causes excess foliage to the detriment of flowering. They will tolerate dry soil, but must have good drainage to grow well. Start plants in July or August in order to develop husky plants for wintering over in locations where they are to flower the following season. Space 8 to 12 inches apart.

Propagation: By seed. Seeds germinate in 14 to 21 days at 60°F. Too high a temperature will inhibit germination.

Uses: Echiums can be used to add a vertical note to beds, borders, walkways, and paths in the garden. The pastel colors combine well with other pastels and white, and strike a happy contrast with sunny, warm colors.

Related species: *Echium fastuosum,* known as "pride of Madeira," is a tender, shrubby perennial for Zones 8 and 9. Great clusters of blue-purple flowers stand well above the foliage in May and June.

Related varieties: 'Blue Bedder' grows to 12 inches high and has cup-shaped flowers. 'Dwarf Mixed' has a mix of colors in purple, lavender, lilac, light blue, mauve, salmon rose, pink, and rose.

Everlastings, Strawflowers

Helichrysum, Everlasting

Helichrysum bracteatum

These double daisy-shaped flowers grow on long stems 18 to 36 inches tall. They come in a wide range of colors: white, yellow, pink, crimson, and bronze. They must have a long season of growth to develop the flowers before fall. Cut for drying before the yellow centers are visible; use wire stems. Air dry upside down in the dark.

Statice

Statice sinuatum

Statice has clusters of small flowers on long stems up to 36 inches in height and bears off-centered flowers in blue, yellow, rose, and white, with other shades less available. Cut the flowers when blooms are at least ¾ open. Air dry them upside down in the dark.

Honesty, Silver Dollar Plant

Lunaria annua

The seedpods of this plant are often used for dried arrangements. The flowers, which bloom on 2- to 3-foot stems, are mauve or white and can be used in fresh arrangements. Cut the stems for drying when the seedpods are beginning to dry, but before the seeds turn yellow. Air dry upside down in a dark place.

Xeranthemum

Xeranthemum annuum

These flowers, also known as "immortelles," grow from 18 to 24 inches tall and have single or double flowers. Flowers are white, pink, rose, violet, and purple. For drying, flowers can be cut at different stages—from half-open buds to fully open flowers. They retain their colors for a long time after drying. Air dry upside down in the dark.

Firecracker Plant

Cuphea ignea

This plant first became popular as an indoor plant, but it's a good tender annual outdoors, too. Its slender, tubular flowers of bright red have a contrasting black band at the tip. It is a native of Mexico.

Description: Firecracker plants form a bushy subshrub up to 1 foot high with an equal or greater spread. Its compact mounding form is heavily covered with tiny, red flowers that appear at all the leaf axils. Leaves are long and narrow.

How to grow: Grow the firecracker plant in full sun in average but well-drained soil. Plant out after all danger of frost is over. Apply an all-purpose, slow-release fertilizer at planting. When planting out, pinch out the tips to increase bushiness. Space them 6 to 12 inches apart, depending on the length of the growing season. They are perennial in frost-free areas and can be sheared back to maintain their shapeliness.

Propagation: By seed or by cuttings. Seeds may be sown in the garden after the soil has warmed. They need light to germinate well—so barely cover them. For earlier bloom, sow seeds indoors 8 to 12 weeks prior to planting out. Seeds germinate in 8 to 10 days at 70 to 85° F. Cuttings root easily in 10 to 14 days.

Uses: Use them as edging plants for borders or in rock gardens. They are also good container plants, with growth flowing over the edges of hanging baskets, window boxes, or other planters. Branches can be cut and used in flower arrangements.

Related species: *Cuphea hyssopifolia*, or "Mexican heather," is a tender perennial used primarily for bedding out, except in frost-free areas. Leaves are tiny, and the plant is nearly obscured by the small white, lavender, or lilac-colored flowers that bloom over a long season. Growing to 1 foot, it spreads wider than its height.

Floss Flower

Ageratum houstonianum

Originally from Mexico and Central America, these fluffy flowers in blue-lavender, white, and pink are favorites for window boxes and edging in summer gardens. One interesting aspect of *ageratum* is that the eye sees the color of so-called blue varieties differently than film, which registers them as pink.

Description: Ageratum is covered with fuzzy flowers about ½ inch in diameter on compact, mounding plants from 6 to 10 inches high. They will spread about 10 inches by season's end. Ageratum blooms continuously from planting out after all chance of frost has passed (it is very frost-sensitive) until fall.

How to grow: Grow in any well-drained soil in full sun or partial shade. Space 6 to 10 inches apart for solid color. Occasional deadheading will improve their performance. They need ample water to make sure that leaves never wilt.

Propagation: By seed. Start seeds indoors 6 to 8 weeks before planting. Cover seeds very lightly, since they need some light to germinate well. Germination time will be 5 to 8 days at 70° F.

Uses: Plant in the front of borders and beds. They also grow well in hanging baskets, window boxes, and other containers. Most of the newer varieties form compact mounds that provide the scarce blue color so seldom found in annuals. Taller, older varieties make good cut flowers.

Related species: Golden ageratum or *Lonas inodora* has the same flower effect in bright yellow.

Related varieties: Several of the popular blue varieties ranging from light tones to deepest violet are 'Adriatic,' 'Blue Danube,' and 'Blue Blazer.' 'Summer Snow' is white, and 'Pink Powderpuffs' is as its name describes. 'Wonder' is a tall variety useful for cutting.

Foliage Plants

Tropical plants are often used for summer planting outdoors in many parts of the country. In frost-free Zones 9 and 10, they may be used as permanent plantings.

Dracaena
Dracaena marginata
This dracaena is used in outdoor container plantings surrounded by geraniums and asparagus fern. It is grown from cuttings.

Polka Dot Plant, Freckle Face
Hypoestes phyllostachya
This plant is used as a ground-covering plant in shade or partial shade during the summer. It is a subshrub that will grow from 1 to 2 feet high. Each leaf has markings in white or pink. It is propagated by seed or by cuttings. The variety 'Pink Splash' has much larger pink markings and is grown from seed.

Moses-in-a-Boat, Moses-in-a-Cradle
Rhoeo spathacea
This semisucculent plant has sword-shaped, metallic-green leaves with purple undersides. The flowers peek out from boat-shaped bracts that appear from leaf axils. This plant is widely used in beds in public plantings in warm parts of the country. They grow in sun or partial shade, resist drought, and flourish in any soil. They are also used as a summer annual in colder climates. A variegated form, *R. spathacea vittata*, has its leaves streaked with pale yellow.

Purple Heart
Setcreasea pallida
This purple-leafed plant is semisucculent and usually a trailer. Native to dry and semi-dry areas of Mexico, setcreasea is a tough plant. The dramatic, purple foliage contrasts beautifully with chartreuse-colored foliage plants as well as with creamy yellow flowers. Use it in large beds or in front of borders.

Forget-Me-Not

Myosotis sylvatica

A bed of spring bulbs—such as tulips or daffodils—underplanted with forget-me-nots is a sight to behold. Biennials native to cool, moist areas of Europe and northern Asia, they are usually grown as annuals.

Description: Forget-me-nots are small plants seldom reaching more than 12 inches in height and an equal diameter. The tiny flowers are clustered together in racemes at the top of plants.

How to grow: Forget-me-nots relish cool, moist weather with sun or partial shade. In Zones 8, 9, and 10, seeds can be sown in the fall where plants will bloom in the spring. When planting in the spring, plant as soon as the soil can be worked. When plants have finished blooming, replace them with summer annuals. Forget-me-nots will reseed, but seedlings in colder climates will not bloom until late spring or summer.

Propagation: By seed. For early bloom in cold climates, seed indoors in January, planting seedlings outdoors as soon as the soil can be worked. Seeds germinate in 8 to 14 days at 55 to 70° F. Be sure to cover seeds; they need darkness to germinate. When removing plants that have bloomed, shake the ripened seeds onto the ground where you want blooming plants the next spring.

Uses: Plant forget-me-nots in masses for best results. They're suited for rock gardens, as an edging, or in the front of a border. Try them in window boxes and patio planters with spring bulbs. Grow forget-me-nots in meadows, along stream banks, or by ponds.

Related varieties: 'Indigo Compacta' is a darker-colored selection that stays smaller than most varieties. 'Blue Ball' is a compact form with bright blue flowers. 'White Ball' is similar in form but has white blooms. 'Victoria Mixed' combines blue-, white-, rose-, and pink-flowered forms.

Chinese Forget-Me-Not, Hound's Tongue

Cynoglossum amabile

This plant is of special value for the clear, sky-blue color of the flowers. They bloom all summer, and are especially good in cool climates. The Chinese in its common name comes from its origin in Asia, although it also resembles the true forget-me-not (*Myosotis*). "Hound's tongue" refers to its leaves, which have a furry surface and are shaped like a dog's tongue.

Description: Chinese forget-me-not is a biennial most often grown as an annual. The plants grow to 2 feet tall with flowers appearing as sprays above the plant. The foliage is gray-green. There are also pink and white forms that are not widely available.

How to grow: Grow in full sun or partial shade in a rich, well-drained soil, high in organic matter. Except in regions with cool summers, they are more successful in full sun if the soil is kept evenly moist, but not soggy. Feed lightly or mix a slow-release fertilizer into the soil before planting. They may be planted outdoors in spring as soon as the soil is workable. Space 8 to 12 inches apart.

Propagation: By seed. Sow outdoors as early as the ground can be worked. For best color during cool weather, sow seeds indoors 6 to 8 weeks prior to transplanting outside. Germination takes 5 to 14 days at 70° F. Plants will reseed profusely if not kept in check. Seeds stick tightly to clothes and animals that carry them far from the planned location.

Uses: Grow them as a source of sky-blue color in beds or borders. They're also striking in beds all by themselves or mixed with other flowers to tone down hot colors or to complement a range of pastels.

Related variety: 'Firmament,' an award-winner, is widely available.

Summer Forget-Me-Not, Cape Forget-Me-Not

Anchusa capensis

The flowers of this South African native resemble forget-me-nots—resulting in anchusa's common names. Flowers with a bright, true blue color are a rarity for the summer garden. For sheer intensity of color, anchusa matches or exceeds every other blue available. A biennial, it is most often grown as an annual.

Description: Clouds of flowers cover the dwarf plants that grow 12 to 18 inches tall and 10 inches in diameter. Flowers are tiny and held on stems above the plant. Branches are rather top-heavy. A pink and white form is not widely available.

How to grow: Anchusa grows best where summers are cool. In hot areas of the country, they do best in spring or fall bloom, although hot days followed by cool nights suit their needs. They perform best in full sun, but will grow in partial shade on open, well-drained soil. Do not fertilize. Bloom will appear in flushes. When flowering diminishes, shear back to 6 inches to encourage repeat bloom that will take about 3 weeks. Repeat for copious bloom until frost. In mild winter areas, anchusas can be started the summer or fall before and grown outdoors over the winter for early flowering. Elsewhere, sow seeds outdoors several weeks before the last frost, or start in pots indoors and transplant outside after frost danger has passed.

Propagation: By seed. Germinates in 10 days at 60° F.

Uses: A splendid source of blue in the garden, use anchusa wherever you want to soften the strident tones of hot colors such as orange and yellow. It combines well with white. Because summer forget-me-not is compact, use it as an edging for beds and borders.

Varieties: 'Blue Angel' is 10 inches tall, and 'Blue Bird' grows to 18 inches. Both form compact mounds.

Four O'Clock, Marvel of Peru

Mirabilis jalapa

This is a plant whose flowers you wait to see until afternoon—hence, the common name "four o'clock." The name *mirabilis* is from the Latin "wonderful." They open in mid- to late-afternoon and close again the next morning (except on dull days).

Description: Four o'clocks form a well-branched, bushy shrub from 1 to 3 feet tall. Flowering is generous, with plants covered with white, yellow, red, purple, and unusual bicolored flowers. Sometimes different flower patterns appear on the same plant. When closed, the flowers curl up tightly.

How to grow: Full sun in average-to-rich garden soil is ideal for four o'clocks. They will also bloom in partial shade, although plants will become lankier. They are very tolerant of humidity, air pollution, heat, and drought. Plant them outdoors once the danger of frost has passed. Since they are vigorous growers, space them 18 to 24 inches apart. Four o'clocks form tubers which, after frost, can be dug up and stored for replanting the following year. Four o'clocks reseed.

Propagation: By seed or by tubers. In warm climates with a long growing season, you can seed outdoors after the last frost. For shorter season gardens, you'll get earlier bloom by starting them indoors 4 to 6 weeks ahead of planting out. Seeds germinate in 7 to 10 days at 70° F.

Uses: Four o'clocks make a neat, low hedge. They can be used for edging walks and borders or grouped in the center of the border. Because the flowers stay open at night, they're attractive when planted near evening activities—such as lighted pools and patios. Four o'clocks also grow well in large containers.

Related varieties: 'Jingles' bears white, rose, red, yellow, and crimson flowers, many of them splashed with contrasting colors.

Foxglove

Digitalis purpurea

The widely used heart medicine comes from this biennial plant, but its garden value is the bell-shaped flowers in late spring. It's a native of western Europe.

Description: Foxglove grows for months as a rosette of gray-green leaves; then a tall spike surrounded by buds quickly arises, growing from 3 to 7 feet tall. Most flowers, which are white, cream, pink, salmon, lavender, or red, are marked with blotches of contrasting color.

How to grow: Foxglove thrives in light woodlands or at the fringes of tree or shrub plantings. It will grow in average soil if kept moist. When flower spikes appear, fertilize with a general fertilizer. The sturdy spikes normally do not need staking. The seeds are tiny and widely distributed by the wind. To prevent reseeding, cut flower spikes after bloom.

Propagation: By seed. To grow as a biennial, sow seeds outdoors in June or July so husky plants will overwinter. For bloom the first year, sow indoors 8 to 10 weeks prior to planting outdoors. Except for selected varieties, these will bloom in late summer or fall. Seeds germinate at 70° F in 15 to 20 days.

Uses: Foxglove deserves a place in the mixed cottage garden. Plant it in groups at the back of the border, against fences, near tall shrub hedges or woodlands. They're also useful in the perennial border, providing the height that early perennial gardens often lack. They make useful cut flowers.

Related species: *Digitalis lutea* brings yellow flowers to the foxglove clan. It grows to 3 feet.

Related varieties: 'Foxy' has a full range of colors and grows to 3 feet tall. 'Excelsior Mixture' contains many colors of tall-growing foxgloves. 'Apricot' is a buttery, copper color, and 'Alba' is pure white.

Fuchsia, Lady's Ear Drops

Fuchsia hybrida

There are hundreds of named varieties of fuchsias, the beautiful plants with pendulous blossoms that bloom heavily from spring to fall. Most of them have been developed from two species. The name "lady's ear drops" is self-evident, but the name *Fuchsia* is more commonly used. The name honors Fuchs, a German botanist.

Description: Garden fuchsias are all more or less woody plants, some having a more erect, bushy habit; others with long, trailing stems from which blossoms hang. The flowers themselves are composed of a calyx, a brightly colored cylinder or tube that points downward, which is topped by flaring, petal-like lobes called sepals. The calyx can be single or double, and the sepals are either the same color or contrasting. The calyx and sepals may also be wavy and ruffled.

How to grow: Fuchsias bloom more freely when they get some shade. They're at their best in cool coastal or mountain regions with good humidity, but can be grown successfully in most places as long as they are kept moist. Fuchsias are heavy feeders. Apply a slow-release fertilizer at planting or feed biweekly with a water-soluble fertilizer. For large-blooming plants by mid-May, plant 3 to 5 rooted cuttings in a 10- to 12-inch basket. To develop full and shapely plants, pinch out tips as soon as two sets of leaves have formed and continue this process until March 1. Fuchsias are not winter-hardy except in Zones 9 and 10, but they can be stored over winter in temperatures above freezing but below 50° F. Water only enough to keep the root ball from drying out. Light is unnecessary. In January, bring into the light, cut back plants by at least 50 percent, and resume normal watering.

Propagation: By seed or by cuttings. Seeds germinate in 21 to 28 days.

Uses: Fuchsias are at their best in hanging baskets where the pendulous flowers can be viewed from below. They are most often placed where they can be seen frequently—on decks, porches, or beside walkways. Upright varieties are eye-catching in containers raised on railings or porch steps. Fuchsias are also grown as standards or in tree form, with foliage and flowers flaring out from a single stem grown to the desired height.

Related species: *Fuchsia magellanica* is a small-flowered, hardier species.

Related varieties: Selections are so varied that it is best to choose them in bloom at a nursery or garden center. 'Swingtime,' with double, white calyxes and red sepals, is by far the favorite variety. Double 'Indian Maid' has blue-violet calyxes and red sepals. 'Lena' bears double purple and white flowers. 'Jack Shahan' is a single, pink flowered variety with a trailing form. 'Marinka,' with a multitude of small, red, single flowers, has a counterpart, 'Golden Marinka,' with variegated leaves. 'Gartenmeister Bonstedt' is an old upright variety with numerous firecracker-shaped red flowers.

Gazania, Treasure Flower

Gazania ringens

This South African flower likes hot, dry summers and cool winters. Gardeners treasure it for its daisylike flowers.

Description: Gazanias grow in rosette form with attractive notched leaves. In many varieties, these are gray-green on top and silver beneath. Flowers rise 8 to 12 inches on short stems. They're white, pink, bronze, red, yellow, orange, and white, contrasting with bright yellow centers. Some varieties have contrasting stripes in the ray petals.

How to grow: Gazanias prefer full sun and moderately fertile but well-drained soil. The only thing they don't like is heavy soil in hot, humid climates. In Zones 9, 10, and sometimes 8, they'll winter over as perennials. In those areas they'll bloom for 8 or 9 months. Elsewhere, plant out as soon as the danger of frost has passed. Space 8 to 15 inches apart.

Propagation: By seed, cuttings, or division. Sow seeds outdoors after final frost or plant them indoors 4 to 6 weeks earlier. Barely cover seeds, as they need light to germinate. Seeds germinate in 15 to 20 days at 70° F. Cuttings taken in the summer root quickly. In Zones 9 and 10, division can be accomplished by cutting clumps apart and replanting the pieces.

Uses: Plant gazanias in the front of beds and borders. Use them as a ground cover in sunny, dry areas or in rock gardens. They're good cut flowers. Gazanias can be potted for bloom indoors. They are good in containers and window boxes.

Related varieties: The 'Daybreak' series blooms in 'Yellow,' 'Orange,' and 'Garden Sun,' combining yellow and orange. The 'Daybreak Mixture' includes pink and white colors. 'Chansonette' has many contrasting colors between the centers and tips of petals. 'Ministar' has a separate 'Yellow' and 'Tangerine,' as well as a mix.

Ivy-Leaf Geranium

Pelargonium peltatum

Ivy-leaf geraniums have an entirely different character than their zonal geranium cousins. Long, trailing stems make them ideal for containers of all kinds. Their flowers are generally less strident and more toned to the pastel range of their hues. Older varieties are somewhat intolerant of long periods of heat and humidity, but newer varieties are more heat-resistant. The common name springs from the shape of the leaves.

Description: Two distinct groups of ivy-leaf geraniums are available to home gardeners. All of them have the cascading form of ivy geraniums, but a group of single-flowered varieties from Europe are proving more floriferous and heat-tolerant. Semi-double flowered varieties have less bloom, but still make real impact all summer. Many varieties are available—from miniatures with a spread of only 12 inches through vigorous ones that can grow to 5 feet tall.

How to grow: Ivy-leaf geraniums grow best in cool, coastal, or mountain climates with lots of sun. In other locations they may need partial shade. Ivy-leaf geraniums in containers relish full sun if temperatures are not above 85° F for long stretches. Where this occurs, give them northern or eastern exposure where they can be protected from hot midday and afternoon sun. Do not let them dry out. Plant ivy-leaf geraniums outside after danger of frost has passed and the soil is warm.

Propagation: By cuttings or by seed (only one variety so far is seed-grown). Take cuttings from stock plants 10 to 12 weeks prior to planting outside. Pinch tips once or twice to encourage branching.

Uses: Ivy-leaf geraniums are excellent container plants. They develop into shapely hanging baskets clothed with foliage and flowers. As window box plants, they excel and are ideal in patio planters. The single-flowered varieties are also good plants to use as sunny ground covers.

Related varieties: Among the heavy flowering, single-flowered varieties (so-called European types), the 'Cascade' series is representative. 'Sofie Cascade' is a light pink with darker shading toward petal centers. 'Bright Cascade' is a glowing red. 'Lila Compact Cascade' is lavender. Good semi-doubles include 'Yale,' rich crimson; 'Galilee,' a very vigorous hot pink; 'Salmon Queen'; 'Snow Queen'; and 'Beauty of Eastbourne,' cherry red. The seed-grown variety is 'Summer Showers' and includes red, white, pink, lavender, and plum-colored varieties.

Regal, Martha Washington or Lady Washington Geranium or Pelargonium

Pelargonium domesticum

Regal pelargoniums like mild weather and sunny days to perform their best. These plants have large, open-faced flowers above light green, pleated leaves. Exceedingly colorful, they include clear colors of pink, red, white, lavender, and burgundy, with the flowers of many varieties marked with bright patches of contrasting colors. Where nights do not go above 60° F, they will continue blooming all summer. In warmer areas, they will take a midsummer hiatus until cooler nights prevail in the fall. Plant in the garden in the spring when the weather has settled.

Variegated Zonal Geranium

A number of varieties of zonal geraniums are grown for their fancy leaves. Culture is the same as for regular zonals. Probably the most colorful are 'Skies of Italy,' 'Mrs. Cox,' and 'Dolly Varden.' The leaves of 'Ben Franklin,' 'Wilhelm Langguth,' and 'Mrs. Parker' are similar in appearance, rounded with distinct margins of white on the edges.

Scented Geranium

A variety of species pelargoniums have distinctly fragrant leaves when the surface is rubbed. Some have attractive foliage, but in most the bloom is modest. *Pelargonium crispum* has lemon-scented leaves. *P. grossulariodes* is coconut-scented, while *P. nervosum* has the fragrance of lime. *P. fragrans* smells like nutmeg. One of the most popular is *P. tomentosum*, which has a strong peppermint scent. Its foliage is especially attractive, with felted leaves of a rich green. Less common varieties include those with the scent of roses and strawberries.

Zonal Geranium

Pelargonium x hortorum

Many gardeners consider zonal geraniums the epitome of summer flowers. Named for the dark, horseshoe-shaped color in the leaves of most varieties, these stalwart garden beauties are tender perennials that must be replanted each year except in the most favored climates. Most *pelargonium* species (true geraniums are hardy perennials) come from South Africa, but through hundreds of years of breeding, the parentage of today's varieties is obscured.

Description: Zonal geraniums are upright bushes covered with red, pink, salmon, white, rose, cherry red, and bicolored flowers on long stems held above the plant. Flower clusters (or umbels) contain many individual flowers and give a burst of color. Plants from 4-inch pots transplanted to the garden in spring will reach up to 18 inches high and wide by the end of summer.

How to grow: Zonal geraniums benefit from sun. They develop into shapely hanging baskets clothed with foliage and flowers. As window box plants, they excel and are ideal in full sun and moderate-to-rich, well-drained, moist soil. Incorporate a slow-release fertilizer into the soil at planting time. Plant after all danger of frost has passed and the soil is warm. Space them 12 inches apart. The only other care requirement is deadheading spent blooms.

Propagation: By seed or by cuttings. So far, the only readily available semi-double, flowered varieties are grown from cuttings. The cuttings root easily. Make cuttings 8 to 10 weeks prior to planting out for husky plants. Seed-grown varieties should be started 10 to 12 weeks prior to garden planting. Seeds germinate in 7 to 10 days at 70 to 75° F.

Uses: Zonal geraniums are among the best plants for formal beds. They can provide pockets of color in any sunny spot. Group 3 or more together for color impact in flower borders or along walks and pathways. They're classics in containers, all by themselves, or mixed with other kinds of plants. Geraniums are also grown as standards—a single stem is trained to the desired height with a bushy canopy of flowers and leaves. Zonal geraniums will bloom through the winter in sunny windows.

Related varieties: There are many varieties available at garden centers in the spring. A few popular semi-doubles are: 'Tango,' a bright orange-red with dark foliage; 'Forever Yours,' a vigorous red; 'Blues,' cherry blossom pink with unique rose and white markings near the center of petals; 'Schone Helene,' a 2-toned salmon; and 'Snowmass,' pure white. Seed-grown singles are generally found in series of many colors. Widely planted are 'Orbit,' 'Elite,' 'Ringo,' 'Bandit,' and 'Hollywood' varieties.

Gladiolus, Glad

Gladiolus hybridus

The name *gladiolus* means "little sword" in reference to the sword-shaped leaves of the plant. Every flower color but blue is represented in modern hybrids, and the flowers themselves vary immensely. They are members of the iris family.

Description: The erect spikes of flowers, from 1 to 4 feet tall, grow through the swordlike leaves from the corm, a modified stem planted underground. The individual flowers are classified by size by the North American Gladiolus Council, from miniatures with flowers under 2½ inches in diameter to giants over 5½ inches in diameter.

How to grow: Gladiolus grows best in well-drained soil high in organic matter, in full sun. Shelter from heavy winds. Where the ground does not freeze, corms may be left in the ground from year to year. Elsewhere, plant each spring in succession to assure continuous bloom. Plant the first about the time deciduous trees are sprouting new foliage, continuing about every 2 weeks until the first of July. Bloom occurs 60 to 70 days after planting. Fertilize a month after planting and again just before the first flowers open. Water regularly if dry.

Propagation: By corms. The tiny corms that form around each corm can be saved at digging (keep separate and label by variety), then planted in the spring for size increase.

Uses: Glads can be used to provide a succession of color, especially in perennial borders when early blooming perennials have finished. Plant them in clusters or groups. They make superb cut flowers, and if wanted primarily for cutting, can be planted in rows in the cutting garden.

Related varieties: There are named varieties by the hundreds.

Godetia, Farewell-To-Spring, Clarkia

Clarkia amoena

The name of this genus honors Captain Clark of the Lewis and Clark expeditions. The species (formerly called *Godetia* botanically) has been improved to produce varieties for spring gardens as well as for cool coastal and mountain locations in the summer.

Description: Godetias produce cup-shaped blossoms in clusters at the tips of strong stems. Flowers are white, pink, red, or lilac with contrasting colors in most. There are also double varieties. Foliage is gray-green. Height ranges from 10 inches up to 2½ feet, and they grow about 10 inches wide. Shorter varieties have a mounding habit.

How to grow: Godetias grow best during the cool weather. In Zones 9 and 10, sow outdoors in the fall for earliest bloom in the spring. In other zones, seed in the garden as early as a seedbed can be prepared. Grow in light, sandy loam in full sun or partial shade. Space plants 12 inches apart. Taller varieties may need staking.

Propagation: By seed. Because they do not transplant well, sow seeds directly in the soil outdoors. Barely cover; they need light to germinate.

Uses: Plant in beds and borders, grow in rock gardens, and naturalize in open meadows. Tall varieties make good cut flowers.

Related species: Many of the flowers usually referred to as clarkias are hybrids of *C. unguiculata* and *C. pulchella* (*Clarkia elegans*). Each species has a variety of garden forms, including double-flowered varieties. Generally, the flowers of clarkias grow along the stem, facing outward, and are about 1 inch in diameter. Colors include white, pink, salmon, and purple.

Related variety: F_1 hybrid 'Grace' is available in red, shell pink, rose-pink, and a mixture of colors.

Ornamental Gourds

Yellow-Flowered Gourd
Cucumis pepo olifera

These are closely related to squash. Hard-shelled fruits of many shapes and colors (both solid and striped) grow on long-stemmed vines.

White-Flowered Gourd
Lagenaria siceraris

This is a rapidly growing vine with large fruits of many sizes and shapes. Depending on the shape, they are often known as bottle gourd, calabash, dipper gourd, siphon gourd, snake gourd, and sugar-trough gourd. Besides being used as ornaments and as containers, they are also used as musical instruments.

Dishrag Gourd, Vegetable Sponge
Luffa aegyptiaca

The long, gourdlike fruits have a fibrous skeleton, which, once the skin is removed, can be used for scrubbing purposes. They grow on a vigorous vine.

How to grow: Full sun, a rich soil high in organic matter, and plentiful moisture are important for good growth by gourds. Sow outdoors when the ground is well-warmed and all danger of frost has passed. Plant seeds in hills of 6 to 8 seeds to a group. Thin seedlings to 4 per hill, selecting the strongest ones. Space hills 8 feet apart.

Propagation: By seed. Roots of gourds resent disturbance, so sow in place outdoors. If started earlier indoors, plant in peat pots that can be transplanted into the ground, pot and all. Seeds germinate in 4 to 8 days at 70° F.

Uses: The vines of gourds can be used to grow over arbors, trellises, pergolas, fences, and arches, or may be left to grow on the ground. Their rapid growth will allow them to reach 15 to 30 feet. After harvesting mature fruit, wash well, dry, then coat with floor wax or varnish before using in ornamental arrangements.

Cloud Grass, Wild Oats, Quaking Grass, Job's Tears, Golden Top, Wheat Grass

Agrostis nebulosa, Avena sterilis, Briza maxima, Coix Lacryma-Jobi, Lamarkia aurea, Triticum aestivum

Ornamental grasses have long been a primary ingredient in dried flower arrangements and winter bouquets. Recently, their use as ornamentals in the landscape has grown dramatically. There are about 10,000 species of grasses, and most of them are perennial, including the bamboos. The following is just a small sampling of the annual varieties that are widely grown both for adornment of the garden and for enduring pleasure in the home. Perhaps 150 different ornamental grasses are used in gardens, with more being tamed for this use all the time.

Description: Cloud grass (*Agrostis nebulosa*) from Spain, growing to 15 inches tall, is grown primarily for its airy flower heads, which are much larger than the sparse foliage. The flower heads dry well but aren't suitable for dyeing.

Wild oats (*Avena sterilis*) from the Mediterranean are now naturalized in the United States. Favored by flower arrangers, they're also a lovely feature in the garden, especially when light strikes from behind so that the hanging spikelets are highlighted. They grow up to 18 inches tall.

Quaking grass (*Briza maxima*) from the Mediterranean was one of the first grasses grown for its ornamental value. The loose flower heads shake at the slightest breeze. They grow to less than 1 foot tall.

Job's tears (*Coix Lacryma-Jobi*) from the tropics have large, tear-shaped grains that are used for making bead necklaces and other ornaments and crafts. As garden plants, they are grown for their seeds. They grow up to 3 feet tall.

Golden top (*Lamarkia aurea*), another Mediterranean import, has erect, silky plumes on

one side of the stalk like a toothbrush. The flower heads range from whitish to yellow and tones of purple. It grows up to 1 foot high; clumps are effective in the front of a border. It is very good for drying.

Wheat grass (*Triticum aestivum*) grows to 3 feet tall and is topped with grains evenly spiraled around the stem. A cereal grain in real life (but not the common one we know), wheat grass is prized by floral arrangers.

How to grow: All the annual grasses thrive in full sun on well-drained soil. They'll survive and seed in poor soil even under dry conditions, but growth will be richer and flowering more luxuriant in fertile soil with adequate moisture. In order to prevent reseeding, harvest the flower heads before they're fully dry.

Propagation: By seed. Sow in place in the spring when soil becomes friable. Plant 12 to 15 seeds in an area 1 foot square in well-worked soil and cover ½ to 1 inch deep. Most varieties will tolerate frost, but wait to plant tropical kinds until the soil is warm and frost danger has passed. Save some of the harvested seed stalks for replanting the following year.

Uses: Ornamental grasses are indispensable to many harvest arrangements, door hangings, and other crafts. The tall spiky kinds add line, and the feathery, soft heads of others provide a graceful note to arrangements. In the garden, plant grasses in clumps so their impact is heightened. Short varieties gracefully tie down the front of the border. Taller ones, unless their foliage is especially attractive, deserve middle of the border position where flower heads can be treasured beginning in July. Varieties grown only for flower arrangements can be planted in the cutting garden. Ornamental grasses are also showing up in container gardens, by themselves, or combined with flowers. In northern climates, many varieties of annual grasses remain attractive in the garden until heavy snows cover them.

Héliotrope, Cherry Pie

Heliotropium arborescens

Fragrance is one of the most alluring attributes of heliotrope. Flowers are deep blue, violet, lavender, or white in copious quantities during the summer. A perennial shrub in South America, we use it in the United States, except in frost-free areas, as an annual.

Description: Heliotrope is a branched shrub with long, gray-green leaves with deep veins. In nature it grows to 4 feet, but as a summer plant a height of 1 foot and equal spread is reasonable. Many tiny flowers are clustered in the large heads carried well above the foliage. The most commonly available varieties are deep blue and white.

How to grow: Any good garden soil with medium fertility in full sun will grow good heliotropes. Normally, plants are started early indoors (from seed or cuttings) and transplanted outdoors when danger of frost has passed and the ground is warm. Depending on the size of transplants, space from 8 to 15 inches apart.

Propagation: By seed or cuttings. Sow seeds 10 to 12 weeks before planting out. Seeds germinate in 7 to 21 days at 70 to 85° F. Root cuttings in 4-inch pots in February in order to have husky plants for planting outdoors in May. Pinch the tips of both seedlings and cutting varieties to create bushy plants.

Uses: Tuck heliotropes into rock gardens, or grow them in the front of borders. Plant them by doorsteps where the fragrance will be appreciated. They are superb as container plants. Grow them indoors if you can provide enough sunlight. To use as cut flowers, plunge the stems and necks deep in water and hold in a cool, dark place for several hours before arranging.

Related varieties: 'Marine,' grown from seed, has dark violet-blue flowers.

Chinese Hibiscus, Hawaiian Hibiscus, Rose of China

Hibiscus rosa-sinensis

Hardy only in frost-free parts of Zones 9 and 10, hibiscus is widely used as an annual elsewhere. It is a member of the mallow family and is found throughout the year in garden centers as a blooming pot plant for indoor enjoyment, but it can be used outdoors as well.

Description: In nature, they're shrubs up to 15 feet tall, but for summering outdoors they will probably reach a maximum of 3 feet tall and wide. The glossy, evergreen foliage is a handsome background for the large—up to 6-inch—flowers. These flaring bells with a distinctive column of yellow stamens in the center are red, yellow, pink, salmon, orange, or white.

How to grow: Hibiscus needs full sun for best bloom production, but it can tolerate partial shade. Soil should be rich, high in organic matter, and be well-moistened. Hibiscus also grows best in high humidity. Primary use in all but frost-free areas is as a container plant. Apply slow-release fertilizer to the soil before planting in the container. Hibiscus can be pruned to make it more shapely by pinching out the tips of young growth to induce branching.

Propagation: By cuttings. Semi-hardwood cuttings root quickly in summer under mist.

Uses: Hibiscus is best used in containers. It can be cut back severely in the spring to maintain its size.

Related species: *Hibiscus rosa-sinensis cooperi* has brightly variegated leaves in pink and white; blooms are red. *Hibiscus schizopelalus* has finely divided, pink blooms. *Hibiscus moscheutos*, or rose mallow, is a perennial with large flowers. 'Disco Belle Mixed,' grown from seed, has large flowers in red, pink, and white.

Related varieties: There are hundreds of named varieties of *Hibiscus rosa-sinensis*.

Hollyhock

Alcea rosea

These tall, stately plants have long been favored by artists when painting scenes of romantic cottage gardens. Hollyhocks have also been a favorite children's plaything—the flowers can be turned into "Southern Belles" complete with long, ruffled skirts.

Description: Most varieties will grow to 6 feet or taller, the stems surrounded by hibiscuslike flowers in every color except blue. Flowers can be single, semi-double, or double, and are waved or fringed. Leaves are large, round, and coarse.

How to grow: Plant in full sun where there's good air movement to avoid rust. Water and feed heavily and spray with a fungicide if rust develops. Staking may be necessary with very tall varieties or if the site is very windy. Plant 12 to 15 inches apart in clumps. Hollyhocks are prolific reseeders, although they will not come true to type this way. To prevent undesirable colors, deadhead the spent flowers.

Propagation: By seed. Most varieties are biennial but, if seeded early enough indoors, can be treated as annuals for the garden. Sow seeds indoors in February or March for flowers the first year. Barely cover seeds (they need light to germinate) and expect germination in 10 to 24 days at 70° F. Plant outdoors after final frost where they'll bloom from July until frost.

Uses: Since hollyhocks are bold in scale, they add height to the rear of a border. They can also be used as a bright clump beside garden paths or at doorsteps.

Related varieties: 'Powderpuff Mixed' provides a wide range of colors with very double flowers. 'Majorette' produces semi-double and laced flowers on 3-foot stems. 'Summer Carnival' with double blooms will flower as an annual if sown early indoors.

Impatiens, Busy Lizzie, Patience

Impatiens wallerana

Impatiens flower in all colors (except true blue and yellow). Their tidy and mounding habit makes them ideal low-maintenance plants. Impatiens were stowaways on trading ships from Africa and naturalized in Central and South America.

Description: Breeders have developed compact, self-branching plants whose flowers are borne above the foliage. Flowers are white, pink, rose, orange, scarlet, burgundy, violet, and many variants. Other varieties have star-shaped patterns of white against colored backgrounds. Double varieties are also grown. Foliage is deep, glossy green or bronze in color. Most varieties grow 12 to 15 inches high in dappled shade. Heavy watering encourages vigorous growth; higher light dwarfs them.

How to grow: Impatiens will grow in any average soil. In cool or coastal areas, impatiens will grow and bloom well if their roots are kept well-watered. In deep shade, bloom diminishes.

Propagation: By seed or by cuttings. Sow seeds 10 to 12 weeks before the last frost date. Impatiens need light to germinate; do not cover seeds, but keep moist. Germination takes 10 to 20 days at 75° F. Use a sterile soil mix, because young impatiens seedlings are subject to damping off disease. A fungicide is recommended. Cuttings root in 10 to 14 days.

Uses: Impatiens can be used in beds, borders, planting strips, and containers. Their mounding habit is beautiful in hanging baskets and planters. Impatiens can be grown indoors in bright, filtered light.

Related varieties: There are many varieties: 'Accent,' 'Dazzler,' 'Impulse,' 'Super Elfin,' and 'Tempo,' to mention a few. Vigorous series such as 'Blitz' or 'Showstopper' are ideal for containers. Double varieties include 'Rosette,' 'Duet,' and 'Confection.'

New Guinea Impatiens

Impatiens species

When a plant hunting expedition went to Southeast Asia, they made significant discoveries. Species impatiens found there are now being developed into varieties quite different from traditional impatiens.

Description: New Guinea impatiens form compact, succulent subshrubs with branches growing 1 to 2 feet tall by summer's end. Leaves are long and narrow, green, bronze, or purple. Flowers, growing up to 2 inches in diameter, are white, pink, lavender, purple, orange, and red.

How to grow: Fertile, moist soil high in organic matter is preferred by New Guinea impatiens. They are more sun-loving than the other impatiens. They will tolerate more sun if their roots are kept moist. Incorporate a slow-release fertilizer into the soil before planting. They should only be planted after the danger of frost has passed and the ground has warmed. Space 9 to 15 inches apart.

Propagation: By seed or by cuttings. Only two varieties of New Guinea impatiens are available from seed so far. Sow 10 to 12 weeks before planting outside. Germinate at 75 to 80° F. Do not cover, since seeds need light to germinate, but mist to keep moist. Cuttings root quickly and easily in 2 to 3 weeks.

Uses: Impatiens should be used in masses of color in beds and borders. Cluster three or more in groups beside garden features. Plant them in containers and in hanging baskets.

Related varieties: 'Tango,' grown from seed, has fluorescent-orange flowers. 'Sunshine' hybrids, grown from cuttings, are a series that include many with variegated foliage and flowers in all colors—white, pink, red, orange, lavender, and purple. They also have bicolors. Look for constellation and meteorological names: 'Cirrus,' 'Gemini,' etc.

Joseph's Coat, Love Lies Bleeding, Prince's Feather

Amaranthus tricolor, A. caudatus

Brightly colored foliage in yellow, red, and orange is the appeal of various ornamental varieties of *A. tricolor;* hence the common name of "Joseph's coat." *A. caudatus* is known as "love lies bleeding" for its brightly colored ropes of flowers in red, white, or bright green.

Description: These tropical foliage and flowering plants with their bright plumage vary in different, visually stimulating ways. Because they grow rapidly in hot weather, choose different amaranthus for specific needs of color and texture.

How to grow: Plant in warm soil after all chance of frost has passed and in full sun to develop the most vibrant color. Amaranthus tolerates poor soil, heat, and drought. Poor drainage or excessively wet soil may cause root rot.

Propagation: By seed. Start indoors at 70° F 6 weeks prior to planting out or sow directly in place.

Uses: Because of its height, *A. tricolor* makes a good background plant. The shorter *A. caudatus* is useful grouped in mid-border. Several plants together will effectively highlight their tassels. They make striking container plants. The flowers may also be cut and dried.

Related species: Prince's feather (*A. cruentus*) has purple or red spikes that will reach 5 feet by season's end.

Related varieties: Plants of *A. tricolor* can grow to 4 feet high and spread 2 feet wide. Varieties include 'Flaming Fountains,' with long, willowy, crimson leaves; 'Joseph's Coat,' with yellow, scarlet, and green foliage; and 'Illumination,' which adds bronze to the previous colors. Varieties of *A. caudatus* are shorter, up to 2 feet high with a 2-foot spread and include 'Green Thumb,' with upright, green spikes; 'Pigmy Torch,' with erect, maroon spikes; and 'Love Lies Bleeding,' with blood-red flowers.

Lantana

Lantana hybrida

These shrubby plants are abundantly covered through the summer with brightly colored blossoms. The garden varieties bear white, yellow, gold, orange, and red flowers; usually the older flowers in each cluster are a different color than the younger ones.

Description: Lantanas are woody shrubs with large, rough leaves. They grow about 3 feet tall and as wide over a summer's growth. When protected against frost, they can grow to 15 feet or more in height over a period of years.

How to grow: Lantana needs full sun and hot weather to perform best. It is actually best in poor soil. It is very frost-sensitive, so plant outdoors after the ground has warmed thoroughly. Space the plants about 18 inches apart. Pinch the tips of plants as soon as they have made 2 sets of leaves and repeat 3 or 4 times. This will promote bushiness. Plants may be dug 6 weeks before frost, cut back, and potted for indoor bloom in sunny locations.

Propagation: By cuttings. For May or June planting outdoors of 4-inch pots, take cuttings in February or early March. For larger hanging baskets, take cuttings in January. Dipping in a rooting hormone speeds rooting. Root under mist or keep from wilting during rooting.

Uses: Lantanas are most often used in containers. They grow well in sunny window boxes, hanging baskets, or patio planters. They can be used in ground beds if soil is not too rich.

Related species: *Lantana montevidensis* is a widely grown, pink-lavender flowering variety. Its growth is more trailing.

Related varieties: 'Confetti' has flowers with pink, white, and red colors intermixed. 'Radiation' has tones of orange and red, while 'Pink Caprice' combines pink and yellow in the same flower clusters. There are many other varieties.

Larkspur, Annual Delphinium

Consolida ambigua

Larkspur resembles the delphinium, with its stately spikes of flowers in cool pastel colors. Formerly lumped with delphiniums, botanists split them off and named them *Consolida,* an old Latin term for "an undetermined plant."

Description: Larkspur grows up to 4 feet tall with delphiniumlike flowers, single or double, evenly spaced around the long stem above lacy, gray-green foliage. Although blue is favored, larkspur also flowers in pink, salmon, rose, lavender, purple, and white.

How to grow: Grow in moist but well-drained soil in full sun. If exposed to high winds, larkspur may need staking. It performs best in cool weather. In Zones 7 to 10, seeds may be sown early enough in the fall so that young plants would bloom early in the spring. In other zones, seeds can be sown late in the fall so that they would germinate in the spring. Remove spent blossoms to encourage bloom.

Propagation: By seed. Sow in place because larkspur does not transplant well. Sow in the fall or as soon as the ground can be worked in the spring. For summer and fall blooms in cool climates, successively sow 2 to 3 weeks apart until mid-May.

Uses: Groups of delphinium backing informal annuals can give a cottage garden look. Group them at the side or at the back of the flower border or center them in island beds to lend height. They're good cut flowers and may be dried for winter bouquets.

Related species: Many of the true perennial delphiniums may be grown as summer annuals. 'Pacific' hybrids are widely grown and hybrids of *Delphinium belladonna* are also planted. Compact hybrids (2 to 3 feet high) grown from seed are 'Blue Springs' and 'Blue Fountains.'

Related varieties: A favorite is the 'Imperial' series that branches freely from the base.

Lisianthus, Prairie Gentian

Eustoma grandiflorum

This native plant of the Midwest to Mexico has come into vogue recently because of widespread breeding efforts. New hybrids have been developed for flowering pot plants, cut flowers, and garden use. The primary color is a bluish-purple, but it also blooms in pink or white.

Description: Prairie gentians grow up to 3 feet tall, are branched, and are surmounted with cup-shaped, poppylike blooms that open wide in full sunlight. Flowers are about 3 inches in diameter. Although most are single-flowered, semi-doubles are also available.

How to grow: Prairie gentians can be grown as annuals by starting them early; otherwise, they are biennials, grown by seeding them the summer before, then wintering them over as small plants in cold frames or heated greenhouses. Grow them in full sun in moist soil. Space 8 to 12 inches apart. Pinch out the growing tips to induce branching and more flowers.

Propagation: By seed. Sow seeds 3 months before planting out when danger of frost has passed. Germination takes 10 to 12 days at 75° F. Because they form a taproot that makes transplanting difficult, prairie gentians should be transplanted to individual pots when they reach the 3-leaf stage. Early growth is slow, picking up when weather warms.

Uses: Grow prairie gentian where you want a strong show of color in moist soils. Because the flower form is so attractive, plant them where they can be viewed close up. They grow well in containers. They are superb as cut flowers.

Related varieties: Varieties include: the 'Yodel' series, with blue, deep blue, mid-blue, lilac, pink, rose, and white flowers. It is also available as a mixture of all colors. The 'Lion' series is semi-double, offered in white, pink, and blue.

Lobelia

Lobelia erinus

Few flowers have the intense blue provided by some varieties of lobelia. They are perennials, but too tender to live over the winter in most parts of the country and are grown as annuals.

Description: These lobelias have small, round leaves and flowers up to ½ inch in diameter. Some varieties are compact and mounding; others are definite trailers. The most prominent flower color is blue, but there are also crimson, pink, and white varieties. The trailing ones will reach 12 to 18 inches by summer's end; the mounding ones grow 6 to 8 inches high.

How to grow: Lobelia grows best in cool areas or where cool nighttime temperatures moderate the weather. They will bloom well in partial shade if their root areas are mulched and kept moist. Space 4 to 6 inches apart in the garden or in containers.

Propagation: By seed. Seeds are tiny and need light to germinate, so they should not be covered. Start plants indoors 10 to 12 weeks before planting outdoors. Seeds germinate in 20 days at 70 to 80° F. Seedling growth is slow, and the early stages should be watched carefully to prevent damping off. A fungicide is recommended. Don't try to separate individual seedlings at transplanting; instead, plant clumps of several seedlings.

Uses: Use the mounding forms for edgings, as pockets in rock gardens, between patio stones, or in the front of taller plantings beside walks and pathways. The trailing varieties can cascade over rock walls and are among the best for containers of all kinds.

Related varieties: Mounding forms include: 'Crystal Palace,' deep blue flowers and bronze foliage; 'Cambridge Blue,' sky-blue flowers; 'Mrs. Clibran,' dark blue with white eyes; and 'Rosamund,' cherry-red. Some trailers are: 'Sapphire,' deep blue with white eyes; 'Blue Cascade,' light blue; and 'White Cascade.'

Lotus Vine, Parrot's Beak

Lotus berthelotti

The scarlet flowers from which the name "parrot's beak" is derived are a short-term bonus from this lovely plant. It's the smoky gray, feathery foliage that makes this plant such a beautiful addition to summer container plantings. A native of the Canary Islands, it's a member of the legume or pea family. It is only hardy in frost-free parts of the United States.

Description: Lotus vine (which is really a trailer) can grow up to 3 feet in length by the end of the season. It has many-branched segments covered with very fine, gray-green leaves. In sun, they're almost iridescent. The blossoms that appear in June or early July are up to 1 inch long with curved petals. They're scarlet to crimson, lightening to an orange-red as they fade.

How to grow: Grow lotus vine in full sun. Normally, it is used in containers and will be satisfied with any commercial potting soil mix. In the wild, it will tolerate summer drought and periods of moisture shortage, but will grow more lushly if given adequate water. Add a slow-release fertilizer to the soil at planting time for continuous feeding during the summer. Space 8 to 12 inches apart in containers.

Propagation: By cuttings. Take cuttings 8 to 10 weeks prior to planting out (after all danger of frost has passed). Strip the foliage off the bottom 1 inch of cuttings and insert in a soil mix. Keep humidity high during rooting. Pinch tips to induce branching.

Uses: Lotus vine is one of the best plants for dressing up mixed container plantings. The trailing habit covers containers, adding color to window boxes, hanging baskets, and planter boxes. Lotus is especially good with white or pastel colors and combined with geraniums of all kinds in planters.

Love-in-a-Mist, Devil in a Bush

Nigella damascena

These frothy, quick-to-bloom annuals add an airy note to garden plantings with their soft colors combining well with other flowers. Nigellas are native to Mediterranean areas.

Description: Love-in-a-mist grows up to 2 feet tall and has many branches. The finely cut foliage is lacy, and the flowers float above the foliage, which is highlighted by large bracts on which the flowers sit. Flowers are most often powder-blue, but there are also pink, rose, and white varieties.

How to grow: Nigella thrives in any sunny location in soil of average fertility or better. Sow the seeds outdoors in the spring as early as the ground can be worked. Thin to a spacing of 5 to 15 inches. For continuous bloom all summer, make successive sowings until early July. Protect them from high winds and stake the plants if necessary.

Propagation: By seed. For earlier bloom, start them indoors 4 to 6 weeks before outdoor planting. Because they are difficult to transplant, start them in peat pots that can be transplanted into the garden, pot and all. Seeds germinate in 10 to 15 days at 65 to 70° F.

Uses: Nigella is a good see-through plant, allowing the plants behind to peek through. Consider using it with other pastels and creamy whites. It's best in informal situations. The seedpods are widely used for winter arrangements. Cut them off after they have ripened and dry them upside down in a dark place.

Related species: *Nigella hispanica* has mid-blue flowers with black centers and red stamens.

Related varieties: 'Persian Jewels' combines the most popular blue with white, pink, rose, mauve, lavender, and purple. 'Miss Jekyll' has semi-double flowers in sky-blue. 'Miss Jekyll Alba' is similar, but with white flowers.

Lupine

Lupinus species

There are many kinds of lupines, both annuals and perennials (some are grown as annuals because they are short-lived in many regions). The most widely planted are hybrids grown under the name of *Lupinus regalis*, which have stout spires of many colors. Lupines are members of the legume or pea family and bear the typical pea-shaped flower.

Description: The best known are Russell hybrids, which, under favorable conditions, can grow up to 5 feet tall. Compact varieties topping out at 18 inches are also available. A rosette of foliage is composed of many leaves resembling bird's feet. The flower stalk appears in late May or early June surrounded with many flowers of varied colors—white, pink, red, blues of many hues, yellow, and apricot. Many have bicolored flowers, usually including white contrasting with another color.

How to grow: The so-called perennial lupines grow best in areas with cool summers and mild winters. Elsewhere, they are best treated as annuals, planted into the ground in spring as soon as the soil can be worked. They resent root disturbance and should be planted out from 4-inch or larger pots in order to bloom the first season. Lupines want full sun; moderately rich, well-drained soil; and continuous moisture. They grow best in acid or neutral soil. The tallest varieties should be planted in areas protected from high winds, or staked to prevent toppling. Plant largest varieties 12 to 15 inches apart; shorter ones in a 3- to 5-inch spacing.

Propagation: By seed. For husky plants, start seeds in January to transplant outdoors as soon as the ground is workable. Since seeds are very hard, soak them overnight or cut a small nick in the seed coat prior to planting. Germination takes 15 to 25 days at 55 to 70° F.

Uses: The tall lupines are unparalleled for bright color in late May and June. They add a vertical note to the mixed border, as well as in planting beds. Plant them in groups of at least three. Use them at the ends or centers of plantings, fronted by lower-growing varieties.

Related species: The Texas bluebonnet (*L. carnosus* or *L. texensis*) is an annual that covers thousands of square miles of southwestern countryside in the spring. Flower color is mostly blue with some whites. Seeds are available. *L. luteus* is a yellow-flowered, fragrant, annual species. The blue lupine (*L. hirsutus*) is an annual variety native to Europe that is sometimes grown in gardens.

Related varieties: The tall Russell varieties are available as separate colors: 'Yellow,' 'White,' 'Red,' 'Pink,' 'Carmine,' as well as bicolors of blue and white, cream and white, and pink and white. Mixtures of all colors are also available. 'Minarette' is a dwarf mixture of colors.

167

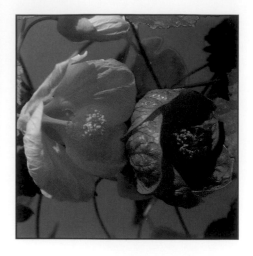

Magic Carpet Plant

Polygonum capitatum

This nonhardy creeping plant makes a lovely ground cover for sun or shade. It deserves to be more widely grown for the carpet it creates over rolling terrain. A member of the buckwheat family, it comes from the Himalaya mountains of Asia.

Description: This charmer creeps across the ground and seldom reaches more than 3 inches in height, but each plant can reach up to 2 feet in diameter from its long trailing stems. Each bright green leaf is marked with a V-shaped purple band. The flowers, lifted above the foliage on short stems, are round, fluffy balls of pink, up to ½ inch in diameter.

How to grow: In frost-free areas, magic carpet plant can make a permanent ground cover. Elsewhere, it is good for covering large amounts of ground quickly. Grow it in either sun or partial shade in average or richer soil that is well drained. Space plants 8 to 10 inches apart for summer coverage. Plant outdoors as soon as all danger of frost has passed. Pinch the tips of small plants to induce branching.

Propagation: For good-sized plants that will grow quickly to cover the ground, start indoors 8 to 10 weeks prior to planting in the garden. Seed germination takes 15 to 25 days at 65 to 75° F.

Uses: Plant it in small pockets for its small, cloverlike blossoms. Use it like any ground cover—underplanted near bushes and shrubs—for providing a carpet of green. Plant it beside walks and pathways or next to ponds or streams. Its trailing stems are especially attractive creeping over rocks or walls. It's also a good trailing plant to use in flowering containers. Plant near the edges so the small stems will cover the maximum outside surface of the container. It's a charming indoor plant in hanging baskets. Give it medium-to-high light and pinch the tips to make it bushy.

Mallow, Cheese

Malva sylvestris

Although in nature it's a biennial and occasionally a perennial, malva is usually grown as an annual in gardens. Related to hollyhocks, this native of Europe is now naturalized in parts of the United States. The purple-pink-lavender flowers are often veined with a darker color.

Description: This mallow grows up to 4 feet tall and has round or kidney-shaped, lobed leaves. The flowers on 2-inch stalks come from the leaf axils of the upper stalk. The flowers are up to 2 inches in diameter.

How to grow: Grow this mallow in full sun. It's indifferent to soil, growing equally well in average and rich fertility. Keep well watered to ensure lush growth. Protect from high winds to prevent toppling. Space plants 10 to 15 inches apart.

Propagation: By seed. Sow seeds in place where plants are to grow. Thin to 10 to 15 inches apart. For earlier growth and bloom, start indoors 6 to 8 weeks prior to planting out after frost danger has passed. Seeds germinate in 10 to 15 days at 70° F. Barely cover seeds; they need light to germinate.

Uses: This mallow can be used in beds and borders. Plant mid-border or at the ends. Use it at the edge of woodlands in full sun. It can be cut and used for arrangements, especially if the entire bloom spike is used in bouquets.

Related species: *Malva nicaeensis* is similar but shorter, growing up to 2½ feet tall, with slightly smaller blooms. *M. verticillata crispa* is a tall species with curled and crisped, round leaves. It grows up to 6 feet tall.

Related varieties: *M. sylvestris* ssp. *mauritiana* has rich purple-pink flowers with dark purple veins. Some of the flowers are loosely doubled.

Flowering Maple

Abutilon hybridum, A. megapoticum variegatum, A. striatum thompsonii

Once considered houseplants, flowering maples are being used increasingly for summer color in the garden. Their common name comes from their leaf shape—roughly maple-shaped. Flowering maples are semiwoody shrubs, hardy only to Zone 9. They'll grow about 2 feet high by summer's end.

Description: *A. megapoticum variegatum* has leaves marked with light and dark green patches, bearing yellow and red flowers with large, dark purple, pollen-bearing anthers. Older plants trail. *A. striatum thompsonii* is upright with orange-salmon flowers. Varieties of *A. hybridum* bear white, yellow, salmon, or purple flowers.

How to grow: Plant in well-drained soil and water only if dry. Incorporate a slow-release fertilizer into the soil before planting. Plant 12 to 15 inches apart. In Zones 9 and 10, flowering maples will benefit from partial shade, otherwise full sun and eastern exposure are preferred. During vigorous growth, pinching tips will encourage branching. Dig and bring indoors before frost.

Propagation: By cuttings or by seed. Start seeds indoors in winter (germination time is 3 to 4 weeks) with bottom heat at 70° F for outdoor bloom. They are also easily propagated from semi-mature cuttings.

Uses: Use in small spaces where the attractive foliage and dainty bells can be viewed close up. They also make ideal container plants especially in raised situations where their flowers can be seen more easily. For indoor use, repot before frost and cut back by half before bringing indoors. Provide at least 4 hours of direct sunlight indoors for good blooming. Pinch tips to induce bushiness.

Related varieties: Varieties from seed include 'Benary's Giant,' with drooping, crimson-rose bells.

Cape Marigold, African Daisy, Star-of-the-Veldt

Dimorphotheca **hybrids**

A member of the composite or daisy family, these are sometimes called *Osteospermum*, depending on which botanist classified closely related plants. They are not closely related to true marigolds.

Description: Cape marigolds grow up to 1 foot tall, in a loose mound heavily covered with flowers during cool seasons or in cool climates. Flowers are 3 to 4 inches in size in yellow, white, salmon, or rose. The reverse sides of the petals are colored in shades of blue or lavender.

How to grow: African daisies thrive in light, sandy soil and will tolerate drought. They prefer cool, dry weather in full sun in coastal or mountain climates. They turn scraggly in hot, humid parts of the country during summer. In such locations, plant them as soon as the ground can be worked for cool season beauty, replacing them later with heat-tolerant plants. They flower best when temperatures are 45 to 50° F. They are good winter annuals (actually semi-hardy perennials) in areas with only a few degrees of frost (Zones 8 to 10). Space 8 to 12 inches apart. Do not fertilize.

Propagation: By seed or by cuttings. Sow outdoors in spring after the last frost or start indoors 6 to 8 weeks in advance of planting out. Seeds germinate in 10 to 15 days at 60 to 70o F.

Uses: Tuck Cape Marigolds into chinks of rock walls or plant them in sunny rock gardens. Use them for large drifts of color through borders and beds. Plant them at the edges of containers. Cape Marigolds combine well with other container plants. They're good cut flowers, too.

Related varieties: 'Starshine' bears flowers of pink, rose, carmine, and white. 'Tetra Pole Star' is a white variety with violet centers. 'Tetra Goliath' is an orange-flowered variety with unusually large blooms.

French Marigold, American Marigold

Tagetes patula, Tagetes erecta

These all-American plants come in such an array of bright colors over a long season that they're a mainstay of gardeners everywhere.

Description: American marigolds can be tall plants, growing up to 36 inches high, although breeding has produced shorter heights. They have large, fully double flowers in yellow, gold, and orange. French marigolds are bushier and more compact with smaller flowers. Their flowers come in many colors and forms. They usually grow no more than 12 inches. Triploids, a cross between French and American marigolds, resemble French marigolds, but have larger flowers.

How to grow: Marigolds grow best in full sun with moist, well-drained soil, although they will tolerate drier conditions. Plant them outdoors as soon as all danger of frost has passed. Space French marigolds 6 to 10 inches apart; Americans 10 to 18 inches apart. They require no deadheading.

Propagation: Seeds may be sown in place. For earlier bloom, start indoors 4 to 6 weeks prior to outdoor planting. Seeds germinate in 5 to 7 days at 65 to 75° F.

Uses: Grow taller ones to the center or rear of beds and borders, or as planting pockets in full sun. Plant them in containers.

Related species: *Tagetes tenuifolia*, or signet marigolds, bear many small, yellow or orange flowers. 'Lemon Gem' and 'Tangerine Gem' are two examples.

Related varieties: The flat-petaled, double, French marigolds include many series: 'Aurora,' 'Sophia,' and 'Early Spice.' Fully double, crested series include 'Boy,' 'Bonanza,' 'Hero,' 'Little Devil,' and 'Janie.' Single-flowered series are 'Disco' and 'Espana.' American marigold series include: 'Inca,' 'Perfection,' 'Voyager,' and 'Discovery.'

Pot Marigold, Field Marigold

Calendula officinalis

These beauties bloom in all shades of white, gold, yellow, and orange. Some varieties have flower petals tipped in contrasting colors. They're known as stalwarts of the cool season garden, growing all winter in Zones 8 to 10.

Description: Cultivated calendulas grow 12 to 24 inches tall with rich green leaves. Plants will spread 12 to 18 inches. Flowers can be single daisies, semi-double, or fully double. Flower size ranges up to 4 inches in newer varieties.

How to grow: Calendulas thrive on poor to medium soil in full sun with moderate moisture. They will survive several degrees of frost, and if properly hardened off, can be planted in the spring as soon as soil is workable. Plant 10 to 15 inches apart. Pick off the spent blooms for continued bloom. For fall bloom, sow seeds in July. In cool damp weather, mildew is occasionally a problem.

Propagation: By seed. For earliest bloom, sow seeds indoors 4 to 6 weeks early at a temperature of 65 to 70° F. Germination takes 10 to 14 days. After transplanting, the seedlings grow in cooler temperatures (50 to 55° F) until planting outside. Seeds can also be sown outdoors when the soil is workable, then thinned to a 10- to 15-inch spacing. For winter bloom in Zones 8 to 10, seeds should be sown in late fall.

Uses: Plant in beds, borders, planting pockets, and containers in full sun. Calendulas also make good long-lasting cut flowers.

Related varieties: The 'Bon Bon Series' has separate shades of yellow and orange, and a mixture that also includes apricot and soft yellow. The 'Fiesta Gitana Series' bears semi-double flowers in yellow, orange, and a mixture, with most of the flowers having dark centers. Taller 'Pacific Beauty' has large flowers on strong stems and is good for cutting.

Meadow Foam, Fried Eggs

Limnanthes douglasii

Here's a West Coast native with many of the attributes of flowers from Mediterranean climates. As the weather warms, rain triggers germination, and the flowers quickly come into bloom. It's at its best for spring bloom. *Limnanthes* comes for the Greek word for "marsh." "Fried eggs" (sunny side up) typifies its look of a great yellow center surrounded by white.

Description: Meadow foam grows up to 1 foot tall with many branches, giving it the appearance of a low mound or bush. It has finely divided, green leaves. The flowers are up to 1 inch in diameter. Typically, they are golden-yellow surrounded by white, but in some forms the petals are all yellow—still others are all white or white with pink veins.

How to grow: Meadow foam prefers full sun and moist, medium-rich soil. In coastal or mountain areas where the summers remain cool, it will continue blooming all summer. In other climates, enjoy it for spring bloom before weather gets torrid. In nearly frost-free areas of Zones 8, 9, and 10, seeds may be sown in the fall and allowed to overwinter for earliest spring bloom. Space plants 4 to 6 inches apart. Plants will reseed for next year.

Propagation: By seed. Sow seeds in fall in mild climates or as soon as ground can be worked elsewhere. For earlier bloom, start seeds indoors 6 to 8 weeks prior to planting out. Seeds germinate in 14 to 21 days at 65 to 70° F.

Uses: Grow it in rock gardens, near pools or ponds, and along walks and pathways. Use it as an edging for beds or in front of borders.

Related varieties: Named varieties of the typical form are not available. Special forms include: *Limnanthes douglasii sulphurea*, with all-yellow flowers; *L. d. nivea*, all white; and *L. d. rosea*, white flowers veined with rose.

Melampodium

Melampodium paludosum

Large, bright green leaves have many perky, little yellow, daisylike flowers peering forth all summer long. A member of the daisy family, it hails originally from Mexico and Central America. *Melampodium paludosum* is one of 36 species in the genus. The name *melampodium* comes from the Greek and literally translated means "black foot," referring to the color of the stalks.

Description: Melampodium forms a vigorous, bushy plant 10 to 15 inches high in the garden. It will be 15 to 20 inches in diameter by the end of summer. The leaves are large and rough. They are paired, and each pair is at right angles to the next. The flowers are small, up to 1 inch in diameter.

How to grow: Melampodium needs full sun. An average-to-rich, moist but well-drained soil is satisfactory. Plants should not be allowed to dry out. Plant outdoors as soon as all danger of frost has passed and the ground is warm. Space 10 to 15 inches apart.

Propagation: By seed. Sow seeds indoors 7 to 10 weeks prior to planting outdoors. Seeds germinate in 7 to 10 days at 65° F. For easier transplanting, grow in peat pots that can be transplanted into the garden, pot and all.

Uses: Plant melampodium where you want some contrast between flowers and foliage. Melampodium can be used as a sunny ground cover or be planted in rock gardens in the front of flower borders. Grow in window boxes, patio or deck planters, and in hanging baskets.

Related varieties: 'Medaillon' is the most planted variety. It grows up to 20 inches tall and as wide, covered all summer with small, golden-yellow flowers.

Mignonette

Reseda odorata

Here's a plant of little apparent virtue until a bit of its sweet aroma wafts your way. Its wonderful aroma has brought it a long way from its native home in North Africa to its place in the gardens of kings, presidents, and common folks.

Description: Mignonette is a spreading plant that grows up to 2 feet high and is covered with spikes of many small flowers—greenish-white or yellowish-green in color. The flowers are very fragrant and are able to perfume large areas.

How to grow: Mignonette grows best in well-drained, moderately rich, slightly alkaline soil. It does best in partial shade in the hottest parts of the country. Transplant it into the garden as soon as the soil can be worked. Space 10 inches apart. Pinch the tips of young plants to encourage branching. Mignonette reseeds itself in the garden.

Propagation: By seed. In mild climates, seeds can be sown in place the previous fall. Otherwise, sow in the spring and thin to the proper spacing. In other areas of the country, an early bloom can be developed by sowing seeds indoors 5 to 6 weeks prior to planting out. Do not cover seeds; they need light to germinate. Seed germination takes 5 to 10 days at 70° F. Seedlings do not like transplanting; grow them in peat pots that can be planted in the garden, pot and all. Because there is a short season of bloom, repeat sowings for several weeks for continuous flowering.

Uses: Plant mignonette where the spicy scent will be noticed—tucked into a corner of the flower bed, near paths and walks, and under windows. Do the same with containers on decks, porches, and patios. Cut flowers maintain the same fragrance.

Related varieties: 'Fragrant Beauty' has red-tipped, lime-green flowers. 'Red Monarch' has more red in the flowers. Both are very fragrant.

Monkey Flower

Mimulus hybridus

The name "monkey flower" comes from the physical appearance of the flowers or from the name *mimulus,* stemming from a root word meaning "mimic." In either case, the low-growing flowers are a good way to brighten up the shade.

Description: Mimulus forms neat, compact mounds seldom reaching over 10 inches in height, but spreading wider. The open-faced flowers are frequently painted with contrasting color markings on the background of yellow, pink, red, burgundy, and other warm-hued tones.

How to grow: Mimulus is not frost-tolerant, but prefers cool weather. It will thrive in moist soil, even in boggy conditions with occasional flooding; it will also bloom beautifully in dappled shade. Plant out after all danger of frost has passed, spacing plants 6 inches apart. Work a slow-release fertilizer into the soil at planting for feeding all summer. Where keeping an even soil moisture level is a problem, a mulch is suggested. Deadheading spent flowers occasionally will improve their appearance.

Propagation: By seed. Sow seeds indoors 10 to 12 days prior to planting outdoors. Do not cover the fine seeds. Germination takes 7 to 14 days at 70 to 75° F.

Uses: Mimulus thrives nears ponds, pools, and streams. Grow it in shady borders and, because of its small stature, in front of a border or as an edging. Mimulus is also a perfect container plant. It will bloom indoors under cool conditions (and high indoor light).

Related varieties: 'Calypso' is a mixture of many colors of 2-inch flowers, both solids and marked bicolors. 'Malibu' is another mixture in shades of red, yellow, and orange. 'Viva' is a single variety with yellow flowers marked with bright red.

Morning Glory Vine

Ipomoea nil, purpurea, tricolor

A group of twining vines with bell-shaped flowers, they have also become intertwined botanically under the name "morning glory." The name comes from the flowers, which last a single day. These rapidly growing vines are closely related to the sweet potato. Flowers are white, blue, pink, purple, red, and multicolored. There are even double forms. Because they're quick, easy, and dependably colorful, they're the most popular annual vine.

Description: The vines grow quickly to 10 feet or more only two months after seeds sprout. The leaves are heart-shaped, and the flowers are normally open from dawn to midmorning, but new varieties will stay open longer, especially on overcast days.

How to grow: Requirements are undemanding. Morning glories will thrive in full sun in any soil, especially if it is not too fertile or too moist. Sow the seeds outdoors when all danger of frost has passed. Provide support. Because they grow by twining, they need extra help if planted around large posts. Plant 8 to 12 inches apart.

Propagation: By seed. Soak the seeds in water for 24 hours before planting to speed germination. In the North, earlier bloom can be achieved by starting indoors in peat pots 4 to 6 weeks before planting out. Germination takes 5 to 7 days at 70 to 80° F. Transplant the peat pots to the garden—pot and all—without disturbing the roots.

Uses: Morning glories are splendid for enhancing fences or for covering up eyesores. They will rapidly cover fences, arches, pergolas, and trellises or can be made into their own garden feature with stakes and twine. They don't have to grow up. They're just as effective as trailers from hanging baskets and window boxes.

Related species: Moon flower (*Ipomoea alba*) has large, fragrant, white flowers that open in the evening and close before midday. *Convovulus tricolor,* known as "dwarf morning glory," forms bushy plants with pink, blue, purple, and rose flowers. 'Blue Ensign' is a selection with blue flowers and contrasting yellow and white centers. *Evolvulus glomeratus* is a prostrate plant, 10 to 15 inches in diameter, with many small, morning glorylike flowers in bright blue. 'Blue Bird' is one selection.

Related varieties: Most famous is 'Heavenly Blue' for refreshing azure color. 'Scarlet Star' has a strong pattern of red and white. 'Pearly Gates' has large, white flowers. 'Early Call Mixture' has white, pink, crimson, lavender, blue, and violet flowers.

Nasturtium

Tropaeolum majus

Nearly every kid who's been near a garden has grown a nasturtium. And today's salad-conscious adult has certainly enjoyed the peppery tang of nasturtium leaves and flowers among the greens. A native of Mexico, they're among our garden favorites.

Description: Nasturtiums started out as vigorous, vinelike plants, and many of them still are. Breeders have altered them so that some are now bushy, compact plants only 12 inches tall. The leaves are nearly round. Flowers with bright, open faces have long spurs behind them.

How to grow: Don't overdo the care with nasturtiums. They need full sun in a dry, sandy, well-drained soil. They're at their best in regions with cool, dry summers, although they will grow elsewhere, too. Sow seeds outdoors in the ground after the last frost. Depending on variety, space them 8 to 12 inches apart. The vigorous varieties can only be trained upward by tying them to supports; they have no means of attachment. Nasturtiums will reseed vigorously but will not be the same colors you planted.

Propagation: By seed. Seed germination takes 7 to 12 days at 65° F. Do not cover the seeds; they need light to germinate.

Uses: Dwarf varieties are good for flower borders, beds, edging paths, and walks. Vining varieties can be tied to fences or posts and trailed from window boxes, hanging baskets, or other containers. Nasturtiums are good cut flowers, too.

Related species: *Tropaeolum peregrinum,* or canary creeper, is a vigorous vine with bright yellow flowers.

Related varieties: 'Dwarf Double Jewel,' in separate colors and a mix, has light yellow, gold, orange, rose, crimson, and brownish-red flowers. It grows 1 foot high. 'Double Gleam' grows to 3 feet with similar flower colors. 'Climbing Mixed' will grow to 6 feet.

Nemesia

Nemesia strumosa

Nemesias are spectacular in cool, maritime areas or mountain gardens where nights remain cool throughout summer. In other places, enjoy them early since they fade in the hot, humid days of summer. They are originally from South Africa. They resemble snapdragons and linaria, to which they're related.

Description: Nemesias grow from 1 to 2 feet tall, with sparsely branched plants. They grow erect, with the flowers carried in large clusters at the top. There's a wide color range, including yellow, orange, brown, pink, red, and lavender-blue.

How to grow: Nemesias like fertile, well-drained soil and prefer full sun, although they will tolerate partial shade. Transplant started plants after the last frost date. Space them 6 inches apart. Pinch the tips of seedlings to increase branching.

Propagation: By seed. Sow seeds indoors 4 to 6 weeks before the last frost date. Seeds germinate in 7 to 14 days at 55 to 70° F. In areas with cool, dry summers, seeds can be sown outdoors as soon as the ground can be worked for later bloom that will continue until fall.

Uses: Use them for edgings, in rock gardens and walls, and for borders. They're splendid container plants and make good cut flowers, too.

Related species: *Nemesia versicolor* is a similar, more compact species. It has a variety of colors including truer blues. 'Blue Gem' is a very compact variety growing to 10 inches high with blue flowers.

Related varieties: 'Carnival' is a mixture of colors on plants that grow up to 2 feet tall. 'Tapestry,' in addition to a wide range of colors, has a good balance of blue and white. 'Fire King' is a scarlet-flowered variety.

Nicotiana, Flowering Tobacco

Nicotiana alata grandiflora

Related to the tobacco plants of commerce, flowering tobacco has been bred for its ornamental value. The flowers are in a variety of colors, including an intriguing lime-green. In addition, flowers have a rich, pervasive scent.

Description: A low rosette of large, flat leaves supports the tall flowering stems covered with star-shaped flowers. Flower colors include white, pink, maroon, lavender, green, red, and yellow. The plants grow up to 3 feet tall.

How to grow: Nicotiana grows best in fertile, humus-rich, moist, well-drained soil in partial shade, or full sun in cooler areas. They are tough plants that will tolerate high temperatures. Before planting out, incorporate a slow-release fertilizer in the soil. Transplant to the garden when all danger of frost has passed, spacing 8 to 12 inches apart.

Propagation: By seed. In areas with a long growing season, seeds may be sown in place, thinning the seedlings to the right spacing. Elsewhere, start the plants indoors 6 to 8 weeks prior to planting out. Seeds germinate in 10 to 20 days at 70° F. Don't cover seeds; they need light to germinate.

Uses: Nicotiana is a plant that can give much-needed height to beds and borders. Group them in clusters for more impact. They're also good for containers.

Related species: *Nicotiana sylvestris* is a very fragrant species with white flowers. It grows up to 4 feet tall.

Related varieties: The most popular series is 'Nicki' hybrids with separate colors of 'White,' 'Rose,' and 'Pink,' as well as a mixture. 'Limelight' is a lime-green variety. More compact varieties growing up to 18 inches are the 'Domino' series. Included: 'White,' 'Purple,' 'Red,' 'Lime-Green,' and 'Pink with White Eye,' as well as a mixture.

Nierembergia, Cup Flower

Nierembergia hippomanica violacae

The name "Cup Flower," although not much used, refers to the shape of the flower, which is somewhat like an open-faced bowl. Native to Central and South America, they are tender perennials grown like annuals in most of the country. In frost-free areas, they will winter over with good drainage.

Description: Nierembergia has attractive thin, narrow leaves topped at the ends with bluish or purple flowers. A small yellow spot in the center of each flower highlights the display. The plants grow outward rather than up, to 6 inches high, and will spread a foot.

How to grow: Grow nierembergia in full sun in well-drained soil with adequate moisture. Medium fertility is adequate to grow them well. Flowers hold their color without fading in full sun. Transplant to the garden when all danger of frost has passed. Pinch them to encourage more branching and a higher production of flowers. For full coverage, plant them 5 to 6 inches apart.

Propagation: By seed. Sow seeds indoors 10 to 12 weeks prior to planting in the garden after the last frost. Seeds germinate in 14 to 21 days at 70 to 75° F. Plants will not grow rapidly until the soil is warm.

Uses: Grow nierembergia as a flowering ground cover in full sun, massed in large patches or beds. It's an ideal edging plant for beds and borders, traveling along paths and walkways with ease. It's also a good plant for rock gardens. Use it in window boxes, hanging baskets, and patio planters, usually with other plants for height and mass.

Related species: *Nierembergia repens* is a creeping species with creamy white flowers.

Related varieties: 'Purple Robe' is the only variety widely available. It has been selected for uniformity and has glowing violet-blue flowers.

None So Pretty

Silene armeria

Small patches of sticky fluid on the stems of these flowers entangle flies and are the reason for the common name. A native of southern Europe, it's now naturalized in parts of North America. The most prevalent color of these annual plants is pink, but there is a white-flowered one, too.

Description: The plants grow a clumplike rosette with narrow leaves and flowering stems rising 1 to 2 feet tall. The many flowers are in branched clusters, with each flower about ¾ inch in diameter. The 5-petaled flowers faintly resemble a star.

How to grow: Grow silene in full sun in ordinary garden soil with good drainage. Transplant well-hardened plants to the garden as soon as the ground is workable in the spring. Space plants 6 to 9 inches apart.

Propagation: By seed. Sow seeds indoors 8 to 10 weeks before transplanting to the garden. Seed germination takes 15 to 20 days at 70° F.

Uses: Their modest size adapts well to rock gardens and in planting pockets. Use them in beds and borders, planting them near the front for the best show. Silenes bloom over a long season and look good in mixed plantings and old-fashioned cottage gardens. They'll also grow well in containers, preferably combined with other flowers with more substance. However, the airy stems with small clusters of flowers will give an open look to the container garden. They are not long-lasting as cut flowers.

Related species: *Silene gallica* ssp. *quinque-vulnera* has white flowers with ruby-red centers. This plant grows 12 to 18 inches high. *Silene pendula* has drooping sprays of flowers in pink, shell pink, rose, and white. It grows up to 12 inches high.

Ornamental Corn

Zea mays

The same corn species that brings the world field corn, popcorn, and sweet corn has turned up some ornamental varieties that are worth growing in the garden for their statuesque beauty. Corn belongs to the grass family, a widely diversified group that includes bluegrass and bamboo.

Description: A single seed of corn grows a tall stalk with long, broad leaves topped by a tassel. Pollen from the tassel fertilizes the ears of corn growing from the stalk below. It can grow up to 10 feet tall.

How to grow: Corn needs rich, fertile soil and full sun. The soil must be well drained and moist. Wait to plant corn until after the last frost-free date and the soil is warm. Plant seeds 1 inch deep. Space plants 6 to 15 inches apart. Corn forms a series of brace roots to support it, so it will not need staking.

Propagation: By seed.

Uses: Corn is tall and requires space to accommodate it. It's useful as a fast-growing screen and as a plant for the back of the border. Ears of ornamental corn are used in many kinds of dried arrangements—from door hangings to centerpieces.

Related varieties: Some corn are grown for their ornamental leaves. *Zea mays gracillima variegata* is a dwarf (3 to 4 feet high) with leaves having long stripes of white. *Z. m. japonica variegata* and *Z. m. j. quadricolor* are tall, with long stripes of yellow, white, or pink running lengthwise on the leaves. Corn grown for its unusual ears include: 'Rainbow,' whose ears have kernels of deep red, yellow, orange, and blue and 'Strawberry Ornamental Popcorn,' bearing small ears with cranberry-colored kernels. It pops like conventional corn but has flecks of ruby-red throughout.

Ornamental Cabbage, Ornamental Kale

Brassica oleracea

The fancy-leaved cousins of our familiar vegetables make a bold statement in the cool season garden. In fact, the ornamental forms are edible, too, but the cabbage is bitter, and when the white, pink, red, and purple leaves are cooked, they turn an unappetizing gray. Tolerant of mild frosts, they're colorful all winter in mild climates.

Description: Bold, round plants whose center leaves (not flowers) color up in cool or cold weather, ornamental cabbage and kale grow 18 to 24 inches in diameter and can grow 18 to 24 inches tall.

How to grow: Their primary use is in the fall because the period of cool weather in spring after hard freezes cease is too short. Grow in large pots in a soil mix and feed weekly with a water-soluble fertilizer as recommended on the package. Transplant to the garden or display container in September. Before transplanting, remove tatty bottom leaves. Plant into the ground so that the crown of leaves is flush with the soil surface (roots will grow along the buried stem).

Propagation: By seed. Sow 6 weeks in advance of outdoor planting at 65° F. Do not cover the cabbage seeds since light aids germination. Conversely, cover kale seeds with ¼ inch of soil.

Uses: Kale or cabbage are best planted in areas where you can peer into the center—on slopes, doorsteps, decks, and patios. They're also successful in ground beds and in large plantings.

Related varieties: 'Dynasty Series' cabbage in pink, red, or white have semi-waved leaves. Ornamental kale in red or white include: 'Chidori Series,' heavily fringed and especially uniform, and the 'Peacock Series,' which is more compact than others.

Ornamental Peppers

Capsicum species

Ornamental peppers are the only summer annuals grown primarily for the attractiveness of their fruit. That, combined with their contrast of foliage and form, is what makes them popular in the summer garden.

Description: Ornamental peppers grow into small bushes 12 to 18 inches high and as wide. Their dark green leaves are topped by bright-colored fruits that form in July and hold on the plant until frost. Depending on variety, fruits may be red, purple, yellow, or orange; the shapes range from conical to slim and tapered. There are even twisted forms. The small, white flowers that appear prior to the fruit are pretty but inconspicuous.

How to grow: Ornamental peppers prefer full sun in rich, well-drained soil and perform best in hot weather. They're remarkably drought-tolerant, but will grow better if watered when soil becomes dry. A slow-release fertilizer should be incorporated before planting. Plant when the soil is warm and the weather has settled down.

Propagation: By seed. Sow seeds 8 weeks prior to planting out after last frost date. Cover seeds, germinating at temperatures above 70° F. Germination time is approximately 12 days. Sow in June or July for potted plants in late fall.

Uses: Bright-colored fruits on glossy, green plants decorate borders or bed edges. Ornamental peppers have been used traditionally as an indoor pot plant for holiday enjoyment.

Related varieties: 'Fireworks' is a variety whose cream-colored, cone-shaped fruits turn a brilliant red. 'Holiday Cheer's' fruits start out cream-colored, then turn orange and bright red with all colors mixed on the plant. 'Holiday Flame,' an F_1 hybrid, has tapered, yellow fruit that turns red. Fruits of F_1 hybrid 'Masquerade' start out purple, then turn consecutively yellow, orange, and red.

Pansy

Viola x *wittrockiana*

Pansies are the ultimate in cool season color, blooming until weather turns torrid. They are related to violets.

Description: Pansies grow on sprawling plants that produce flowers continuously as they grow. Flowers range from 2 inches in diameter up to giants of 5 inches or more. Some have clear colors, but many have the unique faces that are so appealing to kids of all ages. The color range is complete.

How to grow: In mild winter areas, plant as soon as the weather cools in late summer. Even areas with short freezes can enjoy winter pansies; once the weather warms, they'll start opening blossoms. Elsewhere, enjoy them for a short season in the spring. Plant in the garden as soon as the ground can be worked. Space 6 to 9 inches apart. If plants become lank and leggy, shear back halfway to force new growth and bloom. Pansies prefer full sun and cool, moist soil. A bit of shade will help them extend the season in hot climates.

Propagation: By seed. Start seeds 6 to 8 weeks prior to planting out. They will germinate in 10 to 15 days at 68° F. Do not cover seeds; they need light to germinate.

Uses: Plant them anywhere you want spots of color. They are suitable for the front of borders and beds, in small groups among other flowers, in cottage garden plantings, and in containers.

Related species: Several varieties of violas, which are derived from *Viola cornuta* and *V. tricolor* include 'King Henry,' deep violet with a yellow eye; 'Helen Mount,' often called 'Johnny Jump Up' for its yellow and violet-faced flower; and 'Prince John,' a clear yellow.

Related varieties: The largest flowers of all are in the 'Super Majestic Giant' series. 'Majestic Giants' are somewhat smaller. The most widely planted include these series: 'Crown,' 'Crystal Bowl,' 'Imperial,' 'Maxim,' and 'Universal.'

Perilla, Beefsteak Plant

Perilla frutescens

A member of the mint family, its foliage and stems have a pungent fragrance when the leaves or stems are crushed. It is widely used as a flavoring in Oriental cuisines and can be used to dye rice pink.

Description: Perilla has the square stems typical of mint family members. The oval leaves can be green, purple, or bronzy, although the most common are a deep purple. They also have a most attractive, metallic sheen. The leaves are deeply veined and crinkled, adding to its attractiveness. Plants can grow as tall as 3 to 4 feet. Flowers are not noteworthy and appear at the end of summer.

How to grow: Perilla will grow equally well in sun or in shade, but low light will create a lankier plant. Average garden soil is satisfactory. Since they are tender annuals, plant them in the garden after all danger of frost has passed, spacing them 12 to 15 inches apart. Pinch the tips once or twice to form a bushier plant.

Propagation: By seed or cuttings. Sow seeds outdoors after the last frost date. Thin to the desired spacing when the seedlings are 3 or 4 inches tall. For larger plants earlier, sow seeds indoors 4 to 6 weeks prior to transplanting into the garden. Because perillas are difficult to transplant, grow them in peat pots to prevent root disturbance when transplanting. Seeds germinate in 15 to 20 days at 65 to 75° F. Cuttings root quickly and easily, even in water. Plants in the garden will self-sow readily.

Uses: Plant it in beds or borders. Use it as a ribbon to contrast with other foliage and flower colors. Its bushy habit makes a good edging for pathways and along walks. Try it as a low hedge.

Related variety: 'Crispa' has attractively curled leaves and grows 2 to 3 feet tall.

Petunia

Petunia x *hybrida*

Anyone who's been close to a garden is familiar with petunias, a longtime favorite for undiminished color through a long season. Actually tender perennials, they will flower through the winter in nearly frost-free climates. The name "petunia" comes from a South American word for "tobacco," to which they're related along with tomatoes and potatoes. A plant that has long had the eye of breeders, petunias have flowers with charming variations —open bells, crisped, curled, waved, and doubled up into fluffy balls. The enormous color range even includes a yellow.

Description: Garden petunias are divided into two types: multifloras and grandifloras. Each has single and double forms, with grandiflora petunias being larger in each case. Recently, the distinction has become blurred as seed companies have introduced larger-flowered multiflora petunias named 'floribundas.' Always more flowerful and weather-tolerant in the garden than their larger cousins, they were never as popular as the bigger-flowered kinds. Now these new hybrid 'floribundas' are capturing the hearts of gardeners everywhere.

How to grow: Well-drained soil in full sun suits petunias best. They grow well in cool temperatures and will stand a few degrees of frost if plants have been well-hardened before planting. Incorporate a slow-release fertilizer into the soil before planting. Space petunias 12 inches apart. To promote more branching and increased bloom, shear plants back halfway in midsummer. Deadheading is extremely important as the plants set seed, flowering is greatly reduced.

Propagation: By seed. Start seeds indoors 10 to 12 weeks prior to planting outdoors. Seeds are very fine and can be more evenly sown by mixing thoroughly with a pinch of sugar. Do not cover the seeds as they need light to germinate. Seeds germinate in 10 to 12 days at 70 to 75° F.

Uses: Beds, borders, walkways, paths, containers—all will accommodate an abundance of petunias. Some varieties are especially recommended for containers, since they mound up and billow over the edges. The multifloras (and 'floribundas') are especially recommended for mass plantings because they give the most flowers per plant, nearly undaunted by drenching rains and high winds. The intricate, double varieties are probably best in containers for greatest enjoyment of their complex flowers. Petunias also make good, informal cut flowers.

Related varieties: Grandifloras: 'Super Cascades,' 'Super Magics,' 'Falcons,' 'Ultras,' and 'Flashes.' All of these are series petunias and are available in many colors—some are veined. Multifloras: 'Madness,' 'Carpet,' and 'Celebrity' are three of the newer series with larger flowers and good garden habits.

Annual Phlox, Texas Pride

Phlox drummondii

These bright-colored plants originally hail from Texas, but breeders have civilized them to be some of the most dependable garden performers. The name *Phlox* comes from the Greek word meaning "flame," identifying its bright colors.

Description: Annual phloxes grow from 6 inches to 1½ feet tall. The flowers are in large clusters of many colors and many shapes. Colors include pink, red, rose, white, lavender, scarlet, crimson, and yellow.

How to grow: Annual phloxes grow best in well-drained, sandy soil, high in organic matter. They require full sun and must receive continuous moisture during the growing season. Good air movement around the plants will prevent mildew. Plant in the garden as soon as the danger of frost has passed. Space 6 inches apart. Pinch the tips to encourage branching. At midsummer, shear the plants back halfway to reinvigorate flowering.

Propagation: By seed. Sow plants outdoors where they are to grow after the last frost is due. Thin to the desired spacing. For earlier bloom, start plants indoors 4 to 6 weeks before setting out. Seeds germinate in 15 to 20 days at 55 to 65° F. Transplant in clumps of several plants to get a full color range.

Uses: Grow phlox in beds or at the front of borders. Use them as edgings. Intermix them with other flowers in informal plantings and cottage gardens. Phlox are good container plants and hold well in water when cut.

Related varieties: 'Petticoat Mix' is very dwarf with a mix of all colors. 'Cecily' is a mixture with a high number of bicolors with contrasting eyes. It is also a dwarf variety. 'Tall Finest Mixed' has large flower heads on plants up to 20 inches tall. 'Twinkle,' an award winner, is a mix of ringed, pointed, starlike flowers.

Pocketbook Plant

Calceolaria herbeofruticosa

The shape of the flower, resembling a little pouch, is the origin of both the common name and the botanical name of this plant. It comes from the Latin *calceolus* or "slipper."

Description: Flowers appear like clusters of small grapes, although they're held upright rather than trailing and cover the foliage when in full bloom. In their preferred cool climates, they bloom all summer but can be used for fall, winter, and spring bloom in frost-free areas. Their ultimate height is 8 to 12 inches by 10 inches wide.

How to grow: Pocketbook plant grows best in moist soil with partial protection from intense summer sun. For spring and fall use, full sun will increase flowering. To induce repeat flowering, cut back plants when blossoms fade.

Propagation: By seed or by cuttings. Sow seeds 6 to 8 weeks prior to last frost without covering. They germinate in 8 to 18 days at 60o F. They may also be sown outdoors. Seedlings must be thinned to 6 inches apart.

Uses: Plant them near water—by stream banks, at pool edges, or near bogs and moist woodlands in partial shade. So long as their roots are kept moist, they will also make good container plants.

Related species: Good for the partially shaded rock garden is *Calceolaria falklandia,* a dwarf, tufted native of the Falkland Islands with purple spotted, primrose-yellow flowers. It survives winter only in frost-free gardens. *Calceolaria mexicana* is an annual with typical yellow flowers that bloom all summer.

Related varieties: 'Goldcrest,' 'Golden Bunch,' and 'Midas' are all sunshine-yellow in color. 'Goldcrest' has larger flowers than the others.

California Poppy

Escholtzia californica

California hillsides are covered in spring with the golden-orange of California poppies. Gardeners now have a choice of color—white, rose, scarlet, crimson, or salmon.

Description: Perennials in mild winter areas, California poppies have finely cut, blue-green foliage in contrast to silky flower cups on slender, wiry stems 12 to 15 inches tall.

How to grow: The best planting location for California poppies is sandy, slightly alkaline soil in full sun. They tolerate poor and dry soils as well. In all but Zones 8, 9 and 10, treat them as annuals that bloom best during the cool weather. In cool seasons and maritime climates, they will continue blooming all summer if dead flowers are picked off.

Propagation: California poppies are tap-rooted plants that don't transplant well, so they should be sown in place. In mild winter areas, this is best done in the fall, as small plants will winter over for earliest spring bloom. Elsewhere, sow as early in the spring as the ground can be worked. (If you want to start them indoors, transplant before the taproot is established.) Seeds will germinate in 4 to 10 days when the soil temperature is at 60° F. Water well.

Uses: Grow them in rock walls or rock gardens or as part of naturalized meadow plantings. Reseeding will occur and the offspring of hybrids will revert to the golden-orange colors of their ancestors.

Related varieties: 'Aurantica Orange' is the golden-orange color of the original, although the flowers are larger. 'Ballerina' is composed of semi-double and double flowers in yellow, rose, pink, scarlet, and orange. 'Milky White' is a creamy white selection. 'Thai Silk Pink Shades' has flowers with petals enhanced by wavy edges and fluted form.

Horned Poppy, Sea Poppy

Glaucium flavum

This flower is a native of maritime Europe, North Africa, and eastern Asia. It is also naturalized in parts of North America. Although each flower only lasts a day, the succession of bloom lasts for several weeks.

Description: Several branched stems grow from a rosette of leaves. The crinkly, gray-green leaves also appear on the stems and below each flower. The golden-yellow flowers are open and about 2 inches in diameter. Occasionally, there are orange or red flowers. The roots of the horned poppy are poisonous.

How to grow: Horned poppies need to be grown in full sun in well-drained soil. Space 12 to 18 inches apart. The easiest way to grow them is seeding where they are to bloom and thinning them to the desired spacing.

Propagation: By seed. Glaucium can be grown as a biennial by sowing seeds in the ground the previous fall. For earlier bloom, sow indoors 8 to 10 weeks prior to planting in the garden, after danger of frost has passed. Germination takes 8 to 15 days at 60 to 65° F. Transplant the seedlings to individual pots when three leaves have formed, but before the taproot has developed. Then transplant to the garden without disturbing the root system.

Uses: Plant in clusters in mid-border or grow them at the sides. Use them at the end of a path, or at the corners of beds. The contrast of the gray-green foliage should be mixed with other greens, including chartreuse. The dramatic seedpods can be used in dried arrangements.

Related species: A showy, red-flowered species is *Glaucium grandiflorum*, native to the Middle East. The poppies are large and held well above the olive-green foliage.

Iceland Poppy

Papaver nudicaule

The glistening, translucent flowers of Iceland poppies are a glowing sight when backlit by the sun. The petals look like tissue paper or crinkled silk. Their spring and early summer splendor in warm parts of the country can be enjoyed throughout the summer in cooler climates. They're short-lived perennials that are best started fresh each year.

Description: A rosette of thin, narrow leaves forms the base. The tall, slender stems are topped by flowers virtually in all colors of the rainbow but blue, with many hues in between. The ring of prominent yellow stamens enhances the colorful blooms. Stem height varies widely from 1 to 2 feet. There are semi-double forms as well.

How to grow: Iceland poppies prefer full sun and a fertile, well-drained soil; otherwise, their requirements are not demanding. Early flowers during cool weather will be the largest. To encourage continued flowering, remove seed heads when they form.

Propagation: By seed. Seeds sown indoors in January will bloom the first season. Plants may also be started the previous summer and overwintered in the garden. In mild winter areas, bloom can start in the winter. Seeds germinate in 10 to 15 days at 55° F. Poppies are tap-rooted plants that do not transplant easily once the tap root is formed. Grow in peat pots and transplant into the garden, pot and all.

Uses: A whole bed of poppies is spectacular. They can also be grown as clumps, groups, or ribbons of plants in mid-border. They're especially beautiful backed by the foliage of hedges or other green plants. They also make good cut flowers. Cut the flowers in early morning just as the buds are showing color, sear the cut ends in an open flame or plunge the stems in hot (not boiling) water for a few moments.

Related species: *Papaver rhoeas*, the Shirley poppy, is the cultivated form of the Flanders poppy, a deep scarlet with black centers. There are many new forms including doubles in pink, white, rose, salmon, as well as red. 'Mother of Pearl' is a selection of pastel shades including gray, blue, lilac, dusty pink, and bicolors.

Related varieties: 'Wonderland' series offers separate colors of white, orange, yellow, pink, and a mix. They're more compact than most, blooming on 1-foot stems. 'Oregon Rainbows' are a mixture of exceptionally large-flowered Iceland poppies, including peach, apricot, cream, picotee bicolors, green, and lavender, as well as more conventional colors.

Mexican Tulip Poppy

Hunnemannia fumariaefolia

This Mexican native is a tender perennial grown as an annual in most of the United States. Named for John Hunneman, an English bookseller and plant collector, it's a member of the poppy family, and will bloom all summer through autumn with its sprightly, yellow, poppylike flowers.

Description: Mexican tulip poppy grows from 1 to 2 feet tall. The finely divided leaves are a handsome, blue-gray color. The long-stalked flowers are yellow, 2 to 3 inches in diameter, with bright orange stamens. There is also a double form.

How to grow: Mexican tulip poppies must have full sun to grow and bloom well, and they tolerate drought. Any garden soil is satisfactory as long as it is well-drained. In frost-free or nearly frost-free areas of Zones 9 and 10, it will live as a perennial. In other areas, plant in the spring as soon as danger of frost has passed. Space 10 to 12 inches apart.

Propagation: By seed. Like so many members of the poppy family, it forms a taproot that makes it difficult to transplant. Sow seeds outdoors in place after frost danger has passed. Thin the seedlings to desired spacing. For earlier bloom, start indoors 4 to 6 weeks prior to planting outside. Germinate at 70 to 75° F, which will take 15 to 20 days. When seedlings have three leaves, transplant to individual peat pots that can later be planted into the garden, pot and all.

Uses: Group them in beds and borders, in rock gardens, and beside paths. They grow well in containers on decks, patios, or by doorsteps. Because they tolerate drought, they're good for containers where watering is not regular, although flower size will diminish somewhat. They can be used for cutting.

Related varieties: Glossy, yellow blossoms that set off against the gray-green foliage are the highlight of 'Sunlite.'

Portulaca, Moss Rose

Portulaca grandiflora

Portulaca's profusion of sunny flower colors combined with its toughness make it a natural for difficult garden sites. It will do even better under less difficult conditions. It is a native of Brazil.

Description: Moss roses grow nearly prostrate. They grow as a mat of fleshy leaves with stems topped by flowers. The flowers of newer varieties can reach 2 inches in diameter and are in a myriad of jewel-like colors—lemon-yellow, gold, orange, crimson, pink, lavender, purple, and white. They're enhanced by the bright button of yellow stamens in the center. There are both single and double varieties. The latter is sparked by extra rows of petals.

How to grow: Full sun; light, sandy soil; and good drainage are musts for portulaca, although they respond to adequate moisture with lusher growth and more flowers. Very frost-tender, they should not be planted outdoors until the danger of frost has passed and the ground is warm. Space them 1 to 2 feet apart. The flowers close at night and on cloudy days. Moss rose reseeds vigorously.

Propagation: Sow in place as soon as danger of frost has passed and the soil is warm. For earlier bloom, start indoors 4 to 6 weeks ahead. Seeds germinate in 10 to 15 days at 70 to 80° F.

Uses: Reserve your problem areas for portulaca. They're good container plants that do not languish if you forget to water them one day.

Related species: *Portulaca oleracea* has ornamental varieties with flowers in white, yellow, rose, and red. 'Wildflower' is a mix grown from seed; selections with even larger flowers are grown from cuttings.

Related varieties: 'Sundance' is a mixture of double-flowered varieties. 'Calypso' and 'Sunnyside' are double-flowered varieties.

Primrose

Primula species and hybrids

Primroses are favored in mild winter areas. They're also spectacular additions to other gardens for early spring color during cool weather. The two most popular varieties for gardens are *P.* x *polyantha,* which is bred from a number of species with long stems topped by multiple flowers, and *P. malacoides,* the fairy primrose, which is often grown as a pot plant in the spring.

Description: Primrose flowers grow from a rosette of long, narrow leaves. The color range is immense—from a sky color to midnight blue, pinks, reds of all hues, yellow, orange, and lavender. Many of them are centered with a contrasting yellow eye; still others have narrow bands of color in the petals. *Polyanthus* primroses will grow up to 1 foot high.

How to grow: Where climate is favorable, including the maritime West Coast, primroses can be grown as perennials. Blooms will start in mid-winter through spring with a reprise of color in the fall when weather cools. Elsewhere, they must be grown for spring bloom. Transplant well-hardened plants into the garden as soon as the ground can be worked. They should be spaced 6 to 10 inches apart. Grow them in soil rich in organic matter and keep them moist. In most places, they're happiest with a canopy of high shade. *P. malacoides* is hardy in California and other mild areas.

Propagation: By seed or by division. To break seed dormancy, store in the refrigerator for 3 to 4 weeks before sowing. Sow seeds 8 to 10 weeks before planting in the garden. Seeds germinate in 10 to 20 days at 70°F.

Rose Mallow

Lavatera trimestris

Salpiglossis, Painted Tongue

Salpiglossis sinuata

Uses: Primroses can be a highlight of the spring garden in moist, woodland settings and along woodland paths and walkways. Plant them in pockets by streams or ponds. Interplant them with spring bulbs that bloom at the same time. They're also nice with pansies, forget-me-nots, and other spring flowers. In containers, they can be beautifully combined with all of the above and others. An extra bonus is the delightful fragrance many of them have.

Related species: There are between 400 and 500 species and much interest in growing them, including a Primrose Society for aficionados. *P. auricula* is often grown for its variety of flowers, both in the garden and for exhibition at flower shows. *P. japonica* is one of the *candelabra* species with several whorls of flowers growing on tall stems. It is hardy and is a perennial.

Related varieties: The favorite *polyanthus* types are the 'Pacific Giant' series.

Lavatera is an annual originally from the Mediterranean. It is related to both hibiscus and hollyhock.

Description: Rose mallow grows to 3 to 5 feet by the end of summer. It branches vigorously to form a sturdy bush. Lower leaves are rounded, but upper ones are lobed and toothed. The flowers, borne in leaf axils, are 3 to 4 inches in diameter.

How to grow: Grow rose mallow in full sun in average soil. Make sure soil is well-drained. Soil too rich grows excess foliage to the detriment of flowering. Plant outdoors as soon as the ground can be worked in the spring. Make sure to provide plenty of moisture. Space 1 to 1½ feet apart. Remove spent flowers to prevent seed formation.

Propagation: By seed. Sow in the ground outdoors. Space the seeds thinly to 1- to 1½-foot spacing because thinned seedlings will probably die. For earlier bloom, sow indoors 6 to 8 weeks prior to outdoor planting. Sow in individual peat pots and transplant, pot and all, into the ground outdoors. Seeds germinate in 14 to 21 days at 70° F.

Uses: Lavatera can be used along pathways or walks. Cluster groups of three or more at the end or sides of borders, or grow a row of them mid to rear of the border, depending on border height. Rose mallows make good container plants. Individual specimens make a rounded bush in urns, tubs, and other planters. The pink and white colors also mix well with other flower colors. Lavatera makes good cut flowers.

Related varieties: 'Mont Blanc' has pure white flowers; 'Mont Rose' is rose-pink; and 'Silver Cup' has large, pink flowers.

A kaleidoscope of color, each flower is dipped in shadings of color and strong veins. Related to petunias, salpiglossis have the same open-faced, trumpetlike flowers. Natives of Chile, they're well worth extra effort to grow.

Description: Unlike petunias, salpiglossis is a relatively upright grower, reaching up to 3 feet in the garden. Flowers are about 2½ inches in diameter. The colors are cream, lemon-yellow, gold, orange, brown, red, scarlet, violet, and near blue. Most of them are overlaid with veins and other patterns of color, making them look like stained glass.

How to grow: Salpiglossis grows best where summers are moderate, in full sun and fertile, well-drained soil. They must have a continuous supply of moisture. Transplant them outdoors in the spring as soon as all danger of frost has passed. Protect them from high winds. As an alternative, push brushwood into the ground around a young plant; the foliage will hide the support as it grows.

Propagation: By seed. Sow seeds indoors 8 weeks prior to planting out. This will allow good-sized plants for setting into the garden after the danger of frost has passed. Seeds should be covered; they need darkness to germinate. Seeds germinate in 15 to 20 days at 70 to 75° F.

Uses: Salpiglossis are ideal for the center of beds or borders as long as other plants cover their somewhat untidy feet. Do the same with containers. Locate them in the center and surround them with lower-growing plants and trailers. They make good cut flowers.

Related varieties: 'Bolero' is a tall strain growing to 2½ feet, with many different flower colors and variants. 'Dwarf Friendship Mixture' blooms on 15-inch plants. 'Kew Blue' has been selected for blue flowers laced with gold veins.

Salvia, Scarlet Sage

Salvia splendens

Salvias are best known for their spiky color that is dependable in any climate. Adaptable to full sun or partial shade with equal ease, these tender perennials grown as annuals are related to some of the best perennial plants for the garden as well as to sage, which is used for culinary purposes. A native of Brazil, salvia comes in brilliant red, creamy white, rose-colored, and purplish variants.

Description: The native plants are reported to grow up to 8 feet high. In the garden, 3 feet is about as tall as the largest ones grow. There are dwarf variants that grow only 8 to 12 inches. The spikes of flowers are composed of bright bracts with flowers in the center of each. They are either the same color or contrasting.

How to grow: Salvia is a good dual-purpose plant that will perform dutifully in full sun or partial shade. It needs average soil and continuous moisture to perform its best. Transplant plants to the garden after danger of frost has passed and the soil is warm. Depending on variety, space from 8 to 12 inches apart.

Propagation: Although seeds can be sown directly in the garden, earlier sowing indoors will bring earlier flowering. Be sure to use fresh seeds, since they lose their viability quickly. Sow the seeds 6 to 8 weeks before the final frost. The seeds germinate in 12 to 15 days at 70 to 75° F. Do not cover the seeds; they need light to germinate. After germination, reduce the temperature to 55° F.

Uses: Salvia provides some of the purest reds and scarlets in the garden world, and their vertical growth makes them superb accents in the garden. Plant them as spots of color against other colors. They're a classic combination with blue and white for patriotic plantings. Their ability to bloom well in light shade makes them especially useful with pastel colors that tend to fade in the sun. They also make good container plants.

Related species: *Salvia farinacea* is a perennial in milder climates that is now widely used as an annual throughout the country. Its common name is "mealycup sage" for the grayish bloom on its stems and foliage. It grows 18 to 24 inches tall and produces either blue or white flowers. 'Victoria' is the most popular blue; its counterpart is 'Victoria White.' *Salvia patens,* gentian sage, is named for its rich indigo-blue flowers that have a long blooming season.

Related varieties: 'Carabiniere' grows to 12 inches and, in addition to red, has separate colors of coral, shrimp pink, orange, blue-violet, and creamy white. 'Red Pillar' is taller and somewhat later. Tallest reds are 'America' and 'Bonfire,' which will grow to 2 feet in the garden.

Sanvitalia, Creeping Zinnia

Sanvitalia procumbens

Although not a zinnia, sanvitalia has enough resemblance to it to fit its common name of "creeping zinnia." Bright, golden-yellow flowers bloom nonstop all summer until frost. A native of Mexico, it is a member of the daisy family.

Description: The plant is a creeper, growing up to 12 inches in diameter with flowers above topping out at 6 inches. The flowers aren't large, but they're so abundant that they nearly obscure the foliage. The purple or brown centers are a pleasing foil to the yellow petals. Most sanvitalias are singles.

How to grow: Sanvitalia prefers full sun but will adapt to partial shade with less flowering. It is tolerant of most garden conditions. Plant outdoors when all danger of frost has passed and the soil is warm. Space plants 4 to 6 inches apart. Do not overwater or fertilize.

Propagation: By seed. Sow seeds in place when ground has warmed. For earlier bloom, start indoors 4 to 6 weeks before outdoor planting. Seeds germinate in 10 to 15 days at 70° F. Do not cover the seeds; they need light to germinate. Because they do not transplant easily, grow sanvitalias in peat pots that can be planted in the garden, pot and all.

Uses: Since sanvitalia is an annual that likes dry conditions, grow it in rock gardens. Use it as an edging for the front of borders or along sidewalks and paths. It will even bloom near the sunny foundations of houses. It will tolerate dappled shade. Sanvitalia trails well from containers.

Related species: *Wedelia trilobata,* native to Florida and South America, is somewhat similar in appearance with its sunny yellow flowers. It makes a good ground cover in full sun, where it roots as it grows.

Related variety: 'Mandarin Orange' brings a new color to sanvitalia.

Sapphire Flower

Browallia speciosa, viscosa

Sapphire flowers bloom heavily from early spring to fall frost; year-round in sunny windows or greenhouses. They're at their best in cool or coastal gardens, but with partial shade or an eastern exposure they will consistently grow well elsewhere.

Description: *B. speciosa* varieties grow in a loose mound to 18 inches high and as wide, their lax habit allowing them to trail. The most-planted variety of *B. viscosa* ('Sapphire') is a compact, rather stiff plant that doesn't trail.

How to grow: Plant in rich, well-drained soil but keep moist. Plant larger varieties 10 inches apart; dwarf ones 6 inches apart. Browallia is a good shade plant, although with looser habit and sparser flowers. Feed lightly on a biweekly schedule or incorporate a summer-long, slow-release fertilizer in the soil at planting.

Propagation: By seed or by cuttings. Start seeds indoors 6 to 8 weeks prior to planting out after the last frost. Seeds need light to germinate, so do not cover. At temperatures of 70 to 75° F, they'll take 14 to 21 days to germinate. Softwood cuttings taken in the spring or fall root promptly. For large plants in 10-inch hanging baskets, add 4 weeks to the growing time.

Uses: Sapphire flowers are grown in beds, borders, or rock gardens. Compact plants make good edges for a tall border. They are also excellent container plants.

Related varieties: Most planted *speciosa* varieties are the 'Bells': 'Blue Bells Improved,' mid-blue and most popular; 'Marine Bells,' a deep indigo blue; 'Sky Bells,' a clear azure blue; and 'Silver Bells,' pure white. *Viscosa* varieties include 'Sapphire,' deep blue with a white eye; 'Blue Troll,' a dwarf variety in mid-blue; and its counterpart, 'White Troll.'

Scabiosa, Pincushion Flower, Mourning Bride

Scabiosa atropurpurea

This native of southern Europe is like a pincushion with flowers up to 3 inches in size and scores of yellow or white stamens. The original flowers had a sweet scent.

Description: Scabiosa can grow up to 2½ feet tall; modern varieties are shorter. The many branched plants are topped with flowers in white, pink, lavender, and deepest maroon (almost black), from which the name "mourning bride" comes. Both double and single forms are found.

How to grow: Scabiosas grow well in any moderately fertile, well-drained soil. They need full sun. Plant outdoors after all danger of frost has passed, spacing them 8 to 15 inches apart, depending on variety. The taller varieties will need staking, but the shorter ones do not if protected from high winds. Scabiosas are sensitive to water. Apply water in the morning so that it can dry off before night.

Propagation: By seed. Sow outdoors as soon as all danger of frost has passed, thinning seedlings to the proper spacing. For earlier bloom, sow seeds indoors 4 to 6 weeks prior to outdoor planting. Seeds germinate in 10 to 15 days at 70 to 75° F.

Uses: Scabiosa is a delight in cottage gardens and mixed borders. It can also be grown and flowered in greenhouses or in sun rooms through fall and winter. Scabiosa makes good cut flowers.

Related varieties: 'Blue Cockade' has double flowers of rich, lavender-blue. It is a tall, 3-foot variety. 'Dwarf Double' is a mix of colors in white, lavender, lavender-blue, and rose, growing to 18 inches. 'Giant Imperial' features large flowers on long stems, ideal for cutting. They are a mix of lavender-blue, white, rose, and pink. 'Double Mixed' are fragrant, fully double flowers that include the darker colors of purple and deep crimson as well as white and pink.

Scarlet Flax

Linum grandiflorum

This showy annual provides bright red flowers with virtually no care. Each flower lasts a few hours and is followed daily by a procession of new ones. Originally from North Africa, it has become naturalized in parts of the United States.

Description: Scarlet flax grows to 2½ feet tall on slender, branched stems with narrow leaves. The round flowers, up to 1½ inches in diameter, have 5 broad petals. The primary color is shades of red.

How to grow: Grow scarlet flax in full sun in any garden soil, preferably somewhat low in fertility. They perform best in cooler climates. Plants will tolerate mild frosts; in colder climates they can be planted in the fall for late spring bloom. Otherwise, sow in place as soon as the ground can be worked in the spring. Space 4 to 6 inches apart. Water during dry spells. Each plant blooms approximately 4 to 6 weeks. For all season display, reseed at 4- to 6-week intervals.

Propagation: By seed. For earliest bloom in most locations, start seeds indoors 6 weeks prior to outdoor planting. Grow in peat pots to aid in transplanting. Seed germination takes 5 to 12 days at 60 to 70° F.

Uses: Scarlet flax is a good addition to wildflower or meadow gardens. Grow it in clumps in borders or beds and in mixed plantings such as cottage gardens. Plant it also in rock gardens.

Related species: *Linum usitatissimum* has sky-blue flowers that are breathtaking when planted in masses. Height is up to 3 feet. *Linum bienne* is another blue-flowered species that can be grown in the garden.

Related varieties: *Linum grandiflorum rubrum* is a deep red flowered form. 'Bright Eye' is ivory white with chocolate-brown eyes.

Scarlet Pimpernel, Poor-Man's Weather Glass

Anagallis arvensis

The name "Scarlet Pimpernel" was widely popularized by a novel of the French Revolution by Baroness Orczy, whose hero, Sir Percy Blakeney, used the flower as a trademark when he rescued victims from the Reign of Terror. The petals fold up when skies darken before storms or at twilight, not opening again until morning light triggers their rebloom—hence its other common name. A native of Europe and Asia, it is sparingly naturalized in parts of the United States.

Description: A plant whose low-spreading habit causes it to creep over the ground rather than grow upright, scarlet pimpernel's bright flowers provide a twinkling cloud of color. A blue form (*A. a. caerulea*) gives the same light, airy effect. It will rarely grow more than 4 to 5 inches high.

How to grow: Scarlet pimpernel thrives in full sun in ordinary garden soil, but favors sandy, well-drained conditions. Plant 6 inches apart after danger of frost has passed. It will continue blooming all summer.

Propagation: By seed. Seeds germinate in about 18 days indoors at 60° F and may be planted when the danger of frost has passed. They're easily grown by sowing seeds in the garden, then thinning plants to 6 inches apart. They also reseed.

Uses: Scarlet pimpernel is ideal for color in a rock garden. It also makes a good edging for paths or flower borders. Grown in pots on a sunny windowsill, it will continue flowering during fall and winter.

Related species: *A. monellii*, which grows up to 1 foot high, can be grown as an annual. The flowers range from blue with red undersides to pink. *A. tenella*, from the moist soils of southern Europe, bears small, scarlet, bell-shaped flowers on longer stems.

Scarlet Runner Bean

Phaseolus coccineus

In many parts of the world—especially in England and France—the scarlet runner bean is cultivated both as an ornamental and a vegetable. Until recently, the United States has embraced only its ornamental qualities. The lush, thick vines produce clusters of red flowers that are followed by the edible green beans. The Dutch runner bean, *P. c. alba*, has white flowers.

Description: Scarlet runner beans are quick-growing vines with typical, 3-leaflet bean leaves. They grow 6 or 8 feet tall. The bean flowers are borne in clusters like sweet peas. The edible pods that follow are long, slender, green beans.

How to grow: Scarlet runner beans need fertile soil and adequate moisture in full sun. Plant them where they can grow up some kind of support. The beans don't need to be tied—they twine around posts or poles. For covering fences, some kind of twine or netting will be needed for beans to climb. If allowed to grow over the ground, they will form a tangled mass of leaves, and the flowers will be hidden.

Propagation: By seed. Plant the large seeds directly in the ground after danger of frost has passed and the soil is warm. Plant seeds about 3 inches away from fences or posts, spacing them 2 to 3 inches apart. Thin the seedlings to a spacing of 6 to 8 inches. Seeds germinate in 5 to 10 days.

Uses: These quick-growing vines are beautiful when trained up posts, arches, pergolas, or arbors. They make quick-growing screens to break up the garden.

Related varieties: Most seed catalogs list them only as scarlet runner beans and do not select them for special eating qualities. 'Butler' has stringless beans; 'Painted Lady' bears red and white flowers; 'Kelvedon Wonder' is an early variety with long pods; and 'Scarlet Emperor' is named for the color of its flowers.

Schizanthus, Butterfly Flower, Poor Man's Orchid

Schizanthus x wisetonensis

Schizanthus revels in cool-weather climates, blooming well in late winter and spring in frost-free climates and other regions with long periods of cool weather in the spring and summer. Where they grow well, the flowers are spectacular. Although flowers are large and open, somewhat resembling butterflies and orchids, they're related to petunias and tomatoes and are native to Chile.

Description: Large clusters of flowers open above the finely cut, fernlike foliage. Compact varieties can grow up to 2½ feet tall and, when loaded with flowers, tend to tumble. The range of flower color is wide: pink, white, lavender, blue, gold, red, and magenta, with many flowers marked with other colors.

How to grow: Schizanthus likes cool, sunny conditions and a rich, moist soil high in organic matter. Under warmer conditions, light shade is good. They must have perfect drainage. Because they bloom best with root restriction, they are most often grown in containers. For garden planting, space them 12 inches apart. Plant outdoors after all danger of frost has passed.

Propagation: By seed. Sow seeds indoors 12 weeks prior to the last frost. Cover seeds; they respond to darkness. Seeds germinate in 20 to 30 days at 60 to 65° F.

Uses: Schizanthus is a natural for containers. It also makes a superb cut flower.

Scotch Thistle

Onopordum acathium

Like ghostly sculptures, Scotch thistles are attention-getting. They are also invasive enough to be considered noxious weeds in some states. Not scotch at all, they're biennials that grow from a small rosette of leaves the first season to tall, silvery branched columns the next year, bloom, and die. Related to both artichokes and true thistles, they have the same distinctive, light purple flowers (perhaps the model for the Scottish national emblem).

Description: The leaves are covered with white, cottony hairs that reflect the light and give it its ghostly appearance. The first year's basal rosette has leaves up to 1 foot in length. The following summer, a large flowering stalk with numerous branches arises from the center of the leaves. The thistlelike flowers are purple when open.

How to grow: Full sun in any garden soil will accommodate Scotch thistle. Despite their great height, their sturdy stems require no staking support. Because they're so large, they need plenty of room. Scotch thistles will reseed invasively and present some danger of taking over your garden. To avoid this, cut off flowerheads when they lose their purple flower. Like true thistles, they also have sharp spines, so take care when handling Scotch thistles.

Propagation: By seed.

Uses: Scotch thistle is hard to control once it establishes itself, growing in dense patches that outcompetes its neighbors and earns it the status as a weed. Due to its aggressive nature, it is not recommended as a cultivated plant.

Snapdragon

Antirrhinum majus

Children love snapdragons because they can snap open the flowers. They are also prized because of their columnar stateliness. Snapdragons endure cool weather and are widely planted for winter color in mild-winter areas.

Description: Snapdragons uniformly bear a whorl of flowers atop slender stalks. The best known are ones with snappable flowers, but new kinds have open-faced flowers including double forms. Colors include white, yellow, burgundy, red, pink, orange, and bronze.

How to grow: Plant in rich, well-drained soil with high levels of organic matter. Grow in full sun, fertilize monthly, and water moderately. Space tall varieties 12 inches apart, small varieties 6 inches apart. Pinch tips of young plants to encourage branching. Tall varieties may need staking. After first bloom is finished, pinch off flower spikes to induce new growth and repeat flowering. For cool season bloom in Zones 9 and 10, plant in September.

Propagation: By seed. Germination takes an average of 8 days at 70° F soil temperature. Keep seeds moist, but do not cover, since light is required for germination. For early bloom, sow seeds indoors 6 to 8 weeks before setting outdoors after last frost. Snapdragons may also be sown directly in the garden 6 weeks prior to the last frost when soil is friable.

Uses: Use the tall varieties for the back of the floral border and for cut flowers. Short varieties are good in borders and as edgings for beds. All varieties can be used in containers.

Related varieties: Tall snapdragons include 'Rocket' and open-faced 'Double Madam Butterfly.' Medium varieties, up to 18 inches, are 'Princess' and 'Coronet.' The most popular "mini" is 'Floral Carpet.'

Snow-in-Summer, Ghost Weed

Euphorbia marginata

This annual is a native of the eastern United States. The names "snow-in-summer" and "ghost weed" come from the white, variegated margins on the edges of its leaves. The sap can be irritating.

Description: Snow-in-summer grows rapidly from seedling stage, branching to a small bush 1 to 3 feet tall. The lower leaves are virtually all green, but progressively toward the top, more white appears on leaf edges. When flowering begins, the top leaves are mostly white. The real flowers are tiny, the color coming from the modified leaves called bracts.

How to grow: Snow-in-summer grows well anywhere in full sun—from cool, moist locations to dry, rocky places. It reseeds vigorously. Space plants 12 inches apart.

Propagation: By seed. Sow seeds outdoors after danger of frost has passed. Thin to desired spacing. Or start indoors 7 to 8 weeks prior to planting out. Seeds germinate in 10 to 15 days at 70 to 75° F.

Uses: Plant where large drifts of the green-white combination are wanted to cool the landscape. Snow-in-summer also makes a nice border or temporary hedge for pathways and sidewalks.

Related species: *Euphorbia heterophylla,* "summer poinsettia," has bright red bracts about 4 inches in diameter on plants 2 feet tall. It is also called "Mexican fire plant," "painted leaf," and "fire-on-the-mountain." *Euphorbia lathyrus,* with the common name of "mole plant" or "gopher plant," is often planted because it is supposed to keep moles away, a hotly disputed claim. Other names include "caper spurge." A handsome plant growing up to 5 feet tall, it has long, narrow leaves.

Related varieties: 'White Top' and 'Summer Icicle' are two available selections. 'Summer Icicle' is a dwarf, more compact form growing to 2 feet tall.

Southern Star, Star of the Argentine

Oxypetalum caeruleum

Southern star is worth looking at closely—its buds are pink, opening to a silvery blue star that fades to purple and then to lilac as it ages. The shape of the flower is an exquisite 5-pointed star. A shrubby perennial plant from Argentina, it's used here as an annual except in nearly frost-free parts of Zones 9 and 10 where it will winter over in permanent plantings. It's a member of the milkweed family.

Description: Used as an annual, it has a somewhat different character than its subshrub form in permanent plantings. Young plants have somewhat twining stems topped by clusters of flowers 1 inch in diameter. It can grow to 3 feet in nature, but rarely tops 18 inches in the garden.

How to grow: Southern stars do best in rich, well-drained loam in full sun. Space plants 6 to 8 inches apart. Pinch the plants once or twice to induce bushiness. In midsummer, they can be cut back about halfway to force new growth and extra bloom. Just before frost, plants from the garden can be dug, cut back, repotted, and grown for winter color on sunny windowsills.

Propagation: By seed or cuttings. Plants will bloom about 8 weeks after germination. For early bloom, sow indoors 6 to 8 weeks prior to planting in the garden after all danger of frost has passed. Seeds will germinate in 10 to 15 days at 70°F. Seeds may also be sown directly in the ground outdoors, although this will delay bloom until late summer, except in milder areas.

Uses: Plant them beside pathways and sidewalks or at eye level on banks or above walls for close-up viewing. Use them in containers. Because their growth is upright and somewhat spreading, trailing plants make an attractive addition to containers. Southern stars may also be brought indoors for winter bloom.

Stock

Matthiola incana

Stock is appreciated for its cool, distinctive colors and exceptional fragrance in cool season gardens. In mild winter regions, it's grown as a winter/early-spring annual for bloom before the weather gets torrid. In maritime or cool mountain climates, it makes a good flower for late spring or summer flowering. A biennial treated as an annual, it's a native of the Mediterranean coast and a member of the mustard family.

Description: Most stock varieties have become well-bred doubles, an upgrade from their wild, single nature. Modern varieties vary in height from 12 to 30 inches, but they're all rather stiff columns surrounded by flowers. The flowers are pink, white, red, rose, purple, and lavender in color.

How to grow: Stock is at its best in the cool, humid weather of foggy, coastal areas, even though some varieties are more heat-tolerant for a longer flowering season elsewhere. Stock will tolerate light frost and is useful for winter bloom in mild climates. Elsewhere, plant as early in the spring as ground can be worked. Moist, well-drained soil high in organic matter is preferred. Stock should be planted in full sun. Space them 8 to 15 inches apart, depending on the size of the variety.

Propagation: By seed. For winter use in mild climates, sow stock in the fall. In other places, sow seeds indoors 6 to 8 weeks prior to when ground can be worked outdoors. Seeds germinate in 7 to 10 days at 70° F. Don't cover the seeds; they need light to germinate. A percentage of seedlings are singles. Doubles are usually the most vigorous seedlings and are lighter in color than the singles.

Uses: Stock is relatively precise in appearance, best suited to formal beds where it can be lined up like soldiers. Plant them where the fragrance reaches passersby—near walks, by doorsteps, and close to heavily frequented places. They're also adaptable to containers, especially if you combine them with informal flowers to break up the rigidity. They're also superb cut flowers, with the scent pervading an entire room.

Related species: *Matthiola bicornis* has a particularly strong scent at night; the daytime flowers are unexceptional, so plant them discreetly.

Related varieties: 'Trysomic Seven Week' stock is the earliest bloomer. It is more tolerant of heat, offering a complete range of stock colors. It grows 15 inches high. 'Dwarf Stockpot' has separate colors of 'Red,' 'Purple,' 'Rose,' 'White,' or all together in a mix. It grows 8 to 10 inches tall.

Sundrop

Oenothera biennis

Oenotheras are perennials, biennials, and annuals. They can all be grown as annuals. Those whose flowers open at night are called evening primroses; day-bloomers are sundrops.
Description: This plant forms a basal rosette of long, narrow leaves from which rises a flower stalk, bearing blooms that open from the bottom of the stem to the top. It grows up to 3 feet tall. The flowers, up to 1½ inches in diameter, are open cups of a gold color. Sometimes they are scarlet in bud.
How to grow: Oenotheras require average soil with good drainage in a fully sunny location. Good drainage helps improve winter hardiness of the short-lived perennial species. They are relatively tolerant of dry soils, but steady moisture will improve their growth. Sturdy plants, they do not require staking unless grown in locations with high winds. Plant them in the garden in the spring as soon as the ground can be worked easily. Space them 12 to 15 inches apart.
Propagation: By seed or division. For blooming plants the first year, sow them indoors 10 to 12 weeks prior to outdoor planting. Seeds germinate in 15 to 20 days at 68 to 85° F. Biennial and perennial kinds can be sown directly into the garden the preceding autumn, early enough to develop husky plants prior to freezing weather. Sundrops will reseed vigorously.
Uses: Grow sundrops in the middle or at the back of the border. Group them at the center or at the back of beds. They can also be used in front of low hedges.
Related species: *Oenothera erythrosepala* has yellow flowers. Mature blossoms slowly turn red. It grows to 3½ feet tall. *O. texensis* has rose-colored flowers. Compact plants grow up to 12 inches.
Related variety: 'Highlight' is a selection of the perennial species of *O. tetragona*.

Sunflower

Helianthus annuus

Whether giants of the garden at 15 feet tall or barely topping 1 foot, these natives of North America come in a variety of colors and forms. *Helios* is the Greek word for "sun."
Description: Typically growing from 10 to 15 feet tall, sunflowers have coarse leaves and flower heads up to 1 foot or more in diameter. Although they started out as yellow flowers with brown or purple centers, there are now variations with magenta, white, and orange flowers and still others that are fluffy doubles.
How to grow: Sunflowers prefer full sun and will grow in any soil, except one that is light and well-drained. They're very tolerant of heat and drought. The tall varieties may need staking to prevent the wind from toppling them. Plant the tall varieties 12 to 18 inches apart; dwarf ones at 9- to 12-inch spacing.
Propagation: By seed. Sow seeds outdoors after final frost. However, for earlier bloom, start indoors 4 to 8 weeks ahead. Seeds germinate in 10 to 20 days at 70 to 85° F.
Uses: The dwarf kinds can be used in beds and borders, while the taller varieties are best at the back of the border. They can be used as a screen or as a clump at the end of driveways or along fences. The smaller-flowered varieties can also be used as cut flowers.
Related species: *Helianthus debilis* grows 4 to 5 feet tall with yellow or creamy white flowers. *H. giganteus* is the monster sunflower, growing up to 15 feet tall with dinner plate-sized flowers, 12 to 15 inches across.
Related varieties: 'Piccolo' grows to 4 feet and bears rather graceful, 4-inch, semi-double, gold flowers centered in black. 'Sunspot' has 8- to 12-inch blooms on plants only 18 to 24 inches high. 'Large Flowered Mixed' has yellow, red, bronze, and orange flowers on 5-foot plants.

Sweet Pea

Lathyrus odoratus

In cool maritime or mountain climates, sweet peas will bring their beauty all summer. In Zones 9 and 10, they're best in cool seasons, winter, and early spring. Natives of Italy, the original purple or white flowers now come in many hues.
Description: Sweet peas are vining plants that climb vigorously 6 to 8 feet over fences and other supports. The flowers are pink, white, red, lavender, purple, and almost (but not quite) blue.
How to grow: In mild winter areas, sow seeds outdoors in the fall. Elsewhere, plant as soon as ground can be worked. Sweet peas need full sun and a deep, rich soil. Dig a trench and fill with fertilizer and humus-rich soil. When seeds are up, mulch thoroughly to keep soil cool. When seedlings are 4 inches high, pinch the tips to develop strong side branches. Provide support for them to climb. The shortest varieties need no support. Keep blossoms picked to ensure continuous flowering.
Propagation: By seed. Nick seed coats with a knife and soak seeds overnight in water. Before planting, treat with a culture of nitrogen-fixing bacteria available at garden stores. For earliest plants, start in peat pots 4 to 6 weeks before planting outside. Plant pot and all. Seeds germinate in 10 to 14 days at 55 to 65° F.
Uses: Grow them against fences, over trellises, arches, and pergolas. Plant them on a tepee composed of stakes in the center or at the back of the bed. The dwarf varieties can be planted in the border. As cut flowers, sweet peas are superb.
Related varieties: 'Early Mammoth Mixed' has many colors. 'Bijou' is a variety with a bushy habit, growing to 12 inches and a number of colors. 'Super Snoop,' an early flowering dwarf, grows to 2 feet with a full range of sweet pea colors.

Thunbergia, Black-Eyed Susan Vine, Clock Vine

Thunbergia alata

This quick-growing vine boasts many open-faced flowers, usually with dark centers (hence the name "black-eyed Susan"). Where not struck down by frost it is a perennial, but most climates of the United States grow it as a beautiful annual. The name *Thunbergia* honors a Swedish botanist named Karl Pehr Thunberg.

Description: Black-eyed Susan vine can grow 6 to 8 feet tall in a season and has rough, hairy leaves. The blooms have 5 distinct petals and are symmetrical. Flower color can be white, yellow, orange, or cream. Most of them have dark centers.

How to grow: Generally, it grows best in full sun. It needs average, well-drained soil. Plant seedlings 3 inches away from supports. Space plants 5 to 8 inches apart. Pinch the tips to encourage branching. Since thunbergias climb by twining, netting or strings make good trellising materials. They will need a trellis to climb large posts or solid fencing.

Propagation: By seed or by cuttings. Sow seeds outdoors after the last frost or start seedlings indoors 6 to 8 weeks before outdoor planting. Seeds germinate in 10 to 15 days at 70 to 75° F. Cuttings root easily in a commercial soil mix.

Uses: Thunbergias can be used to cover posts, porches, arbors, pergolas, or fences. They also make good container plants. Plants in containers will also bloom over winter in sunny windows.

Related species: *Thunbergia gibsonii* has somewhat larger flowers in a bright orange color. *Thunbergia fragrans* bears 2-inch wide, white, fragrant flowers. The most available variety is called 'Angel Wings' and blooms in about 12 weeks from seed.

Related varieties: 'Susie Mix' is composed of orange, yellow, and white blooms, either with or without dark centers.

Tidy Tips

Layia platyglossa

This annual is native to southern California. A member of the aster family, it has bright, daisylike flowers—a strong, golden-yellow, with every petal tipped with white. This is where the name "tidy tips" arose.

Description: Tidy tips forms a semi-prostrate bush 1 to 2 feet high and as broad. It becomes more or less mounding in form because of frequent branching. The long, narrow, hairy, green leaves are usually entirely covered by the flowers.

How to grow: Tidy tips needs full sun. It is relatively indifferent to soil, growing well in average, well-drained garden soil. It will survive if drought occurs, although it will benefit from watering. Tidy tips is less tolerant of hot, humid weather and in such climates will perform best in the spring and early summer. Otherwise, it will bloom continuously until fall. Space plants 4 to 9 inches apart in the garden. They need no staking, standing up well to wind and rain.

Propagation: By seed. In mild winter climates, seeds may be sown in the fall for earliest bloom in the spring. Elsewhere, sow seeds outdoors as early in the spring as ground can be worked. To start indoors, sow seeds 6 to 8 weeks prior to planting outside. Do not cover; seeds need light to germinate. Seeds germinate in 8 to 12 days at temperatures of 65 to 70° F. Temperatures above 70° F inhibit germination.

Uses: Plant tidy tips in mixed borders and cottage gardens. They're also ideal in wildflower or meadow plantings. They can be used in containers. Tidy tips make good cut flowers.

Related varieties: Named selections are not available. However, a variety, *L. p. campestris,* is more erect, less branched, and has grayer leaves. Flower petals are typically longer, but they have the same yellow color with white tips.

Tithonia, Mexican Sunflower

Tithonia rotundifolia

Tithonia, along with sunflowers, are the largest, most dramatic annuals for the garden. Some varieties can grow up to 8 feet tall. A native of Mexico and southward, its area of origin is the reason for its common name. Members of the daisy family, they are also related to the sunflower.

Description: Tithonias have rough, hairy leaves on tall, vigorous plants. Shorter varieties are now available that will stay approximately 4 feet tall. The flowers are single and up to 3 inches in diameter. The color is a deep orange-red, even though there is now a variety with chrome-yellow flowers.

How to grow: Tithonia must have full sun, but it will grow in average soil with good drainage. It is one of the most heat- and drought-resistant plants, growing reasonably well in soils of low fertility. Plant in the garden after all danger of frost has passed. Space plants 2½ to 3 feet apart. Do not overwater. Protect the plants from high winds and stake them—this is particularly important in late summer and fall when they are tall and top-heavy.

Propagation: By seed. Seeds may be sown outdoors; for earlier flowering, start them indoors 6 to 8 weeks earlier. Seeds germinate in 7 to 21 days at 70° F.

Uses: Its size and coarseness of the foliage dictates planting it at the back of the border. The color is so intense that it only takes a few plants for impact. It is also useful for covering fences and shielding background eyesores in the garden. Tithonias make good cut flowers as long as the hollow stems are seared after cutting and plunged into 100° F water.

Related varieties: 'Torch' is a medal winner that grows 4 to 6 feet tall, bearing the classic, deep orange-red flowers. 'Yellow Torch' has yellow flowers.

Toadflax

Linaria maroccana

Toadflaxes have flowers that pop open when squeezed—just like snapdragons. Native to Morocco, which their species name reflects, these plants should be better known for their cool season color in warmer climates and all summer blooms in cool locations.

Description: Toadflax grows upright and branches, with flowers covering the upper third of the stems. Leaves are long and narrow. The species has blue-violet flowers with white or yellow markings, but new selections include many other colors as well: blue, lilac, pink, yellow, red, and white. They're still marked with a contrasting lip. They grow up to 1 foot tall, but often stay shorter.

How to grow: Toadflax requires full sun and well-drained soil. Low fertility is preferred over a rich soil. Plant as early as the ground can be worked. Seeds can be sown indoors early or directly in the ground outside. They grow and bloom so quickly that an earlier start is not necessary, except in those areas where early heat would diminish their bloom time. Because they are small, plant or thin them to a spacing 3 to 4 inches apart. Linaria self-sows readily.

Propagation: By seed. Sow outdoors as early as ground can be worked. Indoors, seed 4 to 6 weeks earlier. They germinate in 10 to 15 days at 55 to 60° F.

Uses: Toadflax look great in the rock garden. They can also be planted in drifts in the front of borders or beds. They're lovely overplanted with bulbs. Planting them together with snapdragons combines the same flower type with an interesting contrast in size.

Related varieties: 'Fairy Bouquet' and 'Fairy Lights' are both mixtures containing the linaria colors of white, pink, purple, lavender, and yellow.

Torenia, Wishbone Flower

Torenia Fournieri

Torenia is a colorful, modest-sized plant that thrives in shade and hot, humid weather as a result of its original habitat in Vietnam. The common name comes from the two yellow stamens that arch over the center of the petals.

Description: Torenia forms a compact mound about 1 foot high with many branches. Leaves are oval or heart-shaped. The flowers look a bit like open-faced snapdragons with prominent markings on the petals. The most predominant color in the past was blue, but new varieties are pink, rose, light blue, and white. Most carry yellow, but some may have deep blue or purple markings.

How to grow: Torenias grow best in rich, moist, well-drained soil. They're widely used in frost-free areas for winter and spring display. Elsewhere, they thrive during summer in partial shade. They like high humidity and won't tolerate being dry. Plant outdoors after all danger of frost has passed. Space 6 to 8 inches apart.

Propagation: By seed. Sow seeds 10 to 12 weeks prior to outdoor planting. The seeds are tiny; they are more easily sown evenly if mixed with a pinch of sugar before sowing. Germination takes 10 to 15 days at 70° F.

Uses: Torenia is a good addition to plants that bloom well in semi-shade. Plant them in groups of three or more in woodland bowers; grow clumps along paths or walkways. Because it grows evenly, it's a good candidate for formal beds in sun or partial shade. Torenia is well-adapted to containers.

Related species: *Torenia concolor* is a tender trailing perennial. Its flowers are blue to purple without markings.

Related variety: 'Clown Mixture' has flowers of blue, light blue, rose-pink, and white.

Tuberose

Polianthes tuberosa

The cloying tropical fragrance of tuberoses is pervasive on warm summer evenings—reason enough to grow them but with an added benefit of beautiful white flowers. Reputedly, it was cultivated by the Aztecs in pre-Columbian times, then sequestered in a monastery in France until it was released for wider cultivation. Sharing the secret has been a boon to centuries of gardeners ever since.

Description: Tuberoses grow from bulbous rootstocks with a rosette of leaves, centered by a flowering stem that is surrounded by tubular flowers of exquisite fragrance. Flowering stems are from 1 to 2 feet tall. Both single and double varieties are planted. Not hardy, bulbs must be dug up each fall in cold climates and replanted in the spring.

How to grow: Grow tuberoses in rich, well-drained soil that is high in organic matter and in full sun. Plant in the garden after all danger of frost has passed and the soil is warm. Plant the bulbs 2 inches deep and 6 inches apart. Water them thoroughly during dry weather.

Propagation: By offsets. Smaller bulbs will have formed when you dig the bulbs in the fall. They may be replanted the next year and will bloom the second year. For earlier plants, start them indoors 5 to 6 weeks prior to planting in the garden.

Uses: The pure white flowers on long stems combine well with any garden plants. To enjoy their fragrance, plant groups of them where people pass or congregate. Plant them in containers for the lovely flower form and haunting scent. They're good as cut flowers.

Related varieties: 'Mexican Everblooming' is the widely available, single-flowered tuberose. 'Double Pearl' is the widely planted double form, with each blossom packed with many extra flowers.

Venidium, Monarch of the Veldt, Cape Daisy

Venidium fastuosum

The foliage of this plant is nearly as beautiful as the flowers—a shimmery, silvery reflection of light from the hairy leaves and stems. The large, bright orange flowers have darker centers. There are also less strident colors including yellow, cream, ivory, and white. Natives of South Africa, they belong to the daisy family.

Description: Plants grow about 2 feet tall, are branched, and have long flower stems. The large daisies are up to 5 inches in diameter and have a double row of ray flowers. The dark centers are brownish-purple to almost black. Leaves are finely cut and covered with long, shaggy hairs that create the silvery appearance.

How to grow: As perennials, venidiums grow best in mild, maritime climates with cool, dry summers and frost-free winters. They can be used for winter and spring flowering in parts of Zones 9 and 10. Where summers are hot, venidiums are best grown as spring annuals—to be replaced when humidity and temperatures soar. They must have well-drained soil and full sun. Transplant plants to the garden after the last frost date when the soil is warm. Space them 12 inches apart. Stakes may be necessary if they are not shielded from high winds.

Propagation: By seed. Start seeds indoors 6 to 8 weeks prior to planting in the garden. Seeds germinate in 15 to 20 days at 70 to 75° F. Do not cover the seeds; they need light to germinate.

Uses: Plant venidiums in beds and borders. Grow them in groups at a turn or the end of a pathway. They make good cut flowers, although they will close at night.

Related species: A more compact species is *Venidium decurrens*, with bright yellow flowers.

Related varieties: Each seed company makes its own selection.

Verbena

Verbena x hybrida

Verbenas are garden treasures in areas where few other plants would grow. Some varieties trail; others form mounds of color. Parentage is from species found in subtropical and tropical South America.

Description: The trailing varieties may reach 18 inches in diameter, while the mounding types will grow to about 1 foot high and wide. The flowers are in clusters. The leaves are long, narrow, and notched.

How to grow: Verbenas prefer well-drained, sandy soil with good fertility. They will not grow well in shade or with wet feet. They also need air movement around their leaves to prevent mildew. Plant after all danger of frost has passed. Space plants 12 (upright types) to 18 (trailing types) inches apart.

Propagation: By seed or by cuttings. Verbenas are slow in the early stages. Sow seeds 12 to 14 weeks prior to planting in the garden. Chill the seeds in the refrigerator for 7 days before sowing. Cover the seeds; they need darkness to germinate. They are also sensitive to dampness. Wet the seed flat 24 hours before sowing, sow the seeds without watering, and cover with black plastic until germination. Germination takes 3 to 4 weeks at 75 to 80° F.

Uses: The trailing types are ideal for rock gardens, trailing over walls, and as edgings for garden beds and borders. Use mounding types in beds and borders. Verbena also trails nicely from containers.

Related varieties: 'Showtime' and 'Springtime' series are available as separate colors and as mixes. 'Blaze' is a red variety; 'Crystal,' a white; and 'Delight,' a salmon-pink. These are all trailers. Mounding verbenas include the 'Romance' and 'Sandy' series and 'Trinidad'—a fluorescent-rose color. There are also selections grown from cuttings.

Vinca, Madagascar Periwinkle

Catharanthus roseus

These tropical plants, native to Madagascar, stand up well to heat and humidity. Research is now developing new varieties with additional colors beyond the familiar white, pink, and rose of the past.

Description: Flowers are round, 1 to 2 inches in diameter, and borne at the tips of branches or shoots that bear glossy, green leaves. The flowers of many varieties also have a contrasting eye in the center of the bloom. Two forms are grown: somewhat erect types that form moundlike bushes and virtually recumbent trailers.

How to grow: Vinca is at its best in hot conditions—full sun, heat, and high humidity. Grow in warm, rich, well-drained soil. Avoid overwatering to prevent soil-borne diseases. Plant bush types 8 to 12 inches apart; trailing types 12 to 15 inches apart. Avoid planting outdoors before soil is warm.

Propagation: By seed. Sow seeds 12 weeks prior to setting out after last frost. Germination takes 14 to 21 days at a temperature above 70° F. Maintain warm temperatures after germination and be careful not to overwater.

Uses: Trailing types make colorful ground covers and are good edging plants. More upright plants can either back up trailers in the border or combine with other plants. Both types are good container plants. Their heat tolerance makes them ideal for challenging locations.

Related varieties: Creeping kinds include the 'Carpets': 'Dawn,' pink with a rose eye; 'Pink'; 'Snow,' pure white; and 'Magic Carpet Mixture' of all three colors. Uprights include the 'Little' series: 'Blanche,' pure white; 'Bright Eye,' white with a red eye; 'Delicata,' white with a pink eye; and 'Pinkie,' a rosy pink. A new color in vinca is 'Pink Panther,' a fluorescent coral color.

Persian Violet

Exacum affine

Neither a violet nor from Persia, this plant with jewel-like flowers makes a good garden plant. Actually, Persian violets are from Socotra, a small island near the entrance to the Red Sea, and belong to the gentian family.

Description: As a summer flowering plant in the garden, Persian violets can reach 1 foot or more in height, and are very branched, forming a tightly packed clump. The many small leaves are topped by flowers ½ inch in diameter, most often violet-blue in color, although there are also pink and white varieties. Flowers are sweetly scented.

How to grow: Persian violets are easily grown in sunny, warm, humid locations. They prefer moist, well-drained soil and partial protection from the hottest afternoon sun. Since they are very tender, they can only be planted outside after all danger of frost has passed and the ground has warmed. Space 6 to 9 inches apart.

Propagation: By seed or by cuttings. Sow and cover seeds in a seed flat 4 to 5 months prior to planting out in the garden. The very fine seeds take 14 to 21 days to germinate at a temperature of 70° F. After germination, maintain a temperature not below 65° F.

Uses: Plant Persian violets in formal beds or at the front of borders. They also look good along paths and walkways. Plant in containers where their fragrance as well as their color can be enjoyed. Group them in clusters or plant in window boxes.

Related varieties: The 'Midget' series contains blue- and white-flowered varieties. They're dwarf, growing to 10 inches in the garden. 'Tiddly Winks' is a larger variety. The 'Rosendal' series is compact and, in addition to blue and white, has a variety with lilac-rose color.

English Wallflower

Cheiranthus cheiri

These relatives of mustard are perennials in mild winter areas. But they are most often grown for cool season display. Sweetly fragrant, they're grown by the millions in England.

Description: Wallflowers grow from 1 to 2½ feet tall. Many-branched, they're topped by showy terminal spikes in many colors—ranging from creamy white through yellows, oranges, tans and browns, to chestnut red. Some varieties are double.

How to grow: Wallflowers do best in average, moist soil in sun or partial shade in areas where the nighttime summer temperatures are below 65° F. Space 12 to 15 inches apart. Elsewhere they are best for cool season display in spring or fall. They winter over in Zones 8, 9, and 10.

Propagation: By seed. When grown as annuals, sow seeds indoors 6 to 8 weeks before the last frost is expected. Germination takes 5 to 7 days at 55 to 65° F. When transplanting to individual pots, pinch out the tip of the tap root to encourage a bushy root system. Sow seeds in July or August so that plants can winter over for the earliest spring flowering.

Uses: Plant wallflowers in rock gardens, beds, and borders. They are also pleasant by sidewalks and doorsteps. Wallflowers will bloom all winter in a cool room in sunlight. They make good cut flowers, too.

Related species: *Erysimum hieraciifolium* (*Cheiranthus allioni*) is the closely related Siberian wallflower. There are a number of varieties, including 'Early Wonder Mixed Colors.'

Related varieties: Separate, named varieties include: 'Blood Red,' 'Cloth of Gold,' 'Eastern Queen' (salmon-red), 'White Dame,' and 'Fire King' (orange-scarlet). Available mixtures are: 'Bedding Mixed,' growing up to 18 inches and 'Double Dwarf Mixed,' staying below 15 inches.

Zinnia

Zinnia elegans

Zinnias are among the favorite American garden flowers, loved for their variety of colors, which ranges from bold and brassy to muted pastels.

Description: Zinnias are generally grouped into three classes: tall (up to 2½ feet), intermediate (up to 20 inches), and dwarf (up to 12 inches). Leaves and stems are coarse and rough like sandpaper, while the flowers are in almost every color except blue.

How to grow: Zinnias need full sun and rich, fertile soil high in organic matter. They're best in hot, dry climates. Powdery mildew can be a problem in humid locations. Try to avoid watering from above; plant where there is good air movement. Plant them after the final frost when the soil is warm. Space 6 to 12 inches apart, depending on the size of the variety.

Propagation: By seed. Zinnias grow fast, and early bloom can be achieved in most climates by sowing seeds directly into the soil. For earlier bloom, sow seeds indoors 4 weeks prior to planting out. Seeds germinate in 5 to 7 days at 70 to 75° F.

Uses: Dwarf and intermediate varieties can be used in beds and borders or in container plantings. Taller varieties should move to the back of the border or the cutting garden. Zinnias make good cut flowers.

Related species: *Zinnia angustifolia* is a ground-covering species with a prostrate form and single, golden flowers.

Related varieties: Tall varieties: 'Zenith,' hybrids in many separate colors and a mix and 'Giant Flowers, Mixed Colors,' with a variety of colors and flower forms. Medium varieties: 'Border Beauty,' hybrids in separate colors and a mix and 'Cut and Come Again,' with double flowers on long stems. Dwarf varieties: 'Peter Pan,' hybrids with large flowers on short stems and 'Thumbelina,' tiny plants with miniature flowers.

PERENNIALS

Perennials are the backbone of any garden.
Reliable and beautiful, these plants require minimal
maintenance. Every spring, perennials
will come alive once again to fill in your garden with
attractive foliage and beautiful flowers.
With care and planning, your garden can provide an
array of form, texture, and color.

This perennials border, tucked in against a white picket fence, illustrates the beauty of flowers and foliage. The contrast of ground-hugging foliage, arching leaves and blooms, and spiky foxgloves is indeed a sight to behold.

CHAPTER 1

HOW TO PLAN FOR LASTING COLOR

Perennials are plants that survive winter outdoors to produce new growth and flowers each summer. Unlike annuals that flower continuously for several months, most perennials only bloom for two to three weeks. Therefore, it's necessary to plan your garden carefully, in order to have color in perennial beds during selected periods. By carefully working out a plan in advance on paper, you can be assured of a colorful show all season long.

It would be a mistake to place emphasis exclusively on perennial flowers. There is much beauty in the textures and subtle colors of perennial *foliage* as well. Spreading silver-gray mats of cerastium; bold hosta clumps in various shades of blue-green, green and white, and gold; the fine-laced fern fronds—the list of attractive foliage goes on and on. Those who grow perennials tend to be as aware of, and enthusiastic about, foliage as they are about flowers!

Whether you use just a few perennials in bold masses among shrubs or under trees, mix them in with annuals, or specialize in the many varieties of one particular kind, you'll find that perennials provide dependable beauty year after year.

Color

There are several aspects of color that need to be considered when planning perennial plantings. The primary source of color is, of course, from flowers. But another equally important consideration is the color provided by existing backgrounds: fences, house walls, flowering shrubs, or the blossoms in neighboring gardens. If, for example, the background is painted white, white flowers planted against it will become virtually invisible. If the background contains bright red flowers, you may not want the vivid contrast that purple blooms would add. If the area is backed by dark woods or evergreens, you should keep in mind that dark shades of blue and purple will disappear; whites, yellows, silver-grays, and yellow-greens will stand out.

In addition to such physical considerations, there are also emotional ones: Color can be mood setting. Red, yellow, and orange shades are bright, warm, and cheering. On the other hand, blues, silvers, and whites are calming and cooling—they can be very soothing during the heat of summer. A nostalgic, romantic look can be achieved by using pale pastels; a modern, upbeat style results when pure bright colors are mixed. Think about the mood and atmosphere you'd like to create in each area of your garden; it may differ from one location to another and even from one season to the next.

If you feel uncertain about color, you may want to use proven combinations with the help of a color wheel. There are three basic winning combinations. The first is monochromatic—it combines all of the various shades, tints, and tones of a single color. The second is complementary, and includes all of the variations of two colors exactly opposite each other on the color wheel. The last is analogous—those variations of three colors that are found adjacent to one another on the color wheel. These are not the only possible combinations, but they are the easiest to use and the most certain to succeed.

Two final hints on color: 1) White flowers will blend easily with any other colors you select; and 2) Varying the intensity of different flower colors in your design will often help add vitality and interest to the planting.

Although you'll want to plan the colors for your garden with care, inevitably some of your choices will not work out as happily as you'd envisioned. Don't be *too* worried about getting it all exactly right in advance. You can always move or remove those plants that do not blend well. Part of the fun in gardening is to make adjustments and changes from season to season.

This planting of perennials has a nostalgic, romantic look.

Full Color Wheel

A color wheel can be a helpful tool in choosing flower colors that blend well together. All of the shades, tints, and tones, as well as the pure color of any spoke on the color wheel, will automatically combine well.

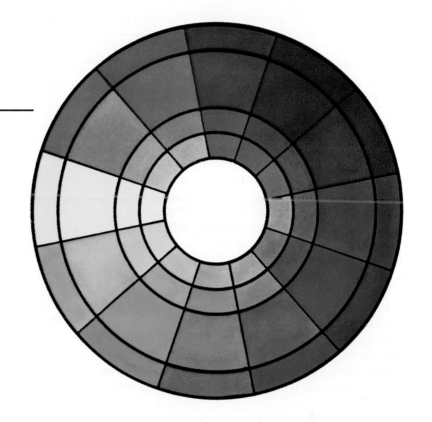

Monochromatic Colors

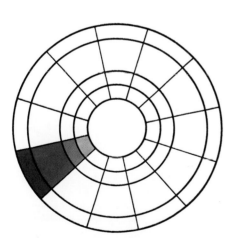

A monochromatic design is one in which all of the flower colors are in a single color line. The only variety will be in their range—from dark, to intense, to pastel shades of that one color: i.e., from navy blue, to bright blue, to baby blue.

Analogous Colors

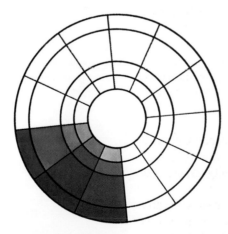

Analogous designs include flowers of any of the hues in any three spokes that are side-by-side on the color wheel: for example, all the blue shades, plus all of the blue-violet shades, and all of the violet shades.

Complementary Colors

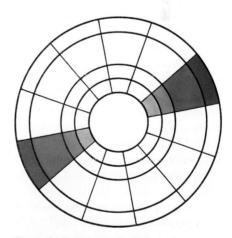

Using two colors opposite each other on the color wheel will produce a complementary color scheme. Starting again with blue, this would blend all of the clear blues with all of the clear oranges.

Form & Texture

Contrast of color, form, and texture can be very pleasing.

Most people give little thought to the forms and textures of plants, even though they are important aspects of perennials because, for a good part of the growing season when they're not in bloom, that's all that is to be enjoyed. In fact, in the case of some perennials, form and texture are *all* that matters: fern clumps take us from the early spring unfolding of their fiddleheads through the fully open filigree of their fronds and on to their golden autumn color. Flowers are not used for this effect at all. Many hostas, stonecrops, and ornamental grasses are also better known for their foliage effects than for their flowers. In other cases, plants may have two very different forms, depending on whether or not they are in bloom. In these instances, it is better to use the forms of these plants when they are not in bloom.

An extra bonus to be savored and utilized in the landscape is a plant that has lovely blossoms as well as an attractive growth habit. The flowers themselves vary in form and texture, too: the huge, airy clouds of baby's breath; tall, handsome spires of delphinium and foxtail lilies; the round pompoms of chrysanthemums and peonies; and the graceful arches of bleeding heart—each bloom perfectly heart-shaped.

Among perennials, there are some outstandingly handsome examples of foliage and form. Peonies have a rugged, bold leaf cluster that turns to wonderful shades of pink or bronze in the autumn; hostas provide dramatic low clumps that can be used alone or combined with other plants; the blue-gray globe thistle foliage makes a handsome bush; and the tall, slender Japanese and Siberian iris foliage provides a wonderful spiky contrast to round-leaved neighbors.

Fortunately, many perennials offer this added bonus of interesting texture and/or form to the garden. In many instances, they also offer a color contrast as well. Use plants with these bonuses wherever possible, although it doesn't mean you should completely bypass those that only have attractive blooms to their credit. Instead, intermix the outstanding stars with the duller kinds. A good idea is to intermingle the various forms and textures of perennials or to repeat forms at regular intervals for a sense of rhythm and flow. In a smaller garden, finer, feathery textures should dominate; in a larger garden, there is sufficient space for coarse textures to be prevalent. Using these simple hints, you'll produce a completed planting, which is interesting throughout the growing season—whether in bloom or not.

The Varied Forms of Perennials

The form, or shape, of perennials is important to consider when designing a garden. By selecting plants with varying forms, the garden will be more interesting to look at. Ground-hugging mats; tall, spiked growth; as well as arching and rounded plants provide a visual variety you'll enjoy even when the plants aren't in bloom.

Ground-hugging

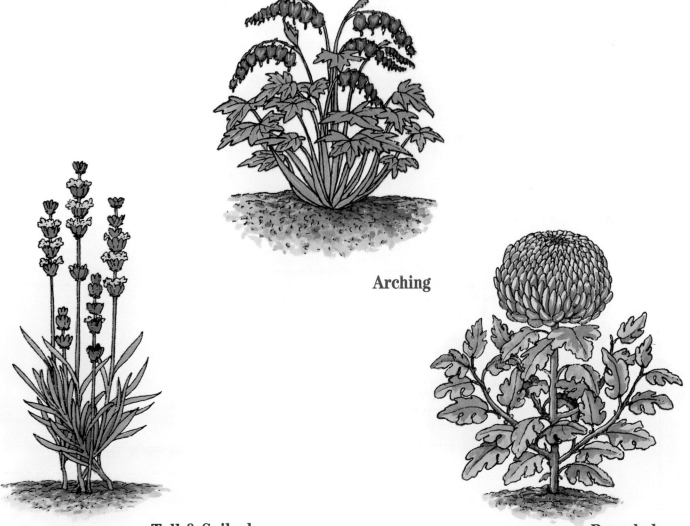

Arching

Tall & Spiked

Rounded

Textures of Perennials

A variety of textures adds to a garden's beauty. Placing plants with feathery foliage or flowers next to ones that have coarse, bold characteristics will produce a dramatic-looking garden. It's helpful to pretest how plants will look together by placing potted samples side by side. Another way to discover good plant partners is by studying how they look together in other people's gardens or in magazine and book photos. Don't be ashamed to copy a good idea!

Feathery

Coarse & Bold

Some plants add interest with patterned foliage or flowers: stripes, spots, or splotches of color all provide variety to the basic forms. Some flowers are two-toned, with outer petals of one color and inner ones of another; other plants have lower petals (iris, for example) of one shade and upper ones of another shade. Used in a limited way, these patterns can be an asset. Beware of adding too many plants with patterned foliage or flowers in a small area—it's possible to have too much of a good thing! In that case, you'll end up with a hodge-podge collection instead of a pleasing design.

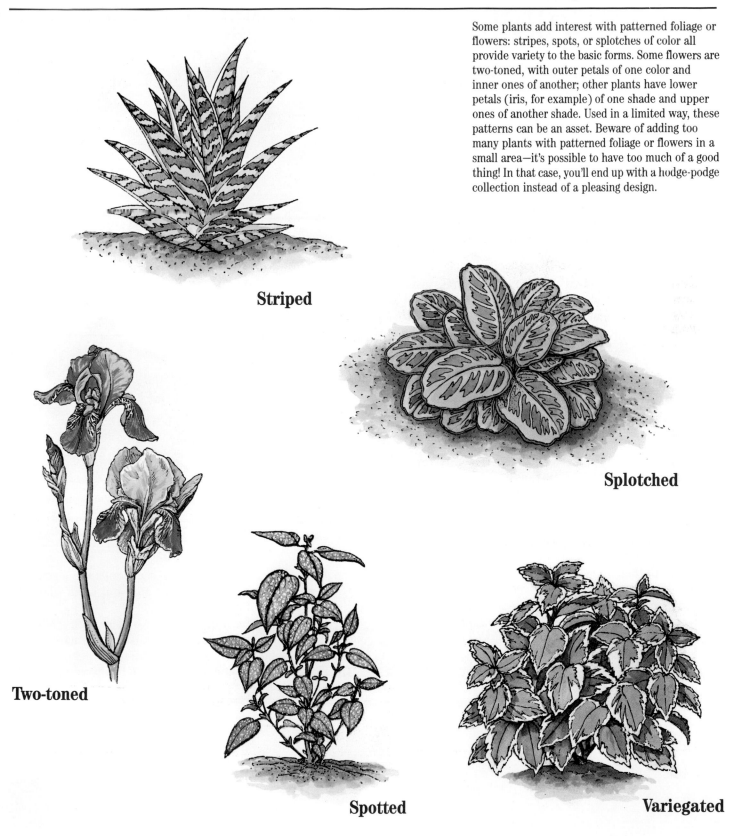

Striped

Splotched

Two-toned

Spotted

Variegated

Selecting Perennials for Color & Characteristics

Gardening with perennials is certainly a rewarding undertaking. The plants are very long-lived, versatile, and undemanding. However, if a gardener is planning to use more than one kind of perennial for a planting, certain factors must be taken into consideration.

Most people prefer to mix different perennial varieties in their gardens, even though it requires a bit more work and planning. Available colors, height of plants, shade or sun preference, soil requirements—all of these factors have to be given attention. Perennial plant textures and forms are two other factors that need to be considered.

Planning a perennial garden in advance is the only way to make sure that a perennial bed is balanced and that the plants work well together in terms of sun or shade, height, soil, form, and texture. For those gardeners who are willing to put in more time and effort, underplanting a perennial garden with bulbs and annuals is another approach that may be considered.

If you list your favorite plants on paper first, noting their available colors and cultural requirements, you're off to a good start. As you narrow down those that work well together, you can actually see a workable garden emerge in front of you. By taking this extra bit of time, you can save yourself from being disappointed later.

The charts that follow are a quick reference for selecting plants for your garden. However, it should be kept in mind that they give only a simplistic first screening. When scanning these lists, you may find many plants that seem appropriate for your garden. However, on further investigation, you'll find that some of them aren't appropriate after all. Use the charts to narrow down the choices; then refer to the more detailed description in the "Encyclopedia of Perennial Favorites," starting on page 248, to identify those best-suited to your climate, soil, and light conditions.

It's important to remember that the "Multicolor" category lists those plants that come in nearly every color range (any perennial that comes in more than three color ranges has been

Perennials of different colors, shapes, and textures can be planted together successfully.

put into this category). Because it contains the most universal and versatile perennials, be sure to use it often when making your selections.

Whether you are a novice or a gardener with many years of planting experience, using a chart with information on color, light, soil, and height can be the difference between a picture-perfect garden and one that just doesn't quite work.

MULTICOLOR FLOWERS

	Dry Soil	Average Soil	Moist Soil	Full Sun	Part Shade	Full Shade	Under 12 Inches	12-24 Inches	Over 24 Inches	Vining
Astilbe		•	•	•				•	•	
Balloon Flower		•	•	•	•			•	•	
Beard Tongue	•			•				•		
Bergamot			•	•					•	
Bergenia, Heartleaf			•		•			•		
Bishop's Hat		•	•				•			
Chrysanthemum		•		•				•	•	
Columbine		•	•		•			•	•	
Coralbell		•	•	•	•			•		
Crane's-Bill		•		•				•	•	
Daisy, Michaelmas		•		•			•	•	•	
Daylily		•	•	•	•			•	•	
Delphinium		•	•	•					•	
Fleabane		•		•				•		
Indigo, False	•	•		•	•				•	
Iris		•	•	•			•	•	•	
Knapweed	•	•		•				•	•	
Lungwort			•		•	•		•		
Lupine			•	•					•	
Mallow, Rose		•	•	•	•				•	
Peony		•		•	•				•	
Phlox, Garden		•		•	•				•	
Pincushion Flower		•		•	•		•			
Pink		•		•			•	•		
Poppy (Oriental)		•		•					•	
Primrose, Japanese			•		•			•		
Rose, Rock		•		•			•			
Rue, Meadow			•	•	•				•	
Self-heal		•	•	•	•	•				
Speedwell		•		•	•			•		
Spiderwort		•		•	•			•		
Stonecrop	•	•		•			•	•		
Thrift	•			•		•				
Yarrow	•	•		•	•			•	•	

BLUE TO PURPLE FLOWERS

	Dry Soil	Average Soil	Moist Soil	Full Sun	Part Shade	Full Shade	Under 12 Inches	12-24 Inches	Over 24 Inches	Vining
Ageratum, Hardy			•	•	•			•		
Aster, Stoke's		•		•				•		
Bellflower		•	•	•	•		•	•	•	
Bluestar	•	•		•	•				•	
Bugleweed		•		•	•	•				
Bugloss, Italian		•		•					•	
Bugloss, Siberian			•	•	•	•	•			
Cardinal Flower			•		•				•	
Clematis, Bush		•	•	•	•				•	

BLUE TO PURPLE FLOWERS (continued)

	Dry Soil	Average Soil	Moist Soil	Full Sun	Part Shade	Full Shade	Under 12 Inches	12-24 Inches	Over 24 Inches	Vining
Coneflower, Purple		•		•					•	
Cupid's Dart		•		•				•		
Forget-Me-Not, Chinese	•	•	•	•				•	•	
Holly, Sea	•			•				•	•	
Hosta		•	•	•	•	•	•			
Lavender	•	•		•				•		
Lavender, Sea	•	•		•				•		
Lily, Toad		•	•		•				•	
Lily Turf, Big Blue		•		•	•		•	•		
Loosestrife, Purple		•	•	•	•				•	
Periwinkle		•	•	•	•		•			
Rockcress (*Aubrieta*)	•	•		•			•			
Sage, Russian	•	•		•					•	
Salvia		•		•					•	
Thistle, Globe		•		•	•				•	

RED FLOWERS

	Dry Soil	Average Soil	Moist Soil	Full Sun	Part Shade	Full Shade	Under 12 Inches	12-24 Inches	Over 24 Inches	Vining
Avens		•	•	•				•		
Blanket Flower		•		•				•		
Cardinal Flower			•		•				•	

PINK TO FUCHSIA FLOWERS

	Dry Soil	Average Soil	Moist Soil	Full Sun	Part Shade	Full Shade	Under 12 Inches	12-24 Inches	Over 24 Inches	Vining
Anemone, Japanese		•	•	•	•				•	
Baby's Breath		•		•			•	•	•	
Blazingstar		•		•					•	
Bleeding Heart			•		•		•			
Butterfly Weed	•	•		•					•	
Coneflower, Purple		•		•					•	
Gas Plant		•	•	•					•	
Knotweed		•	•	•				•		
Mallow	•	•		•	•				•	
Meadowsweet		•	•	•	•				•	
Nettle, Dead		•			•		•			
Obedient Plant		•	•	•	•		•			
Pea, Perennial	•	•		•	•					•
Poppy, Plume		•	•	•					•	
Rockcress (*Aubrieta*)	•	•				•				
Rock Cress (*Arabis*)	•			•			•			
Rodgersia			•		•				•	
Rose, Christmas			•		•			•		
Soapwort		•	•	•					•	
Turtlehead			•	•	•				•	

These cultural recommendations are intended to suggest the average conditions over a wide geographical area. It is important to be aware of local requirements.

YELLOW TO ORANGE FLOWERS

	Dry Soil	Average Soil	Moist Soil	Full Sun	Part Shade	Full Shade	Under 12 Inches	12-24 Inches	Over 24 Inches	Vining
Aster, Golden		•		•	•			•		
Avens		•	•	•			•			
Basket-of-Gold		•		•		•				
Blanket Flower		•		•			•			
Buttercup, Creeping			•	•	•		•			
Butterfly Weed	•	•		•				•		
Coneflower, Yellow		•	•	•			•	•		
Coreopsis		•		•			•	•	•	
Foxglove, Yellow			•		•				•	
Globeflower			•	•	•		•			
Goldenrod		•	•	•				•		
Goldenstar			•	•	•		•			
Inula		•		•			•			
Lady's Mantle		•	•	•	•		•			
Leopard's-bane		•	•		•		•			
Ligularia			•		•				•	
Lily, Blackberry		•		•					•	
Loosestrife, Gooseneck			•	•					•	
Lupine, Carolina		•		•					•	
Ox-Eye		•	•	•					•	
Sneezeweed			•	•					•	
Sundrop		•		•			•			
Sunflower, Perennial		•	•	•					•	

GRASSES AND FOLIAGE

	Dry Soil	Average Soil	Moist Soil	Full Sun	Part Shade	Full Shade	Under 12 Inches	12-24 Inches	Over 24 Inches	Vining
Bugleweed		•		•	•		•			
Goutweed	•	•	•	•	•	•	•			
Grass, Blue Oat		•		•					•	
Grass, Fountain		•		•					•	
Grass, Japanese Blood		•		•	•			•		
Grass, Zebra		•		•					•	
Hosta		•	•	•	•	•		•	•	
Houttuynia			•	•	•		•			
Lamb's-Ear		•		•			•	•		
Lily Turf, Big Blue		•	•	•			•	•		
Nettle, Dead		•		•			•			
Oats, Sea		•		•	•				•	
Pachysandra			•		•	•	•			
Spurge, Cushion		•		•	•		•			

GRASSES AND FOLIAGE (continued)

	Dry Soil	Average Soil	Moist Soil	Full Sun	Part Shade	Full Shade	Under 12 Inches	12-24 Inches	Over 24 Inches	Vining
Stonecrop	•	•		•			•	•		
Wormwood	•	•		•				•		

WHITE TO GREEN FLOWERS

	Dry Soil	Average Soil	Moist Soil	Full Sun	Part Shade	Full Shade	Under 12 Inches	12-24 Inches	Over 24 Inches	Vining
Anemone, Japanese		•	•	•	•				•	
Aster, Stoke's		•		•				•		
Baby's Breath		•		•			•	•	•	
Bellflower		•	•	•	•		•	•		
Blazingstar		•		•					•	
Bleeding Heart		•	•		•			•		
Boltonia		•		•					•	
Bowman's-Root		•		•	•				•	
Bugleweed		•		•	•		•			
Candytuft		•		•			•			
Chives, Chinese		•		•	•			•		
Clematis, Bush		•	•	•					•	
Cohosh, Black		•	•	•					•	
Coneflower, Purple		•		•					•	
Cupid's Dart		•		•				•		
Edelweiss	•			•			•			
Everlasting, Pearly		•		•				•		
Gas Plant		•	•	•					•	
Gaura		•		•					•	
Goat's Beard			•	•	•				•	
Hosta		•	•	•	•	•		•	•	
Houttuynia			•	•	•		•			
Lily Turf, Big Blue		•		•	•		•	•		
Loosestrife, Gooseneck			•	•					•	
Mallow	•	•		•	•				•	
Meadowsweet		•	•	•	•				•	
Nettle, Dead		•		•				•		
Obedient Plant		•	•	•				•	•	
Pea, Perennial	•	•		•	•					•
Periwinkle		•	•	•	•		•			
Poppy, Plume		•	•						•	
Rock Cress (*Arabis*)	•			•			•			
Rodgersia			•		•				•	
Rose, Christmas			•		•		•			
Soapweed		•		•					•	
Soapwort		•	•	•					•	

These cultural recommendations are intended to suggest the average conditions over a wide geographical area. It is important to be aware of local requirements.

Gardening in Color

These six pictures illustrate the various colors of perennials. Plantings of one color can be mood-setting—from dramatic and bold, to cheerful and sunny, to soft and delicate. A gardener can make a strong statement by the color selected for each specific planting.

Bluish-purple delphiniums look cool on a hot summer day.

This planting of red stonecrops is bold and eye-catching.

Pink flowers provide a soft and delicate touch.

Yellow coreopsis and blanket flowers are certainly cheerful.

Zebra grass has a windblown beauty all its own.

White blooms in a perennials garden are dainty and airy.

Sequence of Bloom

Color throughout the growing season is achieved by planning a succession of bloom provided by different species.

Because individual perennials have a limited season of bloom, it's important to know when you can expect each of them to flower. If you want color throughout the entire growing season, you'll need to plan on a succession of bloom provided by different species. With proper planning, it's possible to do this entirely with perennials, even though perennials don't have to stand alone. To obtain summer-long bloom, it's possible to intermix annuals with perennials—the annuals will provide additional flower color from midsummer to late summer.

Also remember that perennial and annual bulbs offer additional summer color possibilities. Gladiolus, tuberoses, fritillarias, resurrection lilies, and, in warm climates, creeping buttercups, can be tucked into small spaces between other plants to provide additional color. Most varied and beautiful are the many hardy lilies that provide an outstanding display of different colors and forms throughout the summer.

Summer isn't the only season when bulbs add beauty to the landscape. All of the spring-flowering bulbs—tulips, daffodils, flowering onions, crocuses, scillas, snowdrops, hyacinths, anemones, etc.—are certainly well known, popular, and easily grown perennial additions to most gardens.

Plant bulbs so the flower stems will be taller than the adjacent plants—this way, their lovely display will be fully visible. After the blooms die, remove the dead flowers in order to direct as much plant energy as possible back into forming large bulbs for next year's growth and blooms. As the flower stems and leaves die back, they'll disappear below the level of adjacent plant foliage and be hidden from view.

When developing your garden plan, avoid clumping all of the plants that bloom at the same time in one part of the garden. Be sure to have a balance of early, mid-season, and late bloomers mixed throughout the planting area.

At first, the idea of intermixing and underplanting may sound too complex. Don't become discouraged. Although it's difficult to plant a well-balanced perennial garden by simply digging holes in the ground and poking plants into them, the job becomes fairly simple if you take the time to draw up a plan on paper in advance. This lets you detect any problems and change them before you ever buy or plant anything. There will probably still be some changes to be made from year to year as you discover new plants you'd like to add, existing plants that you decide to abandon and replace because they never seem to prosper, and others that you feel would look better in a different location.

The Four Seasons
of a Perennials Garden

These four photographs show the same perennials garden during the four main blooming seasons, with different plants in flower during each period.

Spring Border: Pinks (*Dianthus* 'Essex Witch'), bellflowers (*Campanula latifolia* 'Brantwood'), and Siberian irises (*Iris sibirica* 'Ruffled Velvet').

Early Summer Border: False indigo (*Baptisia* species) and early daylilies (*Hemerocallis* species).

Late Summer Border: Daylilies (*Hemerocallis* 'Green Flutter'), shasta daisies (*Chrysanthemum* x *superbum*), meadowsweet (*Filipendula rubra*), and purple loosestrife (*Lythrum Salicaria*).

Fall Border: Stonecrop (*Sedum spectabile*), sunflowers (*Helianthus* x *multiflorus*), Japanese anemone (*Anemone* species), golden asters (*Chrysopsis mariana*), wormwood (*Artemisia* species), and big blue lily turfs (*Liriope Muscari*).

Selecting Perennials by Bloom Date

T his bloom date chart is designed for Zone 7. Bloom time is approximately 10-14 days earlier for each zone south and 10-14 days later for each zone north for each given entry.

EARLY SPRING

February–March

Christmas Rose; Lenten Rose; Hellebore	*Helleborus* species

LATE SPRING

April–May

Avens	*Geum* species
Basket-of-Gold; Goldentuft; Madwort	*Aurinia saxatilis*
Heartleaf Bergenia	*Bergenia cordifolia*
Bishop's Hat; Barrenwort	*Epimedium* species
Bleeding Heart	*Dicentra* species
Bluestar; Blue-Dogbane; Blue-Star-of-Texas	*Amsonia tabernaemontana*
Creeping Buttercup	*Ranunculus repens*
Candytuft	*Iberis sempervirens*
Bush Clematis; Upright Clematis	*Clematis recta*
Columbine	*Aquilegia* species
Coralbell; Alumroot	*Heuchera sanguinea*
Crane's-Bill	*Geranium* species
Painted Daisy	*Chrysanthemum coccineum*
Edelweiss	*Leontopodium alpinum*
Fleabane	*Erigeron hybridus*
Chinese Forget-Me-Not	*Cynoglossum nervosum*
Gas Plant; Burning Bush	*Dictamnus albus*
Globeflower	*Trollius* x *cultorum*
Goat's Beard; Wild Spirea	*Aruncus dioicus*
Goldenstar	*Chrysogonum virginianum*

LATE SPRING

April–May

False Indigo; Wild Indigo	*Baptisia australis*
Iris	*Iris* species
Knotweed; Himalaya Fleece Flower	*Polygonum affine*
Lady's Mantle	*Alchemilla* species
Leopard's-bane	*Doronicum cordatum*
Lungwort; Jerusalem Sage	*Pulmonaria officinalis*
Carolina Lupine; Aaron's Rod	*Thermopsis caroliniana*
Dead Nettle	*Lamium maculatum*
Peony	*Paeonia* species
Periwinkle; Myrtle	*Vinca minor*
Pink; Carnation	*Dianthus* species
Poppy	*Papaver orientale*
Japanese Primrose	*Primula Sieboldii*
Rockcress	*Aubrieta deltoidea*
Rock Cress	*Arabis caucasica*
Meadow Rue	*Thalictrum aquilegifolium*
Sundrop; Evening Primrose	*Oenothera* species
Thrift; Sea Pink	*Armeria maritima*

SUMMER

June–August

Japanese Anemone	*Anemone* species
Golden Aster	*Chrysopsis mariana*
Stoke's Aster	*Stokesia laevis*
Astilbe; Garden Spiraea	*Astilbe* species
Avens	*Geum* species
Baby's Breath	*Gypsophila paniculata*
Balloon Flower	*Platycodon grandiflorus*
Beard Tongue	*Penstemon barbatus*
Bellflower	*Campanula* species
Bergamot; Bee-Balm; Oswego-Tea	*Monarda didyma*
Blanket Flower	*Gaillardia* x *grandiflora*
Blazingstar; Gayfeather	*Liatris* species
Bleeding Heart	*Dicentra* species
Italian Bugloss	*Anchusa azurea*
Creeping Buttercup	*Ranunculus repens*
Butterfly Weed; Milkweed	*Asclepias tuberosa*
Cardinal Flower	*Lobelia Cardinalis*
Cinquefoil	*Potentilla thurberi*
Bush Clematis; Upright Clematis	*Clematis recta*
Black Cohosh	*Cimicifuga racemosa*
Yellow Coneflower; Black-eyed Susan	*Rudbeckia fulgida*
Coralbell, Alumroot	*Heuchera sanguinea*
Coreopsis	*Coreopsis* species
Crane's-Bill	*Geranium* species
Cupid's Dart	*Catananche caerulea*
Michaelmas Daisy	*Aster* species
Painted Daisy	*Chrysanthemum coccineum*

SUMMER

June–August

Shasta Daisy	*Chrysanthemum* x *superbum*
Daylily	*Hemerocallis* species
Delphinium; Larkspur	*Delphinium* species
Pearly Everlasting	*Anaphalis* species
Feverfew	*Chrysanthemum Parthenium*
Fleabane	*Erigeron hybridus*
Chinese Forget-Me-Not	*Cynoglossum nervosum*
Yellow Foxglove	*Digitalis grandiflora*
Gas Plant; Burning Bush	*Dictamnus albus*
Gaura	*Gaura Lindheimeri*
Goat's Beard; Wild Spirea	*Aruncus dioicus*
Goldenrod	*Solidago* hybrids
Feather Reed Grass	*Calamagrostis acutiflora stricta*
Fountain Grass	*Pennisetum alopecuroides*
Sea Holly	*Eryngium* species
Inula	*Inula ensifolia*
Iris	*Iris* species
Knapweed	*Centaurea* species
Ladybells	*Adenophora confusa*
Lavender	*Lavandula angustifolia*
Sea Lavender	*Limonium latifolium*
Ligularia	*Ligularia* species
Blackberry Lily; Leopard Lily	*Belamcanda chinensis*
Big Blue Lily Turf	*Liriope Muscari*
Gooseneck Loosestrife	*Lysimachia clethroides*
Purple Loosestrife	*Lythrum Salicaria*
Lupine	*Thermopsis caroliniana*
Carolina Lupine; Aaron's Rod	*Lupinus polyphyllus*
Mallow	*Malva Alcea*
Rose Mallow; Swamp Mallow	*Hibiscus Moscheutos*
Dead Nettle	*Lamium maculatum*
Sea Oats	*Chasmanthium latifolium*
Obedient Plant; False Dragonhead	*Physostegia virginiana*
Ox-Eye; False Sunflower	*Heliopsis helianthoides*
Perennial Pea; Sweet Pea	*Lathyrus latifolius*
Garden Phlox	*Phlox paniculata*
Pincushion Flower	*Scabiosa caucasica*
Plume Poppy	*Macleaya cordata*
Rodgersia	*Rodgersia aesculifolia*
Rock Rose; Sun Rose; Frostweed	*Helianthemum nummularium*
Russian Sage	*Perovskia* species
Salvia; Meadow Sage	*Salvia* x *superba*
Self-heal	*Prunella Webbiana*
Sneezeweed; Swamp Sunflower	*Helenium autumnale*
Soapweed	*Yucca glauca*
Soapwort; Bouncing Bet	*Saponaria officinalis*
Speedwell	*Veronica spicata*
Spiderwort	*Tradescantia* x *Andersoniana*

SUMMER

June–August

Perennial Sunflower	*Helianthus* x *multiflorus*
Globe Thistle	*Echinops Ritro*
Red Valerian; Jupiter's-Beard	*Centhranthus ruber*
Yellow Waxbell	*Kirengeshoma palmata*
Wormwood	*Artemisia* species
Yarrow	*Achillea* species

FALL

September–Frost

Hardy Ageratum; Mist Flower	*Eupatorium coelestinum*
Japanese Anemone	*Anemone* species
Golden Aster	*Chrysopsis mariana*
Siberian Aster	*Aster* species
Beard Tongue	*Penstemon barbatus*
Bleeding Heart	*Dicentra* species
Boltonia	*Boltonia asteroides*
Chinese Chives; Garlic Chives	*Allium tuberosum*
Chrysanthemum	*Chrysanthemum* species
Bush Clematis; Upright Clematis	*Clematis recta*
Coralbell; Alumroot	*Heuchera sanguinea*
Coreopsis	*Coreopsis* species
Michaelmas Daisy	*Aster* species
Shasta Daisy	*Chrysanthemum maximum*
Feather Reed Grass	*Calamagrostis acutiflora stricta*
Fountain Grass	*Pennisetum alopecuroides*
Maiden Grass	*Miscanthus sinensis* 'Gracillimus'
Zebra Grass	*Miscanthus sinensis* 'Zebrinus'
Gaura	*Gaura Lindheimeri*
Ladybells	*Adenophora confusa*
Toad Lily	*Liriope Muscari*
Big Blue Lily Turf	*Tricyrtis hirta*
Mallow	*Malva Alcea*
Rose Mallow	*Hibiscus Moscheutos*
Obedient Plant; False Dragonhead	*Physostegia virginiana*
Ox-Eye; False Sunflower	*Heliopsis helianthoides*
Sea Oats	*Chasmanthium latifolium*
Russian Sage	*Perovskia* species
Salvia; Meadow Sage	*Salvia* x *superba*
Sneezeweed; Swamp Sunflower	*Helenium autumnale*
Soapwort; Bouncing Bet	*Saponaria officinalis*
Speedwell	*Veronica spicata*
Stonecrop	*Sedum spectabile*
Perennial Sunflower	*Helianthus* x *multiflorus*
Wormwood	*Artemisia* species

This pleasing garden shows the variety of perennials that can be planted together. The different hues, forms, and textures combine to produce a garden that is soothing to the eye. This garden is truly a perennials oasis.

CHAPTER 2

GETTING YOUR GARDEN OFF TO A GOOD START

Unlike beds for annuals or vegetables, perennial plant beds are not dug up and replanted every year. Once perennials are planted, there will be no need to do more than routine weeding, feeding, cultivation, and mulching for several years.

This chapter contains instructions for proper flower bed preparation, as well as information on plant propagation. Strong, healthy plants are better able to survive such difficulties as drought, insect infestations, and diseases. Learn how to get your garden off to a good start. This will almost certainly result in less work in the long run!

Also included is information about how to properly handle pre-grown, potted, and bare-root plants. The hints in these sections will help you to reduce plant loss during the critical transplanting stages. You'll also learn what to look for when selecting plants at the nursery or garden center, so that you can be sure that the plants you buy are in good, healthy condition.

Study the information contained here before laying out and tilling your perennial planting areas or purchasing any plants. You'll find the time spent studying this information in advance will save much future effort.

Transplanting from Pots

Many garden shops and nurseries offer an extensive variety of perennials planted in containers. Whereas in the past there were just a few mail-order specialists from whom the more unusual perennials could be purchased, it's now possible to obtain what you want locally. This allows you to select the individual plants you prefer and to see their condition before you buy.

Potted perennials are offered in a number of sizes from small plants in 3- to 4-inch pots to mature plants in gallon-sized, metal or plastic containers. The small plants are usually only a few months old. In most instances, these will not produce blooms the first season. Those in large containers are often in bloom at the time of purchase and can be expected to quickly become established in their new sites. Smaller plants usually cost less than larger ones; when small plants are priced high, it's because they're rare or exceedingly slow or difficult to propagate. Containerized plants should be planted outdoors as promptly as possible after purchase. The longer they're kept in containers, the more likely they are to dry out and become pot-bound. If you *must* hold plants for a long time prior to planting, place them where they'll be under light shade, and be sure to water them. When you're ready to plant container-grown plants, thoroughly moisten the soil before knocking them out of the pot. Plunge the container into a pail of water to above the pot's rim for a few minutes. Snap off any roots sticking out of the pot bottom. The plant should slide out into your hand. If it doesn't, run a knife blade around the inside of the pot to help release the root ball. If all else fails, break off the pot by knocking it against something solid; in the case of plastic or metal containers, cut them open and peel them off, avoiding damage to the roots as much as is reasonably possible.

Loosen and remove any excess soil from around the roots. Most soil-less mixes will fall away on their own. If the mix adheres to the roots, take away only as much as comes off easily with your fingers. Soil-less mixes dry faster than garden soil, so you want to eliminate what you can without badly disturbing the root ball.

Always place the plant in the ground at the same depth as it was in the pot and provide a water-holding area by forming a soil dam a few inches away from the stem. Transplant in the evening or on a cloudy day; otherwise, provide shade for three to four days by setting an overturned box or a newspaper cone over each plant. Tuck a 2-inch mulch layer around the plants and deep water as needed the first growing season.

These nursery-grown perennials are well cared for.

Transplanting Potted Plants

1 Submerge potted plants in water before transplanting; this helps the plant to slide out of the container more easily. To avoid damage to the plant top and help keep the root ball intact, spread your hand over the top of the pot with stems and leaves poking out between your fingers. Then turn the pot upside down and gently tap its rim against something solid to loosen the root ball from the sides of the pot. The plant will slide out of the pot into your hand.

2 If the plant root ball is tightly packed with roots, these should be gently loosened. They need to spread out after planting, rather than continue to grow in a tight mass. If they resist loosening with your fingers, cut up into the sides of the root ball in several places with a sharp knife or scissors, then shake the roots loose a bit more with your fingers before planting. If roots are not tightly packed, skip this step. **Note:** Knock only one plant out at a time to avoid exposing the roots to the drying qualities of air and light.

 3

The plant hole should be somewhat larger in diameter than the root ball and deep enough to allow you to plant at the same depth as the plant was growing in the container. Fan out the loosened roots over a small soil mound in the center of the hole to encourage spreading root growth.

4 Refill the hole with soil, then firm the soil around the plant stem and roots. Create a soil dam around the plant and fill it with water. As the water soaks in, it will help settle the soil and remove any remaining air pockets around the roots—air pockets can cause delicate feeder roots to dry out and die. Lay a 2-inch layer of mulch around the crown and under trailing foliage.

Setting Bare-Root Plants

The term "bare-root" is self-explanatory: There is *no* soil around the plant roots when you unpack the plant, although there is often a bit of moist excelsior packing. Plants sent by mail order are usually packed bare-root; you can also occasionally find perennials in garden centers that are packed this way.

This technique of packing works perfectly well and is in no way harmful to the plants, as long as the roots have remained moist in transit. If you find the roots are bone dry when you receive your shipment, there is some cause for concern. If this happens, thoroughly soak the plant roots immediately, then plant them outdoors after they've had an hour or so to take up water. Most will revitalize; report any that don't show signs of new growth after three weeks, explaining the dry condition upon arrival. Plant supply houses are so experienced in packing bare-root plants that there is seldom a problem; when there is, it's usually because the shipment was somehow delayed in transit.

Ideally, bare-root plants should be planted immediately. If that's impossible, unpack them right away and place their roots in a container of water (do not submerge the tops). The sooner they're planted, the less energy they lose. If you must delay planting, pot the plants in containers and grow them as potted plants until you're ready to plant them in the ground.

Most perennials are best transplanted in the spring or, as a second choice, in the fall. Bearded irises, oriental poppies, and peonies usually fare better if moved only in the fall. The best planting periods for bare-root plants are: Northeast coast, spring and early to late fall; inland Northeast, spring and early fall; middle-Atlantic coast, mid- to late fall; Southeast, mid- to late fall and early spring; Midwest, spring and late summer to early fall; the Plains, spring and early to mid-fall; eastern side of the Rockies, spring; Pacific Northwest coast, early spring and fall; California, early spring and mid- to late fall; and the Southwest, early to mid-spring.

Place bare-root plants at the same depth as in the nursery—look for the soil line on the stem as a guide. However, those that arrive as dormant roots have no stems or top growth as indicators. The depths at which to plant these types are: oriental poppy—top of root 2 to 3 inches below soil surface; peony—lay root flat with top of clump 1 inch below soil surface; bearded iris—lay flat with top of clump right at, or very slightly above, the soil surface.

Oriental poppies are perennials that are often planted bare-rooted.

When planting bare-root plants, don't just dig a small hole and jam the roots into it. Make the hole large enough so you can carefully spread the roots out in all directions. Aftercare is the same as for containerized plants from this stage onward.

Planting Bare-Root Plants

1 Unpack bare-root plants as soon as they arrive, planting them as quickly as possible. Always keep the roots moist and away from the wind and sun—they don't have any soil around them to help protect their feeder roots from drying out! Trim any extra long or damaged roots with sharp scissors before planting. Inspect, trim, and plant one transplant at a time to avoid extended exposure to air and sun.

2 Set the plant in the hole so the soil line on the plant is at the same level as it was in the nursery. Spread out the roots evenly over a soil mound to help encourage well-rounded root growth.

3 Fill in the soil firmly around the roots, then fill the dam with water, and mulch. Provide shade to the new transplant for one day with an overturned box, newspaper cone, or similar shading.

214

Buying Healthy Plants

Although most garden centers try very hard to supply healthy plants in peak condition—free of disease and insect infestations—it's still possible for problems to escape their notice. A reputable retailer will certainly replace any plants that you may purchase and find to be sick after getting them home. However, by then the damage of passing the problem on to other plants in your garden may already have been done. It is far better to learn what to look for, so that you can protect yourself as much as possible from this kind of problem!

First and foremost, observe the degree of care or neglect that the plants receive at each nursery or garden center. If plants appear wilted, leaves are sun-scorched, or the soil is bone dry, it's probably not a one-time happening. Each time a plant wilts badly, it loses strength. If the retailer doesn't water regularly and does not provide shade for the more vulnerable and shade-loving plants, it's very likely that the plants will be in a weakened condition when you buy them. This, in turn, makes them more susceptible to disease and insect infestations, because they have less strength with which to survive such problems.

Unless you buy the plants very early in the season before they've gone through many wilting cycles, it's best not to purchase plants from a source where they haven't received proper care. There are many alternative sources where good care is given. Look for strong, vital, healthy new growth, and plants that have been handled properly.

You also want to inspect each plant carefully for signs of infestation. Signs of problems include: stippled holes dotting leaves (leafhoppers); squiggly trails on leaves (leaf miners); extremely fine webs on underside of leaves (red spiders); stickiness on plant stems and leaves (red spiders or aphids); colonies of tiny, soft-bodied bugs on flower buds and growth tips (aphids); ants busily running up and down stems (aphids); whitish fluff that turns sticky if pinched (mealybugs); hard, round or oval, shell-like formations on stems (scale); clouds of tiny white insects rising from the plant when you touch it (white flies); leaf edges chewed (caterpillars); grayish-white powder on leaves (mildew); and plant tips wilted, while lower stems and leaves are not (stem borers). More detailed descriptions of insects and diseases can be found in the "Annuals" section, pages 106 to 109 ("Pest & Other Problems"); this list simply provides the primary warning signals to heed when screening plants in the garden center. If you think you see any of these signals, point them out to your retailer. Especially during their busy spring season, it's difficult for retailers to spot the begin-

Perennials will thrive if they are healthy when planted.

ning of every possible problem. Good plantsmen will want to take steps to combat an infestation as early as possible.

It's always helpful to be able to see the plants you're buying in advance. If you're unable to find the particular kinds you want, you can be reassured that there are many, very reliable mail-order sources of high-quality perennials. Frequently, these growers are the only source of the newest and less well-known varieties; it would be a shame to miss growing the many beautiful perennials they offer.

How can you identify which companies can be relied upon to provide top quality plants? Probably the best way is to talk to other gardeners to learn which companies have given them consistently good service and quality plants, and which have not. Another is by reading the fine print on the guarantee the company offers; reputable firms will stand behind their product. If wild claims and rave notices are given to every plant listed in their catalog, and the prices at which they're offered are far lower than from any other sources, chances are you're either going to receive an extremely small plant or a close-to-weed variety. In the plant world, you get what you pay for!

CONTAINER-GROWN
PLANT

GOOD SIGNS

BAD SIGNS

What to Look for
in Container-Grown Plants

Look for these signals when selecting plants grown
in containers. They'll go a long way toward indicating
how long the plant has been in the container and
how it's been cared for during that time. Strong,
vital plants that have been given good care have a
far better chance of surviving when transplanted
into the garden.

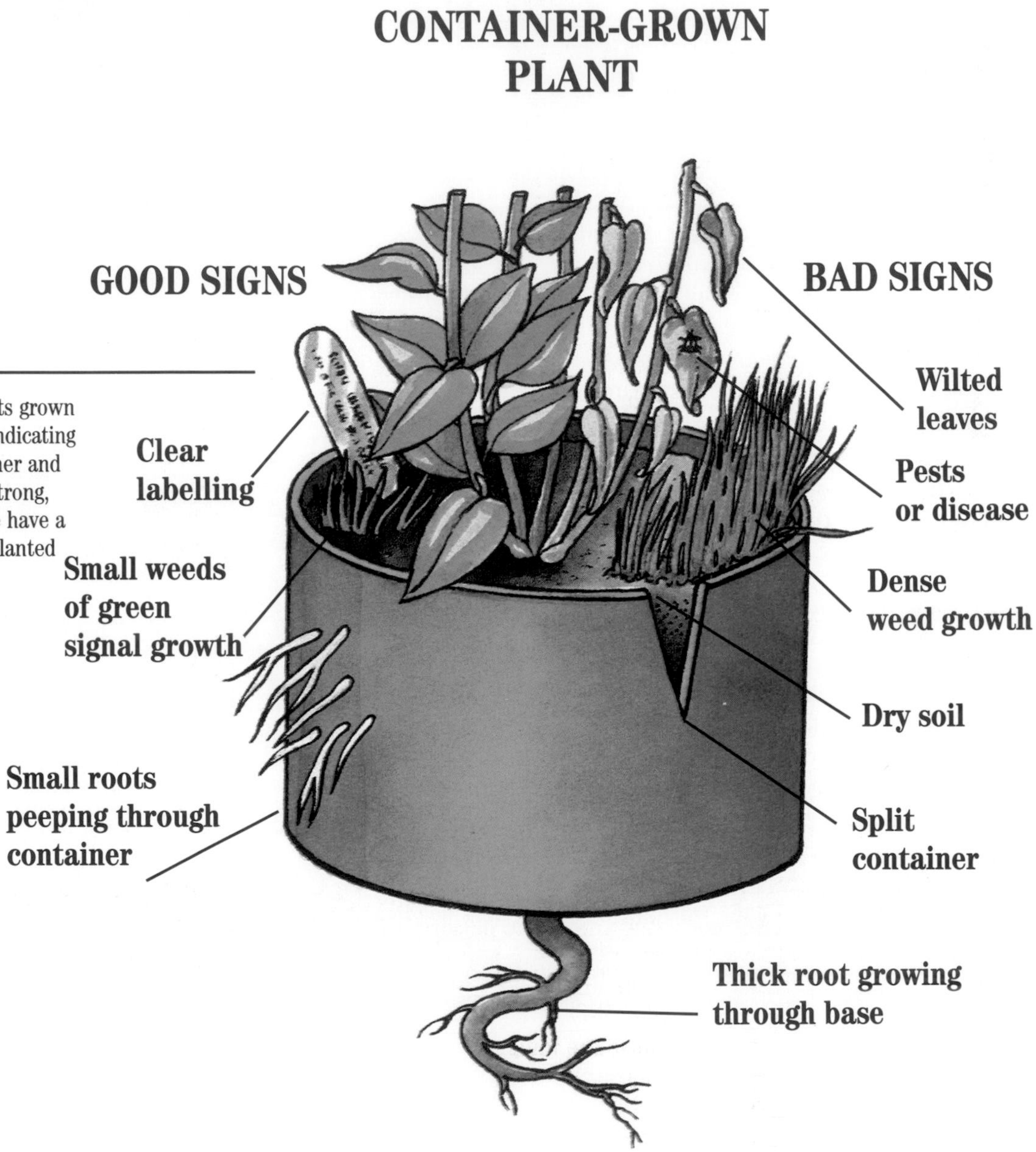

**Clear
labelling**

**Small weeds
of green
signal growth**

**Small roots
peeping through
container**

**Wilted
leaves**

**Pests
or disease**

**Dense
weed growth**

Dry soil

**Split
container**

**Thick root growing
through base**

Here is a brief list of mail-order suppliers of perennial plants:

Kurt Bluemel, Inc.	Canyon Creek Nursery	Miliaeger's Gardens	Wayside Gardens
2740 Greene Lane	3527 Dry Creek Road	4838 Douglas Avenue	1 Garden Lane
Baldwin, MD 21013	Oroville, CA 95965	Racine, WI 53402	Hodges, SC 29695
Bluestone Perennials, Inc.	Carroll Gardens	Prairie Nursery	White Flower Farm
7211 Middle Ridge Road	P.O. Box 310	P.O. Box 306	P.O. Box 50
Madison, OH 44057	Westminster, MD 21158	Westfield, WI 53964	Litchfield, CT 06759
Busse Gardens	Holbrook Farm & Nursery	Andre Viette Farm & Nursery	
13579 10th St. NW	P.O. Box 368	Route 1, Box 16	
Cokato, MN 55321	Fletcher, NC 28732	Fishersville, VA 22939	

Watering, Weeding, & Feeding

Watering hostas will encourage vigorous growth.

If you feed and water perennials well and keep weeds from intruding on their space, they'll respond with vigorous growth and numerous blooms. Here's how to keep them at their best:

Watering—Water, soil, and sun are the most essential ingredients for plants. It's necessary to water perennials the first season after planting whenever nature doesn't supply enough rain. After the first year, most perennials can sustain themselves without watering, except during exceptionally dry spells.

When watering *is* necessary, always water deeply in order to encourage deep root growth. When only the surface inch or two is moistened, the plant's roots are encouraged to grow primarily in that area. Then, as soon as the soil surface dries, they quickly wilt. Shallow-rooted plants are also not anchored well enough to survive strong winds or winter's freezing and thawing action.

Deep watering is done most easily, and is least wasteful of water, when applied with a soaker hose laid around the plants. Allow water to slowly seep from the hose into the soil over a period of several hours. Dig down into the soil to be sure it has soaked in to a depth of 6 to 8 inches. Don't water again until a bit of soil pinched between your fingers feels nearly dry.

Weeding—Mulching helps retain soil moisture. It also greatly reduces the need for weeding, because the mulch layer inhibits many weed seeds from sprouting. Lay on the mulch to a depth of 2 inches right after planting. As you spread the mulch, take care to lift trailing foliage so it lies on top of the mulch, and be sure to keep space open around each plant's growth center to avoid smothering.

When a mulch is used, only a bit of hand weeding will be required around perennials. However, if for some reason a mulch is not used, hand cultivation of the top 1 inch of soil will be needed frequently throughout the summer to stir up the soil and discourage weed growth. Care must be taken not to damage roots or leave them exposed to sun and air, and not to scratch so deeply that hidden bulbs are damaged.

A third alternative for weed control among perennials is to sprinkle a pre-emergent chemical weed control on the soil between the plants. This should not be used in areas where seeds or young plants are growing; once plants are 4 to 6 inches high, they will not be harmed by these chemicals.

Feeding—Perennials profit from two or three light applications of general fertilizer each summer. Most important is a side-dressing of granular fertilizer each spring as growth starts; one or two additional lighter applications at 3- to 4-week intervals are helpful but not essential.

Use a commercial mixture of 5-10-5 or 10-10-10. If you prefer to use an organic fertilizer, simply apply more heavily, or at more frequent intervals to supply the same level of nutrition to the plants.

Many other elements also go into growing and maintaining healthy perennial plants. Soil and light and the proper tools are essential. Increasing or controlling growth can help make your perennial garden fit into your overall landscape. Staking is sometimes needed to keep perennials visible and healthy. See the "Annuals" section pages 56 (soil and light), 72 (tools), 102 (growth), and 104 (staking) for more information on these topics.

Watering with a Soaker Hose

A soaker hose allows water to slowly seep into the soil, allowing deep, thorough watering. At the same time, it applies water directly to the root zone without waste in runoff. It provides the additional advantage of not wetting down the foliage, which in turn cuts down on disease and mildew problems, as well as bending and breakage of plant stems from water weight. Weave the hose through the bed early in the season, leaving the end with the quick-connector attachment near the outside edge. The regular garden hose can then easily be hooked up to it whenever deep watering is needed to supplement nature's supply, and disconnected and stored away between uses.

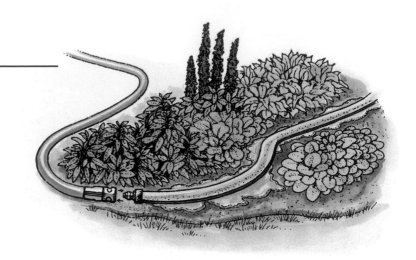

Bubbler Wand for Watering Individual Plants

To water a few individual plants rather than the entire flower bed, a bubbler wand can be connected to the garden hose. This device breaks the pressure of the water as it hits the ground, allowing slow watering without water runoff or erosion of the soil. You can water with a bubbler wand while standing upright; or you can lay it down in an area for a while and let the water soak in, moving it to another section when needed.

Drip Irrigation Watering

In areas where there is little natural rainfall, a drip irrigation system run by a timer may be the appropriate, carefree watering method. Tiny tubes or sprinklers apply the water to each individual plant, or small groups of plants, with minimal water wastage.

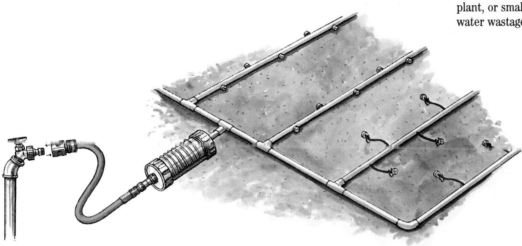

Benefits of an Automatic Sprinkler

An automatic sprinkler is not the best method for routinely watering perennials: Plant stems and flower heads are easily knocked over from excess water weight, and fungi and plant diseases flourish and spread most easily when foliage is frequently wet. However, it can be useful for certain jobs—especially after sidedressing the bed with granular fertilizer.

Sidedressing

Granular fertilizer is applied by sprinkling it over the root zone of each plant—this is known as sidedressing—taking care to avoid contact with the foliage. Apply just before a rainfall, or water after application, in order to start the feeding process.

Feeding with Foliar Fertilizers

Plants are capable of absorbing nutrients through their foliage as well as their roots. A way to supply fertilizer quickly is by spraying it directly onto the plant foliage with a sprayer, watering can, or hose feeding attachment. Buy foliar fertilizers that are specially formulated for this purpose, following the manufacturer's instructions carefully to avoid burning of the foliage.

Feeding with a Garden Hose Attachment

Another feeding alternative is to add nutrients by way of an attachment to the garden hose. This way, watering and feeding go on simultaneously. This is particularly easy to do if a drip irrigation system or soaker hose is the primary water source. Follow the manufacturer's recommendations regarding the frequency and rate of application.

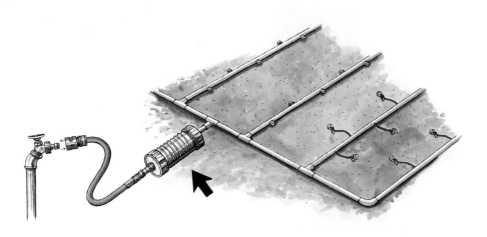

Mulching

A mulch layer on top of the soil keeps down weeds, almost entirely eliminating the need for weeding. It helps retain moisture in the soil, reducing the need for watering, and gives the garden a neat, cared-for appearance. It also evens out soil temperatures, so plants suffer less damage from extremes of heat and cold—it insulates plant roots over winter, allowing them to avoid damage from heaving. Use any mulch material that's readily available and inexpensive in your area: shredded bark, leaves, peanut shells, buckwheat or cocoa bean hulls, pine needles, wood chips—even shredded newspaper.

Hand Weeding

When a mulch is used, little weeding is required—simply pull out the few weeds that are present by hand. Without a mulch, there will be more weeds to control; stir the top 1 to 2 inches of soil with a hand cultivator frequently to kill young weed seedlings as they emerge. Use a weeding tool to root them if they are larger and better established.

Starting from Seed

Perennials can be started from seed indoors during the winter months, or directly in the garden during the growing season. Those started indoors in advance of the growing season will often bloom during their first season in the garden; those started outdoors probably will not.

Outdoor planting can be done almost any time of the year, although in colder climates seeds started in early fall may not develop deep enough roots to survive the winter. Generally, seed starting in spring and early summer is more successful.

Seedbeds should be of a good light loam with moist peat moss or other humus mixed in. They should be located in light shade; if this is not possible, some shading should be provided for the first few weeks after planting. When starting small amounts of seed, a good approach is to sow them in shallow boxes filled with seed starter mix, just as you would if starting them indoors (this sterile soil-less mix eliminates the problem of losing young seedlings to disease or to crowding out by weeds), and placing the boxes in a location where they receive plenty of light but little direct sun.

Sprouting plants will first unfold their seed leaves; within these will be the growth bud for producing their true leaves. When the young seedlings reach the stage where they have their first set of true leaves, they're ready to be carefully transplanted to individual clay, plastic, or peat pots. When they become large enough to survive without special care, they're ready to be planted permanently into the garden.

When starting seeds indoors, it's often difficult to provide enough natural light for them to thrive. As a result, they become leggy and weak. It's easy to avoid this problem by installing grow lights over the plants. Grow lights are special fluorescent tubes that provide the full spectrum of light necessary for good plant growth; they're only slightly more expensive than regular fluorescent lights and can be obtained at most garden shops.

Use a regular fluorescent fixture and hang it in a way that will allow you to easily raise and lower it—ideally, it should be kept 6 to 8 inches above the tops of the plants at all times. Seedlings do best with 16 to 18 hours of light each day; the easiest way to consistently provide this is by plugging the grow light fixture into a simple on-off lamp timer. Remember that although you want to extend the day length, plants also require some hours of darkness in each 24-hour cycle.

This vibrant perennial garden is the result of proper care and handling.

Perennial seeds sprout and grow best at a temperature of about 70° F. Water them with lukewarm rather than ice cold water—it's less shocking and helps the seeds thrive. Be sure to keep the planting mix moist, but avoid having it continuously soaking wet; young plants can drown just as easily as they can die from drying out. Once the seeds have sprouted and seedlings have several sets of true leaves, care regarding watering can relax; it's from the time of planting and during the time of sprouting that seedlings are most vulnerable to improper watering.

Planting Seeds

A seedbed for starting perennials should be raked smooth and have all dirt clumps broken so that a fine, even surface is formed. Mark rows with tautly pulled string between stakes, then dig shallow furrows using the side of a trowel or a thin board. Use the string as a guide. Furrows should vary in depth according to seed size—they should be about three times the size of the seed to be planted.

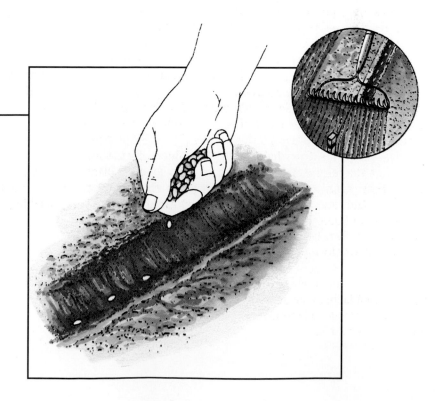

2 Drop individual seeds into the furrow, spacing them ¼ to ½ inch apart. Cover them with very fine, sifted soil or with seed starting mix purchased from a garden supplier—this mix is inert and therefore free of both competing weed seeds and molds or diseases. Since it is very lightweight, tiny seedlings push through it easily. Cover the seeds to a depth of two to three times their diameter. Very fine seeds require no covering.

3 Newly planted seeds should be watered very carefully with a fine spray—use a small bulb sprinkler or something similar to avoid displacing the soil or seeds. From the time they are planted until the young seedlings have formed their second set of true leaves, they are most vulnerable to drying out. Be sure to check the seedbed several times a day, spraying the seeds with a fine water spray as needed to keep the soil moist but not soaked.

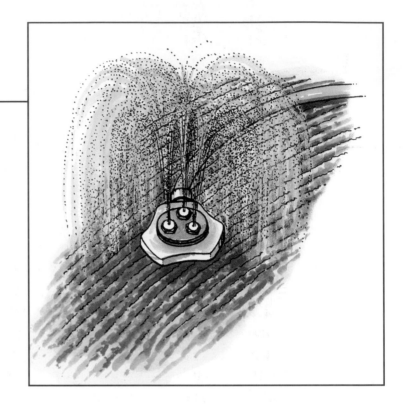

4 When the seedlings reach the stage where they have their second set of true leaves—the first leaves they'll grow are seed leaves; the next set is the first set of true leaves—thin them by pulling out the extra seedlings so they're spaced 2 inches apart. These can be replanted elsewhere, given to other gardeners, or thrown away.

Starting Seeds in Peat Pots

As an alternative to starting seeds directly in an outdoor seedbed, it's possible to start them in peat pots or packs. Plant two or three seeds per individual cube, then thin to the sturdiest one when the seedlings are at the proper stage. Start seedlings this way either indoors or outside.

Starting Seeds Under Growlamps

Seeds can be started during any season if they are grown indoors under growlamps. The main requirement is that they receive enough hours of light—from the sun or from a light fixture—to grow sturdy plants. They need between 16 to 18 hours of light a day. This is easily managed by plugging grow lights into a lamp timer. Seedlings started in late fall or early winter can easily be grown to a sufficient size for spring planting and blooming.

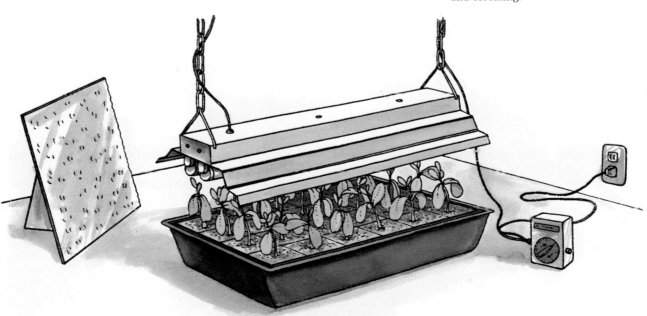

Starting Seeds in a Greenhouse

Those who have a greenhouse available will have plenty of space for growing perennials to sufficient size. You'll still need to supply adequate hours of light for them to grow well—this may mean extending the daylight artificially with grow lights during the shortest days of the year for those living in northern climates.

Hardening off Seedlings

Potted or boxed seedlings should be hardened off for a week or so before transplanting into the garden. This can be done by carrying them outside and leaving them there for a longer time each day before bringing them in overnight. Start by having them outside only one hour, increase to two hours, then four hours, then six hours, etc. This will wean them away from the indoor, hothouselike growing conditions without setting them back from shock. Once the plants have been hardened off in this way, follow planting instructions for container-grown plants.

Starting Stem & Root Cuttings

Many perennials cannot be grown from seed because the plants that result will not be exactly like the parent plant. Instead, these perennials must be propagated asexually—this is known as vegetative reproduction.

One way of doing this is by taking pieces of plant stems or roots and growing them into new plants. Gardeners call these pieces *cuttings*. Not all perennials will generate whole new plants from pieces of themselves, although many do this easily.

Stem Cuttings—Stem cuttings should be taken from the active growing tips of the plant. Cuttings should be between 3 and 6 inches in length, and removed from the parent plant in the evening or in early morning when they're in peak condition. Use only healthy plants that are free from insects and diseases and are in an active growing stage.

Gather cuttings for only five minutes, bringing them indoors to process immediately. This will cut down on the possibility of wilting and the energy loss that accompanies it. After one batch of cuttings has been completed, you can gather additional batches, preparing each and inserting the cuttings into the rooting medium before picking a new group.

Rooting hormone powders, though not absolutely essential, do speed up the rooting process and generally help produce a higher percentage of successful "takes." They're long lasting and inexpensive; the smallest packet is all you'll need for hundreds of cuttings.

A rooting medium must provide good drainage and air circulation. At the same time, it must supply support to the plant stems and enough compaction to keep the stems moist. Coarse sand is the traditional rooting medium, but most growers today use some combination of sand, vermiculite, perlite, and peat moss. A mix of perlite combined with an equal amount of either peat moss or vermiculite provides good drainage and moisture retention capability.

Always make a hole first before inserting the prepared cutting into the medium. Firm the medium around the stem. Once all the cuttings are inserted, water them to help them settle into the medium, covering them with a plastic bag to form a tent. The cutting leaves should not come in contact with the plastic. If they do, this is a prime environment for rot that will kill the cuttings. To avoid this problem, insert stakes in the medium in such a way that they will hold the plastic away from the cuttings.

Place this tent in a location where the cuttings will receive good light but no direct sun; keep the medium moist but not wet. The temperature should be about 70° F. Check for roots by gently lifting a cutting from the rooting medium. When roots are ¼-inch

Oriental poppies can be propagated by root cuttings.

long, transplant them into small pots filled with potting mix and grow them until they're sturdy enough to plant outdoors.

Root Cuttings—For just two or three root cuttings, simply dig down beside the parent plant and cut off one or two roots with a knife or hand pruners. For a larger number of root cuttings, dig up the parent plant and trim off all of the side roots. Discard the parent plant, or trim the top back heavily and replant it.

For best results, root cuttings should be taken in early spring (except for oriental poppies, which seem to do better if cuttings are taken in the fall). To help identify the top of the cutting (that part closest to the plant's main root or crown) from the bottom, make cuts straight across the top end and a slanted cut at the bottom end of each segment. Cut fine roots into 1-inch lengths; fleshy ones into 1½- to 2-inch pieces.

Cuttings of fine roots can be scattered horizontally over the surface of the rooting medium (rich sandy loam is best) and covered with about ½ inch of soil or sand. Fleshy roots are planted upright in the medium, 2 to 3 inches apart, with the top ¼ inch of the cutting sticking out of the ground.

Unlike stem cuttings that root within weeks, root cuttings are slow to generate new top growth. Keep them in a sunny location out of direct sun, and continue to water them whenever the rooting medium begins to dry.

How to Start Perennials from Stem Cuttings

1 Cut 3- to 6-inch growth tips from the parent plant with a small, sharp knife. Make a clean, slanted cut just above a leaf node, side shoot, or growth bud. The parent plant should be in a stage of active growth with young and succulent stems. If the stems are woody and difficult to cut, try recutting closer to the tip. Bring cuttings indoors immediately and recut them just below the bottom node. Use a single-edged razor blade or a sharp knife to give the cleanest possible cut. Crushed stem cells and hanging strands of tissue cause problems you want to avoid. Remove side shoots, leaves, flowers, and flower buds from the lower half of the stem. Trim any large leaves, leaving between one-third and one-half of their surface.

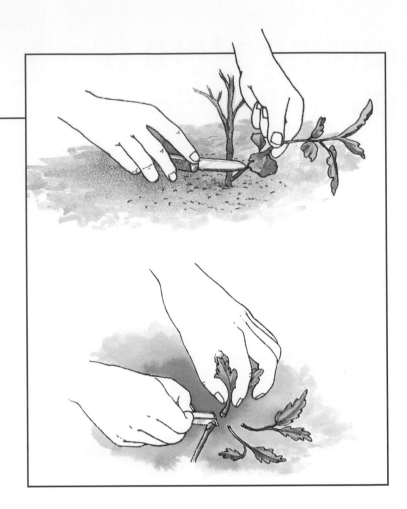

2 Dip the lower one-third to one-half of the stem in rooting powder; this is a hormone stimulant that helps encourage root growth. Gently tap the stem to knock off excess powder.

3

Poke a hole in the rooting medium and insert a cutting to between one-third and one-half of its length. Firm the rooting medium around the stem with your fingers. When all the cuttings are inserted, water them in place.

4 A large, clear plastic bag forms a mini-greenhouse over the cuttings. Insert sticks or stakes around the container edge to hold the plastic away from the cuttings. Lift the edge of the plastic for an hour or so each day to allow air circulation. Water the rooting medium with lukewarm water as needed—this won't be often since the plastic cover helps retain moisture. To avoid rot, take care not to keep the cuttings continually soaking wet.

5 Gently lift out a cutting to check for roots. Some plants root more quickly than others: It may take from one week to one month for roots to show. When roots are ¼-inch long, use a spoon or fork as a small trowel for lifting out cuttings. Plant them in small 1½- to 2-inch pots filled with potting mix. Wait and replant them into larger pots or into the garden when a good strong root system has formed.

Planting Root Cuttings Vertically

Root cuttings are made from 1- to 3-inch sections of the parent plant's roots. When planting them vertically for rooting, be sure that the part that was nearest the main root is up and the part that was farther out is at the bottom. As you cut the root into sections, you can distinguish "up" from "down" by cutting the "up" side straight across and the "down" side on a slant. Plant so that the top of the cutting is ¼-inch above the surface of the medium—potting soil is a good rooting medium for root cuttings.

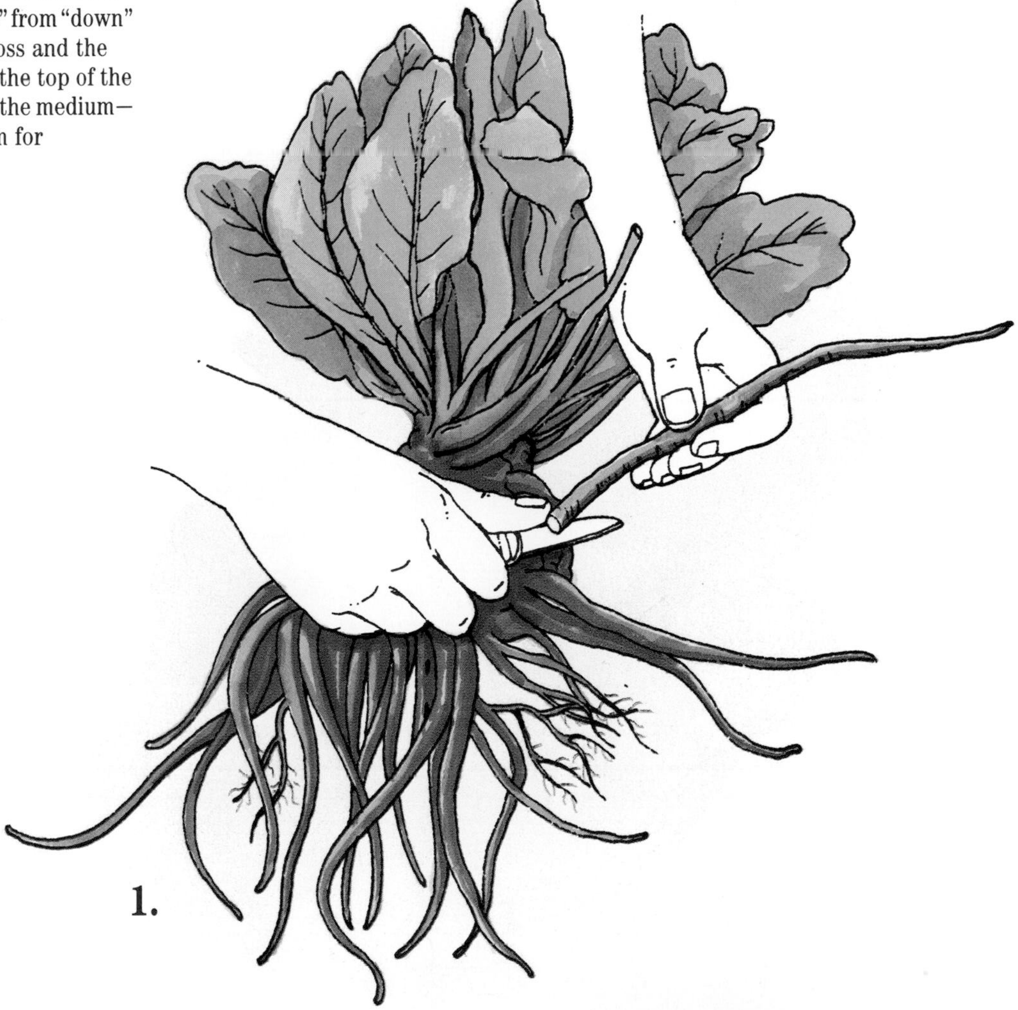

1.

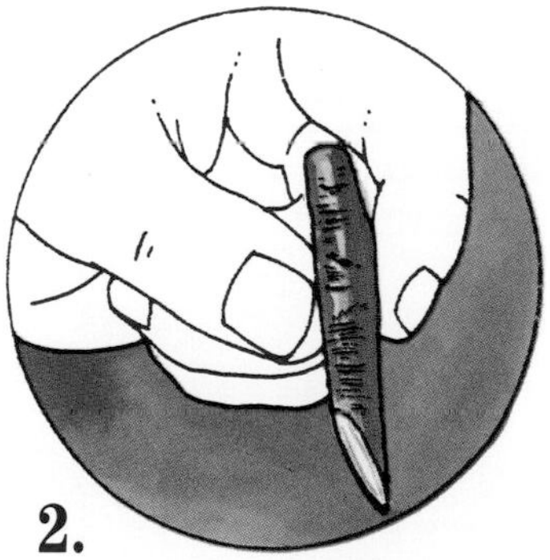

2.

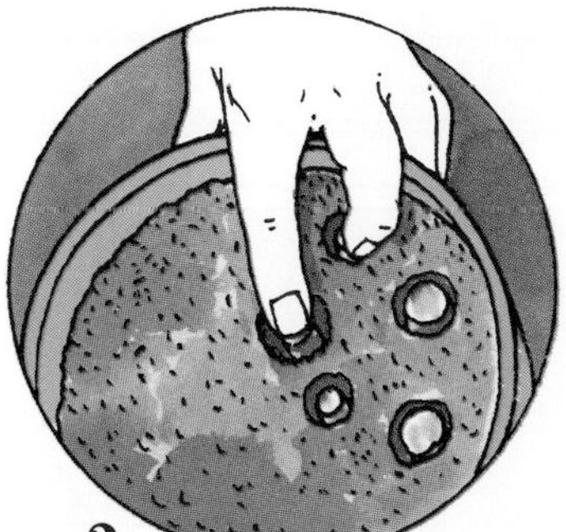

3.

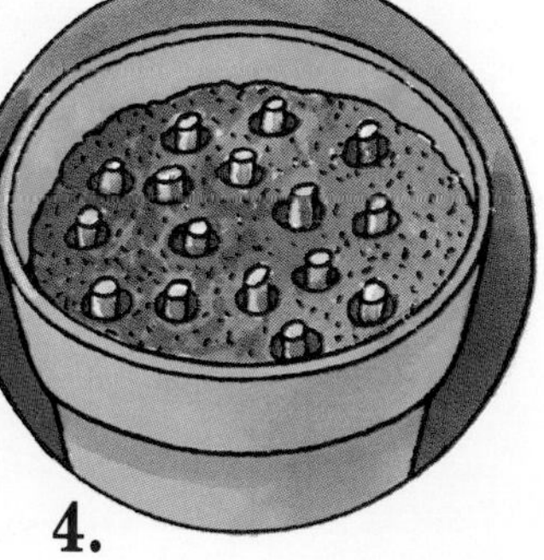

4.

Planting Root Cuttings Horizontally

Many perennials grow well from root cuttings that are laid out horizontally. The pieces are simply strewn on top of the soil surface in a shallow tray, then covered with more soil to a depth of 1 inch or less. Be mindful that root cuttings are much slower to grow than stem cuttings. Therefore, don't be concerned when no activity occurs in the first weeks. Place the cuttings in a shaded location outdoors and keep watering them as needed until you see signs of growth. Once growth appears, feed them with a water-soluble fertilizer for several weeks before transferring them to small pots or into the garden.

2.

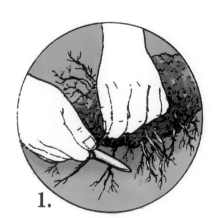

1.

3.

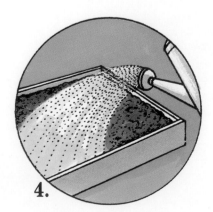

4.

Dividing Perennials

Plant division provides the gardener with additional plants.

Perennials—especially those that thrive and spread abundantly—need to be dug up and divided every few years. This provides the opportunity to keep the plant within bounds and to remove older, less vital portions, as well as any diseased sections. A natural by-product of this plant division is additional plants, which can be replanted in other parts of your own yard or shared with other gardeners.

Perennials can be divided by taking pieces away from their outer edges—separating them from the main plant by cutting through the crown with a knife or a sharp-bladed spade. You can also lift the entire plant from the ground and pull or cut it apart.

Some plants divide very easily. They're loosely interwoven and can be separated into chunks simply by pulling them apart with your hands. Others are so tightly held together that it becomes a real challenge to break them up. Fortunately, the tough ones are also very hardy and will survive even if you ultimately have to resort to using a meat cleaver or machete! Japanese irises, lupines, and gas plants fall into this latter category.

The primary concerns here are to keep as many of the roots intact as possible, and to have some roots and some foliage in each division. Trim back excess top foliage to balance the loss of feeder roots that takes place when the plants are dug up and torn apart. Avoid the impulse to get as many separate clumps as possible: larger clumps will thrive, while small divisions are likely to struggle and grow very slowly.

Everywhere but in the South, the best time to divide most perennials is early spring. All but those that flower in early spring should be divided then. Divide the early-spring bloomers right after they've finished blossoming. In warm climates, fall is a better time to divide all perennials except oriental poppies.

There are a few plants—peonies, irises, and oriental poppies—which, even though they bloom in summer, do better if they're divided after they've finished flowering and have begun to change color.

Always plant the new divisions at the same depth as they were growing before lifting. Firm the soil around each new plant and water well to help settle the soil closely around the roots. The addition of enough water-soluble fertilizer to make a weak feeding solution during this watering will help get the new plants off to a good start. If nature doesn't provide adequate water during the first several weeks after division, be sure to deep water as needed.

When dividing plants that have large fleshy roots, such as dahlias and bearded irises, it's sometimes confusing to know how to approach them. Dahlias, for instance, hold together in a sort of fan. All of the growth "eyes" are clustered close together at the center of the fan. Divide them in the spring before replanting. Use a sharp knife and carefully cut the cluster apart, making sure there is at least one "eye" with each subgroup of tubers. Iris clumps also need to be cut apart with a sharp knife. Let the divisions air dry for a half hour or so after cutting before replanting them—this will give the wounds some time to seal over, thus cutting down on the possibility of rot or infection.

Division of Perennial Clumps by Hand

The simplest way to divide loosely woven perennial clumps is by pulling them apart with your hands, or by digging off a portion with a trowel or spade. Divide them into several large clumps rather than into many very small ones; this will provide fewer plants, but they'll be more vital and sure to produce flowers the first season after division.

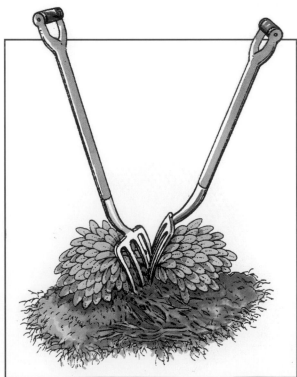

Using Spading Forks to Divide Perennial Clumps

When the perennial clump is more tightly bound together, two spading forks can be stuck through it back-to-back while it's still in the ground. By pushing out on the fork handles, it's usually possible to pry the clump apart. Some are so tenacious, however, that they must be hacked into chunks with a heavy knife, cleaver, or hatchet. Don't be afraid of doing the plant any harm—those that are this tough won't be fazed by such treatment!

Dividing Rhizomes

Some perennials have large, fleshy underground stems called rhizomes. Bearded irises are one example. To divide these types, dig up the entire clump and shake out the dirt. Then use a sharp knife to cleanly cut them into smaller clumps containing three or more buds. Let the pieces air dry for about an hour so the wounds can seal over before replanting them.

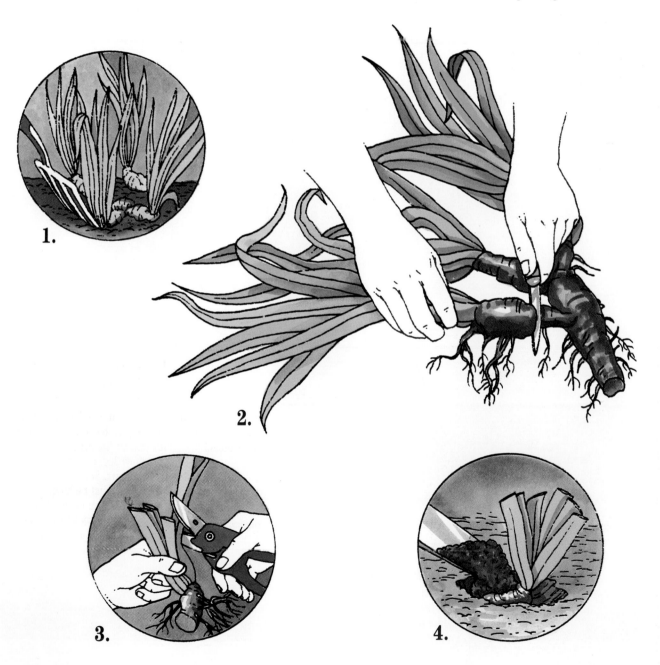

1.

2.

3.

4.

This beautifully landscaped perennials garden combines colorful blooms in various sizes and shapes with foliage of different textures and forms. The pond and garden sculpture contribute to the peaceful look.

LANDSCAPING WITH PERENNIALS

Because of the permanence of perennials, it pays to give advance consideration to where to plant them and which ones to use. You'll do some shifting and adjustment as you see the plantings develop, but you'll want to keep this to a minimum. It's certainly easier to make changes on paper!

Instead of buying the plants first, and then looking at your site for a place to put them, you should reverse the order. *First* study the site. Walk around the yard and take note of its special features: a steep bank, shaded areas, a wet low spot, or a sun-filled alcove. Jot down notes of areas you plan to landscape.

If you have difficulty envisioning how an area might look when planted, create a three-dimensional mock-up: poke sticks or pieces of leafy brush into the ground where you want bushes and trees, and mark out flower beds and patio areas with stakes linked together by twine. Sit in the patio area and look out at the make-believe landscape. Study it from wherever you'll view it. Move the markers around until they produce the best arrangement. Install a permanent label in each location.

In this chapter you'll find information on how to plan perennial plantings for various situations.

Putting a Garden on Paper

This well-planned perennials garden combines blazingstars, ribbon grass, lavender, daylilies, and shasta daisies.

Planning a perennial flower garden for a succession of bloom all season long is a fairly complex undertaking. There are so many details that must be considered: light and soil preferences, the size and height of plants, the color and form of blooms, foliage texture, and plant growth habit all are important. And then there are those plants that can be planted under and between others to give two seasons of bloom in the same space: spring bulbs under summer- and fall-blooming plants, and summer lilies under plants that flower in spring or fall.

Initially, the thought of laying out such a plan can be daunting, but, taken one step at a time, it becomes less overwhelming.

The first step is to make a list of your plant favorites. Research the characteristics of each plant on the list to learn what size they'll grow to, when they bloom, what colors they come in, what kind of soil and light they prefer, etc. This will help you to select the best plant from your list for each spot you've marked in the yard.

Sketch the layout on a piece of paper and note your choices. For flower beds, lay out detailed plans of exactly which plants will go where.

First, plan locations of the basic year-round perennials as we've done in our sample layout. Then take a piece of tracing paper and lay it over the basic planting plan. Mark those areas where bulbs can be interplanted and choose suitable varieties. Finally, make up "proof sheets," as we have done, identifying which portions of the garden will be colorful during each segment of the growing season. Check to see whether or not it's well balanced. If not, make switches and changes as necessary. Double check to be certain no tall plants are in front of shorter ones, that there are no colors that are likely to clash, and that no shade lovers have been placed in a sunny bed, or vice versa. Inevitably, there will be a need for a few changes and substitutions as your garden grows, but by carefully studying your advance plan you can at least avoid the obvious mistakes.

From these plans you can then determine how many plants you need of each kind. With this information, you're ready to make your purchases and do your planting.

How to Plan a Garden

1 Mark out the locations for each kind of plant you want in the border using a list of your favorites as a reference. Keep in mind that tall plants should be at the back and low ones in front, the colors and blooming seasons should be mixed throughout the garden for balance, and a mixture of foliage colors and textures will help add interest to areas not in blossom. Select plants suitable for the amount of light and moisture available.

Colors

Pink = P
Blue = B
White = W

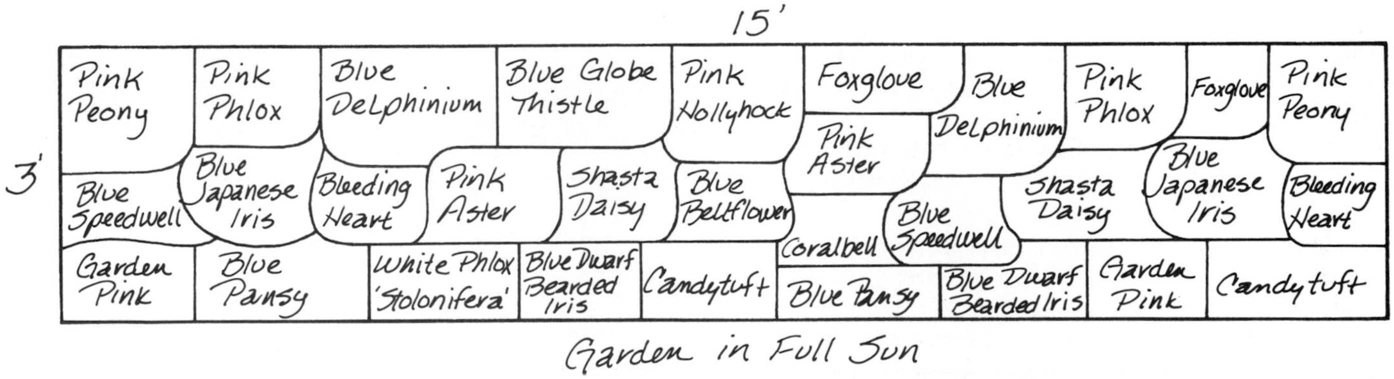

15'

| Pink Peony | Pink Phlox | Blue Delphinium | Blue Globe Thistle | Pink Hollyhock | Foxglove | Blue Delphinium | Pink Phlox | Foxglove | Pink Peony |

3'

Blue Speedwell · Blue Japanese Iris · Bleeding Heart · Pink Aster · Shasta Daisy · Blue Bellflower · Pink Aster · Coralbell · Blue Speedwell · Shasta Daisy · Blue Japanese Iris · Bleeding Heart

Garden Pink · Blue Pansy · White Phlox 'Stolonifera' · Blue Dwarf Bearded Iris · Candytuft · Blue Pansy · Blue Dwarf Bearded Iris · Garden Pink · Candytuft

Garden in Full Sun

Favorites

Bleeding Heart: P, W	Pansy: B, W
Candytuft: W	Peony: B, W
Delphinium: B, W	Phlox: P
Foxglove: B, W	Speedwell: B
Japanese Iris: B, W	Tulip: P, B, W
Madonna Lily: W	

2 Once all of the garden is laid out, place a sheet of tracing paper over the plan and mark those areas in which a double season of bloom is possible—by underplanting with spring flowering bulbs or summer flowering lilies, or by intermixing plants that die back early in the season with others that will expand and cover the same space after they're finished for the year.

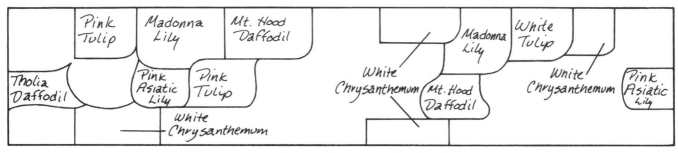

Bulbs and Mums Overplanting Overlay

3 Using the basic plan and the overlay as a guide, create a separate "proof" sheet on tracing paper for each portion of the flowering season: spring, early summer, late summer, and fall. Do this by marking each section of the garden that will be in flower and what colors they will be during that season. Study these to see what changes are needed to improve the balance of color through the entire growing season.

Colors
Pink = P
Blue = B
White = W

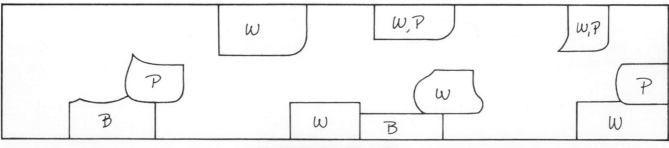

Early Spring "Proof"

Colors
Pink = P
Blue = B
White = W

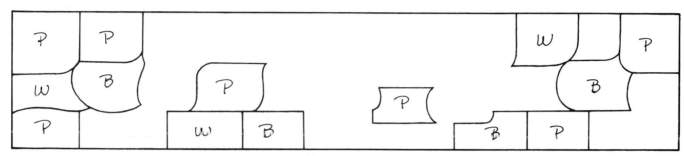

Late Spring "Proof"

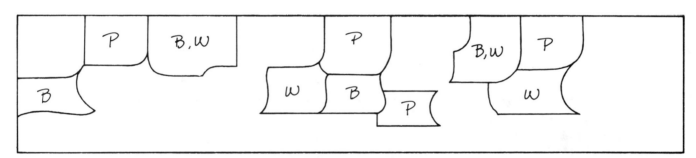

Early Summer "Proof"

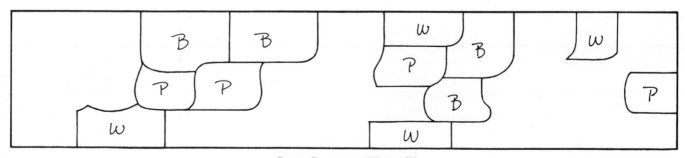

Late Summer "Proof"

Entrance Gardens, Borders, & Island Beds

This island bed incorporates tulips, Spanish Hyacinths, and Japanese anemones in a way that allows each element to be clearly seen.

The border layout we used as an example in the preceding section is a simple rectangular one suitable for use in front of a fence, hedge, side of a building, or row of flowering shrubs. But this is not the only setting and these are not the only proportions suitable for perennial plantings.

Nor do you have to exclusively use perennials in a planting. It's perfectly acceptable to mix annuals with perennials, and even—when the bed space is large enough to allow it—to include trees and evergreen or flowering shrubs in the design.

Because they're not demanding, perennials are ideally suited for use as often as possible in entrance gardens, as well as in borders and island beds.

The approach for laying out such plantings is similar to that shown for our side border, but there are some additional points that must be considered.

For example, the unique aspect of an entrance garden is that it will be viewed very briefly. This is an area people are likely to move through quickly rather than linger in or sit and view for an extended period. Therefore, it must be planted simply and for immediate impact. This is not the place for subtle combinations and rare species; it's where a bold, eye-catching display is needed.

This doesn't necessarily mean that it must be bright or garish; repeated or massed groups of white or pastel flowers can be effective, too. Even an all-foliage display can be dramatic when well chosen. Ornamental grasses, ferns, hostas, rosemary, stonecrops, bergenias, Japanese irises, wormwoods, and many others offer wonderful foliage colors and textures to work with.

Plants with strong perfumes are also more likely to be enjoyed in this situation where more subtle perfumes might go unnoticed. Sometimes these strong perfumes, which can be overpowering adjacent to an outdoor sitting area where they're constantly being inhaled, are ideal for short-term enjoyment.

In contrast to entrance gardens, flower plantings that will be enjoyed at leisure either while sitting among them outdoors or viewing them from inside, may be more low-key in their design. They should invite the eye to keep coming back for another look to perhaps discover additional aspects that weren't obvious at first. Here, of course, the plantings will be more interesting if there are contrasts of flowers, foliage textures, and colors.

Island beds—plantings that are centrally placed and viewed from all sides—require a somewhat different design approach than side beds. In order to be effective from every direction, it's necessary to lay them out so that the tallest plants are located in the middle of the bed rather than at the rear. It is therefore necessary to have many more plants of low and intermediate heights in these plantings than tall ones.

Flower beds come in all sizes and outlines; they can be shaped asymmetrically to fit any corner or contour desired. Squared off symmetrical beds have a rather formal appearance; curving meandering ones are more natural and informal looking. Choose a layout that best suits the surrounding garden, your house style, and your personal preferences.

Eye-Catching Entrance Garden

Entrance gardens should be simple in layout yet eye-catching. Otherwise, they may not be noticed during the brief moments they're viewed.

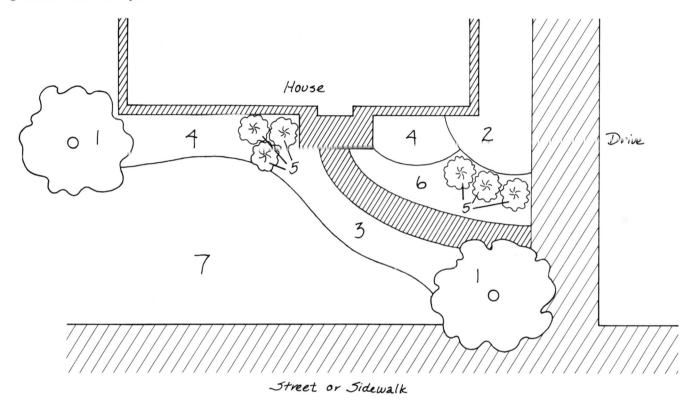

Note: The lists below are to be used for making a selection of *one* variety for each area. Entries should be kept simple for best results and greatest impact.

1 Attractive specimen shrub or small tree:
   Golden Arborvitae (columnar variety)
   Cutleaf Red Maple
   Redbud
   Silverbell

2 Broadleaf evergreens:
   Boxwood
   Ilex
   Pieris
   Rhododendron

3 Low, neat-growing perennials:
   Candytuft
   Hosta
   Lavender
   Lily Turf
   Stonecrop

4 Medium-height perennials or flowering shrubs:
   Azaleas
   Daylilies
   Peonies
   Roses

5 Dramatic grass clumps:
   Fountain Grass
   Maiden Grass
   Variegated Molinia

6 Second choice from group #3

7 Lawn

Corner Beds & Side Borders

Borders come in a wide variety of sizes and shapes.
Their outline and plant content depends on the
surrounding landscape, the land contours, and
your own personal tastes.

■ = **Tall plants**

□ = **Intermediate plants**

■ = **Low plants**

Corner Bed

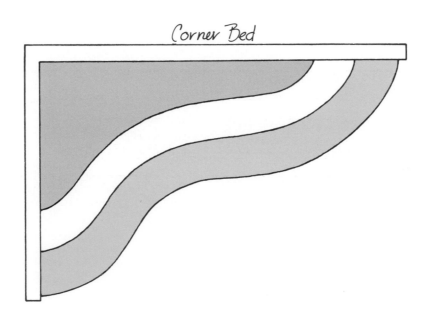

Side Border

Wall, Fence, or Other Solid Background

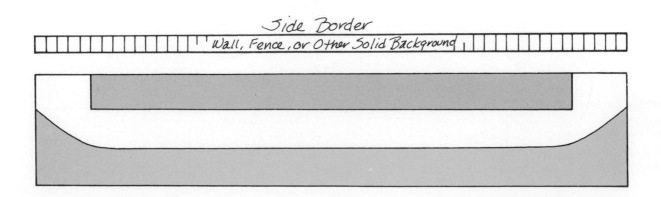

= Tall plants

= Intermediate plants

= Low plants

Island beds are surrounded on all sides by lawn or paving, so they are seen from every direction. It becomes a challenge to have them looking nice from all sides. Planning the layout of an island bed differs from a side border because the tallest flowers are clustered in the center of it, rather than arranged along the back edge.

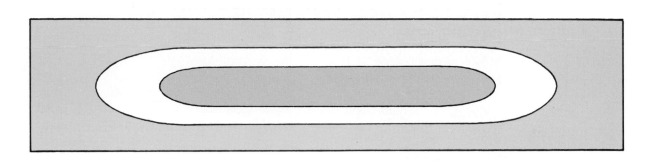

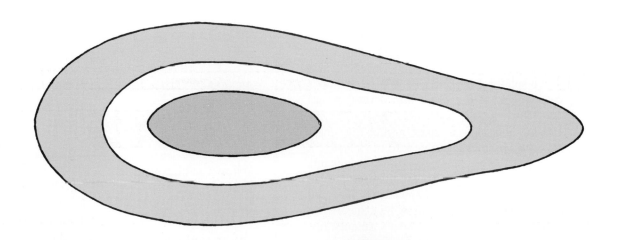

Perennials in Containers

Using garden troughs as containers for perennials planting is a novel idea.

I n most instances, perennials are best grown directly in the ground. However, there are occasions when it's desirable to grow them in containers as potted plants.

When the garden soil is so poor that it's nearly impossible to successfully grow plants in it, container plantings can be the solution. They can also be the answer for soil-less locations such as an apartment balcony, a deck, or a patio.

A third reason for raising container-grown perennials is to allow you to have those varieties that are not winter hardy in your climate. By growing them in containers, it's possible to easily move them into the house or a special shelter over the winter, then back into the garden in the spring.

Finally, it's sometimes nice to grow perennials as indoor plants, providing attractive displays within your home. After all, most houseplants are, in fact, perennials that are tropical and therefore not hardy for growing outdoors in most parts of the country. Some gardeners enjoy the novelty of growing various perennial bulbs in containers for winter bloom: tulips, daffodils, hyacinths, amaryllis, and lilies are popular choices.

Because of the extra care and space year-round container-grown plants require, you'll probably limit yourself to growing only those that are your special favorites—perennials that look beautiful both while they're in bloom and when they are not and those that add appreciably to the decor of your home and garden.

In order for plants to prosper in containers, a primary rule is that the pots must have adequate water drainage capability. Other major needs of potted plants are frequent watering, regular feeding, and repotting when they show signs of becoming rootbound. An easy way to check is by knocking the plant out of the pot every six months to see how jammed with roots it has become—when they're solidly matted, it's time to shift into a slightly larger pot, or to divide the plant into several pieces and repot.

To carry warm weather plants successfully through the winter in cold climates, it's necessary to bring them into the house or a greenhouse where warmth can be maintained. For those plants that are half-hardy or require only slightly milder winters than those you have, it's possible to place them on an unheated enclosed porch or other similar location where daylight sun can reach them, but they're not subjected to extremely low temperatures. If sub-zero temperatures persist, a small space heater on a low setting will provide enough heat to prevent damage. Don't make it so warm that tender new growth is encouraged to sprout—just fend off the very coldest conditions for the brief periods that they last.

Remember that potted plants overwintered under these conditions will require periodic watering in order to keep them from drying out. Such waterings should be infrequent as the plant's metabolism is much slower in cold conditions.

GOOD PLANT CHOICES TO GROW IN CONTAINERS

Asparagus Fern	Ferns
Rex Begonia*	Geranium
Bleeding Heart	Kalanchoe*
Chrysanthemum	Lavender
Clivia*	African Lily
Yellow Coneflower	Big Blue Lily Turf
Daylily	Purple Loosestrife
Espalier and Tree	Rose Mallow
Forms of	Marguerite*
Chrysanthemum,	Oxalis*
Fuchsia, Geranium,	Poinsettia*
Lantana*, and	Russian Sage
Rose Mallow	Stonecrop

* = Not winter hardy

Gardening in Containers

This cross-section drawing shows the best way to plant in a container. To grow plants successfully in containers, good drainage is essential. Drainage holes need to be covered to keep in soil: Pieces of broken pottery, fine screening, or a coffee filter may be used. If additional drainage is needed, add a layer of small stones, perlite, or coarse sand in the bottom of the container. If the container is located where dripping water would do damage, place a drip tray under the container to catch excess water.

Using Decorative Containers

When using a decorative container that has no drainage holes, place a well-drained pot inside of it and actually grow the plants in this inner pot. Raise the inner pot on a layer of pebbles to keep it above water level. The space between the inner and outer pots can be filled with peat moss to provide insulation that helps stabilize soil temperatures.

How to Care for Container-Grown Plants

Perennials in containers must receive special care over winter in cold climates. Keep them in the house or a greenhouse if they are tropical varieties. Those that withstand freezing can be kept in an unheated area such as an enclosed porch and will only require some heating during prolonged, extreme cold spells. Watering should be cut back severely during this dormant period.

A unique planting of perennials adds beauty to an entrance gate. These lovely purple Siberian irises certainly draw attention to themselves. Their intense color is softened by the white daisies behind them and by the profusion of foliage around them.

ENCYCLOPEDIA OF PERENNIAL FAVORITES

Perennials are certainly versatile plants. They can grow in good soil and poor soil; some flourish in full sun, and others are quite content with deep shade. The sizes and shapes nature provides them with are so diverse that any gardener can select perennials to suit his or her garden location and conditions.

The following encyclopedia was designed in order to help gardeners in all regions of the United States make the best perennial selections possible. Botanical and common names, descriptions, ease of care, how-to-grow techniques, propagation, uses, and related species and varieties are all dealt with in depth. Color bars identifying zones that each specimen is congenial to are provided. For example, if a perennial is listed under Zone 5, this means that Zone 5 is the coldest zone at which the plant is hardy. Photos are included for each entry.

The adaptability of perennials truly makes them all-purpose plants. Whether you want to design a garden strictly with perennials, add color to an annuals garden in certain seasons, create a unique rock garden, or try your hand at a wet garden, you will find plants here that will work for you. And if you like what you created, you have the satisfaction of knowing that with a little bit of work your garden can flourish year after year.

Hardy Ageratum, Mist Flower

Eupatorium coelestinum
Zone: USDA 6

The fuzzy, blue flowers of this plant resemble those of the annual bedding ageratum or floss flower. The genus is named for King Eupator of Pontis, who discovered one species was an antidote to a poison.

Description: Hardy ageratums are 2-foot mounds of triangular, coarsely-toothed leaves and flat-topped flower clusters that bloom early in the fall.

Ease of care: Easy.

How to grow: Eupatoriums prefer a good, well-drained but moist garden soil in full sun or partial shade. They like a bit of shade in places with hot summers. Plants appear late in the spring; digging them up by mistake should be avoided.

Propagation: By division in early spring or by seed.

Uses: The showy blue flowers are welcome in early fall and the plants are excellent in a border or used as edging.

Related species: Both *Eupatorium maculatum* and *E. purpureum* are handsome American wildflowers called joe-pye weed. *E. maculatum* grows to 6 feet tall and bears rounded heads of many small, thinly fringed, purple to light purple flowers on stems that are shaded or spotted purple. *E. purpureum* has stems that are usually green, and the flowers smell of vanilla. Both are spectacular in the back of a border. Although adaptable to average garden soil, they prefer an evenly moist spot.

Japanese Anemone

Anemone species
Zone: USDA 5b

The genus comes from the Greek word for "wind," and many of the plants in this family are called wind flowers. They are listed as *Anemone* x *hybrida*.

Description: The strong-stemmed and showy flowers have 5 or more petal-like sepals that enclose numerous golden stamens with compound and very attractive leaves. Mature clumps can reach a height of 5 feet.

Ease of care: Easy.

How to grow: These plants are not difficult to grow but do need a fertile, moist soil with plenty of organic matter mixed in as the roots (or rhizomes) resent heavy clay and wet earth and will rot in those conditions. Anemones enjoy full sun in northern gardens but will easily adjust to partial shade. In southern gardens, they need partial shade. In areas that have severe winters with little snow cover, plants should be mulched in late fall. In colder areas of the country, many flowers are destroyed by early frosts, so they must be protected.

Propagation: By division in early spring or by root division.

Uses: Anemones are especially beautiful when grown in large clumps.

Related varieties: A number of varieties are found, including 'Alba,' with white flowers; 'Mont Rose,' with deep rose flowers; and 'Queen Charlotte,' bearing semi-double, pink flowers. *Anemone vitifolia* is similar, but the pink-blossomed plants are hardier and more tolerant both of sun and of drier soil. It is usually sold as 'Robustissima' and blooms a month earlier than *Anemone* x *hybrida*.

Golden Aster

Chrysopsis mariana
Zone: USDA 5

This is an American native flower spreading from eastern New York to Ohio and then south to Texas and Florida. The genus name means "golden aspect" and refers to the color of the flowers.

Description: Silky stems, often with a purplish stain, grow to 3 feet in height with leaves that are woolly when young, becoming smooth with age. The leaves have a pronounced midrib. Flower sprays are bright yellow, blooming in late summer and on into fall.

Ease of care: Easy.

How to grow: Golden asters like full sun or just a bit of shade, doing well in hot weather with average garden soil. This is a good drought-resistant plant found growing in sandy soil in the wild.

Propagation: By division or by seed.

Uses: The golden aster is fine for the wild garden or planted in borders. It makes a fine addition to the autumn garden, where it will mix well with other asters. Seeds sown in early spring will produce flowering plants the first year.

Stoke's Aster

Stokesia laevis
Zone: USDA 5b

Stoke's aster is a native American wildflower that resembles a China aster, originally found from South Carolina to Florida and Louisiana. It is surprisingly hardy as far north as Rochester, New York. It is named in honor of Dr. Jonathan Stokes, an English botanist.

Description: Leaves are alternate, spiny-toothed toward the base, with the upper leaves clasping the stem. Fluffy blue to lavender flowers are 2 to 5 inches across on well-branched, 1- to 2-foot stems.

Ease of care: Easy.

How to grow: Stokesias need full sun and a good, well-drained soil. New plants take a year or two to settle in before maximum bloom. They should be mulched in areas with bad winters and little snow cover. Remove spent blooms for flowers to continue blooming until September.

Propagation: By seed or by division in spring.

Uses: Stokesias are very decorative flowers for the front of the bed or border. Plants can also be forced for winter bloom in the greenhouse. They are good cut flowers, and the seedpods are excellent in dried arrangements.

Related varieties: 'Alba' is the pure white form; 'Blue Danube' is blue; and 'Silver Moon' is icy white.

Astilbe, Garden Spiraea

Astilbe species
Zone: USDA 5

Beautiful plants for the garden, the astilbes available to gardeners today are usually the result of hybridizing and listed as *Astilbe* x *Arendsii* in garden books and nursery catalogs. The botanical name means "without brilliance" and refers to the lack of punch in the individual flowers.

Description: Astilbes are lovely plants both for their dark green, fernlike foliage growing on polished stems and their long panicles (or spikes) of flowers that resemble feathery plumes. Individual blossoms are small, but as each head contains dozens of branches and each branch bears hundreds of flowers, the total effect is one of beauty. Depending on the type, they can bloom from midsummer to the end of August.

Ease of care: Easy.

How to grow: Astilbes do well in full sun but are best with partial shade, especially in the southern parts of the country. Soil should be good and moist with plenty of organic matter mixed in. Divide the clumps every third year.

Propagation: By division.

Uses: The larger varieties work well in the garden border as specimen plants, even though most of them should be set out in groups of three or more. Colors include white, pink, red, rose, and lilac. Heights vary from 12 to 40 inches. The white forms are especially effective against a shrub border or a line of bushes. They also make an effective ground cover. Astilbes turn a lovely shade of brown in the fall, with the dried flower heads persisting until beaten down by heavy snow. They can be used as cut flowers in the summer and then dried for winter floral arrangements. Finally, astilbes can be forced for winter flowering by potting them in the fall, rooting them, and bringing them into greenhouse heat with plenty of water.

Related species: *Astilbe chinensis* 'Pumila' originally came from China and Japan. The flowers are a mauve-pink on 8- to 12-inch stems, perfect along the edge of a border and in the rock garden as they can tolerate a drier soil than others. *Astilbe tacquetii* 'Superba' is also from China and bears large plumes of rose-pink flowers resembling cotton candy on 4-foot stems.

Related varieties: 'Bridal Veil' bears white flowers on 2-foot stems; 'Peach Blossom' has salmon-pink flowers on 26-inch stems; pink 'Erica' is on 30-inch stems; and 'Montgomery' is a clear red on 28-inch stems.

251

Avens

Geum species
Zone: USDA 6

The avens are members of the rose family. They produce brilliant flowers and plants with attractive leaves coated with silky down. *Geum* is the original Latin name for the herb Bennet (*Geum urbanum*), a plant with an astringent root once used in medicine. Most of the garden forms are hybrids of two or more species.

Description: Avens have clumps of attractive, lobed, shiny green leaves covered with silky down on hairy stems. The plants grow to 2 feet tall and bear single flowers about 1½ inches across. Flower colors are red, yellow, or white. They bloom in spring and summer.

Ease of care: Easy.

How to grow: Avens are plants for cool summers. They prefer full sun and a well-drained but moist soil with plenty of humus. The plants should be divided every two years. In areas subject to below zero temperatures without snow cover, these plants should be mulched.

Propagation: By division in spring or by seed.

Uses: Avens are attractive in the front of a border and in a rock garden where the bright flowers are very showy.

Related varieties: 'Mrs. Bradshaw' is a double, brilliant scarlet and 'Lady Stratheden' is a warm yellow.

Baby's Breath

Gypsophila paniculata
Zone: USDA 5

Almost everyone has given or received a bouquet of flowers from the florist that contained a few sprays of baby's breath. The genus is Latin for the phrase "friendship with gypsum," because one species, *Gypsophila repens*, has been found growing on gypsum rocks.

Description: Small, blue-green leaves, almost fleshy, on stems with slightly swollen joints bear a profusion of many-branched panicles containing numerous ⅛-inch wide flowers. Plants bloom in June and July.

Ease of care: Easy.

How to grow: Baby's breath require full sun and a good, deep, well-drained garden soil with humus. Even though the plants have tap roots, they still require liberal amounts of water. If the soil is at all acid, a cup of ground limestone per square yard should be added into the soil surrounding these lime-loving plants. Tall plants will probably require staking. They will rebloom if spent flowers are removed.

Propagation: By seed. Propagation by cuttings requires patience, skill, and luck.

Uses: Baby's breath are wonderful for filling in gaps in a bed or border. They are especially lovely when tumbling over rock walls or falling out of a raised bed.

Related species: *Gypsophila repens* is a creeping baby's breath that grows 6 inches high, but covers an area to a width of 3 feet. 'Alba' is white; 'Rosea' is pink.

Related varieties: Two popular varieties are 'Bristol Fairy,' with pure white, double flowers, that grows to a height of 4 feet, and 'Pink Fairy,' reaching 18 inches in height with pink doubles.

Balloon Flower

Platycodon grandiflorus
Zone: USDA 4

A one-species genus, balloon flowers are so named because the unopened flowers look like small and rounded hot-air blimps. They are originally from Japan. The genus is named for the Greek word for "broad bell" and refers to the flower shape.

Description: Balloon flowers are clump-forming perennials with alternate leaves of a light green on stems usually between 1½ and 3 feet tall. They bear balloon-shaped buds that open to bell-shaped flowers with 5 points and are 2 to 3 inches wide. The sap is milky.

Ease of care: Easy.

How to grow: Balloon flowers like moist, well-drained soil in full sun or partial shade. They prefer places with cool summers. Plan the plant's position carefully as it is not until late spring that the first signs of life appear.

Propagation: By division in mid-spring or by seed.

Uses: Blooming for most of the summer, balloon flowers are attractive in borders, with the smaller types growing best along garden edges. They are especially effective when used in conjunction with white pansies or the white obedient plant.

Related varieties: 'Album' bears white flowers, and 'Hakona Blue' has two layers of petals, both on 16-inch stems. 'Mariesii' has blue flowers on 12- to 16-inch stems, and 'Shell Pink' bears larger flowers of a soft-pink on 2-foot stems and is best in some shade.

Basket-of-Gold, Goldentuft, Madwort

Aurinia saxatilis
Zone: USDA 5

Originally included in the *Alyssum* genus, these charming flowers of spring have now been moved to an older genus named after a chemical dyestuff used to stain paper. They belong to the mustard family.

Description: Attractive and low gray foliage growing in dense mats gives rise to clusters of golden-yellow, 4-petaled flowers floating 6 to 12 inches above the plants.

Ease of care: Easy.

How to grow: Aurinias need only well-drained, average soil in full sun. Plants will easily rot in damp locations and resent high humidity. They can be sheared after blooming.

Propagation: By cuttings or by seed.

Uses: Aurinias are quite happy growing in the spaces between stone walks, carpeting the rock garden, or growing in pockets in stone walls where their flowers become tumbling falls of gold.

Related varieties: *Alyssum montanum*, 'Mountain Gold,' 4 inches tall, with silvery, evergreen leaves and fragrant, bright yellow flowers makes a dense ground cover. 'Citrina' bears lemon-yellow flowers; 'Flore Plena' has double, yellow blooms; and 'Compacta' has a denser habit of growth.

Beard Tongue

Penstemon barbatus
Zone: USDA 4

There are so many kinds of penstemons that the American Penstemon Society publishes a newsletter and illustrated guides for choosing these plants. Except for one species from Asia, all the rest are native to North America, with most coming from the West Coast. The genus name refers to the presence of a fifth stamen.

Description: Basal foliage is evergreen in warmer climates. The leaves are sometimes whorled. Flowers are tubular in airy, terminal clusters atop strong stems, blooming from spring into summer.

Ease of care: Moderately easy.

How to grow: Penstemons come from areas with rough growing conditions and should never be exposed to wet or damp earth. A thin, rocky soil in full sun is best. Of all the species, *P. barbatus* seems to do the best in the East.

Propagation: By division in spring or by seed.

Uses: Penstemons are exceedingly attractive in the garden and have a long season of bloom. Plants are best set out in groups so that a mass of flowers is in view. For those who succumb to their beauty, entire specialty gardens can be made of only this genus. They are excellent as cut flowers.

Related varieties: 'Alba' has white flowers; 'Elfin Pink' has clear pink flowers on 1-foot high branches, making it perfect for the front of the border; 'Prairie Fire' is a vivid orange-red on 22-inch stems; and 'Prairie Dusk' has purple flowers on 20-inch stems.

Bellflower

Campanula species
Zone: USDA 4

The botanical name is from the Latin word for "bell" and refers to the shape of the flowers. The genus includes annual flowers, biennials, and perennials suitable for the formal garden and the wild garden. *Campanula rapunculoides* is a wild weed and should be avoided. *C. rapunculus* can be considered for the vegetable garden, since the rampion has roots that are used in salads.

Description: Bellflowers are usually in various shades of blue, and many are available in white. Flowers bloom from late spring into early summer. Basal leaves are usually broader than the stem leaves and form rosettes or mats.

Ease of care: Easy.

How to grow: Bellflowers need a good, moist, but well-drained soil with plenty of organic matter mixed in. In the North, plants will tolerate full sun as long as the soil is not dry, but elsewhere a spot in semi-shade is preferred.

Propagation: By division or by seed.

Uses: According to the species, plants are beautiful in the border, useful in the rock garden, and fine for the shade or wild garden. Many species, including *Campanula isophylla*, the star-of-Bethlehem, also do well when grown in pots.

Related species: *Campanula carpatica* is from the Carpathian mountains of Europe, blooming at a height of 10 inches with solitary blue flowers. It is effective as an edging or tumbling over a small rock cliff. Among the many varieties: a white form called 'Alba' as well as 'Blue Carpet,' a smaller, more compact form. *Campanula Elatines* var *garganica*,

(continued)

Bellflower (continued)

Bergamot, Bee-Balm, Oswego-Tea

Heartleaf Bergenia

Monarda didyma
Zone: USDA 4

Bergenia cordifolia
Zone: USDA 4

originally from the Mount Gargano region of Italy, is a plant best set in partial shade where it will flower at a height of 6 inches with bright blue, star-shaped flowers. *Campanula glomerata,* or the clustered bellflower, usually bears a dozen blossoms in tight clusters at the top of a 14-inch stem. 'Crown of Snow' bears large, white flowers. *Campanula persicifolia,* or peach bells, bear flowers on stems up to 3 feet high and prefer moist soil. They are most effective when naturalized at the edge of a wood or shrub border. Flowers are either white or of various shades of blue. 'Grandiflora Alba' bears large, white flowers; 'Blue Gardenia' has deep silvery blue blossoms; and 'Telham Beauty' has larger-than-usual, china-blue flowers. *Campanula Poscharskyana* is a ground creeper with star-shaped, 1-inch blossoms of lavender-blue, perfect for the rock garden or in a hanging basket. *Campanula rapunculoides,* or the creeping bellflower, is a weed from Eurasia that is now naturalized along roadsides from Canada south to Delaware, then west to Illinois. *Campanula rapunculus* is native to the fields of Italy. Its fleshy roots were once cultivated as a salad crop. It bears small blue flowers in long chains that bloom over a long period.

These are stunning, native American plants that have been garden favorites for decades. They are closely related to culinary mint and all have aromatic foliage. Bergamots are named for Nicolas Monardes.
Description: Sturdy, square stems growing to 4 feet tall have simple leaves. They are topped by crowns that are studded with lipped, usually bright red flowers blooming from summer into fall.
Ease of care: Easy.
How to grow: At ease in almost any soil, bergamots prefer a slightly moist spot and full sun, becoming somewhat floppy when grown in the shade. Extra water during dry periods is appreciated. The plants are spreaders, so excess plants should be removed from time to time. Spent flowers should also be removed for extended bloom. Clumps must be divided every few years to keep them healthy.
Propagation: By seed or by division in early spring.
Uses: Useful for the wild garden in moist soil or by the waterside, they are also beautiful in beds or borders because of their long season of bright bloom. Flowers are beloved by hummingbirds and butterflies.
Related varieties: 'Blue Stocking' is not really blue, but a brilliant, deep violet, and 'Mahogany' is a deep wine red. Both are on 36-inch stems. 'Cambridge Scarlet' is an old type with brilliant, scarlet flowers; 'Croftway Pink' is a clear rose-pink; and 'Snow White' is white—all are on 30-inch stems.

Bergenias are plants from Siberia and Mongolia. As such they are perfectly happy in low temperatures when covered with snow. They are named in honor of Karl August von Bergen, a German physician and botanist.
Description: Thick, rounded, evergreen leaves, often 1 foot long, grow from a single crown and are edged with red in cold weather. Flowers are pink with waxy petals, blooming in drooping clusters.
Ease of care: Easy.
How to grow: These plants prefer light shade and, without snow cover, protection from bitter winds. They also need a good, moist soil with plenty of organic matter.
Propagation: By division or by seed.
Uses: Excellent as an edging in the border or planted in groups on slopes, bergenias are also a fine addition to the rock garden. The leaves are often used in floral arrangements and will last a month in water.
Related species: The winter begonia, *Bergenia ciliata,* hails from West Pakistan and has large, rounded leaves that are densely hairy on both sides. *Bergenia purpurascens* (often called *B. Delavayi*) has dark green leaves that turn a beetroot-red in winter.
Related varieties: The bergenias have been hybridized over many years, leaving parentage often confused. Among the varieties available are 'Evening Bells,' with bright red winter foliage and rose-pink flowers; 'Evening Glow,' with maroon-colored leaves in winter and flowers of a magenta-crimson said to be hardier than most; and 'Silverlight,' bearing blush-white flowers.

Bishop's Hat, Barrenwort

Epimedium species
Zone: USDA 5

Distinctive foliage and delicate flowers make epimediums a wonderful addition to any garden. The genus is named for the land of the Medes, a country in ancient Persia.

Description: Epimediums have sturdy, heart-shaped leaves with a toothed edge on wiry stems that closely resemble a jester's hat or, in some species, a bishop's miter or biretta. They bloom in April and May.

Ease of care: Easy.

How to grow: Epimediums like good, well-drained, somewhat moist garden soil in open shade, although they will tolerate some sun. They do well under tree canopies. Cut the foliage off in early spring before the new growth begins.

Propagation: By division or by seed.

Uses: Classified by most nurseries as a rock garden ground cover, epimediums are also excellent for the edge of a border. Some of the species are evergreen where the climate allows.

Related species: *Epimedium grandiflora* grows about 1 foot high with white flowers tinged with pink at the tips of the spurs. 'Album' has white flowers and new leaves are tinged with red that slowly turns green. *Epimedium* x *rubrum* has red leaves when young and pale red flowers on 12-inch stems. *Epimedium* x *versicolor* 'Sulphureum' produces the densest foliage and yellow flowers on 10-inch stems. *Epimedium* x *Youngianum* 'Niveum' has white flowers on 8-inch stems and 'Roseum' bears lilac flowers.

Blanket Flower

Gaillardia x *grandiflora*
Zone: USDA 4

Cheerful and bright daisylike flowers, gaillardias are named in honor of Gaillard de Clarentonneau, a French botanist.

Description: This particular species is a hybrid of two others, more vigorous than the native types and often blooming the first year from seed. Slightly hairy leaves are usually basal; 3- to 4-inch flowers have purple centers (disk flowers) and notched petals (ray flowers) in a number of bright colors. They bloom throughout the summer.

Ease of care: Easy.

How to grow: Blanket flowers need full sun and a good, but not too fertile, well-drained garden soil. Sometimes shortlived, the plants will not survive a winter in wet soil. Each year, the center of the crown dies back and new plants appear off center. They are easily transplanted to bloom that summer. Blanket flowers bloom over a long period even if spent blossoms are not removed.

Propagation: By division in early spring or by seed.

Uses: Gaillardias are suited for the front of a border, particularly if grouped in threes or fives. They also provide marvelous cut flowers. The dwarf varieties are fine as edging plants.

Related varieties: There are a number of varieties available with new types showing up every year. The 'Monarch Strain' has a good choice of reds, yellows, and browns, and 'Goblin' is a dwarf reaching a 12-inch height and bearing red flowers with yellow borders.

Blazingstar, Gayfeather

Liatris species
Zone: USDA 4

Blazingstars are good garden plants native to North America. They are especially valuable since they bloom from late summer into fall when the bed or border can use the color. The botanical name is of unknown derivation.

Description: Simple, linear leaves on usually stout stems grow in clumps from thick rootstocks. Flower heads are set along tall spikes and bear fluffy disk flowers, resembling feathery staffs. They bloom in late summer.

Ease of care: Easy.

How to grow: Blazingstars want only good, well-drained soil in full sun to succeed. Winter wet will usually kill the plants. The taller varieties sometimes require staking. They are especially valuable as cut flowers.

Propagation: By division of older plants in spring or by seed.

Uses: Clumps of liatris are perfect for the bed and border. Mix them with white garden phlox or plant taller types behind fountain-type ornamental grasses.

Related species: *Liatris pycnostachya*, the cattail or Kansas gayfeather, grows up to 5 feet, and bears spikes of purple flowers. *Liatris scariosa*, or the button snake-root, bears purple or white fluffy disk flowers on spikes from 3 to 6 feet tall. 'White Spire' has white flowers and 'September Glory' has deep purple flowers on 4-foot stems. *Liatris spicata* 'Kobald' bears rose-purple flowers on 2-foot stems and is perfect for the front of the border. 'Silvertips' has lavender flowers with a silvery sheen on 3-foot stems.

Bleeding Heart

Dicentra species
Zone: USDA 4

These heart-shaped pendant flowers with spurs at the base (the genus name means "two-spurred") have attractive foliage until midsummer.

Description: Bleeding hearts have clusters of rose, pink, or white flowers on arching sprays and bluish, fernlike foliage. Roots are fleshy and sold by the number of eyes present on plant starts.

Ease of care: Easy.

How to grow: Bleeding hearts need open or partial shade with an evenly moist soil on the acid side containing plenty of humus. Plenty of peat moss must be used when planting; mulching is done with pine needles or pine bark.

Propagation: By division in early spring or by seed.

Uses: This plant is a lovely sight when planted next to a moss-covered log with ferns in the background or between the gnarled roots of a large tree.

Related species: *Dicentra eximia*, or the fringed bleeding heart flowers, do best in late spring, but if protected from hot sun and given plenty of moisture, will bloom until frost. Their height is 18 inches. 'Alba' has white flowers. *Dicentra formosa* is a rose-colored species found from British Columbia to California and usually is about 18 inches high. *Dicentra spectabilis* is the old garden favorite from Japan with deep pink flowers blooming from May to June on 24-inch stems. Except in rare instances, this plant will go dormant by midsummer, so it is best screened.

Related variety: *Dicentra* x 'Luxuriant' is a hybrid that will bloom throughout the summer, especially if old flowers are removed.

Bluestar, Blue-Dogbane, Blue-Star-of-Texas

Amsonia tabernaemontana
Zone: USDA 5b

Bluestars are native wildflowers found in woods and on banks from New Jersey to Tennessee and south to Texas. The genus is named in honor of Dr. Charles Amson, an American physician of the 18th century.

Description: Blooming in May and June, bluestars have 5 petals and are a lovely pale blue. After flowering has passed, the upright stems with narrow leaves are still attractive. In the fall, the foliage turns a beautiful butterscotch-yellow.

Ease of care: Easy.

How to grow: Plants should be established in any reasonably fertile garden soil. They grow between 2 and 3 feet tall and are somewhat tolerant of dry soil, remaining shorter when located in such situations. Blossoms are better when given full sun, but bluestars will tolerate just a bit of shade. They will self-sow, with seedlings becoming bushy clumps in a few years.

Propagation: By division in the early spring.

Uses: Bluestars belong in any wild garden and in the perennial bed or border, being especially attractive mixed with wild or garden columbines (*Aquilegia* spp.) and planted in the vicinity of tree peonies.

Related species: A variety called *A. salicifolia* bears very narrow leaves.

Boltonia

Boltonia asteroides
Zone: USDA 4

Boltonias are American native wildflowers found in poor or damp soil as far north as Manitoba and south to Florida, then west to Texas. They are named in honor of James B. Bolton, an English botanist.

Description: Plants resemble asters, with sturdy stems, narrow leaves, and dozens of white flowers in clusters. Blooming from late summer into fall, a well-situated boltonia will be covered with bloom.

Ease of care: Easy.

How to grow: Boltonias prefer average garden soil in full sun. Like many wildflowers, they will be larger in moist, fertile soil.

Propagation: By division in spring or fall.

Uses: Since boltonias grow 5 to 8 feet high, they are best at the rear of the garden. A line of these plants will become a flowering hedge of great charm. They can be used with ornamental grasses or mixed with fall asters.

Related species: *Boltonia latisquama* is listed by some authorities as a variety of *B. asteroides* or by others as a distinct species from the West.

Related variety: 'Snowbank' is a 4-foot selection of the species.

Bowman's-Root

Porteranthus trifoliata
Zone: USDA 5

Bowman's-root is an American wildflower from the Northeast growing south to Alabama. It was formerly called *Gillenia* in honor of Arnoldus Gillenius, a German botanist of the 17th century.

Description: Terminal clusters of thready, white blossoms about 1 inch across on bushy plants with compound leaves bloom in late spring to early summer.

Ease of care: Easy.

How to grow: Bowman's-roots need a good, well-drained garden soil on the acid side in full to partial shade. The roots appreciate plenty of humus or peat moss when planting. Watering is necessary during periods of drought. If the first round of spent blossoms is removed, the plants will bloom again.

Propagation: By seed or division in spring.

Uses: The flowers are quite showy, and the white petals move in the slightest breeze. Sometimes there is a pink tinge to the blossoms. Bowman's-roots work as accent plants in shady gardens and look lovely when planted beneath shrubbery where they can get half a day in shadow.

Bugleweed

Ajuga species
Zone: USDA 3b

Bugleweeds are excellent both for the color of the leaves and the attractive flowers. The botanical name refers to the shape of the leaves that cover the flower.

Description: Plants grow along the ground, the flat, rounded leaves forming mats that can keep weeds from making headway. They bloom in May and June with irregular flowers in spiked clusters.

Ease of care: Easy.

How to grow: Bugleweeds are easy to grow in ordinary, well-drained garden soil, with full sun or partial shade. As a ground cover, plants should be placed 10 inches apart; they will soon fill in. In areas with mild winters or under good snow cover, they are evergreen.

Propagation: By division in spring or fall.

Uses: Bugleweeds are excellent as ground cover and are also beautiful when used as edgings at the front of a border. In a rock garden, they are perfect for tumbling over rock edges. Although they grow quickly, plants are easily uprooted.

Related species: Two species are generally available. *Ajuga pyramidalis* bears brilliant blue flowers on 6-inch spikes, hovering above deep green leaves, and stays bushy, not spreading as widely as others in the clan. In the fall, the leaves turn to purple-bronze. *Ajuga reptans* is the ground cover of note.

Related varieties: 'Metallica Crispa' has purplish-brown leaves with crisped edges, and 'Alba' bears white flowers. 'Burgundy Glow' bears blue flowers with leaves in three colors: new growth is burgundy-red, but as the leaves age, they become creamy white and dark pink. 'Rosea' has rose flowers.

Italian Bugloss

Anchusa azurea
Zone: USDA 4a

A member of the forget-me-not family, it is regrettable that *Anchusa azurea* bears the ponderous common name of Italian bugloss. The genus refers to anchusin, a chemical used for a brilliant-red coloring (derived from plant relatives), and *azurea*, of course, refers to the clear, lovely blue of the flowers.

Description: The blossoms are a brilliant true blue and belong in every garden, flowering in June.

Ease of care: Easy.

How to grow: Bugloss is easy to grow, needing at least a 4-inch depth of well-drained, reasonably fertile garden soil in full sun; however, it will tolerate partial shade. Since plants sometimes reach 4 feet of rangy growth, it is often necessary to stake them. Young plants bloom with more exuberance than old ones.

Propagation: By division or by seed.

Uses: These plants are quite beautiful in large clumps or in a border.

Related varieties: 'Little John' has deep blue flowers on 18-inch stems; 'Loddon Royalist' blooms with purple-blue flowers; and 'Royal Blue' bears intense blue flowers on plants up to 3 feet high.

Siberian Bugloss

Brunnera macrophylla
Zone: USDA 4

From western Siberia, these plants are perennial forget-me-nots, named in honor of Swiss botanist Samuel Brunner. Some catalogs still call it *Anchusa myosotidiflora*.

Description: Showy blue flowers about ¼-inch across bloom in clusters during spring. The leaves are large and heart-shaped on slightly hairy stems. Plants can reach 2 feet in height but usually remain at 18 inches.

Ease of care: Easy.

How to grow: Brunneras prefer a deep, moist soil with plenty of organic matter in full sun (only in the North) or partial shade. They will, however, do reasonably well in a dry spot if they have shade.

Propagation: By division or by seed.

Uses: They are lovely in the front of a border but are exceptionally attractive when naturalized at the border of a wooded area or in a wild garden along a stream or by a pool. After blooming, the large leaves make an effective ground cover.

Creeping Buttercup

Ranunculus repens
Zone: USDA 4

Years ago, children held buttercups under their noses to test their fondness for butter, even though they were warned not to chew the flowers or the leaves because they are capable of raising blisters. Centuries ago, beggars used the sap to ulcerate their feet to arouse pity. Creeping buttercups, originally from Europe, are now naturalized over much of the Northeast. The genus is named from the Latin for "little frog," an allusion to the aquatic habitat of some species.

Description: Buttercups have long, creeping stems. Rooting at nodes are 3-lobed, cut, basal leaves, often with pale blotches. In spring, 5-petaled, yellow flowers, 1-inch wide, appear on 2-foot stems. The plants are poisonous to cattle.

Ease of care: Easy.

How to grow: Any good moist soil will do in full sun or partial shade.

Propagation: By division in spring.

Uses: Creeping buttercups are only for the wild or natural garden. They are not attractive enough for the formal garden.

Related varieties: 'Flore Pleno' is the preferred form of the creeping buttercup, since the double yellow flowers on 18-inch stems are quite beautiful. Although somewhat invasive, they can be easily controlled. *Ranunculus acris,* or the common buttercup, is available in a double form called 'Flore Pleno' that is not a runner but grows in a clump with flowers on 2- to 3-foot stems. Plants require moist soil in full sun to partial shade.

Butterfly Weed, Milkweed

Asclepias tuberosa
Zone: USDA 4a

Butterfly weed is a native American wildflower that is not only at home in the wild garden but contributes to the perennial border as well. The genus is named after the Greek god of medicine.

Description: Bloom time is late spring on into summer. Flowering plants resemble a dish full of orange candy on a 3-foot stem. The individual flowers are striking in their beauty. The plants bear thin leaves and are most attractive when in flower.

Ease of care: Easy.

How to grow: These are easy plants to grow and tolerate a wide variety of soil types, surviving in the thinnest of poor soils but generally doing their best in an average garden setting with full sun and good drainage. Once a butterfly weed develops a good root system, it becomes a great drought-resistant plant, but until mature, watering must not be neglected in a prolonged dry spell.

Propagation: By division in early spring or by seed.

Uses: Butterfly weed does well in meadows and in wild gardens. The flowers can be cut for fresh bouquets. They can also be pressed or dried, retaining their brilliance over a long period of time. The seedpods are also used in dried arrangements.

Related species: The swamp milkweed, *Asclepias incarnata,* has pinkish flowers on 2- to 4-foot stems and will do well in very wet situations. The common milkweed, *Asclepias syriaca,* is beautiful when growing in a nearby field or sequestered in a wild garden, but it is too invasive to bring into the garden proper.

Candytuft

Iberis sempervirens
Zone: USDA 4

Many species of candytuft originally came from Iberia, the ancient name of Spain—hence the genus of *Iberis*. They bloom in the spring.
Description: Candytuft is a many-branched, small, evergreen shrub with smooth, oblong leaves about 1½ inches long. In the spring, it bears flat-topped clusters of white flowers, sometimes flushed with pink. Height can reach 10 inches, spreading to about 20 inches.
Ease of care: Easy.
How to grow: Candytufts need a good, well-drained garden soil in a sunny spot. They are usually evergreen, but in most areas of Zone 4, winter results in severe damage to the leaves. Mulching is necessary if snow is lacking. Dead branches need to be cut off for growth to begin again. Pruning back after spring flowering is recommended.
Propagation: By division or by seed.
Uses: Candytufts are great for a rock garden where they can tumble about and over rocks. They are also excellent as edging in a border and are well-suited to growing in pots.
Related varieties: 'Autumn Snow' stays about 10 inches high and blooms twice—in spring and in fall. 'Little Gem' is a dwarf at a 6-inch height.

Cardinal Flower

Lobelia Cardinalis
Zone: USDA 4

Cardinal flowers are native American wild-flowers of great beauty. The genus is named in honor of botanist Matthias de l'Obel.
Description: Basal foliage, evergreen in mild climates, and oblong leaves on stout stems produce 2- to 4-foot spikes of truly brilliant red flowers that can be seen in the summer over a great distance because of the intense color. They are often found growing at the edge of stream banks in the open shade of tall trees.
Ease of care: Moderately easy.
How to grow: Cardinal flowers will be killed in the winter if they are not properly protected. They must have plenty of moisture in the soil and a good winter mulch in areas without adequate snowfall. They grow best in a light shade in humus-rich, well-drained soil. Divide the plants every two years. Remove flower stalks after blooming, leaving one or two seed-pods for new plants.
Propagation: By division or by seed.
Uses: Unexcelled for waterside planting, the bed, border, and for wild gardens.
Related species: *Lobelia siphilitica*, great blue lobelia, is a plant with similar requirements, but has smaller blue flowers on stout stems 1 to 3 feet high, blooming from late summer into fall.
Related variety: 'Royal Robe' has ruby-red leaves.

Chinese Chives, Garlic Chives

Allium tuberosum
Zone: USDA 4

Usually bulbs are thought of as something separate from perennials because they seldom persist throughout the garden season. Chinese chives, or garlic chives, can be lifted and divided like any other perennial and, even when not in bloom, the foliage is attractive. In addition, they provide blossoms in late summer when most other plants are through. The botanical name is taken from the Latin word for "garlic." The plants only smell of garlic if the leaves are broken or bruised. The flowers are lovely when cut for bouquets.
Description: Plants have narrow leaves and many small, starlike flowers with white petals, each with a green nerve down the center. The root is a bulb.
Ease of care: Easy.
How to grow: Chinese chives are easy to grow in a fertile, well-drained garden soil in full sun or partial shade. If not deadheaded, they will seed about the garden—this is usually only a problem in warmer zones.
Propagation: By division in early spring or by seed.
Uses: In partial shade, garlic chives can be used as underplantings with a border of hostas, so the flowering stalks rise above the other plants long after the latter have ceased to bloom. The dried blossoms persist well into winter, the petals turning a straw color in stark contrast to shiny black seeds, thus making a fine addition to dried bouquets. Since the stems are hollow, they can be slipped over other stems and used in tall arrangements. In Asia, Chinese chives are grown for salads.

Chrysanthemum

Chrysanthemum **species**
Zone: USDA 4 to 6

Chrysanthemums are members of the daisy clan, numbering over 200 species of ornamental plants. One member of the species is the source of the insecticide pyrethrum; another is eaten in the Orient in salads. The genus is Greek for "golden flower."

Description: Leaves are usually divided, often aromatic, and sometimes in basal rosettes. Stems are strong and flowers are showy—either with yellow centers (tubular flowers) surrounded by a row of petals (ray flowers) or a flower head entirely covered with petals as in the florist's mum.

Ease of care: Easy to moderately difficult.

How to grow: As a class of plants, chrysanthemums want good, well-drained soil in full sun. Most have shallow roots, so the soil should be evenly moist with frequent applications of fertilizer. The majority of chrysanthemums are late-blooming, short-day plants with flowers initiated by decreasing day length. They benefit from frequent pinching, which promotes bushy growth. Without adequate snow cover, these plants benefit from mulching in the North.

Propagation: By cuttings, by division, or by seed.

Uses: Garden mums (*Chrysanthemum* x *morifolium*) come in a number of styles including incurved, where petals form a perfect globe; single-flowered, with 5 or less rows of petals around a central disc; and pompons, with small, button-shaped blossoms. Football and spider mums are always popular. Blue is the only color not available. Seeds sown in early spring will flower around October.

Mums can be purchased as rooted cuttings from nursery suppliers to be set out after all frost danger has passed. They are pinched back for bushy growth and bloom in the late summer and fall. In the fall, potted mums can also be purchased from garden centers and transplanted around the garden where they will continue to bloom until severe frost cuts them down. They also do well in containers.

Related species: *Chrysanthemum coccineum*, or the painted daisy, is a minor source of pyrethrum and a major source of cut flowers. Leaves are fernlike, and blossoms come in a number of shades of red, pink, and white on 30-inch stems, blooming in June. They must be cut back to the ground after blooming for a second crop of flowers. *Chrysanthemum* x *superbum*, or the shasta daisy, produces 4-inch flowers on 1- to 3-foot stems. They prefer cool summers and need some shade in the South. Spotted throughout the border, they bloom from summer to fall and make excellent cut flowers. 'Miss Muffet' has white flowers in early summer; 'Aglaya' is a double, white flower on 26-inch stems blooming from June to September; and 'Cobham Gold' has large, double, cream-colored flowers blooming in summer. *Chrysanthemum nipponicum*, or the Nippon daisy, bears white flowers on 2-foot woody stems, which bear thick, scalloped leaves. They resemble small bushes. These plants cannot be divided, but new plants do grow about the base. Early frost will ruin the flowers, so care must be taken to cover them. The foliage is very aromatic. Nippon daisies are excellent in seaside gardens. *Chrysan-*

themum pacificum is a new plant on the nursery scene. It forms a dense, low-growing ground cover with succulentlike foliage. Its leaves have distinct silver-green margins, on plants 4 to 6 inches high. Clusters of golden-yellow flowers resembling the common tansy appear in October but are often cut down by frost in the North. Runners of one plant are said to cover a 3 × 4-foot area in three years. *Chrysanthemum Parthenium*, or feverfew, is still called *Matricaria* in some catalogs. It is an old medical herb, the common name referring to the plant's use as an aid in reducing fever and curing headaches. Bushy plants grow to 3 feet with aromatic leaves. 'Double White' bears double, white flowers on 2-foot stems, and 'Aureum' bears little white flowers on leaves of a golden-yellow color. *Chrysanthemum Weyrichii* is a fairly recent Japanese import that flowers in very late fall with 2-inch single flowers with a yellow eye. 'Pink Bomb' bears flowers with soft, pink petals on 12-inch stems. 'White Bomb' has white flowers in great profusion. *Chrysanthemum Zawadskii*, or the Korean chrysanthemum, is often called *C. rubellum* and is usually available only as 'Clara Curtis.' This plant bears clear pink, single-flowered blossoms that are very hardy.

Cinquefoil

Potentilla thurberi
Zone: USDA 5

This is a large genus, including a number of shrubby plants with foliage and flowers often compared to those of the strawberry—a fact that is not too surprising since both plants belong to the rose family. The genus name refers to the word "potent" because the plants were once thought to be the source of miraculous medicines.

Description: Plants have compound leaves comprised of 5 to 7 leaflets and are coarsely toothed. They bloom in summer with 5-petaled, mahogany-red flowers about ⅜-inch across.

Ease of care: Easy.

How to grow: Potentillas need excellent drainage, a spot in full sun, and good soil.

Propagation: By division or by seed.

Uses: Cinquefoil is a fine plant for the edge of the border or in the rock garden.

Related species: *Potentilla nepalensis*, originally from the Himalayas, is a sprawling plant best seen as a border edging plant or in the rock garden. The plant usually offered is 'Miss Willmott,' with flowers of a warm cherry-pink.

Bush Clematis, Upright Clematis

Clematis recta
Zone: USDA 4

Most gardeners think of clematis as vines that twine around a trellis or arbor, producing large flowers in great profusion. The plants described here are the shrub clematis, which are excellent for the bed or border. *Clematis* is a Greek word for "brush wood" and refers to the plant's branches.

Description: These are the tall shrubby plants with handsome, compound leaves and showy flowers are followed by silky seed heads.

Ease of care: Easy.

How to grow: Plants like full sun to partial shade, requiring good, well-drained but moist soil with plenty of organic matter mixed in. The phrase "a cool root run" is often used to describe the wants of these plants, since clematis roots resent hot sun, dryness, and heat.

Propagation: By stem cuttings or by seed.

Uses: Planted on a low bank, these plants can tumble down to the ground in a white cascade. They can also wander over low shrubs and small conifers. If neatness is desired, the plants can be ringed with a low wire fence, where the foliage will soon cover the support. The white, star-shaped flowers are fragrant and produce silky seed heads. A plant will grow in a large pot if kept out of the hot sun.

Related species: *Clematis recta* 'Purpurea' has white flowers with rosy foliage. *Clematis heracleifolia Davidiana* bears lightly scented, blue flowers on bushy plants up to 4 feet high in the summer. 'Robert Brydon' bears pale blue flowers and will grow to 10 feet. It can be tied to a trellis or allowed to fall over the other plants in the garden.

Black Cohosh

Cimicifuga racemosa
Zone: USDA 4

Black cohosh is an American native wildflower. *Cimicifuga* is Latin for "driving bugs away," referring to the unpleasant, but not offensive, smell of the flowers. It was erroneously thought to repel insects.

Description: Enormous leaves divide into three parts and are very attractive. In summer, flower spikes often reach a height of 8 feet in a perfect location. There are many tiny, white flowers that glow like candles if the plant is in the shade.

Ease of care: Easy.

How to grow: Cimicifugas like partial shade and a good, fertile soil on the acid side. In evenly moist soil, they will take more sun. A good mulch of compost every spring is appreciated. Clumps enlarge slowly and can be left alone for years.

Propagation: By division of mature plants in spring or by seed.

Uses: When not in bloom, these plants are attractive in the garden, but when flowering, these are the stars of the back of the border.

Related species: *Cimicifuga americana,* or American bugbane, is another member of the genus that is shorter, with flowering stalks up to 4 feet tall and blooming in late summer. *Cimicifuga simplex* comes from Japan and bears white flowers on 4-foot stems in the fall, often succumbing to frost before blooming.

Related varieties: *Cimicifuga racemosa* 'Atropurpurea' has dark purple foliage and can be grown from seed (remember to discard the lighter-leaved seedlings). Plants are shorter. *Cimicifuga racemosa* 'Brunette' is another new addition to the purplish foliage forms.

Columbine

Aquilegia species
Zone: USDA 4

Columbines are beloved by hummingbirds, are perfect for cut flowers, and have a very long season of bloom. The genus is from the Latin word for "eagle," probably referring to the spurred petals of the flowers.

Description: The leaves are compound with rounded lobes and are susceptible to insects called leaf-miners that tunnel about and produce tracings that often resemble nonsense writing. They do not harm the plants. Flower seasons can be extended by removing all of the spent blossoms before plants go to seed.

Ease of care: Easy.

How to grow: Columbines are easy to grow, adapting to almost any reasonably fertile garden soil, although the thick, black roots must have good drainage. They will do well in full sun or partial shade, especially in the South.

Propagation: By division in early spring or by seed.

Uses: Since the flowers are both attractive and will bloom over a long period, columbines are excellent in beds and borders. An entire garden could be composed of these blossoms. Flower season can be extended by removing all of the spent blossoms before plants go to seed.

Related species: *Aquilegia caerulea* is the Colorado columbine, with sky-blue blossoms with white centers on wiry stems growing to 2 feet. *Aquilegia canadensis* is the wild Eastern columbine, with graceful flowers having long, red spurs and yellow faces on 1- to 2-foot stems. It is one of the easiest wildflowers to cultivate. Plants want partial shade and well-drained but not too rich soil. The foliage lasts all year and is often evergreen in milder climates. Perfect in a rock garden, these plants will often seed about in the thinnest layers of soil. They bloom in spring. *Aquilegia chrysantha* is another American native from the Southwest that bears yellow flowers on plants up to 3 feet high and blooms over a long season. There is a dwarf called 'Nana' that remains about 1 foot high. *Aquilegia flabellata* come from Japan and are excellent in the rock garden or as an edging for a border, since the plants are usually 14 inches high or smaller. 'Nana Alba' has pure white flowers on plants under 1 foot high that come from seed.

Related varieties: The hybrid plants vary between 1 to 3 feet in height and are available in many varieties and in many colors. Among the best are the McKana hybrids, with 2-foot plants bearing blossoms of blue, pink, maroon, purple, red, and white, and the Music hybrids, with 20-inch plants producing flowers of intense yellow, blue and white, red and white, and pure white. 'Nora Barlow' has fully double flowers in combinations of red, pink, and green. 'Dragonfly' has flowers with longer than average spurs.

Purple Coneflower

Echinacea purpurea
Zone: USDA 5

This lovely American native was once found naturally from Ohio to Iowa and south to Louisiana and Georgia. The genus is named in honor of the hedgehog because the receptacle (the part that holds the flower proper) is prickly.

Description: Cone-shaped, prickly heads of a bronze-brown are surrounded by rose-purple petals (really ray flowers) on stout stalks from 2 to 4 feet high. Leaves are alternate, simple, and coarse to the touch.

Ease of care: Easy.

How to grow: Coneflowers will take almost any well-drained garden soil in full sun. If soil is too good, the flowers must often be staked. Spent flowers should be removed to prolong blooming.

Propagation: By division in spring or by seed.

Uses: Coneflowers are beautiful plants for the back of a small garden border and they are a welcome addition to a wildflower garden. They are especially fine when mixed with gloriosa daisies (*Rudbeckia* sp.) and many of the ornamental grasses. They make excellent cut flowers.

Related species: *Echinacea pallida* is a similar wildflower species from the Midwest with thinner and more graceful petals.

Related varieties: 'White Lustre' and 'White Swan' are two varieties with white flowers; 'Bright Star' bears maroon flowers; and 'Magnus' has rosy purple petals with a dark disk.

Yellow Coneflower, Black-Eyed Susan

Coralbell, Alumroot

Coreopsis

Rudbeckia fulgida
Zone: USDA 5

Heuchera sanguinea
Zone: USDA 4

Coreopsis species
Zone: USDA 5

All the members of the genus are native American wildflowers, known collectively as coneflowers. The genus is named in honor of Olaf Rudbeck and his son, both professors of botany.

Description: Coneflowers have hairy, 2- to 3-foot stems with simple, saw-toothed edges. They bear daisies with yellow ray flowers, slightly orange at the base, and purple-brown disk flowers, blooming in July and on to frost.

Ease of care: Easy.

How to grow: Although best with a good, moist soil, orange coneflowers will adapt to any good garden soil that is not too dry or too wet, in full sun. Divide plants every three years.

Propagation: By division or by seed.

Uses: Great flowers for the wild garden or for naturalizing in the meadow garden, 'Goldsturm' is best for the formal bed or border and should be planted in drifts. These flowers are perfect when used in combination with the variegated ornamental grasses. They are also excellent for cutting.

Related species: *Rudbeckia laciniata,* or the green-headed coneflower, is valuable for a wild garden. 'Goldquelle' or, as it's sometimes called, 'Gold Drop' has big, double flowers on 24- to 30-inch stems.

Related varieties: 'Goldsturm' is the plant usually offered by nurseries. About 24 inches high, the golden-yellow flowers bloom profusely in July and August. 'Golden Glow' is found in old-fashioned gardens, with its moplike golden heads on 6-foot stems.

Coralbells are American wildflowers originally from New Mexico and Arizona and south to Mexico.

Description: Coralbells are mounds of basal leaves that are rounded and lobed, rising from a thick rootstock. The flowers are tiny bells on 1- to 2-foot slender stems, blooming from spring into summer.

Ease of care: Easy.

How to grow: In areas of hot summers, these plants like a bit of shade, but usually they prefer as much sun as possible. They should be planted in good, well-drained garden soil with a high humus content and kept somewhat moist. In winter, coralbells resent wet soil and often will die. Every three years they must be divided to prevent crowding. Spent flowers should be removed.

Propagation: By division in spring or by seed.

Uses: Coralbells are lovely in a border or when planted among rocks, rock walls, and in the rock garden. They are also good cut flowers.

Related varieties: 'Bressingham Hybrids' produce flowers in shades of pink to deep crimson and white on 20- to 24-inch stems; 'Chatterbox' has rich, rose-pink flowers on 18-inch stems; 'French White' are white; and 'Pluie de Feu' (or rain of fire) bears cherry-red flowers. 'Purple Palace' has deep mahogany-purple foliage with pale pink flowers.

Coreopsis is a Greek word for "buglike," referring to the shape of this plant's seeds, which were thought to look like ticks. The comparison is not particularly apt.

Description: Small daisies in various shades of yellow and orange grow on wiry stems up to 3 feet high. Leaves vary from simple, oval shapes in basal rosettes to foliage that is decidedly fernlike.

Ease of care: Easy.

How to grow: Coreopsis are happy in almost any well-drained garden soil in full sun. They are drought-resistant and an outstanding choice for hot, difficult places.

Propagation: By division in spring or by seed.

Uses: Excellent for the wild garden and in the formal border, these flowers are prized for cutting. The smaller types are also good for edging plants. Coreopsis are suited for patio containers and in hanging baskets. Tying up is often indicated.

Related species: *Coreopsis grandiflora* and *C. lanceolata* are freely interchanged. *Coreopsis auriculata* 'Nana' is a dwarf form that stays about 1 foot tall and bears orange flowers. *Coreopsis grandiflora* 'Sunray' bears double, golden-yellow flowers on 2-foot stems. *Coreopsis lanceolata* 'Goldfink' has golden-yellow flowers on 9-inch stems. 'Brown Eyes' has a ring of dark brown close to the center of golden flowers on 20-inch stems. *Coreopsis verticillata* bears bright yellow flowers on 2-foot mounds of foliage. 'Moonbeam' is a light-cream yellow; 'Golden Showers' bears dozens of yellow flowers on 24- to 30-inch stems; and 'Zagreb' is a long-blooming type with yellow flowers on 18-inch stems.

Crane's-Bill

Geranium species
Zone: USDA 5

Crane's-bill is the common name for this plant because the female part of the flower resembles the shape of a crane's beak. *Geranium* is the genus and is Greek for the same similarity. These plants are not to be confused with the common summer or florist's geranium that is really a *Pelargonium* and at home in South Africa.

Description: Usually low-growing plants with lobed or deeply cut leaves on forked stems, crane's-bills bear 5-petaled flowers in great profusion. They bloom from spring to summer.

Ease of care: Easy.

How to grow: Garden geraniums need good, well-drained garden soil in full sun or light shade in areas of hot summers. The larger types will sometimes need staking.

Propagation: By division or by seed.

Uses: In a border or a rock garden, crane's-bills are lovely plants. They make an excellent ground cover and are striking when grown along a wall, letting the stems and flowers tumble over the edge. In many of the species, leaves turn red in the autumn.

Related species: *Geranium cinereum* is a low-growing plant usually reaching about 8 inches in height with pink flowers 1 inch across. 'Ballerina' is deep pink, and 'Splendens' is a vivid crimson. *Geranium dalmaticum* grows 6 inches high with rose-colored flowers. *Geranium himalayense* (sometimes called *G. grandiflorum*) produces 2-inch wide, violet-blue flowers on 15-inch stems. 'Johnson's Blue' has bright, blue-violet flowers that bear dozens of blossoms in June and July. *Geranium sanguineum* reaches 1½ feet in height, with violet-red flowers that bloom most of the summer.

Cupid's Dart

Catananche caerulea
Zone: USDA 5

One species of this small genus is at home in the garden. The botanical name is derived from a Greek word that means "a strong incentive," since ancient Greek women used it for a love potion.

Description: The blue or white flowers resemble annual bachelor's buttons. They grow about 2 inches across on 20-inch stems with narrow, woolly leaves.

Ease of care: Easy.

How to grow: Plants need a location in full sun with perfectly drained soil. Winter wet will rot the roots.

Propagation: By division or by seed. Seeds sown early will flower the first year.

Uses: Use the plants in the front of the garden in a grouping to provide a drift of flowers. Cupid's dart makes both a good cut flower and a fine everlasting flower for winter bouquets.

Related variety: 'Alba' bears white flowers.

Michaelmas Daisy

Aster species
Zone: USDA 5

The genus name of the asters is the Greek word for "star," and if ever a group of plants deserved such a bright appelation, this is the one.

Description: Daisylike flowers, usually about 1 inch wide with yellow centers, are carried on stiff, branched stems with long, narrow leaves. Bushy plants vary from 6 inches to 6 feet high, blooming from late summer into fall. The yellow centers are actually disk flowers, and the petals are really ray flowers.

Ease of care: Easy.

How to grow: These plants do not need pampering other than good drainage and full sun. They want reasonable garden soil, preferring one that is slightly acid. Although asters in the field can take a great deal of dryness, those in the garden will need water in periods of drought. Plants should be divided every two years as the center of the clump begins to look tattered. Plants can be pinched to produce neater clumps of flowers or be left alone. Sometimes the taller types require staking.

Propagation: By division in spring. Seedlings of many species can be variable both in growth habit and bloom, but adventurous gardeners might enjoy the challenge.

Uses: Originally the English took the American New York field aster, *Aster novi-belgii*, and the New England aster, *A. novae-angliae*, and produced the Michaelmas daisy through hybridizing. Today the resulting varieties are stalwarts of the late summer and fall garden. The smaller types can be used as edgings for borders; the middle-sized asters are beautiful when grouped according to color; and the largest asters become effective backdrops to

Daylily

Hemerocallis species
Zone: USDA 4

other plants. Asters mix well with ornamental grasses—also blooming in the fall—and late-blooming perennial sunflowers (*Helianthus* species) and sneezeweeds (*Helenium* species).

Related species: The alpine aster, *Aster alpinus*, is a dwarf species with gray-green leaves and yellow-centered, purple-blue flowers, from 1 to 1½ inches wide. They are excellent in the rock garden or in the front of a border, blooming in summer. There are a number of colored forms available. The wild asters, *Aster novae-angliae* and *A. novi-belgii*, the parents of the Michaelmas daisies, are usually too rangy for the formal garden, although variations do occur in the wild that deserve some attention. They are also excellent for the wild garden. The Siberian aster, *Aster tataricus*, is hardy to USDA Zone 3 and produces light blue flowers on very tall plants, sometimes reaching 7 feet.

Related varieties: From the original *Aster novae-angliae* line come, among others, 'Alma Potschke,' 3 feet tall and bearing deep pink flowers that bloom for almost six weeks; 'September Ruby,' with deep crimson flowers on 40-inch stems; and 'Harrington's Pink,' featuring pure pink flowers on 4-foot stems. For shorter plants look for the *Aster novi-belgii* varieties: 'Alert,' with red flowers on 15-inch plants; 'Pink Bouquet,' with pink flowers on 14-inch plants; and 'Snow Flurry,' with white flowers on 15-inch plants.

The scientific name of the wild daylily is *Hemerocallis fulva*—*hemero* being Greek for "beautiful" and *callis* Greek for "day," since each individual blossom opens, matures, and withers in 24 hours or less. *Fulva* is the Latin word for "tawny."

Daylilies first reached England in 1575: Originally they were brought over the trade routes from China. Settlers in America from Europe and England brought these hardy plants to brighten their colonial gardens. Almost every home had tawny daylilies and a clump of lemon lilies, *Hemerocallis Lilio-asphodelus* (once known as *H. flava*). Today there are well over 30,000 varieties with more on the way every year.

Description: Tuberous and fleshy roots with mostly basal, sword-shaped leaves usually grow up to 2 feet long with tall, multi-branched stalks, each containing many 6-petaled lilylike flowers. Once blooming only in summer, new varieties now begin to bloom in May and on into September and include some rebloomers.

Ease of care: Easy.

How to grow: Daylilies are literally carefree, wanting only good, well-drained garden soil in full sun. They benefit from partial shade in the South.

Propagation: By division in spring or fall. The species is also propagated by seed.

Uses: Entire gardens can be created using these marvelous plants—dwarf types for rock gardens, species for beds and borders, and varieties for edging. By mixing types, bloom can be present from late spring to fall. The common tawny daylily can be used to hold dry, rocky banks together and for plantings in meadows or wild gardens. The lemon lily is

indeed a valuable garden plant. Flower sizes vary from 3 to over 6 inches, with as many as 30 to 80 flowers on a stem or scape.

Related species: *Hemerocallis citrina* blooms in summer with arching 3½-foot leaves and fragrant, yellow blossoms on 4-foot stems that open in the early evening and last to the following day. *Hemerocallis fulva* is the tawny daylily, too rough for today's perennial bed or border, but still excellent for a ground cover or for a wild or meadow garden. *Hemerocallis Lilioasphodelus* is the old-fashioned lemon lily with fragrant blossoms for late May and June. *Hemerocallis minor* is a dwarf species with yellow, fragrant flowers and grasslike leaves reaching a height of 18 inches.

Related varieties: There are hundreds of daylily varieties available every year from nurseries. The following are noteworthy: *Hemerocallis* 'Bertie Ferris' has midseason blossoms of deeply ruffled persimmon on 15-inch stems; 'Catherine Woodbery,' with flowers of a pale, orchid-pink blooming in July on 30-inch stems; 'Chicago Fire,' a brilliant red hybrid, with 6-inch blossoms on 24-inch stems for midseason; 'Evergold,' bearing deep gold flowers on 40-inch stems and blooming in August; 'Ed Murray,' with deep black-red flowers on 28-inch stems for midseason; 'Hyperion,' a fragrant lemon lily blooming midseason on 42-inch stems; and 'Stella de Oro,' with 2½-inch, golden-yellow flowers that bloom from late June into autumn.

Delphinium, Larkspur

Delphinium species
Zone: USDA 4 to 6

The genus of this plant comes from the Greek word for "dolphin" and is suggested by the shape of a gland in the blossoms that secretes nectar. Many delphiniums are poisonous to cattle.

Description: The alternate leaves are cut and divided. Plants produce tall spikes of showy flowers, usually in shades of blue, each having a long spur behind the petals.

Ease of care: Moderately difficult.

How to grow: Delphiniums are worth almost any effort to grow because they are so beautiful. They need full sun and a good, deep, well-drained, evenly moist soil that has a high humus content. If the soil is too acid, agricultural lime should be added. They are hardy feeders that must be supplied with compost or well-rotted manure, benefiting from feedings of a 5-10-5 fertilizer every year. The area where they grow should have some protection from high winds because the hollow flower stalks, though strong, are often so covered with flowers that they can easily break in the breeze. Many gardens use delphiniums in front of stone walls for this reason. Without such protection, the gardener will have to resort to staking. After flowering, flower heads should be removed unless seeds are wanted. Surprisingly, these plants are very cold-hardy and resent hot climates and long, blistering summers. Delphiniums are short-lived perennials that lose their vitality after two to three years. Since they grow easily from seeds and cuttings, propagation is never a problem.

Propagation: By cuttings, by seed, or by careful division.

Uses: Short delphiniums can be used in the front of a garden, the Belladonna hybrids in the middle, and the tall Pacific Coast hybrids in the rear. They are excellent cut flowers, too.

Related species: Only hardy to USDA 8, *Delphinium cardinale,* or scarlet larkspurs, are lovely flowers for the summer garden. *Delphinium elatum,* or the candle larkspur, is one of the sources for many of the most beautiful delphinium hybrids today. Reaching to 6 feet, the flowers are now available in white, lavender, blue, and purple. The Belladonna hybrids are light blue with 5-foot stalks and, if spent flowers are removed, they will usually produce blooms all summer long. 'Casa Blanca' is pure white. The Blackmore and Langdon hybrids were first developed in 1905. Today's plants bear pastel blue, lavender, white, violet, and indigo flowers on 4- to 5-foot stems. The Pacific Coast hybrids produce 7-foot stalks that must be staked even when given protection; the flowers in various shades of blue and pink are spectacular. 'Magic Fountain' is a dwarf version growing to 30 inches with double blooms. 'Connecticut Yankee' is a bush delphinium with single flowers of mixed colors on 30-inch stalks. *Delphinium grandiflorum* (sometimes called *D. chinensis*), or the Siberian larkspur, has finely cut foliage and blue flowers on 2- to 3-foot stalks, blooming the first year from seed if started early. 'Blue Mirror' has gentian-blue flowers, and 'Alba' is white.

Edelweiss

Leontopodium alpinum
Zone: USDA 5

Edelweiss means "noble white" in German. This is the plant that supposedly has led to the death of stalwart youths who, when reaching from mountain crags for the blooms, missed their footing and fell into the abyss. The genus name means "lion's foot" and refers to the shape and woolly aspect of the flower.

Description: Tufted plants with gray and woolly leaves grow to about 12 inches in height. Small flower heads are surrounded by starlike clusters of white, woolly bracts.

Ease of care: Easy.

How to grow: Edelweiss want full sun, well-drained sandy or gritty soil, and will not survive wet soil in the winter. In areas without snow cover, protect the plants from rain and sleet with glass.

Propagation: By seed sown in spring.

Uses: Edelweiss are perfect for the rock garden, as the woolly plants look best when used in conjunction with stone.

Pearly Everlasting

Anaphalis species
Zone: USDA 4a

Pearly everlastings bear the genus name of *Anaphalis*, said to be an ancient Greek name for a similar plant. They are members of the daisy family. Their common name refers to their everlasting quality when dried, and many a farmer's mantlepiece held winter bouquets using this American wildflower.

Description: The American species, *Anaphalis margaritacea*, grows as a wildflower over much of the country. It is 2 feet tall and has slender, pointed leaves that are green on top and gray underneath. Small clusters of ¼-inch white flowers bloom in the summer. *Anaphalis triplinervis* comes from the alpine Himalayas. It has silvery gray leaves in the spring that turn green as summer progresses. Flowers bloom in clusters from midsummer until frost.

Ease of care: Easy.

How to grow: Both species are easy to grow, adapting to most soil conditions, but *Anaphalis triplinervis* is not as rangy as *A. margaritacea* and better for the perennial border. It will also adapt to a moist soil. Plants grow up to 18 inches in height bearing 6-inch leaves of a silvery gray color. *Anaphalis margaritacea* will grow to 20 inches and is especially valuable in dry situations as it will survive and bloom on dry hillsides. It is also a welcome addition to the wild garden.

Propagation: By division in spring or fall or by seed.

Uses: The gray leaf color adds a welcome change from the greens found in the typical summer garden. In late summer, the plants begin to bloom and bear many clusters of small, white blossoms with petals—really bracts—that feel and look like shiny paper. They are easy to dry for winter bouquets. After autumn winds blow away the seeds, only the attractive outer bracts are left.

Fleabane

Erigeron hybridus
Zone: USDA 5

Fleabanes are members of the daisy family that closely resemble asters. Their common name is a salute to the belief that they once controlled the ravages of fleas. The genus name is from the Greek and means "an early old man," probably referring to the early flowering and fruiting of some species.

Description: Fleabanes have narrow leaves that are smooth above and woolly underneath. The flowers are densely fringed in clusters on 18-inch stems.

Ease of care: Easy.

How to grow: Fleabanes prefer good, well-drained garden soil in full sun. They prefer slight shade in areas of hot summers.

Propagation: By division in early spring, by cuttings, or by seed.

Uses: Fleabanes are excellent in the rock garden, the formal bed or border, and the wild garden. Plant them in drifts as the flowers look best when more than one plant is used. They are excellent as cut flowers.

Related species: *Erigeron speciosus* 'Azure Fairy' has semi-double, lavender flowers on 30-inch stems.

Related varieties: 'Foerster's Liebling' has double, pink flowers; 'Double Beauty' bears double, violet-blue flowers; and 'Prosperity' has semi-double, mauve-blue flowers.

Chinese Forget-Me-Not

Cynoglossum nervosum
Zone: USDA 5

Cynoglossum, the Greek word for "hound's tongue," and "Chinese forget-me-not" are both aptly chosen names. The delightful flowers resemble the common garden forget-me-not (*Myosotis sylvatica*), and the leaves indeed look like Fido with an open mouth.

Description: Large, hairy, rough leaves grow on stems up to 30 inches high. They are topped with many sprays of ³/₅-inch, gentian-blue flowers that bloom in July, lasting well into August.

Ease of care: Easy.

How to grow: Cynoglossums want full sun and a good, well-drained but moist soil. They will also do surprisingly well in dry soils. In good soil, growth will be exuberant and stems will flop over.

Propagation: By division in spring or by seed.

Uses: While the flowers are welcome in the formal garden bed or border, these plants seem better suited for the wild garden as the leaves can be quite unruly. Stems should be cut off in the fall.

Related variety: 'Dwarf Firmament' produces sky blue blossoms on 18-inch plants.

Yellow Foxglove

Digitalis grandiflora
Zone: USDA 4

Most foxgloves are biennial plants, but *Digitalis grandiflora* (still called *D. ambigua* in some catalogs) is a true perennial for the garden. The genus is named for the Latin word for "finger" in reference to the shape of the flower. The common name alludes to the belief that a fox could become invisible and make off with the chickens if it wore blossoms on its paws.

Description: Yellow foxgloves are strong-stemmed plants with simple alternate leaves. Their nodding bell-like flowers usually line up on one side of the stem and bloom in summer.

Ease of care: Easy.

How to grow: Yellow foxgloves want a good, moist, well-drained garden soil in partial shade. If dead flower stalks are removed, plants sometimes bloom a second time.

Propagation: By division or by seed.

Uses: Foxgloves are superb in the wild garden and among plants that have naturalized along the edge of a wooded area. They are also lovely in front of a line of shrubbery or small trees.

Related species: *Digitalis lutea* is a perennial from 2 to 3 feet high that bears many small, creamy yellow fingers on one side of each blooming stalk, flowering in May and June.

Gas Plant, Burning Bush

Dictamnus albus
Zone: USDA 4

There is only one species in this genus, and rumor has it that its leaves, if lighted with a match on a breathless summer evening, will produce a gas and burn with a faint glow. Many have tried, but few have reported success. The genus is named in honor of plants that grew on Mount Dicte in Crete.

Description: A handsome plant resembling a small bush, gas plants grow between 2 and 3 feet high with glossy, compound leaves and attractive white flowers. The leaves have a faint, lemony scent.

Ease of care: Easy.

How to grow: The location of a gas plant must be chosen with care. Once planted it will persist for decades, although it cannot be moved as its roots resent any disturbance. A spot in full sun with good, humus-rich, moist, and well-drained soil is needed. Plants are usually purchased as 2-year-old seedlings. Allow 3 feet between plants if grouped.

Propagation: By seed.

Uses: In flower or out, this is an attractive plant for the border since, even after flowering has passed, the seed heads provide visual interest.

Related varieties: 'Purpureus' bears pink flowers, and 'Rubra' has flowers of a rosy-purple.

Gaura

Gaura Lindheimeri
Zone: USDA 6

There are a number of gauras that are native American wildflowers; however, this particular species is the best for the garden. Found naturally from Louisiana to Texas and south to Mexico, the white flowers slowly fade to pink as they age. The genus is a Greek word for "proud," since many of the species are showy when in bloom.

Description: Gaura has alternate, lance-shaped leaves up to 3 inches long on stout stems. It blooms with 1-inch, white, 4-petaled flowers that age to pink and persist throughout the summer. Stems can reach to 6 feet.

Ease of care: Easy.

How to grow: Gauras need full sun in good, deep, well-drained garden soil as the tap root is very long. They are both drought- and heat-resistant.

Propagation: By division in spring or by seed.

Uses: Perfect for both a dry garden and a wild garden, they are also very attractive in a formal border. In northern climates, they bloom late in the season and are charming when planted with asters and ornamental grasses.

Globeflower

Trollius x *cultorum*
Zone: USDA 5

Globeflowers resemble large, double butter-cups or florist's ranunculus, with blossoms sitting like golden-yellow balls atop 30-inch stems. The genus name is from the Hungarian, *torolya*, a native name for the flower.
Description: Thick rootstocks slowly form large clumps that produce many strong stems with coarsely toothed leaves and one showy 2-inch flower per stem. Each flower has many waxy, rounded sepals and 5 or more petals, blooming in late May and June.
Ease of care: Easy.
How to grow: Globeflowers need a good, moist garden soil with plenty of humus. In the North, full sun will do as long as the soil is moist. They are better in partial shade. Remove spent flowers to promote further bloom.
Propagation: By division in fall or by seed.
Uses: Globeflowers are beautiful when planted in masses—both in sunny or shady borders. They are excellent waterside plants, doing well where others might not succeed. They make good cut flowers.
Related species: *Trollius europaeus* forms a compact clump and bears clear yellow flowers on 24-inch stems, blooming in late April and May. 'Superbus' is usually offered.
Related varieties: 'Byrne's Giant' is pure yellow, and 'Etna' is a dark orange—both are on 24-inch stems; 'Lemon Queen' is lemon-yellow on 28-inch stems; 'Orange Nassau' has orange flowers, and 'Prichard's Giant' bears large, deep golden-yellow flowers. It is one of the first to flower.

Goat's Beard, Wild Spirea

Aruncus dioicus
Zone: USDA 4

Goat's beard has been revered for years; the genus was named by Pliny, the Roman naturalist.
Description: Plants can grow as high as 6 feet and look like a bush. Then in early autumn, the plants come into bloom, producing many showy plumes of tiny, white flowers. The plants bring color to the garden after the usual spring show has passed.
Ease of care: Easy.
How to grow: Goat's beard is easy to grow as long as the gardener provides light shade and a moist soil. The plants are *dioecious,* meaning that male and female flowers grow on separate plants, but there is little difference between them, and most nurseries never mark the distinction. Goat's beard does very well in moist bottomland and should never lack for water in the summer.
Propagation: By division in the spring (difficult with older plants) or by seed.
Uses: Because it wants light shade rather than deep shadow, goat's beard is a fine choice for areas under groups of high trees. A waterside planting is also a good choice, especially when the plants have a background of trees.
Related species: *Aruncus aethusifolius* is a dwarf variety from Korea that makes a 6- to 8-inch mound of feathery leaves and 1-foot spires of white, plumelike blossoms, making an excellent edging for the garden border.
Related varieties: 'Kneiffi' is the cut-leaf goat's beard, reaching a height of 4 feet with leaves that are cut into narrow segments. 'Zweiweltenkind' bears white plumes of flowers on 4-foot plants.

Goldenrod

Solidago hybrids
Zone: USDA 5

Glorious flowers of the American fall, gold-enrods have suffered from bad press due to the mistaken belief that they cause hay fever and the fact that a few can become weedy when brought into the garden. Since most of the 130 or so species found in the wild cross-pollinate with ease, the plants described are unspecified hybrids. The genus name is from the Latin *solidare*, "to join," and refers to reputed healing properties.
Description: Goldenrods are strong-stemmed plants, often growing to 6 feet tall, with either smooth or lightly toothed alternate leaves arising from a root crown or rhizome. They bloom in late summer or fall with sprays of small, usually golden-yellow flowers.
Ease of care: Easy.
How to grow: Goldenrods are happy in full sun or partial shade with good, well-drained garden soil. They will also do well in moist conditions.
Propagation: By division in spring or by seed.
Uses: Great for the wild garden, stream side, or naturalized in meadow gardens, goldenrods are striking in the open bed or border. They are excellent for cutting.
Related varieties: 'Golden Mosa' has golden-yellow flowers on 2- to 3-foot stems. 'Cloth of Gold' has golden-yellow flowers, while 'Crown of Rays' bears yellow flowers—both are on 18-inch stems. 'Laurin' bears bright yellow flowers on 16-inch stems, and 'Golden Dwarf' has bright yellow blossoms on 1-foot stems.

Goldenstar

Chrysogonum virginianum
Zone: USDA 6

From Pennsylvania and West Virginia, south to Florida and Louisiana, the goldenstar is an American native and the only species in this genus. The genus name means "golden joint" and refers to the blossoms rising from stem nodes.

Description: Yellow daisies about 2 inches across nod above hairy leaves on stems that creep and make a mound about 10 inches high, blooming from spring into summer. The leaves are evergreen and are not particularly attractive.

Ease of care: Easy.

How to grow: If trying to grow this plant in the North, a sunny spot with protection from winter winds must be chosen. Lack of snow cover in Zone 5 will usually do it in. Well-drained, humus-rich soil is best and, while it does well in full sun, partial shade is best. When the plants first bloom, they are only a few inches high, but the last flowers of the season might be on stems 12 inches high. Nursery-grown specimens are often shorter than those from the wild.

Propagation: By seed or by division (only in the spring).

Uses: A star in the wild garden, goldenstar is also an excellent ground cover and perfect for the rock garden.

Related varieties: Both 'Mark Viette' and 'Australis' are long-blooming clump forms. 'Allen Bush' is a rapid-spreading form that blooms heavily in the spring.

Ornamental Grasses

Gramineae **family**
Zone: USDA 5

Ornamental grasses are a distinct family of plants unexcelled for the perennial garden. They are popular in English and European gardens. The grasses have no need for petals because they are fertilized by pollen grains that are carried from plant to plant by the wind. Still, grass flowers possess all the necessary sexual parts to produce seeds, and many of the seed heads of the grasses are very beautiful and have long been popular.

Description: The grass family (*Gramineae*) runs the gamut—from 120-foot giant bamboos (*Dendrocalamus giganteus*) to the tiny, dwarf fescues (*Festuca* spp.) only a few inches high. The stems, or culms, of the true grasses are usually round and hollow (although corn is solid), and the stem sections are joined by solid joints, or nodes. Root systems are very fibrous, growing deep into the ground, making them excellent plants in dry summers and invaluable for holding soil together. The leaves are always parallel-veined and consist of a blade and a sheath. The flowers are usually feathery or plumelike and feature an awn, or a barbed appendage, that is often quite long.

Ease of care: Easy.

How to grow: Unless specified, grasses need only a good, well-drained garden soil in full sun. A few will do equally well in moist or wet soil. The only chore connected with the perennial grasses is the annual pruning of the larger types in early spring. That is the time to cut the dead stems and leaves to within 6 inches of the ground before new growth begins. Division for the larger clumps is best effected with hearty digging and using an ax to divide the roots.

Propagation: By division in spring or by seed.

Uses: The large grasses make superb specimen plants. Both their seed heads and leaves provide interest until finally beaten down by winter snows. Ornamental grasses make excellent ground cover. The miscanthus grasses can also be used as valuable screens. Miscanthus types can also produce an astounding amount of flowers to be used in dried or winter bouquets.

Related species: *Calamagrostis acutiflora stricta,* or feather reed grass, reaches a height of 5 to 7 feet. It makes an upright stand of slender leaves and a narrow panicle up to 12 inches long that quicky turns a light tan. Although preferring sun, this grass will accept some open shade and will do well in damp situations. *Chasmanthium latifolium,* or sea oats (the genus means "gaping flower" in Greek), is one of the most valuable ornamental grasses that will do well in partial shade. It usually grows about 3 feet high. After the first frost, the leaves and flowers turn a rich, tannish-brown and remain on the plant well into December. If the flowers are picked while still green, they will retain their color. *Helictrotrichon sempervirens,* or blue oat grass (the genus is Greek for "twisted awn"), is valuable for its blue color and the form of the leaves. It usually grows about 2 feet in height. The flowers are attractive. *Imperata cylindrica rubra,* or Japanese blood grass (the genus is named for *Ferrante Imperato*), consists of blades from 1 to 2 feet high that begin the season as green but quickly turn a deep, rich red. Happy in full sun or a bit of shade, the color is a startling addition to the flower garden or the rock garden. In areas with winter temperatures below

Sea Holly

Eryngium **species**
Zone: USDA 6

0°F and a lack of snow, mulching is necessary. *Miscanthus sinensis* 'Gracillimus,' or maiden grass (Greek for "flower on a stalk"), varies from 5 to 8 feet in height, forming a tight clump of grass at ground level that quickly becomes a fountain of thin, arching leaves. In the fall, tall seed heads are formed that open into plumes persisting well into winter. The color is light tan after frost. *Miscanthus sinensis* 'Zebrinus,' or zebra grass, looks like a tropical plant that has adapted to the North. Reaching a height of 8 feet, the arching leaves are dashed with horizontal bands of a light and creamy golden-brown that only appears as the summer heats up. Massive clumps are formed over the years. Flowers are large and showy, tinted with an iridescent maroon until they open to silver, and evenually white. While full sun in required, zebra grass will persist in damp or dry soil and is an excellent waterside choice. *Pennisetum alopecuroides,* or fountain grass (Latin for "feathered bristles"), produces leafy fountains about 3 feet high and blossoms on arching stalks. These plants are best when planted singly rather than in masses. *Carex siderostica* 'Variegata', or variegated sedge, is an easy-care plant with ribbonlike leaves up to 8 inches that are lined with white stripes. The leaves form dense clumps, which emerge in early spring along with the insignificant fuzzy yellow flowers. By summer, the broad clumps are very showy. Plant them in moist, rich soil in light to full shade. Slugs may chew the foliage. Use the plants as an edging or as an accent among bold, textured plants such as hosta and bloodroot. They are also lovely when planted with ferns. *Hakonechloa macra,* also

known as Hakone grass, is an adaptable plant for sun or shade. The arching, 1- to 2-foot stems are loosely clothed in 6-inch pointed ribbonlike leaves. The plant has the appearance of a delicate bamboo. The brown flowers are borne in sparse clusters at the tips of the stems in summer. The foliage is this plant's main attribute. 'Aureola' has bright yellow-striped leaves. Plant in rich, moist soil. Use it as a specimen or groundcover in formal beds or informal woodland settings. These plants are lovely in decorative pots on a patio or terrace. Though it thrives in Zones 4 to 9, 'Aureola' needs shade from hot sun to keep the foliage from burning and thus needs protection in Zone 4. *Molinia caerulea,* or purple moor grass, is a dense clumping grass to 2 feet that has stiff, spiky, bright-green leaves. The airy flower heads grow a foot or more above the foliage in summer. Plant in moist, rich soil in full sun or partial shade. Use it as a specimen among perennials or as fronting for a shrub bed. 'Variegata' has yellow-striped leaves and is very showy. The subspecies *arundinacea,* or tall moor grass, is more robust, with blue-green leaves to 3 feet and tall flower spikes 5 to 8 feet in late summer. *Schizachyrium scoparium,* or little bluestem, is a native prairie grass with dense clumps of thin-leaved blades. The flower spikes rise in late summer, and the silvery flowers emerge soon after and persist through the autumn. The dried stems turn golden. Plant in average, well-drained soil in full sun or light shade. Use in prairie and meadow gardens or in beds and borders with perennials and other grasses.

Sea hollies resemble teasels, with compact heads of long-lasting, small blossoms surrounded by spiny petals that are actually leaves, or bracts. They belong to the carrot family, as evidenced by their thick taproots. The genus is an ancient Greek name for a species of *Eryngium.*

Description: Sea hollies have simple, spiny-toothed leaves on stout stems from 2 to 6 feet tall, with clusters of teasel-like blossoms. They bloom in July and August.

Ease of care: Easy.

How to grow: Sea hollies need full sun and a good, well-drained soil worked to sufficient depth for the growth of the taproots. Their deep roots make them difficult to transplant.

Propagation: By cuttings or by seed.

Uses: For a bold stroke in the formal garden or a fascinating addition to the wild garden, sea hollies are a good choice. The flowers are not only excellent when cut, they are also valuable when dried for winter bouquets.

Related species: *Eryngium alpinum* grows to 2 feet tall with 1¼-inch long, silvery-blue flower heads. 'Donardt's Blue' bears blue flowers on 2-foot stems. *Eryngium amethystinum* is one of the best species, bearing small, blue flowers on plants to 3 feet high. *Eryngium giganteum* grows to 3 or 4 feet with silver-blue flower heads to 2 inches long. This species dies after flowering, although it usually produces abundant seedlings. *Eryngium planum* has many round, ½-inch long, blue flowers on 3-foot stems. It is not as pretty as the other species, making it better suited to a wild garden.

Hosta, Plantain Lily

Hosta **species**
Zone: USDA 4

Next to daylilies, the most-common garden perennial plants are the hostas. The original species came from Korea, Japan, and China where they have been cultivated for centuries. The Japanese grow them in deep shade and full sun in pots, gardens, rock gardens, and temple gardens. They even use them cut up in stir-fry. In 1894, William Robinson called these plants *Funkia*. They were named in honor of Heinrich Christian Funck, a German doctor. By the turn of the century, the genus had been changed to *Hosta* in honor of Nicolaus Host, another German doctor. Both names still remain.

Description: Usually large clumps of basal leaves with pronounced veining and smooth or wavy edges distinguish hostas. Leaf colors come in various shades of green, often with many variegations. Lilylike flowers on tall stems (or scapes) in white and many shades of blue bloom from late spring to late summer.

Ease of care: Easy.

How to grow: Hostas do best in good, well-drained, moist garden soil with plenty of humus. They require some sun to partial shade to deep shade, depending on the species and variety. Many hostas can take a great deal of sun and adapt to dry spots in the garden. They dislike wet soil in winter. Once in place, hostas can survive for generations. The plants are very tough and only slugs present a problem that, if left unchecked, can produce large holes in the leaves.

Propagation: By division or by seed (some species).

Uses: There is a place in every garden for hostas. The smaller types are excellent in the border or as ground cover. The larger varieties become elegant specimen plants forming gigantic clumps of leaves over the years. Although usually grown for the leaves, the flowers are often beautiful, too. Hostas are the backbone of the shade garden, since many of them are happiest in full or open shade protected from the rays of the sun. They are also excellent in pots.

Related species: Some hosta suppliers will stock well over 200 different species and varieties of this adaptable plant. The following list is only a sampling of what's available, and the list grows every year. Those named enjoy shade to partial sun. *Hosta Fortunei* forms mounds about 14 inches high and 2 feet wide. It has oval leaves 5 inches wide and 12 inches long with pale purple flowers in early summer. 'Aureo-marginata' has a yellow-gold margin on a dark green leaf; 'Albo-marginata' has white edges on its leaves; and 'Albo-picta' has a bright yellow leaf with a crisp, dark green margin. *Hosta lancifolia* has small, spear-shaped, dark green leaves about 6 inches long, forming clumps about 1 foot high and 18 inches wide. Flowers are light purple on 22-inch stems blooming in summer. *Hosta montana* has dark green leaves 11 inches wide and up to 20 inches long, forming a mound 30 inches high and up to 4 feet wide. Flowers are off-white and bloom in early summer. 'Aureo-marginata' has wavy leaves of a glossy green with irregular, yellow margins. *Hosta plantaginea*, or the fragrant hosta, has large, heart-shaped leaves and produces sweet-smelling, white flowers in late summer or early autumn that can be killed by early frost if not protected. 'Grandiflora' has larger-than-species flowers in clumps that can reach 3 feet in diameter. *Hosta Sieboldiana* has round, blue-green, and seersuckered leaves 12 inches wide and 14 inches long in mounds that can reach 30 inches high and 4 feet wide. 'Frances Williams' has blue-green leaves with broad, golden-yellow margins that deepen in color as the summer progresses. Lilac flowers appear in early summer. *Hosta Sieboldii* is a smaller plant with dark green, lance-shaped leaves a bit over 1 inch wide and 4 to 5 inches long. Flowers are white with purple veins and bloom in August. 'Kabitan' has leaves with a greenish-yellow base and a narrow, green margin. *Hosta undulata* has wavy leaves about 6 inches long and pale purple flowers in early summer. 'Variegata' has leaves with more white than green. *Hosta venusta* is a small plant from Korea with slightly wavy, green, heart-shaped leaves, 1 inch long and 1 inch wide. Flowers are violet and bloom in early summer.

Houttuynia

Houttuynia cordata
Zone: USDA 5

This plant became popular in the last few years. It is the only species in the genus and is named in honor of a Dutch naturalist. The plants are called *Dokudami* in Japan.

Description: Houttuynia resembles English ivy, with red stems and blue-green leaves somewhat metallic in appearance. It grows about 1 foot high and produces small, white flowers in summer that resemble begonia blossoms. When bruised, the plants smell of Seville oranges.

Ease of care: Easy.

How to grow: Plants grow well in sun and in shade but need good, well-drained garden soil that is always moist. Houttuynias will also grow in shallow water.

Propagation: By division or by seed.

Uses: These plants are a fine ground cover in beds, borders, and for the edge of a water garden. Plants spread by underground runners and can be quite invasive. Houttuynias adapt readily to potting.

Related varieties: 'Chameleon' has leaves variegated with blotches of green, red, yellow, and pink. 'Plena' has double flowers.

False Indigo, Wild Indigo

Baptisia australis
Zone: USDA 5

A beautiful plant in leaf, in flower, and after going to seed, false indigo was originally planted to produce a blue dye for early American colonists. Unfortunately, the dye wasn't fast. The name of the genus is from the Greek word for "dipping," which is also the root word for baptism.

Description: This is a large plant that grows to 4 feet in height. The blue-green, compound leaves on stout stems are attractive all summer, and the dark blue, pealike flowers that eventually become blackened pods are very showy.

Ease of care: Easy.

How to grow: It needs well-drained soil in full sun, but will accept some partial shade. Being a member of the legume family, baptisia will do well in poor soil. The root systems of older plants become so extensive that they are difficult to move.

Propagation: By division or by seed.

Uses: One baptisia will in time cover an area several feet in diameter with gracefully arching foliage. Because they die down to the ground in winter, a line of these plants makes a perfect deciduous hedge when spaced 3 feet apart. Because of the extensive root system, these plants are perfect for holding banks of soil in place. One plant makes a perfect specimen in the border. In addition, these plants are excellent for a meadow garden, a wild garden, or planted along the edge of the woods. The flowers are also beautiful when cut. After the fall frost, the leaves, as well as the inflated seedpods (often called Indian rattles), turn black. Expensive florist shops often gild these pods.

Related species: The prairie false indigo, *Baptisia leucantha*, has white flowers. It does well in the shade, although it is best in the wild garden as it's too rangy for a formal spot. *Baptisia perfoliata* is only reliably hardy to USDA Zone 7. The stems arch gracefully to the ground. The flowers are small and yellow, bloom in July, and appear surrounded by the gray-green leaves that resemble eucalyptus plants in growth habit. This plant is drought-resistant.

Inula

Inula ensifolia
Zone: USDA 4

Most gardeners think of the inulas as represented by elecampane (*Inula Helenium*), a large and raucous herb used in past centuries to heal both men and horses. But *I. ensifolia* is beautiful in the garden and available from most large nurseries.

Description: Inula is a clump-forming plant with thin, narrow leaves on thin stems growing to 16 inches, topped with bright yellow, 1½-inch wide daisies. They bloom in July and August.

Ease of care: Easy.

How to grow: Inulas want only a sunny spot in good garden soil in order to succeed. Seeds sown in early spring will bloom the first year.

Propagation: By division or by seed.

Uses: These yellow daisies are perfect for the front of a bed or border and also make excellent cut flowers.

Related variety: 'Gold Star' produces flowers up to 2½ inches wide.

Iris

Iris species
Zone: USDA 4

Just as gardeners could create a fascinating garden using nothing but daylilies and hostas, the same approach would also work for the iris. This large genus contains over 200 species in the northern hemisphere and is most abundant in Asia. The plants are responsible for a marvelous array of flowers plus, in many cases, fine foliage.

Description: Irises usually have basal leaves in two ranks, linear to sword-shaped, often resembling a fan, arising from a thick rootstock (or rhizome) or, in some species, from a bulb. There are three groups in the rhizomatous species: Bearded iris has a "beard" or pattern of hairs on the bottom half of the falls (the lower petals); the crested iris has a cockscomblike crest on the falls; and the beardless iris has no hairs on the bottom petals. They come in shades of pink, blue, lilac, purple to brown, yellow, orange, dark to almost black, and white. There are no true reds.

Ease of care: Easy.

How to grow: Most irises need sunlight. Except for those like the water flag (*Iris Pseudacorus*) that delights in a watery spot or the Japanese iris (*I. ensata*) that wants a humus-rich, moist soil, they also prefer a good, well-drained garden soil. In the North, rhizomatous irises should have the tops of the rhizome showing when planted; in the South, they should be covered slightly. The fan of leaves is to be pointed in the direction you wish the plants to grow.

Propagation: By division in the fall or by seed.

Uses: Even though bloom period is short, a bed of irises is ideal for a flower garden. There are irises for the poolside and the pool, the wild or woodland garden, the early spring bulb bed, and the rock garden.

Related species: Tall, bearded iris, hardy to USDA 4, sometimes called *Iris germanica*, usually comes to mind when people think of irises. The flowers come in a multitude of color combinations and sizes, with hundreds of new varieties introduced every year. The fanlike leaves are a lovely gray-green, browning at the tips in a hot summer. There are varieties that bloom both in the spring and the fall. Tall bearded irises are over 25 inches tall; intermediate bearded ones are between 16 and 27 inches tall; the standard plants are between 8 and 16 inches, and the miniatures grow to 8 inches tall. As with daylilies and hostas, there is a bewildering number of varieties and colors. Perhaps the best suggestion for the beginning gardener is to order a mix of colors, a choice frequently offered by most nurseries. *Iris cristata*, the dwarf, crested iris that is hardy in USDA 5, wants partial shade and a humus-rich soil and blooms in early spring. It is lavender-blue with a 2-inch, yellow crest across a 6-inch stem. The leaves are attractive after bloom. In areas of bad winters with little snow, these plants need mulching. 'Alba' is white and 'Summer Storm' is deep blue. *Iris foetidissima*, or the Gladwin iris, has a distinct smell of roast beef or boiled meat when bruised and does not deserve its other common name of "stinking gladdon." Hardy to USDA 6 and doing best in good soil in partial shade, it is grown for its seedpods on 18-inch stems which, upon bursting open in autumn, reveal beautiful orange-red shining seeds that are used for indoor arrangements. *Iris Kaempferi* is the nursery name for the Japanese iris, and *I. ensata* is the official botanical term. They are hardy in USDA 6. Blossoms are often over 6 inches wide on stiff, 8-inch stems, blooming in June and resembling layers of colored linen

Knapweed

Centaurea species
Zone: USDA 4

Knotweed, Himalaya Fleece Flower

Polygonum affine
Zone: USDA 4

waving in the wind. Plants prefer evenly moist soil and do well near the water's edge. There are many color choices: 'Gold Bound' is a double white with a golden band on each petal; 'Eleanor Parry' has reddish-purple flowers; and 'Great White Heron' is a white, semi-double up to 11 inches in diameter. The Higo Strain from Japan includes 'Nikko' with petals of pale purple-blue and a gold throat. *Iris pallida,* or the orris iris, grown primarily for foliage, produces flowers on 3-foot stems with fragrant, lilac flowers. It is hardy in USDA 6 and prefers partial shade. 'Albo-Variegata' has white-striped leaves and 'Variegata' has yellow, vertical stripes. *Iris Pseudacorus,* the yellow flag, is a beautiful plant for the bog or at the edge of a pond or pool. The flowers, blooming in late May to June, are yellow on 40-inch stems. 'Light Yellow' is lemon-colored, and 'Flore Plena' has double, yellow flowers. *Iris pumila,* the dwarf bearded iris, grows 4 to 6 inches high, blooming in early May, and is suited for the rock garden in full sun. 'Blue Frost' has light blue flowers; 'Red Dandy' is a wine-red; and 'Golden Fair' is a deep gold. *Iris sibirica,* the Siberian iris, is a plant that has beautiful 3- to 4-inch flowers on 30-inch stems and great foliage—the swordlike leaves stand erect and eventually form a large clump. They need full sun, prefer a good, moist soil, and are hardy in USDA 4. 'Blue Brilliant' is as named; 'Ruffled Velvet' has deep plum-purple flowers; and 'Snow Queen' is pure white. *Iris tectorum,* the Japanese roof iris, is supposedly used as a living binding material for thatched roofs in the Orient. Plants are hardy in USDA 5; grow about 1 foot high; and are covered in June with 6-inch, lilac-blue flowers. Soil should be good and moist, with mulch used in areas without winter snow. 'Alba' is white.

Four useful garden perennials—*Centaurea dealbata, Centaurea hypoleuca, Centaurea macrocephala,* and *Centaurea montana*—belong to this genus, all resembling the popular annual bachelor's buttons. The genus derives its name from a species, which, according to mythology, was used to cure the foot of a Greek centaur called Chiron.
Description: Knapweed has large leaves; the usually stout-stemmed plants bear thistlelike flowers.
Ease of care: Easy.
How to grow: Knapweeds like full sun and any good garden soil that is dry and well drained.
Propagation: By division or by seed.
Uses: Grouped in the border or set throughout the garden, these flowers are bright and cheerful, bearing attractive seed heads.
Related species: *Centaurea dealbata,* or the Persian knapweed, bears bright, rose-purple flowers typical of the genus that bloom over a long period on 2-foot stems. The coarsely cut leaves are gray and hairy underneath and green on top. Plants sometimes need staking. *Centaurea hypoleuca* blooms from June to August with 2- to 3-inch flowers of rich rose on 18-inch stems. Leaves are green above and silvery white beneath. The seed heads are very attractive. *Centaurea macrocephala* has no common name. The plants have large, coarse leaves with stout stems often reaching 4 feet in height. The blossoms are bright yellow and resemble thistles. They make good cut flowers and are excellent when dried. They only bloom for a short time. *Centaurea montana,* or the mountain bluet, has cornflower-blue flowers that bloom over a long period on 18-inch stems. Young foliage is silvery white.

One of the most pernicious weeds in America is the so-called Japanese bamboo, *Polygonum cuspidatum,* a plant that is as happy along a roadside as it is in a garden. Luckily, the plant described below is small and attractive. The genus name is from the Greek for "many knees," referring to the large number of joints found on the stems.
Description: Himalaya fleece flower is a tufted ground cover plant with dark green, tapered leaves on creeping stems. Tiny, bright rose flowers bloom in dense spikes about 8 inches high from late summer into fall.
Ease of care: Easy.
How to grow: Knotweed requires good soil, preferably slightly moist, in full sun.
Propagation: By division in spring.
Uses: The plant is good as a ground cover or as an edging plant for the bed or border. It is especially valuable because the plant sends up new flowers over a long period.
Related species: *Polygonum Bistorta* 'Superbum' is a very attractive plant for the border that bears 6-inch pinkish spikes of flowers on 2-foot stems. Plants prefer light shade in areas with hot summers. Soil should be moist. *Polygonum cuspidatum* var. *compactum* is a dwarf form of Japanese bamboo that grows under 2 feet in height, wants full sun, and makes a good ground cover.
Related varieties: 'Darjeeling Red' has pale pink flowers when new, turning to a deep rose-red as they mature; 'Donald Lowndes' has flowers of a light pink.

275

Lady's Mantle

Alchemilla **species**
Zone: USDA 3b

Lady's mantles are beautiful plants usually grown for both their foliage and the unusual chartreuse flowers. The botanical name is a Latinized term for an old Arabic name.

Description: Plants grow between 8 and 14 inches high, with lobed leaves of gray-green that bear silky hairs.

Ease of care: Easy.

How to grow: Lady's mantles are easy to grow in average garden soil where summers are cool and moist, preferring some protection from hot sun in midsummer. In warmer parts of the country, they need a moist, fertile soil and light shade. As the summer progresses, the plants become larger and have a tendency to flop about. Flowers should be removed before the seeds ripen, as they can seed about.

Propagation: By division in spring or by seed.

Uses: The flowers appear in clusters in early summer, standing well above the leaves, and last for several weeks. They are excellent when cut. These plants can be used in the front of the garden border or along the edge of a low wall where the leaves are easy to see.

Related species: Three species are usually offered: *Alchemilla alpina,* the alpine lady's mantle, grows about 8 inches high; *Alchemilla erythropoda* grows about 6 inches high; and *Alchemilla mollis,* the most common, grows to 14 inches high.

Lamb's-Ears, Lamb's-Tongue

Stachys byzantina
Zone: USDA 5

Some plants beg to have a finger run along their surface; among such plants, lamb's-ear is one of the best. The common name is precisely on the mark, since the gray-white, woolly leaves feel exactly like a lamb's skin. The genus name is Greek for "a spike of grain."

Description: The 4-inch-long leaves and sturdy stems of this plant are covered with dense, white wool. Plants grow to about 6 inches tall. Flower spikes up to 2 feet tall bear small, pink to purple flowers hidden by silvery bracts.

Ease of care: Easy.

How to grow: Lamb's-ears require full sun and a good, well-drained soil. They are drought-resistant.

Propagation: By division in spring or by seed.

Uses: Try this plant along the edge of a sunny border, in the rock garden, or as an effective ground cover. Even though the flowers are insignificant, the dried spikes are very effective in dried arrangements. It also does well in pots for terrace decoration.

Related variety: 'Silver Carpet' is a non-flowering form of the same plant.

Lavender

Lavandula angustifolia
Zone: USDA 4

These are species of aromatic herbs originally from the Mediterranean. The genus name is from the word *lava,* which originally referred to a torrential downpour of rain and then became the word *lavare,* "to wash." It alludes to the ancient custom of scenting bath water with oil of lavender or a few lavender flowers.

Description: Plants are shrubby, usually with square stems and narrow, evergreen leaves that are white and woolly when young. Flower spikes have terminal clusters of lavender or dark purple flowers, blooming in late June and bearing a pleasing scent.

Ease of care: Easy.

How to grow: Lavender plants want full sun and well-drained, sandy soil—preferably not acid. In colder areas, prune back the dead wood in the spring. In areas with lots of rain, grow lavender in elevated beds, troughs, or pots. Prune back to 6–8 inches in spring to encourage lush growth. In colder areas where there is no snow cover or the snow cover is inconsistent, the plants should be mulched. Protect plants with a covering of evergreen bows, or turn a bushel basket over the clump to keep the stems from being damaged. Straw is also an effective covering.

Propagation: By soft cuttings in spring or by seed.

Uses: Lavender is perfect as a low hedge and in clumps next to rocks. It is also suitable in front of stone walls that face away from the wind. These plants are also lovely in herb gardens or in perennial beds and borders. Lavender plants tolerate seaside conditions.

Related varieties: 'Hidcote' has deep violet flowers on 20-inch shrubs; 'Munstead Dwarf,' a

Sea Lavender

Limonium latifolium
Zone: USDA 4

Leopard's-bane

Doronicum cordatum
Zone: USDA 5

shorter type, has deep purple flowers at a 12-inch height. 'Jean Davis' is a pink-flowered selection with blue-green foliage; plants grow to 15 inches.

Related Species: Lavandin (*Lavandula* x *intermedia*) is a hybrid resulting from crosses between *L. angustifolia* and *L. latifolia*. Selections of this hybrid are some of the most fragrant lavenders. It is sought after for scenting perfumes, bath oils, and sachets. Plants have long narrow spikes of flowers that stand above the rich green foliage. 'Grosso' has deep violet flowers on 24-inch stems in summer and fall. The flowers stand well above the dense crown of foliage, making them perfect for cutting and drying. 'Provence' is taller, to 36 inches, with silvery, spiky mauve flowers. Spanish lavender (*Lavandula stoechas pedunculata*) is a curiously beautiful plant that is fairly new to American gardeners. The dark, buttonlike flower heads have a crown of rabbit-ears, which give the plant a startled look. The dense, needlelike leaves are rich green. These plants are hardy in Zones 6 and warmer.

There are many annuals in this genus—flowers that are dried and used in winter bouquets. But one perennial, *Limonium latifolium,* is especially effective for its branching sprays of tiny flowers that resemble baby's breath in character. The genus name is from the Greek word for "meadow" and refers to the frequent occurrence of some species in salt meadows.

Description: Large, leathery leaves to 10 inches long form a basal rosette, which, in late July and August, sends up 2-foot stems that branch out into huge clouds of tiny 1/8-inch lavender-blue flowers.

Ease of care: Easy.

How to grow: Plants need full sun and a good, well-drained garden soil with plenty of sand for drainage. They do well in seaside gardens.

Propagation: By division or by seed.

Uses: Since they bloom in summer, sea lavenders are excellent choices for beds and borders, where their airy cloud of flowers has a lovely effect.

Related variety: 'Violette' has brilliant, violet-blue flowers that keep their color when dried.

All the plants in this genus were once thought to be poisonous to animals, hence the common name of "leopard's-bane." The genus is from an old Arabic name for the flowers. Some catalogs list it as *Doronicum caucasicum.*

Description: Bright yellow, daisylike flowers bloom 2 inches across, reaching a height of up to 2 feet. Leaves are heart-shaped with a toothed edge; they clasp the stems. Plants bloom in the spring.

Ease of care: Easy.

How to grow: Leopard's-banes prefer a good, well-drained soil in partial shade. Since their roots are shallow, they also benefit from a moist situation. These plants prefer cool summers. In hot climates, they must have some shade.

Propagation: By division in early spring or by seed.

Uses: Since these flowers bloom in spring and usually go dormant by midsummer, they should be planted where their absence will not be missed. They make fine border plants when massed and are beautiful in front of a low wall. They also make excellent cut flowers.

Related varieties: 'Magnificum' has larger-than-average heads, and 'Finesse' bears bright yellow blooms 3 inches in diameter on 18-inch stems.

277

Ligularia

Ligularia species
Zone: USDA 4 to 6

The plant's name comes from the Latin word *ligula,* which means "little tongue," and refers to the tonguelike shape of the large petal on each of the ray flowers.

Description: Basal leaves on stout stems are either round or kidney-shaped. They bear tall spires of yellow or orange flower heads. The flowers smell of chocolate.

Ease of care: Easy.

How to grow: Ligularias do best in partial shade and good, humus-rich garden soil that is kept evenly moist. Even with plenty of water, the leaves will wilt in hot summer heat, but they quickly recover as the sun sets and temperatures fall. Since the roots form large clumps, plenty of space should be allowed between plants.

Propagation: By division in spring or by seed.

Uses: Ligularias are great in the back of shady beds, along borders, in bogs, or planted at the edge of water gardens.

Related species: *Ligularia dentata* 'Orange Queen' and 'Othello' each has leaves up to 1 foot wide. The first is green throughout with flowers of a deeper orange, while the second has leaves that are green on top and purple underneath. *Ligularia Przewalskii* 'The Rocket' and *Ligularia stenocephala* 'The Rocket' both bloom in late July and early August with large, serrated leaves and tall spires of bright yellow flowers on purple stems. *Ligularia tussilaginea* 'Aureo-maculata' has leaves splotched with areas of yellow or white. It is hardy only to USDA 7. *Ligularia Veitchiana* forms large clumps that can reach 7 feet if growing conditions are good. Flower heads are bright orange and are about 2½ inches across.

Blackberry Lily, Leopard Lily

Belamcanda chinensis
Zone: USDA 6 (zone 5 with protection)

Belamcanda is an East Indian name for this genus of irislike plants that are native to China, Japan, and Korea. They have escaped from gardens and are now established in pastures and along roadsides in many northeastern states.

Description: Blackberry lilies have 10-inch long, sword-shaped leaves that give rise to 2-foot stems. Each stem holds many 6-petaled, orange flowers speckled with red. Flowers only last for a day, drying with a twist into tight spirals, then falling as pods develop. They are, however, soon followed by other blossoms, flowering during July and August. Eventually the oval, green pods split open to reveal attractive, shiny black seeds.

Ease of care: Easy.

How to grow: Belamcandas prefer well-drained and fertile soil in full sun. They resent heavy clay soils where the roots have a tendency to rot.

Propagation: By division of the rhizomes in early spring or by seed.

Uses: A large grouping of these plants looks especially attractive when backed by a stone wall or in company with gooseneck plants (*Lysimachia clethroides*) or planted among mounds of two ornamental grasses.

Related species: *Belamcanda flabellata* has 8-inch leaves and bears yellow flowers. 'Hello Yellow' grows to 15 inches.

Related variety: 'Freckle Face' produces flowers of a light orange that bloom the first year if planted early.

Toad Lily

Tricyrtis hirta
Zone: USDA 5b

It's unfortunate that such an attractive and unusual flower should have the common name of "toad lily." The amphibian reference really refers to the blotches and markings on the flowers. The genus name is from the Greek for "three" and "convex" because the 3 outer petals have tiny bags or swellings at the base.

Description: Plants have alternate, 6-inch leaves on arching, hairy stems that are usually 2 feet high. They bear single, creamy white flowers, often in clusters, which open to purple-spotted petals and centers resembling pieces of chenille. They usually bloom in late September or October.

Ease of care: Moderately easy.

How to grow: Toad lilies need a moist, fertile soil with a high humus content and partial shade, or the open shade found beneath trees. In higher elevations of Zone 5b where fall frosts arrive early, the plants must be protected.

Propagation: By seed or by division in spring.

Uses: Toad lilies should be planted where they are easily seen. The plants are especially valuable for the shade garden and are among the few that bloom so late in the garden year.

Related species: *Tricyrtis formosana* has flowers spotted with mauve on a lighter background with yellow in the throat.

Big Blue Lily Turf

Liriope Muscari
Zone: USDA 6

Lily turf is a grasslike plant belonging to the lily family. It is often used as a low-maintenance ground cover in institutional landscapes. The genus name is derived from Liriope, who was the mother of Narcissus.

Description: Firm, evergreen, grasslike leaves, often over 1 foot long, grow in tufts. They produce terminal spikes of small flowers that bloom in late summer with violet or dark blue flowers, which are followed by glossy black seeds.

Ease of care: Easy.

How to grow: Liriopes respond well to any good, well-drained garden soil either in sun or shade. They require no special care.

Propagation: By division in early spring.

Uses: Liriopes are unexcelled as a ground cover. They are also excellent along paths and walkways or massed in the front of a border, where their evergreen leaves are attractive in the fall and winter.

Related varieties: 'Christmas Tree' has larger-than-type lavender flowers on 8-inch plants; 'Majestic' grows to a 15-inch height with large, deep lilac flowers; and 'Monroe's White' is 12 inches high with white flowers.

Gooseneck Loosestrife

Lysimachia clethroides
Zone: USDA 5

Few plants deserve such a descriptive common name as this particular species does—a number of them in bloom truly look like a gaggle of geese ready to honk at an intruder. The genus is named after King Lysimachus of Thrace.

Description: Gooseneck loosestrifes have alternate, simple leaves on stout stems that grow to 3 feet tall. They end in nodding whorls of small, white flowers that bloom in the summer.

Ease of care: Easy.

How to grow: This particular member of the loosestrifes prefers a good, well-drained, moist soil in full sun or partial shade. If the site is to its liking, it will quickly spread—so contain the roots if necessary.

Propagation: By division or by seed.

Uses: Put these plants in a moist part of the bed or border or use them unrestrained in the wild garden. They are also excellent cut flowers.

Related species: *Lysimachia punctata,* or the garden loosestrife, is an old-fashioned garden plant with bright yellow flowers that whorl around the stem among the leaves. Height is between 2 and 3 feet, blooming in early summer. It will tolerate drier soil if given partial shade.

Purple Loosestrife

Lythrum Salicaria
Zone: USDA 4

Purple loosestrife has become naturalized throughout the Northeast, especially in marshy lands. Unfortunately, it has recently been discovered to be aggressive and invasive. Once established, it is hard to control and can choke out competing plantlife. The genus name comes from the Greek word for "gore" and refers to the dark color of some flowers.

Description: Purple loosestrifes have strong stems growing to 6 feet high with willowlike leaves and flowers in terminal spikes. They are hardy plants, growing in boggy and wet places.

Ease of care: Easy.

How to grow: Preferring moist soil in full sun, loosestrifes will easily adapt to streamside locations, as the roots can grow in water. They can also adapt to a fairly dry spot in the shade.

Propagation: By division.

Uses: Because of its invasive nature, some states have passed laws banning the sale and purchase of purple loosestrife. Considered by many to be a noxious weed, it is not recommended as a cultivated plant.

Lungwort, Jerusalem Sage

Pulmonaria officinalis
Zone: USDA 4

One of the first flowers of spring, the lungworts are exceptional plants for both their blossoms and foliage. Because the leaves are dotted with white spots, the plant was thought to be a medicine for lungs. The genus name is from the Latin word for "lung."

Description: Lungworts have simple basal leaves growing to 1 foot long, which are spotted with silver-white splotches. Terminal coiled clusters of 5-lobed flowers, which in many species open as pink and then fade with age to blue, bloom in the spring.

Ease of care: Easy.

How to grow: While lungworts will persist in poor soil, they are truly lovely when planted in a good, moist garden soil in partial to full shade. Water must be provided during times of drought.

Propagation: By division in fall or by seed.

Uses: Lungworts are lovely plants for the shade garden, the wild garden, and even as ground covers on banks under the shadow of trees and bushes. Plants can be potted in late fall and forced into greenhouse bloom.

Related species: *Pulmonaria angustifolia* 'Azurea' is a European plant that bears brilliant blue flowers; 'Johnson's Blue' has gentian-blue flowers. *Pulmonaria montana,* often called *P. rubra,* has plain green leaves and bears salmon-red flowers. *Pulmonaria saccharata,* or the Bethlehem sage, is usually represented by 'Mrs. Moon,' which has very attractive leaf spotting; 'Janet Fisk' has much silver on its foliage. 'Sissinghurst White' bears white flowers.

Lupine

Lupinus polyphyllus
Zone: USDA 5

Some authorities think that *Lupinus* comes from the Latin word for "wolf," as it was an ancient belief that lupines destroyed the fertility of the soil. Others, however, think the name is from the Greek *lype* for "bitter," because the seeds have a bitter taste and were considered a food of the downtrodden.

Description: Attractive alternate, gray-green leaves are fingerlike, with many leaflets beginning at a central point. In early summer, plants produce 30-inch spikes of pealike flowers followed by silky seedpods.

Ease of care: Moderately easy.

How to grow: Lupines require a lot of water and a spot in full sun or in the lightest of shade. Plants resent areas with hot summers. Soil must be well-drained with additional grit or sand.

Lupines do not adapt to alkaline soil. Remove the dead flowers to prevent seed formation and to conserve the plant's strength. Cutting back to the ground after flowering will often produce a second crop of blossoms.

Propagation: By seed or division in early spring.

Uses: Lupines should be planted in large groups where their flowers make a spectacular sight. The plants are especially suited to seaside gardens.

Related varieties: The Russell strain of lupines is the variety that is usually offered by nurseries. It can be purchased in mixed colors that include blue, pink, red, purple, maroon, white, and mixed colors. Some nurseries offer individual colors.

Carolina Lupine, Aaron's Rod

Thermopsis caroliniana
Zone: USDA 4

Carolina lupines are native American wildflowers originally from North Carolina and Georgia. They closely resemble *Baptisia australis;* both are members of the pea family. The genus is Greek for "resembling a lupine."

Description: Leaves have 3 leaflets on stems growing to 5 feet and bear spikes of yellow, pealike flowers in late June and July, followed by small pods resembling small string beans that are covered with short hairs.

Ease of care: Easy.

How to grow: Plants grow in almost any good, well-drained soil in full sun. Without full sun, the stems will lean to the light and then flop over. In rich soil, plants will be very tall and need staking. New plants take a few years to form sizable clumps. If given adequate moisture just before flowering begins, plants are very drought-resistant.

Propagation: By division in early spring or by seed.

Uses: The spikes of yellow flowers are very attractive against a dark background, so keep them at the back of the border, especially in front of bushes or shrubbery. They bloom at a time of the garden year when yellows are mostly absent. The light green leaves remain attractive until frost.

Related species: *Thermopsis montana* grows to 2 feet.

Mallow

Malva Alcea
Zone: USDA 4

Malvas are lovely flowers that bloom in late summer and into fall. *Malva* is the ancient Latin name for "mallow," used by Pliny and derived from the Greek name *Malachi,* "to soften," in reference to its emollient qualities.
Description: Mallow is a bushy perennial with stout stems growing to 4 feet. Soft green, fingered leaves and 5-petaled flowers in the leaf axils bloom over a long period.
Ease of care: Easy.
How to grow: Malvas are not fussy about soil, and any good garden soil will do. They adapt to dry conditions, but do require full sun or, at best, a bit of shade.
Propagation: By seed or by division in early spring.
Uses: Malvas mix beautifully with white phlox and in the midst of ornamental grasses. They are most effective when planted mid-border.
Related species: *Malva moschata* 'Alba' is similar to *M. Alcea,* with white flowers on slightly shorter stems.
Related variety: 'Fastigiata' has pink flowers with darker veining. It requires no staking and can be used for cut flowers.

Rose Mallow, Swamp Mallow

Hibiscus Moscheutos
Zone: USDA 5

This native American genus contains many plants including roselle (*Hibiscus Sabdariffa*), from which carcade, a beverage that Mussolini wanted the Italians to drink, is made. *Hibiscus* is Latin for "marsh mallow."
Description: Hollyhocklike flowers up to 10 inches across bloom in pink, purple, or white with a dark red eye. Plants have alternate leaves, green above and white and hairy beneath, on stems to 7 feet in height. Plants bloom most of the summer.
Ease of care: Easy.
How to grow: Rose mallows prefer good, moist garden soil in full sun, but the plants will adapt to dry soil. All the members of the clan make big clumps in time, so plenty of room for growth must be allowed. The mallows seem to be unaffected by salt, making them an excellent choice along highways. Without a snow cover, a mulch must be provided in cold areas.
Propagation: By division or by seed.
Uses: Mallows are fine for wild gardens and places with damp soil. They are also excellent for the back of a bed or border and can easily be grown in pots. When planted in groups, the flowers will make the backyard look like a tropical paradise.
Related species: *Hibiscus coccineus* bears bright red flowers on 4-foot plants and is native to the southern United States. It is not hardy north of Philadelphia.
Related varieties: 'Southern Belle' produces huge flowers often up to 10 inches across in colors of red, rose, pink, and white on 4-foot plants. 'Poinsettia' is a rich red, and 'Silver Rose' is pink. Both reach 5 feet in height.

Meadowsweet, Queen of the Prairie

Filipendula rubra
Zone: USDA 3

Meadowsweet is an American native at home at the edge of woods, in wet prairies, and in meadows from New York to Minnesota and south. A member of the rose family, the genus name means "hanging by a thread" and is said to refer to tubers that hang on the roots of one species.
Description: Meadowsweet is a tall plant, growing to 7 feet with large clusters of tiny, pink flowers. Together they are reminiscent of a ball of cotton candy. They sit on top of stout stems and bloom in July.
Ease of care: Easy.
How to grow: Meadowsweets prefer a good, well-drained, moist garden soil in full sun, although they will succeed in partial shade. Plants eventually form a good-sized clump.
Propagation: By division in early spring or by seed.
Uses: Meadowsweet is best toward the back of a border and against a dark background such as low trees or shrubs.
Related species: *Filipendula purpurea* 'Elegans,' sometimes listed as *F. palmata,* is from Japan. Plants reach between 30 and 40 inches in height and bear pale pink flowers in clusters, blooming in July. *Filipendula Ulmaria* grows between 3 and 5 feet tall. Flowers resemble feathery plumes and appear in June. 'Plena' grows to 3 feet, with double flowers, and 'Variegated' has green leaves with creamy yellow stripes in the center. *Filipendula vulgaris,* or *F. hexapetala,* has finely cut leaves and bears loose panicles of small, white flowers on 18-inch stems, blooming in June. 'Flore Pleno' has double flowers.

Dead Nettle

Lamium maculatum
Zone: USDA 5

The nettles are generally weedy plants, with only this genus valued for the garden. The term "dead" refers to the fact that these perennials do not cause pain in the manner usually reserved for the stinging nettles (*Utrica dioica*), plants which they somewhat resemble. *Lamium* is the ancient Latin name for plants in this genus.

Description: Dead nettles are sprawling plants with square stems, toothed oval leaves, and 1-inch long flowers that resemble small snapdragons. They bloom in May and June.

Ease of care: Easy.

How to grow: Lamiums are not fussy, doing well in a good, well-drained garden soil. They are more robust in partial shade and moist soil, yet they are reasonably drought-resistant.

Propagation: By division in spring.

Uses: Lamiums are excellent ground covers and border edgings both in the formal garden or the wild or woodland garden. Their variegated leaves are as attractive as the flowers.

Related varieties: 'Aureum' has a golden leaf with a white center and lavender-pink flowers; 'Album' has dark green leaves with silvery white splotches; 'Beacon Silver' has leaves of a silvery green with dark green edges and pink flowers; 'Chequers' has deep pink flowers and marbled leaves; and 'White Nancy' is a white-flowered form of 'Beacon Silver.'

Obedient Plant, False Dragonhead

Physostegia virginiana
Zone: USDA 4

A member of the mint family, obedient plants are native American wildflowers, still called *Dracocephalum* in some reference books. The genus name is from the Greek for "swollen bladder" and refers to the inflated body of the flower.

Description: Basal rosettes are evergreen in milder climates. Square, strong stems are from 1 to 3 feet tall and have narrow, toothed leaves, bearing rose-purple flowers that resemble a snapdragon. The individual flowers can be pushed around the stem without harm and will remain pointing in the same direction as when last touched.

Ease of care: Easy.

How to grow: Plants like full sun and will tolerate most soils, preferring the addition of some organic matter. They are at their best in moist conditions. The common types are invasive and should be either fenced at ground level or divided every two years.

Propagation: By division in spring or by seed.

Uses: Because they flower late in the season, these are valuable plants for beds and borders. They will often bloom into October. They should be planted in groups and are excellent for naturalizing in the wild garden.

Related varieties: 'Alba' is pure white and blooms in late summer on 24-inch stems; 'Bouquet Rose' has rose-colored flowers on 3-foot stems; and 'Vivid' stays about 15 inches high with flowers of a brilliant lavender-pink.

Ox-Eye, False Sunflower

Heliopsis helianthoides
Zone: USDA 5

Ox-eyes are native American plants found from New York to Michigan and south to Georgia. Members of the daisy family, they are similar to sunflowers but bloom earlier in the season. The genus is Greek for "like the sun."

Description: Ox-eyes are bright yellow daisies, often 4 inches in diameter on stout stems that grow between 3 and 5 feet tall. The leaves are simple and toothed. Flowers bloom from summer to frost.

Ease of care: Easy.

How to grow: These plants will bloom the first year from seed. Although they want full sun, ox-eyes will tolerate partial shade. They need a good, well-drained garden soil and will require extra water during periods of drought.

Propagation: By division in spring or by seed.

Uses: Since their cheerful flowers bloom over such a long period, ox-eyes are valuable in a bed, a border, and in a wild garden. The flowers are excellent for cutting.

Related species: *Heliopsis scabra* is a subspecies sometimes offered by nurseries.

Related varieties: 'Gold Greenheart' has double, yellow-green flowers with a green center when newly opened. 'Golden Plume' has double, yellow flowers about 2½ inches across.

Pachysandra, Japanese Spurge

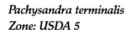

Pachysandra terminalis
Zone: USDA 5

Pachysandra is the quintessential ground cover. The genus name is from the Greek and means "a thick man," in reference to the filaments in the flower.

Description: Fleshy stems about 1 foot high have simple, toothed, evergreen leaves. These are often crowded at the tips of branches, which bear small, greenish-white flowers in erect spikes in the spring.

Ease of care: Easy.

How to grow: Any good, moist garden soil is sufficient for pachysandra. The plants are especially valuable since they will grow in shady areas where few other plants survive. The leaves will yellow in full sun.

Propagation: By division or by cuttings.

Uses: Pachysandra is great under bushes and in the open shade found under evergreen trees. It can be used to carpet banks and as edging along shaded walkways. Plants can also be set in pots for the terrace.

Related species: *Pachysandra procumbens,* or Allegheny spurge, is a native American wildflower that is usually evergreen as far north as Zone 5. Stems have a purplish tinge and bear toothed leaves flecked with silver that becomes more pronounced in the spring. The spring flowers are off-white and quite beautiful. Good soil should have additional humus.

Related variety: 'Silver Edge' has a narrow, silvery white edge around the light, toothed, green leaves.

Perennial Pea, Sweet Pea

Lathyrus latifolius
Zone: USDA 5

These vines are perennial wildflowers imported from Europe and now naturalized over much of the Northeast. The word *Lathyrus* is Latin for a "thick pottage" and refers to the use of pea seeds in porridge.

Description: Perennial pea is a vining plant with paired leaflets of light green with winged stems. It bears tendrils and sweet-pealike flowers of pink, bluish-red, or white and blooms in August.

Ease of care: Easy.

How to grow: Perennial peas do well in any good garden soil, often reaching a length of 10 feet in one season. In fact, they sometimes do too well and can become a garden pest.

Propagation: By division or by seed.

Uses: They are perfect for ground covers, especially for hard-to-plant slopes and banks. They also grow on trellises. The flowers are excellent when cut.

Related varieties: 'Albus' has white flowers, and 'Splendens' has dark, reddish-purple flowers.

Peony

Paeonia species
Zone: USDA 5

Not only are peony flowers beautiful, the plants are especially attractive, too. Throughout history, peonies have been famous—they have inspired poetry, been the subjects for tapestry and wall paintings, and been included in witches' brews. They are named for the Greek physician Paeon, who first used the plants for medicinal purposes.

Description: Herbaceous peonies are shrubby plants with thick roots and large, compound, glossy green leaves on reddish stems. They bear large, many petaled, showy flowers with a pleasing fragrance. They bloom in June and are followed by large, interesting seedpods. Ants are often seen in company with peony buds. Herbaceous peonies die down to the ground for the winter. Tree peonies have branches with obvious bark. Like small trees, tree peonies remain in evidence all year and should not be cut down.

Ease of care: Easy.

How to grow: Autumn planting is best. This means full sun (except in the South) and a proper hole with good, well-drained, moisture-retentive soil rich with humus. If soil is excessively acid, add one cup of lime per plant. Keep manure and added fertilizers away from direct contact with the roots. Plant with the "eyes" or growing points to the top about 1½ inch below the soil surface. Water well. Mulch the first year to protect from severe cold.

Propagation: By division of the roots or by seed (seedlings will take 3 years or more to bloom).

Uses: As specimen plants, in hedges, beds or borders, and even in the cutting garden, peonies should be an important part of any garden. Remember that even if they did not bloom, the attractive shape and gloss of the

(continued)

Peony (continued)

Periwinkle, Myrtle

Vinca minor
Zone: USDA 5

Garden Phlox

Phlox paniculata
Zone: USDA 5

leaves and their shrubby aspect would make them valuable.

Related species: *Paeonia Mlokosewitschii,* or the Caucasian peony, bears yellow flowers about 5 inches across. *Paeonia suffruticosa* is the Japanese tree peony (originally Chinese but refined—not discovered—by the Japanese), which is actually a bush, usually reaching a height of 5 feet and a spread of 6 feet. Flowers are between 6 and 8 inches across. 'Chinese Dragon' has semi-double blossoms of a rich crimson; 'Age of Gold' has large, double, golden blossoms; and 'Gauguin' has yellow petals inked with rose-red lines.

Related varieties: Various crosses of peony species have led to a large number of double varieties. According to type, they will bloom early, midseason, or late in June. Some of the more attractive are 'Bowl of Cream,' with pure white, double blossoms 8 inches across, blooming in midseason; 'Emma Klehm,' with double, deep pink flowers that bloom late in the season; 'Coral Sunset,' with flowers of intense coral, blooming early; and 'Sarah Bernhardt,' which has deep pink petals, lighter toward the edge, with a marvelous fragrance. It blooms late in the season.

This charming plant has a long history. Originally a native of southern Europe, plants were brought over by the colonists, and now it has naturalized over much of the Northeast. "Periwinkle" is thought to be an old Slavic word, *pervinka,* meaning "first" and referring to the early spring flowers.

Description: Periwinkle is a trailing plant about 6 inches high with small, oval, opposite, dark green, shiny, evergreen leaves. In spring, 5-petaled flowers, about ¾-inch in diameter, are borne on short stems in a lovely shade of blue.

Ease of care: Easy.

How to grow: Periwinkles will grow in full sun, but they prefer light or partial shade. Good, well-drained garden soil is best.

Propagation: By division or by cuttings.

Uses: An excellent ground cover, periwinkle is also a welcome change when planted along the edge of beds or borders and lining flagstone or brick walks.

Related varieties: 'Alba' has pure white flowers, larger than the species. 'Bowles' Variety' is more compact than the species, with profuse flowering into May.

Phlox are very popular plants since they are easy to grow, great for color, and marvelous for cutting. By far the most popular are the garden phlox and, over the years, a number of lovely kinds have been developed. The genus is named for the Greek word for "flame" and refers to some of the brightly colored flowers.

Description: Clump-forming perennials with very strong stems, phlox bear simple, lance-shaped leaves. These are topped with clusters of usually fragrant, showy, 5-petaled flowers arising from a narrow tube. They bloom over a long period.

Ease of care: Easy.

How to grow: Garden phlox need good, well-drained soil in full sun or light shade, and plenty of water during the summer. Plants are often prone to powdery mildew. Keep individual plants 18 inches apart to promote air circulation. Divide plants every three years to keep them vigorous, and deadhead to prolong bloom.

Propagation: By division or by seed.

Uses: Phlox can be bunched by color or mixed, the taller types best at the rear of the border.

Related species: *Phlox carolina* (once called *P. suffruticosa*) are native American flowers from North Carolina west to Missouri and then south, hardy to USDA Zone 5. They bloom from June into July. Soil should be good and well-drained in full sun. 'Miss Lingard' bears clear white flowers on 30-inch stems, while 'Rosalinde' has clear pink flowers on 36-inch stems, often blooming from late June into

Pincushion Flower

Scabiosa caucasica
Zone: USDA 4

Pink, Carnation

Dianthus species
Zone: USDA 5

September. *Phlox divaricata*, or the wild sweet William, is another American native and a low-growing species, flowering in May and June, preferring partial shade. Hardy to USDA Zone 4, plants usually bloom at a height of 14 inches. 'Fuller's White' has pure white flowers. *Phlox stolonifera*, or creeping phlox, is another native wildflower, which crawls along the ground and bears purple or violet flowers on 6-inch stems in late spring. Plants are hardy to USDA Zone 4 and prefer light shade, but will take a half day of sun. 'Blue Ridge' has sky-blue flowers and 'Osborne's White' is pure white. *Phlox subulata*, or the mountain pink, is a creeping phlox used as a ground cover or in rock gardens, blooming in early spring. It is hardy in USDA Zone 4. Soil should be well-drained with full sun. Height is 6 inches.

Related varieties: 'Dodo Hanbury Forbes' is clear pink on 3-foot stems; 'The King' has deep purple flowers; 'Starfire' is a brilliant red; and 'White Admiral' is a pure white. All are on 30-inch stems. The Symons-Jeune strain of phlox was developed both for strength of stems and resistance to fungus—a problem that most of the phlox are susceptible to. Notable varieties are 'Blue Lagoon,' with large heads of lavender-blue flowers on 40-inch stems; 'Dresden China,' flowers of a soft shell-pink on 4-foot stems; and 'Gaiety,' with salmon blossoms with a cherry-red eye on 42-inch stems.

The pincushion flower was introduced to England in 1591 and has been a popular garden flower ever since. The common name refers to the flower heads that when closed resemble pincushions full of pins. The genus is named for "scabies," an itch that some species were said to cure.

Description: Plants have simple, lance-shaped, deeply cut leaves, with long, graceful flower stems growing to 2 feet high. They bear domed flower heads up to 3 inches across.

Ease of care: Easy.

How to grow: Scabiosas want good, well-drained garden soil in full sun. In areas of hot summers, light shade is welcomed. Remove dead flowers for a long period of bloom.

Propagation: By division in spring or by seed.

Uses: Plant scabiosas in drifts and along the edge of the bed or border. They are excellent as cut flowers.

Related varieties: 'Alba' has pure white flowers; 'Fama' has flowers of a true lavender; 'House's Hybrids' produce flowers about 2 inches in diameter in colors of blue, lavender, and white; and 'Miss Willmott' bears flowers in ivory white.

Pinks are the hardy flowers of the garden, and carnations are usually thought of as being the flower of the buttonhole or the bouquet, although the terms are often mixed. Regardless of the name, these flowers are known for both their blossoms and for the marvelous sweet and spicy scent that many produce. The genus is a Greek word for "divine flower."

Description: Plants have narrow leaves on jointed stems that end with 5-petaled flowers with fringed edges, often having a distinct odor.

Ease of care: Easy.

How to grow: Plants want full sun and a good, well-drained garden soil. Except for some of the alpine species, these plants are short-lived perennials and benefit from division every two or three years.

Propagation: By division, by cuttings, or by seed.

Uses: Pinks are excellent choices for a rock garden, hanging over the edges of a wall, or for the front of a garden, especially as edging plants. They make wonderful cut flowers, and many will bloom all summer if spent flowers are removed.

Related species: *Dianthus barbatus*, or Sweet William, produces clusters of varicolored flowers that are lovely in the border. They are usually thought of as biennials, but with self-seeding produce flowering plants year after year. *Dianthus deltoides*, or the maiden pink, forms low mats of leaves usually covered with

(continued)

Pink (continued)

Poppy

Papaver orientale
Zone: USDA 5

Plume Poppy

Macleaya cordata
Zone: USDA 4

delightful single flowers on 6- to 12-inch stems perfect for the rock garden. It needs good drainage. 'Brilliant' bears bright, double crimson flowers. *Dianthus gratianopolitanus*, or the cheddar pink, produces clouds of flowers on 6- to 8-inch stems perfect for the rock garden. The flowers are about 1 inch wide and beloved by butterflies. They are hardy in USDA 4. *Dianthus Knappii* comes from Yugoslavia and, unlike the other pinks in the clan, bears yellow flowers on 18-inch plants.

Related varieties: *Dianthus* x *Allwoodii* are hybrids produced years ago in England. The foliage is bluish-green, with flowers of red, pink, or white, often with darker centers, reaching a height of 18 inches. They must be divided every few years to survive. There are many cultivars available. 'Alpinus' is a dwarf growing up to 12 inches high; 'Blanche' is a glorious double white; and 'Robin' has bright red, double flowers.

Papaver is the ancient Latin name for the flowers and is thought to refer to the sound made in chewing the seeds.

Description: Basal leaves are covered with hairs. Graceful stalks grow to 4 feet and bear single or double flowers with petals of crepe paper texture surrounding many stamens. They flower in late May and June. Seedpods are attractive. Any part of the plant will bleed a milky sap when cut.

Ease of care: Easy.

How to grow: Poppies are very undemanding, wanting only good, well-drained soil in full sun. Drainage is especially important in the winter, as water will rot the roots. Place the crown 3 inches below the soil surface and mulch the first winter to prevent heaving. During heavy spring rains, try to cover the plant with Reemay cloth, a commercially available material that is very light and offers some protection. Plants go dormant in late summer, so their spaces should be filled with annuals or summer bulbs.

Propagation: By division in the fall or by seed.

Uses: Use poppies in beds or borders in combination with other perennials or in single groupings.

Related species: *Meconopsis cambrica*, or the Welsh poppy, has 4-petaled, orange or yellow flowers that close at night; adapt to light shade; and seed about the garden.

Related varieties: 'Carmen' bears brilliant red flowers; 'Harvest Moon' has flowers of orange-yellow; 'Lavender Glory' has deep lavender flowers with large, black basal spots; 'Maiden's Blush' has ruffled petals of white with a blush-pink edge; and 'White King' is white.

The plume poppy is a plant that every border should have. Even when not in bloom, it is lovely. Older books call it *Bocconia*. The genus is named in honor of Alexander Macleay, a Colonial Secretary for New South Wales.

Description: Large, lobed leaves, gray-green on top and white and downy underneath, are often 8 inches across on stems to 8 feet tall. Small, white flowers have up to 30 stamens that wave in the wind and bloom in late summer.

Ease of care: Easy.

How to grow: Plume poppies do well in average garden soil in full sun and partial shade in areas with very warm summers. If soil is fertile and dug deeply, plants will quickly spread. The stems are very strong and plants do not need staking.

Propagation: By division or by cuttings.

Uses: Unlike many plants in their height range, plume poppies look great from the ground up and should not be set behind other plants. They are great as specimen plants and also do well in pots.

Related species: *Macleaya microcarpa* 'Coral Plume' has coral-pink flowers with 8 to 12 stamens.

Japanese Primrose

Primula Sieboldii
Zone: USDA 5

In the garden world, there are over 400 species of primroses. Most primroses revel in an English climate calling for cool temperatures and plenty of rainfall and are at a loss in the often short spring and variable summers found over much of the United States. The species listed below performs well in this country. The genus name is a diminutive of the Latin *primus,* "first," alluding to the early flowering of certain European species.

Description: The basal foliage is a rosette with dark green, heart-shaped leaves with a scalloped edge. The plant bears tight bunches of 2-inch wide, pink or purple deckle-edged flowers on 12-inch stems. Each has a white "eye."

Ease of care: Easy.

How to grow: Japanese primroses require partial shade and a good, moist soil. Unlike other primroses, the leaves disappear and plants become dormant in the summer and are spared the rigors of drought and heat.

Propagation: By division or by seed.

Uses: Primroses are unexcelled for the woodland garden or for planting among spring wildflowers in a shady spot of the garden—even without bloom the foliage is very attractive. They make excellent cut flowers. Dormant plants may be potted up in late winter and forced into bloom at normal room temperatures.

Related varieties: The Barnhaven hybrids come in colors of frost-white, rose-red, lilac, China blue, and pink. Blossom shape varies from perfectly round to fringed to a snowflake form.

Rockcress

Aubrieta deltoidea
Zone: USDA 5

Rockcresses are trailing perennials that usually burst into glorious bloom in late April and May. Plants originally came from Greece and Sicily. The genus is named in honor of Claude Aubriet, a French botanical artist of the 1700s.

Description: Rockcresses are creeping and trailing plants with small and simple leaves covered with tiny hairs. They bear a wealth of 4-petaled flowers, each about ¾-inch wide and typically in blues, lilacs, and purples. Plant height is between 4 and 6 inches. The leaves are evergreen when given snow cover, but turn brown without.

Ease of care: Easy.

How to grow: Rockcresses prefer good soil with perfect drainage and a location in full sun. They will also do well in some shade and a very lean soil mix with a great deal of sand. After blooming is finished, they can be cut back.

Propagation: By division, by seed, or by cuttings.

Uses: Rockcresses are great for rock gardens, where they form large carpets of bloom. They can also be planted in pockets of stone walls and do well in trough gardens. In addition, they are fine for the edging of borders.

Related varieties: 'Purple Gem' bears purple flowers on 6-inch stems; 'Bengel' produces larger-than-average flowers in rose, lilac, and deep red; 'Dr. Mules' is an old garden favorite with violet-purple flowers. 'Novalis Blue Hybrid' is a new cultivar with a mid-blue color that comes from seed.

Rock Cress

Arabis caucasica
Zone: USDA 4

The rock cresses are charming plants that hug rock surfaces like rugs. The genus means "Arabia" and could refer to the fact that the plants revel in warm sand and sun.

Description: These creepers are made up of tufted rosettes of oval leaves covered with white down. In spring, they send up 1-foot stems covered with dozens of 4-petaled flowers, ½ inch wide and with a sweet scent.

Ease of care: Easy.

How to grow: The plants resent hot and damp summers and must have perfect drainage. Spent blossoms should be cut to neaten up the plants.

Propagation: By division in early spring or fall or by seed.

Uses: Rock cresses are best suited for a rock garden or for cultivation in a wall garden.

Related species: *Arabis Ferdinandi-Coburgi* 'Variegata' bears its white flowers on 5-inch stems and has creamy white and green leaves with a faint touch of pink. 'Flore-Pleno' is the double, white-flowered form with 10-inch stems; 'Snow Cap' is a single form with flowers on 8-inch stems; and 'Compinkie' bears rose-red flowers on 6-inch stems.

Rodgersia

Rodgersia aesculifolia
Zone: USDA 5

These are extremely handsome plants primarily grown for their foliage. The plants are named in honor of a United States admiral, John Rodgers, who commanded an expedition to Japan at the end of the 19th century, where one species (*Rodgersia podophylla*) was discovered.

Description: Rodgersia has large, compound leaves that resemble those of a horse chestnut. Each leaflet is about 7 inches long, coarsely toothed, and grows on 4-foot high plants that are usually tinted with bronze. Small, 5-petaled white flowers appear in July, blooming in flat clusters on 2-foot stems.

Ease of care: Moderately easy.

How to grow: Rodgersias need specific conditions that include a good, moist soil with plenty of organic matter mixed in and a location with the crowns at least 1 inch below the surface. They want partial shade with sun only part of the day, preferably in the morning. In areas of severe winter without snow cover, mulch is necessary.

Propagation: By division in spring or by seed.

Uses: Like ferns, rodgersias are special plants perfectly suited for the wild garden, the edge of the water garden, or the shade garden. They do especially well in open shade under tall trees.

Related species: *Rodgersia pinnata*, the feathered bronze leaf, has large, toothed, emerald-green, fanlike leaves tinged with bronze. Flowers are pink, and plants grow to about 36 inches high.

Christmas Rose, Lenten Rose, Hellebore

Helleborus species
Zone: USDA 4 to 5

Myth has it that an angel gave a Christmas rose to a young shepherdess who had no present for the infant Jesus. The genus is an ancient Greek name for the plant. The entire plant is deadly poisonous.

Description: Deeply divided, usually evergreen leaves grow from a thick rootstock, producing flowers with thick petals (really sepals) appearing in late fall, winter, or very early spring.

Ease of care: Easy.

How to grow: Hellebores require a good, deep, well-drained soil with plenty of humus and partial shade. When temperatures fall below 15° F, blooming is usually put off until the weather warms. At low temperatures, some protection is needed.

Propagation: By division or by seed.

Uses: The foliage alone is worth growing and makes an excellent ground cover. Flowers are good for cutting, and the plants can be grown in pots or in a greenhouse.

Related species: *Helleborus niger,* or the true Christmas rose, bears white or pinkish-green flowers, and blooms in late fall, winter, or early spring depending on the climate. Although hardy in USDA Zone 4, winters often make growing difficult. *Helleborus orientalis,* or the Lenten rose, is the easiest of the species to grow, with cream-colored flowers fading to brown amidst palmlike foliage. This variety is hardy in USDA Zone 5.

Related variety: 'Atrorubens' blooms in late winter or early spring, with deep maroon flowers.

Rock Rose, Sun Rose, Frostweed

Helianthemum nummularium
Zone: USDA 6

Even if the individual flowers of the rock rose last only one day, there are always more to come. The genus name is from the Greek for "sunflower."

Description: Sprawling and trailing evergreen shrubs with 2-inch leaves that are gray and woolly underneath bear lovely 5-petaled flowers that bloom from late spring into July.

Ease of care: Easy.

How to grow: Rock roses are undemanding plants, wanting only full sun and good, well-drained soil. They should be given winter protection in colder parts of Zone 6. If soil is too acid, add a cup of ground limestone per square yard into the soil surrounding the plant. If cut back after the first blooming, they should bloom again in late summer.

Propagation: By cuttings or by seed.

Uses: Since these plants are real sun-lovers, they are best in rock gardens, along flagstone paths, tumbling over the edge of a low wall, or set in the crevices between and alongside garden steps.

Related species: *Helianthemum apenninum* 'Roseum' has pink flowers on 10-inch stems.

Related varieties: 'Buttercup' bears golden-yellow flowers on 10-inch stems; 'Fire Dragon' has large, copper-red flowers in stark contrast to the gray-green foliage; and 'St. Mary's' blooms with pure white flowers.

Meadow Rue

Thalictrum aquilegifolium
Zone: USDA 5b

Meadow rues are tall and lovely plants with flowers that lack petals but have dozens of fluffy stamens. The English word "rue" refers to the resemblance between the leaves of these plants and the herb rue (Ruta). *Thalictrum* is an old Greek name for this genus.

Description: The leaves are compound (the species name means "leaves like an *Aquilegia* or columbine") on stout-branched stalks growing up to 4 feet tall. Plants bear clusters of rosy purple, petal-less flowers with many stamens, resembling balls of fluff. They bloom in late May and June.

Ease of care: Moderately easy.

How to grow: Soil for meadow rues should be moist with plenty of additional organic matter in partial shade. In cool gardens in the North, they can take full sun. In hot summers, they must have additional moisture.

Propagation: By division in early spring or by seed.

Uses: Use these plants in the wild garden where they naturalize with ease. They are also excellent at the back of a bed or border. Both flowers and foliage are good for bouquets.

Related species: *Thalictrum polygamum*, or tall meadow rue, is an American native wildflower often reaching a height of 10 feet when conditions are to its liking. The flowers are white. It works well in the back of the garden or in a swampy area of the wild or water garden. *Thalictrum speciosissimum* blooms in June with bright yellow flowers on 6-foot stalks and plants with very attractive blue-green foliage.

Related variety: 'Album' has white flowers.

Russian Sage

Perovskia species
Zone: USDA 5

A plant of great charm, originally from Afghanistan and Pakistan, Russian sage is aromatic in addition to being beautiful. The genus is named in honor of a provincial Russian governor, V. A. Perovski.

Description: A subshrub with a woody base produces gray-white stems up to 4 feet tall, bearing small, oval, aromatic leaves with gray-white hairs on the undersides. Sprays of small ¼-inch, violet-blue flowers appear in late July and August.

Ease of care: Easy.

How to grow: Well-drained soil and a spot in full sun are the requirements for these plants. They are not at all fussy. Cut any branches that remain after winter to the ground in early spring.

Propagation: By cuttings.

Uses: As a specimen, as a hedge, or planted in a mass, these late-flowering plants will always elicit comments from garden visitors. The flowers are excellent when cut.

Salvia, Meadow Sage

Salvia x *superba*
Zone: USDA 4

When people think of salvia they think of 'Blaze of Fire,' the variety of *Salvia splendens* from Brazil, with its blatant scarlet blossoms found in almost every public planting in America. But there are other perennial salvias with better colors and greater charm available for gardens. The genus name is the ancient Latin word *salveo,* "to heal," from the alleged medicinal qualities of some species.

Description: Salvia is a sterile hybrid found only in cultivation. It has gray-green, paired leaves covered with tiny hairs underneath on square stems growing up to 3 feet high. They bear spikes, or bracts, of violet-purple flowers that contain smaller, true flowers.

Ease of care: Easy.

How to grow: Salvia are not fussy except that they need full sun and a good garden soil with excellent drainage.

Propagation: By division or by cuttings.

Uses: Use salvias in drifts—the effect will be one of many flower spikes.

Related species: *Salvia azurea,* or the blue salvia, is a native American plant reaching 5 feet in height and bearing deep blue flowers. 'Grandiflora' is a variety of the species. It has larger flowers.

Related varieties: 'Blue Queen' has deep violet flowers through June. 'East Friesland' (or 'Oestfroesland') has 18-inch spikes of violet-blue flowers of particular beauty. 'May Night' (or 'Mainacht') bears indigo flowers with purple bracts on 18-inch stems. Spent flowers should be cut back for rebloom.

Self-heal

Prunella Webbiana
Zone: USDA 5

The self-heals include a very common wildflower from Europe and Asia, *Prunella vulgaris,* believed to be a remedy for curing wounds and other ailments. The genus is named after *brunella* or *braune,* the German word for "quinsy," a disease of the throat the plants were thought to cure.

Description: Self-heals have simple leaves with prominent veins on the underside and square stems. Small flowers resembling snapdragons bloom in the summer in round spikes.

Ease of care: Easy.

How to grow: Self-heals prefer a good garden soil. In the cooler North full sun is fine, but in warmer areas of the country, partial shade and a moist soil are best.

Propagation: By division in spring or by seed.

Uses: Self-heals are a good ground cover in the wild garden and in shady areas along walkways, under taller plants, and in the rock garden.

Related varieties: 'Loveliness' has lilac flowers on 9-inch stems; 'Pink Loveliness' bears pink blossoms on 1-foot stems; 'Purple Loveliness' is a rich purple and has a vigorous habit that makes it a good ground cover; and 'White Loveliness' has pure white flowers on 8-inch stems.

Sneezeweed, Swamp Sunflower

Helenium autumnale
Zone: USDA 4

There are many plants that begin blooming in early fall in bright colors that can often match those of autumn leaves. Sneezeweed is one such flower. The genus name is from an ancient Greek word for a plant named after Helen of Troy. The common name refers to a profusion of golden pollen that could cause problems for allergy sufferers. They are native American plants.

Description: Small daisies have downturned ray flowers on stout stems that branch toward the top and can reach 6 feet. Basal rosettes of leaves are evergreen in areas of mild winters. Plants bloom from late August through September.

Ease of care: Easy.

How to grow: Although the plants are often found in dampish spots in the wild, swamp sunflowers can easily adapt to ordinary garden soil, especially in a low spot. During periods of drought, they need extra water. Nipping off the growing tips in the spring will help produce bushier plants.

Propagation: By division in spring or by seed.

Uses: Sneezeweed provides beautiful color for the back of a border or for an autumn or wild garden. They should be planted with ornamental grasses and with fall asters. They are excellent for cutting.

Related varieties: 'Riverton Beauty' has yellow flowers with a maroon eye; 'Butterpat' has flowers of clear yellow; and 'Moerheim Beauty' is bronze-red. All are on 4-foot stems.

Soapweed

Yucca glauca
Zone: USDA 5

These evergreen plants with swordlike leaves are hardy where the ground freezes and snow falls. The flower buds are edible and the fruits and roots can be substituted for soap. The genus is named for an entirely different Haitian plant.

Description: Short, prostrate stems form clumps of leaves, ½-inch wide and up to 36 inches long with narrow, white margins. Stems growing to 8 feet bear bell-shaped, greenish-white flowers 2 inches long, which turn up at night and become fragrant to lure moths for pollination. Fruits are pods.

Ease of care: Easy.

How to grow: Yuccas are adaptable to most situations, preferring full sun and good, well-drained garden soil. They have tap roots, so once planted they are best left alone.

Propagation: Seeds or occasional offsets on mature plants.

Uses: Since they have tap roots, yuccas are very drought-resistant and, once ensconced, can be left alone. They are excellent as specimen plants. Since they are evergreen, they should also be considered for the winter garden. The flowers are spectacular.

Related species: *Yucca filamentosa,* or Adam's needle, has 2½-foot leaves, their margins bearing threads. Flowers are creamy white and bell-shaped, on stalks often up to 12 feet high, but usually growing to about 6 feet. 'Gold Sword' has evergreen leaves with soft green margins and bright yellow centers.

Soapwort, Bouncing Bet

Saponaria officinalis
Zone: USDA 5

A European immigrant that has now naturalized over much of North America, soapwort was brought over by the colonists to be used as a soap substitute. When bruised or boiled in water, the leaves produce a lather with detergent properties that even removes grease. The genus name refers to the Latin word *sapo,* meaning "soap."

Description: Soapwort has stout, 24-inch stems, swollen at the joints, with oval and opposite leaves. It bears pink or white 1-inch flowers in clusters, each with 5 united petals that are especially fragrant at night.

Ease of care: Easy.

How to grow: Saponarias want a good, well-drained soil in full sun, but they will also do well in a moist spot.

Propagation: By division or by seed.

Uses: Saponarias are useful in the wild garden, in the bed or border, and even to carpet a slope or bank.

Related species: *Saponaria Ocymoides,* or the rock soapwort, is a branching, trailing plant for the edge of the border or a rock wall, needing full sun and good drainage. Plants are usually 6 inches tall and covered in June with 5-petaled rose-pink flowers. 'Alba' has white flowers, and 'Splendens' bears deep rose-pink blossoms on 4-inch plants.

Related variety: 'Rubra Plena' is a form with double pink flowers.

Speedwell

Veronica spicata
Zone: USDA 5

Speedwell is a plant of the roadside with pretty flowers that "speed you well." In Ireland, a bit of the plant was pinned on to clothes to keep the traveler from accident. The flowers were named for St. Veronica.

Description: Plants have simple, oblong, 2-inch leaves usually opposite on strong stems. They grow to 18 inches, often bending, bearing densely branching spikes of small, blue or pink, 5-inch long flowers that bloom in summer.

Ease of care: Easy.

How to grow: Speedwells will succeed in any good, well-drained garden soil in full sun or partial shade. Be sure to deadhead for repeat bloom. Plants will not usually survive wet feet in winter.

Propagation: By division or by seed.

Uses: The taller varieties are beautiful in both bed and border as well as in the rock garden. They are good cut flowers.

Related species: *Veronica latifolia* is usually available only as 'Crater Lake Blue,' bearing flowers of a deep gentian-blue on 18-inch stems. *Veronica prostrata* is a mat-forming type with deep blue flowers on 4-inch stems. 'Heavenly Blue' is usually offered.

Related varieties: 'Blue Peter' bears deep blue flowers in July and August on 24-inch stems; 'Icicle' is pure white on 18-inch plants; 'Minuet' has silvery green leaves and bears pink flowers on 1 foot stems in June; 'Nana' has blue flowers on 8-inch stems; 'Red Fox' blooms with deep rose-red flowers on 14-inch stems; and 'Sunny Border Blue' has violet-blue spikes that bloom from June until hard frost.

Spiderwort

Tradescantia x Andersoniana
Zone: USDA 5

Spiderworts can be compared to daylilies and dayflowers—each blossom lasts only one day. The common name refers to the many glistening hairs on the sepals and the buds. They resemble a spider's nest of webs, especially when covered with dew ("wort" is an old English word for plant).

Description: Spiderworts are weak-stemmed plants that grow up to 1 foot long. They produce a watery juice and have folded, strap-like leaves. The 3-petaled flowers, opening at dawn and fading by mid-afternoon, are surrounded by many buds.

Ease of care: Easy.

How to grow: Spiderworts want a good, well-drained garden soil in full sun or partial shade. In dry summers, they will need extra water. In too-rich soil, they grow quickly and tumble about. Even the newest types can become floppy by midsummer—so when flowering is through, cut the plants to the ground, and they will often flower again.

Propagation: By division in spring or by seed.

Uses: Although fine in the sunny border, the newer spiderworts are best in areas of open shade, especially under tall trees.

Related species: *Tradescantia virginiana* is the original species and is still found in many old country gardens. The flowers are usually 1 inch wide, violet-purple, and often very floppy.

Related varieties: 'Red Cloud' has deep rose-red flowers; 'Zwanenberg' has very large, blue flowers; 'Snow Cap' is pure white; and 'Valor' is a deep red-purple. All grow to a height of 20 inches.

Cushion Spurge

Euphorbia epithymoides
Zone: USDA 5

These flowers are in the same genus as the familiar Christmas poinsettia. In both plants, the flowers are very small and what we perceive to be petals are really colored leaves (called bracts), in various reds and white in poinsettias and bright yellow in the spurges. They are named in honor of a Greek physician called Euphorbius.

Description: Cushion spurges are plants with a milky sap (irritating to some people), with oblong, green leaves, growing in a clump 12 to 14 inches high and covered with yellow to chartreuse bracts in spring—the color itself looks as though it were applied with an artist's airbrush. The leaves turn red in the fall.

Ease of care: Easy.

How to grow: Spurges prefer a good, well-drained garden soil in full sun and partial shade in hot climates.

Propagation: By seed.

Uses: The yellow glow of this plant is startling in spring. Plants are best in front of a low wall or grouped on a low bank.

Related species: *Euphorbia Myrsinites,* or the donkeytail spurge, has bright yellow bracts in early spring and bluish-gray leaves on 10-inch stems that turn pink in the summer. Plants sprawl and are best when tumbling over a low stone wall.

Stonecrop

Sedum spectabile
Zone: USDA 4

There are perhaps 600 species of these succulent herbs—mostly in the North Temperate Zone. Many make excellent garden subjects, but they are usually not found in most nursery centers and are only available from the various rock garden societies. The genus name is from the ancient Latin term, *sedere,* "to sit," referring to their low-spreading habit or possibly from *sedare,* "to quiet," alluding to their supposed sedative properties.

Description: Sedums have strong stems with succulent, usually alternate leaves. Terminal clusters of small, star-shaped flowers have 5 petals.

Ease of care: Easy.

How to grow: Sedums need only a good, well-drained garden soil in full sun. They withstand drought and do amazingly well in very poor soils.

Propagation: By seed, by leaf cuttings, or by division.

Uses: The tall sedums, like *Sedum spectabile,* are excellent when planted in the bed and border, especially when planted in masses. The shorter, sprawling types are best for the rock garden. Most make excellent cut flowers.

Related species: *Sedum Aizoon* reaches a height of between 12 and 18 inches with yellow to orange flowers in summer. *Sedum kamtschaticum* is only 4 inches high and has deep green, scalloped leaves. It bears orange-yellow flowers from July to September. *Sedum Sieboldii* is often called the "October Daphne." It's a trailing plant with lightly scalloped leaves and lovely pink flowers appearing in late fall. Bloom is often killed by frost. *Sedum spurium*

Sundrop, Evening Primrose

Oenothera species
Zone: USDA 5

is a creeping sedum, evergreen even in Zone 5, and makes an excellent ground cover. 'Bronze Carpet' has leaves that are tinted bronze and bears pink flowers, while 'Dragon's Blood' has dark red flowers.

Related varieties: Probably one of the top ten perennials in the garden world today is 'Autumn Joy.' It is also known as 'Herbstfreude' or 'Indian Chief.' Although best in full sun, plants will take light shade. They are always attractive: whether in tight buds of a light blue-green atop 2-foot stems; rosy pink in early bloom; in late bloom as the flowers turn mahogany; or a russet-brown during the winter. *S. spectabile* 'Brilliant' opens its flowers a month ahead of 'Autumn Joy'; 'Meteor' bears carmine-red blossoms on 18-inch stems; and 'Variegatum' has carmine flowers and leaves variegated with areas of creamy white.

The day-bloomers in this genus are the sundrops, and the common name is a perfect choice for petals that look like molten gold. The night-bloomers are called the evening primrose. They are often found in old-time gardens. The genus is named for the Greek word *oinos,* "wine," and *thera,* "to hunt," because of confusion regarding this flower and another genus with roots possessing the aroma of wine.

Description: Simple alternate leaves on strong stems grow up to 2 feet high. They are topped by clusters of bright yellow, 4-petaled flowers up to 2 inches across that bloom in the summer. Basal rosettes are evergreen in colder areas.

Ease of care: Easy.

How to grow: Sundrops are extremely tolerant of poor soil and are very drought-resistant, but the ground must be well-drained and full sun is necessary. If given a spot in good soil, they become quite pushy, but are easily controlled since they are shallow-rooted.

Propagation: By division in spring or by seed.

Uses: Sundrops are perfect for the wild garden and can hold their own at the edge of a field or meadow. Most of the flowers can be gathered for winter bouquets because the seedpods are very attractive.

Related species: There are a number of species useful for the garden. *Oenothera fruticosa* is a wildflower of the eastern United States, with 2-inch yellow flowers on 1½- to 2-foot stems and is the type usually found in old gardens. 'Youngi' is offered by nurseries today. *Oenothera missourensis* stays about 1 foot high, but the blossoms are often showy and 4 inches wide. The trailing stems carry a succession of lemon-yellow flowers opening in early afternoon. They are especially suited for the rock garden where the stems can tumble about and because their soil must never stay wet for any length of time. The seedpods are very attractive. *Oenothera speciosa* is another wildflower that is a rampant spreader in the wild garden; 'Rosea,' with light pink flowers 2 inches in diameter on high stems, is excellent for border edging. *Oenothera tetragona* is often confused with *O. fruticosa.* Its chief claim to fame is the splendid 'Fireworks,' with brilliant yellow flowers on 18-inch stems.

Perennial Sunflower

Helianthus x multiflorus
Zone: USDA 5

Perennial sunflowers are very valuable for their late season bloom, as their bright yellow flowers combine well with goldenrods and fall asters in September. The genus is Greek for "sun flower."

Description: Perennial sunflowers are tall, robust plants with fibrous roots and large, rough, simple leaves on stout stems. Large, yellow, daisylike flowers bloom in September and October.

Ease of care: Easy.

How to grow: Sunflowers want full sun and good, moist garden soil with water provided during periods of drought. Some of the wild species can be invasive.

Propagation: By division or by seed.

Uses: Perennial sunflowers are best grown in the back of the border or in the wild garden.

Related species: *Helianthus angustifolius,* or the swamp sunflower, is native from New York to Florida and west to Texas where it grows in wet or boggy areas. If moved to good garden soil and provided with extra water during periods of drought, the 6-foot plants will bloom in September with 3-inch wide, yellow daisies. *Helianthus salicifolius,* or willow-leaved sunflowers, are American natives from the Midwest. Although the 2-inch wide sunflowers are pretty when blooming in the fall, this plant is used for its attractive foliage. Plants grow about 4 feet high and want only good, well-drained garden soil with a bit of lime added if necessary.

Related variety: 'Flore Pleno' is the typical cultivar with double blossoms that look more like chrysanthemums than sunflowers.

Globe Thistle

Echinops Ritro
Zone: USDA 4

Globe thistles are large and stalwart plants for beds and borders that produce attractive balls of small, individual flowers. The genus name is in honor of the hedgehog because of the plant's prickly aspect.

Description: Globe thistles are 1½-inch balls of metallic-blue blossoms on stout, ribbed stems and, depending on the variety, grow from 3 to 7 feet tall. The leaves have spiny edges and are white-woolly beneath. They bloom in July and August.

Ease of care: Easy.

How to grow: Globe thistles are not fussy as to soil and will do well in full sun or open shade. Once established, they are very drought-resistant. They seed about with ease.

Propagation: By division in the spring or by seed.

Uses: The larger species are impressive when used in background plantings or when grown as specimen plants. The smaller types are attractive in a bed or border or when spread throughout a wild garden. All look especially lovely when mixed with a planting of conifers.

Related species: *Echinops sphaerocephalus* is a species that is much taller, sometimes reaching 7 feet and best used where a strong statement is needed.

Related variety: 'Taplow Blue' has a more intense blue color in the flowers.

Thrift, Sea Pink

Armeria maritima
Zone: USDA 4

Thrifts are excellent for the rock or wall garden. The derivation of the genus name is supposedly Celtic, a fact not too surprising, as the plants are found naturally along the maritime shores of Europe, in addition to the Pacific Northwest and Newfoundland.

Description: Low, basal rosettes of grasslike, evergreen leaves form carpets. Plants bloom in the spring with tightly packed globes of pink flowers, often sending up a few pink flowers all summer long.

Ease of care: Easy.

How to grow: They are very easy to grow as long as the soil is well drained with a location in full sun. If the soil is too fertile or too moist, the plants will begin to rot in the center. Older plants frequently do.

Propagation: By division in early spring or by seed.

Uses: Thrifts can be used to carpet a sandy bank or a seaside garden and do well in terra-cotta pots in a cool greenhouse.

Related varieties: 'Vindictive' bears deep pink flowers on 6-inch stems; 'Launcheana' has flowers of deep rose; and 'Alba' exhibits white flowers.

Wormwood

Artemisia species
Zone: USDA 3

With the exception of *Artemisia lactiflora*, or mugwort, the rest of the wormwoods are best used for their foliage. The genus is named for the wife of Mausolus, an ancient king who built a giant tomb. Surprisingly, these plants are members of the daisy family and include sagebrush, common wormwood (the source of absinthe), and the herb tarragon.

Description: Wormwoods are shrublike plants usually with attractive silver-gray foliage and sprays of small, mostly unattractive flowers. The leaves and other plant parts are often aromatic.

Ease of care: Easy.

How to grow: Plants prefer poor and sandy soil over deep and fertile earth. They must have full sun and good drainage or the roots will soon rot. Do not bother with these plants in areas of high humidity and damp summers. In warmer gardens, they can become weedy.

Propagation: By division or by seed.

Uses: The larger plants can be used as backgrounds to perennial borders; individual plants can be set about the garden to act as foils to bright and colorful blossoms, especially those with white, pink, or lavender flowers. When dried, they are excellent in winter bouquets.

Related species: *Artemisia Abrotanum*, or southernwood, can be used as a deciduous hedge as it can grow to a height of 5 feet. *Artemisia Absinthium*, or common wormwood,

has shiny, silvery, cut foliage on 4-foot stems. 'Lambrook Silver' has leaves of a finer cut. *Artemisia lactiflora*, or white mugwort, is the only one of this group grown for the flowers, which are not really white but more of a cream color. Masses of these tiny blossoms crowd 5-foot stems, starting in late summer and on into autumn. This plant needs better soil than the others. Even though the stems are strong, they might need staking in areas with gusty summer storms. They make excellent cut flowers. *Artemisia ludoviciana*, or white sage, bears willowlike leaves of silvery grayish-white on 3-foot stems. The variety *albula* has a cultivar 'Silver King,' with beautiful foliage on 2-foot stems. *Artemisia Schmidtiana* 'Silver Mound' is a cultivar from Japan that grows in rounded balls with feathery, cut foliage about 20 inches wide. The mounds tend to spread with maturity and will eventually need to be divided. *Artemisia Stellerana*, or beach wormwood, is the only member to be somewhat inclined to humidity and is often found naturalized along sandy beaches of the Northeast. Plants grow about 2½ feet high with tiny, yellow flowers.

Yarrow

Achillea species
Zone: USDA 3b

Most people have seen the wild form of yarrow, *Achillea Millefolium*, a wildflower originally from Europe and western Asia. The botanical name refers to *Achilles*, the hero of Greek legend, who is said to have used a species to heal battlefield wounds.

Description: Yarrow will grow between 1 and 3 feet high, blooming from June until August, and often until frost. Flowers are small and arranged in flat heads on top of stout stems. The foliage is finely cut and resembles a fern. Most species are aromatic and smell of chamomile.

Ease of care: Easy.

How to grow: Yarrows are especially valuable as they are tolerant of drought and suitable for any reasonably fertile garden soil that has good drainage. Plants revel in full sun, although they will tolerate a small amount of shade. New plants should be spaced about 12 to 18 inches apart.

Propagation: By division in spring or fall.

Uses: Yarrow are especially suitable for the garden border and look well in masses. They are excellent both as cut flowers and dried for winter bouquets.

Related species: 'Coronation Gold' bears large heads of golden-yellow flowers and is excellent for drying. The wildflower *Achillea Millefolium* is suited for the meadow or wild garden; the cultivar *Achillea* 'Crimson Beauty' bears rose-red flowers on 2-foot stems; 'Moonshine' has sulfur-yellow flowers on 2-foot stems; *Achillea Ptarmica* 'The Pearl' blooms with small, round, white flowers like its namesake on 3- to 4-foot stems. This plant has unbroken, weedy leaves.

TREES, SHRUBS, & VINES

Every yard needs more than just pretty flowers to make it
complete. You'll want the grandeur of trees
arching overhead; shrubs provide privacy and protection;
vines can fill in bare walls or fences.
Find out how woody plants fit into your landscape.

This lovely blooming accent tree really stands out from the surrounding green foliage and grass. Accent plants make for pleasant viewing when strolling through a well-planned garden.

CHAPTER 1

GETTING COZY WITH WOODY PLANTS

Woody plants—that is, trees, shrubs, and woody vines—form the background of your home's landscape. Without them, beds and borders would seem to float on a sea of grass. Woody plants define the landscape, indicating its limits and breaking it up into separate parts.

Many other plants are seasonal: They grow in spring, bloom through summer, and then disappear in fall and winter. But wood, by its nature, is permanent. Even woody plants that lose their leaves are still visible during the winter months, their trunks and branches continuing to define the landscape.

That doesn't mean woody plants only offer interest when other plants are absent. From the flush of spring green on conifers to the successive bloomings of deciduous shrubs, from the magnificent fall colors and beautiful berries of trees and vines to the colorful bark and graceful silhouettes of the winter landscape, woody plants bring life and movement to the garden all year long.

Woody plants tend to dominate the areas where they grow. They outcompete weeds, resist drought, and are generally able to recover readily from even severe insect attacks and other pests. As a result, woody plants require far less care than any other plant group. Once well-established, in fact, most of them literally take care of themselves.

Woody Plants in the Landscape

Autumn color is just one of the many attractive features of woody plants.

Woody plants are a permanent, year-long presence in the landscape. This permanence helps determine their major uses.

Consider the landscape as if it were a living room. The floor would be formed by low-growing plants and ground-hugging constructions, like lawns and ground covers, patios and pavement. They form the base of any landscape. But what about the rest of the landscape, the walls and ceiling? That's where trees, shrubs, and climbing plants come in.

Walls—Shrubs and vines, as well as related constructions such as fences, form the walls of the room. They help define its boundaries, separating your yard from your neighbor's and one garden area from another. This is most obvious when plants are grown as a hedge, but even informal plantings of shrubs will help define bounds between various areas.

A simple cluster of shrubs, for example, can separate the children's play area from a quiet rest area or the service area with its shed, garbage cans, and clothesline. Formal hedges, because of the obvious barrier they create, are most often used to define property lines.

Shrubs can also offer a screen for privacy, or they can block unsightly views. Deciduous shrubs are good choices for screening: They offer privacy during the summer months yet allow a maximum amount of winter sunlight to penetrate your yard at a season when light is at a premium. If the goal of the screen is to block an undesirable view, evergreens—both conifers and broad-leaf—are the plants of choice, since their cover is permanent. Taller shrubs can also be used as windbreaks or to create a bit of shade in an overly sunny spot.

Vines are used much like shrubs, except they must grow on some sort of support, such as a fence or trellis. A hedge may need many years to grow high enough to block a view. You can create the same effect in a year or two by planting a vining plant at the base of a fence. If you can't put up an attractive fence, a simple chain-link one with vines planted at the base will offer security without being obtrusive.

Vines are also useful in places where space is lacking. Most shrubs quickly attain a diameter of three to five feet; this can seem a waste of space in a tiny urban yard. Vines grow vertically: Most cling so closely to their support that they take up only inches of horizontal space.

For security purposes, you might want your wall to be composed of plants with spiny leaves or branches. A fire thorn or barberry hedge, for example, can be as effective a barrier as a chain-link fence but far more attractive.

Ceilings—After the "floor" and "walls" have been taken care of, the outdoor living room needs a ceiling. Although the sky can serve as a ceiling, it can be too much of a good thing. The vastness of the sky makes it too dominant.

Trees block out part of the sky, defining the sky's borders. Trees also contribute structure to the garden. Trunks and branches act as posts and beams to bring the sky down to a more human scale. For this management of the sky, trees have a purpose in every landscape, even the smallest one.

Trees have other uses as well. No other characteristic of trees is as obvious in the landscape as the shade they provide. Through their ability to filter sunlight and to cool the air through evapotranspiration, leaves can reduce the temperature by up to 10 degrees Fahrenheit on a hot summer day. Shade also protects from excess sun that can annoy your eyes and be dangerous for the skin. So every garden should have at least one shady nook. Some trees are known as "shade trees." These are usually taller trees with a broad crown. Smaller trees can also provide plentiful shade, although you may prefer to remove some of the lower branches for sitting.

Putting It all Together—With the structure of your "living room"—floor, walls, and ceiling—now clearly defined by the lawns and woody plants it contains, you have the base on which to build your landscape. All you have left to add is the "furniture": flower beds, accent plants, and the like.

Defining
Woody Plants

The attractive bark of this birch also provides year-round protection.

Woody plants come in all shapes and sizes, from tall and upright to low and creeping. Aside from producing wood, these plants have one thing in common: persistent stems, meaning the stems survive from one year to the next. This distinguishes woody plants from herbaceous (nonwoody) plants like perennials, which die back to the ground each year. Although many woody plants lose their leaves in the winter or dry season, the stems survive and produce new leaves the following year. Trees, shrubs, and most vines are woody plants, but the boundaries between each group are not always clear.

Trees Versus Shrubs—Although most people recognize a tree when they see one, defining what does and does not constitute a tree is not easy. This is particularly the case when distinguishing between a tall shrub and a small tree.

One common definition of a tree is a perennial plant that bears only one single woody stem (the trunk) at ground level. Size is not a determining factor in this definition. A tree can reach 100 feet or more in height or only one foot. In practice, however, a very small tree is likely to be treated as a shrub. Woody shrubs have several stems rising from ground level. Shrubs are also usually smaller. There are many obvious exceptions, such as trees with multiple trunks that can be very hard to distinguish from tall shrubs. Other plants can be either trees or shrubs depending on how they are grown. These general definitions, however, do help to distinguish between the two groups.

Humans also influence plant growth by pruning and other practices. For example, a gardener may prune off all the secondary stems of a shrub, leaving only one main trunk, thus creating a "standard" (tree-form shrub). A gardener may also repeatedly cut back young trees, forcing them to branch at their base, turning them into shrubs. Nature does the same thing. Some plants that normally grow as trees will take on a shrub form at the northern limits of their range. Each winter their top growth is pruned back by cold, causing them to develop multiple branches rather than a main trunk. Subshrubs are plants with woody stems, yet they die back at least part way to their roots each year. Subshrubs are usually treated as perennials. Some true shrubs, such as butterfly bush, will behave as subshrubs in cold or extreme climates.

Vines—Vines can be separated into three main categories: woody vines, with permanent above-ground stems; perennial vines, which die back to the ground each winter and then sprout again in spring; and annual vines, which start anew from seed each year. A woody vine can be considered a shrub that needs some sort of support to grow well. Some woody vines (including many types of clematis) die back to the ground each year, just as subshrubs do, especially under harsh climatic conditions. Only woody vines are covered in this section.

Deciduous or Evergreen?—Trees, shrubs, and woody vines are classified as either deciduous or evergreen. Deciduous woody plants usually lose their leaves in the fall. In warmer climates leaf loss can occur at other times in the year, notably at the onset of the dry season. Evergreen plants remain clothed in foliage throughout the year. They do lose their leaves, but gradually rather than all at once; they are never completely barren. Some woody plants are classified as semievergreens. Their leaves are persistent in most conditions but fall off in harsh ones, especially in cold or very dry climates. Deciduous plants often have attractive fall colors. Evergreens present a continuous display of green foliage, even when deciduous plants are bare.

The term "evergreen" is often mistakenly thought to pertain strictly to conifers (cone-bearing plants). This is not the case. There are broad-leaf evergreens, including boxwoods and most rhododendrons, and deciduous conifers, such as larches and bald cypress. In many plant catalogs, woody plants are divided into three categories as to their foliage: deciduous, broad-leaf evergreens, and needled evergreens.

Anatomy of a Tree

All trees are made up of many parts, from leaves above ground to roots below ground.

Any attempt to divide Mother Nature's work into convenient categories for human discussion is bound to have a few exceptions. Such is the case with plants. For example, many bamboos have persistent leaves and stems but don't produce true wood. Although some plants may not be true woody plants, gardeners tend to classify such plants according to the group they most resemble. Thus bamboos, at least the taller ones, are treated as shrubs.

1. **Leaves:** Produce food and release water and oxygen.

2. **Buds:** Contain embryonic leaves, shoots, and flowers for the next season.

3. **Scaffold branches:** Give the tree its main structure.

4. **Lateral branches:** Secondary branches that fill in the tree's form.

5. **Trunk:** The main structural support for the tree.

6. **Bark:** The outer protective layer of the tree.

7. **Inner bark (phloem):** Carries organic compounds to the roots.

8. **Cambium:** A thin layer that produces new inner bark and sapwood. All tree growth in girth occurs in this layer.

9. **Sapwood (xylem):** Carries nutrients and water to the leaves.

10. **Heartwood:** Inactive sapwood that serves mostly to strengthen the trunk. Heartwood makes up most of the woody part of mature trees.

11. **Taproot:** A downward-growing root mainly used to anchor the tree. Not all trees have taproots.

12. **Lateral roots:** Spread out in all directions around the tree, mainly in a horizontal direction, to help anchor the tree. They also store food reserves for future use.

13. **Feeder roots:** Secondary roots usually covered in root hairs.

14. **Root hairs:** Microscopic growths produced by feeder roots. They are essential for the absorption of water and nutrients and in the exchange of gases.

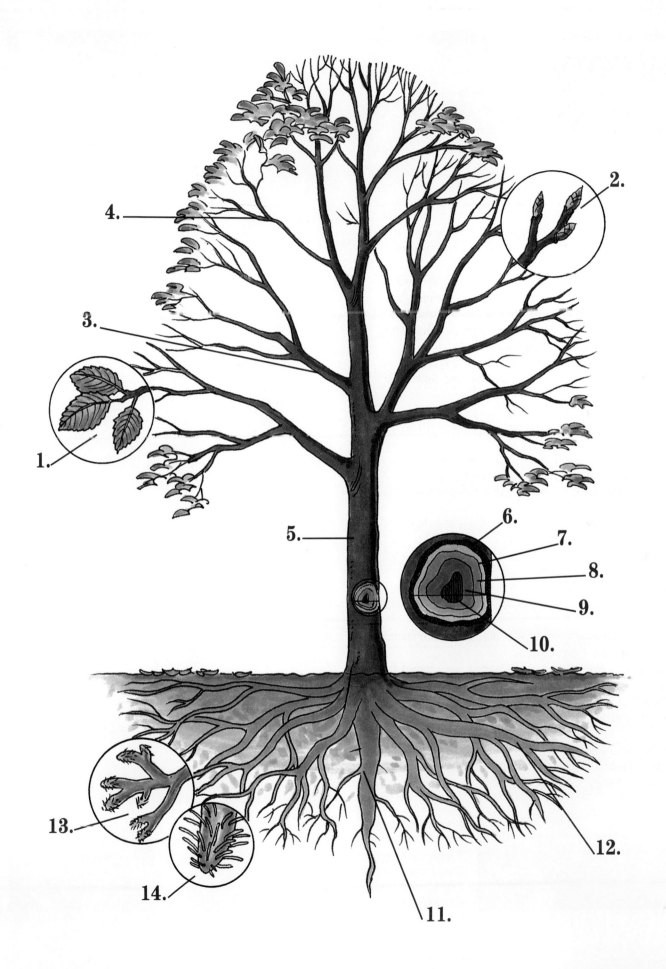

Of all trees, sugar maples
have some of the most
spectacular fall colors.
These yellow-orange leaves
can brighten up your
backyard on even the
dreariest autumn day.

CHECKING OUT THE OPTIONS

Trees, shrubs, and vines make up a vital part of the landscape, yet many people purchase them with no more thought than deciding what to eat for dinner that night. They go to the nursery, pick out a plant that looks interesting, and plant it where they think it will look good. Never for an instant do they consider its needs or its eventual size or shape. With annuals, that's not such a bad mistake. If annuals do poorly or look awful in the spot where you planted them, you can always try something else next year. Woody plants don't offer the same option. Trees, shrubs, and vines are comparatively expensive, and they are permanent or nearly so: You can't just dig them up and move them with ease. You may even find you can't cut them down if they are in your way. Most municipalities now require permits for tree removal. Usually, they do not allow you to cut one down without a valid reason; invoking the fact that you planted it in the wrong place is rarely a good one. You should know how each woody plant will behave under present conditions before you make your purchase.

In this chapter you'll learn the different uses for trees, shrubs, and vines so you won't make mistakes when planning your landscape. How can woody plants be put to best use? Which are well-adapted to your conditions and which should be avoided? These are just some of the questions to consider in selecting trees, shrubs, and vines for your landscape.

Designing with Trees, Shrubs, & Vines

This Clematis x Jackmanii *vine adds color in a spot that may be bare otherwise.*

Designing your landscape is much like decorating your home, but you need to plan even more carefully. After all, you can always move the sofa or change the picture on the wall until you get just the right effect. However, you can rarely move a tree, shrub, or vine once it is established. You should plan your landscape on paper first if you want it to be effective.

Start by mapping out your yard. Graph paper is perfect for planning: It takes much of the difficulty out of measurement (each square can be a precise measurement, say 1 foot by 1 foot) and makes drawing straight lines a snap. Draw in the permanent structures first: the house, the garage, the sidewalk, the driveway, and anything else you will not be moving or changing in a major way. Include such features as windows in your house, which help determine special views you'll want to enhance. Draw these in pen. Next consider any plants or secondary constructions (fences, garden walls, lights poles, and the like) that are already in place and not likely to change. These can be either penciled in or inked in, depending on how sure you are that they really will be conserved. Remember to add utilitarian constructions such as telephone poles, tool sheds, and fire hydrants that you may want to make less visible, as well as any features of your neighbor's yard that you want to either continue to enjoy or hide from sight. Don't include anything you intend to remove. You now have the base on which to develop your plan.

The next step is to start testing your landscape ideas. Pencil in a few shrubs or trees (or cut out their forms in paper and paste them in place). If the initial results look good on paper, try putting more plants elsewhere. Any time something you add doesn't please you, just erase it and start again. Consider your family's needs both now and in the future; the plantings should mesh with these requirements. For example, if you have young children and intend to install an above-ground pool to keep them busy for the summer, don't plan to plant tall trees nearby because their shade simply won't be welcome.

Once you have your plan, it is time to start shopping for plants, but again, only on paper. At this point, look for shapes, forms, and heights rather than specific species. Try to visualize the height of the plants you want, and the space they'll take up. Include some variety in your plan but don't hesitate to use the same plant in different places or in mass plantings. The pattern

thus created will help unify the landscape. Plantings of totally disparate trees, shrubs, and vines will look like a hodgepodge collection. Consider contrast and balance, texture and color, scale and form. If you have large trees on your lot, remember that the scale of your plantings will have to be much larger than in a yard with no trees or only young ones. Large trees tend to dwarf other plants unless the other plants are large also. You might want to color in your plan at this point with different shades of green or spots of color to represent flowering shrubs, trees, and vines.

Planning on Paper

Use graph paper to develop a scale drawing of your house and yard. Ink in permanent structures, then pencil in those features that you are considering planting. Make ample notes to help you better organize your thoughts. When you've developed a plan that seems to meet all your needs, you can begin to look for the proper species to plant. Pencil in potential plantings until you have a design that suits your needs.

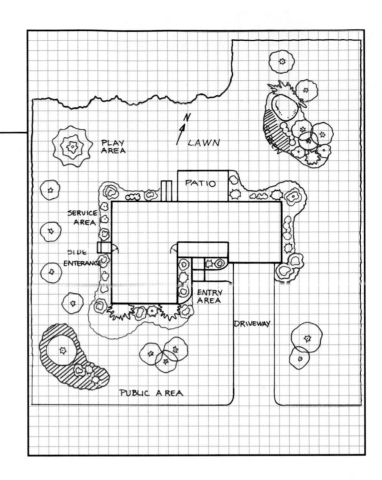

Accent Plants

An accent plant usually stands out from the other plants surrounding it because of an unusual feature. Don't overdo accent plants, or they lose their effectiveness. They are designed to draw the eye, and the eye can't look in several directions at once. One accent plant per major garden feature per season is plenty.

Putting Woody Plants to Use

Shrubs can serve excellently as a hedge.

Accent Plants—Many woody plants are well-suited to serve as garden accents: incidental features that highlight part of the landscape and draw the eye to it. Unlike annuals and perennials, which certainly make excellent accent plants when they are in bloom, many woody plants can offer season-long interest. It may be a special shape or texture or foliage of a contrasting color. It could simply be a plant that would be quite ordinary in other circumstances but stands out because it is different from the surrounding plants. For example, an upright shrub would make a good accent in a bed of low, spreading ground covers. Small weeping trees often make excellent accents, since they are tall enough to be visible year-round, and their pendulous branches look intriguing even when they are not clothed in leaves.

Shade Trees—Shade trees need to be carefully placed, or they will quickly crowd each other out. Check eventual width and plant them so they will barely touch at maturity. Try planting shade trees about 20 feet from the house on the southwest or west sides. They make convenient air conditioners, lowering the indoor temperature by as much as 20 degrees Fahrenheit. Deciduous shade trees have the advantage of blocking excess summer sun but, when their leaves fall, they let in light during the winter when it is most needed. Place them at the corners of the house rather than directly in front of the windows. This ensures they don't block your view, and trees that frame a house make it look more attractive.

When planting shade trees, remember to leave some room for sunlight in your yard, especially if you have or intend to have a swimming pool or a flower, water, or vegetable garden. You can plant shade trees to the north or northeast of these features.

Flowering Trees—These are usually smaller than shade trees and are not as likely to overpower the landscape. They make excellent accents when planted singly, and this is often their best use on small lots. On larger ones, you can try mass plantings or repeating them to define a straight or curved line. Many flowering trees offer all-season interest, with spring flowers, green or bronze summer foliage, colorful leaves in the fall, and bright berries or attractive bark in the winter.

Shrubs—Shrubs are quite easy to incorporate into the landscape as long as their eventual height and width are taken into account. Don't fill up a planting space with young shrubs for an immediate effect. Although it will look good at the moment and perhaps for a year or so after that, it won't take long before the area is terribly overcrowded. Instead, place the shrubs so they will create the best effect when mature; fill in the gaps with mulch or temporary plantings (annuals, perennials, bulbs, and the like). When used as hedges, shrubs can be planted much closer together than they normally would be.

Shrubs can be planted singly, as accent plants, or in borders, often to form a background for other garden plants. Although the shrub border can be composed of mixed plants, you'll get better results by grouping several of a given type together or by repeating a particular shrub elsewhere in the border rather than by using one of a dozen different types of shrubs. Mass plantings of the same shrub are also attractive.

Foundation Plantings—Most houses, with their rigid construction and geometric outline, look peculiar if surrounded by lawn only. Houses can best be integrated into the surrounding land through foundation plantings. Plant shrubs and vines, possibly even small trees, near the walls of the building. Do not place foundation plants too close together or too close to the walls. Find out their full diameter at maturity and space them appropriately. Shrubs, even narrowly upright ones, should be planted at least three feet from the walls.

Low-growing and spreading shrubs are ideal subjects for foundation plantings. Vines growing up trellises also make excellent foundation plants.

Vines—Climbing plants are ideal for landscaping because their height and width are limited by the structures on which they grow. Unless climbing plants "escape" by reaching into nearby trees or other structures, they'll remain within bounds. Be careful about planting clinging vines, such as English ivy, up against the house itself. If the mortar is weak, the vine can damage the house's structure. (Scrape at the mortar with a key: If it resists, there will be no danger of damage.) Just in case, consider training vines up trellises set about a foot away from the house.

The Size & Shape of Woody Plants

This graceful Malus *species is just part of an overall landscape design.*

Woody plants, as opposed to herbaceous plants, build on their growth of previous years, becoming bigger and bigger with time. There is a limit of course—a small shrub will never become a tall tree—but most woody plants will continue to increase in size throughout their lives. Growth is modest, however, once they attain their full size.

The "full size" of any woody plant is a highly variable point. A tree growing in ideal conditions will become much larger than the same species growing in a spot for which it is poorly adapted. Protection from strong winds will also help woody plants attain a larger size, since branches are not as subject to breakage. In general, trees and shrubs grown in full sun will be much broader and fuller yet often not as tall. If the same species has to compete with other trees and shrubs (for instance, in a forest), it will often grow beyond its "maximum" height but have a narrow growth habit with fewer branches. Size and breadth are also dependent on the space available. A shrub that can reach ten feet in height and eight feet in diameter in an open space will reach less than half that if it is planted in a container, which restrains its roots.

Vines differ from other woody plants in that they adapt to the size of their support. A climbing plant may have the potential to reach 50 feet in height, but if it is growing on an eight-foot trellis, it won't get much higher than the trellis.

The ultimate size and shape of trees and shrubs can be controlled by pruning. Often, the plants in a moderate-size hedge would actually grow to become trees, but their growth can be maintained indefinitely by judicious trimming. For more information on pruning, see chapter 4 of this section, "Caring for Your Woody Plants," page 326.

For these and other reasons, the sizes given here are only approximate. If a tree is said to eventually attain a height of 50 to 60 feet, that is what it can be expected to reach under average growing conditions.

Some trees and shrubs are fast-growing: They can put on several feet of new growth a year. Fast-growers are ideal when quick results are desired. Most fast-growing woody plants, however, are also short-lived. You may be better off planting fast-growing trees and shrubs to quickly give your landscape the proper volume. At the same time, you can plant slower-growing but longer-lived plants that will one day comprise the backbone of your landscape after the short-lived plants are removed.

Trees and shrubs can be divided into groups based on different growth habits. Many trees and shrubs may have one growth habit when young and another when mature. Vines can be divided according to the way in which they climb and the kind of support they need. However, all vines can also be grown as ground covers. Just plant them in an open space with no objects to climb, and they will spread nicely. As soon as the vine finds a likely support, the plant will climb it.

Prostrate Shrubs

These shrubs grow low to the ground, since their branches offer little support. Prostrate shrubs can easily be trained up walls or trellises and, when so used, can be considered vines.

Globular Shrubs and Round-head Trees

Globular shrubs have a distinct globular shape. They are often relatively small plants and are ideal choices where space is limited. Round-head trees have a similar globular appearance, but on top of a trunk. Many trees naturally have a rounded head, but others are pruned that way. Round-head trees generally make excellent shade trees.

Spreading Shrubs or Trees

These plants have a vase-shaped silhouette. Depending on the degree to which their branches arch, they can be called low-spreading, open-spreading, rounded-spreading, or even weeping. Most of these shrubs will eventually cover quite a bit of space, so choose spreading shrubs according to the space you have available. Trees, such as the American elm, can also be vase-shaped.

Weeping Trees

The weeping willow is the most typical example of a weeping tree. They have an upright trunk but long, pendulous branches, which often touch the ground. Weeping trees are rare in nature—most of those seen in gardens are selections created by humans. Some species of trees do have secondary branches that are naturally somewhat pendulous. Full-size weeping trees, such as a weeping willow or a weeping beech, usually take up a lot of space and are suitable only for large yards. Others, however, are so weak-stemmed they cannot support themselves if left to grow on their own. These are usually grafted on top of straight trunks or trained up a support to the desired height and then allowed to hang downward. These "dwarf" weeping trees never get very large.

Pyramidal Trees or Shrubs

These plants have a triangular growth pattern, with a broad base and a relatively narrow top. This, along with the round-head form, is one of the most common patterns for mature trees. Pyramidal trees that have lost their lower branches are usually good shade trees.

Conical Trees or Shrubs

Conical trees and shrubs are also triangular in outline, but even more narrow in growth. This is the typical shape of "Christmas trees" such as spruces, firs, and other young conifers.

Columnar or Fastigiate Trees

These trees and shrubs have a very narrow, entirely upright growth pattern. This occurs when the plant either produces only very short branches or all the branches fork upward at a very narrow angle. These are ideal trees and shrubs for planting where height is desired but little horizontal space is available.

Dense or Open Growth

Trees and shrubs can also have either **dense growth,** in which leaves and secondary branches are so heavy that limbs are almost hidden from view during the growing season, or **open growth,** in which the main branches are well separated and leaves tend to be concentrated at the ends of the branches. Many trees have dense growth in their youth and become more open with age. Trees with dense growth tend to make good shade trees. Open growth trees let more light penetrate to the ground, making it easier to set other plants at their base.

Scramblers

Also called leaners, scramblers have long flexible stems and climb simply by leaning against other objects. Climbing roses are a typical example. These plants usually push their way up through the tangle of branches of existing trees or shrubs. In the case of roses, the thorns help them hook on to their hosts. In culture, scramblers need to be attached to their support: They will not climb without some help.

Twiners

These vines wrap themselves around their support in order to climb. While some can twist their way around moderately thick tree trunks, most of these vines cannot climb unless a much thinner support is provided. Most of these plants have twining stems, but others produce tendrils, which are special growths that wrap themselves around objects. In still other plants, such as clematis, the leaf stalk (petiole) acts as a tendril, wrapping itself around the object it is climbing. Plants that climb by twining require a trellis, fence, or similar support to climb in culture.

Clingers

These are vines that have no need for a trellis.
One group of clinger vines, including English ivy,
climbs by means of aerial roots. Another group,
typified by Boston ivy, has special adhesive disks
at the end of their tendrils. Plants of either of
these two groups will climb just about any nearby
object, even walls, with no special means of
support.

Selecting for Hardiness

This combination of trees, flowering and green shrubs, and border plants shows the potential of mixing different plants.

The term "hardiness" is generally considered by most gardeners to apply to cold hardiness, which is the ability of a plant to adapt to a given degree of cold. But the subject is actually much more complex than that. Many supposedly "hardy" trees and shrubs from the Pacific Northwest, for example, do poorly in the Midwest and Northeast: not because of the cold but rather because of the hot, dry summers. Plants adapted to cold conditions often will not grow well in the South. These plants need cold temperatures to signal a time of dormancy or a time to flower. Many apple and crabapple varieties, for example, will produce foliage in the South, but they will neither bloom nor bear fruit: They need a certain number of days of cold temperatures for their flower buds to develop.

Local nurseries or botanical gardens are good sources for information concerning cold hardiness as well as whether a given plant will do well under local conditions. Always ask before you buy. It can be frustrating to plant a sapling believing it will become a large shade tree only to discover it barely grows under local conditions.

Cold Hardiness—Woody plants are far more susceptible to temperature change than perennials since they don't die back to the ground. Instead, their branches and buds are exposed to winter's coldest temperatures. It is important to choose woody plants that are adapted to your climatic zone.

There are several different hardiness zone maps, but the one most used in North America was created by the United States Department of Agriculture (USDA). This map lists 11 different zones, based on the average annual minimum temperature. Zone 1 is the coldest: The average mean winter temperature drops to -50 degrees Fahrenheit or lower. Zone 11 (a new zone not appearing on older maps) is the warmest: Temperatures almost never drop below freezing, making the zone essentially tropical. See pages 112 and 113 for the USDA zone map.

The zones are further divided into parts a and b, representing respectively colder and warmer parts within the zone. Zone 6a, for example, experiences colder temperatures than zone 6b. These subzones are important in making precise decisions concerning the plants you want to grow.

Most North American garden plants have been classified according to their adaptability to cold and have been assigned a particular hardiness zone based on the coldest temperatures at which the plants can be expected to do well. For example, the silk tree (*Albizia Julibrissin*) is considered hardy to zone 6: It will do well in that zone and in zones with higher numbers, such as zone 7 or zone 8, but not in zone 5b, which is colder.

Pushing the Limits—Remember that hardiness classifications are indications only. It is not always necessary to follow them to the letter. For example, if you can offer good snow cover, excellent growing conditions, and protection from dominant winds, you might be able to grow a plant a half zone, or even a full zone, beyond its normal classification.

Within a species, individual plants may be hardier than the average. Such extra hardy plants are often used to breed even hardier plants. The USDA, for example, has been working on developing hardier varieties of crape myrtle (*Lagerstroemia indica*), holly (*Ilex* sp.), camellia (*Camellia* sp.), and many others. Cuttings or seeds taken from plants already growing beyond their normal range often yield hardier plants and are well worth experimentation if one of your favorite plants doesn't normally grow in your area. Specialist nurseries also often offer clones of trees, shrubs, and vines adapted to colder climates.

Trees to Avoid—Not all trees are desirable under all circumstances, and some are barely interesting even under the best of circumstances. These trees should be avoided, at least under the conditions in which they cause problems.

Some trees have evolved far-reaching root systems that seek out water wherever it can be found. These roots can cause serious damage by clogging drainage pipes, strangling piping, and pushing their way into foundations. It can be costly to repair any damage on your property, and you may be liable for any damage done to a neighbor's or city property. Such trees are best reserved for large properties where they can be planted far from buildings or drains of any sort. Many municipalities have ordinances prohibiting their use. Most poplars (*Populus* sp.) and willows (*Salix* sp.) fall into this category, as does the silver maple (*Acer saccharinum*).

Some trees, including poplars (*Populus* sp.) and staghorn sumac (*Rhus typhina*), are unwanted because of the numerous suckers (plantlets) they produce, often at great distances from the main trunk. This is not a major problem when the main tree is surrounded by lawn, since the young trees are easily removed by mowing. However, it would be unwise to plant these trees in gardens where limited maintenance is the desired goal.

Still other trees produce seeds or berries in such abundance that they become quite an annoyance. In some cases, such as the white mulberry (*Morus alba*), the fruit falls off the tree, staining clothes and lawn furniture and attracting wasps. Sometimes, for example the ginkgo (*Ginkgo biloba*), the fruit simply has a very unpleasant smell. Some trees produce so many seedlings that the sheer abundance is the main inconvenience (ashes [*Fraxinus* sp.] and the Siberian elm [*Ulmus pumila*]). This problem can be entirely avoided by choosing nursery-grown stock; selections are available that produce no fruit or seeds at all.

In some areas of the country, popular landscape plants, such as buckthorn (*Rhamnus* sp.) and Norway maple (*Acer platanoides*), are escaping into the wild and crowding out native species. Finally, there are several trees that are considered to have little use under any circumstances, usually due to a combination of poor growth habits, messy leaves and fruit, and extreme invasiveness. Among the "black-listed" species are the tree of heaven (*Ailanthus altissima*); box elder (*Acer Negundo*), although its variegated forms are highly useful; and the Brazilian pepper tree (*Schinus terebinthifolius*).

Gardeners in colder zones often wrap their rhododendrons and other broad-leaf evergreens in burlap for the winter. This provides extra protection from cold, drying winds and allows them to be grown up to a full zone colder than they normally would be. Coldframes are another way of providing a bit of extra heat for relatively tender shrubs. Tender plants grown in containers can always be stored in a partly heated garage or cool basement for the winter.

Shopping: The Nursery Versus Buying Mail-Order

When buying seedlings, mail-order houses and nurseries each have advantages and disadvantages.

Once you've studied the situation in your garden and have a good idea of the trees, shrubs, and vines you wish to purchase, it's time to go shopping. The question is where.

Most amateur gardeners look no further than local nurseries for their plants. These growers offer a wide variety of sizes of the most popular plants, and you can pick exactly the specimen you feel would look best on your property. Furthermore, nursery employees are usually very knowledgeable about which plants do best in your area. Don't hesitate to ask questions.

The main difficulty with local nurseries is a lack of choice. They tend to stick to the tried-and-true. If you are looking for a specific species or variety, the nursery may not be able to help you. If you live near a major urban center, you may find among the local nurseries a few that specialize in less common trees, shrubs, and vines. Those nurseries are good places to shop for more unusual varieties.

It may surprise novice gardeners to discover that many nurseries operate by mail order. Mail order is an excellent way to find particular species and varieties that are not available locally. Mail-order nurseries are generally reputable companies with many years of experience in serving customers. But beware of those that seem to offer too much for your money. They often fail to mention the original size of the tree, which may be barely more than a rooted cutting, or they may offer seedlings of unproved value. When dealing with this sort of nursery, you may find the money you saved would have been better spent on a smaller number of larger or better-quality trees and shrubs bought from a more trustworthy source. With nurseries, as with any business, you get what you pay for.

Some mail-order nurseries are specialists. They may deal only in dwarf conifers, windbreaks, trees with variegated foliage, or some other specialized category. Their plants are often expensive (some of the offered plants are extremely rare and hard to multiply), but they are often the only source of many less common trees, shrubs, and vines. They usually offer a wide range of sizes. If you are looking for a rare but expensive plant, you might be willing to buy a smaller specimen and watch it grow. Whenever possible, try to buy from a mail-order nursery that is located in a climate similar to yours: The plants you buy will already be well-adapted to your growing conditions. If you can't buy from a nursery in a climate similar to yours, give your new tree, shrub, or vine ample winter protection for its first season or so. When ordering outside of your area, spring is the best time. Plants ordered in fall, especially from Southern nurseries, may not go dormant in time for early autumn freezes in the North.

Be sure to check state regulations regarding plant purchases: You may find some plants cannot be sent to your area. Most citrus-producing states, for example, will not allow citrus produced in other states to be brought within their borders. You can import plants from foreign countries, but check first for information on importation permits and fees.

The dark green of evergreens creates a striking and beautiful contrast with a blanket of newly fallen snow. Woody plants offer year-round possibilities for attractive landscaping.

318

CHAPTER 3

THE CULTURAL NEEDS OF YOUR PLANTS

While an annual can be a temporary planting, woody plants are another story. Most woody plants should be considered permanent parts of your landscape. Keep this in mind not only when deciding how to incorporate them into your landscape plan but also when determining what conditions are present in the site.

The real secret to success with plants is not in taking meticulous care of them but in planting them in the right place at the start. You can, of course, use all your available time and effort keeping a weeping willow alive in a desert or growing an acacia in a swamp, but neither will ever really thrive. However, if you plant the willow in the evenly moist soil it prefers and the acacia in the dry conditions it loves, chances are they will thrive almost in spite of your care.

This chapter will help you analyze the conditions in your yard. Once you understand the situation—soil type, drainage, exposure, and the like—you're dealing with, it will be far easier to choose trees, shrubs, and vines that will adapt well to your yard's conditions. The plants will thrive and become a beautiful part of your landscape. And if you have a problem, such as poor drainage or excess shade, there are often a few simple techniques that can improve conditions permanently.

Soil, Water, & Drainage

Water and drainage are as vital for woody plants as for container plants.

When we look at a tree or shrub, we generally only consider the aspects above ground: shape and size, leaf color, flowers, and the like. We rarely stop to think that at least half the plant—its extensive root system—is underground. The underground portion, more than anything else, determines whether the plant will thrive or fail. Before you begin choosing the proper trees, shrubs, or vines for your yard, you must analyze the soil, water, and drainage conditions in your yard. You then must determine whether any changes should be made. It is always easier to do this before you begin planting. It's also less costly: You won't find yourself having to replace dead or dying plants.

The soil in which your plant grows serves four basic purposes. It helps, through its structure, to hold the plant upright, and it supplies food, water, and air to the roots. Most soils are already capable of meeting these purposes and can be used with little amendment. Called loam soils, they contain a mixture of large and small soil particles plus abundant organic matter.

Some soils, however, may be extremely dense, with little air space between the particles. This type of soil, called clay, is made up of particles of rock so tiny and close together they allow little air circulation. Clay holds water well, sometimes perhaps too well. Sandy soil, on the other hand, contains larger particles of rock. Air is present in abundance in sandy soils, but water runs straight through. This creates dry growing conditions, even in a moist climate.

To determine which type of soil you have, squeeze some slightly moist soil in your hand. Clay soils will form a compact lump and retain their shape. Loam soils will form a ball but fall apart if poked at. Sandy soils won't hold their shape at all.

Both sandy and clayey soils can be improved in the same way: by adding organic amendments. Add about one-third peat, compost, well-rotted manure, or other organic matter, and mix carefully. Clay soils also require the addition of sand to open up air spaces. If possible, do this for the entire lot or at least the entire planting area. You don't want to create a single pocket of good soil surrounded by poor soil because your plant, as it grows, will want to send its roots further afield, beyond the original planting site. Roots may be hesitant to leave the pocket of good soil to penetrate the surrounding inhospitable soil.

It is also worthwhile before planting to test your soil's pH level. This is a measure of acidity and alkalinity. The pH scale runs from 1 to 14, with 7 being neutral. Anything above 7 is increasingly alkaline, anything below, increasingly acid. Most soils in North America fall in a pH range of 6 to 7, from slightly acid to neutral. This is ideal for most plants.

Garden centers and local Cooperative Extension offices usually offer an analysis service and will explain how to collect a soil sample. You can also buy a pH kit and do your own testing, but the results will be less specific than with a professional test.

If your soil is on the alkaline side (7 or above), consider either planting plants that tolerate alkaline soils or amending it with peat moss or sulfur. If your soil is very acid (below 5.5), try either planting acid-loving plants or adding ground limestone. The exact quantities of amendment needed to change your soil's pH to the one you want depends on a great many factors, notably its original pH and the type of amendment used. A professional soil analysis will indicate the exact amount.

Water makes up about 90 percent of the tissue in leafy plants. Woody plants have an advantage over perennial ones in that they generally have extensive root systems that reach down and out for great distances, often far beyond the circumference of the plant's branches. Thus, woody plants can seek out moisture and continue to grow even as other plants suffer from lack of water. But there are limits to this ability. Most woody plants

Soil Profile

The soil your plants grow in serves many purposes. Be sure to analyze your soil before purchasing any plants.

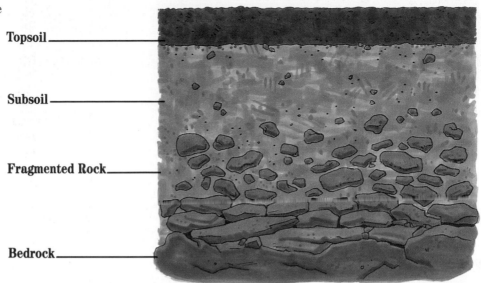

Topsoil

Subsoil

Fragmented Rock

Bedrock

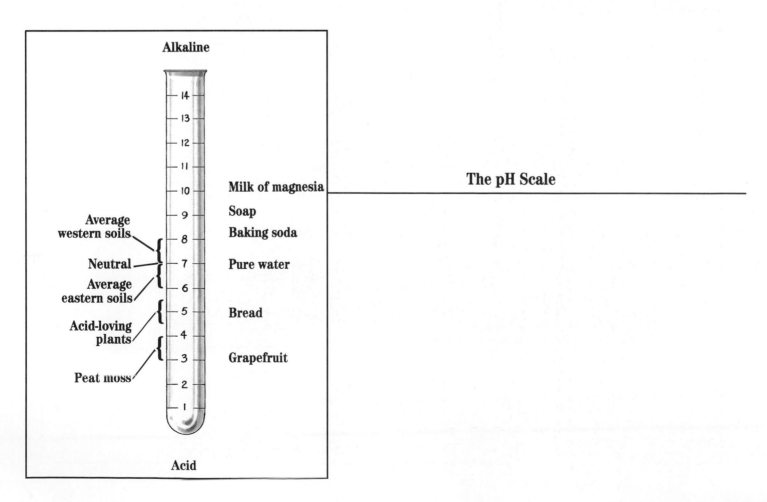

Alkaline

14
13
12
11
10 Milk of magnesia
9   Soap
8   Baking soda
7   Pure water
6
5   Bread
4
3   Grapefruit
2
1

Average western soils

Neutral

Average eastern soils

Acid-loving plants

Peat moss

Acid

The pH Scale

prefer soils that are evenly moist, meaning soils that may dry out on the surface but remain slightly moist underground.

If your area is subject to regular or prolonged droughts, you should consider planting trees, shrubs, and vines that are naturally drought-tolerant. But even drought-tolerant plants don't appreciate extreme drought. You might want to consider installing an irrigation system to facilitate watering. Newly planted trees and shrubs will need extra care in watering since their root systems are quite limited, especially during the first year.

Some soils suffer from chronically poor drainage. They are spongy and moist at all times and may even be inundated for days on end. Since few woody plants will tolerate such conditions, it will be necessary to improve the drainage of your yard before you begin to plant.

There are several reasons why soils drain poorly. Often, their clay content is too high, a condition best improved by adding abundant organic matter and sand. Sometimes the soil is located in a depression or at the bottom of a slope. Other times the soil is simply too shallow. Shallow soils do not allow roots to grow downward and properly anchor the plant, and they may prevent excess water from draining away. If your garden is underlaid with hardpan, a nearly impervious layer of clay about a foot beneath the soil's surface (a common problem in dry climates), you can solve the problem by breaking through the hardpan in several places and filling the resulting holes with porous soil. In many cases, however, the best solution for poorly drained soils is to install drainage tiles. You can also consider planting woody plants in raised beds or mounds to give them a few extra feet of soil in which to grow. This will provide enough well-draining soil for good air circulation, and the moister soil beneath will ensure that roots never lack water.

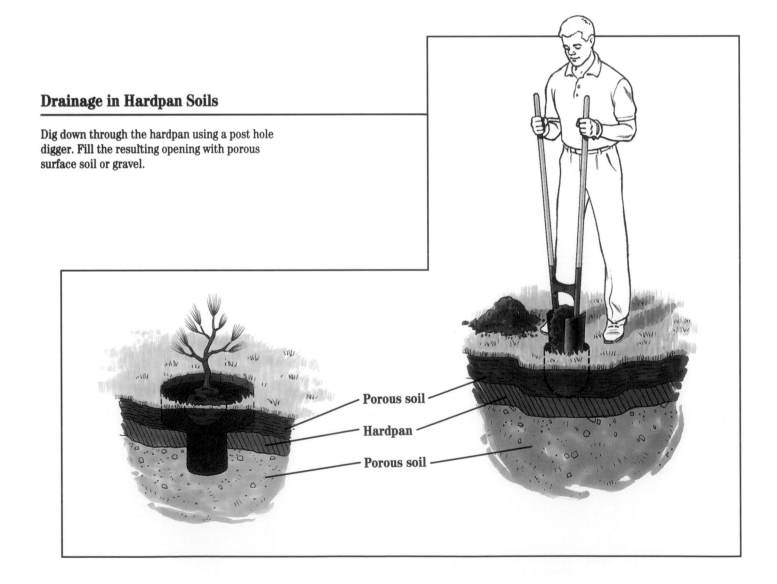

Drainage in Hardpan Soils

Dig down through the hardpan using a post hole digger. Fill the resulting opening with porous surface soil or gravel.

Porous soil

Hardpan

Porous soil

Drainage in Shallow Soils

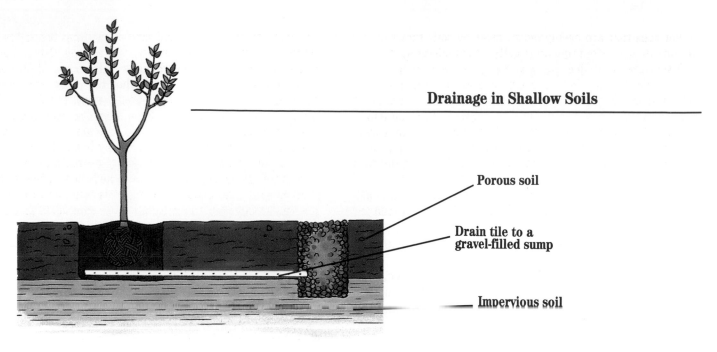

Porous soil

Drain tile to a
gravel-filled sump

Impervious soil

Raised Beds

Raised beds allow good drainage even in moist
soils.

Mounding

Mounding soil into berms can be a solution for
moist soils.

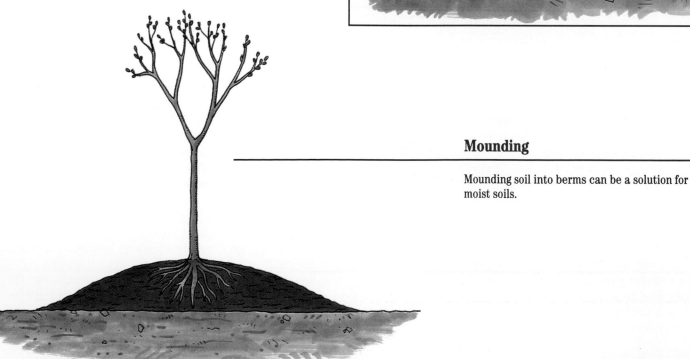

Sun, Shade, & Wind

These ponderosa pines are well-adapted to their environment.

Each plant in the wild fits perfectly into its own niche. Some trees rise high into the air, basking in the sun while being pummeled by harsh, drying winds, and they thrive under such conditions. At the feet of these tall trees, small trees and shrubs live in a different environment: no harsh wind and no brilliant sun. These plants trade abundant solar energy for protection from the elements.

The same pattern is repeated in your yard. Some parts are shady much of the day, others are sunny. Some parts are exposed to dominant winds, others are protected. These elements are in constant flux. As trees and shrubs grow, they modify the environment around them, creating more shade and a greater barrier against the wind.

Plants gather energy from sunlight. It would seem reasonable that most plants should grow faster and denser with full sun. But with nearby walls, fences, and trees, full sun is rare in the average backyard. Most "full sun" plants actually grow well enough with fewer than 12 hours of intense sunlight per day.

Most woody plants grow almost equally well in full sun or partial shade. Full sun tends to stimulate increased flowering and helps bring out more brilliant fall colors. Some protection from hot afternoon sun is good for even "full sun" plants.

In general, deciduous flowering shrubs and trees need the most light, broad-leaf evergreens the least. Silver- or gray-leaved plants are also avid sun lovers. Variegated plants generally prefer bright shade (ample light with little direct sun); they can burn in full sun. Most conifers grow best in partial shade to full sun, although a few, such as yews, do well in shady conditions as well. Most shade plants require some sunlight.

The best shade for most plants is dappled shade, which is sunlight piercing through the leaves of tall trees. Such shade provides good light all day while keeping out the burning effects of full sun. The least hospitable shade is that found to the north (to the south in the Southern Hemisphere) of walls and other structures with much dense vegetation nearby. In such places, sunlight can be cut out entirely, allowing only reflected light to reach the plants. Even so, there are trees, shrubs, and vines that will grow there.

Of all the exposures, an eastern one provides the most sun with the least burning rays. It offers bright morning sun for several hours per day, but it never becomes too hot. Western exposures offer a similar number of hours of sun, but the site will be much hotter. Southern exposures offer full sun for six hours or more a day, but the intense heat can be harmful to many plants. Northern exposures are the coolest of all, which is a major plus on hot summer days, but receive little direct sun. They are best reserved for foliage plants.

Mature conifers and broad-leaf evergreens create the deepest shade. They cut off sunlight for the entire year.

The form trees and shrubs take on will vary according to the light they receive. Full sun creates dense growth, with branches well-cloaked in foliage. Deepening shade will cause the plants to develop a lankier look, as if stretching for the light. Extra light can be brought into a shady spot by thinning out overhanging branches.

Strong winds can do severe damage to plants, especially during the winter months. As the wind blows through the leaves and buds, it dries the air, causing leaves to burn on the edges and flower buds to abort. The windier it is, the more damage cold temperatures will do: This is the "windchill factor" so well known to those who live in cold climates. Plants that are borderline hardy in a given zone should always be planted where they won't be affected by strong winds.

The best protection from strong winds is offered by other plants. They buffer the wind rather than cut it off entirely.

Conifers and wind-resistant broad-leaf evergreens are the best choices for softening wind year-round, although even the leafless branches of deciduous trees are surprisingly efficient at buffering strong winds. Fencing can also help buffer winds.

Protection from Wind

In sites with severe wind, an actual windbreak (a row of wind-resistant trees or shrubs) may be necessary for plants to thrive.

These azaleas, blooming beneath a canopy of trees, offer bright color amidst the peaceful shade. With proper care, all your woody plants can be just as attractive.

CHAPTER 4

CARING FOR YOUR WOODY PLANTS

L earning about woody plants and their needs and taking into account the conditions in your yard are just the first steps in growing trees, shrubs, and vines. You also need to know how to plant them and how to care for them once they are in the ground.

Planting a tree, shrub, or vine properly is the most important step in growing it. How well a woody plant does in its first few years depends directly on the way it was handled when it was placed in the ground. If the plant gets off to a poor start, it may never recover enough to become a useful element of your landscape. Put extra effort into those first few hours of care, and your plant will have a long, healthy existence.

Once planted, woody plants need little care: much less than most other plants. However, if you want your plants to give their best performance, you do have to meet their needs. Careful mulching, feeding, and pruning as necessary will ensure that your trees, shrubs, and vines always look their best.

Planting & Transplanting

Even if you're experienced at planting woody plants, it is worth reviewing planting techniques. Studies have shown that some former methods were not helpful, notably planting depth and soil improvement.

The new rule in planting trees and shrubs is to dig a hole three times as wide as the root ball but no deeper. This is a major change compared with previous recommendations, which promoted deep digging before planting. The theory behind the new method is that roots should be resting on solid ground so they can support the plant's weight. Loose soil beneath the root ball causes it to sink too deeply into the ground, burying the crown of the plant. Don't improve the soil by adding amendments unless you are doing the same for the rest of the sector. Loosen the earth on the side of the hole as well. The goal is to produce a wide but shallow space with loose soil into which the roots can grow for many years to come.

Set the plant in the hole so that the soil line (a distinct mark at the base of the stem showing the point where the plant was originally covered in soil) is slightly above its previous level. In sandy soils, the plant can be placed level with its original mark. Do not plant too deeply.

Nurseries offer trees, shrubs, and vines in three basic forms: bare-root, balled-and-burlapped, and container. Each has its own requirements at planting time. Balled-and-burlapped and bare-root plants should be planted as soon as possible after purchase.

Contrary to popular belief, it is not necessary to thin one-third of the branches of trees after planting. It is certainly not recommended to cut back the main leader. If there are competing leaders, however, prune to remove all but one. Damaged branches or ones that grow at awkward angles can also be removed.

Shrubs and young trees can easily be transplanted from one part of the garden to another as long as care is taken to remove as large a root ball as possible. The general rule is to dig up one foot diameter of root mass for every inch of trunk, with trunk measurement starting six inches above the soil level. Transplanting is best done in early spring or in fall, when the plants are dormant. If you cannot transplant immediately (within the next few hours), make sure the root ball is covered with an old blanket or similar cover and watered thoroughly. The roots must never be allowed to burn in the sun.

During their first year of growth, newly planted trees, shrubs, and vines need to be watered more regularly than established plants. Water thoroughly, soaking the ground entirely, then let the soil nearly dry before watering again.

A well-conceived plan can bring intriguing results when planting or transplanting woody plants.

Bare-root Planting

This should only be carried out when the plant is dormant, usually in early spring.
1. Trim off any broken or twisted roots.
2. Spread roots evenly, setting the plant so the soil line is at the correct level.
3. Work the soil in and around roots, firming carefully.
4. Water slowly but thoroughly to settle the soil.

1.

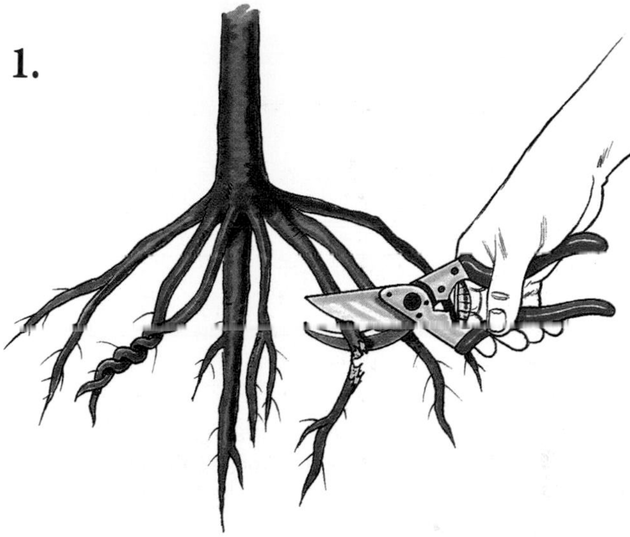

2.

3.

4.

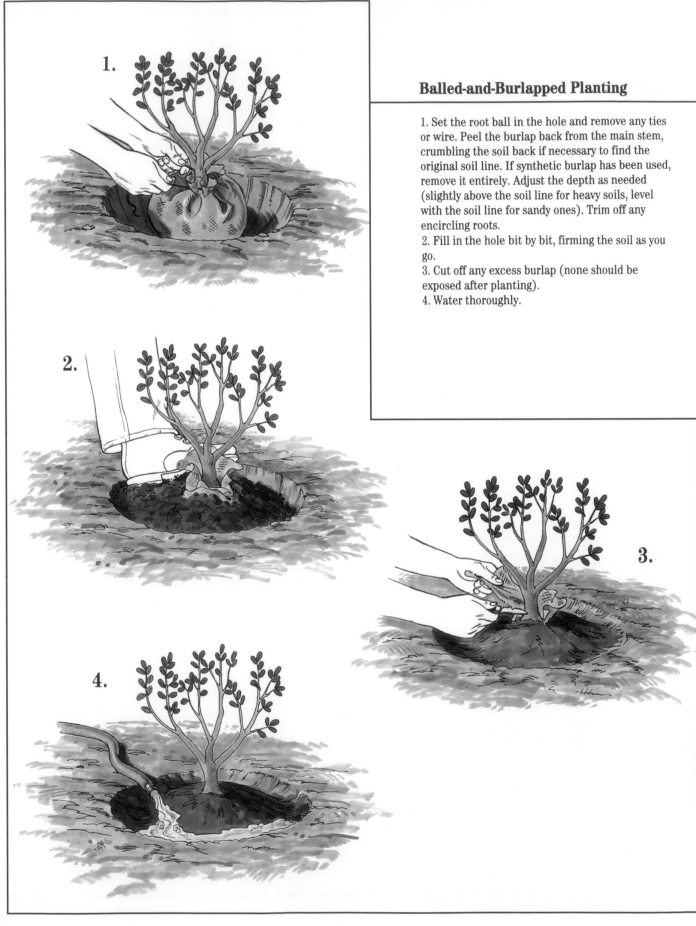

Balled-and-Burlapped Planting

1. Set the root ball in the hole and remove any ties or wire. Peel the burlap back from the main stem, crumbling the soil back if necessary to find the original soil line. If synthetic burlap has been used, remove it entirely. Adjust the depth as needed (slightly above the soil line for heavy soils, level with the soil line for sandy ones). Trim off any encircling roots.
2. Fill in the hole bit by bit, firming the soil as you go.
3. Cut off any excess burlap (none should be exposed after planting).
4. Water thoroughly.

Container planting

1. Carefully remove the plant from its container,
even if the pot is biodegradable.
2. Loosen the roots, especially those that encircle
the root ball, pruning them back if necessary.
3. Add soil gradually, firming it as you go.
4. Water thoroughly.

1.

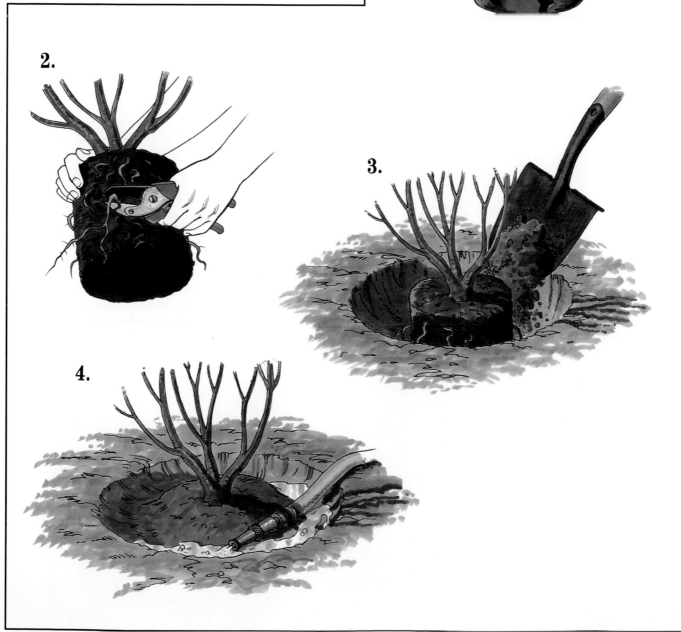

2.

3.

4.

Building an Irrigation Basin

To ensure the quick establishment of a newly planted tree, shrub, or vine, make sure it is well-watered. To do so, build a catch basin of soil around the root ball. This will help direct rainfall or irrigation to the plant's roots rather than allowing it run off.

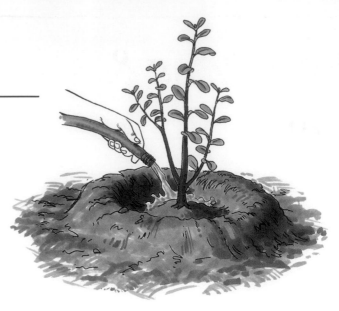

Staking

After the plant is in the ground, stake carefully if it seems unstable. In most cases, two or three stakes set into the ground just outside the root ball will suffice. Taller stakes may be necessary to support trees with thin trunks, especially bare-root plantings. Staking is not recommended unless the tree is unstable or in a high-wide zone. Use ties made of an elastic material, such as old nylon hose or wide flat straps, that will not dig into the trunk. Do not pull the ties too tightly. The stem should be able to move somewhat in the wind. These stakes should be removed as soon as the plant is solidly anchored, usually within a year.

Pruning

Shrubs can be pruned back after planting, but trees need no major pruning until they are established.

Fertilizing & Mulching

Mulching is a key element to protecting woody plants from severe weather.

Like all living organisms, woody plants need various nutrients and minerals, but unlike animals they do not need to be "fed" on a regular basis. They draw what they need from the sun's rays, the air that surrounds them, and the soil in which they grow. In most cases, a single annual fertilization is sufficient, starting the year after planting. Fertilizer is best applied in spring or early summer. Avoid fertilizing woody plants in late summer or fall. They have to harden off at that time of year, and a late application of fertilizer may stimulate rapid, weak growth that will not overwinter well.

Nurseries offer a wide variety of fertilizers, including some specifically designed for woody plants. Choose a slow-release fertilizer, which will ensure that your plant's needs are met over a long period of time rather than all at once. Most organic fertilizers naturally liberate minerals slowly, making them excellent choices.

Fertilizer should be applied evenly throughout the area covered by the plant's root system. The root system often stretches beyond the spread of the plant's branches, especially on established plants. As a rule of thumb, calculate that the roots reach at least a foot beyond the plant's branches.

Granular fertilizers are easy to apply either by hand or by spreader. Carefully follow the directions on the package; you can apply less fertilizer than recommended, but never more. Water thoroughly after application to carry the fertilizer to root level. In the case of large trees, especially those that have to compete with grass for minerals, professional arborists often drill into the ground beneath and around the tree's canopy and fill the holes with fertilizer. This ensures that the fertilizer reaches the tree's roots rather than being used by the grass above. Specially conceived fertilizer stakes do much the same and can be applied by punching them into the soil with a hammer.

In the wild, most woody plants grow with a deep layer of fallen leaves covering their soil and roots. This layer keeps the soil from overheating in summer or freezing too hard in winter. It also keeps the soil from drying out too much and reduces or prevents the growth of weeds. The leaves also keep grasses in check, so woody plants in natural settings almost never have to compete with grasses. For these reasons, it is well worth your time to cover the soil at the base of woody plants with an organic mulch.

Many materials can be used as a mulch: chopped autumn leaves, buckwheat hulls, wood chips, bark nuggets, garden com-
post, conifer needles, and the like. Any fresh materials, such as sawdust, manure, or grass clippings, should be allowed to compost for several weeks before use. In dry climates, spray dry mulches frequently with water to prevent them from becoming a fire hazard.

Applying Fertilizer

Fertilizer should be applied from near the base of the plant to a foot or so beyond the spread of the outer branches.

Applying Mulch

Apply mulch over the entire root area of the plant, if possible. The larger the area covered with mulch, the healthier the plant likely will be. A few inches of mulch is sufficient. Mulch is biodegradable: As it breaks down while feeding the plant, you will have to add more mulch on a regular basis.

Maintaining Your Trees, Shrubs, & Vines

This garden is a charm for the eye; woody plants don't require much labor to maintain.

W oody plants are considerably easier to maintain than most landscape plants (such as annuals and perennials). In fact, once established, most need little care at all, especially if they are planted in fertile soil and their root zone is protected by mulch. Beyond an occasional pruning and fertilization, watering as needed, and replacing the mulch at their base, woody plants should thrive with little care on your part. But there are a few special pointers for specific cases that you may apply for even better performance.

Woody plants need water less frequently than other ornamental plants because of their deep roots. When woody plants do need water, however, they require greater quantities of it at once. To water them efficiently, set the sprinkler or irrigation system at a relatively low pressure but leave it on for a longer period of time. As a result, the tree or shrub receives roughly the same amount of water as other plants, but slowly, soaking the root zone to a greater depth. Superficial waterings, such as those for lawns, do more harm than good to woody plants.

Exposure of woody plants to cold winter winds can cause problems due to desiccation, even among plants that are fully hardy. The damage is most evident in conifers and broad-leaf evergreens, which can turn brown by spring, especially on the side most exposed to winter winds. Damage to deciduous plants may be obvious only when they green up in spring. Leaf or flower bud damage can be seen by the dieback in different areas.

This damage is most easily prevented by making sure the plant does not lack water. If rain is lacking, keep watering throughout the autumn even though the plants appear dormant. If there is a mid-winter thaw, make sure the plant is well watered. This will help keep the flower and leaf buds supplied with moisture.

Woody plants of marginal hardiness or those grown beyond their normal hardiness zone will require special winter protection. Surround them with burlap or snow fencing (or a combination of both) to filter winds and help collect snow. Fill enclosures with straw or oak leaves packed around the stems. You can also use the branches of conifers to cover them, especially on sides exposed to dominant winds. Vines can be taken down from their trellis, tied together, laid on the ground, and covered with a thick mulch of leaves.

Trees and shrubs that bloom in spring are highly appreciated because they bring color to the garden so early in the season. However, this also leaves their buds particularly susceptible to damage from late frosts. As long as the flower buds are dormant, little danger of damage exists. If frost threatens when the buds have begun to swell or open, turn on the sprinkler and set it so the plant is soaked from top to bottom overnight. This method works because moving water rarely freezes and, when it does, it actually gives off heat. Often, flowers entirely cloaked in ice will suffer little or no damage, while those subject to the same degree of frost alone will die.

Any tree extending much beyond the height of surrounding trees will be subject to lightning damage, especially if it is the only tall object in the vicinity. Damage can range from scarcely noticeable to severe, killing the tree outright. Since a large tree not only has considerable value but is also impossible to replace, you may want to consider protecting it with a lightning rod. Consult an arborist for recommendations and installation.

Watering

Woody plants need approximately one inch of water a week, less if their roots are covered in mulch or the soil is very heavy.

Winter Protection

Marginally hardy plants should be protected from drying winter winds.

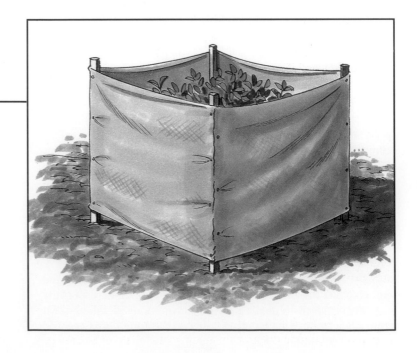

Pruning

Perhaps no other aspect concerning trees, shrubs, and vines confuses amateur gardeners as much as pruning. When to prune? What to prune? How to do it? These are just a few of the questions asked.

When To Prune—When to prune depends on several factors, notably the species being grown and the reason you are pruning. Pruning can actually stimulate growth. Pruning back a weak branch in late winter or early spring will often cause the new growth that replaces it to grow much faster. To slow growth down, prune in early summer. These are the two basic principles of pruning, but there are numerous exceptions.

Trees and shrubs that bloom in spring (blooming on branches formed the previous year) are usually pruned immediately after they finish blooming. This stimulates greater flowering the next year. Those that bloom on new wood (usually summer-bloomers) can be left until the following spring. Most formal hedges can be pruned at any season, as needed. It is preferable not to prune at the very end of summer since this can produce new growth that will be susceptible to winter damage. Informal hedges are pruned after blooming.

There are two kinds of coniferous plants that require different types of pruning. The first are those that put out their entire year's new growth all at once, in late spring. This group includes pines, spruces, and firs. They can be pruned by removing up to two-thirds of the new growth while it is still fresh and pale green. Do not prune them back to old wood because they will not produce new shoots from those sections. Conifers that grow throughout the summer, such as yews, arborvitae, and junipers, are pruned once in early summer and again, if necessary, later in the season. They can also be pruned more heavily, down to old wood if necessary.

What To Prune—What to prune depends a great deal on the effect you want to create. There are major differences between the way to prune shrubs and the way to prune trees.

Except under rare circumstances, ornamental trees should be left to take their natural shape and appearance, resulting in little need for pruning. They are usually pruned only to remove damaged or diseased branches or ones that cross, rub together, or form an overly acute angle with the trunk. Sometimes the upper limbs of overly dense shade trees can also be thinned to open them up, allowing more light to reach the garden below. Two other circumstances requiring pruning are when two leaders form (remove one) and when suckers (also called water sprouts) appear. Suckers are upright, unbranched sprouts that appear at the base of the tree or on the lower trunk.

Young trees should be pruned as little as possible at planting time because hormones released by leaf buds and newly emerging shoots stimulate the growth of new roots. Weak and damaged

This blooming pear tree is a good example of espalier.

branches, however, can be removed. Once young trees are established, they can be pruned to remove weak growth and give them a better form. When the tree has attained a fair height, any lower branches that interfere with human movement can be removed, preferably over a two- to three-year period.

One common pruning technique in tree pruning is topping, or heading. This is not recommended. Topping involves pruning back the large branches of deciduous trees in an indiscriminate fashion to change the tree's natural shape into that of a round ball. This causes all sorts of problems, including wounds that heal poorly, severe dieback, and increased danger of wind damage. It also destroys the tree's natural symmetry. The process must be repeated, since topped trees will grow back even more vigorously.

Different pruning techniques are used on shrubs, depending on the desired effect. Formal hedges, topiaries, and other closely clipped forms are sheared, which means all branches are clipped to the same length. Some shrubs that bloom on new wood are also sheared back annually to the base to encourage a maximum number of branches and thus more flowers. Subshrubs, which die back nearly to the ground anyway, should also be sheared back annually.

When a more natural shape is desired, shrubs are generally thinned. Older or excessively long branches and weaker secondary branches are removed down to a main branch or to the base of the plant. This allows room for younger branches to grow to their best advantage. Thinning is usually the preferred method for spring-flowering shrubs (those that bloom on old wood) and is done after the year's flowers have faded.

Even nicely formed shrubs may need pruning. If left on their own, some flowering shrubs will bloom heavily only one year out of every two because much of their energy will go into seed production. Unless the plant is also grown for either the edible or decorative nature of its fruit, it should also be deadheaded (pruning flower stalks off at their base). This will prevent seed formation and ensure better bloom.

There is no ideal solution to pruning fruit-producing shrubs. If you trim before they bloom, you'll reduce their display of flowers. If you prune after blooming, they'll produce less fruit. One partial solution is to thin after blooming. This removes enough branches to encourage future development without entirely sacrificing the show of fruits for the year.

Vines should be treated like shrubs. Those blooming on old wood (spring bloomers) should be pruned back after blooming, and those blooming on new wood (summer or fall bloomers) should be pruned back in late winter or early spring. Vines grown for their foliage often produce overly exuberant growth and need to be pruned regularly. They can be pruned back any time except late summer or early fall; pruning at that time of year can result in new growth that doesn't harden properly.

Large branches require a pruning saw and should be removed back to the trunk or a main branch. Cut neatly down to the collar (the ring of growth where one branch joins the trunk or another branch) without wounding it. Do not leave a stub, or the healing process will be long. For major branches, use the 3-cut method. Do not apply tree paint to wounds. Always sterilize pruning tools by dipping them in rubbing alcohol or other disinfectant between cuts. In most cases, major pruning on a large tree should be left to a professional arborist.

Special Effects—Most pruning and training is done strictly on a utilitarian basis: just enough to produce a healthy, attractive tree, shrub, or vine. But pruning can also be artistic, actually changing the shape of the plant according to human whim. Which type of pruning you prefer depends on your tastes. If you enjoy experimenting, you might want to try some ornamental pruning techniques.

Hedging is the most common form of ornamental pruning. Shrubs or small trees, often evergreens, are planted closely together—only one to two feet apart—forming a wall or screen.

Informal hedges, usually planted with flowering shrubs, are the easiest to maintain; thin occasionally so new, healthy growth is produced. Formal hedges are trimmed into geometric shapes and require frequent shearing, often up to four times a year (less for conifers). The base of the hedge should be wider than the top, or the lower branches will be shaded out and die.

Topiaries take pruning one step further, turning shrubs into living sculptures. The plants can be pruned into animal shapes, geometric forms, or anything you want. Slow-growing but dense evergreen shrubs are the best choices for topiary.

Pleaching is accomplished by weaving and pruning trees and shrubs to form an arched tunnel. Two rows are planted with a wide path between them. When the plants reach the desired height, the tops are bent and woven together. This technique is usually applied on large estates.

Pollarding involves severely cutting branches back to the same point each year, usually on a large tree, forming pom-pom growths on the ends of thick branches. This technique has never been popular in North America, although it is widespread in continental Europe. Trees to be used for pollarding should be chosen with care since few species can survive such harsh pruning for long periods.

Espalier involves pruning small trees and shrubs into a two-dimensional form, usually against a wall or trellis. It can be geometric or free-form. Espalier can be used to give a formal look to your garden or, by training trees and shrubs up a south wall, to allow tender plants to grow in a hostile climate. Firethorn and fruit trees are frequent subjects for espalier.

Trees

Trees usually only need pruning to eliminate damaged or diseased branches or branches that cross, rub together, or form an overly acute angle with the trunk.

Topping

Topping is not a recommended pruning technique.

Shearing

Shrubs that bloom on new wood can be sheared.

Thinning

Spring-flowering shrubs should be thinned

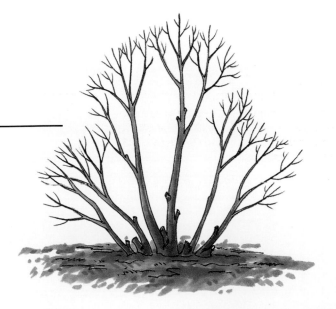

339

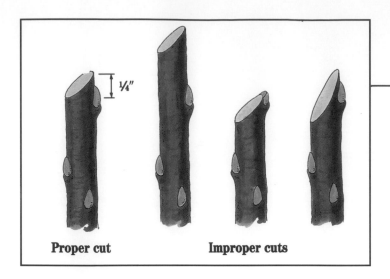

Proper cut   **Improper cuts**

How To Prune

Small branches can be pruned with pruning shears. Cut back to just ¼ inch above a healthy side bud, at a 45° angle.

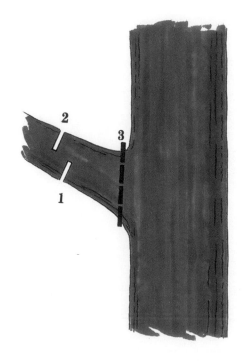

Three-Cut Method

1. Undercut the branch halfway through to prevent tearing.
2. Cut from above, slightly beyond the first cut.
3. Cut from above, parallel to the collar, to remove the stub.

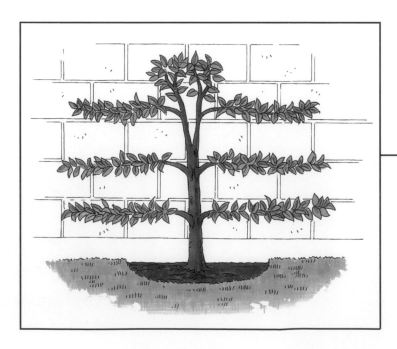

Espalier

Use the espalier technique to give a more formal look to a garden.

Hedges

Always prune formal hedges so the base is wider than the top.

Pollarding

Trees used for pollarding must be able to survive harsh pruning.

The blooms of this Japanese flowering cherry may make this tree look delicate, but in general woody plants are tough plants that usually don't require much care.

KEEPING AHEAD OF THE CHALLENGES

Trees, shrubs, and vines are generally easy to grow and maintenance free. In the best of all possible worlds, it would be nice to say, "Just plant them and let them grow!" Unfortunately, that isn't always possible. Occasionally things go wrong. They may be the result of mistakes you yourself have made, but more often they result from accidents or natural phenomena beyond your control. A lawn mower damages a trunk, a hungry insect moves in, or you wake up one morning to find your favorite shrub is white with mildew. These are all things that can occur, and you should be prepared for them.

Some damage to trees, shrubs, and vines can be prevented as long as you are aware of the problem. Other damage may occur despite your best efforts, but the harm can be reduced by preparing ahead of time. Of course, some damage—usually the worst and most disfiguring—often seems to appear almost overnight. It really can't be prevented, but it can sometimes be predicted. Get to know your plants, inspect them regularly, and treat problems as soon as you notice them. This will keep damage to a minimum.

Fortunately, woody plants by their nature are fighters. They will tenaciously try to struggle through even the worst injuries or infestations. With you alongside, doing what you can, woody plants can live through some of the worst of gardening calamities and thrive again.

Environmental Hazards

These conifers are suffering from drought damage.

Something is obviously wrong with your plant. Your natural reaction is to reach for the nearest can of insecticide. Don't do it. It is important to analyze the situation first to determine what is causing the problem. Only afterward should you search for a solution. Most problems with trees, shrubs, and vines are not caused by insects or disease, but rather by an inappropriate environment. Spraying a chemical pesticide on a plant already suffering from one problem is more likely to finish it off than to cure it.

Salt Toxicity—Spring is supposed to bring fresh new leaves and bright flowers, yet the opposite sometimes happens. Evergreens may show browning leaves or needles. On deciduous plants, new leaves may be yellowish, branches and twigs may die back, and growth is weak. Damage tends to be on one side of the plant rather than equally around the entire plant. In late summer, deciduous plants go into a dazzling display of color; except this occurs about a month too early. The problem is not a pest or disease, but salt damage from de-icing salts.

Salt toxicity is common in areas where de-icing salts are used in the winter. The worst damage occurs right where the salt is applied, such as on sidewalks or roads. However, salt spray—stirred up from fast-moving vehicles—can drift well away from the road and into your front yard.

The first step in controlling the problem is to stop using de-icing salts yourself. Environmentally safe compounds are now available that, although more expensive than rock salt, are not harmful to plants. You can also use lawn fertilizer to melt accumulated ice. Since you cannot control what your city or town applies on nearby roads, hose down shrubs and trees near the road first thing in the spring. Also thoroughly water the ground at their feet so any salts will dissolve and be carried safely beyond the range of their roots. In areas where the problem is severe, consider planting a buffer zone of salt-resistant plants nearest the road. These plants will absorb the salt spray with little impact, protecting the plants inside your yard. Salt-tolerant plants need to be washed in the spring, as would other plants.

Runoff—Some areas seem chronically dry. Even when rainfall has been abundant, plants suffer from scorched and brown leaf margins, wilt frequently, and branches and twigs die back. This problem is frequent with newly planted trees and shrubs as well as on slopes and in clay soils. It is caused by not enough water reaching the roots.

New transplants dry out more quickly and need more water than established plants. When planting, leave a basin (a ring of raised soil) around the root ball for the first year or so. This will help hold the water in place so it can soak in.

Clay soils hold water readily when damp but are hard to remoisten once they dry. Try watering slowly—you don't want the water to simply run off into another section of the garden—over a long period of time (up to 24 hours) to make sure the root ball is thoroughly moistened.

Slopes often suffer from chronic drought problems. Trees and shrubs planted there can have a permanent ring of soil built around them to trap run-off, or the slope can be broken up with retaining walls. If the slope must be maintained as is, consider installing a separately controlled irrigation system for the affected sector.

Girdling—When established trees and shrubs stop growing after having done well for a long time, especially if the top branches die back and the leaves yellow and decrease in size, girdling is a possible cause. The roots of the plant wrap completely around the base, in effect, choking itself to death. Usually, the root is hidden from sight, and the cause of the problem is discovered only when the plant dies and is removed. Sometimes you can see the girdling root at the surface.

This problem can be prevented at planting time by removing or straightening any encircling roots. These types of roots are especially prevalent with container-grown plants. They should always be carefully inspected at planting time. A girdling root on an established plant, especially a large tree, can be difficult to remove and requires the assistance of an experienced arborist.

344

Salt Toxicity

Salt damage to a plant often becomes apparent in spring. If not taken care of, large parts of the affected plant can be permanently disfigured. It may even die.

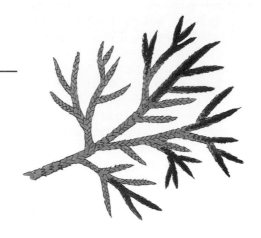

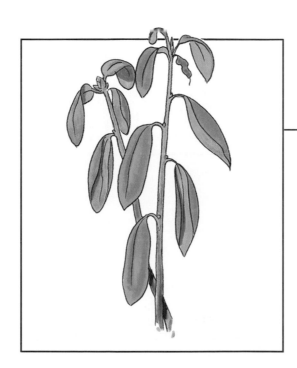

Runoff

Scorched leaves, wilting, and dieback on plants are often caused by not enough water reaching the roots.

Girdling

Girdling occurs when a plant's own roots wrap completely around its base. Sometimes the girdling root is visible at the surface of the soil, but often it is hidden from sight.

Soil Compaction—If slowly over a period of years growth is poor, leaves are yellowed, and dieback occurs, there could be many different causes. However, if various species all seem to be suffering from the same problem in the same spot, the likely problem is soil compaction. This problem is especially frequent after a new construction, such as a swimming pool or a building extension, is added to an established yard. Try pushing a bamboo stake into the ground at the spots where you suspect compaction might be occurring. If this is difficult or impossible to do, the soil is seriously compacted.

Compaction is difficult to correct around established plants, although verticutting or aerating may loosen up the soil in the surface area if that is where compaction has occurred. Machines can be rented or lawn specialists hired to do the job. Both verticutting and aerating will damage surface roots, but compaction is worse. If the plant is healthy, it will grow new roots.

It is better to prevent compaction by making sure the soil is well loosened at planting time. Thereafter, whenever heavy vehicles or machinery are used in the yard, make sure that a predetermined path is followed and that trees and shrubs requiring special protection are roped off. Do not allow constructors to pile soil or debris over the root area of plants, even for a short time. Such materials should always be carried off site.

Winter Injury—Several types of winter injury can occur. The most common is due to the drying effects of cold winds (windburn). It is especially obvious on needled and broad-leaf evergreens. Windburn is best prevented by planting susceptible plants in a protected area. Another option is to set up burlap barriers to the windward side of these plants for the winter months. The problem can become worse if the plants do not receive generous amounts of water throughout the fall and winter seasons. If windburn is a recurring problem, try planting a windbreak.

Vertical cracks may form on the south side (north side in the Southern Hemisphere) of a trunk or branch in winter, especially on trees or shrubs with thin bark. These cracks provide a path for diseases and insects. The cause is sunscald: The bark heats up on a warm winter's day and freezes rapidly at night. Sunscald can be prevented by whitewashing the bark, which was formerly a popular treatment but not particularly aesthetic. Wrapping the trunk in a protective covering for the winter is another form of protection. Special spiral tubes are sold for this purpose (they also prevent damage by rodents), but simple aluminum foil is also effective.

Winter Injury

The most common type of winter injury to plants is windburn. Leaves and needles turn reddish brown and fall off in spring or summer. In severe cases, branches die back.

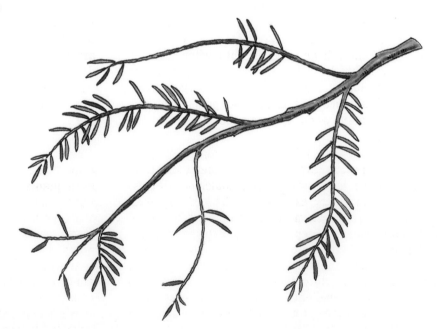

Mechanical & Other Types of Damage

One way to a protect woody plant from mechanical damage is to surround it with a circle of mulch.

Lawn mowers and weed-trimmers are among the major killers of trees and shrubs. Even a slight bump from a lawn mower that leaves barely a mark on the bark can damage a plant's ability to transfer carbohydrates to its roots. If this kind of injury is repeated entirely around the trunk, the plant's survival is threatened. Scrapes and other injuries where the bark is actually torn off are much worse. These injuries open a pathway to pests and disease. One form of protection from such damage is to surround the base of woody plants with a wide circle of mulch. With no grass or weeds to cut, you will not need to approach the trunk with a mower or trimmer. Trunks can also be surrounded with a protective barrier; commercial trunk protectors are widely available. Be sure the protector isn't so tight that it girdles the tree.

Snowblowers can also do major damage to bark and buds. The rasping action of snow and ice blowing against trunks and branches can pierce thin bark and destroy the previous season's buds. The branches of conifers—many of which don't have the ability to resprout from older wood—can die back entirely after a single winter's damage. Other trees and shrubs have dormant buds and will sprout again, but a witches'-broom pattern of short, stubby branches sprouting yearly from the same spot can develop. If snowblowers must be used, direct them away from shrubs and trees. If that's not possible, place a solid barrier, such as plywood, between the plants and the snowblower's path.

Many animals can do much harm to your plants. Rodents such as field mice and voles are especially problematic in winter. They tunnel under the snow or through mulch or tall grass and nibble on soft young bark, especially the bark of fruit trees. Wrapping the trunk in ¼-inch mesh hardware cloth or a commercial trunk protector will keep them away. Rabbits and hares nibble on tender buds in winter, causing setbacks and aesthetic damage to shrubs and young trees, but rarely permanent damage. Only during severe winters will the animals do serious injury to bark. Special repellents are available to keep these animals away. Although they prefer vegetables and other more succulent meals, woodchucks and gophers will attack young woody plants if nothing else is available. The animals can be trapped and moved elsewhere, or plants can be protected by a tube of hardware cloth.

Deer are not as easily dissuaded and cause damage year-round. They are becoming increasingly common in suburban areas and are difficult to control. There are several commercial deer repellents. Although there have been several attempts to publish lists of plants deer do not like, they are often contradictory. Check with your county Cooperative Extension office to see if they have any suggestions for your area. The only truly effective deer repellant is an eight-foot-high fence.

Herbicides are made to eliminate plants. Not only can they damage or kill plants you want to get rid of but they can also harm plants you want to keep. Herbicides are of two types: selective, such as those used on lawns to kill broad-leaf weeds, and nonselective, such as those that kill all vegetation in driveways, sidewalks, patios, and the like. Either kind can harm woody plants if absorbed by the plant.

Always be extremely careful when applying such products. Apply only as recommended on the label. Heavy applications soak into the soil and can easily enter the roots. Avoid spraying on windy days or in extreme heat; herbicides can evaporate and travel to the foliage of nearby plants. Even "weed-and-feed" formulas can create fumes that are toxic to woody plants. The best rule is to put mulch underneath trees, shrubs, and vines so you will not need to apply pesticides.

Injury from Machines

Young trees and shrubs and woody plants with thin bark are most susceptible to injury from lawn mowers and other lawn care equipment.

Injury from Animals

The damage to trees and other plants caused by rodents and deer is a major problem in many areas.

Herbicide Damage

Herbicide damage is characterized by curled, puckered, or deformed leaves and, in serious cases, by dieback of branches and twigs.

Pests & Diseases

There are a great many potential pests and diseases of trees, shrubs, and vines. Fortunately, most are relatively innocuous, causing no long-term damage and only minor aesthetic damage. This is just as well since it can be difficult to treat pests on woody plants, especially large trees, because sprays don't reach the upper branches.

The first step in treating any pest problem is prevention. Give your plants the best conditions possible and that includes planting them in places where they are likely to grow healthily. Buy varieties noted for their disease resistance, notably for plants in the rose family, which suffer from many serious diseases. When a problem does become noticeable, try to determine what is causing it. The chart below should be of some help in this regard. If you can't determine the cause of an infestation, have it identified by an expert. Applying pesticides indiscriminately can do more harm than good.

The following pests and diseases include those most commonly found on a variety of ornamental trees, shrubs, and vines in North America. There are a great many others that are specific either to certain types of plants or to certain parts of the continent. Your local garden center or county Cooperative Extension office should be able to help in identifying pests and suggesting cures.

This viburnum is suffering from insect damage.

INSECTS AND ANIMALS

SYMPTOM	CAUSE	CURE	PLANTS
Small brown spots appear on leaves, often coalescing, giving the leaf a scorched look. Leaves may drop.	*Anthracnose*	Keep trees growing healthily. Remove badly diseased foliage. Apply Bordeaux mixture when buds are first opening.	Flowering Dogwood, Sycamore, Weeping Willow, Others
Tiny pear-shaped, soft-bodied insects in green, brown, red, or black appear in clusters on stems and leaves. They often leave sticky secretions on the ground below.	*Aphids*	Spray with insecticidal soap, repeating as necessary.	Most trees, shrubs, and vines

INSECTS AND ANIMALS

SYMPTOM	CAUSE	CURE	PLANTS
Stems and shoots die back. Holes, sawdust, or droppings are visible on trunks or branches. Wormlike, legless, cream-colored larvae are found in holes.	 *Borers*	Keep plant healthy. Prune off infested branches. For insecticide treatment, check with county Cooperative Extension office to determine proper product and period.	Fruit trees, Birch, Dogwood, Lilac, Mountain Ash, Rhododendron, Others
Enlarging discolored spots on stem, becoming dry and dark or light. Black fungal spots appear in dead areas. Stems or trunk may die back.	 *Canker*	Avoid pruning during wet weather. Prune out and destroy infected stems. Sterilize pruning shears between cuts.	Apple, Ash, Beech, Honey Locust, Mountain Ash, Pear, Poplar
Leaves are partly or entirely consumed; the entire plant can be defoliated. Soft-bodied, wormlike insects, which can be smooth or hairy, are seen. Weblike tents may be visible. Adults are moths or butterflies.	 *Caterpillars*	Cut down and burn webs. Spray with *Bacillus thuringiensis.* Direct spray toward offending organisms only.	Most trees, shrubs, and vines
Blackened terminal shoots. Oozing stem cankers. Plant death.	 *Fireblight*	Avoid pruning during wet weather. Prune out and destroy infected stems. Sterilize pruning shears between cuts. Select resistant varieties. Spray with bactericide.	Plants in the rose family: Apple, Cotoneaster, Hawthorn, Mountain Ash, Pear, Others
Leaves and shoots wilt suddenly and turn brown. Plant growth is stunted.	 *Fungal Blight*	Avoid moistening foliage. Improve air circulation around plants. Prune out infested sections.	Clematis, Lilac, Others
Leaves chewed, even skeletonized. Flowers may be frayed. Hard-shelled, oval to oblong insects may be visible.	*Leaf-feeding Beetles*	Spray with insecticidal soap, repeating as necessary.	Grape, Linden, Rose, Others

INSECTS AND ANIMALS

SYMPTOM	CAUSE	CURE	PLANTS
Papery, meandering paths and blotches are found in leaves. Leaves may drop. Small, soft-bodied grubs are found within leaf. Adults are flies or beetles.	*Leaf Miners*	Damage is largely aesthetic since plants are rarely weakened, even by heavy infestations. Remove severely infested leaves. Chemical sprays are largely ineffective.	Ash, Boxwood, Holly, Lilac, Privet
Leaves and stems covered with grayish, powdery coating. Leaves may be deformed or fall off.	*Powdery Mildew*	Increase air circulation. Regularly thin infected trees and shrubs. Treat with appropriate fungicide.	Apple, Euonymus, Lilac, Rose, Others
Stems covered with small, waxy, soft- or hard-bodied "scales" (stationary insects) in shades of white, brown, black, or gray. Growth stunted. Leaves yellowed.	*Scale Insects*	Spray in spring with dormant oil spray before growth begins.	Beech, Camellia, Euonymus, Horse Chestnut, Magnolia, Others
Leaves appear pale and dry from a distance; up close they are seen to be covered with small yellow dots. Fine webs may be present. Tiny eight-legged arachnids are seen in profuse numbers on leaves and stems. Plant may be stunted.	*Spider Mites*	Spray regularly with water, attaining both sides of leaf.	Arborvitae, Peach, Others
Plant growth stunted. Leaves crinkled, mottled, or deformed.	*Viruses*	No cure. Destroy infested plants. Buy only disease-free plants.	Many trees, shrubs, and vines
Progressive wilting. Leaves turn yellow. Infected branches or even entire plant may die. Often transmitted by insects.	*Wilt (fungal or bacteria)*	If only a few branches are infected, remove them. Destroy heavily infested plants.	Maple, Smoke Tree, Sumac

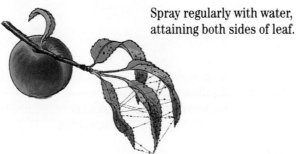

This Japanese garden contains maples, conifers, and Japanese anemones. The wooden bridge adds charm to this tranquil autumn scene. Use a variety of trees, shrubs, and vines to gain an engaging effect in your own landscape.

ENCYCLOPEDIA OF TREES, SHRUBS, & VINES

Once you have an idea of your yard's conditions, your landscaping needs, and the amount of care that will be required, the only thing left to do is actually pick out the trees, shrubs, and vines you'd like to use.

The following section provides scores of selections of trees, shrubs, and vines you might be interested in trying. The choice covers varieties suitable for all climates in North America (from tropical to near arctic, from dry to moist) as well as growing conditions of all sorts (from deep shade to full sun). Also included are the types and categories of woody plants: flowering and foliage, deciduous and evergreen, needled and broadleaf.

Carefully read the profiles, taking notes on the plants that seem best suited to your needs. Then visit a local garden center and ask plenty of questions. Most nurseries will have information and suggestions. You shouldn't have any trouble finding plants that would fit in perfectly with your property.

Common Alder

Alnus glutinosa
Zone: USDA 3 to 8

This easy-to-grow European native is not particularly striking. It is appreciated, however, for its rapid growth and ability to thrive in wet soils where few other trees will prosper.

Description: The common alder has an upright, pyramidal growth habit reaching about 50 feet in height. It has lustrous, green bark that becomes brown with age. The deciduous, dark green leaves are shiny above and dull underneath, and turn bright yellow in fall. They are oval in outline with a toothed margin. The catkins, although not particularly colorful, add some interest because of their early appearance, often while snow is on the ground. The conelike brown fruits are mostly of interest because they are present throughout the fall and winter, when most other trees are totally barren.

How to grow: The common alder prefers light shade but will tolerate full sun or moderate shade. It also tolerates wet soils but will not grow well in dry ones.

Uses: This is one of the choicest trees for wet conditions, since it is not as invasive as most other wetland species.

Related varieties: There are several varieties with ornamental leaves, including *Alnus glutinosa* 'Aurea,' with yellow-green leaves, and *A. glutinosa* 'Imperialis,' with deeply cut, almost lacy leaves.

Common Apple

Malus pumila
Zone: USDA 3b to 7a

Although apples are considered orchard trees, there is no reason they can't also be used in the landscape. They offer a pleasing form and colorful flowers, not to mention colorful and edible fruit.

Description: The apple is a small to medium (15 to 40 feet tall) round-topped tree with a short, often crooked, trunk and spreading branches. The ovate, tooth-edged, deciduous leaves are green, sometimes offering moderate fall color. Its numerous white spring flowers—often flushed with pink—are followed, in the case of the species itself, by small yellow or red fruit. Cultivated varieties, of course, include all the forms and colors of apples we know today.

How to grow: Apples need full sun to light shade to do well. They tolerate most soil conditions except extreme wetness. Prune to develop strong branches and to open the center for better light penetration. Most are strongly susceptible to various diseases and insect pests. Apples need a certain number of cool nights during the winter in order to bloom, so they perform poorly in warm climates. Many apple trees sold today are grown on dwarfing rootstocks.

Uses: Apples make attractive, ornamental flowering and fruiting trees. They are suited to medium-size yards and larger. Dwarf apples can suit smaller yards. Apples also make good choices for espalier.

Related varieties: There are literally hundreds of varieties to choose from. Check with your local Cooperative Extension office for recommendations as to disease-resistant varieties well adapted to your climate.

American Arborvitae

Thuja occidentalis
Zone: USDA 3a to 7b

Native to northeastern North America, this tree has become one of the most widely distributed of all conifers in culture and is grown in temperate climates throughout the world. It has given rise to innumerable varieties of various shades and forms.

Description: This tree shows a narrow columnar form in youth, eventually broadening to conical at maturity. It is extremely slow-growing, especially under dry conditions, although it can eventually reach 40 feet in height. The bark is attractive and reddish brown but is only noticeable on mature plants, since young ones are clothed in foliage right to their base. Its persistent leaves are scalelike, forming flattened, horizontal sprays. They are dark green in the summer in the species, turning brownish green in the winter. Most selected forms, however, retain their green coloration all winter. The small cones are of little decorative use.

How to grow: The American arborvitae is easily transplanted and grows in a wide range of soils, from moist to quite dry and acid to alkaline. It does best in full sun and should be watered regularly during periods of drought. This tree needs a humid atmosphere, so it is a poor choice for areas with dry summers.

Uses: The tree is often used as a hedge or windbreak and can be pruned as needed. It is a good accent plant and has been widely used as a foundation plant.

Related species: The oriental arborvitae (*Thuja orientalis*, actually *Platycladus orientalis*) is similar but with vertical fans of scales, not horizontal ones. It is less hardy than the American form, but a better choice for warm climates.

Related varieties: These are too numerous to mention. Some have an extremely narrow, columnar form, others can be shrubby or globular. They range in color from green to golden to variegated.

White Ash

Fraxinus americana
Zone: USDA 4a to 9a

The white ash is probably the most popular of all ashes for landscaping purposes. It is a fast-growing, low-care, multipurpose landscape tree that adapts to almost any conditions.

Description: This eastern North American native is oval in outline in its youth, becoming open and rounded at maturity. The bark is gray to brown with a distinct diamond pattern. It bears deciduous pinnate leaves, usually with 7 leaflets, that are dark green above and paler below. They take on yellow to purple shades in the fall. Female trees produce hundreds of messy seeds and should be avoided.

How to grow: White ash is easy to grow and adaptable, although it reaches its full height (well above 100 feet) only in moist, deep, well-drained soils in full sun. It dislikes dry or rocky soils. It is susceptible to many diseases when grown in poor conditions but relatively pest free when properly placed.

Uses: This is a fast-growing but long-lasting tree, best used in large spaces because of its eventual size. It makes a good shade tree and an excellent city tree.

Related species: The green ash (*Fraxinus pennsylvanica*) is another popular ash for landscaping use and is somewhat smaller than the white ash. 'Marshall's Seedless' is a good green ash.

Related varieties: There are many male selections of this tree, which do not produce seeds; these are the choicest varieties for landscaping. 'Autumn Purple,' the most popular seedless variety, produces reddish purple fall leaves and has a pyramidal habit.

American Beech

Fagus grandifolia
Zone: USDA 4a to 9a

This majestic species is one of the most remarkable trees of eastern North America, where it forms dense groves in deciduous forests.

Description: A tall, massive tree, the American beech can grow to more than 80 feet high and nearly as wide, providing dense shade. It has a beautiful ghost gray bark, the nicest coloration of all the beeches. The deciduous leaves are oval and pointed, toothed on the edges. They are dark green in summer, turning golden bronze in fall and often persist much of the winter. The edible nuts are protected by a prickly outer coating.

How to grow: The American beech does best in full sun but tolerates partial shade. It likes relatively moist, yet well-drained, soils.

Uses: The size of this tree limits its use to large gardens, where it quickly becomes the focal point. It is a dominating tree, and its dense shade and shallow roots eliminate all competition, including anything you try to plant under its boughs.

Related species: The European beech (*Fagus sylvatica*) has smaller leaves and darker gray bark and is less hardy. It is best known for its numerous varieties with variously colored and contorted leaves, often with a striking weeping habit.

Paper Birch

Betula papyrifera
Zone: USDA 2b to 5a

This popular tree is remarkable for its papery white bark. It is found in cooler locations across the continent.

Description: Generally a medium-size tree, paper birch grows to about 40 feet in height. In good conditions it can reach 75 feet or more. The bark is reddish brown on younger plants, becoming creamy white with dark horizontal lines called lenticels in the third or fourth year. The bark peels back readily, revealing a reddish orange inner bark. Its deciduous leaves are dark green and lightly toothed, becoming golden in the fall. The catkins offer little special interest.

How to grow: Paper birch grows in a wide variety of conditions, from full sun to moderate shade, and from dry soils to moist ones—although it will not tolerate waterlogging. Like most white-barked birches, it is susceptible to insects and diseases in warmer climates or prolonged drought.

Uses: A popular landscape tree, paper birch is used both as a single specimen and in clumps. Its fall color and white bark in winter make an unbeatable combination.

Related species: There are many species of white-barked birches, including the popular, but short-lived, European birch (*Betula pendula*), which offers several cutleaf, weeping, and bronze-leaf varieties. *B. jacquemontii* is a good choice for those looking for particularly white bark. *B. nigra* 'Heritage' is becoming increasingly popular as a substitute for paper birch in warmer zones. Its bark is light tan with a distinct salmon tinge.

Deodar Cedar

Cedrus deodara
Zone: USDA 7 and 8

Affectionately known as "California Christmas tree," the majestic deodar cedar has charm with its sensuous, weeping branchlets and soft, touchable foliage. Native to the Himalayas, this pine family member is just as comfortable planted in moderately mild American climates.
Description: This cedar is distinguished from other conifers by its larchlike needles, a curious arrangement of dense bunches. Its display includes fragrant wood, downy twigs, and graceful, spreading branches, which are among the most elegant of evergreens. It has longer leaves than other cedars and grows up to 70 feet in cultivation, but much more in the wild.
How to grow: The deodar cedar will thrive in average garden soil in zones 7 and 8. Avoid wind-ravaged and soggy sites. To avoid transplant shock, plant balled-and-burlapped or from a nursery container. Give this large evergreen plenty of room to grow. Pests and diseases are minimal.
Uses: Use as a specimen tree, or plant a trio of these wide-spreaders for screening.
Related varieties: Hardy varieties include 'Shalimar' and 'Kashmir.'

Sargent Cherry

Prunus sargentii
Zone: USDA 5a to 9a

The Sargent cherry is possibly the best of all the ornamental cherries, which is saying quite a lot considering their great beauty. It is also considerably hardier than most oriental cherries.
Description: The Sargent cherry, from Japan and Korea, is fairly large for a cherry tree, growing up to 50 feet high. It forms a dense upright tree with a rounded top. The bark is singularly attractive—rich, polished chestnut—and its deciduous leaves are a shiny dark green, turning a vivid red in the fall. It produces striking clusters of deep pink flowers a week or so before the double-flowering Japanese cherries. These are followed by the black fruits, which attract birds when they ripen in summer.
How to grow: This is a full-sun tree that is well adapted to varied conditions, although it prefers well-drained soil. It is easily transplanted and, in a genus where 20 years or so represents old age, remarkably long lived. Some Sargent cherries are still going strong at 50.
Uses: It makes a spectacular specimen tree, a good shade tree, and can even be used as a street tree. The only limitation is that it is a bit large for smaller terrains. The Sargent cherry is the only reliable oriental cherry for colder climates.
Related species: For slightly warmer climates, the true Japanese cherries, such as the double-flowered, deep pink *Prunus serrulata* 'Kwanzan' or the light pink, semidouble columnar cherry, *P. serrulata* 'Amanogoawa,' are good choices.
Related varieties: 'Columnaris' is a columnar form which, due to the limited horizontal space it requires, is better adapted to city conditions.

Crape Myrtle

Lagerstroemia indica
Zone: USDA 7b to 9a

This is a dazzling summer-flowering tree with showy flower panicles in electric colors that sizzle across the branches.
Description: The crape myrtle is a broad-crowned tree that is variable in size, averaging about 20 to 25 feet, but potentially taller. Often multistemmed, it has smooth, sculptured gray bark that gently exfoliates, showing multishaded underbark. Dappled shade allows for the growth of complementary ground covers beneath its leaf canopy. The petals are crinkled, like crepe paper, and vary from white to red, pink, lavender, or purple. They appear recurrently from July through September.
How to grow: Transplant container-grown or balled-and-burlapped plants into slightly acid, well-drained soil. The crape myrtle will not flower well in the shade, and it is subject to powdery mildew there. It can get tip blight if planted north of zone 7b. Encourage recurrent blooms by tip-pruning spent flowers.
Uses: Used as a tree or shrub, crape myrtle is a good choice as a specimen plant, for borders, or to plant near a corner of the house.
Related species: Recent crosses of *L. indica* with *L. Fauriei* at the U.S. National Arboretum have led to the development of about 20 cultivated varieties, most of which exhibit increased hardiness and better mildew resistance than *L. indica* without losing any charm and color. Among the new introductions are 'Choctaw' (bright pink, tree-type), 'Tonto' (medium lavender, semidwarf), and 'Sioux' (dark pink, intermediate height).

Bald Cypress

Taxodium distichum
Zone: USDA 5 to 11

The bald cypress, often overgrown with Spanish moss (*Tillandsia usneoides*), is the tree that gives the Louisiana bayous and the Florida everglades their exotic atmosphere. Despite its association with the South, the bald cypress is hardy and adaptable to many parts of the continent.

Description: The bald cypress has a pyramidal shape similar to other conifers, with a broad buttressed base. It reaches up to 100 feet in height in its native environment, but rarely more than 70 feet in culture. In wet situations it develops 'cypress knees': curious growths which rise out of the ground or water and are believed to help the tree breathe in swampy conditions. The short green needles turn brown and drop off in the fall. Its bark is fibrous and an attractive reddish brown. The small, rounded cones are of little decorative effect.

How to grow: Considering its origins in the Louisiana bayous and other warm, wet places, the bald cypress is surprisingly adaptable. It grows well in dry soils and has been grown in climates as diverse as northern Minnesota and southern Canada. It grows best in full sun on rich, sandy loams.

Uses: This stately tree makes a good specimen for parks and large lots. It is a good street tree and, of course, is particularly choice for swampy areas where few other trees will grow.

Related varieties: There are a few selections with narrow pyramidal habits or more weeping growth than the species.

Flowering Dogwood

Cornus florida
Zone: USDA 5b to 8b

This native of the eastern United States is perhaps the king of all the flowering trees. It is certainly popular wherever it can be grown and offers an attractive appearance throughout the year.

Description: The flowering dogwood is a tall deciduous shrub or a tree of medium size (20 feet high in most areas, but sometimes reaching 40 feet) with a spreading, layered growth habit. It produces large white bracts surrounding small yellow flowers. The blooms appear before the foliage, making for a spectacular display. The dark green leaves are showy all summer, but even more so when they turn bright scarlet in the fall. The red berries are attractive to birds. The tree's unique oriental silhouette makes it an attractive specimen plant even in winter.

How to grow: The flowering dogwood grows best in an acid, rich, but well-drained soil in partial shade or full sun. It will not tolerate prolonged drought.

Uses: The flowering dogwood's year-round beauty makes it a perfect accent plant. Because of its modest size, it suits the smaller lots of modern homes. Its susceptibility to dogwood anthracnose has limited its use in recent years, but plants given good care are rarely bothered by this disease. Borers may also be a problem.

Related varieties: There are many varieties of flowering dogwood, including some with light to dark pink bracts. 'Cherokee Chief' offers flowers in a deep shade of pink. 'Cloud Nine' is an especially profuse white bloomer. 'New Hampshire' is the hardiest form, often flourishing where other flowering dogwoods have failed.

Related species: The Japanese flowering dogwood (*Cornus kousa*) is similar to its American cousin but blooms about three weeks later. It is supposedly less susceptible to anthracnose.

Dove Tree

Davidia involucrata
Zone: USDA 6b to 8b

This rather slow-growing tree is somewhat of a collector's item. It is rarely available but is a choice selection for those with patience and lots of space. It can take 10 years or more before reaching flowering size and eventually attains 20 to 40 feet in height and width.

Description: A broadly pyramidal shade tree, it has large, toothed, deciduous leaves, medium green above and silvery below. It has no notable fall color. The dove tree's main attraction is its blooms, or rather the bracts that surround them. Two pure white leaves, one longer than the other, hang down gracefully around a central ball of small, yellow true flowers. The effect is quite unique, like a flock of birds in flight or a series of handkerchiefs set out to dry. It is the bracts that give the tree its common names of dove tree, ghost tree, and handkerchief tree.

How to grow: This tree does best in rich, deep loam and prefers partial shade when young, full sun at adulthood. It is often grown with a fast-growing but short-lived tree, such as a poplar, which will fill in for the slow-growing dove tree until it reaches maturity.

Uses: This is a tree of great beauty and grace, deserving a spot of special merit, and is used almost uniquely as an accent or specimen tree.

Related varieties: *Davidia involucrata vilmoriniana* is a hardier form (zone 5).

Douglas Fir

Pseudotsuga Menziesii
Zone: USDA 4b to 6a

Douglas fir is native to western North America, a cone-bearing member of the pine family, and favored as a cut Christmas tree in some areas of the country.

Description: This pyramid-shaped ornamental tree has wingy branches and a unique habit in which the upper branches are ascending while the lower branches descend. It is distinguished from other narrow-leaved evergreens by its scaly, long, pointed terminal buds and curious cones. No other cones of native conifers have persistent scales with conspicuous, protruding three-pointed, forked bracts. The Douglas fir has flat, blunt needles with two white lines on the underside of the leaf, which are variable in color.

How to grow: This tree needs humid conditions and moist, well-drained acid to neutral soil. It will not survive dry, thin, infertile soil or dry atmospheric conditions.

Uses: Douglas fir makes a fine specimen tree and can be used as a screen. It holds its short needles when used as a Christmas tree.

Related varieties: *P. Menziesii glauca* has bluish needles. It is often grown from seed, and therefore the intensity of blue is variable. There are also dwarf, weeping, and pyramidal forms of Douglas fir.

White Fir

Abies concolor
Zone: USDA 4a to 8a

A classic American beauty native to the Rocky Mountains, this stiffly pyramidal evergreen is also know as Colorado fir. A member of the pine family, white fir does well in cool, humid environments in Midwestern, East Coast, and Pacific coastal gardens.

Description: The white fir grows symmetrically up to 40 feet or more in height in cultivation and sports airy, ascending branches. The flat, 2-inch long, aromatic needles are grayish green or bluish, with two whitish or pale lines on the underside. After the needles fall, circular scars remain on the twigs. Its upright cones are purplish or yellow-green, growing mostly near the top of the tree on spreading branches.

How to grow: Provided with well-drained, acid soil, the white fir is widely adaptable in full sun or partial shade. It can take more abuse from climatic extremes and city stress than other firs. This popular concolor fir is trouble-free and low-maintenance.

Uses: Massive at maturity, the white fir is used as a specimen on large properties, or as a screen or background plant.

Related species: The Fraser fir (*A. Fraseri*) is similar to the Douglas fir, but with dark green needles. Other interesting species are the noble fir (*A. procera*) and Veitch fir (*A. Veitchii*).

Golden-chain Tree

Laburnum x *Watereri*
Zone: USDA 6a to 7b (cool sites in zone 8)

This is a stunning, small tree noted for its long, pendulous clusters of flowers. A member of the pea family, *Laburnum* x *Watereri* is a hybrid cross between the common and Scotch laburnum. Golden-chain tree is native to Europe and widely planted there. All plant parts contain cytisine, an alkaloïd that is toxic to children, adults, and livestock if eaten.

Description: This vase-shaped tree grows about 10 to 15 feet high in cultivation. Short-lived, pealike, yellow blossoms, 6 to 10 inches long, cascade from its branches. Its bright green foliage is composed of three leaflets, and the bark is pleasantly olive green.

How to grow: Plant laburnum in well-drained soil. Find a sheltered spot away from windy spots and hot, noonday sun. Its bark is prone to sunscald in winter if poorly placed, and its foliage can get burned if used in dry or windy sites.

Uses: This plant is best used as an accent plant in the shrub border. Avoid street use.

Related varieties: + *Laburnocytisus Adamii* is a true botanical curiosity. It occurred when a plant of *Cytisus purpureus* was grafted onto a stalk of *Laburnum anagyroides* and produced a single branch showing characteristics of both parents. Cuttings taken from this branch produced a small tree that moves back and forth between both parents. Its flowers can be pinkish purple, yellow, or purple and yellow; its foliage is sometimes like that of a golden-chain tree, sometimes like that of a broom (*Cytisus*), and sometimes intermediate between the two.

Golden-rain Tree

Koelreuteria paniculata
Zone: USDA 5b to 9a

This 40-foot-tall tree of Asian origin is justly popular since it is one of the few yellow-flowered trees. It is doubly interesting because it blooms in summer, when most other trees only have foliage to show.

Description: The golden-rain tree forms a regular, rounded outline on a short trunk. The deciduous leaves are bright green and bipinnately lobed, with irregular but often deeply lobed leaflets. The fall color is an attractive yellow but is not consistent in all years. Its yellow flowers are borne in tall, wide panicles at the ends of the branches in early summer. They are followed by attractive, bladderlike, yellow to brown pods.

How to grow: This tree prefers full sun and tolerates a wide range of soils, even dry ones. It is best transplanted while still young. The golden-rain tree is resistant to air pollution and does well on crowded urban boulevards.

Uses: This tree is a good choice as a specimen plant for medium-size gardens. It makes a good street or shade tree where space is limited.

Related varieties: 'Fastigiata' has a narrowly upright growth pattern.

Common Hackberry

Celtis occidentalis
Zone: USDA 3b to 8b

The common hackberry is particularly resilient, making it ideal for use in situations where other trees will not thrive. A tree of simple beauty, it is being used more and more widely as a landscape specimen.

Description: As a young tree, the hackberry is roughly pyramidal. As it matures, it takes on a vase-shaped profile, with arching branches much like the American elm. In fact, it is commonly used as a replacement for that tree where Dutch elm disease is a problem. It can reach 100 feet in height but usually does not exceed 60 feet in culture. The bark is gray-brown with characteristic corky ridges. The deciduous leaves are elmlike and bright green with toothed edges. They become yellow in the fall. The berries ripen in midfall and vary in color from red to dark purple.

How to grow: This is a good city tree, able to take hot, dry winds and drought. On the other hand, it does equally well in moist, cool situations. Grow in full sun. The tree is generally pest free, although it can be affected by witches'-broom. Infected sections can be pruned out. The leaves often bear harmless nipple galls that form green lumps.

Uses: The common hackberry makes a good street tree and is adaptable to a wide variety of landscape situations. It is also a good tree for attracting birdlife.

Related varieties: The variety 'Prairie Pride' is a good selection, offering denser growth and excellent resistance to witches'-broom.

Washington Hawthorn

Crataegus Phaenopyrum
Zone: USDA 4b to 8b

The Washington hawthorn is quite possibly the best of all the ornamental hawthorns—and that's saying a great deal, since they are a particularly showy and useful group of trees. It is especially interesting because of its resistance to fireblight, a disease that severely limits the use of many hawthorns.

Description: A tall shrub or small tree, it grows to about 25 feet. Growth is rather columnar at first, eventually becoming rounded. The clustered spring flowers are white and numerous. The Washington hawthorn forms a thorny, horizontally branched crown clothed in a dense mass of dark green, lustrous foliage. The leaves turn orange-red in the fall, then drop to reveal an abundant crop of bright red berries.

How to grow: Full sun and most soil conditions suit it well, although it does poorly in dry soils.

Uses: An excellent city tree, it is important to prune away thorny lower branches so they will be out of the way of human contact. The tree's thorny nature makes it a good hedge for security purposes. The fruits not only attract birds but are delicious to eat.

Related species: There are many other hawthorns of interest with white to pink, single or double flowers and edible, attractive fruit.

Eastern Hemlock

Tsuga canadensis
Zone: USDA 3a to 8a

The eastern hemlock is native to northeastern North America, where it starts its life as an understory tree. Eventually, it pushes its way up through the broad-leaf trees that surround it until it reaches full sun. It can reach more than 100 feet in height but is frequently kept pruned to shrub size in culture.

Description: The eastern hemlock is a gracefully pyramidal evergreen conifer with horizontal to drooping branches. The furrowed bark is brown and the needles are short and soft, not pointed like relatively similar firs and spruce. Some conifer specialists rate it as highly as the eastern white pine for landscape use.

How to grow: Hemlocks prefer rich, moist, well-drained soils somewhat on the acid side. They do poorly in dry, windswept locations. Among the few trees that will grow in full shade, they will have a nicer, denser appearance in light shade to full sun. They can be pruned to any size, from low hedges to tall screens. To maintain the tree's naturally lacy effect, do not prune by shearing, but rather by cutting back on overly long branches each year. The plant is extremely susceptible to a foliage pest that has rendered this tree useless as a landscape plant throughout much of its range.

Uses: This is truly a multipurpose tree, equally useful as a large specimen plant or a low hedge.

Related varieties: The Sargent hemlock (*Tsuga canadensis* 'Pendula') is an attractive, low-growing, weeping form.

Shagbark Hickory

Carya ovata
Zone: USDA 4b to 8b

This native of northeastern North America is a tall deciduous tree, growing to 80 feet and forming dense shade at maturity. It is not commonly known as an ornamental tree despite several interesting characteristics.

Description: The growth of the shagbark hickory is upright at first, but at maturity it forms a round-topped tree. Its most striking characteristic is its bark—gray to brown, but broken into plates that curve at the ends, giving it a 'shaggy' appearance. The leaves are pinnately compound with five leaflets and shaded a deep yellow-green. In the fall they become yellow or golden brown. The fruits are large, oblong, and contain large edible nuts.

How to grow: The shagbark hickory does best on deep, rich loams but will tolerate poorer soils. It is best grown in full sun or light shade. The tree produces a deep taproot, which makes it particularly hard to transplant. It is often most easily grown from seed sown where you want the tree to grow.

Uses: The shagbark hickory is an excellent shade tree with good fall color. Not only are its nuts edible but its wood is highly esteemed for many uses. This is the tree used in producing hickory-scented foods.

Related species: The shellbark hickory (*Carya laciniosa*) is similar but is better adapted to damp, even wet, soils.

American Holly

Ilex opaca
Zone: USDA 6a to 9a

This is the best of the native evergreen hollies. It has been widely planted both within its native East Coast range and well beyond it, where it supplies cut branches for the Christmas decoration industry.

Description: The American holly is extremely variable, both in the wild and in culture. More than 1,000 varieties have been named. It is generally a slow-growing tree, reaching up to 50 feet in height (although dwarf, shrublike clones exist). Densely pyramidal in youth, it becomes more open with age. The leaves are typical of our image of a Christmas holly—thick and dark green, with spiny edges. The berries are red and produced on female plants in the fall. They last through much of the winter, attracting birds.

How to grow: Like many evergreen hollies, this tree is particular about its needs. It prefers deep, rich, well-drained soils, preferably acid, since it becomes chlorotic (yellowed) in alkaline soils. Partial shade or full sun are fine, but drying winds should be avoided. One male should be planted for every three females so fruit will develop.

Uses: Smaller clones are often used as evergreen shrubs and patio trees; standard size selections can become outstanding landscape specimens. The American holly makes an excellent privacy screen and security fence and can easily be pruned to hedge form. It also does well in city conditions as long as it is not exposed to strong winds.

Related varieties: These are too numerous to mention. Variations include brighter, more abundant berries; yellow, orange, and red fruits; and denser growth.

Related species: There are many evergreen hollies, but few species are as adaptable as the American one. Among the hybrid types, the Meserve hollies (*Ilex* x *meserveae*) are particularly choice because of their great hardiness.

Honey Locust

Gleditsia triacanthos inermis
Zone: USDA 4b to 9a

Honey locust is a tall, pod-bearing shade tree with striking, ornamental foliage. It gets its common name from the sweet, gummy sap found in the pods.

Description: This short-trunked, leaf-losing tree bears lacy, medium- to fine-textured foliage. Its mature size is variable, growing in the 30 to 70 foot range, taller in the wild. Honey locust is a rapid-growing tree whose fall foliage is clear yellow to yellow-green. The fruit is a long, reddish brown, straplike, curved pod produced in late summer.

How to grow: Plant honey locust in full sun and limey soil. It's adaptable to a range of conditions including drought and high pH, and is tolerant to road salt spray.

Uses: To avoid thorns and litter problems, use an unarmed, podless selection as a shade tree. Webworm is this plant's worst enemy.

Related varieties: *G. triacanthos inermis* 'Shademaster,' a superior podless variety with a vaselike form, is fairly resistant to webworms. *G. triacanthos inermis* 'Skyline' is noted for its golden fall color and upright form.

European Hornbeam

Carpinus betulus
Zone: USDA 5a to 7a

An outstanding small, multipurpose landscape tree, the European hornbeam is unfortunately little planted in North America. It is attractive in all seasons, adaptable, and easy to grow.

Description: European hornbeam attains only 40 (rarely up to 60) feet in height. Allowed to grown naturally, the plant takes on a pyramidal form in youth, becoming rounded at maturity. It is, however, so often used in hedges and as a geometrically pruned topiary that just about any form is possible. The deciduous foliage is dark green and oval with toothed edges. Unlike most European imports, it has an attractive fall color—golden yellow. The bark on old specimens is a handsome gray.

How to grow: European hornbeam is quite tolerant of most soils, including moderately acid and alkaline ones, but prefers well-drained conditions. It does best in full sun to light shade.

Uses: This species makes an excellent small landscape tree and is useful for screens, hedges, and patio boxes. It can be pruned heavily if needed and, in Europe at least, is often trained into an arbor form.

Related species: The American hornbeam (*C. caroliniana*), native to eastern North America, is a choice plant for fall color—a bright yellow to orange-red. It can be difficult to transplant.

Related varieties: 'Columnaris' and 'Fastigiata' are two varieties with particularly narrow growth patterns. 'Asplenifolia' and 'Incisa' have delicately cut leaves. There are also weeping and purple-leaf forms of this tree.

Ruby Horse Chestnut

Aesculus x *carnea* 'Briotii'
Zone: USDA 5a to 9a

This is a particularly choice clone of a hybrid horse chestnut, resulting from a cross between the European horse chestnut (*Aesculus Hippocastanum*) with white flowers and an eastern North American native (the shrubby *Aesculus Pavia*) with red ones. It is a better landscape plant than either of its parents and should be planted more widely. 'Briotii' originated in 1858 from seed grown at the Trianon in France.

Description: The ruby horse chestnut is a medium to large tree, reaching from 40 to 60 feet in height at maturity. It has gray-green bark and dark, palmately compound, deciduous leaves, which are dark green above and silvery below. Its foliage turns bright yellow in fall. Upright panicles of deep rose flowers, nearly red, appear in the spring. These are followed by gray-green fruit, each bearing two large seeds.

How to grow: The ruby horse chestnut is a tough, easy-to-grow tree. It thrives in just about any soil that is not waterlogged. The plant prefers full sun but will tolerate considerable shade.

Uses: This variety is much less susceptible to disease than the more common horse chestnuts. It makes a good street tree and provides ample shade.

Related species: The European horse chestnut (*Aesculus Hippocastanum*) is the most widely planted of the horse chestnuts. Unfortunately, it is more susceptible to disease.

Related varieties: The variety *Aesculus* x *carnea* 'Plantierensis' is similar but with paler pink flowers. The plant is sterile—bearing no fruit—which makes it the preferred choice where fruit drop is undesirable.

Juneberry

Amelanchier arborea
Zone: USDA 3b to 8a

The juneberry is native to eastern North America but has abundant and similar relatives in other parts of the continent. It hosts a wide variety of common names, from juneberry to serviceberry to shadblow, to cite only a few.

Description: This small, often multistemmed, deciduous tree or tall shrub grows to 25 feet tall. It offers color in all seasons: in winter, with smooth gray bark delicately streaked with longitudinal fissures; in spring, with its numerous clusters of delicate white flowers, appearing just as the leaves start to burst out; in summer, with its red berries that gradually turn black; and finally, in fall, with its beautiful orange-red oval leaves. The berries are delicious and often used in cooking.

How to grow: Juneberry is tolerant of various soils and exposures, although it blooms most heavily in full sun.

Uses: It can be trained as a small tree or encouraged to develop multiple trunks by pruning. An increasingly popular landscape plant, it is adaptable to just about any use where its modest size is not a problem. Juneberry is often planted in naturalistic landscapes, not only for its appearance but because it attracts birds.

Related species: There are several similar *Amelanchier* species, some more shrublike than the species mentioned. They are all interesting landscape plants.

Kentucky Coffee Tree

Gymnocladus dioica
Zone: USDA 4b to 7b

Native to the central United States, Kentucky coffee tree is a member of the pea family. Its name—from the Greek, meaning "naked branches"—refers to the fact that it loses most of its leaves in the winter. It is also one of the last trees to leaf out in the spring.

Description: A tall, handsome, somewhat slow-growing tree, the Kentucky coffee tree can reach cultivated heights of 60 to 75 feet (taller in the wild). Its stout branches carry large, compound leaves with many leaflets. The bark is rough, scaly, and dark grayish brown. The reddish brown pealike pods of female trees hang on into the winter.

How to grow: Kentucky coffee tree likes full sun and moist, fertile soil. It is a tough tree that can adapt to dry soils and city stress, and insects are not usually a serious problem.

Uses: Use a male for a street tree to avoid pod litter. The Kentucky coffee tree is too big for the small landscape but is a park or large garden candidate. It has a bold winter silhouette.

Related species and varieties: There are no related species or varieties.

Lawson Cypress

Chamaecyparis lawsoniana
Zone: USDA 6b to 8a

This native northwestern United States tree is a popular landscape subject and a valuable commercial timber source.

Description: The Lawson cypress is a striking columnar evergreen that grows up to 50 feet in height. Its soft leaves range from steely blue/green to green or yellow, depending on selections. Juvenile leaves are awl-shaped, while mature, scalelike leaves, with telltale white markings on their undersides, hug the fan-shaped branchlets. The interesting bark is warmly reddish brown and tends to shred. This tree is often confused with its near-lookalike, arborvitae, but the false cypress has globular cones while arborvitae's are bell-shaped.

How to grow: The Lawson cypress is limited to cool areas with high humidity and moist, well-drained, slightly acid soil. Shield new plants from drying wind and hot afternoon sun. The tree is subject to mite infestation where summers are hot and dry. Mulch plantings with wood chips to protect shallow roots.

Uses: It is best used as a specimen tree, vertical accent, or screen.

Related species: The Hinoki cypress (*Chamaecyparis obtusa*), the Nootka cypress (*C. nootkatensis*), and the Sawara cypress (*C. pisifera*) are all widely grown and, like the Lawson cypress, offer an almost infinite variety of different forms and foliage colors.

Related varieties: There are literally hundreds of selected clones of Lawson cypress, ranging from upright pyramidal trees to dense, rounded or spreading shrubs, often with golden, silver, or bluish needles.

American Linden

Tilia americana
Zone: USDA 3a to 8a

This is the native eastern North American species of linden, also known as basswood. It is just one of many lindens used in ornamental horticulture.

Description: The American linden is a tall, stately tree, growing to more than 100 feet high. Pyramidal in youth, the tree develops a more rounded crown at maturity. It has gray to brown bark and large, toothed, heart-shaped, deciduous leaves. They are dark green above and pale beneath, turning yellow or yellow-green in the fall. The yellow flowers would not be particularly noticeable without their pervading fragrance. They are considered among the best flowers for honey. The winged fruits are of little ornamental value.

How to grow: This tree transplants readily and does best in deep, rich, moist, well-drained soils. It can also be grown on drier, heavier soils, but grows more slowly there. It does well in full sun or partial shade. Never plant the American linden over a parking lot; the sticky nectar dripping from the flowers can damage car paint.

Uses: American linden is a good choice for a specimen tree or naturalizing in large lots and parks.

Related species: A smaller-leaved linden, the European linden (*Tilia cordata*), is the most widely planted ornamental species and offers many varieties.

Related varieties: The variety 'Redmond' is a superior clone with a beautiful pyramidal form.

Maidenhair Tree

Ginkgo biloba
Zone: USDA 4b to 8b

According to fossil records, this ancient oriental, single-species genus is believed to be the oldest flowering plant in existence, although it is now apparently extinct in the wild.

Description: Variable in height from 40 to 80 feet, the ginkgo's foliage has the unusual habit of hugging spur branches instead of forming a broad crown. This results in branches that grow in every direction. An impressive specimen, its exotic, parallel-veined, green leaves are fan-shaped, but often deeply notched at the outer margin's center. They turn butter-yellow in autumn. Male and female flowers are on separate trees. Naked seeds, produced in late summer and fall, are plum-shaped with a fleshy outer coat that smells like rancid butter when decomposing. The seeds are considered gourmet fare and highly touted in the Orient.

How to grow: A survivor this tough has to tolerate differing soil pH, many soil types, moisture variations, and light exposures. The ginkgo needs little pruning and is virtually free of pests and diseases.

Uses: To avoid fetid fruit, plant only male trees as specimen or shade trees.

Related varieties: There are several selected clones of maidenhair tree, including 'Autumn Gold,' a male selection with an improved fall coloration, and 'Princeton Sentry,' also a male selection but with a narrowly upright form.

Southern Magnolia

Magnolia grandiflora
Zone: USDA 7 to 9

This is a splendid, broad-leaf evergreen tree or shrub, native to the southeastern United States. Standout qualities of the magnolia include its large, flamboyant flowers and attractive, tropical-looking leaves, adding distinction to the garden landscape.

Description: The southern magnolia is a handsome, low-branching tree, reaching heights of 60 to 80 feet. It displays wooly young buds, and 8-inch long, thick, shiny leaves. The huge, solitary blooms are white and exude a lovely fragrance. Its fruit is 3 to 4 inches long and cone-like, opening to reveal red seeds.

How to grow: Plant container-grown or balled-and-burlapped plants in spring. The soil should be fertile, deep, well-drained, and slightly acid. This tree tolerates high soil moisture, but should be protected from wind. Avoid transplanting once it is situated. It can be pruned after flowering, if needed. Pests are not a particular problem.

Uses: The southern magnolia is used in the South as a street tree, but it does have a good deal of leaf litter. It is best used as a specimen where it has ample room to develop.

Related species: The deciduous magnolias are choice trees for cooler climates; they bear large flowers in white, pink, red, purple and, most recently, yellow, usually before the leaves appear. Among the hundreds of varieties, the saucer magnolia (*M.* x *Soulangiana*), with large white or pink to purplish flowers, and the extra-hardy star magnolia (*Magnolia stellata*), with smaller but more numerous flowers, are especially popular.

Related varieties: There are several selections of southern magnolia offering larger or smaller leaves, better or repeat blooming, increased hardiness, and other options. Ask a local nursery for varieties best suited to your climate.

Amur Maple

Acer Ginnala
Zone: USDA 3a to 6b

This small deciduous tree is native to China and Japan. It does particularly well in colder climates, where many other trees fail.

Description: The amur maple makes a small tree or tall shrub, growing to 25 feet high with smooth, light-gray bark on young branches. The leaves are small for a maple, only 3 inches long, toothed, and have three main lobes. They turn scarlet red in the fall. The seeds vary in color but, in the best clones, are bright red. The plant is one of the rare maples with flowers of any interest. Yellow and fragrant, they appear in spring before the leaves.

How to grow: Plant the amur maple in just about any conditions, although it prefers good, well-drained soil and full sun or, at best, partial shade. It tolerates alkaline soils particularly well. It can be trained as a small tree through pruning or allowed to grow as a tall shrub. The tree grows relatively upright when young, but it eventually takes on a round-headed appearance.

Uses: A good tree for small lots and patio plantings, the amur maple is tolerant of city conditions and is relatively pest free. It makes an excellent screen or small specimen tree.

Related species: The tartarian maple (*Acer tataricum*) is similar and can be distinguished from the amur maple by its barely-lobed leaves. Some experts consider them two variants of the same species.

Related varieties: A number of varieties have been chosen for their brighter fall colors or red fruit. 'Flame' is a particularly choice selection with bright red fall leaves.

Sugar Maple

Acer saccharum
Zone: USDA 3b to 7b

One of America's favorite trees, the sugar maple, also called hard or rock maple, is a popular choice for its razzle-dazzle red, orange, or yellow fall color. Native to the northeastern United States, this selection is best known as the source of maple syrup.

Description: A short-trunked, large, and spreading tree, the sugar maple can reach heights of 50 to 70 feet or more, but grows somewhat slowly. The United States grand champion, in Norwich, Connecticut, is a massive 93 feet tall and has a spread of 80 feet. The pointed leaves are 4 to 6 inches across, with five lobes. Nonshowy, chartreuse flowers appear in early spring preceding the leaves. Horseshoe-shaped fruit—paired winged seeds called "samaras"—mature in fall.

How to grow: The sugar maple is soil fussy and requires a well-drained, fertile soil and plenty of room to grow. Do not plant in dry, compacted soil, too close to streets, or where road salt is used.

Uses: This plant is best used as a shade or specimen tree. It is resistant to storm damage.

Related species: Among the larger-growing maples, the Norway maple (*Acer platanoides*) is particularly popular. It offers many varieties, including some with deep purple, red, or variegated leaves all summer long. The silver maple (*A. saccharinum*) has a lighter silhouette due to its deeply cut leaves with a silver backing. Neither of these maples offers the amazing fall coloration of the sugar maple, but the red maple (*A. rubrum*) is every bit as brilliant with its almost luminous moderate red leaves in the fall.

Related varieties: There are several selected clones of sugar maple: Some offer improved fall color, others unusual forms, and still others better resistance to specific climatic conditions. Check with a local nursery for varieties recommended for your area.

Mountain Ash

Sorbus aucuparia
Zone: USDA 3b to 7b

The mountain ash is actually not an ash but a member of the rose family. *Sorbus aucuparia* is a European native and the most widely planted of a large group of similar shrubs and trees. The native mountain ashes are just as beautiful, but tend to be shrubby in nature. The European mountain ash has a more distinctly treelike form.

Description: This small to medium tree (up to 50 feet tall) has light grayish bark and an oval, open head at maturity. It produces clusters of white flowers in spring followed by bright, long-lasting, orange-red berries in fall that attract birds. The deciduous leaves are toothed and pinnately compound. They are dark, dull green in summer and yellow to reddish in fall.

How to grow: Grow in full sun in rich, well-drained, acid soils. It is short-lived under alkaline conditions. The tree transplants well. Mountain ashes are highly susceptible to borers and fireblight, among other pests. They are best grown in the northern part of their range where cool summers are not conducive to these problems.

Uses: Mountain ash is a good small tree for home landscapes and is especially appreciated for its long-lasting berries.

Related species: The white beam mountain ash (*Sorbus aria*) has the same form and berries as the more common mountain ashes, but with totally different leaves. They are not compound and the undersides are covered with attractive white felt.

Related varieties: There are many selections of this tree with variously colored berries, from red to pink to yellow, weeping or upright forms, or doubly compound leaves.

Fruitless Mulberry

Morus alba 'Striblingii'
Zone: USDA 5a to 9a

This Chinese tree was first introduced to North America as a food source for a potential silkworm industry. The industry never got off the ground, but the tree has since become widely naturalized. The original form is considered undesirable in most landscapes because of its messy fruits, which stain clothes and furniture. They are also weedy because birds love to eat them and carry the seeds far and wide, spreading the tree as they go. Fruitless clones, like 'Striblingii,' offer none of those disadvantages and are becoming popular as landscape plants.
Description: The fruitless mulberry develops an extremely dense, round-topped crown and reaches 30 to 50 feet in height. Its deciduous, toothed leaves, yellow-green to lustrous dark green, are extremely variable in form, with some being nearly heart-shaped and others deeply-lobed—often all on the same plant. Young branches have an orange tinge to them, which they lose as they age.
How to grow: The seedless mulberry is an easy tree to grow in every respect; it will even grow in nearly pure gravel. It is drought-resistant and fast-growing, preferring full sun to light shade.
Uses: This tree is ideal where fast shade is needed. Pollution resistant, it is a good choice for urban conditions and succeeds near the ocean as well.
Related varieties: There are several weeping mulberries, including 'Chapparal,' a choice small-growing, fruitless variety.

White Oak

Quercus alba
Zone: USDA 3a to 9a

This oak grows to a massive size—up to 150 feet high with an 80-foot spread—and can reach a great age: Specimens 800 years old are known. Even in culture it can reach 80 feet in height with an equal spread. It is native to eastern North America.
Description: The white oak has a pyramidal form when young, becoming broadly rounded with massive branches at maturity. The bark is gray and rough, breaking into scaly blocks. The leaves, narrow at the base, have five to nine rounded lobes. They are dark green in summer, turning red to wine before falling. They often remain on the tree much of the winter. The nuts are typical acorns: chestnut brown and ½ to ¾ inch long with a bowllike cup.
How to grow: The white oak is slow-growing and must be planted as a small tree, since its deep taproot makes transplantation difficult. It needs full sun and prefers a deep, moist, well-drained soil that is slightly acid. Its leaves tend to acidify the soil over time and, in the wild, oaks are often found in association with acid-loving plants, such as rhododendrons.
Uses: The white oak makes a splendid specimen tree for parks and large terrains.
Related species: The swamp white oak (*Quercus bicolor*) is similar but has entire leaves that are broad and undulated on the edges rather than lobed. As the common name suggests, it makes a good substitute for white oak on moist soils.

Willow Oak

Quercus phellos
Zone: USDA 6a to 9a

If it weren't for the acorns it produces, this southeastern tree would scarcely be recognizable as an oak. Its graceful, willowlike leaves are a far cry from the broad, deeply-lobed leaves usually associated with this genus.
Description: Other than having narrow, pointed, shiny leaves, this is a typical deciduous oak, with as massive a trunk and branches as any and a similar round-headed form at maturity. It reaches 60 feet in height. In the extreme southern part of its range, the leaves may be partially evergreen, but generally they turn yellow or reddish brown before dropping in fall.
How to grow: The willow oak is faster growing than many oaks and much easier to transplant, since it doesn't have as deep a taproot as most of its cousins. It takes full sun or light shade and needs a well-drained soil, preferably rich and on the acid side.
Uses: The willow oak is widely used as a street and shade tree, especially around its native habitat, and has shown itself quite pollution resistant. It makes an excellent specimen tree for a vast lawn.
Related species: The shingle oak (*Quercus imbricaria*) is similar, with slightly broader leaves, and can be considered a northern variant of the willow oak.

Sweet Orange

Citrus sinensis
Zone: USDA 9 to 11

Oranges, with a long season of bloom and colorful fruit, are hard to beat for attractive foliage year-round. Their dual use as fruit and ornamental tree is a major plus.

Description: Most sweet orange sold are grafted onto dwarfing rootstock, keeping them less than 15 feet tall at maturity. They form a rounded tree or large shrub with glossy leaves. The white flowers are highly scented and attract many pollinating insects. Fruit is present much of the year since it takes many months to mature, but only takes on its characteristic orange color when it is nearly ripe.

How to grow: Oranges are suitable for sunny spots in most soil conditions, but will not tolerate wet soils. It is important to choose a variety adapted to your local climate, since some oranges need a great deal of heat to bring their fruit to maturity while others are more adaptable. Many are also surprisingly frost tolerant, although they will not support long periods below freezing.

Uses: Oranges are usually planted where both ornamental qualities and usefulness are important. Birds are also attracted to the flowers. Oranges, especially dwarf varieties, make excellent container plants.

Related species: Other citruses (lime, lemon, grapefruit, and others) also make good landscape trees.

Related varieties: 'Valencia' is the best known juice orange and is widely grown as an ornamental tree. 'Washington,' a naval orange, is a good choice for eating fresh off the tree.

Bradford Pear

Pyrus Calleryana
Zone: USDA 5 to 9

A member of the rose family, the Bradford pear is one of the best of the smaller, spring-flowering, shade trees. Originally from China, this hardy tree has found overwhelming favor in the United States. It is grown both for its ornamental value and its tasty fruit.

Description: The Bradford pear usually grows no taller than 35 feet in cultivation. It has a pyramidal shape in youth, spreading with age. Its fall color is scarlet to purple. White clouds of flowers are followed by russet pears.

How to grow: Use container-grown or balled-and-burlapped transplants in spring before its leaves emerge. Be sure to plant in full sun. An easy-growing, adaptable tree, it can tolerate various soils, including dry ones.

Uses: The Bradford pear is appropriate as a small shade tree, a street tree, a lawn accent, or even on the patio or planted in a large tub.

Related varieties: *P. Calleryana* 'Aristocrat' has attractive, crinkly-edged leaves that turn red in fall.

Pecan

Carya illinoinensis
Zone: USDA 5b to 9a

The pecan is a tall, massive tree, ideal for large spaces. It is a dual-purpose tree, grown both as a shade tree and for its delicious nuts.

Description: This majestic tree is the largest of the hickories—growing 70 to 100 feet high—with a symmetrical, broadly oval crown. The compound deciduous leaves are dark green and bear 11 to 17 leaflets. It has good fall coloration.

How to grow: Transplant when young, since the tree has a deep taproot that is easily damaged. Plant in deep, organic, well-drained soils in full sun.

Uses: The pecan makes a good skyline tree or shade tree for large spaces. Selected varieties are prolific nut producers. Check with local growers, since each seems to be best adapted to a specific region.

Related varieties: There are many pecan clones, but most seem to be site-specific: They grow or produce poorly outside a narrow climate range. Always choose a variety from among those that have a reputation of doing well locally.

Common Persimmon

Diospyros virginiana
Zone: USDA 5b to 9a

The common persimmon is native to the eastern United States but is planted widely beyond that area as a fruit tree with landscape possibilities.

Description: The persimmon is slow-growing but eventually becomes quite large for a fruit tree—from 35 to 60 feet high. It has a rather oval form, usually symmetrical and densely cloaked in foliage. The deciduous leaves are dark green and elliptic. They turn yellow to reddish purple in fall where summers are long, but often drop while still green in colder climates. The edible fruits are up to 1½ inches in diameter and yellow to orange. They mature in the fall. The bark is one of the most striking features of this tree. It is dark gray and, on mature specimens, divided into uniform squares. The fragrant flowers are whitish but not often visible among the foliage. The craggy winter appearance of the branches is another plus.

How to grow: Plant as a young tree, since mature ones resent transplanting. It grows well on most soils, including poor, dry ones, but prefers moist, well-drained, sandy soils. Individual plants usually bear only male or female flowers; plant at least one male for every four females to ensure pollination. Where there is room for only one tree, try to locate a variety carrying both sexes.

Uses: The persimmon is a good choice for naturalizing and for home orchards. Only harvest the fruit after a hard frost; they are astringent until cold weather increases their sugar content.

Related species: The Japanese persimmon (*Diospyros Kaki*) keeps its bright orange fruits well after the leaves fall for an interesting display. Although it is of limited hardiness (zones 7 to 9), it can be grown as a container plant in cold climates and given frost protection in the winter.

Eastern White Pine

Pinus Strobus
Zone: USDA 3a to 9a

At more than 200 feet in height, this was once the tallest tree of eastern North American forests, a good 50 feet taller than its nearest competitor, the tulip tree. Unfortunately, the original giants—some known to be more than 450 years old—were wiped out in the 19th century by the search for tall, straight masts for sailing vessels. Today it is rare to see one any taller than 100 feet.

Description: Young white pines are pyramidal in shape, but lose their lower branches as they age and take on a wind-beaten look, rather like giant bonsais. The tree is attractive at both stages. The bark on younger trees is grayish green and smooth. Old specimens have grayish brown, scaly bark. Its persistent needles, soft for a pine, are grouped by fives and are bluish green in color. The cones are large and decorative.

How to grow: This pine is easily transplanted. It grows best in fertile, moist, well-drained soils and, although it prefers full sun, can tolerate some shade. It can be pruned into an attractive evergreen hedge.

Uses: The eastern white pine is an exceedingly handsome landscape tree. Some rate it the best ornamental conifer of all. Given lots of room, it makes an unforgettable impression as a landscape plant. It is not a good city tree, since it is susceptible to pollution and salt damage.

Related species: The Japanese white pine (*Pinus parviflora*) is similar but is a slow-growing, smaller pine.

Related varieties: There are many dwarf and weeping varieties of white pine, too many to list here.

Southern Yellow Pine

Pinus palustris
Zone: USDA 7b to 9a

Also known as the longleaf pine, the southern yellow pine does indeed have very long needles, three to a bundle, that are often put to good use as Christmas decorations when cut.

Description: Young trees go through a long 'grass stage' in which they remain at ground level, with no trunk, until their long taproot is fully developed. They then produce a trunk and branches and, for another few decades, have a triangular growth pattern. At maturity, they lose their lower branches and form a rounded top on a straight trunk that reaches up to 80 feet in height. The persistent needles are striking in length: up to 18 inches long, although 8 to 15 inches is the average. The cones, up to 12 inches long, may remain on the tree for 20 years.

How to grow: The southern yellow pine prefers full sun and sandy soils with good drainage. It grows poorly in heavy soils and is difficult to transplant.

Uses: This tree is interesting for backgrounds and windbreaks.

Related species: The pitch pine (*Pinus rigida*) has an appearance similar to the Southern yellow pine, but with shorter needles. It is a better choice for colder climates.

Western Yellow Pine

Pinus ponderosa
Zone: USDA 3b to 8a

Perhaps no other name is so well known. It rings a bell with millions of people world wide who may not have seen the tree or even known it is a pine. But it was made famous by the popular television show *Bonanza*. *Ponderosa* is Spanish for ponderous (heavy, enormous), a name given for the tree's huge size at maturity.

Description: This western pine bears bundles of two to three persistent needles from 5 to 11 inches long. They are an attractive yellow-green. The ponderosa pine grows as a narrow pyramid when young, then develops a bare trunk with a cluster of branches at the tip forming a cone or flat-topped crown. It reaches more than 100 feet in ideal conditions.

How to grow: This pine is easily transplanted and prefers a deep, moist, well-drained loam. It needs full sun and is tolerant of alkaline soils.

Uses: This is a good tree for shelter belts and windbreaks, as well as a specimen plant for dry climates.

Related species: The lodgepole pine (*Pinus contorta*) is a closely related species with a straight trunk once used by Native Americans of the plains to construct their tepees. It gets its botanical name, *contorta*, from its needles, which are twisted rather than straight. It is a better choice for damp soils than the ponderosa pine.

Eastern Red Cedar

Juniperus virginiana
Zone: USDA 3b to 9a

This is the common upright juniper of the eastern half of North America. It is a highly variable plant, but always forms a relatively conical silhouette of up to 50 feet. Many choice selections are popular in landscaping.

Description: The species generally has dark green, scalelike needles that persist throughout the year, although they may take on a reddish tinge in winter. Cultivated forms have been selected that remain the same shade year-round. The berries, borne on female plants only, are blue. The attractive reddish bark, peeling off in long strips, is most visible on mature specimens.

How to grow: The eastern red cedar requires full sun to grow well and prefers rich, moist, well-draining soils. It is, however, surprisingly adaptable and will even thrive on poor, gravelly soils. It appears to do equally well in acid or moderately alkaline soils. The plant can be pruned as needed.

Uses: This tree offers a wide range of uses. It is most popular as a columnar tree for landscape planting, but is also excellent for hedges and screens, even for topiary. It is also quite tolerant of seashore conditions. The wood is highly valued for its rich red color and fragrance.

Related species: The western counterpart of the eastern red cedar is the Rocky Mountain juniper (*Juniperus scopulorum*). It is available in many varieties of varying shades of green and bluish green.

Related varieties: The varieties of the eastern red cedar are too numerous to mention. The most popular ones are narrowly upright with grayish to bluish needles.

Russian Olive

Elaeagnus angustifolia
Zone: USDA 3a to 7a

The Russian olive is a short, tough, sturdy tree of Old World origin, distinctive for its silvery foliage.

Description: This deciduous, shrubby tree never gets much more than 12 to 20 feet high, but it can get as wide as it is tall. Its form is open but irregular in growing habit. Gray-scaled twigs support ½-inch thorns. Fine-textured, willowlike leaves hold their silvery green color through most of summer and fall. Its small, fragrant flowers appear in spring. Small, plastic-foam-like fruits are processed in the Orient for dessert making.

How to grow: The Russian olive prefers sunny, open locations and sandy, light soil, but it is adaptable. This plant can tolerate drought, cold, wind, and salt, but is vulnerable to ice storms and canker disease. Judicious pruning keeps it vigorous.

Uses: Well suited to the Midwest and Northern prairies, this tree is good for screens, hedges, and windbreaks. The silvery foliage gives added desirability as an accent plant in borders. To avoid disunity, use colorful foliage with restraint.

Related species: There are several similar species of *Elaeagnus*, most of them shrublike. The native silverberry (*E. commutata*) has particularly colorful leaves: almost pure silver. As the name suggests, the berries are also silvery. It is a spreading shrub to 6 to 12 feet. For warmer climates, the thorny elaeagnus (*E. pungens*) has glossy dark green leaves lacking the silvery sheen that makes the other species so attractive. It makes up for this lack of being evergreen. There are several variegated clones available.

Sassafras

Sassafras albidum
Zone: USDA 5b to 9a

This medium-size tree, native to the eastern part of North America, is grown for its curiously variable leaves, beautiful fall color, and ability to adapt well to poor soil conditions. It is used in the production of sassafras tea.

Description: The sassafras usually starts off its life as a shrub, forming a thicket of saplings all around the mother plant. It eventually forms a flat-topped tree with an irregular head, reaching about 40 to 60 feet in height. The bark is reddish brown with corky ridges. Its leaves are smooth-edged and bright medium green, turning various shades of yellow, orange, scarlet, and purple in the fall. The leaf form is variable, ranging from unlobed to mittenlike to three-lobed, often all on the same branch. The dark blue berries are borne on bright red stalks.

How to grow: Plant when young, since this tree resents transplanting. It prefers a rich, moist, acid soil, although it is often found in rocky soils in the wild. If a treelike shape is desired, prune out suckers as they form. It is relatively pest free.

Uses: This is a good choice for naturalized plantings, roadsides, and small lots.

Related species and varieties: There are no related species or varieties.

Silk Tree

Albizia Julibrissin
Zone: USDA 6a to 9a

This deciduous Asian tree is the hardiest of the mimosas, adding an exotic, almost tropical, touch to cold-climate gardens. It needs to be placed in a well-protected spot when grown toward the northern part of its range.

Description: The silk tree is a short, flat-topped tree or tall shrub, growing 20 to 25 feet in height (rarely 35 feet). It is grown for both its fernlike, dark green leaves and its fragrant powderpuff clusters of pink stamens up to 1 inch across. They appear in mid to late summer.

How to grow: Grow in full sun to very light shade in just about any soil. Although it is frost resistant, the silk tree does not tolerate low temperatures or prolonged periods below zero. Its use in zones 6, 7, and even 8 is limited to spots where subzero temperatures are rarely prolonged.

Uses: The silk tree can be grown as a curiosity in more northerly zones. It also makes a good plant for patio containers. In the South, it is a popular accent plant.

Related varieties: The smaller-growing *Albizia Julibrissin* 'Rosea' appears to be much hardier than the species (up to −15 degrees Fahrenheit) and may be somewhat resistant to wilt.

Carolina Silverbell

Halesia carolina
Zone: USDA 5a to 9a

The Carolina silverbell, native to the southeastern United States, is little known in its native country, but it is very popular abroad. That's a shame, since it is one of the best North American flowering trees.

Description: This small tree or large shrub—40 to 60 feet high in the wild—often grows multistemmed, but can be pruned to tree form when young. It is pyramidal in youth, but matures to a round-headed form. The smooth gray to black bark eventually becomes covered in scaly plates. The deciduous leaves are elliptic and dark yellowish green in the summer, turning to yellow in the fall. The entire tree is often covered in inch-long, wedding-bell-shaped white flowers in the spring. The seed pods, with two to four wings, are decorative in the fall.

How to grow: The Carolina silverbell is best suited to sun or semishade and rich, well-drained soils. It prefers slightly acid soils and becomes yellowed in alkaline conditions.

Uses: This small tree is a good understory tree in tall forests and fits well into shrub borders and woodland settings.

Related varieties: 'Rosea' is a pink-flowered form.

Sour Gum

Nyssa sylvatica
Zone: USDA 5a to 9a

The sour gum is a beautiful shade tree with fire engine red fall foliage. Native to the eastern United States, it is a favorite plant of bees. A water-loving plant—named for Nyssa, water nymph of Greek mythology—this plant is also known as tupelo, pepperidge, and black gum.

Description: Sour gum is pyramidal in youth, but with maturity forms an irregularly rounded crown. In cultivation it grows to about 25 feet by 30 years. One of the first trees to color up in fall, sour gum's glossy, green leaves turn scarlet. Its bitter, fleshy, blue-black fruit is favored by bears and birds, and follows pollination of female trees. Older trees have dark, blocky bark.

How to grow: Moist, acid soil is required. This tree needs protection from the wind, and light shade will decrease its autumn leaf spectacle. For best performance, transplant in spring, using local stock. Taprooted sour gum transplants poorly unless balled-and-burlapped or container-grown plants are used.

Uses: Sour gum is used as a specimen, shade, or street tree, also naturalized or en masse.

Related species: The water tupelo (*Nyssa aquatica*) is similar but does best in moist or even swampy soils.

Sourwood

Oxydendrum arboreum
Zone: USDA 6 to 9 (marginal in zone 5b)

Sourwood is an outstanding native tree of North America, a sweet sight to see east of the Mississippi River in every season. Its glossy, sour tasting, springtime leaves were once used as a medicinal tonic. Deer love to munch on the bright red, slender, sour twigs.

Description: Sourwood's average height is 30 feet, with a rounded crown and spreading shape, featuring gracefully dipping branchlets. The 10-inch long panicles of nodding, white, bell-shaped summer flowers, similar to the lily-of-the-valley, are fragrant. This tree has vivid red autumn foliage and tiny, woody fruit that persists into fall. The dark, thick, furrowed bark is a major winter asset.

How to grow: Sourwood will be undaunted by pests, diseases, or minor cultural problems if it gets the well-drained, acid soil it requires. Its roots are shallow and easily disturbed, so plant from young, balled-and-burlapped stock. It is best transplanted in spring, and kept well-watered and mulched until established. Avoid air-polluted environments.

Uses: Sourwood is outstanding as a focal point, a patio tree, or fronting taller trees.

Related species and varieties: There are no related species or varieties.

Norway Spruce

Picea Abies
Zone: USDA 3a to 7b

Ask children what this tree is and they'll immediately respond, "A Christmas tree." In actual fact, firs make better cut Christmas trees than do spruce, but the Norway spruce makes a better living Christmas tree for the yard.

Description: The Norway spruce forms a perfectly pyramidal silhouette, never rounding out with age like many pines. It is rather stiffly formal in its youth, but older branches produce pendulous branchlets, giving it more charm as it ages. Its needles are dark green year-round. The cones, borne sporadically, are particularly large for a spruce. It can reach more than 100 feet in height, even under cultivation.

How to grow: Grow in full sun in just about any soil, although moist, sandy, well-drained soils are preferred. The Norway spruce does best in cool climates. Give this tree plenty of space, because it will lose its lower branches—and much of its charm—if crowded or shaded at its base. It can be also pruned as a hedge when young.

Uses: This tree makes a striking specimen plant or, if pruned annually from the time it is young, a dense hedge. It also makes an excellent windbreak.

Related species: The Colorado blue spruce (*Picea pungens* 'Glauca') is renowned for its blue needles. Several selected clones with particularly good form or color are known.

Related varieties: There are many dwarf, columnar, and weeping varieties of Norway spruce. The weeping varieties are trained up a tall stake until they reach the desired height, then are allowed to dangle.

Sweet Gum

Liquidambar Styraciflua
Zone: USDA 5b to 9a

It is difficult to beat this tall, majestic tree for symmetrical beauty in a landscape setting. Although native to eastern North America, it is widely planted throughout the continent in its range.

Description: The sweet gum has a pyramidal habit when young, eventually becoming rounded and tall—up to more than 100 feet. The bark is grayish brown and deeply furrowed. Stems often have corky and attractive wings during the second year. The deciduous leaves are maplelike in outline, with five pointed lobes and lightly toothed margins. They are deep, glossy green in summer and turn yellow to purple-red in the fall. Its fruit cluster is a round ball often persisting in winter, as if the naked branches had been hung with woody Christmas ornaments.

How to grow: Transplant when young—the sweet gum resents root disturbance when it matures. Often, newly planted trees will scarcely grow at all for the first two or three years. Although this tree normally grows on rich, moist soils in the wild, it has proven itself quite adaptable in culture. In fact, it is one of the most pH-tolerant of all trees, thriving equally well in acid or alkaline conditions.

Uses: The sweet gum is a perfect choice for parks, large lots, and street plantings (as long as the tree's massive roots are not in the way). The tree is particularly choice when it changes color in fall.

Related species: The Formosan sweet gum (*Liquidambar formosana*) is similar to the native sweet gum but with three-lobed leaves. It is not as hardy as the native species.

Sycamore

Platanus occidentalis
Zone: USDA 5a to 9a

This deciduous native of the eastern North American forests is second only to the tulip tree in possible height among broad-leaf trees. Specimens well over 150 feet tall are not uncommon. In the wild it grows in moist areas, but it has been widely planted elsewhere.

Description: The sycamore is a tall, massive tree with equally massive white branches. Its striking bark flakes off to reveal plaques of brown, gray, cream, and white. The medium to dark green leaves are large and maplelike, with three to five lobes. The tree's fall color are not especially noticeable. The woody fruit forms a dangling round ball, which hangs on for at least part of the winter.

How to grow: The sycamore prefers full sun to partial shade and thrives in deep moist soils. It will, however, grow well in other conditions and, until recently, was a popular street tree. In the last decade or so, such specimens have often been severely attacked by anthracnose, causing it to be dropped from the list of recommended urban trees.

Uses: The sycamore makes a striking specimen tree but needs lots of space to grow. It never really made a good street tree because of its thick roots, which have lifted pavement, and its rather messy habit. Trees grown in conditions approaching the sycamore's natural one—deep, moist soils—are quite immune to the disease problems afflicting urban trees.

Related species: The London plane tree (*Platanus* x *acerifolia*) resulted from a cross between the native sycamore and the European plane tree (*P. orientalis*). It inherited much of the sycamore's charm, although its bark is not as colorful. It is not as susceptible to anthracnose.

Tamarack

Larix laricina
Zone: USDA 2 to 6b

Larches, including the tamarack, or Eastern larch, are among the few conifers that lose their leaves in the fall. They do so gracefully, taking on a beautiful fall coloration beforehand. The tamarack, native throughout northern North America, is underappreciated as a landscape tree. It is at least as interesting as many of the imported species often used in its place.

Description: This is a conical tree that grows to 40 feet or so in cultivation. It would be a perfect "Christmas tree" if it didn't lose its needles in winter. The stems of the numerous branches are yellowish brown, giving the tree a more than acceptable appearance even without needles. The needles, borne in bundles, are soft and blue-green in color, turning yellow in fall. Its cones are small and egg-shaped.

How to grow: In the wild, the tamarack grows in cool, moist spots, but in culture, it has proven itself adaptable to a wide range of conditions. It prefers slightly acid soils to alkaline ones and is intolerant of shade and air pollution.

Uses: The tamarack makes a good choice for wet soils where other trees will not grow. It creates a handsome effect in groves and rows.

Related species: There are several other species of larch, all quite similar in appearance and use. Some offer dwarf or weeping varieties.

Tulip Tree

Liriodendron Tulipifera
Zone: USDA 5a to 9a

The tulip tree is the tallest of the eastern North American deciduous trees—often well over 150 feet, though 70 to 90 feet is more common. It has been widely planted as an ornamental tree throughout North America and in Europe. It has a stately grace equalled by few other trees.

Description: This tree is fast-growing in youth, taking on a pyramidal form. Later it slows down considerably, eventually developing a rounded head. It tends to develop a tall trunk that sheds old branches as it grows, leaving branches only at the top, especially in a forest setting. The leaves of the tulip tree are unmistakable, looking like someone had cut the top off a maple leaf with scissors. They are deciduous and dark green with a polished appearance, turning yellow in fall. The fragrant flowers, produced in spring, are large, tulip-shaped, and greenish yellow with orange markings inside. Unfortunately, they are generally borne so high that they can scarcely be seen.

How to grow: Rich, moist, well-drained soils and full sun to light shade are ideal for this tree. It prefers a slightly acid soil but is quite adaptable. Give it plenty of root room.

Uses: The tulip tree makes a large specimen tree for parks and large properties. Although often planted as a street tree, it is not really a good choice for this purpose, having little resistance to pollution and soil compaction. Furthermore, its branches tend to be subject to breakage. It has few problems with insects or disease, although aphids may feed on the leaves in summer.

Related species: The Chinese tulip tree (*L. chinense*) is a little known but similar tree of medium size, a good choice for small lots.

Related varieties: There is a pyramidal version of the tulip tree (*L. tulipifera* 'Fastigiatum') that makes a good choice wherever horizontal space is at a premium.

Black Walnut

Juglans nigra
Zone: USDA 4b to 9a

This is an eastern North American form of walnut and perhaps the most adaptable species of its genus. It is an extremely valuable timber tree.

Description: The black walnut is a large tree, often more than 100 feet in height, usually developing a full, well-formed trunk with high branches. The oval crown is quite open. The black trunk and stems add to its winter charms. The large, deciduous leaves are pinnately compound. Its nuts are edible but encased in a thick green covering that stains the skin, making harvesting difficult.

How to grow: It is best to grow this tree from seed, since it has a deep taproot and resents transplanting. The black walnut is fast-growing in its youth, so it makes an interesting landscape specimen within a reasonable length of time, then its growth slows down. It rarely reaches its maximum height of more than 100 feet in culture unless it is supplied with a deep, rich, moist soil. It also grows well, but slowly, in dry soils.

Uses: Due to its large size, the black walnut is best used as a specimen tree. Although tolerant of street conditions, it makes a poor street tree because of its messy leaves and fruit. All walnuts produce juglone, a substance that can be toxic to plants growing in their vicinity.

Related varieties: The variety 'Laciniata,' with finely cut leaves, is the best choice for landscape use.

Related species: The English, or Persian, walnut (*Juglans regia*) produces the walnut of commerce, but it is of limited hardiness. The Carpathian walnut (*J. regia* 'Carpathian') is a hardier selection (zone 5).

Sydney Golden Wattle

Acacia longifolia
Zone: USDA 8 to 11

This native Australian small tree or large shrub is short-lived (20 to 30 years) but fast-growing. It can help to fill in until slower-growing, longer-lived trees can take their place. Ideally suited to warm, dry climates, the plant is highly prized in California as a street tree.

Description: Sydney golden wattle forms a billowy, rounded silhouette that grows to 20 feet in height and width. Unlike many wattles, it is evergreen, holding onto to its bright green 6-inch leaves year-round. It blooms in late winter or early spring, producing numerous golden yellow ball-shaped flowers in loose clusters along its branches.

How to grow: This tree needs full sun and tolerates dry situations and poor soils well. It is ideal for planting in sandy locations, even near the ocean; although if it is buffeted by salt sprays, it will probably take on the form of a prostrate shrub. Prune when young to remove lower branches if your goal is to develop a street tree.

Uses: An ideal accent plant, Sydney golden wattle also makes a good street tree that filters out dust and helps prevent wind erosion. Birds are attracted to its flowers and seeds.

Related species: The broad-leaf acacia (*Acacia latifolia*) is often confused with the Sydney golden wattle, but it is smaller and has a distinctly bluish cast to its leaves. Many other acacias adapt well to similar conditions.

Related varieties: *Acacia longifolia floribunda* is similar but with shorter, narrower leaves.

Golden Weeping Willow

Salix alba 'tristis'
Zone: USDA 3a to 9a

This is the most typical of the weeping willows, although there are many other willow selections with weeping habits. It is unmatched by any other landscape tree for its long, pendant, golden branches, which can literally sweep the ground.

Description: The golden weeping willow is a massive, spreading tree, reaching up to 80 feet in height. Although main branches manage to arch somewhat upward, the secondary ones grow straight down, creating the graceful weeping effect for which it is renowned. The trunk is brown with a distinctly corky bark. The pendant stems are yellow green. The narrow, deciduous leaves are pointed and green to yellow-green above, pale below. They turn yellow in the fall.

How to grow: This tree is well adapted to wet soils and is absolutely charming when planted right beside a lake or pond so its branches can dangle over the water. It does equally well in drier conditions, but in such cases its long-stretching roots can block pipes and drainage tiles in their pursuit of moisture. A branch stuck in moist soil is often all that is needed to reproduce this fast-growing tree.

Uses: The golden weeping willow is only recommended for very large lots and should be planted well away from any structures.

Related species: There are several other weeping willows, but the terminology is hopelessly confused. It is best to consult your county Cooperative Extension office for suggestions as to varieties adapted to your region.

Yellowwood

Cladrastis Kentuckea
Zone: USDA 4b to 8a

The yellowwood is native to North Carolina and Kentucky but is widely used far beyond its native range. The tree gets its name from its yellow heartwood.

Description: Yellowwood is a relatively slow-growing, low-branching tree or large shrub, 30 to 50 feet in height and even more in spread. Eventually, it forms a broad, rounded crown. Its pinnately compound leaves are an attractive bright green, turning yellow before they fall in autumn. The smooth grey bark, similar to that of the beech, and zigzagging branches give it good winter interest. In June it produces pure white, pealike flowers in dangling panicles, much like those of the wisteria.

How to grow: Plant in full sun in ordinary soil. It resents waterlogging and alkaline soils. The tree is drought tolerant and cold-resistant when well established. Extreme heat may cause the foliage margins to brown.

Uses: An excellent tree for both flowers and foliage, yellowwood also makes a good shade tree, especially for small properties.

Related varieties: The variety 'Rosea,' quite rare, has light pink flowers.

Japanese Zelkova

Zelkova serrata
Zone: USDA 6a to 9a

This Asian tree has often been promoted as a substitute for the American elm (*Ulmus americana*), now largely eliminated as a landscape tree because of its susceptibility to Dutch elm disease. While the Japanese zelkova doesn't have quite the charm of the American elm, it is an attractive tree and well worth planting.

Description: This is a fast-growing, round-headed tree in its youth, becoming moderate in growth in middle age and taking on a vaselike silhouette. It can reach up to 50 feet in height. The bark, cherrylike on younger trees, exfoliates on older trees, leaving an attractively mottled pattern. The deciduous leaves are similar to those of an elm, but smaller. They turn yellow or yellow-brown in the fall.

How to grow: The Japanese zelkova is easily transplanted. It prefers moist, deep soil and full sun. It is wind and drought resistant once established and is not bothered by air pollution. Susceptible to some elm diseases and pests, it is generally immune to Dutch elm disease.

Uses: This is a good choice for a lawn or street tree, providing good shade quickly.

Related varieties: 'Village Green' is a selection with a particularly elmlike form and rusty red fall leaves. 'Green Vase' is similar but much faster growing. It has orange fall leaves.

Abelia

Abelia 'Edward Goucher'
Zone: USDA 6a to 9a

This hybrid abelia was created in 1911 at the Glenn Dale Plant Introduction Center by Edward Goucher from a complex cross involving several species. It was the best abelia of its time—and still retains that first place today.

Description: This semievergreen shrub (it loses its leaves in the northern part of its growing area) is small in size: 4 feet is the average maximum, although it can attain 5 feet in a good location. It forms a dense, rounded shrub with lustrous, dark green leaves in summer, taking on a purplish tinge in winter. The fragrant tubular flowers, purple-pink in color, are borne profusely for much of the summer and early fall.

How to grow: Plant in full sun or half shade in moist, acid soil. The shrub should be protected from cold winter winds, especially at the northern limits of its territory. It can be pruned in spring, since it blooms on new wood, although it looks best if pruned selectively rather than sheared.

Uses: Its lacy appearance and long blooming season make it a good choice for a spot of honor in the yard. The abelia makes a good foundation and accent plant and combines well with broad-leaf evergreens. It is sometimes used as a hedge in the South. The plant attracts hummingbirds with its tubular blossoms.

Related species: *Abelia* x *grandiflora* is one of the parents of 'Edward Goucher.' It is just as attractive, with slightly larger white flowers, flushed pink.

Flowering Almond

Prunus triloba multiplex
Zone: USDA 3b to 9a

The flowering almond is an attractive spring-flowering shrub or small tree. The original variety, sent from China in 1855, is the double-flowered form described here. The wild species, with single flowers, is rarely grown.

Description: The plant forms a medium- to large-size shrub. Its small, coarsely toothed, three-lobed leaves have a yellow autumn color. The branches are upright at first, eventually becoming spreading and pendulous, forming a round-topped mounded shrub. The flowers are large, double, and roselike in clear pink. They are produced in abundance in early spring. The double-flowered variety produces no fruit.

How to grow: This shrub does best in full sun to light shade and any soil that is not waterlogged. To control its size, prune by removing older branches. It can also be transformed into an attractive mop-headed tree by selective pruning.

Uses: The flowering almond makes a good accent plant when in flower. It also fits well into shrub borders, especially as a background plant, and makes an excellent screen.

Related species: The dwarf almond (*P. glandulosa*) is a similar but smaller shrub with double white ('Alboplena') or double pink ('Roses Plenn') flowers. The dwarf Russian almond (*Prunus tenella*) has darker pink flowers; *P. tenella* 'Fire Hill,' with intense red flowers, is a particularly choice selection.

Japanese Andromeda

Pieris japonica
Zone: USDA 6a to 8a

The Japanese andromeda is a medium-size Asian shrub with attractive, glossy foliage and white, waxy flowers borne in drooping clusters.

Description: Although it can attain 12 feet in height, Japanese andromeda is slow-growing and is usually seen as a 4- to 6-foot shrub with dense evergreen foliage. The lance-shaped leaves are shiny and dark green at maturity, but display a bright, coppery coloration when they form, a characteristic that has been accentuated in many varieties. The long-lasting, urn-shaped flowers appear in spring in pendulous clusters and are lightly fragrant. The flower buds form the previous summer and add to the attractiveness of the shrub.

How to grow: This plant requires the same general conditions as rhododendrons and azaleas—moist, acid, well-drained, organic soil with a deep mulch—and are often grown with them. Moderate shade is best, especially in the South. Prune after flowering. It needs protection from cold winter winds.

Uses: The Japanese andromeda makes a beautiful specimen plant or can be planted in groups, in shrub borders, and as a background plant for other broad-leaf evergreens.

Related varieties: Literally dozens of varieties are available, most notably with pink or pink-blushed flowers, colorful new growth in scarlet red to bright pink, and diversely variegated foliage.

Bamboo

Bambusa glaucescens (B. multiplex)
Zone: USDA 9b to 10

Are they grasses or are they shrubs? It's hard to tell with bamboos, but those with woody stems that persist from year to year are generally grown as shrubs, although they are grasses. And that is certainly the case with this bamboo, often called the hedge bamboo.

Description: The hedge bamboo has thick, 1-inch-diameter stems, growing up to 10 feet in height. They are green at first, becoming yellow with time. The leaves are grasslike.

How to grow: Plant in full sun or partial shade in average garden soil.

Uses: The hedge bamboo is one of the most shrublike of all bamboos, with a fountainlike growth pattern. It is clump-forming and not invasive. It is a popular hedge plant in its range.

Related species: There are a great many species and varieties of bamboo, some hardy enough for cold climates.

Related varieties: Bamboo varieties are numerous and attractive. 'Alphonse Karr' has green- and yellow-striped stems. 'Fernleaf' has, as its name suggests, fernlike foliage. 'Silverstripe' has white-striped leaves. It is taller than the others and makes an excellent high screen.

Banana Shrub

Michelia Figo
Zone: USDA 8b to 11

The banana shrub gets its name from the scent of its flowers: fruity with a definite banana overtone. This Chinese plant, closely related to the magnolia, forms a dense, evergreen shrub.

Description: The banana shrub produces a dense, rounded form up to 8 feet in height and width, hiding its branches completely with small, dark green, lustrous leaves. The 1½-inch flowers, creamy yellow shaded purple-brown and borne among the leaves, would not be particularly noticeable were it not for their attractive perfume. They are produced from spring through summer.

How to grow: Plant in full sun to partial shade. Give it a well-drained, fertile, acid soil with a high organic content. This shrub is best planted out of strong winds so its perfume can accumulate.

Uses: The banana shrub is used in foundation plantings, as an accent plant, and in group plantings. Place it near a walkway or some other spot where its pervasive fragrance will be noticed. It also makes a good container plant in colder climates.

Related species and varieties: There are no related species or varieties that can be grown outside of the Florida Keys or Hawaii.

Japanese Barberry

Berberis Thunbergii
Zone: USDA 4b to 8b

This small-leaved, spiny shrub is a popular hedge plant, adaptable to a wide range of conditions. It is unequaled in the brilliance of its autumn foliage and bright red berries.

Description: The Japanese barberry is a medium-size shrub, eventually reaching 6 feet in height and somewhat wider in spread (half that for dwarf selections). Its dense branches are liberally covered with smooth, leathery, spoon-shaped leaves and small spines. The deciduous leaves are bright green in summer, becoming orange, scarlet, or reddish purple in fall. The yellow flowers are scarcely noticeable among the foliage, but the berries—long, narrow, and bright red—are a long-lasting fall and winter feature.

How to grow: This shrub is often available as a bare-root shrub for spring planting. It does best in full sun, but is adaptable to various soils, even doing well in dry conditions. Plant 2 feet apart for hedges.

Uses: The Japanese barberry is an excellent plant for hedges and barriers as well as mass plantings. It can be pruned quite harshly if necessary. The red berries attract birds.

Related varieties: There are literally dozens of varieties available, many with compact or dwarf growth habits and variously colored foliage. The purple-leaf varieties (the *Berberis Thunbergii atropurpurea* group) are especially popular. *B. Thunbergii atropurpurea* 'Crimson Pygmy,' a dwarf variety with purple leaves, is the most popular selection.

Crimson Bottlebrush

Callistemon citrinus
Zone: USDA 9

This summer-flowering evergreen shrub with red, bottlebrush flowers is popular in Southern California, where conditions are similar to those in its native Australia. But it is only barely frost-hardy, which makes it of limited use in most other climates.

Description: The crimson bottlebrush is a vigorous, spreading, fast-growing shrub. It can reach 15 to 20 feet in height and spread in a relatively short time. The narrow, rigid leaves are lemon-scented when crushed. Its clustered flowers are covered in bright red, bristlelike stamens, giving the flowers their characteristic bottlebrush shape. They appear year-round, but are cyclical, with periods of intense flowering followed by periods of little or no bloom. The rounded seed capsules persist for years.

How to grow: Plant in full sun in just about any nonalkaline soil, although moist, deep soils are best. Even dry, salty conditions are tolerated. The bottlebrush can be trained into a tree form or an espalier but otherwise needs little pruning.

Uses: An attractive plant that makes a good accent, the bottlebrush is an excellent, informal hedge. It tolerates city conditions well and can be grown as a container plant in colder climates. Hummingbirds love the flowers.

Related varieties: 'Compacta' is a popular dwarf selection. There are numerous other varieties of different size and flower color.

Common Boxwood

Buxus sempervirens
Zone: USDA 5 to 8

The common boxwood forms a large shrub or small tree if left to its own devices, but most people know it as a small, densely-leaved, evergreen hedge. It originated in western Asia but is well established in the wild throughout Europe.

Description: The common boxwood can attain 30 feet in height, but this is rare in culture. It is a densely branched, slow-growing shrub with numerous small, smooth-edged leaves. They are usually dark green and shiny, remaining on the shrub all winter (although they are subject to browning in strong winter winds). The fragrant flowers and tiny fruit offer little of interest.

How to grow: Boxwoods grow best in full sun to deep shade and rich soils. Newly transplanted shrubs should be protected from the summer sun, and even established plants are subject to winter damage if exposed to drying winds. Mulching will help prevent damage to its shallow roots, keeping them slightly moist at all times. Boxwoods can be sheared into just about any shape and respond well to harsh pruning.

Uses: Its evergreen nature and slow, dense growth make this shrub ideal for formal hedges and topiary. It is a good border plant and an excellent choice for foundation plantings.

Related species: The littleleaf boxwood (*Buxus microphylla*) is similar but has smaller leaves. It is somewhat hardier—to zone 4—with some winter protection.

Related varieties: Numerous dwarf and standard varieties with variously colored leaves are available.

Bridal-wreath

Spiraea x *Vanhouttei*
Zone: USDA 3b to 8b

The genus *Spiraea* is a highly popular one in the garden. Most are spring-bloomers with numerous tiny white flowers. Bridal-wreath is one of the best of this group.

Description: The Vanhoutt spiraea grows 6 to 8 feet in height, spreading 10 to 12 feet in diameter. It has a distinctly fountainlike growth habit, with a round top and arching branches recurving to the ground. Its leaves are simple or slightly lobed and less than 1½ inch in length and diameter. They are greenish blue, turning plum color in the fall. The tiny white flowers appear in dense clusters in midspring.

How to grow: Although the shrub will grow well in medium shade, full sun produces more flowers. The bridal-wreath adapts well to most soils. To keep the shrub in top shape, prune back one-third of the old flowering wood annually after it finishes blooming.

Uses: An excellent accent plant, the bridal-wreath is also good for informal hedges or screens and is well suited to mixed shrub borders.

Related species: The garland spiraea (*Spiraea* x *arguta*) is similar to the bridal-wreath but has less pendulous branches and a better covering of flowers in spring. The bumald spiraeas (*Spiraea* x *bumalda*), of which there are many selections, are summer-flowering spiraeas with pink to whitish flowers. Unlike the spring-flowering spiraeas, they need to be pruned in early spring. 'Anthony Waterer,' a low-growing shrub with summer-long flattened clusters of purple-pink flowers, is typical of this group. There are also many colored leaf varieties of bumald spiraea.

Broom

Genista tinctoria
Zone: USDA 3a to 8a

Also known as 'dyer's greenweed' because its green stems were once used as a dye, this shrub is a native of Europe and Western Asia. It is a hardy representative of a genus little known in North America but widely grown in Europe for its beautiful summer flowers and the surprisingly green winter color of its leafless stems.

Description: The broom forms a spreading, low-growing shrub with spiny, gray-green upright branches, eventually becoming flat-topped at about 2 to 3 feet in height and somewhat more in spread. The greenness of the stems is especially striking in winter: Although dormant at that time, they are such a spring green the broom seems to be in full growth. The short-lived, linear leaves are 1 inch long and rich green. Its yellow, pealike flowers are borne in abundance throughout the stems in June and, to a lesser extent, throughout the summer.

How to grow: Grow in full sun in infertile, preferably dry conditions. It does particularly well on neutral or alkaline soils. Plant when young, since established plants resent transplanting.

Uses: The broom makes a good shrub or ground cover for dry soils and slopes where few other shrubs thrive. It can also be used as a low-growing, informal hedge if planted 2 feet apart.

Related species: *Genista pilosa* 'Vancouver Gold' is a prostrate shrub with yellow flowers, making an ideal ground cover for sunnier, dry sites.

Related varieties: 'Royal Gold' is a choice selection with better blooming habits than the species. 'Plena' is a semiprostrate form with double flowers, ideal for rock gardens.

Fountain Butterfly Bush

Buddleia alternifolia
Zone: USDA 4b to 7b

The fountain butterfly bush is a tall shrub or small tree native to China. By far the hardiest of the butterfly bushes, it performs reliably as a true shrub in most conditions (many others die to the ground in winter and are best treated as perennials).

Description: The fountain butterfly bush is a tall, arching, graceful shrub reaching 15 feet in height if unpruned. Its branches are practically pendulous, making it resemble a shrubby weeping willow. The long, narrow, dark green leaves are grayish below. Although deciduous, they offer little in the way of fall color. The ends of the branches are covered in June with dense clusters of delicately-scented, bright lilac-purple flowers.

How to grow: Light, dappled shade or full sun are best. The shrub prefers deep, rich soils. Prune by removing one-third of the old wood after blooming.

Uses: The fountain butterfly bush is an excellent accent plant if given enough space. It can be trained into tree form by pruning, making its pendulous form even more striking. It attracts butterflies.

Related varieties: *Buddleia alternifolia* 'Argentea,' with silvery leaves, is a popular selection and the first to flower.

Related species: The butterfly bush (*Buddleia Davidii*) is better known and more highly scented than the fountain butterfly bush. It is smaller with a less attractive habit and is best pruned to the ground each spring. The cluster flowers come in a wide variety of colors.

Southern Bush Honeysuckle

Diervilla sessilifolia
Zone: USDA 4b to 8a

The southern bush honeysuckle is a low-growing, summer-flowering shrub, native to the southeastern United States. It is similar to the weigela in form, but with yellow flowers.

Description: This is a spreading, suckering, deciduous shrub growing 3 to 5 feet in height and at least as much in diameter. The glossy, dark green, pointed leaves sometimes take on interesting fall colors, especially if planted in full sun. The distinctly two-lipped flowers are tubular and appear in clusters through much of the summer.

How to grow: Grow in full sun to partial shade in moist soils. The shrub dislikes dry conditions. Prune back in early spring to promote fuller growth and better flowering.

Uses: This is an adaptable, useful, and easy-to-grow shrub, although it is not particularly showy. It makes good filler material and a nice addition to shrub borders. It also provides excellent erosion control.

Related species: The dwarf bush honeysuckle (*Diervilla Lonicera*) is shorter (2 to 4 feet) and hardier, with larger leaves.

Camellia

Camellia japonica
Zone: USDA 7b to 9a

Camellias are magnificent evergreen shrubs with large, often double flowers in a wide range of colors. Originating from Japan and China, they are popular in their range: true aristocrats of the garden.

Description: Most varieties form a dense pyramid of lustrous, dark green foliage, although some are laxer. Its leaves are elliptic, lightly toothed, and 2 to 4 inches long. The flowers, usually solitary, range from 3 to 5 inches across and appear from late winter to early spring. They come in shades of white, pink, and red and may be double, semidouble, or single. They are occasionally lightly fragrant.

How to grow: Camellias do best in moist, acid, well-drained soils. They prefer some shade, since they are subject to scalding in full winter sun. Mulch to keep the roots moist. Prune any time, but preferably after flowering is finished. They can be grown as container plants in cold climates.

Uses: Camellias make striking accent plants, especially for wooded areas but should not be overused in the landscape.

Related varieties: There are literally thousands of varieties in every possible shade and form.

Related species: The sasanqua camellia (*Camellia sasanqua*) is quite similar but with smaller flowers. Depending on climate, they can be late fall- to early spring-blooming.

Red Chokeberry

Aronia arbutifolia
Zone: USDA 4b to 9a

Native to the eastern United States, this shrub gets its common name from its bright red, but astringent, fruit. They are edible, but only with lots of sugar.

Description: The shrub has a distinctly upright growth pattern, and would be rather bare at the base if it weren't for the numerous suckers it bears to fill in the gaps. The narrow, dark leaves have a gray, felted underside. They are deciduous, turning a rich crimson or reddish purple in fall. Its white flowers are borne in small clusters. The bright red berries, however, are noticeable. Since birds eat them only when other berries are gone, they last in perfect shape well into the winter.

How to grow: This adaptable shrub is easy to grow and thrives even on poor soils. It will grow well in half-shade, but full sun encourages the best fruit production.

Uses: The red chokeberry is often used in mass plantings, where its rather barren base is not as noticeable.

Related varieties: 'Brillantissima' is a selection with especially brilliant fall color.

Bush Cinquefoil

Potentilla fruticosa
Zone: USDA 2b to 7b

The bush cinquefoil forms a small, dense shrub producing yellow flowers throughout the summer. In the wild it grows throughout much of the Northern Hemisphere. The common name 'cinquefoil' is from old French for five leaflets, a reference to its compound leaves.

Description: This is a bushy shrub, growing up to 4 feet in height and as much in diameter. It is well cloaked in foliage—small pinnately compound leaves with three to seven leaflets. The leaves are silky green when they unfurl, changing to green in the summer. They have little fall interest. The buttercup yellow flowers, which look like tiny 1-inch wild roses, are borne singly or in small clusters from early summer until frost. Few other flowering shrubs for cold climates have this much staying power.

How to grow: The shrub grows well in full sun or partial shade. The latter is the best choice for dark-flowered varieties, which tend to turn pale in full sun. It tolerates most soil types, even poor, rocky ones. Prune either by shearing back to the base in spring, or by trimming off the older branches annually, removing up to one-third of the plant's stems at a time.

Uses: The bush cinquefoil is a good choice for prairies and the North, where so many other ornamental shrubs fail. It makes a fine accent plant, an excellent informal hedge, and can be added to shrub and perennial borders or mass and foundation plantings. It is an all-purpose, easy-care shrub.

Related varieties: There are literally dozens of varieties, mostly color variants on the original buttercup yellow of the species: pale yellow, orange, red, pink, and others.

Related species: The species *Potentilla davurica* is similar to *P. fruticosa* in nearly every way except its flower color, which is white. It also offers a wide range of varieties.

Sargent Crabapple

Malus Sargentii
Zone: USDA 5 to 7

This is a delightful shrub-form crabapple with colorful spring flowers and abundant, cherry-like fruit.

Description: The Sargent crabapple is a true shrub, unlike most crabapples, which are small trees. It produces multiple stems at ground level and rarely attains more than 8 feet high, twice that in spread. The green leaves are simple or three-lobed, sometimes turning yellow in the fall before they drop. The flowers are red in bud, but open white. Typical apple blossoms in form, they are quite fragrant and up to 1 inch across. The fruit is bright red and cherry-shaped. It is important to select a clone known to bloom annually, since seed-grown plants often only flower heavily every other year.

How to grow: The Sargent crabapple needs full sun to light shade to do well and tolerates most soil conditions except extreme wetness. It is susceptible to various diseases and insect pests.

Uses: This crabapple makes an excellent accent plant and fits well into the shrub border. The fruits make good preserves.

Related varieties: 'Rosea' has flowers that are blushed with pink. 'Roseglow' has fruits that are darker red.

Alpine Currant

Ribes alpinum
Zone: USDA 3b to 7b

The alpine currant is an easy-to-grow European native with an attractive form and excellent hedge qualities. It is widely used as a landscape plant in cooler parts of the continent.

Description: The alpine currant is a small- to medium-size shrub with an upright habit in youth, spreading as it ages. The 1- to 2-inch leaves are bright green with three to five lobes, like small maple leaves. The flowers are yellow-green and appear in clusters in spring. Its bright red berries are not poisonous—but not considered edible. Furthermore, they are rarely seen, since most varieties grown are male clones.

How to grow: Grow in full sun or deep shade in nearly any kind of soil. Prune at any season.

Uses: The alpine currant is used almost exclusively as a hedge, either formal or informal. It is also a good choice for mass plantings.

Related species: The clove currant (*Ribes odoratum*), with highly scented yellow spring flowers, and the flowering currant (*Ribes sanguineum*), with rose-pink flowers, are commonly grown.

Related varieties: 'Aureum' is a dwarf type with yellowish leaves. It does best in full sun. 'Green Mound' is one of several dwarf varieties used in low-growing hedges.

Red-osier Dogwood

Cornus sericea (formerly *C. stolonifera*)
Zone: USDA 2a to 8a

The red-osier dogwood gets its name from its purplish red stems and its former use in making wicker baskets (*osier* is French for "wicker"). In various forms it is native to much of North America.

Description: In the wild, the red-osier dogwood is a tall shrub that grows to 10 feet in height and has an even greater spread, though it is usually pruned to much shorter heights in culture. It spreads by underground stems. Young branches are smooth and attractively colored in red; older ones are woody and less charming. Its smooth, pointed leaves are medium green, turning purplish red in fall. The clustered white flowers, followed by white berries, are borne on older branches and are consequentially rarely seen, since the shrub is heavily pruned in culture.

How to grow: Although the red-osier dogwood is most common in wet meadows and swamps in the wild, it seems to adapt to most soils, even dry ones, in culture. It does best in full sun. Older branches can be pruned back to stimulate increased production of colorful young stems.

Uses: Excellent for mass plantings and shrub borders, it is also useful in erosion control and makes a good container plant. Birds are attracted to the berries when present.

Related species: The Tatarian dogwood (*Cornus alba*) is nearly indistinguishable from the red-osier dogwood. Most variegated-leaf varieties, such as the white-margined 'Argenteo-marginata' and the yellow-edged 'Spaethii,' belong to this species.

Related varieties: 'Flaviramea' is a popular yellow-stemmed variety.

  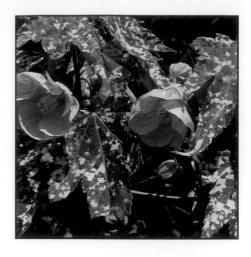

Winged Euonymus

Euonymus alata
Zone: USDA 4a to 8a

This is one of the most reliably colorful of all the shrubs grown for their fall foliage. Its winged branches offer winter attraction as well.

Description: The winged euonymus forms a spreading shrub up to 10 feet in height, eventually becoming flat-topped. The green to brown stems have two to four prominent corky wings. The leaves are dark green, becoming a brilliant crimson-pink in fall—a display that lasts several weeks until the leaves drop. The spring flowers are not showy, and the seeds, although a bright orange-red, ripen just as the leaves turn red, so they are scarcely noticeable.

How to grow: This is an adaptable plant that can tolerate widely varying conditions, although it will not accept waterlogged soils. Unlike many shrubs, the winged euonymus turns as bright a red when grown in shade as in full sun.

Uses: This shrub can be used for just about any purpose: hedges, group plantings, accent plant, screening, shrub borders, foundation plantings, and the like.

Related varieties: 'Compacta' is rounder, smaller, and less hardy than the species.

Scarlet Fire Thorn

Pyracantha coccinea
Zone: USDA 5b to 9a

The fire thorn is a thorny shrub from the Mediterranean basin, well known for its bright red berries that last through much of the fall and winter. It is often trained up walls.

Description: The scarlet fire thorn is an evergreen shrub (semievergreen in colder climates) with stiff, thorny branches, reaching about 10 feet in height in warm climates, much less in colder ones. The narrowly oval, fine-toothed leaves are a dark lustrous green in summer and retain their green color through the winter if protected from cold, dry winter winds. The white flowers are small but extremely numerous, often covering much of the plant. The orange-red fruits ripen in September and last through the winter.

How to grow: Full sun leads to more flowers and therefore more fruit, but it may leave the plant exposed to dry winds. For that reason, semishade is a better choice in cold climates. Most soils that are not waterlogged are suitable, but it is best to start with a young shrub, since mature fire thorns are not easy to transplant. Prune at any time of the year to control the shrub's uneven growth.

Uses: This shrub makes an attractive informal hedge or barrier plant. Fire thorn is often trained up walls as an espalier and makes a beautiful showing in such situations.

Related varieties: There are many varieties with different hardiness levels and fruit colors. Check with your county Cooperative Extension office for suggestions of good varieties for your area.

Flowering Maple

Abutilon hybridum
Zone: USDA 9 to 11

This fast-growing, rather rangy evergreen shrub has one major saving grace—large, colorful flowers. They are produced throughout spring and summer and, in some varieties, practically nonstop throughout the entire year.

Description: The flowering maple can grow up to 8 feet high and just as wide. Its weak green stems, turning woody at their base, bear green, maplelike leaves with three to five lobes. The flowers are bell-shaped and pendant. They range in color from white and yellow to pink, orange, and deep red.

How to grow: Grow in full sun, although partial shade is preferable in hot, dry climates. Moist soil is best. Pinch frequently to keep the shrub within bounds.

Uses: The flowering maple can be trained to make a formal espalier or small standard tree. In northern areas, it is commonly grown as a patio plant and brought indoors for the winter.

Related species: *Abutilon pictum* has leaves heavily speckled with yellow marks. Its light orange, bell-shaped flowers are veined red. *A. megapotamicum*, most often seen in its yellowed-marbled form 'Variegata,' is a weakly stemmed shrub often trained as a vine. It has red and yellow lantern flowers.

Flowering Quince

Chaenomeles speciosa
Zone: USDA 4b to 9a

This medium-size spreading shrub from China is grown for its brightly-colored flowers, which are sometimes followed by edible fruits.

Description: The flowering quince is variable in habit, from rounded spreading to quite rambling. Its twiggy branches are often spiny and tangled. The toothed, pointed leaves are dark green and deciduous but offer little fall color. The strikingly colored flowers, scarlet to red, are borne before the leaves appear. It is winter-blooming in the South, but flowers in early spring in the North. The fruit, not always abundantly produced, is pearlike and yellowish green. It is quite bitter when eaten raw but makes excellent preserves.

How to grow: The flowering quince blooms best in full sun, although partial shade is acceptable. It tolerates most soils, even dry ones. Prune by removing old branches. Aging shrubs can be rejuvenated by shearing them back to the base.

Uses: The flowering quince makes an interesting one-season accent plant and a good hedge, offering excellent security due to its thorns and impenetrable nature.

Related species: The hybrid flowering quince (*Chaenomeles* x *superba*) is similar.

Related varieties: Selected varieties offer a wide range of flower colors, from white to pink, apricot, orange, flame, and red.

Early Forsythia

Forsythia ovata
Zone: USDA 4 to 7a

This Korean shrub is probably the earliest-blooming of all the common forsythias. It is one of the earliest shrubs to bloom in the landscape.

Description: The early forsythia is a low-growing, spreading shrub reaching up to 4 feet (sometimes 6) in height. The bright yellow flowers are borne singly from the nodes. Its leaves are simple, dark green, and toothed, dropping off in the fall while still green.

How to grow: The early forsythia needs full sun for maximum flowers. It grows well in most loose, rich soils. Prune by cutting back the older branches to the ground as soon as the flowers fade. Avoid shearing this shrub into a formal hedge, because this eliminates most of the following year's flowers.

Uses: This forsythia offers greater bud hardiness than most others, blooming abundantly well into zone 4 (where other forsythias often only bloom below the snow line). It is an ideal choice for shrub borders, informal hedges, or as an accent plant.

Related varieties: 'Ottawa' is even hardier than the species and is a good choice for cold climate gardens.

Dwarf Fothergilla

Fothergilla Gardenii
Zone: USDA 5b to 9a

The dwarf fothergilla, native to the southeastern United States, is a low-growing shrub with fluffy, white, bottlebrush flowers in spring. They are intensely fragrant.

Description: The tip of each of the spreading branches, rarely more than 3 feet tall, is decorated in spring with an erect cluster of white, petalless flowers, creating the typical bottlebrush appearance of the shrub. Its leaves, rounded but somewhat irregular, don't appear until later. They are dark green, turning a combination of yellow, red, and orange before dropping in the fall.

How to grow: This shrub requires an acid, peaty, sandy loam with good drainage. Although it does well in partial shade, it only blooms abundantly and colors up well in full sun.

Uses: The dwarf fothergilla is a choice plant for borders, foundation plantings, and mass plantings. It combines well with other acid-loving plants like azaleas and rhododendrons. No pruning is required.

Related species: The large fothergilla (*Fothergilla major*) is similar but, as both the common and the botanical names suggest, is a much larger plant. It can attain heights of up to 10 feet, although 6 feet is more common.

Gardenia

Gardenia jasminoides
Zone: USDA 8b to 9a

This Chinese shrub is extremely popular in its range—and beyond its range, it's grown in pots. Its unmistakable perfume and its white flowers are its main claims to fame.

Description: The gardenia forms a rounded evergreen shrub 4 to 6 feet high. The leaves, attractive year-round, are a glossy, dark green. Its pure white flowers, waxy and rather like wild roses in form, appear over a three-month period in late spring and early summer. They measure 3 inches across.

How to grow: This shrub requires moist, acid, well-drained soil with a high organic content and full sun to partial shade. It requires some protection from drying winter winds and late frosts. Indoors it needs cool temperatures and bright light to do well.

Uses: A good specimen plant, the gardenia is more popularly used as a foundation plant and in shrub borders. Place it near a walkway or some other spot of frequent passage so its fragrance will be noticed by passers-by.

Related varieties: 'Fortuniana' has fully double, carnationlike flowers. 'Radicans' is a low-growing, creeping variety with smaller leaves.

Purple Guava

Psidium littorale longipes
Zone: USDA 9 to 11

This Brazilian shrub or small tree is the purple-fruited form of the strawberry guava (*Psidium littorale*). It is popularly planted in tropical climates for its delicious fruit and attractive form.

Description: When allowed to grow on its own, the purple guava usually forms an 8- to 10-foot-high shrub, but it can be trained to reach a greater height as a small tree. The bark is an attractive greenish gray to golden brown. Its evergreen leaves are a glossy medium green, growing up to 3 inches long. New leaves have a delightful bronze coloration. It produces white flowers with numerous fuzzy stamens that develop into purplish fruit with white flesh in early summer.

How to grow: Grow in full sun to light shade, preferably in rich soil (although it will adapt to most soil types if necessary). The plant is drought resistant once established. Prune as needed to obtain the desired shape.

Uses: The purple guava makes a good accent plant and adapts well to planting near the seashore. The fruit is sweeter to the taste than most guavas and can be eaten fresh or used in cooking.

Related species: The apple guava (*P. Guajava*) is a similar but taller plant with larger leaves. Its fruits are variable in size and color and can have white, pink, or yellow flesh.

Related varieties: The yellow strawberry guava (*Psidium littorale lucidum*) has yellow fruits and denser growth.

Indian Hawthorn

Raphiolepis indica
Zone: USDA 8b to 9a

This native of eastern China is among the most widely planted of all garden shrubs in warm climate areas. They are easy-to-grow, display attractive foliage all year long, and have beautiful flowers.

Description: The Indian hawthorn is generally a densely foliaged, low-growing shrub, less than 6 feet in height and often maintained below 3 feet by occasional pruning. The smooth, glossy, pointed leaves are evergreen and measure about 1½ to 3 inches long. New leaves are attractively tinted in bronze or red. The flowers appear in dense clusters from late fall or midwinter to late spring. They are available in shades of white and pink. Blue berry-like fruits follow the flowers.

How to grow: The Indian hawthorn does best in full sun or light shade and in moist, well-drained soils of average pH. It is somewhat drought-resistant. To retain an interesting form the Indian hawthorn should be pruned regularly, pinching back the branches at least once a year.

Uses: This shrub is used in many ways: hedges, screens, barriers, containers, accent plant, topiary, espalier on walls, and others. It also makes a great tub specimen, both in colder climates and within its range.

Related species: The Yedda raphiolepis (*Raphiolepis umbellata*) is similar, but has nearly round leaves. Offering several interesting varieties, it is hardier than *R. indica* and therefore a better choice at the northern limits of the plant's range. *R. x Delacourii* is an intermediate form, resulting from a cross between *R. umbellata* and *R. indica*. It is the true name of many of the varieties usually attributed to *R. indica*.

Related varieties: Many varieties, differing mainly in vigor, size, and flower color, are available.

Michigan Holly

Ilex verticillata
Zone: USDA 4a to 9a

This shrub, with its deciduous, spineless leaves, is an unhollylike holly. Nevertheless, it's an attractive plant since leaf drop better reveals its spectacularly colored, long-lasting berries.

Description: This densely foliaged shrub has an oval form and numerous branchlets. It grows 8 to 12 feet tall. The leaves, 1½ to 3 inches long, are dark green and shiny, turning yellow in the fall. The flowers are insignificant but are followed by scarlet red berries, which last right through the winter if not eaten by birds.

How to grow: Michigan holly does well in full sun or partial shade and moist, rich soils. This is an acid-loving plant and will do poorly in neutral or alkaline soils.

Uses: The shrub makes a good accent plant for spots where its winter color will be appreciated. It is also a good choice for mass plantings and wildlife gardens. At least one male must be planted for fruiting to occur.

Related varieties: 'Sparkleberry' is one of the more spectacular selections, with numerous, long-lasting berries. But there are many others, including some with more compact growth habits or differently colored berries.

Winter Honeysuckle

Lonicera fragantissima
Zone: USDA 3a to 8a

This is a delightful shrub for extending the seasons: Its winter flowers bring spring to the garden several months early while, at the other end of the year, its foliage lasts well into winter. It is sometimes evergreen in warm climates.

Description: The winter honeysuckle forms a dense, tangled shrub from 6 to 10 feet in both height and spread. The dark bluish green leaves are elliptic, staying on the plant until late fall in the North, into winter in the South, and year-round in near-tropical climates. They have no notable fall coloration. The creamy white flowers—appearing in winter in the South, early spring in the North—are not very showy but are extremely fragrant. The red berries, borne in late spring, are well-hidden by foliage.

How to grow: Plant at any time in good loamy, moist, well-drained soil and full sun to partial shade. Avoid wet conditions. Prune after blooming is finished. To rejuvenate an old shrub, cut nearly to the ground.

Uses: The winter honeysuckle is a good hedge plant and screen, and makes an ideal choice for the shrub border. Plant where its perfume will be noticed, such as near a pathway. Cut branches force easily indoors in winter.

Related species: There are numerous other species of shrubby honeysuckles, all fully deciduous but better adapted to colder climates, including such popular ones as 'Clavey's Dwarf,' *Lonicera tatarica* 'Claveyi,' and *L. Korolkowii*. Most make excellent hedge and accent plants, with attractive flowers and berries, but they lack the winter honeysuckle's heady perfume. Many are invasive pests.

Oakleaf Hydrangea

Hydrangea quercifolia
Zone: USDA 7a to 9a

This shrub is an exception among hydrangeas; it is prized for its autumn colors and its bloom. It is native to the southeastern United States.

Description: The oakleaf hydrangea forms upright, nearly unbranching stems, spreading at the base from stolons to make a mounded colony. Its flowers, borne in terminal clusters in early summer, are of two types: sterile and fertile. The sterile flowers are 1 to 1½ inches in diameter. They are white, changing to purplish pink then brown in the fall, and serve to attract pollinating insects. The fertile flowers are insignificant. As the name suggests, the deeply cut leaves are oaklike. They are dark green in the summer, changing to a spectacular mix of red, orange-brown, and purple in the fall.

How to grow: Plant in partial to half shade, although full sun is tolerated. This shrub does best on rich, moist, well-drained soils. Mulch to maintain the cool, moist conditions the roots prefer. Pruning mainly consists of removing faded flowers and cutting out deadwood, although overgrown shrubs can be rejuvenated by harsh pruning if necessary.

Uses: Oakleaf hydrangea is a good shrub for planting in wooded areas and in shrub borders. It is spectacular enough in fall coloration that it is often grown well to the north of its normal range (to zone 4), even though its flower buds are killed almost every winter in such climates.

Related varieties: 'Snowflake' is a double-flowered form composed almost entirely of sterile blooms.

Peegee Hydrangea

Hydrangea paniculata 'Grandiflora'
Zone: USDA 4a to 9a

This popular old-fashioned shrub is currently undergoing a surge of renewed interest. Its main attraction is its long-lasting flowers, which appear in late summer and last right through fall.

Description: This hydrangea, possibly the showiest of all the large shrubs, reaches 10 feet or more in height and spread. It has an upright, rather coarse habit with large, elliptic, toothed leaves, that are dark green and offer little fall interest. The pyramidal clusters of flowers, often so dense the branches arch gracefully under their weight, are up to 18 inches long and 12 inches wide at the base. Its flowers are mostly the sterile, attractive form, opening white in late summer and gradually changing to purplish pink in fall, brown in winter. The fertile flowers, rarely found on this variety, are insignificant.

How to grow: Grow in full sun or partial shade in a good loamy, moist soil. No harm comes from harvesting the flowers for long-lasting dried arrangements. In fact, this actually helps stimulate bloom the next year while preventing the winter damage that can occur when snow adds to the weight of the already heavy flower clusters. Hard pruning may be necessary every few years in early spring to remove old wood and improve the naturally straggly growth pattern. It can also be pruned into a standard (tree) form.

Uses: The peegee hydrangea makes an attractive freestanding shrub or addition to the shrub border.

Related species: The tree hydrangea (*Hydrangea arborescens*) is similar but has rounded inflorescences that start blooming earlier than the peegee hydrangea. They open greenish white, then turn cream colored and last until fall. 'Annabelle' is a particularly choice clone.

Inkberry

Ilex glabra
Zone: USDA 4b to 9a

This is the hardiest of the evergreen hollies, found in the wild in eastern North America from Florida right up into Canada. Although it does not have the spiny leaves of the "Christmas" holly, it is an attractive and useful plant in the landscape.

Description: Inkberry is a medium-size shrub with an upright, rounded form, often becoming rather open with time if not pruned. It spreads by suckers, forming colonies. The small leaves, oval to almost spoon-shaped, are dark green and lustrous, remaining on the shrub all year. They sometimes turn brown in harsh winters. The insignificant flowers are followed by black berries, which last right through the winter.

How to grow: Plant in sun or shade in moist, rich soils. The shrub tolerates—and even prefers—acid soils, so it can be grown in combination with rhododendrons and azaleas. It can be pruned heavily to rejuvenate older specimens.

Uses: Inkberry makes an excellent choice for foundation plantings, hedges and screens, mass plantings, and container plantings. It is a good city shrub.

Related species: The Japanese holly (*Ilex crenata*) is similar but with tiny leaves. It is offered in many varieties, mostly of denser growth than the species.

Related varieties: 'Compacta' is a female clone with dense foliage and abundant berries. At least one male should be provided to ensure pollination. There are several varieties with showy white berries.

Jacaranda

Jacaranda acutifolia
Zone: USDA 7b to 9a

This small tree is often grown as a shrub in warm-climate areas. It has beautiful blue flowers and ferny leaves.

Description: A rather open shrub or small tree, jacaranda grows to 10 feet or so in height. It is deciduous, with compound, pinnate leaves bearing 5 to 6 pairs of leaflets. The clustered tubular blue flowers (they can be white, but this is rare) are borne in spring and make a spectacular showing. They are followed by long-lasting, beanlike pods. This plant is often confused with *Jacaranda mimosifolia*, but is shrubbier with fewer leaflets per leaf.

How to grow: Plant in full sun in sandy, well-drained but not overly dry soils. Prune mostly to remove deadwood. Young shrubs are fragile and can be killed to the ground by even light frosts, but established plants are somewhat hardier. Jacaranda may flower poorly, even where frost is rare, if summer temperatures are low.

Uses: Jacaranda is commonly used as an accent plant or for shrub borders. It also does well in containers and in urban conditions.

Related species: *Jacaranda mimosifolia* is a tree-shaped version, reaching 40 feet or more in height. It may need to be pruned and staked to form a single trunk.

Mountain Laurel

Kalmia latifolia
Zone: USDA 5a to 9a

This shrub, native to eastern North America, is becoming increasingly popular as a companion plant for rhododendrons, which it resembles on a smaller scale.

Description: A large shrub with dense, evergreen foliage, it can reach 7 to 15 feet in height and spread; but it is slow-growing, so it can be maintained indefinitely at 4 feet with only a little pruning. The smooth, shiny, deep green leaves are borne on thin stems. The flowers, appearing in mid to late spring in terminal clusters, are attractive in bud, opening to reveal a cup-shaped flower, often paler in color than the bud. They range in shade from white to deep rose in wild selections. The choice is even wider among the increasingly vast range of varieties.

How to grow: Easily transplanted, the mountain laurel thrives in moist, cool, well-drained soils with an acidic base. Mulch to keep the soil moist. It grows well enough in deep shade, but full sun encourages better blooming. Provide some protection from drying winter winds.

Uses: Perfect for shrub borders and mass plantings, the shrub is also a good choice for naturalizing in oak woods and other spots that are naturally acid.

Related species: Lambkill kalmia (*Kalmia angustifolia*) is a low-growing evergreen shrub with white to pink to dark purple flowers. It is extremely hardy, a good replacement for rhododendrons in climates where that plant does not thrive.

Related varieties: There are too many different ones to describe here.

Drooping Leucothoe

Leucothoe Fontanesiana
Zone: USDA 5b to 9a

This southeastern United States native is an excellent low-growing shrub or ground cover, offering a combination of evergreen foliage, often with fall color, and attractive flowers.

Description: A graceful evergreen shrub reaching 3 to 6 feet in height and width, the drooping leucothoe gets its name from its spreading, arching branches, which are almost weighted down by the pendulous fragrant clusters of creamy white flowers. The leaves are leathery and dark green, 3 to 6 inches long. They often take on a bronzy to purplish color in fall and winter. The urn-shaped flowers resemble those of the lily-of-the-valley.

How to grow: This shrub is a good choice for partial to full shade, although it will tolerate sun if mulched and protected from drying winds. It prefers moist, well-drained, organic soils and acid growing conditions. To maintain it as a ground cover, cut back all the older branches to the ground after blooming is finished. It will then stay below 1½ feet in height.

Uses: Drooping leucothoe is a good ground cover and is excellent for mass plantings. It nicely hides the base of other shrubs that become leggy over time, especially rhododendrons, since the two require the same growing conditions. Hummingbirds are attracted to its flowers.

Related varieties: 'Girard's Rainbow' is a variegated form with cream, yellow, and pink markings, especially on new growth.

Common Lilac

Syringa vulgaris
Zone: USDA 3 to 7

Just about everyone recognizes the common lilac. Its dense clusters of highly perfumed, lavender flowers are an essential part of the landscape, especially in colder climates. Its delightful scent has been captured in many popular beauty products.

Description: The common lilac is an upright, leggy shrub that grows to about 15 feet with a spread of 12 feet. Its heart-shaped, dark green leaves are up to 5 inches long. The flowers are produced in dense, pyramid-shaped clusters at the end of the branches in spring. They are light lavender in the species.

How to grow: Full sun is best, although lilacs will grow in up to medium shade. They are tolerant as to soil type, but prefer neutral soils with good drainage. Deadhead after blooming to stimulate good flowering each year instead of every second year. Remove old trunks and unwanted suckers occasionally.

Uses: The lilac is a good spring accent plant, offering little interest the rest of the year. It is often grown in shrub borders and makes a good cut flower.

Related species: There are many other species of lilac, some earlier or later bloomers and many with equally interesting perfumes. They are often used to extend the common lilac's all-too-short flowering season.

Related varieties: The so-called French hybrids actually include varieties from several continents. All of the improved forms of *Syringa vulgaris* fall into this category. They differ in flower color—from white to pink to deep purple—and many have double flowers.

Sweet Mock Orange

Philadelphus coronarius
Zone: USDA 4a to 7b

The sweet mock orange is a tall, deciduous shrub with abundant fragrant summer flowers. Originally from Europe, it is a parent of many of the numerous mock oranges grown in gardens around the world.

Description: It forms a large, rounded shrub up to 12 feet in height with an equal spread, although it is often kept much shorter by pruning. The medium green leaves are ovate and lightly toothed, with little fall interest. Its flowers are sweetly scented, much like orange blossoms. They are white and 1 to 1²/₃ inches across, borne in early summer. The seed capsules are persistent but add little to the shrub's beauty.

How to grow: Sweet mock orange is easily transplanted. It needs full sun to partial shade and tolerates most soils, even dry ones, although it prefers moist, organic, well-drained soil. Prune after flowering, either lightly to stimulate new growth, or heavily to rejuvenate older specimens.

Uses: It can be used either singly as an accent plant or in groups, as in shrub borders or mass plantings. It also makes a massive informal hedge for screening purposes.

Related species and varieties: 'Aureus' has bright yellow spring foliage, turning yellow-green in summer. The sweet mock orange is also one of the parents of a great many hybrid mock oranges, most of which retain its sweet perfume. Among them are 'Virginal,' with 2-inch double flowers, and 'Minnesota Snowflake,' a hardier variety, both listed as *P.* x *virginalis*.

Dwarf Myrtle

Myrtus communis
Zone: USDA 9 to 11

This Mediterranean evergreen shrub is pleasantly perfumed when its stems or leaves are lightly crushed. It is often grown for historical reasons, since it is the myrtle so frequently mentioned in ancient writings.

Description: The myrtle forms a densely leaved shrub 5 to 6 feet tall and 4 to 5 feet wide. In truly hospitable sites, it can become a small tree. The fragrant white flowers are numerous and have a fuzzy appearance due to their numerous stamens. They are produced in summer and followed by purple-black berries.

How to grow: Myrtle is normally grown in partial shade but does well in full sun if its watering needs are met. Just about any soil will do as long as it is well-drained. Prune as needed.

Uses: This shrub is often grown for screening or as a hedge and can also be pruned into topiary forms. It is also attractive when trained up a wall as an espalier. It can be grown as a container plant indoors.

Related varieties: There are a great many varieties of this shrub. 'Compacta,' with a low-growing, small-leaved habit, is ideal for low edgings, foundation plantings, and low formal hedges. 'Microphylla,' which has even smaller, narrow leaves, is the most commonly used variety indoors.

Oleander

Nerium Oleander
Zone: USDA 9 to 11

This tall evergreen shrub or small tree is popular in areas where frost is rare because of its long-lasting, colorful blooms and ease of care. All parts of the plant, however, are toxic if ingested, so the oleander should not be placed where children or pets have access to it.

Description: The oleander is an upright-growing shrub eventually forming a rounded crown and can be trained as a tree in frost-free areas. It can be expected to reach 12 feet or more in height. The long, willowlike leaves are shiny and dark green. Its clustered flowers, fragrant and five-petalled, are often double or semidouble. They can be white, pink, yellow, or red and appear on new growth throughout the summer.

How to grow: Plant in full sun or partial shade in just about any kind of soil, from rich to poor and dry to wet. This shrub is killed to the ground by sub-zero temperatures, but usually resprouts from its roots. It makes a good tub plant in northern climates. Prune if necessary to reduce its height.

Uses: The oleander is a good choice for foundations, borders, tall hedges, and screens, as well as individually as an accent plant. It is well adapted to urban conditions and grows well by the seashore.

Related varieties: Numerous oleander varieties are available. 'Hardy Pink' appears hardier than the average oleander, surviving short periods of 0 degrees Fahrenheit temperatures with little damage to its above-ground parts. 'Hardy Red' is similar but with a darker shade of pink.

Oregon Grape

Mahonia Aquifolium
Zone: USDA 5b to 9

A native of western North America, the Oregon grape is only grapelike in its edible blue berries. Otherwise it is a low-growing, shrubby plant with persistent, hollylike leaves.

Description: This is generally a dense, rounded evergreen shrub spreading via stolons and reaching 3 to 6 feet in height, although some selections are distinctly upward-growing and reach 9 feet or more. The leaves are compound, with shiny, spiny-edged leaflets much like those of a holly in shape and texture. They are dark green in summer, often turning red or purple-red in fall and winter. The small, modestly fragrant, yellow flowers are borne in dense clusters in spring. They are followed by blue-black, edible berries that take their full color in August and last until December.

How to grow: Oregon grape will take sun if kept moist, but prefers light to moderate shade. It does best in moist, well-drained, acid soils. It prefers some protection from drying winter winds. Prune back harshly every three to four years to keep it within bounds.

Uses: The Oregon grape makes a good foundation or accent plant, and is well adapted to shrub borders and naturalizing in wooded sites. It also makes a good plant for erosion control.

Related species: There are several species of *mahonia*. Some are ground covers and others upright shrubs.

Related varieties: There are several selections offered that differ from the species by their dwarf habits or leaf color.

Pittosporum

Pittosporum Tobira
Zone: USDA 8b to 9a

This shrub, native to Asia, is often called "mock orange," creating considerable confusion because the plants in the genus *Philadelphus* also go under that name. The reason for the same common name is simple: They both smell like orange blossoms when they are in bloom.

Description: The pittosporum forms a densely leaved, spreading evergreen shrub or small tree that can grow up to 15 feet tall, usually less. The spoon-shaped, leathery leaves are shiny and dark green. They are borne in whorls that completely hide the stem on younger plants, although older specimens display thick, woody, contorted branches. The early spring flowers form in clusters at the end of the stems. They open white, then turn creamy yellow. They are inconspicuous but extremely fragrant.

How to grow: Plant in full sun to heavy shade in just about any soil, including dry ones. Although overly long branches can be pruned out, this shrub does not respond well to shearing and is of little use for formal hedges.

Uses: The pittosporum is excellent for massing, foundation plantings, or accent use. It also makes a good screen and windbreak as well as a superior informal hedge. In cold climates this shrub is often grown in tubs and brought inside for the winter.

Related varieties: 'Variegata' has gray-green leaves with white to cream edges. 'Wheeler's Dwarf' is an extremely compact form, forming a mound of dark foliage.

American Plum

Prunus americana
Zone: USDA 3b to 9a

This native plum is found throughout much of North America east of the Rockies. It is a shrub or small tree of graceful habit, offering both attractive flowers and fruit to the landscape palette.

Description: The American plum is a thicket-forming shrub, often pruned into a small tree. It can reach 15 to 20 feet in height and bears dark green leaves of only limited fall interest. The branches are often moderately spiny. Its fragrant white flowers are 1 inch across and appear in clusters of two to five. They are followed by tart, 1-inch, yellow to red plums, which are commonly used in preserves.

How to grow: This shrub is particularly easy to grow, adapting to nearly all conditions as long as it gets full sun and a well-drained soil. It can be trained as a small tree by removing any suckers and lower branches. Prune out any weak or disease-infested branches.

Uses: The American plum makes an attractive screen and background plant, and is excellent for naturalizing. It is especially recommended in poor soils or other spots where other shrubs are difficult to grow, since it truly thrives on neglect.

Related species: There are many species of plums with potential ornamental value, including many with purple leaves. One of the best of these is *Prunus* x *blireiana*, with double, fragrant, deep pink flowers in spring. Its reddish purple leaves also appear in spring, turning greenish bronze in summer.

Japanese Podocarpus

Podocarpus macrophyllus
Zone: USDA 8b to 9a

This conifer is, as its common name suggests, native to Japan. It makes a slow-growing but tough landscape shrub. The plant is the hardiest species of an otherwise tropical genus.

Description: An evergreen shrub or small tree with a rather columnar habit, it is frequently pruned into other shapes: purposely in warm climates, accidentally (by cold damage) in borderline ones. The needles are long and flat with a rounded tip and grow up to 4 inches long. They are dark green, leathery, and grow densely all around the stem, giving the branches a bottlebrush effect. The berrylike fruit, red to purple and up to ½ inch long, is not commonly seen in culture.

How to grow: Plant in full sun to moderate shade and in any soil that is well-drained. Prune as needed to maintain the desired shape or to remove cold-damaged branches.

Uses: Japanese podocarpus makes an excellent hedge, screen or, through pruning, small specimen tree. It is commonly grown in containers, notably as a bonsai.

Related varieties: 'Maki' has shorter leaves and lower growth than the species and is the preferred variety for container culture. Several variegated forms are also known.

California Privet

Ligustrum ovalifolium
Zone: USDA 5b to 7

This is a fast-growing shrub usually used in hedges. In spite of its common name, it is native to Japan, not California.

Description: The shrub is either deciduous or semievergreen, depending on the climate. It reaches up to 15 feet in height but is usually kept much smaller through pruning. The white flowers are highly scented but rarely seen, since the plant is often grown as a formal hedge and the flower buds are pruned off. Obviously, if the flowers are pruned off, the shiny black berries are as well.

How to grow: Plant in full sun to light shade. Just about any soil will do, but it requires regular watering during periods of drought. Feed heavily to help it maintain its foliage in winter. It can be pruned severely if necessary. Plant 9 to 12 inches apart for hedge use. Plants reseed readily, becoming invasive.

Uses: The California privet is popular as a formal hedge, but it also makes an excellent informal hedge or screen. It's also a good subject for topiary.

Related species: For colder climates, hardier but deciduous species of privet, like the common privet (*Ligustrum vulgare*) and the Amur privet (*Ligustrum amurense*) are better choices. Both offer several interesting varieties.

Related varieties: There are several variegated clones.

Redroot

Ceanothus velutinus
Zone: USDA 4 to 8

Redroot is one of a large genus of underused, showy American shrubs and small trees that have tremendous garden potential. Most species have limited hardiness and are only useful in the mild western states. A few, however, are extremely hardy and are able to thrive in a wider range of the country.

Description: Redroot is a dense, evergreen shrub with deep-green, finely toothed oval leaves. The top of the foliage has a glossy, resinous coating that is sticky to the touch. The lower surface is hairy. The resin is very fragrant, especially in the hot sun. On a warm day, the fragrance will fill the garden. The plants may grow as tall as 15 feet, but generally they are 4 to 6 feet tall with an equal or greater spread. The creamy white flowers are borne in domed to elongated terminal clusters in early to mid summer.

How to grow: Redroot is an easy-care plant if its simple requirements are met. It thrives in average, well-drained soil in full sun or partial shade. Good drainage is essential if this plant is to survive. In rich, moist soils, the plants will succumb to root rot. These plants keep a compact shape without pruning, especially when grown in full sun. In partial shade, the crown may be a bit more open.

Uses: Chose redroot for dry banks, rockeries or gardens with thin, rocky soil. Place them around patios or decks where the fragrant foliage is easily enjoyed. Plant them between pavers in a terrace or around a swimming pool. They can also be used as a dense hedge.

Related species: New Jersey Tea (*Ceanothus americanus*) is a smaller shrub to 3 feet that is more tolerant of moisture and rich soil. It will also thrive on neglect like its larger cousin. These plants are hardy to Zone 3. Inland Ceanothus (*Ceanothus ovatus*) is similar to New Jersey Tea but has a coarser branching habit.

Rhododendron/Azalea

Rhododendron sp.
Zone: USDA 2 to 11

The rhododendron's broad, leathery leaves and large trusses of pink flowers are known by everyone. But these typical 'iron-clad' rhododendrons (mostly *R. catawbiense* hybrids) are only a drop in the bucket in the huge sea of thousands of rhododendron species and hybrids. To further add to the confusion, the genus also includes all azaleas. Fortunately, their culture is similar: If you can grow one rhododendron, you can (if you respect the proper hardiness zone) grow them all.

Description: Rhododendrons have broad, leathery, persistent leaves, while most azaleas have smaller, thinner, deciduous ones. Plants range from low-growing to tall, treelike shrubs. The flowers are generally cup- or funnel-shaped and appear singly or in clusters at the end of the branches. They are often brightly colored: white, pink, orange, red, mauve, purple, and other colors. Most are spring-bloomers, although there are several summer bloomers and even a few that flower in the autumn.

How to grow: The plants in the rhododendron complex, with few exceptions, are acid-loving plants with shallow roots. Plant them in rich, organic, well-drained soils and protect their root system with a mulch. Although they grow well enough in full sun, they need some protection from winter winds and are best planted in dappled or light shade. They are slow-growing and require little pruning.

Uses: Rhododendrons are good choices for shrub borders, mass plantings, and foundation plantings. Some are good container plants. Most are well adapted to intermediate climates, but only a few are good choices for extremely hot or cold conditions.

Related species: There are too many with variable needs to make suggestions. Check with your county Cooperative Extension office for suggestions of varieties for your area.

Reeves Skimmia

Skimmia Reevesiana (S. japonica reevesiana)
Zone: USDA 7b to 8b

Reeves skimmia is a dwarf broad-leaf evergreen with attractive leaves and colorful fall berries.

Description: Reeves skimmia is a low-growing shrub reaching up to 2 feet high by 3 feet in diameter, eventually forming a compact mound. Its narrowly elliptic leaves are light green. The white flowers appear in terminal clusters in spring, followed by oval, crimson fruits that persist until winter. The contrast between the red fruits and the green foliage is a highly decorative one.

How to grow: Grow in partial to full shade in a rich, moist, well-drained, acid soil. Prune only if rejuvenation is necessary. Unlike most skimmias, Reeves skimmia produces bisexual flowers, so it can produce berries with no need for a separate variety for pollination purposes.

Uses: This shrub is good for foundation plantings, borders, rock gardens, and plantings of mixed broad-leaf evergreens.

Related species: The Japanese skimmia (*Skimmia japonica*), of which the Reeves skimmia is probably only a variety, is taller-growing (up to 4 feet) but otherwise similar in appearance and use. At least one male should be planted to ensure berry production on the female plants.

Smoke Tree

Cotinus Coggyrgria
Zone: USDA 5a to 7b

This tall shrub from Europe and Asia is deservedly popular in North America for its often striking summer and fall colors and plumelike inflorescences.

Description: This multistemmed, deciduous shrub has a spreading, open form and is best kept pruned to prevent it from becoming straggly. The smooth, satiny leaves are nearly round and are blue-green in color. The actual flowers, yellow and very tiny, go practically unnoticed. They are borne in large, long-lasting, fawn-color, feathery inflorescences, appearing in summer and lasting through fall. These make up one of the principal ornamental features of the plant.

How to grow: Full sun is best, especially for the purple-leaf varieties. The smoke tree tolerates just about any soil, even poor, rocky ones. Pruning this shrub is a compromise between two goals: obtaining dense foliage growth (best obtained by heavy annual pruning) or stimulating abundant flowering, since blooms only appear on wood three years old. Good intermediate results can be obtained by occasionally removing older, overly long branches.

Uses: The smoke tree is good for shrub borders and mass plantings. The varieties with colorful foliage make nice, if rather dominant, accent plants.

Related varieties: There are many purple-leaf varieties, and these are far more popular than the species itself. 'Royal Purple' is a particularly choice variety, since its purple color doesn't fade in the summer heat and its inflorescences are purplish red.

Sweet Olive

Osmanthus fragrans
Zone: USDA 8b to 9a

This is a large shrub or small tree most noted for its deliciously scented flowers in summer. It otherwise makes an attractive (but not spectacular) landscape specimen.

Description: The sweet olive is a broad-leaf evergreen of considerable interest. It can reach 20 feet or taller, but cold damage (it is harmed at temperatures below 0 degrees Fahrenheit) keeps it much smaller in most North American conditions. The broadly lanced-shaped leaves are finely toothed and are a glossy medium green in color. Hidden among the leaves are tiny white flowers that would go unnoticed if it weren't for the pervasive, sweet, apricotlike fragrance they give off.

How to grow: This shrub is well suited to all kinds of soils, from heavy to light, and is even quite drought-tolerant once established. It will not tolerate wet conditions for long periods. It prefers light to medium shade, although it will take full sun. Prune as needed to keep it within bounds or to train it to tree form.

Uses: The sweet olive is used as a hedge, screen, or background plant and can be trained into an espalier form. In climates outside its range it can be grown as a tub plant.

Related species: There are several other *osmanthus* that make good garden shrubs, all of them hardier than the sweet olive. One of the most popular is the holly osmanthus, or false holly (*Osmanthus heterophyllus*, zones 7 to 9), with leaves so much like those of American holly that most people can't tell the difference. There are several variegated varieties of holly osmanthus.

Related varieties: *O. fragrans aurantiacus* is identical except for its yellow-orange flowers.

Korean Spice Viburnum

Viburnum Carlesii
Zone: USDA 4b to 8a

The viburnums are a vast and varied group of plants. While many are widely planted, the Korean spice viburnum is one of the most popular. It is a medium-size shrub with pure white, highly perfumed flowers and jet black berries.

Description: The Korean spice viburnum forms a rounded, dense shrub with upright, spreading branches. It usually remains well within bounds at about 4 to 5 feet in height and somewhat more in diameter. The leaves are heart-shaped, dull dark green, and fuzzy, turning wine red in the fall. Its flowers appear in dense halfmoon clusters, a form often called "semi-snowball" (in reference to the snowball viburnum, whose flower clusters are perfectly round). The buds are red to pink, opening to reveal pure white, long-lasting, fragrant flowers. Red berries appear in early fall, finally turning black at full maturity, but they are of secondary interest.

How to grow: This shrub does best in full sun to partial shade in a well-drained, moist, slightly acid soil. Any pruning should be done immediately after the flowers have faded.

Uses: The Korean spice viburnum is mainly used to add spring fragrance to the landscape. It works well in foundation plantings, mass plantings, shrub borders, and the like.

Related species: 'Cayuga' is a complex hybrid with smaller leaves, a more compact growth pattern, and both pink buds and white flowers showing at the same time. *Viburnum* x *Juddii* is a descendant of *V. Carlesii* and is similar to it, although faster-growing and taller.

Related varieties: 'Carlotta' is an improved form with larger leaves.

Old-Fashioned Weigela

Weigela florida
Zone: USDA 4b to 9a

The common name for this Asian shrub comes from its great popularity during the Victorian era. That is not to say that it is now out of style. Nothing could be further from the truth: As the 21st century nears, it seems to be rapidly regaining any popularity it may have lost, helped in its growth by some top-quality new hybrids.

Description: The old-fashioned weigela is a dense, spreading, rounded shrub with branches that eventually arch to the ground. Its leaves are elliptic, pointed, and medium green. The pink, funnel-shaped flowers appear in spring at seemingly every axil. After the first flush of bloom is over, most weigelas bloom again (although sporadically) throughout the rest of the summer.

How to grow: Give it full sun and a well-drained soil for best results. Prune off any winter damage in spring.

Uses: This shrub is ideal for the shrub border or as an accent plant. It makes an attractive informal hedge when spaced 2½ feet apart. It is also available as a small grafted tree.

Related varieties: The old-fashioned weigela has many varieties and is the parent of numerous hybrids, with a wide range of flower colors from white to deep pink and even red to yellow. There are also some beautifully variegated selections and others with purple leaves. Most currently common varieties are dwarf ones.

Pussy Willow, Goat Willow

Salix caprea
Zone: USDA 3a to 9a

The pussy willow is a small tree generally treated as a shrub. It is remarkable for its fuzzy catkins, known to children everywhere as "pussies." They appear in late winter to early spring.

Description: There are several different pussy willows, but this is the one most widely grown. Its oval, pointed leaves are medium green above and grey below, turning yellow before dropping in the fall. The upright-growing, light green stems are stout for a willow.

How to grow: Plant in full sun to moderate shade and in average to moist soil—even waterlogged sites. To produce a maximum number of "pussies," prune to the ground every two years.

Uses: This species has only limited use as a landscape plant and can be used as filler material or in the shrub border. It is rarely used for anything but the production of cut branches.

Related varieties: 'Kilmarnock' is a weeping variety, generally seen trained into tree form, although it can also be used as a ground cover. It is spectacular in all seasons—one of the best small weeping trees—and makes an excellent accent plant.

Common Witch Hazel

Hamamelis virginiana
Zone: USDA 4a to 9a

Native to eastern North America, the common witch hazel is grown as an ornamental shrub for its fall flowers. It was once the commercial source of the essence known as witch hazel.

Description: The common witch hazel is a tall shrub or small tree that grows up to 20 feet in height and spread, possibly more in its native environment. It is remarkable for its fall flowers, usually being the last shrub of the year to bloom. The curious flowers are yellow and fragrant, bearing four straplike petals. They are borne in loose clusters and the display can last from two to four weeks in October, November, or December, depending on the local climate. The leaves are irregular in shape—nearly rounded but with toothed margins. They are medium green in summer, turning golden in the fall before dropping. In some climates, the leaves are still on the shrub when the flowers appear, diminishing the floral effect, although the heady perfume is still a drawing card.

How to grow: Witch hazel does best in full sun to light shade and adapts to most soils, even poor ones. In the wild, it most commonly grows in moist situations.

Uses: Due to its size, the common witch hazel is often reserved for large properties or the back of the shrub border. It makes a good choice for naturalizing.

Related species: The vernal witch hazel (*Hamamelis vernalis*) is similar, but blooms in winter, even in cold climates, often while the ground is still covered in snow. The exact blooming period depends on the local climate, but it can start as early as January in the South. Its flowers are yellow to red. The intermediate witch hazel (*H. x intermedia*) offers a wide range of winter-blooming varieties of varying flower color.

American Yew

Taxus canadensis
Zone: USDA 3a to 6b

The American yew is the hardiest of all yews, yet the eastern North American native has been little exploited in ornamental horticulture.

Description: The American yew has the typical flat, dark green needles of the more horticulturally important yews and similar reddish brown bark. It has a variable growth pattern, from spreading to nearly prostrate, often rooting in the ground as it spreads. The shrub eventually reaches 6 feet in height and 8 feet in width. Its needles have a tendency to turn reddish in winter, but careful selection may reveal, as it has for other conifers, superior clones with more attractive winter color. The berries are bright red.

How to grow: The American yew is normally an understory plant in dense, moist forests, so it should do well in similar conditions in culture. It needs cool conditions and winter shade to do well. Like all yews, it is readily pruned at any season.

Uses: This shrub is best used as an evergreen ground cover in shady spots.

Related species: The Japanese yew (*Taxus cuspidata*) and its hybrid (*T. x media*) are the best-known yews for landscaping purposes. Both offer many varieties, from upright to spreading to conical to low-growing. If not pruned, most eventually attain tree size after many years of growth. They are commonly used in hedges, topiary, and foundation plantings.

VINES

Five-Leaved Akebia

Akebia guinata
Zone: USDA 4b to 9a

This semievergreen Asian climber is grown for its dark green leaves and ease of care.

Description: The five-leaved akebia is a twining vine that grows up to 40 feet high. It has dark blue-green, palmately compound leaves, each producing five oblong leaflets with a distinctive notch at the tip. Their small size, unusual among shrubby vines, gives the plant a delicate look. Its deciduous leaves remain green for a long time in the fall but otherwise offer little fall color. The red-purple flowers are fragrant but are too well hidden by the foliage to be of much interest. The 2- to 4-inch purple, sausagelike pods are a curiosity, but they only seem to be produced when conditions are just right.

How to grow: The vine succeeds equally well in full sun or partial shade and in most garden soils.

Uses: Pergolas, arbors, trellises, and the like. It will also grow into trees and shrubs, over stumps, and otherwise cover unwanted views.

Related species: The three-leaflet akebia (*Akebia trifoliata*) is similar but has three leaflets. There is also a hybrid between the two (*A.* x *pentaphylla*) with intermediate characteristics and (usually) five unnotched leaflets.

Bower Actinidia

Actinidia arguta
Zone: USDA 4b to 8a

This Asian vine, a close relative of the kiwi fruit (*Actinidia chinensis*), grows right to the top of lofty trees in its native land. In North America, where it is mostly grown on trellises and pergolas, it is much more controlled.

Description: The bower actinidia is a tough, vigorous twining shrub with woody stems and broadly ovate, sharply-toothed green leaves with little fall coloration. It produces abundant fragrant white flowers in early summer, usually mostly hidden by the leaves. The greenish yellow berries, about 1 inch long, are edible.

How to grow: Full sun or partial shade and average to poor soil are suitable. It can be pruned at any time. Most bower actinidias bear either male or female flowers, although a few selected clones bear both types. If fruit is desired, either choose a bisexual clone or plant a male and a female on the same support.

Uses: This vine is grown for the fast cover it provides on trellises, arbors, and other structures. It has little ornamental value other than its green leaves. It can also grow on trees.

Related species: The Kolomikta actinidia (*Actinidia Kolomikta*) is becoming increasingly popular, especially the male clones, which have leaves whose bottom half is splashed pink and silvery white. It would appear that most plants in culture are male, so it is unlikely most gardeners will be able to grow it for its edible berries.

Related varieties: 'Issai' is a self-fertile selection.

American Bittersweet

Celastrus scandens
Zone: USDA 3b to 8b

This climbing shrub is native to North America east of the Rocky Mountains. It is an extremely rampant grower and care should be taken not to let it "escape" into desirable trees or shrubs.

Description: This woody shrub climbs by twining around its support and is so efficient that it frequently strangles the trees it grows on. It can grow to whatever height its host attains. The stems are woody. Its deep green, glossy leaves are ovate and pointed, turning yellow before dropping in the fall. The male and female flowers, inconspicuous, appear on separate plants. If pollinated, female flowers bear striking orange berries in the fall, lasting through much of the winter.

How to grow: This plant will thrive in nearly any soil that is not constantly wet. It requires full sun or partial shade to get started. Make sure to plant at least one male per group of three females to ensure pollination. Prune severely in early spring to stimulate flowering and also cut off unwanted suckers.

Uses: American bittersweet is often used to cover unsightly fences and rock piles. It can be trained up arbors, trellises, and even mature trees, but should never be allowed to climb young trees or shrubs because the vine's twisting woody stems can cut off their sap as they grow. The seeds, although poisonous to humans, seem to do no harm to the birds that eat them in winter. The fruit-bearing branches are often harvested for dried winter decorations.

Related species: The Loesener bittersweet (*Celastrus Loeseneri* or, more correctly, *C. Rosthornianus*) is similar, but less hardy and not as attractive.

Boston Ivy

Parthenocissus tricuspidata
Zone: USDA 4b to 8b

Although the common name suggests a Boston origin, this climber is actually native to Asia. It is also not an ivy (*Hedera*) or even a close relative, but a member of the grape family.

Description: Boston ivy can climb even smooth surfaces thanks to the sticky discs at the end of its tendrils, eventually reaching heights of up to 60 feet. Its branches are thin and rambling at first, turning woody and thick with age. The same plant will produce two different kinds of leaves: The majority are entire with three lobes and look rather like maple leaves; others, often smaller, are compound with three leaflets. The leaves are shiny and medium green, turning red, yellow, or orange before dropping in the fall. It is only when the leaves fall that the berries, dark blue and clustered like grapes, become noticeable.

How to grow: Plant in sun or partial shade, although branches exposed to full winter sun are subject to severe dieback in the northern part of the plant's range. It tolerates most soils, even dry ones, but for fast growth, supply rich, moist, well-drained organic soil. Attach young plants to their support at first: They'll soon send out new tendrils and begin to climb on their own.

Uses: Boston ivy is generally used on walls and as a ground cover.

Related varieties: 'Lowii' is a smaller-leaf variety with multilobed leaves and a purplish coloration when young. 'Purpurea' has reddish purple leaves throughout the summer.

Jackman's Clematis

Clematis x *Jackmanii*
Zone: USDA 4 to 6

This old-fashioned hybrid is still the most popular clematis in gardens and is a parent of many of the more modern large-flowered varieties.

Description: The plant's 4- to 7-inch, deep violet flowers with flattened sepals are well known by gardeners everywhere. They appear on new wood all summer until frost and can be extremely abundant. The Jackman's clematis climbs by wrapping its leaf petioles around narrow objects and can reach 12 feet in height. Its leaves are dark green and pinnate. The fuzzy seed heads are another point of attraction.

How to grow: Plant so that the roots are in a cool, shady spot but the upper growth is in full sun (for example, at the base of a shrub). The soil should be light, organic, and well-drained, but not constantly wet. Use an abundant cover of mulch. Clematis grows well in alkaline soil but does not require it for healthy growth. In early spring, prune to the ground those plants that, like Jackman's clematis, start anew from their base in the spring. Those that bloom on old wood (usually early spring-bloomers) should only be pruned lightly. In cold climates, mound plentiful soil at the base of the plant for the winter.

Uses: Jackman's clematis is spectacular for use on rock walls, trellises, fences, in shrubs and trees, and other climbing areas.

Related varieties and species: There is an entire series of large-flowered clematis similar to Jackman's clematis, including various hybrids and selections from a wide range of species. They require approximately the same care. The colors range from white to pink, red, purple, and blue. Some have bicolored or double flowers. The genus *Clematis* also includes a wide variety of small-flower species and hybrids, and even some perennials and subshrubs.

Creeping Fig

Ficus pumila
Zone: USDA 8b to 11

This small-leaved, evergreen, Asian creeper climbs by means of clinging aerial roots and can fix itself like cement to the objects it climbs. Don't be fooled by the apparent fragility of this tiny vine. It can climb to 60 feet or more, and a single stem cutting can grow to cover the entire side of a large building in only a few years.

Description: Tiny, thin, heart-shaped leaves in medium green grow flat against the surface of the object it climbs. The stem, thin and weak-looking at first, become thick and woody as the vine grows. At maturity, the vine produces projecting branches and adult foliage—larger, thicker, 2- to 4-inch hairy leaves—and 2-inch pear-shaped figs.

How to grow: Grow in full sun to partial shade in any moist, well-drained soil. Prune off adult branches if fruit is not wanted. In cold climates it is often grown as a houseplant.

Uses: This climber is a top choice for permanently hiding unattractive walls, tree trunks, and garden structures, or where a flat wall of greenery is desired.

Related varieties: *Ficus pumila* 'Minima' has small leaves, while the oak-leaved creeping fig (*F. pumila* 'Quercifolia') has equally tiny, quilted, maplelike leaves. There are also several variegated varieties.

Crimson Glory Vine

Vitis Coignetiae
Zone: USDA 5b to 9a

This Asian species is perhaps the most spectacular of all vines. It is a true grape vine, but its fruits aren't edible or attractive. Instead, it is grown for its colorful foliage.

Description: A fast-growing, woody vine climbing by means of tendrils, the crimson glory vine can reach 50 feet in one season. The rounded leaves measure up to 1 foot across and are heart-shaped with three to five lobes. They are green on top and attractively rust-colored underneath, turning a flamboyant coppery red in the fall. Its "grapes" are purple-black berries most visible in the fall after the leaves drop.

How to grow: For best color, plant in full sun and poor soil. Oddly enough, the more the roots are restricted, the better the plant grows and the more colorful it is. As a result, the crimson glory vine often gives its best results in those tight spots between the sidewalk and the wall where nothing else will grow.

Uses: It is a perfect choice for training up walls, trellises, trees, and other places where a fast-growing, colorful vine is needed.

Related species: Many grape vines can be used ornamentally, including most fruiting types. Two good choices are the fox grape (*Vitis Labrusca*) and the riverbank grape (*Vitis riparia*). Both produce attractive foliage and edible grapes which, while they may not be typical table or wine grapes, are often of eating quality or can be used in cooking.

Cross Vine

Bignonia capreolata
Zone: USDA 5 to 9

This vigorous evergreen or semievergreen vine wants it both ways: Not only does it climb by twining leaf tendrils around narrow objects but each tendril is also tipped with a sticky disc, allowing it to climb up flat surfaces. This climbing shrub is native to the southeastern United States.

Description: The leaves and stems are evergreen in the South, reaching up to 50 feet in the air, but are killed to the ground each year at the northern limits of its culture. Fortunately, it sprouts vigorously from its roots, although it tends to grow back only as a ground cover. The leaf is attractive and composed of two lance-shaped leaflets. It is medium green in summer, sometimes reddening in the fall. The beautiful trumpet-shaped summer flowers, 2 inches long, are red outside and yellow inside. Flat 5- to 7-inch seed pods follow in the fall.

How to grow: Plant it in full sun or partial shade in ordinary garden soil. Hard pruning seems to stimulate bloom.

Uses: As an evergreen vine it screens undesirable views permanently. It climbs smooth surfaces such as walls (weakly), as well as trellises and other plant supports.

Related species and varieties: There are no related species or varieties.

Dutchman's-pipe

Aristolochia durior
Zone: USDA 4 to 8

This is one of the hardy species of an otherwise tropical genus. Native to the eastern United States, it is unmistakable with its large, dark green, heart-shaped leaves.

Description: This twining vine can grow to 30 feet in height and is particularly vigorous once established. (If cut to the ground in spring, it can regain its full former height in a single growing season.) Unfortunately, the heart-shaped leaves half-hide the curious flowers, which—as the common name suggests—are shaped like a Dutchman's pipe. They are yellowish green with a flared brownish purple mouth.

How to grow: Full sun or partial shade and ordinary garden soil seem to suit this climber just fine.

Uses: Dutchman's-pipe is a fast cover for arbors, pillars, trellises, pergolas, stumps, or any other object that has to be hidden from view. This twiner will only climb a smooth surface if string or wire is provided.

Related species: *A. sempervirens*, a similar species, is evergreen in warm climates. In colder climates, it dies to the ground in winter.

Trumpet Honeysuckle

Lonicera sempervirens
Zone: USDA 4 to 9

This climbing shrub, native to south-central United States, is evergreen over much of its range, becoming deciduous only in the coldest sectors.

Description: This twining vine can grow up to 50 feet in height if it has something that high to cling to. Around most homes, it is unlikely to be required to reach more than 20 feet. The opposite blue-green leaves are variable: Even on the same branch, some have short petioles, some have none and join together at the base, and still others are perfoliate (joined so completely the stem seems to pass through the leaf). The tubular red flowers are produced in clusters at the tips of the branches throughout the summer. Unlike many flowering vines, they are scentless. Bright red berries appear at the end of the summer and last through much of the fall.

How to grow: Plant in full sun to partial shade and ordinary to poor but well-drained soil. Overly rich soils tend to promote excessive stem growth while reducing flowering. This species is also quite drought-resistant, although it prefers its soil kept evenly moist.

Uses: Trumpet honeysuckle makes both a good ground cover and a climbing vine for trellises, pergolas, fences, and the like. It requires a strong support on which to grow. Harsh pruning tends to create both more controlled, attractive plant and to stimulate bloom. Hummingbirds are drawn to its flowers.

Related species: There are several different climbing honeysuckles. One of the choicest species is the woodbine honeysuckle (*Lonicera Periclymenum*), with flowers that are purple to yellow outside and cream inside. 'Berries Jubilee' is particularly choice, with red and yellow flowers and bright red berries.

Related varieties: 'Sulphurea' has bright yellow flowers, while 'Superba' has orange-scarlet ones.

English Ivy

Hedera Helix
Zone: USDA 6a to 9a

Probably no other plant offers as much variety in foliage as the English ivy: cut-leaves; rounded leaves; twisted and crinkled leaves; leaves mottled, splashed, and splattered yellow, cream, white, or pink. The list goes on and on. Whatever your need in a climbing plant, there is probably an English ivy to match it.

Description: In its juvenile form, the species has three- to five-lobed, dark, pale veined, evergreen leaves about 1½ to 2 inches long. It climbs objects via sticky aerial roots, reaching 60 feet or more in height. The adult form, which usually does not develop until the ivy has reached the top of the object it is climbing, has outward-growing, nonclimbing stems and larger, rounded or spoon-shaped leaves. The adult form produces yellow flowers and black berries.

How to grow: Full sun to heavy shade suit it wonderfully, but some protection from the drying winter sun is advised. It will grow in nearly any kind of soil, even salty ones, but prefers rich, moist, organic, well-drained conditions.

Uses: English ivy is ideal for cloaking walls and fences. It also makes a good ground cover.

Related species: Algerian ivy (*Hedera algeriensis*, also called *H. canariensis*) is commonly grown in warmer climates (zones 9 to 11). It forms broad, large, evergreen leaves with three to seven shallow lobes. 'Gloire-de-Marengo,' shiny and dark green with patches of white and silver green, is a popular variety.

Related varieties: These are too numerous to mention. Since many English ivies suffer from winter damage in cold climates, it is worth briefly naming a few of the hardiest varieties: 'Baltica,' 'Bulgaria,' 'Hebron,' 'Rochester,' 'Rumania,' 'Thorndale,' and 'Wilsonii.'

Yellow Jasmine

Jasminum nudiflorum
Zone: USDA 6b to 11

If left on its own, this deciduous vine acts more like a ground cover, with its long stems creeping over the ground. But properly trained, it makes an attractive and floriferous climbing vine.

Description: This shrubby vine, growing up to 15 feet, is renowned for its winter flowers: bright yellow trumpets, 1½ to 2 inches long, bursting from waxy red buds. They appear in the middle of winter when the plant is still without leaves. Unlike most jasmines, the yellow jasmine is not fragrant. The pinnately compound leaves, each with three leaflets, appear in the spring and last until late fall, dropping off without much color change. The green stems make an interesting contrast to the woody browns and grays of other deciduous woody plants.

How to grow: For best blooms, grow in full sun, although it will grow and flower in partial shade. For faster growth, plant in good, rich, well-drained garden soil. On the other hand, if you want to restrict its growth (a distinct possibility with this rampant grower), give it poorer soil. Rejuvenate aging plants every three to five years by cutting them back to ground level.

Uses: The yellow jasmine can be trained up structures and trunks or down over walls and fences. It can also be allowed to grow as a ground cover, in which case it will root wherever it touches the ground, providing excellent erosion control.

Related species: The primrose jasmine (*Jasminum Mesnyi*) is similar in habit and form to the yellow jasmine, but larger in all its parts. It blooms later, in spring rather than winter.

Carolina Jessamine

Gelsemium sempervirens
Zone: USDA 8a to 9a

This species, native to the southeastern United States, is an evergreen climber with yellow, funnel-shaped flowers. It is commonly planted in zones 8 and 9.

Description: This vine climbs via thin, wiry twining stems and reaches up to 20 feet in height. Its leaves are lance-shaped and dark, shiny green. The 1-inch-long tubular flowers are produced in spring and early summer and sometimes again in fall. They are highly fragrant.

How to grow: Plant in full sun for best bloom, although it will grow and flower in shade. Moist, well-drained, organic soils are best, but it will adapt to poorer conditions.

Uses: Carolina jessamine can be grown on downspouts, trellises, structures, fences, mailboxes, or even into small trees. It can also be allowed to trail, making a good ground cover.

Related varieties: 'Pride of Augusta' is a double-flowered form.

Blue Passionflower

Passiflora caerulea
Zone: USDA 7b to 9a

The name "passionflower" comes from the use Spanish missionaries made of the plant's complex flower. They used it to describe the passion of Christ, with each of the flower's parts having a special significance.

Description: The blue passionflower grows to 20 feet, climbing by means of tendrils. It is evergreen in warm climates, deciduous in intermediate ones, and is killed to the ground in zone 7, sprouting again from its roots each spring in plenty of time to bloom abundantly through the summer. The shiny, dark green leaves are deeply lobed, with five to nine divisions. The 3- to 4-inch flowers, produced throughout the summer, have white to pinkish petals, but the overall effect is blue due to the numerous blue filaments which fan out in a circle from the center and are almost as long as the flowers. A yellow to orange fruit, 2½ inches long and edible, sometimes forms after the flowers fade.

How to grow: Plant in full sun in a rich, deep, moist, well-drained sandy loam. Prune heavily to remove deadwood and to control excess growth.

Uses: The blue passionflower is good for trellises, fences, pergolas, and the like. It also grows well in tubs and is often grown indoors in the North and placed outside for the summer.

Related species and varieties: The red passionflower (*Passiflora coccinea*) and the hybrid passionflower (*P. alatocaerulea*), with blue, pink, purple, or white flowers, are also commonly grown. Passionflowers have been used extensively in hybridizing, and many new, hardier varieties are being tested.

Silver-lace Vine

Polygonum aubertii
Zone: USDA 4b to 8b

This twining, deciduous vine is a vigorous, rampant grower, ideal for covering eyesores. It is attractive both in leaf and flower.

Description: The shrubby stems can reach 30 feet in height—up to 20 feet in a single season—and are well cloaked in shiny, bright green, 1- to 2½-inch, nearly triangular leaves. They are reddish when they emerge, becoming bright green at maturity. The vines develop 6-inch clusters of fragrant white flowers in the late summer and early fall. The individual flowers are tiny and insignificant, but all together the flowers give the vine a look of a hazy mass of white lace. In zone 4 the silver-lace vine may be killed to the ground in severe winters, but it usually comes back beautifully the following spring.

How to grow: Plant in full sun or partial shade. The silver-lace vine adapts well to most soils, even dry ones. Because of its very rapid growth, it may require heavy pruning.

Uses: Silver-lace vine provides good cover for wire fences, bare banks, old stumps, etc. This vine is especially attractive when grown into small trees. It is pollution-tolerant and well adapted to city use.

Related species: The Russian vine (*P. baldschuanicum*) is similar but with smooth branches.

Trumpet Creeper

Campsis radicans
Zone: USDA 4b to 9a

The trumpet creeper is native to the southeastern United States but has escaped from culture and now grows wild throughout much of the country. It is raised for its orange and scarlet flowers.

Description: This is a vigorous vine, climbing by means of sticky aerial roots to a height of up to 30 feet. It produces pinnately compound leaves with 9 to 11 coarsely toothed leaflets. The trumpet-shaped, scarlet and orange flowers appear at the ends of the branches throughout much of the summer.

How to grow: The trumpet creeper grows well in full sun and literally any kind of soil, even out of cracks in pavement. Attach young plants to their support to get them started; they'll soon climb on their own. Prune heavily in late winter to control the vine's vigorous growth.

Uses: This fast-growing vine climbs just about anything that doesn't move, so it has a wide variety of uses as a climbing plant. This plant also attracts hummingbirds.

Related species: The Chinese trumpet creeper (*Campsis grandiflora*) is similar but less hardy (zones 8 to 11). A hybrid of *C. radicans* and *C. grandiflora*, called *C.* x *Tagliabuana*, is intermediate between the two but quite hardy. 'Madame Galen' is a choice variety with deep red flowers.

Related varieties: 'Flava' is an attractive yellow-flowered version.

Wisteria

Wisteria floribunda
Zone: USDA 5b to 9a

This is one of the most popular flowering vines. It is breathtaking when in full flower.

Description: The twining climbing stems of the wisteria grow quickly and look fragile at first. With time, however, they become woody and even trunklike. (This is not a good vine to grow on a flimsy support.) The pinnate leaves, medium green and glossy, are slow to appear in the spring and drop off without much color change in autumn. The flowers, which appear just as the leaves are emerging, are violet or blue-violet in color and like pea flowers. They are borne in long strands that drip down from the stems like a violet waterfall. The velvety, beanlike pods are more a curiosity than an attraction, but they do add some interest during winter.

How to grow: Container-grown plants that are slightly root-bound seem to be the fastest to establish themselves and to flower, but they can still take a few years before really creating the desired effect. Plant in full sun in a rich, moist, well-drained loam. Soils close to neutral—or even slightly alkaline—are best. Avoid applying nitrogen fertilizer or the vine will tend to produce mostly foliage. If the plant fails to flower after five years, dig into its root zone with a sharp shovel to root prune it (sometimes a sudden shock seems to get it going). Ordinary trellises are often crushed by the weight of this massive vine. Consider something more solid, like metal pipe or PVC.

Uses: Wisterias are great for patio coverage and growing over large structures. They can also be trained to tree form.

Related species: The Chinese wisteria (*Wisteria sinensis*) is similar, but has mauve flowers and 11 leaflets instead of 9.

Related varieties: There are several wisterias in shades of white, pink, lavender, and violet. 'Lawrence,' a very hardy selection with violet-blue flowers, is best for northern gardens.

SPECIALTY GARDENS

A flourish of nothing but glorious roses, an early springtime splash of bulb color, the soothing quiet of trickling water. These are all possible if you decide to design your own specialty garden. It's up to you to decide how special a garden you want.

A collection of flowering and fragrant roses can create a spectacular effect, adding a touch of elegance to any yard. These roses exude charm with a splash of greenery.

CHAPTER 1

THE ROSE GARDEN: ROSES ARE FOR EVERYONE

Roses have been considered special since the dawn of history. The ancient Egyptians grew and appreciated them, as did the Chinese, the Greeks, and the Romans. Empress Josephine, Napoleon's wife, surrounded her palace, Malmaison, with every variety of rose then available. As immigrants flooded into the New World, they often carried rose bushes with them, sometimes bringing them right across the continent in wagon trains.

Roses have traditionally been grown in gardens of their own because they don't particularly like competition from other plants. As recently as the 1800s, though, the beauty of the rose garden was a fleeting thing. Roses burst into spectacular bloom for a short period in early summer and then showed nothing but foliage through the rest of the growing season, although their brightly colored fruits (rose hips) did offer winter color. Modern hybrid roses changed everything. With the perpetual blooming habits of hybrid roses, rose gardens can now bloom through summer and deep into fall, and in warm climates they bloom nearly year-round.

Whatever you're looking for in a flower—beautiful form, vast array of color, exotic fragrance—roses offer it. The rose garden will remain with us for many generations.

Starting Your Rose Garden

Lovely blossoms such as the above can take one's breath away.

Traditional rose gardens are rather formal affairs. The beds are often laid out in geometric patterns, with tree roses at each corner and an arbor of climbing roses at the rear. Your home rose garden doesn't have to be quite so static. As long as proper planting distances are respected, the rose garden can take on any appearance from a near-formal style to a flowing island with an irregular outline. The only rule that really should be followed is that taller plants should go in the center or rear of the bed.

Purists grow only roses in a rose garden. Gardeners with less stringent ideas can introduce spring-flowering bulbs, noninvasive perennials, low-growing annuals, or other plants. The upkeep of these other plants should not damage the roses they are designed to set off. If you're really adventurous, you can develop an entire garden of roses in individual containers on a patio or balcony.

Although roses are quite specific in their needs, you can find a place for them with a little searching in just about any yard. The first requirement is plenty of sun: six hours or more a day if possible. Some roses will do well with less. Early morning sun is better than late afternoon sun since the flowers last longer under cooler conditions.

Roses will adapt to most moderately fertile soils, even sand ones. Just make sure you work in plenty of organic matter: compost, peat moss, well-rotted manure, etc. Test the soil for pH before planting. Roses prefer a pH of 6.5 to 6.8, although they will tolerate levels from 6.0 to 7.5. Any soil that is extremely acid or alkaline should be corrected by adding, respectively, lime or powdered sulphur.

Good drainage is essential in the rose garden. If your soil is constantly damp, consider either adding drainage tiles or raising the bed 8 to 10 inches above ground level. Soil that drains too well can be improved by adding organic material and through careful irrigation.

Proper placement is also essential for a successful rose garden. Avoid areas near large trees and shrubs, since roses are intolerant of root competition. A certain amount of air circulation is beneficial, so avoid low-lying pockets. Windy spots can be moderated by using a windbreak. In cold climates, planting on a slight slope will help prevent damage from a late spring frost.

Bare-root or packaged roses are best planted in spring after all danger of frost has passed. In the deep South, the cooler winter months are the ideal planting time. Container-grown roses can theoretically be planted any time during the growing season. Avoid planting during the dry, hot summer months.

1 Planting Bare-Root Roses

Dig a hole 15 to 18 inches deep and equally wide. Mix an abundant amount of organic matter into the soil removed. Form a firm cone of this improved soil in the center of the hole.

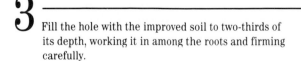

2 Remove packaging from the rose and prune lightly, removing any broken canes and cutting the others back to 8 inches. The pruning cut should be ¼ inch above an outward-pointing bud. Trim the roots to about 8 inches and spread them out. Set the plant on the cone. Make sure the bud union is at the proper depth for your climate.

3 Fill the hole with the improved soil to two-thirds of its depth, working it in among the roots and firming carefully.

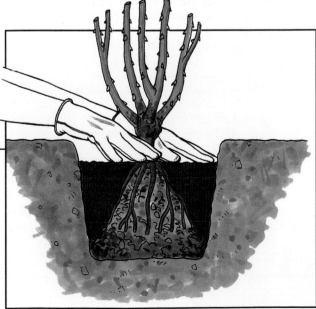

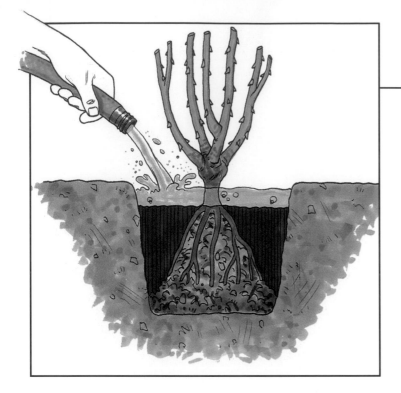

Fill the depression surrounding the plant with water and let drain. Then fill the remainder of the hole with the improved soil.

4

5 Mound soil up around the base of the plant until growth begins. (This may be a few weeks.) After growth begins, remove the mound of soil.

Planting container-grown roses in the garden requires a different planting technique. Dig a hole slightly larger and deeper than the container. Remove the plant and set it at the proper level. Water well when the planting hole has been filled with soil to two-thirds its depth. If the container is biodegradable, it can be placed in the hole but make sure you cut slits in its side. For more information, see the section on planting shrubs, page 328.

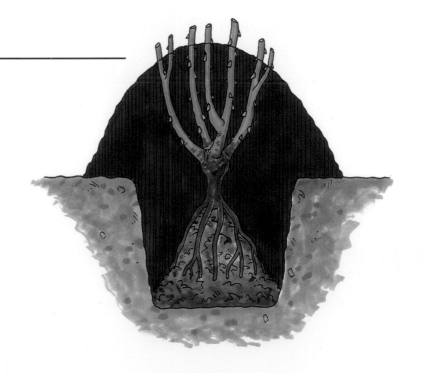

Planting Depth

In warmer climates, plant roses so that the bud union (the knob where the canes join the main stalk) is just above ground level. In climates where temperatures regularly drop below freezing, plant them more deeply, with the bud union covered by one or two inches of soil.

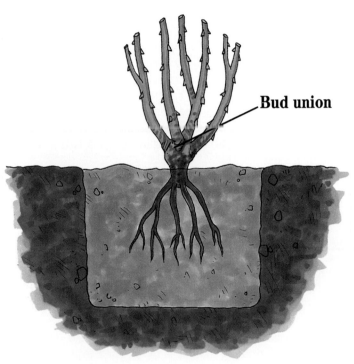

Bud union

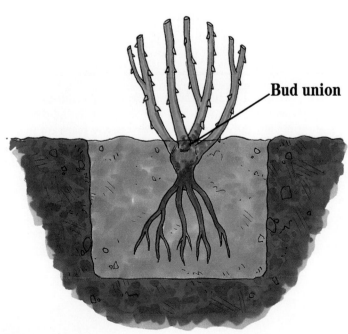

Bud union

Maintaining Your Rose Garden

A climbing rose next to a door or gate makes for a pleasant effect.

Fertilizing—When you mix abundant organic material into the planting soil, you establish a good basis for healthy growth. Occasional applications of fertilizer rich in phosphate, however, can be useful if your soil is low in phosphorous. Wait until growth has begun in spring before fertilizing. A second application can be made in midsummer. Avoid fertilizing in the fall since it can promote late growth, which reduces hardiness.

Watering—Recently planted roses should be watered carefully to make sure they don't dry out. Keep the soil moist but not wet. Established roses are more resilient but still require watering during periods of drought. In dry climates, regular irrigation may be necessary. Apply water slowly over a period of several hours so it soaks deeply into the soil. Frequent, brief waterings will not moisten the plant's entire root system. An organic mulch, applied in early summer at the base of the plant, will help keep roots cool and moist, even during periods of moderate drought.

Pruning Shrub and Climbing Roses—Shrub and climbing roses require less pruning than bush roses. Their pruning needs are limited to pruning out any winter-damaged stems and weak growth. Occasionally, thick, older canes should be removed to allow room for younger, more vigorous ones. Climbing roses can be deadheaded in the same way as bush roses to encourage repeated flowering. Shrub roses, on the other hand, will produce colorful hips for added color in the fall and winter if their faded flowers are not removed.

Winter Protection—In climates where temperatures rarely drop below 10 degrees Fahrenheit, winter protection is not necessary. Where temperatures drop below 10 degrees Fahrenheit but only rarely below zero, protection is optional, but soil-mounding is recommended. The further temperatures drop below 0 degrees Fahrenheit, the greater the protection needed. In zones 4 and colder, surround the entire rose plant with straw or leaves packed into a basket or commercial rose cone.

Pest Management—Roses have the reputation of suffering greatly from pests and diseases. However, a regular program of prevention backed up with prompt treatment of any incipient infestations will keep your roses healthy year-round.

Start by keeping your rose garden meticulously clean. Remove weak, diseased, or dead stems by pruning 1 inch below the damaged section into healthy tissue. Remove fallen petals and leaves without delay. Don't allow weeds to grow; they may harbor insects and disease. Cultivate the soil regularly to expose insect and diseases to the sun. Most insects can be removed with a spray of water or by shaking the bush over a basin of soapy water. Diseases that can't be eliminated by pruning can be controlled by applying appropriate pesticides.

Disease-Resistant Roses—Until recently, bush roses such as hybrid teas and grandifloras were developed strictly for their flowers. As a result, they were often inherently susceptible to disease and required regular, year-long pesticide treatments to remain healthy. This situation is changing, and newer hybrids are often chosen specifically with disease resistance in mind.

It would be impossible to prepare a complete list of disease-resistant roses: Not only are new ones being developed all the time but the same rose can be disease resistant in one area but quite susceptible in another. Check with a garden center or a local rose society to learn which roses are best suited to your locality.

1 Pruning

Pruning is necessary to maintain healthy roses. If
left entirely on their own, rose plants will produce
dense, tangled growth, which opens a path to
disease. Roses are best pruned at the end of the
dormant season, just as buds are swelling but before
new leaves appear. First prune out dead or diseased
growth, then any branches that rub together. Young
plants should be further pruned to about four stems,
which are called canes, by removing weaker canes.
Established plants can be allowed eight or more
canes, especially in warmer climates. Prune the
remaining canes back to about one-half (in cold
climates) to one-third their original height. Pruning
will open up the plant, letting in light and
circulation, and it will also stimulate growth of
young, healthy canes

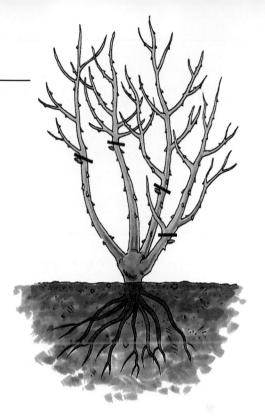

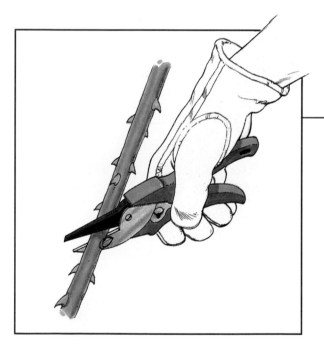

Cut canes ¼ inch above an outward-pointing bud at
a 45° to 60° angle. **2**

3

During the rose's growing period, remove any weak
or dead growth and any suckers growing from the
base. To encourage maximum flower size, many rose
enthusiasts disbud; that is, they pinch out all buds
except one per stem. Deadhead (prune off flower
stems when the blooms fade) to stimulate repeated
flowering.

Winter Protection

1

Mound soil up around the plant to a depth of 12 inches. If necessary, surround the plant with a ring of wire mesh or a rose collar.

2

Once the ground freezes, place a thick mulch of organic matter around the plant. This will help prevent the alternate freezing and thawing of the ground that does so much harm.

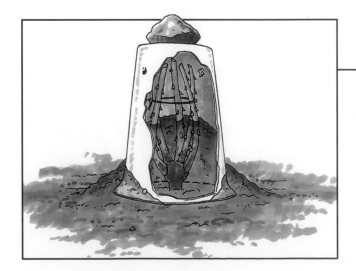

3

In very cold climates, instead of mulch cover the shrubs with a basket or commercial rose cone, pruning just enough so the covering can be put in place. If you use plastic foam rose cones, punch a few air holes to allow some air circulation.

4

All winter protections should be removed when the danger of severe frost is over. If possible, remove protections on a cloudy day so tender, new growing tips are not burned by sudden exposure to strong sun.

1 Protecting Climbers and Tree Roses

Climbing roses need special winter protection in cold climates. Bend the stems over and hold them in place with stakes. Mound soil over the stems. In very cold climates, dig a trench next to the plants and bury the canes for the winter, mounding up even more soil. This method is also used for hybrid tea roses in zones 3 and 4.

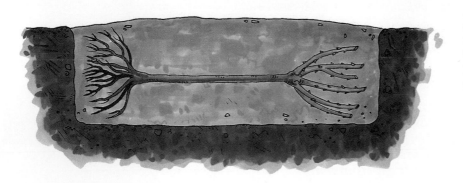

2

A tree rose, whose bud union is even more exposed to cold air than other roses, should be buried entirely in cold climates. Dig up the root ball and place the entire plant in a deep trench. In the spring, delicately remove the soil and place the plant back into its original position.

This rock garden has a bit of everything—rocks, plenty of greenery, water, and even a quaint gazebo—showing the versatility of this type of garden. Imagine passing an afternoon in such a tranquil environment.

CHAPTER 2

THE ROCK GARDEN: AN ALPINE MEADOW IN YOUR YARD

There are as many reasons for building a rock garden as there are people who build them. Rockeries are an easy and unique way to reduce lawn care on a hard-to-mow slope. They can re-create a piece of nature in the back yard. They can add an element of movement to an excessively flat landscape. They make an ideal site for a collection of delicate alpine plants and are also perfect for highlighting less delicate but tiny plants that would otherwise go unnoticed.

A rock garden is more than just a haphazard pile of rocks. It requires adequate planning, an appropriate selection of rocks, and careful placing of stones. Your goal is to re-create, albeit in miniature, a natural mountain slope in your own yard. This is not as easy as it seems, but the next few pages will guide you in preparing and planting the site.

Fortunately, a properly designed rock garden requires little care. Most rock garden plants are drought tolerant, need little fertilizer, and rarely require any pruning. The only main task is weeding, and this can be reduced to a minimum by making sure all perennial weeds are removed from both the site and any soil being added before starting the rock garden.

Planning a Rock Garden

Slopes make an excellent spot for a rock garden.

There are rock garden styles to suit every taste, but great care must be taken that the style chosen suits the site. For example, a huge mound of rocks rising out of nowhere will look very much out of place in a grassy lawn. Flat, craggy limestone, while attractive in its own right, will not suit a yard dominated by a fieldstone house. Remember, a rock garden is essentially a re-creation of a mountain slope. Picture this in your mind and try to create it on a scale that suits your growing space.

The easiest rock garden to plan is always a natural one. If your garden has a natural stone outcropping, you can easily bring out its beauty by cutting back invasive roots, removing a few shrubs and trees to increase sunlight, and possibly digging away some soil to better reveal the natural rock. Even a small rock outcropping can be used to advantage by adding similar rocks to repeat and accentuate the original pattern.

Slopes are ideally suited to rock gardens. Not only are they hard to maintain otherwise (just ask anyone who has tried to mow a hillside lawn) but it is also easy to integrate rocks into a slope and make it look as though they were put there by Mother Nature. Flat surfaces are not obvious choices for a rock garden, but don't rule them out entirely. The next few pages will suggest ways of creating a successfully integrated rockery even in a flat area.

Generally speaking, rock gardens should be placed in full sun; most plants you'll use in a rock garden love sunlight. Although you can create an attractive rock garden in a shady spot, your plant choices will be more limited.

Perhaps no other step is as important in planning a rock garden as choosing the right rocks. All too often, a "rock garden" consists of a pile of rounded river stones of various sizes and colors randomly strewn on the ground: Nothing could look more artificial! Instead, use rocks that are uniform in color and texture; ideally, they should be angular in shape with distinct lines or strata. If these similar rocks are placed at roughly the same angle, it will look as though Mother Nature deposited them.

Rounded rocks, however, need not be banished from the rock garden, but they should be similar in color and texture. For a natural look, set the first ones quite deeply in the ground. As more rocks are added, make sure that about half of each rock is hidden from sight.

Make sure some of the rocks are very large ones: true boulders. These larger rocks are the keystones of the rock garden. One rule of thumb: If it can be moved by one person, it's too small. Once the boulders are in place, medium-size rocks can be added. Smaller rocks will be needed to fill in any gaps.

Rock gardens are also ideal sites for a waterfall. Even a steady stream of water droplets landing in a tiny pond at the garden's base will do. In fact, smaller waterfalls are often the best choice for the home rockery: large cascades of frothy, foaming water are for very massive rock gardens.

Building a Rock Garden

Rocks of the same color and texture help tie a rock garden together.

Once the rocks have been chosen, prepare the site by excavating to the proper depth. Make sure you remove any weeds or lawn grasses now: You don't want them reappearing later between two heavy rocks where you can't get to them.

Most alpine plants require perfect drainage. If your soil is naturally heavy, put down a drainage layer of six inches of gravel or crushed rock. Cover this layer with landscape fabric or two inches of sand so the soil you add later won't percolate through. Unless the soil taken from the excavation already drains perfectly, mix it with an equal quantity of sand. If you don't intend to grow alpine plants, simply add about one-quarter compost or peat moss to increase the soil's organic content. If you intend to grow mostly alpine plants, check the soil's pH and amend it with ground limestone if necessary; alpine plants tend to prefer neutral to alkaline soils. Only a few rock garden plants (heathers and dwarf rhododendrons are among them) need acid soil.

To "anchor" a rock garden to its landscape, consider adding a few minor rock outcrops in peripheral areas. Also, add to the base of the rock garden a flat area of gravel or crushed rock in the same shade as the dominate rock. This is known as a "scree garden." This will help prevent lawn grasses from invading the garden, and the effect will appear quite natural, as if bits and pieces of broken rock had fallen off the rock outcropping over the years.

In regions where droughts are frequent, consider adding an irrigation system from the outset. The simplest method is burying a perforated garden hose just below the surface of the soil: It can then be attached to a supply hose whenever watering is necessary.

Rock Depth

One secret to a natural-looking rock garden is making sure half of each rock is hidden from sight. Rocks with almost all of their surface exposed will look artificial.

Building a Rock Garden on a Level Site

To build a rock garden on a level site, begin by excavating the site for placement of the largest rocks. Make sure they are firmly anchored and properly positioned.

If you want your garden to have a tiered effect—which is ideal when you are using flat sedimentary stone—fill in the center of the garden with rocks that don't match your garden's style. Use crushed rock or gravel to fill in any gaps. Next, place the desired rocks on top of this mound. Any spaces remaining in the construction can then be covered in good, porous soil.

Building a Rock Garden on a Slope

Building a rock garden on an existing slope is not particularly difficult. If the slope is very steep, however, reduce the slope to at most a 45° angle. Set the rocks so they angle slightly inward and downward. Thus, any rain will be carried in toward the plant roots, not away from them. Start by placing the largest rocks—the ones you want to see dominate your rock garden—then add medium-size rocks. Fill in any gaps with soil.

Planting the Rock Garden

Rock gardens are best planted in spring or fall, although container-grown specimens can be planted throughout the growing season. Dig a hole corresponding to the size of the root ball, insert the plant, fill in the gaps with soil, and tamp down. Water well until the plant shows signs of new growth. After planting, you might want to partly cover the soil with a layer of crushed stone for a more natural effect. The stone also helps keep the soil cool and moist. A rich brown humus will look out of place in a rock garden until the plant fills in a bit.

Plant Placement

Upright-growing plants and shrubs should be placed near the base of a large rock, while prostrate or crawling plants can be placed where they will cascade over the edges. Smaller rock garden plants are often wedged into crevices, even at an almost 90° angle: They will quickly readjust themselves to their rather awkward position and give the rock garden a natural look.

Rock Walls

If a rock garden is not your style yet you enjoy alpine plants, consider a rock wall. Simply leave gaps in a retaining wall and fill the spaces with handfuls of soil and alpine plants.

Maintaining a Rock Garden

A pretty array of rock garden plants: stonecrop, basket-of-gold, moss pink, dwarf wallflower, and others.

Rock gardens are not hard to maintain. In fact, most work simply involves removing weeds on a regular basis. Even this task will diminish as the rockery plants establish themselves and fill in any gaps where weeds might grow. By covering any exposed soil with a layer of crushed rock, weed seeds will have a difficult time getting started. In a rock garden, weeds must be removed by hand, preferably as soon as they appear. Herbicides, even when carefully sprayed, tend to drip down rock surfaces and harm desirable plants.

Less hardy rock garden plants can be protected during the winter with spruce or pine branches or some other light mulch. Fallen leaves and other moisture-retentive debris should be removed as soon as it accumulates; most alpine plants rot when in contact with damp materials.

Prune as needed to control any plants that spread beyond their limits. Many low-growing, matting alpine plants can also be cut back hard after flowering to encourage the formation of new, healthy growth. Finally, don't be afraid to move plants that appear unhappy.

Most of the information given above describes the preparing and planting of rock gardens for sunny sites. Although this is the most traditional form of rock garden, there is no reason you cannot produce a beautiful rock garden in shady conditions. Use a richer soil mix with plenty of organic matter since most shade-loving plants prefer a moisture-retentive mixture. For suggestions of shade plants suited to the rock garden, see "The Shade Garden: A Haven of Serenity" on page 426. Most of the lower-growing plants in that section will do wonderfully in a rock garden.

The plants covered in the "Encyclopedia of Specialty Garden Plants"(starting on page 446) are only a partial list of good rock garden plants. Many others have been profiled elsewhere in this book and are listed on the next page. For more information on their care and selection, see the Index.

This collection of various hens-and-chicks is an example of easy-to-maintain rock garden plants.

OTHER SUGGESTED ROCK GARDEN PLANTS

Perennials

balloon flower	(*Platycodon* sp.)
basket-of-gold	(*Aurinia* sp.)
beard tongue	(*Penstemon* sp.)
bellflower	(*Campanula* sp.)
bugleweed	(*Ajuga* sp.)
candytuft	(*Iberis sempervirens*)
columbine	(*Aquilegia* sp.)
crane's-bill	(*Geranium* sp.)
creeping buttercup	(*Ranunculus repens*)
cushion spurge	(*Euphorbia* sp.)
dead nettle	(*Lamium* sp.)
dwarf iris	(*Iris* sp.)
edelweiss	(*Leontopodium* sp.)
goldenstar	(*Chrysogonum* sp.)
lamb's-ears	(*Stachys* sp.)
lavender	(*Lavandula* sp.)
pachysandra	(*Pachysandra* sp.)
periwinkle	(*Vinca* sp.)
pink	(*Dianthus* sp.)
primrose	(*Primula* sp.)
rockcress	(*Aubrieta* and *Arabis* sp.)
rock rose	(*Helianthemum* sp.)
self-heal	(*Prunella* sp.)
thrift	(*Armeria* sp.)

Bulbs

crocus	(*Crocus* sp.)
flowering onion	(*Allium* sp.)
glory-of-the-snow	(*Chionodoxa* sp.)
Iris reticulata	
meadow saffron	(*Colchicum* sp.)
narcissus	(*Narcissus* sp.)
Siberian squill	(*Scilla* sp.)
snowdrop	(*Galanthus* sp.)
tulips	(*Tulipa* sp.)

Shrubs

boxwood	(*Buxus* sp.)
cotoneaster	(*Cotoneaster* sp.)
dwarf conifers	(various sp.)
dwarf myrtle	(*Myrtus* sp.)
firethorn	(*Pyracanths* sp.)
flowering quince	(*Chaenomeles* sp.)
Oregon grape	(*Mahonia* sp.)

The early spring splash of color provided by bulbs—such as the tulips gracing this quiet street—is greatly appreciated when everything else is still dormant.

418

CHAPTER 3

THE BULB GARDEN: NATURE'S SEASON EXTENDERS

Many people believe the flowering season starts in late spring and ends in early fall, but it can actually last much longer. There are a whole series of plants that bloom through the "off season." A few of these are shrubs, but most of the season's extenders are hardy bulbs.

Bulbs are curious plants. While other plants go dormant during winter, bulbs are actually actively growing, underground. Winter is when they send their roots deep into the soil and begin to sprout. Then, in earliest spring, while all the other plants are just beginning to stir, bulbs burst into bloom. When summer arrives and sunlight is abundant, other plants come into their prime, but bulbs lose their leaves and go fully dormant.

Bulbs are most often included in other flower beds. Rock gardens abound with miniature ones; tulips, narcissi, crocus, and lilies find their way into just about every perennial border. But for those who love growing bulbs, there is nothing like giving them a garden of their own. From the earliest bulbs of late winter and spring to the alliums of early summer to a host of lilies throughout summer to fall-flowering bulbs of autumn, you can have bulbs in bloom almost every month of the year.

Planning the Bulb Garden

A few crocuses peek through the snow after an early spring storm.

Any garden designed specifically to showcase bulbs requires special planning, otherwise there will be short bursts of flowering followed by long periods with no bloom. Bulbs are classified according to their flowering season: late-winter and spring flowering, summer flowering, and fall flowering. Within each seasonal group, there are early, midseason, and late bloomers. Among spring-flowering bulbs, for example, late-winter flowering bulbs, such as snowdrops and *Iris reticulata,* are followed by early spring bulbs such as Dutch crocus and Siberian squill. By mid to late season such bulbs as narcissi and tulips are blooming, which are finally followed by very late season bulbs such as alliums. Within each bulb category, there are further divisions. Tulips, for example, are available in early, midseason, and late varieties. In the same way, among the summer bloomers, there are early, midseason, and late lilies. In fact, a bulb garden composed of only lilies can bloom right through the summer if care is taken in selecting varieties.

One advantage of bulbs over many other garden plants is their adaptability. Although most bulbs prefer full sun or only light shade, their leaves generally sprout in early spring before deciduous trees and shrubs leaf out. Thus, they can be grown successfully in spots that are shady much of the year. Just about any soil is acceptable, although a generous addition of organic matter to poor soils is wise. The only thing bulbs will not tolerate is waterlogged soil. If your chosen site stays moist or wet for long periods, consider planting bulbs in raised beds so they get the drainage they need. Bulbs can also be easily grown in containers as long as the containers are placed where they will not freeze solid during the winter.

Most hardy bulbs (lilies are a notable exception) lose their leaves in early summer, so it is important to plan ahead to fill in the gaps. Clusters of annuals and perennials, for example, can be interplanted among groups of bulbs. Ground covers and bulbs make an even better marriage: Bulbs will grow right through the ground cover, bloom, then disappear from sight until the following year. Choose an open, shallow-rooted ground cover to minimize competition with the bulbs.

Bulbs look best planted in groups rather than scattered randomly through the garden or planted in straight rows. Clusters of at least 3 to 5 large bulbs such as lilies; 7 to 10 medium-sized bulbs such as tulips, narcissi, or hyacinths; and 12 or more small bulbs such as crocuses or Siberian squills are fine. Avoid mixing bulbs: They rarely give an interesting display. Leave spaces between each cluster of bulbs to interplant ground covers, annuals, or perennials, which will help cover up the foliage of the bulbs as they fade.

Usually, tall-growing bulbs are planted at the back of the border or in the middle of the bed with smaller bulbs in front and medium-high ones in between. But it is also possible to grow bulbs of all sizes in a single space. Tall bulbs need deep planting, so put them in first. Then add a layer of soil, and place medium-high bulbs directly over them; finally, another layer of soil and then small bulbs. Since small bulbs flower first, the same spot will offer a succession of bloom. A good combination would be early crocuses, midseason hyacinths, and late tulips.

Massive formal plantings of spring bulbs, as commonly seen in public gardens, are also possible in the home garden but require some effort. In such cases, a hundred or more of the same bulb may be required to fill the bed. After blooming, either treat the bulbs as temporary visitors—composting them and replanting the bed with summer flowers—or remove the fading bulbs to an out-of-the way spot where they can ripen. They can then be replanted in the formal bed the following autumn after the summer flowers have finished their display.

The most beautiful bulb gardens often are not formal beds or mixed borders but naturalized plantings. In such cases, bulbs are chosen to suit the present conditions and are then planted permanently so they seem to have always been part of the landscape. In such cases, the elaborately colored, fully double hybrid varieties are usually forsaken for bulbs that more closely resemble wildflowers. Bulbs that are inherently tough and spread on their own are ideal choices.

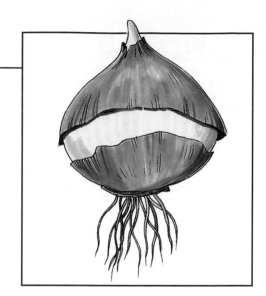

1 What is a Bulb?

Gardeners tend to refer to any plant with an underground storage organ as a bulb, but there are actually many different categories. **True bulbs** are made up of modified leaves that are attached to a flat basal plate and that surround the following season's bud. Many true bulbs, such as tulips and narcissi, are surrounded by a papery outer tunic. In others, such as lilies and fritillarias, the bulb is covered by fleshy scales.

Corms look like bulbs on the outside, including the **2** flat basal plate and the papery tunic. But when they are cut open, they have a solid starchy interior stem. Crocuses are an example of typical corms.

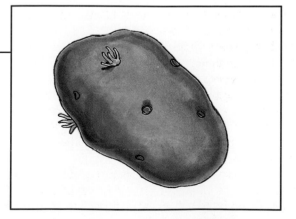

3

Tubers are modified stems with starchy interiors but no basal plate or tunic. Both roots and shoots sprout from the same growth buds, called eyes. The potato is a typical tuber. Tuberous roots are similar to tubers but are really swollen roots. Dahlias produce tuberous roots.

Obviously, rigidly formal plantings are not recommended for naturalized gardens. In fact, one common planting method is to toss bulbs into the air and plant them where they fall. Another method is to lay out a garden hose in an irregular pattern that resembles a meandering stream and then plant bulbs within its limits.

People who enjoy multiplying plants find most bulbs to be obliging: They increase in number on their own. Any time you have to disturb a bulb, you'll find numerous bulbs of various sizes where the original bulb was planted. The largest ones can be replanted immediately and will bloom the following year; the smaller ones should be grown in an out-of-the-way spot for a few years until they reach flowering size. Naturalized bulbs will also multiply prolifically, although it may take several years before the seedlings reach flowering size. Rhizomes, tubers, and tuberous roots can also be divided by cutting them into sections. Each section must have at least one eye.

The discussion has focused on hardy bulbs, but there is a wide variety of tender bulbs. These are hardy only in the warmest parts of the United States. Elsewhere, they are either treated as annuals and allowed to freeze in the fall or dug up and stored indoors in a cool and dry but frost-free spot over the winter. For more information on these bulbs and their care, see the "Annuals" section, page 52; see also specifically the descriptions of tuberous begonias, caladiums, callas, cannas, dahlias, gladiolus, and tuberoses. These are widely used in bulb gardens for summer color.

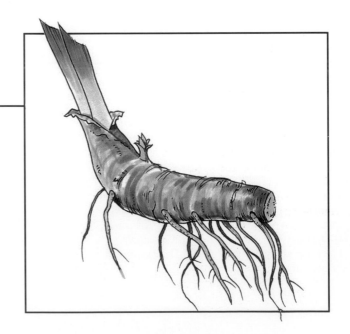

4 **Rhizomes** are thickened underground stems. They grow in a horizontal direction, sprouting new sections as they go. The bearded iris (*Iris germanica*) has a typical rhizome.

Planting

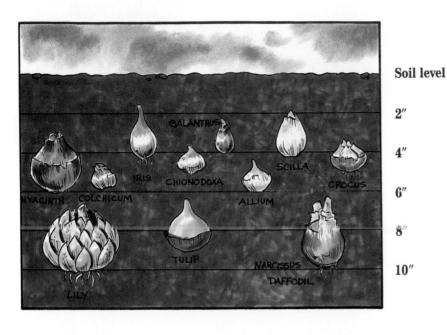

Soil level

2″

4″

6″

8″

10″

GALANTHUS
IRIS
CHIONODOXA
SCILLA
CROCUS
HYACINTH
COLCHICUM
ALLIUM
TULIP
NARCISSUS
DAFFODIL
LILY

Plant bulbs as soon as you receive them, usually in early fall in the case of hardy bulbs and late spring for tender ones. Lilies (hardy bulbs), however, can be planted in either spring or fall. If you can't plant the bulbs immediately, store them in a cool, dry place.

Prepare a planting hole a few inches deeper than the recommended planting depth shown on the planting chart. Mix compost, well-rotted manure, or peat moss into the soil removed. Add a slow acting organic fertilizer to the bottom of the hole; then add enough soil to bring the hole to the proper planting depth. For a maximum effect, space bulbs only a few inches apart. Fill in the planting hole and water thoroughly.

Naturalizing Bulbs

One particularly successful type of naturalized planting is the woodland garden. Most spring bulbs will thrive in areas dominated by deciduous trees, since the trees allow plenty of light in the spring when the bulbs are in leaf. Meadow gardens, composed of bulbs intermingling with grasses that are allowed to grow to their full height, are also attractive. Meadow gardens need to be sheared once a year in fall or early spring to prevent trees and shrubs from taking over. Bulbs can also be naturalized directly into lawns. Just lift up the sod, drop in a few bulbs, pat down, and water. Early spring bulbs, such as snowdrops, crocuses, and glory-of-the-snows, are ideal choices here since they have grasslike leaves and don't mind being mowed.

Bulb Maintenance

Once planted in a permanent spot, hardy bulbs require little care: Water well throughout the fall until the ground freezes to stimulate good root growth. In spring, as bulbs begin to bloom, work bulb fertilizer into the soil at their bases. This will supply nutrition for the development of healthy bulbs and abundant blooms. After the flowers fade, clip off any developing seed pods. Take care not to cut back the foliage as long as it is still green; bulbs need these leaves to absorb energy. Leaves should only be removed and composted once they begin to yellow: generally in early summer for spring- and fall-flowering bulbs and fall for summer-flowering ones.

Most bulb plantings are permanent, so little care is needed during the summer months, when the bulbs are dormant. But be careful not to dig them up accidentally while their leaves are absent. When space is needed for other plantings, hardy bulbs can be carefully lifted after blooming, with roots and leaves intact, and planted elsewhere. After a few years, bulbs tend to become overcrowded and flowering diminishes. When this happens, lift the bulbs just when their leaves begin to fade in early summer. Let the bulbs dry in the sun for a few days, then remove the faded leaves. Store in a dry, warm spot out of sunlight (a tool shed is ideal) until fall planting time.

Resistance to cold winter weather is rarely a problem for hardy bulbs. Planted deep beneath the ground, they are capable of surviving and even thriving in extreme conditions. On the other hand, permanent bulb plantings, especially fresh ones, are subject to frost heaving, which can thrust the bulbs out of the ground. For that reason, cover recently planted areas with a 3- or 4-inch layer of mulch of organic material—shredded bark or leaves, evergreen branches, or the like—once the ground freezes. This mulch should be removed in spring as the bulbs begin to grow and the danger of hard frost decreases. Mulching is most important in areas where snow cover is lacking, particularly in zone 4 or colder. Naturalized bulbs rarely need mulching. Those planted in wooded areas receive an abundant supply of natural mulch from fallen leaves; those planted in lawns or meadows have sod to protect them from heaving.

Lilies require different care than other hardy bulbs since they grow throughout the summer and never really go entirely dormant. They should be lifted only in late fall and then immediately replanted, taking care that their tender bulbs never dry out. In any case, lilies are generally best lifted only when severely overcrowded; they resent any disturbance.

Most hardy bulbs require little in the way of maintenance.

Most bulbs can be "forced," that is, made to bloom indoors in midwinter, well before their regular flowering season. The technique is quite simple. Place up to five bulbs in an eight-inch pot. Use a light, moisture retentive soil mix. Cover the bulbs completely to help keep them anchored. Water thoroughly to settle the soil. Store the bulbs in a cool but frost-free spot (for example, a root cellar or unheated garage) until the bulbs have a solid root system and healthy sprouts are showing. For most bulbs, this can take 12 weeks or more. Bring the bulbs into a warmer, brightly lit location indoors, and they will soon be in full bloom. After flowering, plant the bulbs outdoors; they cannot be forced a second time.

The "Encyclopedia of Specialty Garden Plants" (starting on page 446) highlights some of the most popular hardy bulbs, but there are a great many others of interest. The short list on the next page gives some idea of the vast choice available.

Moving Bulbs

If the space where spring bulbs are grown is needed for some other purpose, carefully lift the bulbs after blooming has ceased and replant them elsewhere. A garden fork is ideal for this job since it causes less damage to tender roots.

OTHER BULBS OF INTEREST

Hardy Bulbs and Bulblike Plants

blackberry lily	(*Belamcanda* sp.)
hardy cyclamen	(*Cyclamen* sp.)
dog-tooth violet	(*Erythronium* sp.)
foxtail lily	(*Eremurus* sp.)
fritillary	(*Fritillaria* sp.)
grape hyacinth	(*Muscari* sp.)
lily-of-the-field	(*Sternbergia* sp.)
lily-of-the-valley*	(*Convallaria* sp.)
snowflake	(*Leucojeum* sp.)
spring meadow saffron	(*Bulbocodium* sp.)
striped squill	(*Puschkinia* sp.)
wake-robin*	(*Trillium* sp.)
windflower	(*Anemone blanda*)
winter aconite	(*Eranthis* sp.)

Semi-Hardy Bulbs †

brodiaea	(*Brodiaea* sp.)
camas	(*Camassia* sp.)
corn lily	(*Ixia* sp.)
florist's anemone	(*Anemone coronaria*)
Italian arum	(*Arum italicum*)
naked lady	(*Amaryllis belladonna*)
hardy orchid	(*Bletilla* sp.)
Persian buttercup	(*Ranunculus* sp.)
Peruvian lily	(*Alstroemeria* sp.)
spring starflower	(*Ipheion* sp.)
star-of-Bethlehem	(*Ornithogalum* sp.)
Tartar lily	(*Ixiolirion* sp.)
wood sorrel	(*Oxalis* sp.)

Tender Bulbs ‡

amaryllis*	(*Hippeastrum* sp.)
Amazon lily	(*Eucharis* sp.)
caladium*	(*Caladium* sp.)
calla*	(*Zantedeschia* sp.)
canna*	(*Canna* sp.)
Cape cowslip	(*Lachenalia* sp.)
Cape lily	(*Veltheimia* sp.)
cardiocrinum	(*Cardiocrinum* sp.)
crinum	(*Crinum* sp.)
dahlia*	(*Dahlia* sp.)
freesia	(*Freesia* sp.)
gladiolus*	(*Gladiolus* sp.)
lily-of-the-Nile	(*Agapanthus* sp.)
magic flower	(*Achimenes* sp.)
montebretia	(*Crocosmia* sp.)
nerine	(*Nerine* sp.)
peacock orchid	(*Acidanthera* sp.)
pineapple lily	(*Eucomis* sp.)
rain lily	(*Zephyranthes* sp.)
summer hyacinth	(*Galtonia* sp.)
tiger flower	(*Tigridia* sp.)
tuberose*	(*Polianthes* sp.)
tuberous begonia*	(*Begonia* x *tuberhybrida*)

* These plants are covered elsewhere, see Index.
† These should be lifted in fall in very cold climates.
‡ These should be lifted in the winter in all but the mildest climates.

Foam flowers and hostas are just two of the many plants that can make a shade garden a place of relaxation and tranquillity. A shade garden offers restful shelter on hot summer days.

CHAPTER 4

THE SHADE GARDEN: A HAVEN OF SERENITY

P eople rarely set out to create shade on purpose, at least not in the garden. Instead, shade is usually something that is forced upon them. It comes from nearby walls that cast a dark shadow over part of a yard, from lovingly planted young trees that mature into giants and block out the sun, or from a neighbor whose fence keeps all the light on his side of the property line.

It is all too easy to look at the negative aspects of shade: the favorite sun-loving plants you cannot grow, the inability to get a suntan in your own backyard, the pervasive greenness rather than the riotous color of the mixed border. Often there is little you can do about shade, so why not accept it and learn to live with it? You'll quickly find that shade gardening, while a bit of a challenge, offers ample advantages as well.

Shade gardens generally look good with less maintenance than a sunny garden. They are also better protected from summer and winter damage because nearby trees and walls make an excellent screen against dry summer heat and cold, drying winter winds. A shady nook is ideal for such restful activities as reading. And with concerns about the dangers of sunlight on tender skin, the shade garden is one place where you can spend time outdoors without overexposure to sunlight.

Coping with Shade

American maidenhair ferns thrive in a shady nook.

Most gardeners consider full sun to be six hours or more of direct, uninterrupted sun per day; beyond that, all definitions fail. To some gardeners, three to six hours of sun is "partial sun" and less than three hours of sun is "light shade." What about gardens that get no direct sun, yet plenty of light filters through overhanging branches over a long period of time? Some people call this "dappled shade" and, while such a site is certainly "shady," it may receive enough light to allow some sun-loving plants to thrive. No direct sun means you have deep shade.

For the sake of simplicity for the purposes of this chapter any garden that does not get full sun will be considered a shade garden. The degree of shade will likely change from spot to spot and season to season. As you work in the shade garden, you'll soon learn what can and can't be successfully grown where. No plant will grow in total darkness, but a great many will grow with only a faint glimmer of natural light. These plants are the ones to choose for the shade garden.

Many shade gardens are naturally cool and moist. They are usually surrounded by deep-rooted trees and copious amounts of natural mulch from fallen leaves. Their soils are normally rich, deep, and easy to dig. These are the easiest shade spots in which to garden, as shade plants thrive under such conditions. In such places, plantings can be made directly into the ground with little special preparation.

Other shade gardens are also cool, but dry rather than moist. These are filled with shallow-rooted trees and shrubs that soak up every drop of rain. The soil is often poor and hard-baked, depleted of nutrients by gluttonous roots. These gardens represent quite a challenge for the gardener. Digging is difficult. If you carefully cut away sections of root-clogged soil and replace it with good humus-rich earth to nurture a special plant, the invasive roots of nearby trees and shrubs will soon be back.

Perhaps the greatest disappointment to the new owner of a shady yard is that lawns are difficult to grow. The lawns grow quickly at first, needing frequent mowing, but they are sparse and subject to dieback. These lawns generally require regular overseeding to retain even a semblance of thickness. Some gardeners believe that fertilizing or watering abundantly will help, but to no avail. The only way to get a reasonably healthy lawn in a shady spot is to use lawn seed mixes designed for that purpose. These mixes contain a larger percentage of shade-tolerant grass species than regular lawn grasses. But even with special lawn seed mixes, results are often mediocre in truly shady spots. Lawns and shade simply do not mix.

It is often because of poor lawns that many people stumble upon the concept of shade gardens. They replace part of the lawn first with one plant, then another, and soon find their yard looking better than ever even though little green grass is left.

If you insist on a low-growing carpet of greenery in a yard where lawns do poorly, consider shade-tolerant ground covers. They make nice, even carpets in various tones of green, and most require little maintenance.

It is sometimes possible, although rare, to increase the amount of light in a shady garden. Painting nearby walls white or using white lawn furniture can dramatically increase the light in the immediate vicinity: White reflects light rather than absorbing it. If overhead foliage is dense, you might be able to remove a few overhanging branches and bring in more dappled sunlight. But new branches will grow back in. There isn't much else you can do to increase the sunlight in the garden. Neither of these methods will create a fully sunny garden, but they can help bring in enough light for you to be able to grow a favorite plant.

How to Beat Roots in a Shade Garden

1 There are three basic ways to beat root competition in a shady garden. However, remember to keep the health and well-being of the trees as a priority; don't disturb too much too fast. One way is to dig down into the soil and insert a solid barrier, such as a plastic barrel with the bottom taken off, to keep the roots out. Fill the space inside the barrier with good soil.

2 Another method is to plant in containers. Pots, trays, and flower boxes set on top of the soil will stymie even the most invasive roots. This is often an ideal way to introduce annuals into the shade garden.

3 The final method is to install raised beds, filling each bed with at least 12 inches of top-quality soil. Do not do this over the entire surface of the garden all at once: The sudden change in soil depth can smother the roots of nearby trees. Instead, add raised beds gradually, in sections, over a number of years. Once the new soil has been added, make sure you water regularly as needed. If not, the water-starved trees will soon send new roots upward in search of water, clogging up the new bed.

Color, Texture, & Naturalizing

Wax begonia is a shade-tolerant annual that adds a nice bit of color to the shade garden.

Even under the best circumstances, a shade garden cannot compete with a sunny garden for bright and gaudy colors. In fact, most shade-tolerant plants offer soft, subtle hues: whites, pinks, pale blues, and lemon yellows rather than garish oranges and reds. On the other hand, these subtle colors, often lost in the sunny garden, really stand out in a shady one. Nothing beats pale hues for adding color to a shade garden, and pure white is the brightest color of all in the shade. Look for these pale shades in the plants you select.

Foliage can also add color to the shade garden. White and yellow striped and marbled leaves, or silvery-mottled ones, can brighten even the shadiest spots. Leaf colors are more durable than those of flowers, lasting through the entire growing season. Variegated shade-tolerant plants can make an excellent long-term solution to overbearing shade. Finally, the shade garden, as subtle as it may be during spring and summer, often turns surprisingly colorful in fall when autumn leaves far outshine the best fall flowers the mixed border can produce.

Truly beautiful shade gardens often rely more on attractive combinations and contrasts of foliage texture and plant forms than on flowers. Light, airy fern fronds stand out from heavy, oblong hosta leaves, which in their turn can be highlighted by the small leaves and prostrate growth patterns of ground covers. Subtle differences in the shades of foliage green become more distinct when there are few flowers to steal the show. Nature provides a vast and pleasing array of foliage colors: blue-greens, apple-greens, dark greens, and more.

Shade gardens can be planted just as formally as any other garden, but a more natural look is usually preferable. Both Oriental gardens, with their sparse appearance, meandering paths, and small pools, and English gardens, with their beds overflowing with mixed plants of all sorts, make ideal styles for shade gardens. If your shade garden is already at least partially a forested one, however, consider establishing a wild garden.

You can easily establish a wild garden by planting hardy yet decorative shade-tolerant plants among the trees in an informal pattern. This technique is known as naturalizing. The goal is to introduce or reintroduce into the landscape plants that will be capable of growing, and even spreading, under existing conditions with minimal help from you. The plants you introduce will depend on many factors, notably your local climate, but look for plants that are capable of taking care of themselves. Consider both native wild flowers that may once have grown there and nonnative varieties of equal ornamental appeal. Avoid plants that are invasive.

Maintaining the Shade Garden—Shade gardens often require quite a bit of effort to establish, but only a minimal amount of upkeep. For example, with sunlight already at a premium, most weeds don't have a chance: Established shade plants and ground covers take what is left of the light, leaving nothing for would-be competitors. In fact, the major weeding effort often consists of simply removing the countless tree seedlings that somehow always seem to manage to break through the plant cover.

Fall leaves often integrate perfectly into a shade garden: Leave them where they fall, and they'll supply a natural mulch that regenerates and enriches the soil while helping to suppress weeds. Large leaves could smother growth, and these should be chopped up into small pieces (run a lawn-mower over them or rent a chipper) before being spread among the shade garden plants.

Shade gardens with heavy root competition will require special help. Water regularly during periods of drought. Remember, you're watering for two: the trees that cause the shade and the plants that grow beneath the trees' boughs. If you let nature take its course, the shallow-rooted understory plants will be the first to go during a drought.

Plants for the Shade Garden—There is no lack of choice plants for specialty and semishady sites. The specialty garden directory of plants, starting on page 446, offers some suggestions. The following lists include some of the good shade-tolerant plants covered elsewhere in this book. See the Index for more information.

PLANTS FOR THE SHADE GARDEN

Shade-Tolerant Perennials

anemones	(*Anemone* sp.)
astilbe	(*Astilbe* sp.)
balloon flower	(*Platycodon* sp.)
bellflower	(*Campanula* sp.)
bergamot	(*Monarda* sp.)
bergenia	(*Bergenia* sp.)
bishop's hat	(*Astrophytum* sp.)
bleeding heart	(*Dicentra* sp.)
bowman's root	(*Gillenia* sp.)
bugleweed	(*Ajuga* sp.)
Siberian bugloss	(*Brunnera* sp.)
creeping buttercup	(*Ranunculua repens*)
cardinal flower	(*Lobelia cardinalis*)
chameleon plant	(*Houttuynia* sp.)
black cohosh	(*Cimicifuga* sp.)
columbine	(*Aquilegia* sp.)
coralbell	(*Heuchera* sp.)
crane's bill	(*Geranium* sp.)
daylily	(*Hemerocallis* sp.)
dichondra	(*Dichondra* sp.)
foxglove	(*Digitalis* sp.)
globeflower	(*Trollius* sp.)
goat's beard	(*Arunucus* sp.)
goldenstar	(*Chrysogonum* sp.)
goutweed	(*Aegopodium* sp.)
hosta	(*Hosta* sp.)
ladybells	(*Adenophora* sp.)
leopard's bane	(*Doronicum* sp.)
ligularia	(*Ligularia* sp.)
toad lily	(*Tricyrtis* sp.)
lily-of-the-valley	(*Convallaria* sp.)
liriope	(*Liriope* sp.)
gooseneck loosestrife	(*Lysimachia clethroides*)
lungwort	(*Pulmonaria* sp.)
dead nettle	(*Lamium* sp.)
pachysandra	(*Pachysandra* sp.)
periwinkle	(*Vinca* sp.)
plume poppy	(*Macleaya* sp.)
primrose	(*Primula* sp.)
rodgersia	(*Rodgersia* sp.)
Christmas rose	(*Helleborus* sp.)
meadow rue	(*Thalictrum* sp.)
self-heal	(*Prunella* sp.)
speedwell	(*Veronica* sp.)
spiderwort	(*Tradescantia* sp.)
turtlehead	(*Chelone* sp.)
yellow waxbell	(*Kirengeshoma* sp.)
violet	(*Viola* sp.)

Shade-Tolerant Shrubs

abutilon	(*Abutilon* sp.)
amelanchier	(*Amelanchier* sp.)
Japanese andromeda	(*Pieris* sp.)
azalea	(*Rhododendron* sp.)
banana shrub	(*Michelia* sp.)
boxwood	(*Buxus* sp.)
camellia	(*Camellia* sp.)
alpine currant	(*Ribes alpinum*)
daphne	(*Daphne* sp.)
red osier dogwood	(*Cornus sericea*)
gardenia	(*Gardenia* sp.)
Oregon grape	(*Mahonia* sp.)
Michigan holly	(*Ilex verticillata*)
hydrangea	(*Hydrangea* sp.)
inkberry	(*Ilex glabra*)
kerria	(*Kerria* sp.)
mountain laurel	(*Kalmia* sp.)
drooping leucothoe	(*Leucothoe fontanesiana*)
dwarf myrtle	(*Myrtus communis* 'Compactus')
sweet olive	(*Osmanthus fragrans*)
Japanese podocarpus	(*Podocarpus macrophyllus*)
rhododendron	(*Rhododendron* sp.)
Reeves skimmia	(*Skimmia reevesiana*)
snowberry	(*Symphoricarpos* sp.)
summersweet	(*Clethra* sp.)
common witchhazel	(*Hamamelis virginiana*)
American yew	(*Taxus canadensis*)

Shade-Tolerant Vines

bittersweet	(*Celastris* sp.)
creeping fig	(*Ficus pumila*)
honeysuckle	(*Lonicera* sp.)
English ivy	(*Hedera helix*)
Dutchman's pipe	(*Aristolochia* sp.)

Water can fit into almost any type of garden. Moving water from a fountain makes a refreshing break in the midst of this rock garden.

CHAPTER 5

THE WATER GARDEN: WATER ADDS LIFE

Water contributes a sense of peace and tranquillity to a garden, making it more inviting, more romantic, more livable. Whether the water garden is little more than an enlarged bird bath or an elaborate aquatic milieu brimming with plant and animal life, its presence alone makes your yard a more pleasant place. Water cools the air on hot days and helps keep frost away on cold ones. Activated by hidden pumps, moving water also supplies a relaxing background of natural music. And water in the garden attracts birds and butterflies.

Many gardeners put off plans for a water garden because they think water gardens require too much effort to start or a great deal of experience to maintain. Actually, water gardens require little care and are no more difficult to maintain than the average flower garden. Some knowledge of the care and maintenance of garden pools and aquatic plants is necessary of course, but all the basics are explained in this chapter.

So why wait? Even the smallest backyard or patio can host a water garden: for example, a half barrel containing a single dwarf water lily. There is no limit to how extravagant the project can be if you have the space: two or three levels interconnected by waterfalls, complete with wooden bridges and garden lighting, and brought alive by sprays and fountains. All that is possible in an average backyard.

Planning a Water Garden

A quaint bridge over water is possible in most backyards.

Until recently, water gardens were beyond the reach of many gardeners. Concrete—expensive and difficult to install—was the main material used in construction. Concrete also required special care to use and maintain. Most people had little choice but to call professionals for planning and installation, adding to the expense. A water garden was something one dreamed of but did not actually own.

Times have changed. With more modern pool lining materials—PVC and fiberglass are currently the main ones—material costs have dropped enormously and installation is easily carried out by anyone. You don't even have to know how to nail two boards together to be able to install a water garden.

Although water gardens can be placed just about anywhere, you may find the choice of sites limited depending on the type of plants you want to grow. If your goal is a simple reflecting pool, the choice of a location is up to you. But most people dream of a water garden brimming with water lilies and other aquatic plants. This places a major limit on where the water garden can be placed, since water lilies require at least six hours of full sun per day to grow well (a few species will tolerate as few as four hours). Most other flowering aquatic plants also require abundant light; plants grown for their foliage alone are more tolerant. If you want to get the most out of your water garden, select a sunny location.

The amount of space available is also a factor. Even the tiniest yards have room for a small water garden (people have been known to raise goldfish and a single dwarf water lily in a tub on a balcony), but a truly balanced water garden with a variety of plants and animals takes a fair amount of space.

Pool depth is also a consideration. For a simple reflecting pool, you'll need only a few inches of water, but very shallow pools are subject to extreme temperature change, which is not conducive to living organisms such as plants and fish. A minimum depth of 18 inches for much of the pond's area is desirable. To overwinter plants and fish in cold climates, at least part of the pond should drop to three feet.

The shape of the pond will depend a great deal on the effect you wish to create. Square, rectangular, round, or oval ponds give a formal appearance to the yard, an effect heightened by using fountains. If you keep your yard neatly mowed, if shrubs and hedges are carefully trimmed, and other plantings are in formal beds, a geometric pond will suit it perfectly. If, on the other hand, your yard is composed of English-style mixed borders and naturalistic plantings, a formal water garden would look out of place. An irregularly shaped pond, perhaps with a border planting of bog plants to soften its appearance even further, would be more appropriate. If you're unsure, try laying out the pool shape of your choice with a piece of garden hose, then look at it from every angle. It is far easier to spend a day or so testing different pond shapes and locations with a hose than to move an established water garden.

The topography of the site should also be considered. Ponds should not be placed in the lowest section of the yard: Any overflow could quickly turn the area into a bog. Make sure there is some possibility for drainage. If you plan to include a naturalistic cascade or waterfall, a yard with a somewhat abrupt slope is most fitting.

Finally, check with your municipality concerning zoning laws and fencing codes. Many cities and towns make no distinction between a water garden and a swimming pool. Security fencing may be required. For further security, you might want to wait until your children are past the toddler stage before you install a water garden.

Installing Your Own Pool

Installing your own water garden is easier than most people expect.

Many people these days choose to install their own garden pools. If that's your choice, there are two main alternatives: flexible liners and prefabricated pools. Both are inexpensive and can be installed by two people in a single weekend. Concrete pools are more expensive and require greater skills: It is generally best to contact a professional landscaper for planning and construction.

The pool surface itself must be perfectly even (one edge can be a bit lower to allow rainwater to drain away). If your yard is on a slope, you may have to dig further down at the higher end or even shore up the lower one to obtain the desired effect. Use a level throughout the installation process to make sure your pool remains on the level.

Installing a flexible liner is the easiest and least expensive process for the nonspecialist. Be sure to use a liner specifically designed for water gardens, not just any sheet of plastic. Currently, PVC liners are most popular; dark shades will give the most natural effect. The thicker your liner is, the longer it will last and the more it will cost. Since light degrades plastic, look for liners with enhanced UV protection, especially if your pond is a shallow one.

To calculate the proper size for your liner, measure the width and length of the planned pool at the widest points, add twice the pool's depth and then tack on an extra foot for overlap. For example, a pool 10 feet long, 6 feet wide, and 2 feet deep would require a liner 15 feet long $(10' + (2 \times 2') + 1')$ and 11 feet wide $(6' + (2 \times 2') + 1')$.

Installing a Flexible Liner

1 Outline the pool with a piece of garden hose. If your pool will be square or rectangular, use string staked carefully into place to do the outline. A framing square will be necessary to get a 90° angle at the corners.

2 Dig out the pond to two inches more than the desired depth. Leave shelves about 6 to 18 inches (9 inches is average) deep in areas where you intend to place emergent plants such as cattails. Don't cut the edges perfectly perpendicular or they may collapse: A slight angle (about 20°) is best. As you dig, use a straight board with a level to make sure the pond's edge is perfectly level. If you'll be edging your pond in field stone, remove a further layer of sod from around its edges so the stones can be set evenly with the surrounding soil.

3 Remove any stones, sticks, or other debris from the pool bottom and sides, then line the entire surface with two inches of damp sand. You may want to install a piece of landscape fabric over the sand for further protection against piercing, especially if you are using an inexpensive grade of liner.

4

Spread the liner carefully over the excavation, folding it carefully at corners or curves. Mold the liner to the hole by pushing with your feet (remove your shoes first). Use stones to hold it in place.

5

Slowly add water, smoothing out wrinkles as the pool fills.

6

Cut away any excess liner, leaving six inches of liner overlapping at all points. Cover the overlap with soil or paving stones.

Installing a Prefabricated Liner

1 Outline the pool's position with a piece of garden hose. Dig out the hole two inches wider and deeper than the required depth, making sure to take into account any built-in shelves. The final excavation should be a perfect image of the liner's form.

2 Line the excavation with two inches of wet sand, checking as you go to make sure the base is level. Place the shell in the hole.

3 Add water slowly, filling in the area around the shell with sand as you go. Add edging if desired.

Movement in the Water Garden

Even formal gardens can benefit from the addition of water and fountains.

Moving water is not required in a water garden—aquatic plants, for example, grow best in still water—but a waterfall or fountain adds several advantages. Moving water is better aerated than still water so fish do better. A filter can easily be added to any pump, making water clearer. But the main reason for including a pump in your water garden is aesthetic: People enjoy the sound and sight of moving water.

Care should be taken to avoid creating strong currents or excessive splashing near aquatic plants or they can be damaged. Fountains especially are not conducive to plant life, as their spray can reach considerable distances under strong winds. Waterfalls can usually be separated from water lilies and other plants by placing the cascade at one end of the pool and installing a few well-placed rocks to diffuse the current.

Choose the form of moving water that best corresponds to your pool. Fountains and other pool ornaments are best for formal pools. Waterfalls cascading over rocks work well for irregular pools in a more natural setting. And simple underwater filter systems suit any kind of pool.

There is no lack of choices among fountains: cones, sprays, jets, bubble effects, or pretty much whatever you want. Pipe heads can also be fitted to ornamental statues, ceramic jars, or bamboo pipes. When installing a fountain, make sure the height of the spray is not more than half the diameter of the pond; otherwise much of the water will end up being sprayed out of the pool during windy periods.

If your yard has a natural slope, consider installing a waterfall: It will help integrate your water garden into the rest of the landscape. Waterfalls can also be used in flat areas, but care should be taken that the resulting raised section doesn't stick out like a sore thumb. Place tall plants or a fence behind the waterfall to ease this potential problem. The combination of rock gardens and waterfalls is a natural one since the waterfall is set off by rocks anyway and rock garden plants, generally low-growing, won't block the view of the resulting stream.

Prefabricated waterfall units are readily available and easily installed. They may consist of an entirely preformed section with several tiers, or they may be individual catch basins designed to be placed so that each one slightly overhangs the previous one. It is also easy to make your own waterfall using a section or sections of flexible liner.

There is a wide variety of pumps available for water gardens. The pump should be chosen according to the quantity of water to be moved, the distance the water has to cover, and the height the water is to be pushed. For example, it requires much more power to pump a fast-moving stream of water five feet up and ten feet from the pool for an extensive waterfall than to simply filter the water in a pond. Pumps generally come with charts detailing their capacity. Ask the supplier to help you choose if you have any doubts.

Always select a pump somewhat stronger than your needs, just in case. The pump should never have a rate of flow per hour greater than the capacity of the pond, but it should be able to circulate nearly half the pool's water per hour. To calculate the approximate volume of your pool, multiply its length by its width by its depth (in inches). This gives the number of cubic inches. Divide this by 231 to obtain the number of gallons. For example, a pool 10 feet (120 inches) by 6 feet (72 inches) by 18 inches deep would have a volume of 155,520 cubic inches, or 673 gallons. A pump rated at 300 gallons per hour would be adequate.

Water filters are not necessary for a healthy pond, but they do help keep the water clear and the pool free of debris. Mechanical filters are still the most popular and need only regular cleaning or replacement of the filter. Biological filters take up more space but need little upkeep.

Choosing a Pump

The most commonly used pump is a submersible pump, which can be placed out of sight under water. For small ponds, a 24-volt pump may be sufficient. Larger ones using a regular 110-volt house current are the norm for larger pools. If there is no electrical outlet near the pond, have one installed by an electrician. Any underground wiring should be placed at least 18 inches deep and run through PVC piping to avoid accidental breakage. A ground fault circuit interrupter is recommended in all cases.

Building a Waterfall with Flexible Liner

1 Dig out individual basins.

Cover excavation with flexible liner.

2

3

Use rocks to conceal liner and edges.

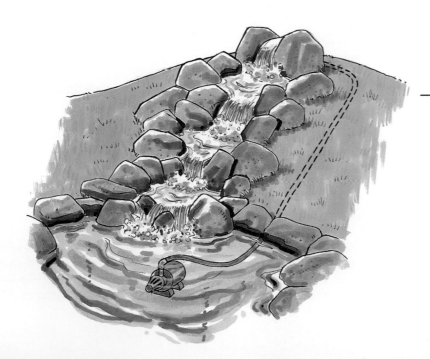

Install pump and add water.

4

Planting the Water Garden

A diversity of water plants creates variety in the pool.

Aquatic plants—aside from being attractive in their own right—offer numerous advantages to the water gardener. They help filter impurities from the water and, by cutting off intense sunlight, they keep the pond cooler for fish and reduce excessive algae build-up. Aquatic plants also help integrate the water garden into the rest of the landscape. There are several different types of aquatic plants, and each has its own use.

Floating plants are the most "aquatic" of all water garden plants. They simply float on the surface of the water. They help filter the water and cut out sunlight, reducing algae. Many of these are tiny plants, and they help nourish the fish in the pool. Typical examples are duckweed (*Lemna*) and floating ferns (*Salvinia* and *Azolla*). Floating plants may be beached by excessively strong currents, so they do best in still waters.

Submerged plants live out most of their life cycle underwater. Although not very visible, they are essential to a healthy pool because they oxygenate and filter the water, competing directly with algae. For maximum effect, calculate about one cluster of submerged plants per square foot of pool surface. Submerged plants are generally sold unrooted in bunches and should be planted in containers that are then placed at the bottom of the pool. For reduced algae development, about one-third of the pool should be filled with submerged plants.

Emergent plants are the largest and most popular group of aquatic plants. Their roots are solidly anchored in the soil underwater, but their leaves and flowers rise above the water level, where they are easily visible. They are generally grown in baskets placed at the proper depth in the pool. Some, like water lilies, have floating leaves. Others have leaves that rise well above the water. Emergent plants help filter and oxygenate the water and, by their shading effect, reduce algae by cutting off sunlight. Typical emergents include water lilies and lotus. Usually, enough floating-leaf emergents should be used to cover more than half the water surface of the pool.

Bog plants differ from emergent plants in that they grow in wet soil but not with their root systems entirely submerged. There is no clear distinction between bog and emergent plants; many plants are equally at home in wet soil (the official realm of the bog plant) and inundated soil (emergent plant territory). Many common "emergent" plants can also grow as bog plants, including cattails, pickerel rush, and arrowhead. They usually do not appreciate dry soil and should be kept constantly moist. On the other hand, many so-called "garden plants" can grow in marshy conditions. This latter group includes such popular perennials as forget-me-not (*Myosotis scorpioides*), bee balm (*Monarda didyma*), moneywort (*Lysimachia Nummularia*), and chameleon plant (*Houttuynia cordata* 'Variegata').

Bog plants are most easily maintained by planting them in pots and placing them on low shelves in the pool itself. It is also quite easy to dig a shallow hole at the lower edge of the water garden and cover it with a piece of leftover liner. Filled with soil again, it will remain moderately moist at all times: a perfect habitat for bog plants of all kinds.

Besides being classified as floating, submerged, emergent, or bog, aquatic plants can also be grouped under the labels tropical or hardy. Hardy aquatic plants are those that can be left outdoors year-round just about anywhere in North America. Tropical ones are either treated as annuals in cold climates or brought indoors for the winter. Most of the latter can be raised outdoors year-round in zones 9 and 10.

Special water lily pots, pans, and tubs (generally made of plastic or rubber) are available, but just about any container of appropriate size can be used for aquatic plants. Plastic dish pans, for example, are an ideal size and shape for water lilies and lotus. Plants with less extensive root systems will grow well

More Than Just Plants in a Water Garden

Goldfish and koi are popular fish for a water garden, and both make colorful and lively guests. They will actually multiply when happy with their conditions.

A Collection of Aquatic Plants

An entire range of water plants can be placed in the water garden: floating, submerged, emergent, and bog. Only under rare circumstances are aquatic plants set directly in the ground (such as in a natural pond with a dirt bottom). Otherwise, they are always planted in containers. This facilitates their care and upkeep; this also allows the water garden itself to be emptied of its plants occasionally for a more thorough cleanup. Container growing also makes it easy to move plants that aren't doing well to another part of the garden.

The larger your water garden, the greater the potential for diversity of plants; biodiversity makes for a healthier garden.

in ordinary flower pots or even plastic pails. Generally, the containers should be wider than they are deep since water garden plants generally have shallow root systems that spread horizontally. There is no need for drainage holes in aquatic plant containers.

Water lilies and lotus need plenty of root space. Although they can grow in containers holding as little as 9 quarts of soil, 11 quarts is better. Larger containers will allow for future expansion without repotting. Other aquatic and bog plants can be planted in any size container suitable to their root system but give them some room for future expansion. Most aquatic plants will rapidly fill up any container you give them.

Avoid artificial soil mixes, which are too light and tend to float away. Even regular garden soil is likely to cloud the water. Instead, use a heavy garden soil with a fair amount of clay. Do not use soil from a natural pond since it may contain weed seeds or host unwanted pests.

Hose off the plant before potting it up. Carefully spread the roots in the container and fill with soil. Place the crowns at or just below the soil surface. Insert a slow-release fertilizer tablet for aquatic plants (about one per five quarts of soil) as you add soil. Cover the soil with a ½ inch layer of rinsed gravel to prevent the soil from floating out. Soak thoroughly before placing the pot in the pool. Containers are easily raised to the required depth by placing bricks or inverted containers under them.

Submerged plants are usually sold as cuttings. Insert the cut ends into sand or soil and cover with gravel as mentioned above. There is no need to add fertilizer tablets since these plants get their nutrients from the water around them.

Animal Life in the Water Garden—Plants are not the only things you'll want to raise in a water garden. Fish are also quite popular. They need surprisingly little care and add so much enjoyment to the experience of water gardening that few water gardens are without them. They also help equilibrate the pool and eliminate unwanted insects.

Don't overstock the pool. You'll need only one inch of fish for every five gallons of water; the fish will grow over time. Don't introduce fish to a freshly filled pond: Wait at least a day for the chlorine to evaporate and preferably two or three weeks. Fish are generally sold in plastic bags of water. Let these bags float in the pool for about 20 minutes before releasing the fish. This allows the fish to adjust to the new water temperature. Feed fish lightly with commercial goldfish food. Fish will get much of their food from the animal and plant life that forms in any pool. Goldfish and koi (Japanese carp) will overwinter nicely in warm climates or in deep ponds in cold ones. Elsewhere, they can be brought indoors and kept in a large container in a cool spot over the winter. Fish remain inactive during cold weather and will not need to be fed during that time.

Most other animals for garden pools are considered "scavengers," meaning they eat detritus and other debris. This helps keep the water clean. Check with your local water garden supplier for snails, tadpoles, freshwater clams, and the like that are suited to your climate.

444

Maintaining the Water Garden

Small pool or large, a water garden is easy to maintain.

Keeping a water garden attractive and healthy is surprisingly easy.

• Occasionally remove plants to prune away dead or dying leaves. While you're at it, insert fertilizer tablets, about one per five quarts, into their containers.

• Remove any dead leaves and other organic material that has accumulated on the pool bottom.

• An occasional spray with a hose will knock any aphids that have developed on plant leaves into the water where fish will eat them.

• Clean the filter occasionally according to the manufacturer's instructions.

• Add water as necessary to maintain the proper water level.

Winter care is also quite simple. In most climates, hardy plants can be left as they are. In cold climates, though, sink even hardy plants in the deepest part of the pond (three feet or more) to prevent freezing. In extremely cold areas, pools will freeze to the bottom. Tropical plants must be brought indoors for the winter in all but the warmest climates.

It is normal for the water in a garden to turn soupy green upon occasion, especially early in the spring or when nutrient-rich fresh water is added, which can cause a rapid increase in the algae population called a "bloom." If the pool is properly balanced, with plenty of oxygenating plants to reduce the carbon dioxide level, abundant floating or emergent plants to absorb nutrients and shade algae out, fish and scavengers to consume the algae, and some water circulation, algae blooms should be of short duration. But don't expect water in a garden pool to be perfectly clear. That isn't any healthier for fish and plants than green water.

This garden with pool, raised beds, and blooming plants shows the immense diversity a gardener can obtain while using specialty garden plants. This garden provides a formal yet relaxing atmosphere.

CHAPTER 6

ENCYCLOPEDIA OF SPECIALTY GARDEN PLANTS

Plants for each specialty garden—rose, rock, bulb, shade, or water—have their own charm.

To distinguish among the literally thousands of roses currently available, it is helpful to divide roses into different classes. Self-supporting bush roses are the most popular today. Bush roses include hybrid teas, grandifloras, floribundas, polyanthas, and miniature roses. Other roses of interest are shrub, climbing, tree, and species. In a rock garden, rocks should dominate. As you choose plants for your rockery, don't forget to take into account their flowering season. The vast majority of alpine plants are spring bloomers. Be sure to take special note of summer and fall bloomers and use them accordingly. There are bulbs for just about every season. This directory includes just a few of the hardy bulbs, tubers, and corms that can be grown in most home gardens. There are literally thousands of shade-tolerant plants to choose from. Anything that can survive and thrive in the understory of a local forest is probably a good choice for the shade garden at home. Water gardens add the finishing touch to any landscape project, but without at least a few aquatic plants to bring it to life, a water garden is just a pool.

Hybrid Teas

Single-stemmed, large-flowered, and delicately perfumed, hybrid teas are the epitome of the perfect rose. They are the class all other roses are compared with. Hybrid teas were originally derived from crosses between tea roses and hybrid perpetuals: two categories of roses popular more than a century ago.

Description: Hybrid teas generally bear one flower per stem and are particularly beautiful in bud, with a long, pointed form that opens delicately into a delightful double flower with a high central cone. The color range is the most complete among roses; there are even "blue" (actually, lilac or lavender) hybrid teas. They are often moderately to strongly perfumed and bloom off and on throughout the season. Plants generally reach about 3 feet in height in cold climates and up to 5 feet in warmer ones.

Planting: Space 24 to 30 inches apart in cold climates, 3 to 4 feet in warm ones.

Special needs: Hybrid teas need harsher pruning than most other roses. They tend to suffer from severe winter kill, and full winter protection is necessary in cold regions. Remove faded flowers to ensure continual bloom.

Propagation: Few hybrid teas grow well on their own roots. They are usually sold in the form of grafted plants.

Uses: Hybrid teas are the cutting rose par excellence: The "long-stemmed roses" of the florist industry are hybrid teas. Since their growing habit tends to be rigidly upright and rather sparse, they are best planted in the center of beds where their flowers, rather than their overall appearance, will be noticed.

Varieties: 'Chrysler Imperial,' dark red; 'Garden Party,' white; 'Mister Lincoln,' dark red; 'Pascali,' white; 'Peace,' yellow blend; 'Tropicana,' orange red.

Grandifloras

Grandifloras combine the vigor and blooming ability of floribundas with the beautiful blooms and long stems of hybrid teas. This is not a surprising combination since they resulted from crosses between the two groups. Their vigorous growth habit makes them more satisfactory garden subjects than hybrid teas.

Description: Grandifloras are tall-growing roses, often reaching 5 feet or more in height even in harsh climates. They are sturdy, upright-growing plants that are generally well-clothed in large, shiny leaves similar to the leaves of hybrid teas. They bear clusters of large flowers that, in the best cultivated varieties, are as attractive in both bud and bloom as hybrid teas, although often not as perfumed. Grandifloras generally bloom continually over the flowering season rather than in bursts.

Planting: Space about 2 to 3 feet apart in cold climates, 4 feet in warm ones.

Special needs: Grandifloras are generally hardier than hybrid teas and suffer less from winter kill. Nevertheless, they require full winter protection in cold regions. Remove faded flowers to ensure continual bloom. Although their tall stems may suggest a need for staking, they are self-supporting.

Propagation: Grandifloras are best purchased as grafted plants, although some grow fairly well on their own roots from cuttings.

Uses: Their tall size makes grandifloras perfect choices for the back of the rose bed. Their long stems make excellent cut flowers.

Varieties: 'Arizona,' bronze; 'Love,' red and cream; 'Prominent,' orange; 'Queen Elizabeth,' medium pink; 'Sonia,' pink blend; 'Sundowner,' copper.

Floribundas

Floribunda roses first became popular in the middle of the 20th century. They resulted from crosses between hybrid teas and polyanthas. They are renowned for their season-long clusters of medium-size blooms.

Description: Floribundas are quite variable in height, ranging from 18 inches to 3½ feet. They generally form more attractive, less rigid plants than hybrid teas. Floribundas bear clusters of small to relatively large flowers (up to 2 to 3 inches across) on moderately long stems and come in a full range of colors. Some are single-flowered or semi-double, but most modern hybrids are fully double. Constant bloom is perhaps the main characteristic of this group; they are rarely out of flower. Although floribundas are not generally reputed for their fragrance, this class does contain several highly perfumed varieties.

Planting: Space about 18 inches to 2 feet apart in cold climates, 2 to 3 feet in warmer ones.

Special needs: Floribundas are considered particularly easy to grow and are quite hardy, but they do require some winter protection in cold regions. Remove faded flowers to ensure continual bloom.

Propagation: Like most modern roses, floribundas are best purchased in the form of grafted plants.

Uses: Their profuse, nonstop blooming over relatively compact, dense-leaved plants and their general ease of care make floribundas truly all-purpose roses. They are ideal for both beds and edging. They are best planted in groups of three or more and produce a stunning effect in mass plantings. They are also an excellent choice for container growing.

Varieties: 'Escapade,' mauve; 'Europeana,' dark red; 'Iceberg,' white; 'Sexy Rexy,' medium pink; 'Sunsprite,' dark yellow.

Polyanthas

Polyantha roses were popular around 1900, but they have been losing ground to more modern rose classes in recent years. They are the parents of the popular floribunda class and thus, indirectly, of the grandifloras. They are still actively used in breeding.

Description: Polyanthas are generally low-growing, bushy plants, averaging 18 to 24 inches in height. They have small leaves and dense clusters of small flowers on short stems in shades of white, pink, red, and orange. The blooms may be single, semi-double, or double. Among the latest roses to bloom in spring, they continue to flower until frost.

Planting: Space about 18 inches apart in cold climates, 30 inches in warmer ones.

Special needs: Polyanthas are hardy plants and tend to be easy to grow. They often outlive the more exotic but delicate roses of the modern hybrid classes. Some winter protection may be necessary in colder regions. Remove faded flowers to ensure repeat bloom.

Propagation: Polyanthas are best purchased in the form of grafted plants.

Uses: Their hardiness and low growth make polyanthas good choices for beds and edging. They are best planted in groups of three or more. They also make good container plants.

Varieties: Few new polyanthas have been released over the last few decades, and most varieties still available date back 75 years or more. Those that remain, though, have withstood the test of time: Any rose that has remained popular for such a long time is bound to be a good one. Popular varieties include 'Cécile Brunner,' light pink; 'China Doll,' medium pink; 'The Fairy,' semi-double, pink; 'Margo Koster,' coral orange.

Miniature Roses

Miniature roses first became popular during the 1800s, then were almost forgotten. Lately, their popularity has been growing rapidly. They are now among the most commonly hybridized of all roses.

Description: Since miniature roses are available in so many different forms, defining them is difficult. Even their height is deceptive: While truly tiny miniatures rarely reach more than 6 inches, many other "miniatures" eventually grow to 3 feet. The major characteristic of this group is a combination of small flowers on thin stems and diminutive foliage. Generally speaking, they either remain or can easily be maintained at less than 18 inches in height. Their flowers can be simple, semi-double, or double; clustered or single; fragrant or odorless. They have as wide a color range as any class of rose and more growth forms, from shrubby to creeping to climbing, than any other. Most are everblooming.

Planting: Spacing will depend on the eventual size of the variety chosen; 10 to 18 inches is usually adequate.

Special needs: Miniature roses are probably the hardiest of the bush roses. Many survive temperatures below 0 degrees Fahrenheit, although they may be killed to the ground. However, some winter protection is recommended in colder regions. Remove faded blooms to ensure continual bloom.

Propagation: Miniature roses are readily reproduced by cuttings.

Uses: Their small size makes miniature roses ideal for edging, mass plantings, and rock or herb gardens. They are ideal container plants and the only roses truly useful as houseplants.

Varieties: 'Cinderella,' white; 'Holy Toledo,' copper; 'Lavender Jewel,' lavender; 'Starina,' orange red.

Climbing Roses

Climbing roses are quite a varied group, some originating as hybrids, others as mutations from bush roses such as hybrid teas, grandifloras, and floribundas. They are especially popular in areas where winters are mild since protecting them for the winter is quite painstaking elsewhere.

Description: Climbers have long, supple canes and would actually become trailers if not trained to a support. They can reach 10 feet or more in height. The range in flower form is quite vast, from large-flowered, hybrid tea blooms to small, clustered, shrub rose blossoms. They are often separated into two groups: large-flowered climbers, which bloom intermittently throughout the summer on thick canes, and ramblers, which have clusters of small flowers that bloom once in late spring or early summer on thinner canes.

Planting: Space about 3 to 4 feet apart. In cold climates, it is important to leave ample room for mounding or trenching the long canes during the winter months.

Special needs: Ample winter protection is needed for these tender plants, although a few of the more recent hybrids derived from shrub roses, such as 'John Cabot,' are fully winter hardy, even in temperatures below 0 degrees Fahrenheit. On varieties that bloom just once, prune some of the older canes to the ground after blooming. On other climbers, remove old canes only when overcrowding threatens. Prune out faded flowers to stimulate repeat flowering. Climbers must be fastened to their support.

Propagation: Large-flowered climbers are best purchased as grafted plants. Many ramblers can easily be grown from rooted cuttings.

Uses: Climbers are ideal for training up walls, trellises, pergolas, and arbors.

Varieties: 'America,' coral; 'Blaze,' crimson; 'Golden Showers,' yellow; 'John Cabot,' medium red; 'New Dawn,' light pink.

Shrub Roses

This vast, hard-to-define group of plants is mostly made up of "leftovers"; that is, roses that don't fit into other categories. Many are "improved" versions of species roses, bearing double flowers or blooming repeatedly. Others result from crossing species roses with bush roses. Many different subclasses could be defined, but the two most obvious are the typical shrub roses with tall, arching canes, and the creeping ground cover roses.

Description: Shrub roses are generally tall (4 to 12 feet), shrubby plants that produce numerous arching canes. Their flowers can be single, semi-double, or double and are borne singly or in clusters both at the ends of the canes and on side branches. Many bloom only once—but very heavily—in the spring, but others are repeat bloomers. Ground cover roses are similar, but they grow flat against the ground, rooting as they grow and covering large areas over time. Both types often produce colorful red, orange, or yellow hips.

Planting: Space about 4 to 6 feet apart, closer when grown as hedges.

Special needs: Most commonly available shrub roses are fully winter hardy. Pruning for the most part consists of pruning any winter kill and removing older canes in spring. Unlike most roses, shrub roses should not be deadheaded, or they will not produce their attractive fruit (hips).

Propagation: Most shrub roses can be readily multiplied by division or cuttings.

Uses: Shrub roses are unrivalled for use in privacy hedges and shrub borders, and many are excellent in seashore plantings. They are grown for both their flowers and their hips, which are rich in vitamin C and are used in cooking, medication, and flower arrangements. The hips also attract birds during the winter.

Varieties: Repeat-blooming shrub roses: 'Blanc de Coubert,' white, semi-double; 'F. J. Grootendurst,' red, double; 'Golden Wings,' light yellow, single. Ground cover roses: 'Max Graf,' pink; 'Sea Foam,' white.

Tree Roses

Tree roses are not actually a class of rose but rather a way of growing them. A bush or climbing rose is simply grafted onto a straight trunk, giving the desired treelike appearance.

Description: Miniature roses are usually grafted onto trunks only 1 to 2 feet high. Floribundas, hybrid teas, and grandifloras are grown on stock about 3 or 4 feet tall. Climbing roses grafted onto a 6-foot trunk gives the weeping tree roses of commerce.

Planting: Space tree roses 3 to 5 feet apart; weeping tree roses, about 6 feet. Plant the same way as other roses; however, before filling in the planting hole, install a sturdy stake that is the same height as the trunk. Attach the trunk to the stake with elastic ties to prevent the trunk from being broken by strong winds.

Special needs: Tree roses are very tender and require careful winter protection in all but the warmest climates. Those grown in containers can be brought indoors when dormant and kept barely watered in a cool space until spring.

Propagation: Tree roses can only be multiplied through grafting onto special stock.

Uses: Tree roses are used as specimen plants, placed strategically where they will be shown off to best advantage. Smaller ones are often used as container plants.

Varieties: Just about any kind of rose—from miniatures to hybrid teas to even climbing roses—can be grafted into tree rose form. Local nurseries usually offer only a limited variety.

Species Roses

More and more gardeners are turning to the simple beauty and ease of care of species roses. These are roses as found in nature, with simple flowers and the kind of inherent ruggedness that makes them thrive where no other roses will grow. There are some 200 species roses, but only a few dozen are commonly grown.

Description: Species roses bear abundant single flowers, but they usually bloom only once a season. They are often fragrant, and most produce colorful hips. The majority are shrub roses, although some are climbers. Most offer excellent resistance to pests and diseases.

Planting: Space about 4 to 6 feet apart, closer when grown as hedges.

Special needs: Winter hardiness is extremely variable. Some, such as *Rosa rugosa*, are hardy virtually everywhere. Pruning mainly consists of removing any winter kill and older canes in spring. There is no need to prune faded flowers.

Propagation: Species roses can be multiplied by division or cuttings. They are the only roses that come true from seed.

Uses: Species roses are used for hedges and borders and as climbing plants. They are ideal for naturalizing. Their hips are used in cooking and flower arranging and to attract wildlife.

Varieties: *Rosa glauca* (*R. rubrifolia*) is probably the only rose grown for its foliage: Lightly thorned red canes bear reddish purple leaves. This hardy plant produces fragrant pink flowers with a white eye in late spring; hips are red. *Rosa rugosa*, a bright pink rose, and its white flowered form, *R. r. alba*, are frequently used in seashore plantings where they often naturalize. The summer-long blooms are followed by large, bright orange hips. The stems are heavily spined. This is the parent of many shrub roses and is extremely hardy. *Rosa wichuriana*, the "memorial rose," makes a hardy climber or ground cover. It bears fragrant white flowers late in the season followed by red hips.

Bird's Nest Spruce

Picea abies 'Nidiformis'
Zone: USDA 2

The Norway spruce, of which this plant is a variety, can attain heights of 150 feet, hardly a rock garden plant. The bird's nest spruce, however, is completely different. Even after nearly three decades, it rarely reaches more than 3 feet in height. It may attain 6 feet or more in spread.

Description: Bird's nest spruce is a low-growing, rounded conifer with a distinctly flat top. It bears dark green needles that are much shorter and daintier than those of the typical species. As the plant ages, the outer section often grows higher than the middle, giving the plant its characteristic central depression: the "bird's nest" shape from which it derives both its botanical and common names.

Ease of care: Easy.

How to grow: Plant in full sun to light shade in soil that remains moderately moist. This plant grows better in cool summer areas than in warm ones.

Propagation: By grafting.

Uses: The bird's nest spruce is a solid, easy-to-grow dwarf conifer. It works well in rock gardens and as foundation plantings or specimen plantings. Its main advantage, unlike so many other "dwarf" conifers, is that it never outgrows its space.

Related varieties: There are several dwarf spruces that can be used in rock gardens. Where some elevation is required in the rock garden, 'dwarf Alberta spruce' (*Picea glauca* 'Conica'), with its densely conical form, is a popular choice. Its new growth is an attractive light green. Dwarf Alberta spruce will eventually reach 10 to 12 feet in height, but only after 30 years or so. Other conifers offering slow-growing varieties of similar appearance to dwarf spruces include firs (*Abies*) and hemlock (*Tsuga*).

Dalmatian Bellflower

Campanula portenschlagiana
Zone: USDA 4

Bellflowers are popular garden flowers with bell-shaped blooms, and they are discussed in more detail in the "Perennials" section, page 190. However, several are of specific interest to rock gardeners, including the beautiful and adaptable Dalmatian bellflower.

Description: This is a low, tufted perennial with somewhat kidney-shaped leaves. The stems grow up to 9 inches in height and bear bluish-purple, 1-inch-long flowers.

Ease of care: Easy.

How to grow: Plant in full sun or partial shade and in well-drained soil with adequate moisture.

Propagation: The Dalmatian bellflower self-sows readily and can also be grown from divisions and cuttings.

Uses: This is an excellent plant for almost all situations in the rock garden: scree gardens, crevices, and the like. It is ideal for rock walls and often self-sows in them.

Related species: There are a great many other rock garden bellflowers, including the similar bluebells of Scotland (*C. rotundifolia*) with round basal leaves and grasslike stem leaves. It also grows in the wild on rock faces in eastern North America. Its flowers are typically bright blue, but purple and white flowered varieties are also available.

Creeping Broom

Genista pilosa 'Vancouver Gold'
Zone: USDA 5

Creeping broom is a low-growing plant with bright yellow blooms from midspring to early summer. It makes an excellent ground cover in sunny spots.

Description: The rather sparse leaves of creeping broom are rounded and measure about ½ inch long. They are borne on intricately twisted grey-green branches. The yellow pealike flowers are quite long-lasting. Although the shrub rarely reaches more than 1 foot in height, it can spread up to 7 feet.

Ease of care: Easy.

How to grow: This plant does perfectly well in poor, even sandy, soil and hot, dry conditions. It requires full sun. Since it dislikes transplanting, set it in its permanent home immediately after purchase.

Propagation: By cuttings and layering.

Uses: This low-growing shrub makes a fine ground cover for drier parts of the rock garden. It also grows well near the seashore since it isn't bothered by salt spray and sandy conditions.

Related species: There are several other species of broom well suited to the rock garden. 'Spanish broom' (*Genista hispanica*) is taller-growing (up to 2 feet) and produces golden yellow flowers in late spring. In winter, although the leaves drop, its branches and heavy spines remain bright green. 'German broom' (*G. germanica*) is similar to Spanish broom, but it has hairier stems and smaller, later-blooming flowers. Most other brooms are too tall for rock gardens.

Creeping Gypsophile, Creeping Baby's Breath

Gypsophila repens
Zone: USDA 3

The best known *Gypsophila* is baby's breath (*G. paniculata*). Although baby's breath, with its thin, multibranching stems and sprays of tiny flowers, looks wonderful at the back of the rock garden or in front of a large boulder, the top choice gypsophile for a rock garden would have to be one of the creeping varieties; the best known is *G. repens*.

Description: Creeping gypsophile is a low-growing, prostrate, or trailing, perennial with narrow gray-green leaves that grow no more than 10 inches high and usually much less. It is covered with airy sprays of tiny white to pale pink flowers from early to midsummer.

Ease of care: Easy.

How to grow: The name "gypsophile" means "lover of gypsum," a reference that *G. repens* grows in alkaline soils in the wild. It is not quite as specific in its needs in culture, but acid soils should certainly be avoided. Creeping gypsophile prefers full sun and a well-drained location.

Propagation: By cuttings or seed.

Uses: Creeping gypsophile is a particularly adaptable rock garden plant and makes a fine ground cover.

Related varieties: The pink-flowered version of creeping gypsophile (*G. repens* 'Rosea') is possibly more attractive and better behaved than the species. 'Rosy Veil,' although generally listed as a variety of *G. repens,* is most likely the result of a cross between *G. repens* and baby's breath. It grows taller (up to 18 inches) and bears pink to white fully double flowers.

Dwarf False Cypress

Chamaecyparis pisifera nana
Zone: USDA 5

The dwarf false cypress is one of a vast selection of dwarf conifers suitable for rock gardens. However, unlike many "dwarf evergreens" that all too quickly become quite large, the growth of the dwarf false cypress is truly slow. It rarely reaches more than 2 feet in height and 6 feet across after 40 years.

Description: The dwarf false cypress is a small, dense-growing conifer, rounded in its youth but becoming flat-topped as it ages. It bears fan-shaped branchlets that are deep green at the tips and blue-green below.

Ease of care: Easy.

How to grow: Although the dwarf false cypress is tolerant of varying conditions, it prefers moister soil than many other rock garden plants. For that reason, it is often planted at the base of the rockery, where it will not be as exposed to drying winds. It does equally well in full sun or partial shade.

Propagation: By cuttings.

Uses: Its year-long coloration and slow, regular growth make this plant a star of the dwarf conifer collection. It is often planted where dense permanent cover is wanted, both in rock gardens and in foundation plantings.

Related varieties: The varieties of dwarf false cypress include rounded or broadly conical versions, pyramidal types, and low-growing ones. These varieties are generally chosen from sports (side shoots with characteristics different from the main plant) appearing on the following species: 'Sawara false cypress' (*Chamaecyparis pisifera*), 'Hinoki false cypress' (*C. obtusa*), 'Nootka cypress' (*C. nootkatensis*), and 'Lawson cypress' (*C. Lawsoniana*). Other than sharing dwarf growth habits, they come in a variety of foliage shades, from deep black-green to blue-green to yellow to variegated. Make sure any varieties selected for the rock garden are true dwarfs and not just slow growing species.

Alpine Forget-Me-Not

Myosotis alpestris
Zone: USDA 2

True forget-me-nots (*Myosotis scorpioides*) are popular in mixed borders and shade gardens where their sky blue flowers are a sure sign of spring. It's nice to know there is also an alpine species that adds just as much beauty to the rock garden.

Description: The alpine forget-me-not is a dainty perennial that blooms in early summer. The flowers are essentially identical to the true forget-me-not and in the same shade of true blue, but alpine forget-me-nots are borne on shorter stalks (about 6 inches high). The plant has small tufted leaves and a loose papery sheath at the base of the stems.

Ease of care: Moderately easy.

How to grow: The alpine forget-me-not does well in both sun and partial shade. It requires a gritty soil that retains moisture.

Propagation: By division or seed. It should be allowed to self-sow since it is rather short-lived and could almost be considered a biennial.

Uses: The alpine forget-me-not looks most at home—and also grows best—in crevices and scree gardens.

Related species: 'Woodland Forget-me-not' (*Myosotis sylvatica*) is often erroneously sold as *M. alpestris.* Woodland forget-me-not requires moderate shade and rich, moist soil to grow well; it is not a good choice for the well-drained soils of most rock gardens. It is an annual or biennial plant and readily self-sows. The flowers range in color from blue to pink and white.

Hens-and-chicks

Sempervivum tectorum
Zone: USDA 4

This old-fashioned plant, also called common houseleek, is undergoing a resurgence in popularity. Its attractive and intriguing shapes and its ability to grow under just about any conditions make it a perfect choice for everything from rock gardens to borders to containers. Its botanic name means "live forever," and it was once planted on rooftops in the belief that neither lightning nor fire would touch a house so adorned. The common name "hens-and-chicks" comes from the numerous plantlets borne on short stolons all around the mother plant.

Description: Hens-and-chicks produces low-growing, 3- to 4-inch rosettes of pointed gray-green leaves. Hens-and-chicks is less commonly planted than the subspecies *Sempervivum tectorum calcareum,* which has purple-tipped leaves. At maturity the rosette forms a thick, hairy flower stalk that rises to 12 inches in height. The star-shaped flowers are pink or red.

Ease of care: Easy.

How to grow: Plant in any kind of well-drained soil in full sun. It will grow in a crack between two rocks even if there is no apparent soil. Hens-and-chicks is so resilient it essentially takes care of itself.

Propagation: By detaching and planting offshoots in any kind of soil.

Uses: This classic rock garden plant makes an attractive display when planted in rock crevices, stone walls, and between paving stones.

Related species: 'Cobweb houseleek' (*Sempervivum arachnoideum*) bears smaller rosettes covered with cobweblike threads. It produces showy red flowers on 4-inch stems. *S. montanum* produces rosettes nearly 2 inches across of hairy, dark green leaves. The flowers are bluish-purple.

Iceland Poppy

Papaver nudicaule
Zone: USDA 2

Although the common name suggests an Icelandic origin, the Iceland poppy is actually native to the mountainous and arctic regions of North America. It is a short-lived perennial often grown as a biennial or, especially in warm climates, an annual.

Description: The Iceland poppy produces a low-growing rosette of toothed, hairy leaves. The plant sends up, for a long period during the summer, thin, hairy stems from 1 to 2 feet high; each stem is topped by a large, solitary, cup-shaped fragile-looking flower in shades of white, pink, orange, yellow, or bicolored. The flowers can be single, semi-double, or double. In warm climates, where it is raised as an annual, it is planted in fall for winter and early spring flowers.

Ease of care: Moderately difficult in warm climates. It is easy to grow in colder areas as long as the plant is allowed to reseed itself.

How to grow: Sow seeds in fall or early spring. Iceland poppies dislike transplanting but can be started in peat pots for later transfer into the garden. They generally bloom the first year from seed. Place in full sun in well-drained soil. Do not overfertilize. Pinch off faded flowers to stimulate repeated bloom and to encourage the plant to perennialize. This plant performs best where summers are cool.

Propagation: From seed. Always allow at least one plant to produce seed to ensure the upcoming generation.

Uses: A good rock garden plant for all situations, the Iceland poppy also makes an excellent cut flower. Sear the cut stem before putting the flowers in a vase.

Related species: 'Alpine poppy' (*Papaver Burseri,* sometimes listed as *P. alpinum*) is similar in appearance and culture, but it is smaller (up to 10 inches) and nearly hairless.

Irish Moss

Sagina subulata
Zone: USDA 4

This plant looks so much like moss that most people cannot be convinced otherwise—until it blooms. The tiny white flowers, though, are proof that this rock garden miniature is not even related to moss, which are primitive plants that never bloom.

Description: Irish moss makes a dense, bright green mat of tiny leaves and tiny stems. Its tiny white flowers are borne singly but are often numerous enough to nearly cover the plant.

Ease of care: Easy.

How to grow: Irish moss grows best in full sun to light shade and in good, well-drained soil. With time, one plant forms an attractive carpet of greenery. Occasionally, growth becomes crowded, pushing sections of the carpet upward. If you consider this less attractive, cut out a slice of the plant and push down until the roots are in contact with the soil. Any empty space resulting from this surgery will be quickly filled with greenery.

Propagation: Cut out sections and press down in moderately moist soil.

Uses: Irish moss makes an elegant and attractive rock garden plant, forming a cushion of greenery in even the shallowest soil or the narrowest of cracks as long as it is not allowed to entirely dry out. It can also be planted between stepping stones or in cracks in pavement since it can tolerate some foot traffic.

Related species: A similar plant, *Arenaria verna,* is also called Irish moss. When not in bloom, the two look virtually identical. Even when flowering, they are similar, although *Arenaria verna* bears its flowers in small clusters. Both have golden green forms (*Arenaria verna* 'Aurea' and *Sagina subulata* 'Aurea') often called Scotch moss.

Lewisia

Lewisia **species**
Zone: USDA 5

Lewisias are among the most spectacular of all alpine plants, with delightfully colored flowers that are large compared with the tiny size of the plant. Lewisias have the reputation of being difficult to grow, but this is less true when they are raised in rock gardens where conditions are similar to their mountainous homeland. They are native to western North America.

Description: When not in flower, lewisias could almost be mistaken for succulents. Their thick, waxy leaves look much like those of the popular hens-and-chicks. In bloom, though, they are quite different from any other plant. The waxy-textured blooms come in bright pink, pink, apricot, white, or red. They bloom in late spring. Their leaves are either evergreen or deciduous, depending on the species.

Ease of care: Difficult.

How to grow: Grow in full sun in well-drained, deep soil. The soil mix should contain at least 50 percent sharp sand for perfect drainage. Surround the base of the plant with rock chips to prevent rot. Lewisias prefer sites with abundant spring moisture followed by a dry, cool summer.

Propagation: By division or seeds in spring.

Uses: Crevices, scree gardens, and other well-drained sites are ideal for this spectacular plant. Plant in groups of three or more for best results.

Related species: The best-known lewisia is undoubtedly *L. rediviva*, also called 'bitter root lewisia'; its starchy roots, once consumed by Native Americans, are bitter to the taste if not harvested at the right season. Bitter root lewisia has thick, fleshy, deciduous leaves and pink to white flowers. *L. Cotyledon* has persistent leaves and grows in the form of matlike rosettes. Its flowers are white with pink veins or red stripes. Hybrid lewisias have become available that are said to be easier to grow.

Moss Campion

Silene acaulis
Zone: USDA 5

This low-growing plant looks much like moss except when it blooms in spring and summer.

Description: Moss campion forms a low mound of narrow, pointed leaves only 2 inches high but up to 18 inches across. The five-petaled, notched flowers are reddish purple and quite large for the size of the plant: ½ inch diameter on 4-inch stalks. The flowers appear from late spring to midsummer.

Ease of care: Easy.

How to grow: Plant in deep, well-drained gritty soil in full sun.

Propagation: By division, cuttings, and seed.

Uses: Moss campion likes dry conditions and does best in tight rock crevices. It is ideally suited to smaller rock gardens where its flowers will garner more attention.

Related species: There are several varieties of moss campion, including a white-flowered form (*Silene acaulis* 'Alba') and a double, purplish-pink form (*S. a.* 'Cenisia'). 'Alpine catchfly' (*Silene quadrifida,* sometimes sold as *S. alpestris*), with white flowers, and 'Schafta campion' (*S. Schafta*), with pink flowers, grow taller (up to 12 inches) but are otherwise similar to moss campion.

Pasqueflower

Pulsatilla vulgaris
Zone: USDA 5

This plant was long considered an anemone and is still listed as *Anemone pulsatilla* in many books and catalogs. It is a popular and easy-to-grow rock garden plant: one of the stars of the early spring garden.

Description: The 2-inch cup-shaped flowers are blue to deep purple with a large cluster of bright yellow central stamens. They appear on short stalks before the leaves emerge in spring, often covering the entire plant in flowers. Cultivated varieties also come in pink, red, and more rarely, white. The leaves are deeply divided and silky. The leaves are attractive in their own right, forming a mound about 8 inches high by 12 inches in diameter. The long-lasting seed heads look like gray pom-poms and add a further decorative dimension.

Ease of care: Easy in cool climates, difficult in warm ones.

How to grow: Plant in sun or partial shade in humus-rich, well-drained soil.

Propagation: By seed sown in late spring or root cuttings taken in fall.

Uses: Pasqueflower is ideal for planting in deep soil pockets in the rock garden and is also suited to low borders.

Related species: This plant was formerly considered an anemone. While there are a great many anemones, some of which can be grown as rock garden plants in shady spots, none has any real resemblance to the pasqueflower. However, one plant in a closely related genus, the *Adonis vernalis,* is similar but with bright yellow 3-inch flowers. It needs the same conditions and flowers at approximately the same period as the pasqueflower.

Moss Pink

Phlox subulata
Zone: USDA 3

This native of North America is one of the most striking flowering plants of spring, forming a dense evergreen carpet entirely covered in blooms.

Description: Moss pink is a ground-hugging plant up to 6 inches in height with evergreen, needlelike leaves on creeping woody stems. The star-shaped flowers are ¾ inch across and come in shades of white, pink, deep pink, red, purple, or blue. They appear from midspring to early summer, depending on the local climate.

Ease of care: Easy.

How to grow: Grow in full sun to partial shade in a well-drained, even sandy, soil. Do not overfertilize. After blooming has ceased, prune harshly (to 1 to 2 inches) to stimulate new growth.

Propagation: By division, layering, or cuttings.

Uses: It's the perfect ground cover plant for the rock garden; it is spectacular in bloom and makes an attractive green carpet otherwise.

Related species: There are several other low-growing phloxes, most of which are best suited to semishady rock gardens. 'Trailing phlox' (*Phlox nivalis*) is so similar to moss pink that, in culture, the two are usually sold as *P. subulata*. The two can be distinguished only by obscure differences in flower structure. 'Creeping phlox' (*Phlox stolonifera*) has rounded leaves and blue to lavender flowers in dense clusters. It reaches a height of 6 to 12 inches. 'Wild sweet William' (*P. divaricata*) grows up to 18 inches and also bears blue to lavender flowers.

Polyanthus Primrose

Primula x polyantha
Zone: USDA 4

Most rock gardens are designed for sunny locations. But if you have no choice except to build one in a shady spot, there's no need to be discouraged: You can always grow primroses.

Description: The polyanthus primrose produces a stemless rosette of fresh green, tongue-shaped leaves. Short flower stalks arise from the center of the rosette, each bearing a cluster of 1- to 2-inch flowers in a wide array of colors. They may be blue, purple, pink, red, yellow, or white and often with a contrasting central eye. The flower stalks can be up to 1 foot in height, but dwarf varieties, with stalks so short they barely rise above the leaves, are currently more popular.

Ease of care: Moderately easy.

How to grow: Plant in cool, moist, humus-rich soil in light to moderate shade. Divide them every three to four years to maintain vigor. In dry, hot climates, treat polyanthus primroses as annuals or potted plants.

Propagation: By division after flowering. Can be grown from seed but germination is irregular.

Uses: Woodlands and shady rock gardens. They combine well with spring-flowering bulbs.

Related species: 'Japanese primrose' (*Primula japonica*) bears stout stems up to 2½ feet high with up to five separate whorls of flowers. It needs consistently moist growing conditions. 'Auricula primrose' (*P. auricula*) is the best primrose for the drier, warmer conditions typical of most rock gardens, although it does prefer some shade. Native to the Alps, it grows perfectly in well-drained, even stony, soils. It has gray-green leathery leaves often covered with a mealy bloom and bears clusters of fragrant flowers in many shades, usually with a yellow or white eye.

Pussytoes

Antennaria dioica
Zone: USDA 2

It is not clear whether this plant gets its name from the soft fuzzy heads of gray flowers, often with pink tips, that it bears in summer or from its woolly gray leaves. In either case, it is a charmer and particularly easy to grow in a rock garden.

Description: The small, woolly leaves, white underneath, form a dense mat across even barren rock surfaces. The stems grow about 2 inches high and spread to about 18 inches. The silvery flowers appear on 10-inch stalks in early to midsummer and are borne in dense clusters.

Ease of care: Easy.

How to grow: This plant is well adapted to full sun and dry, lean soil: conditions similar to those of its natural environment. It will not tolerate competition, so be sure to weed carefully.

Propagation: By division in spring or fall.

Uses: This perennial is ideal for planting in cracks and crevices where it will trail over rock faces. It also makes an attractive ground cover for spring bulbs.

Related varieties: There are several varieties of pussytoes, including *Antennaria dioica* 'Tomentosa,' with especially silvery leaves. *A. rosea* was once considered a variety of *A. dioica* but is now given species status. It is similar to *A. dioica* but with entirely pink flowers on a somewhat larger plant. *A. rosea* and *A. dioica* are often confused in culture.

Rock Jasmine

Androsace sarmentosa
Zone: USDA 2

This low-growing plant is perhaps the epitome of the alpine plant. Its small size would make it hardly noticeable elsewhere, but it really shines when given its own niche in a rock garden.

Description: Umbels of small pink flowers appear on 5-inch stems in spring, almost hiding the foliage. The hairy, silvery 1½-inch leaves form a dense rosette. Rock jasmine produces numerous runners and quickly surrounds itself with offsets so that the plant forms a thick clump up to 2 feet in diameter, although the individual rosettes are quite tiny.

Ease of care: Moderately difficult.

How to grow: Rock jasmine requires perfect drainage and should be mulched with stone chips. It can be grown in full sun in colder climates, but needs partial shade elsewhere since it does not tolerate heat. Water regularly during periods of drought.

Propagation: Separate and root the plantlets that form at the end of stolons.

Uses: The rock jasmine's need for perfect drainage makes it an ideal candidate for scree gardens, rock clefts, and rock walls.

Related species: *A. sarmentosa* is probably one of the hardiest of the genus. *A. lanuginosa* forms a mat with silky, silver leaves; it is hardy to zone 6. *A. sempervivoides* is a much smaller plant, forming clumps only 9 inches across and 2 inches high on 4-inch flower stalks.

Rockfoil

Saxifraga **species**
Zone: Varies with the species; most are hardy to at least zone 6, some to zone 4.

The name *Saxifraga* means "rock breaker." Members of this genus of plants are generally found sprouting out of narrow crevices in rocky outcrops throughout the Northern Hemisphere. There are more than 300 species, many of which are in cultivation. Although the genus is widely grown, no one species could be said to be common. Most sources of rock garden plants offer several different ones.

Description: Most rockfoils are cushion-forming perennials with silvery or succulent foliage growing as clusters of small rosettes. In many cultivated forms the leaves are variegated yellow or white. The flower stalks are held well above the low-growing foliage and bear numerous flowers in shades of white, pink, purple, or yellow.

Ease of care: Moderately easily.

How to grow: Most do best in gritty, well-drained soil and in sun or partial shade. Strawberry geranium (*S. stolonifera*) differs from the others in requiring rich, moist soil.

Propagation: By layering, cuttings, or seed.

Uses: These plants are good choices for planting in rock gardens, even where little soil exists: cracks, crevices, paving, screes, and the like. Strawberry geranium is better used as a woodland plant or a houseplant.

Related species: 'London-pride' (*S. umbrosa*) bears rosettes of green, shiny, tongue-shaped leaves and clusters of pink flowers. *S.* x *urbium* is similar with larger, toothed leaves. It is also called London-pride. 'Jungfrau rockfoil' (*S. Cotyledon*) has spoon-shaped, pubescent leaves with white flowers veined in red. The least typical of the rockfoils is 'strawberry geranium' (*S. stolonifera*). Its needs and uses are quite different, and it bears leaves quite unlike the others: round with silver veining and a red reverse. It also produces long stolons with plantlets at the tip.

Siberian Draba

Draba sibirica
Zone: USDA 3

The Siberian draba is typical of most mound-forming alpine plants except it blooms in fall as well as spring. It grows fast and easily, winning a place of honor in many rock gardens.

Description: Siberian draba is a trailing plant forming loose rosettes of large leaves, often only 2 or 3 inches high. Its bright yellow flowers are borne on drooping stems.

Ease of care: Easy.

How to grow: Plant Siberian draba in just about any well-drained soil. It will grow well in even small pockets of soil as long as there is room for its long taproots to dig in deeply. It appreciates nearly full sun, although some protection from midday sun is best.

Propagation: By division or cuttings.

Uses: It can be grown anywhere in the rock garden from open spaces to narrow cracks. It is also well-suited to scree gardens.

Related species: There are a large number of drabas from Arctic and alpine areas of the Northern Hemisphere, and most of them are good choices for the rock garden. 'Whitlowgrass' (*Draba aizoides*) forms a low-tufted perennial with dense rosettes of linear leaves and clusters of yellow flowers in the spring. 'Arctic draba' (*D. fladnizensis*) produces cushionlike tufts of foliage and greenish white flowers.

Snow-in-Summer

Cerastium tomentosum
Zone: USDA 2

This popular creeping perennial can be grown under many circumstances, but it is best known for its usefulness as a rock garden plant. It adapts to almost all conditions and has the rare quality of thriving equally well in cold and hot climates.

Description: Snow-in-summer bears its name well: icy-looking silvery gray foliage with a profusion of ½-inch white flowers in early spring. The ¾-inch leaves and creeping stems make a dense mat up to 8 inches high and spreading up to 3 feet in diameter.

Ease of care: Easy.

How to grow: Snow-in-summer does well in just about every kind of well-drained soil, from rich humus to nearly pure sand. It prefers full sun except in warm climates where light shade is preferable. It can become invasive if its faded flower clusters are not sheared off.

Propagation: By division or seed.

Uses: Snow-in-summer is perfectly at home growing in cracks and crevices and makes a wonderful border plant for the transition zone between the rock garden and the rest of your yard. It can also be planted between stepping stones, in scree gardens, and in rock walls.

Related varieties: 'Taurus cerastium' (*Cerastium Biebersteinii*) is similar to snow-in-summer, but its white flowers are almost twice as large. It behaves better than its cousin, but its grayish foliage is not as colorful.

Spring Heath

Erica carnea
Zone: USDA 5

Spring heath is a rhododendron relative best known for its long flowering season: from mid-winter to late spring depending on the local climate. The flowers are tiny but so numerous the entire shrub seems blushed with color.

Description: Spring heath is a low-growing shrub, rarely reaching over 1 foot in height or spread. Most varieties are even smaller, and many are only 6 inches or so high. The tiny, persistent leaves are little more than needles. Bell-shaped pink flowers are borne copiously from each branch.

Ease of care: Moderately difficult.

How to grow: Spring heath is unusual among heaths in that it can grow in alkaline soils, although it prefers acid ones. It does best in poor soils; it can become leggy if overfertilized. Spring heath likes full sun in cooler climates, partial shade in warmer ones. The plant doesn't tolerate excessive summer heat. Prune the plant harshly after the flowers fade if it becomes leggy. Good snow cover is important to its survival in the colder parts of its range.

Propagation: By cuttings or root division.

Uses: Individual spring heaths are planted as spring-flowering accent plants for the rock garden. It can also be planted in groups, eventually forming a deep, even carpet.

Related varieties: Numerous horticultural selections of spring heath have been made. Most are hardier, denser, and more floriferous than the wild species. Some popular cultivated varieties are 'Springwood Pink,' bright pink; 'Vivelli,' carmine red; and 'Springwood White,' silvery white. There are also many other heaths suited to the rock garden, including 'bell heather' (*E. cinerea*) with deep pink-purple flowers appearing from summer through early fall. Complete the season with 'Scotch heather' (*Calluna vulgaris*), a close relative that blooms from midsummer through midfall in white, pink, purple, or red.

Stonecrop

Sedum cauticolum
Zone: USDA 3

Although sedums have already been discussed in the "Perennials" section (see page 190), all of them—especially the creeping kinds—are suited to rock gardens. Also, there are so many kinds, it is worth presenting a few others here.

Description: This creeping species has thick succulent leaves in a distinct shade of gray, often with a pinkish tinge in full sun. It bears cherry-red flowers in clusters.

Ease of care: Easy.

How to Grow: Stonecrops prefer full sun and well-drained soil.

Propagation: By division and cuttings.

Uses: All sedums are suited to rock gardens, rock crevices, and stone walls. Many can also be used as houseplants.

Related species: 'Leafy stonecrop' (*Sedum dasyphyllum*) forms mats of gray-blue foliage and bears pink flowers in early summer. *S. lineare* has narrow, light green leaves and a spreading habit. It makes a thick ground cover and bears abundant yellow flowers. It is one of the few stonecrops that grows well in moist shade. 'Capo blanco' (*S. spathulifolium*) bears thick spoon-shaped leaves in dense rosettes on short, trailing stems. The leaf color—blue-green with a purple tinge—is quite spectacular. The flowers are light yellow. 'Gold moss stonecrop' (*S. acre*) is perhaps the tiniest stonecrop, with minuscule green leaves covering a creeping stem. It quickly forms a dense mat. The yellow flowers are so small as to be scarcely visible. There are numerous other species of stonecrop, and many of those above offer variegated, golden-leaved, or purple-leaved varieties.

Hardy Amaryllis

Lycoris radiata
Zone: USDA 7

The hardy amaryllis is a pleasant surprise in the early fall garden. The flower stalks appear out of nowhere, seeming to spring up overnight, and remain in bloom for several weeks.

Description: The straplike leaves of the hardy amaryllis fade away by midsummer, but the flower stalks don't appear until early fall. The blooms are borne in clusters on top of an 18-inch stalk. They are pink to red, rarely white, and are so heavily dominated by long, colorful filaments that the petals themselves are scarcely noticeable.

Ease of care: Moderately easy.

How to grow: Plant bulbs 3 to 4 inches deep and 6 inches apart in a sunny, well-drained area. Plant in fall or spring and, because they dislike being disturbed, leave the bulbs in place for many years. Although heavy mulching can help this plant grow farther north than its normal zone, results are often disappointing: The flowers may be killed by frost before they even open. In colder zones, grow hardy amaryllis as a potted plant, bringing it indoors when frost threatens.

Propagation: By division, in spring or fall.

Uses: Cut flowers, beds, and container planting. Hardy amaryllis naturalizes readily where it is hardy.

Related species: *Lycoris squamigera* is much hardier than *L. radiata* and can be grown successfully in zone 4. It bears trumpetlike flowers of rose-pink on 1½- to 2-foot stems.

Colchicum, Meadow Saffron

Colchicum **species**
Zone: USDA 4

By far the most spectacular of the fall-flowering bulbs, colchicum, or meadow saffron, blooms just as the flower border begins to fade and trees take on their fall colors. Colchicum corms are highly toxic; keep them away from children and pets.

Description: Single-flowered colchicums produce cup-shaped flowers in shades of white through magenta. Double flowered forms have star-shaped blooms. The flowers range in size from 2-inch crocuslike blossoms to giants up to 8 inches across. Flowers arise directly from the ground. The long, shiny, strap-shaped leaves don't appear until the following spring. With time, a single bulb can produce an impressive mound of flowers.

Ease of care: Easy.

How to grow: In late summer or early fall plant corms 4 to 6 inches deep, 8 inches apart, in sunny, well-drained area. Don't delay planting, or the corms will bloom on their own in the sac in which you bought them. Winter mulching is advisable in colder areas. Bare corms are sometimes allowed to bloom on windowsills as a novelty. Colchicums are treated as annuals in warm climates; they need cold winters to establish themselves.

Propagation: By division.

Uses: Beds and borders. Can also be naturalized in lawns and meadows.

Related varieties: 'The Giant,' violet, and 'Lilac Wonder,' lilac, are hybrid colchicums that produce large flowers. 'Waterlily,' deep pink-lilac, has a spectacular double-flower, but the heavy flowers often bend under their own weight. Other fall-flowering bulbs include 'lily-of-the-field' (*Sternbergia*) and 'autumn crocus' (*Crocus* species).

Crocus

Crocus **species**
Zone: USDA 3

Crocuses are the most popular of the late-winter/early spring bulbs. Widely available and easy to grow, they are the first blossoms of spring and offer a wide range of colors.

Description: The cup-shaped flowers of the crocus are upward-facing and come in a vast array of shades, from white to golden yellow to deep purple to bicolor, and may be attractively striped. The flowers appear from late winter to early spring, depending on the variety and the local climate, over grasslike leaves with a white central stripe. Fall-blooming crocuses produce their flowers without any foliage; the leaves appear in spring. Crocus flowers open fully only on sunny days.

Ease of care: Easy.

How to grow: Plant corms 2 to 4 inches deep, 3 to 5 inches apart, in a sunny, well-drained area. Plant winter- and spring-blooming crocuses in fall and fall-blooming crocuses in late summer.

Propagation: By division.

Uses: Crocus are ideal for beds and borders and can also be naturalized in lawns and woodlands. They are excellent for forcing indoors.

Related varieties: The large-flowered Dutch hybrids (generally hybrids of *Crocus vernus*) bear 2- to 3-inch flowers in a full range of colors in early spring. The so-called winter-flowering crocuses, such as *C. chrysanthus*, offer a wide color range. These crocuses are simply very early flowering versions of spring crocuses. While they may bloom as early as January in warm climates, they bloom only a few days earlier than "spring-flowering" crocuses in colder regions. These winter-flowering crocuses bear smaller but more numerous flowers than Dutch hybrids and spread more rapidly when naturalized. *C. sativus,* a fall-flowering crocus, is the commercial source of saffron.

Glory-of-the-Snow

Chionodoxa luciliae
Zone: USDA 3

The bright blue flowers of the glory-of-the-snow are one of the harbingers of spring, often appearing when snow is still on the ground. The colder the weather, the longer they last. These plants actually do best in cold climates, needing a deep winter rest to bloom properly.

Description: Chionodoxas are low-growing plants, 4 to 6 inches high, with grasslike leaves that appear at the same time as the flowers. The flowers are star-shaped and face upwards, unlike many other early spring bloomers. They are generally blue with a central white eye. The flowers can last two weeks or more. The leaves fade away in early summer.

Ease of care: Easy.

How to grow: Plant 3 inches deep, 1 to 3 inches apart, in almost any kind of soil. Full sun to light shade is fine. Moderate shade is necessary in warm climates to keep flowers from fading too quickly.

Propagation: By division or seed.

Uses: A delightful plant for rock gardens or borders, the glory-of-the-snow really shines when naturalized in lawns and woods where it spreads well without ever becoming weedy.

Related varieties: 'Pink Giant' and 'Rosea' have pink blooms. 'Alba' is pure white. Closely related *Puschkinia scilloides* is similar but with very pale blue flowers with a blue central stripe.

Hyacinth

Hyacinthus orientalis
Zone: USDA 5

Colorful as its flowers may be, the true joy of the Dutch hyacinth lies in its delightful, pervading fragrance. Even a few bulbs suffice to instill the garden with a heady scent.

Description: Hyacinths are renowned for their dense 10-inch spikes of star-shaped flowers, generally one spike per bulb, over a vase-shaped rosette of swordlike green leaves. Their bloom is most intense the first year after planting. In following years, the flower clusters are looser and less impressive, although more than one spike may be borne per bulb. The color of the flowers ranges from pure white to yellow, salmon, pink, blue, purple, and near red.

Ease of care: Moderately easy.

How to grow: Plant bulbs 4 to 6 inches deep and 6 to 8 inches apart, in a sunny, well-drained area. Plant the bulbs in early fall. Winter mulching is advisable in colder regions. Hyacinth bulbs don't renew themselves well in cold climates and may need to be replaced every two or three years. They need some winter cold and so do poorly in zones 9 and 10.

Propagation: By division and bulb sections.

Uses: Beds and borders. They are especially appropriate for formal plantings. Plant a few near a doorway so the heady perfume can waft inside with each visitor. They make excellent cut flowers and force well.

Related varieties: Some of the most popular varieties include 'Carnegie,' white; 'City of Haarlem,' yellow; 'Pink Pearl,' pink; 'Delft Blue,' blue; and 'Amsterdam,' deep pink. 'Roman hyacinth' (*Hyacinthus orientalis albulus*) bears looser spikes of white to light blue flowers. It is a bit less hardy than the Dutch hyacinth.

Violet-Scented Iris

Iris reticulata
Zone: USDA 4

Bearded iris and most other garden irises grow from rhizomes and therefore could technically be called bulbous plants. In general, though, gardeners consider them perennials, and they are treated as such in this book. See the "Perennials" section, page 190, for more information. Some of the smaller, generally spring-flowering irises, of which *Iris reticulata* is the main species, do grow from true bulbs and are included here.

Description: *Iris reticulata* is a late winter- or spring-flowering bulb. It bears typical iris blooms in shades of blue and violet with contrasting yellow markings on short 8-inch stems. The grasslike foliage disappears shortly after flowers fade.

Ease of care: Moderately easy.

How to grow: In early fall plant bulbs 4 inches deep, 3 inches apart, in a sunny, well-drained area. Winter mulching is advisable in colder areas. All bulbous irises are easily forced indoors.

Propagation: By division.

Uses: Rock gardens and borders. Can also be naturalized in lawns and meadows.

Related species: *Iris danfordiae*, yellow, and *I. histrioides*, blue, are among the first flowers to bloom in spring; they do not establish themselves well and are best treated as annuals. The taller-growing "Dutch iris" (hybrids of *I. Xiphium*) is available in a wide range of colors. It reaches 15 to 25 inches in height and blooms much later in spring than its smaller cousins.

Lily

Lilium **species**
Zone: USDA 4 to 8, depending on species

Lilies are the mainstay of the summer bulb garden. Although each species has a relatively short blooming period, with careful selection it is possible to have a garden filled with nothing but lilies from early summer until midfall.

Description: There is a wide variety of lilies, and a concise description of the whole group is difficult. Generally, they bear large trumpet-shaped flowers that can face upward, outward, or downward. The latter are often called Turk's cap lilies. Lilies come in just about every color but true blue, and many are attractively spotted or mottled. Stems are usually upright and covered with grasslike leaves and range in height from a few inches to 7 feet or more.

Ease of care: Moderately difficult.

How to grow: Buy only fresh bulbs and plant as soon as possible since lily bulbs never go entirely dormant and cannot tolerate drying out. Plant bulbs 4 to 8 inches deep (2 inches for *Lilium candidum*) and up to 1 foot apart in either late fall or spring. The ideal site is in rich, well-drained soil with humus. The plants need plenty of sun yet some protection from midday rays. Mulching is recommended.

Propagation: By division, bulbils, or bulb scales. Species lilies can be grown from seed.

Uses: Dwarf lilies can be placed in the front of the border, but most others look best toward the middle or back of the garden. Many are readily naturalized in meadows or on the edge of wooded areas. All make excellent cut flowers. Do not cut too much foliage when harvesting the flowers, or the bulb will weaken.

Related varieties: Asiatic hybrids (the Mid-Century hybrids are especially choice) are early flowering; Aurelian hybrids bloom in midsummer; and Oriental hybrids are late blooming. Species lilies include the classic 'Madonna' (*Lilium candidum*), white flowers, and the 'Regal' (*L. regale*), white with a yellow center and lilac-pink exterior.

Narcissus

Narcissus **species**
Zone: USDA 4

Whether you call them daffodils, jonquils, or narcissus (the names are used interchangeably), these bulbs are popular and hardy, providing plentiful flowers for the early to mid-spring garden. True jonquils are small flowered hybrids of the *Narcissus jonquilla*.

Description: The narcissus best known to most people has bright yellow flowers consisting of a ring of flat petals surrounding a long trumpet-like crown or cup. But the central crown can be much smaller and white, yellow, orange, salmon, or red in color. The surrounding petals can also come in yellow or white. Double forms, in fact, may look more like tuberoses than "daffodils." The flowers may be produced singly or in clusters. Many varieties readily produce more than one stalk. Most narcissi are perfumed to some degree, some very strongly. All bear similar straplike leaves that fade away in late spring. Narcissi range in height from 4 to 18 inches or more in height.

Ease of care: Easy.

How to grow: Plant large bulbs 8 inches deep and 6 inches apart in a sunny, well-drained spot. Small bulbs can be planted only 4 inches deep and much more closely. Plant in early fall.

Propagation: By division after leaves fade in spring.

Uses: Cut flowers, beds, and naturalizing. Small varieties are ideal in rock gardens and all narcissi make beautiful, easy-to-grow container plants for forcing.

Related varieties: Narcissi are divided into several categories, including trumpet daffodils (yellow-flowered 'King Alfred' is the typical cut flower "daffodil"), long-cupped narcissi, short-cupped narcissi, multiflowering Tazetta narcissi, and others. The Tazetta narcissi 'Paperwhite' and 'Grand Soleil d'Or' are not hardy and are generally used for forcing.

Flowering Onion

Allium **species**
Zone: USDA 4

Although they're onions, these ornamental plants have no unpleasant scent unless cut. Some are actually sweetly perfumed. Alliums are useful in the garden because they bridge the gap between spring-flowering and summer-flowering bulbs. Most bloom for several weeks in June and July.

Description: Alliums bear spheres or loose clusters of star-shaped flowers in shades of pink, white, blue, purple, or yellow. There are both tall-growing species (to 4 feet or higher) and miniature ones. Their attractive leaves, often a lovely blue-green, appear in early spring but fade away in early summer, often just as the plant is flowering.

Ease of care: Easy.

How to grow: Plant small bulbs 3 to 4 inches deep, large ones 6 to 8 inches deep, in a sunny, well-drained area. Winter mulching is advisable in colder climates.

Propagation: By division or seed.

Uses: Low-growing alliums are ideal plants for borders and rock gardens. Tall-growing alliums make wonderful cut flowers; soak their stems in cold water for 10 minutes to remove any scent of onion. They are also attractive in beds and borders of all sorts.

Related species: *Allium giganteum* produces huge 6-inch globes of purple flowers on top of 3- to 6-foot stems and may require staking. 'Drumstick allium' (*A. sphaerocephalum*) bears 2-foot stems with smaller clusters of reddish purple flowers. 'Blue garlic' (*A. caeruleum*) is similar but with blue flowers. 'Yellow allium' (*A. Moly*) produces yellow flowers in loose clusters on 10-inch stems. *A. neapolitanum* is similar but with beautifully perfumed white flowers; it is hardy only to USDA zone 6.

Siberian Squill

Scilla siberica
Zone: USDA 1

This tiny, delicate-looking plant is actually one of the hardiest of all garden plants, thriving well north of the Arctic circle. It adapts to most conditions and self-seeds readily, forming vast colonies in undisturbed sites over time.

Description: Borne on stems only 4 to 6 inches high, the nodding blue flowers pack quite a punch in the landscape, especially when planted in large numbers. White and double-flowered forms are also available; 'Spring Beauty' has larger, deeper blue flowers. The grasslike leaves fade away shortly after flowering ceases.

Ease of care: Easy.

How to grow: Plant bulbs 2 to 3 inches deep and 3 to 6 inches apart in well-drained soil in fall. Siberian squills are equally at ease in full sun or deep shade. They need winter cold and do poorly in zones 8, 9, and 10.

Propagation: By division

Uses: Although there is no reason this bulb cannot be used in beds and borders, it is so ideally suited to naturalizing that it is generally used that way. Some lawns literally turn blue in the spring due to the number of Siberian squills that grow there.

Related species: *Scilla Tubergiana* bears white flowers with blue stripes. *S. bifolia,* a tiny early-spring bloomer, has blue, white, or pink flowers. An entire category of spring bulbs, the bluebells or wood hyacinths, has been taken out of the genus *Scilla* and put into the genus *Endymion* (sometimes called *Hyacinthoides*). 'Spanish bluebell' (*E. hispanica*) and 'English bluebell' (*E. nonscripta*) are typical of this group, with straplike leaves and 15-inch stalks of blue, white, or pink bell-shaped flowers.

Snowdrop

Galanthus nivalis
Zone: USDA 3

In many gardens, this plant, along with the winter aconite (*Eranthis*), is the first flower of spring, blooming as early as January in the South and as late as April in the North. The flowers often push their way up through the snow. Should a late snowfall occur, snowdrops will remain in suspended animation until the snow melts and then carry on with their display.

Description: Snowdrops bear dainty, 1-inch hanging flowers on 6-inch stems. The flowers are white with greenish inner petals. When grown in large masses, the combined fragrance perfumes the air. The leaves are grasslike, appearing with the flowers and fading away in late spring.

Ease of care: Easy.

How to grow: Plant bulbs 3 inches deep and 3 inches apart in an area where they can grow undisturbed for many years. The plant is easily forced indoors. Snowdrops perform poorly in warm climates.

Propagation: By division.

Uses: Although they can be grown in beds and borders, snowdrops are best used for naturalizing. They adapt readily to lawns, meadows, and woods. Although their stems are rather short, they are popular cut flowers.

Related varieties: 'Flore Pleno' is a double-flowered form of the common snowdrop. 'Giant snowdrop' (*G. Elwesii*) is only slightly larger than its cousin and blooms later.

Tulip

Tulipa species
Zone: USDA 7

The tulip is the most popular of the spring-flowering bulbs. It also offers the greatest variety in color, shape, and form of any bulb. Although tulips are associated with Holland, they actually are not native there; tulips descend mostly from species originating in the Middle East.

Description: Tulips typically bear cup-shaped flowers in almost every shade but true blue. They can be double or single, fringed or twisted, perfumed or nonscented. The plants range in size from rock garden miniatures to 2½ feet or more in height. Most have broad leaves that quickly fade away in summer heat. Individual flowers last barely two weeks. However, since tulips offer various flowering seasons, you can have tulips in bloom from snow melt to the beginning of summer.

Ease of care: Easy.

How to grow: Plant bulbs 5 to 8 inches deep (less for tiny species tulips) and 4 to 6 inches apart in a sunny, well-drained area. Plant in fall, then water well. Divide bulbs every few years when flowering diminishes. Tulips need a period of cool weather to bloom. For that reason, pre-cooled bulbs are available for winter planting in warmer zones. These should be treated as annuals and replaced yearly.

Propagation: By division.

Uses: Cut flowers, forcing, beds, and borders. Species tulips are ideal for naturalizing.

Related varieties: Hybrid tulips are divided into various categories: early tulips, with large flowers on 10- to 14-inch plants; midseason tulips, both medium-high 'Triumph' and the tall, giant-flowered 'Darwin' hybrids; and late tulips, mostly consisting of tall-growing tulips with large flowers. Most species tulips bloom in early spring, often before the earliest hybrid tulips. Species tulips include *T. Greigii, T. Kaufmanniana,* and *T. tarda.*

Bloodroot

Sanguinaria canadensis
Zone: USDA 3

Bloodroot is a beautiful wildflower of the Eastern woodlands that is fast becoming a popular garden flower for shade gardens. Its curious name comes from its blood-red sap, which was once used as a dye by Native Americans.

Description: A thick 6- to 8-inch stem pushes out of the ground in early spring, revealing a single leaf tightly rolled around a large flower bud. When it unfurls, the light green leaf is 4 to 8 inches wide and generally rounded in shape but with an irregular margin and wavy edges. The single white flower is 1½ inches in diameter with numerous yellow stamens. The flower opens in early spring and lasts only a few days, but the foliage remains attractive until the entire plant disappears in late summer.

Ease of care: Moderately easy.

How to grow: Plant in summer just after the leaf has yellowed. Bloodroot prefers moisture-retentive, humus-rich soil. It needs sunlight only in the spring; therefore, the plant will grow in the deep shade formed by deciduous trees. Once established it needs no special care, spreading abundantly. If the soil dries out, the plants go dormant early. Wear gloves when handling this plant and wash your hands afterward; its red sap is somewhat toxic.

Propagation: By rhizome divisions in late summer.

Uses: Bloodroot makes an ideal flower for spring color in shaded areas. Bloodroot does well even when planted at the base of shallow-rooted trees.

Related varieties: 'Multiplex' (*Sanguinaria canadensis*), the most desirable variety, produces pure white, fully double flowers that last much longer than those of the species.

Golden Dead Nettle

Lamiastrum Galeobdolon
Zone: USDA 4

This plant is known by at least three different names: *Lamiastrum Galeobdolon, Lamium Galeobdolon,* and *Galeobdolon luteum.* It is an easy-to-grow, colorful perennial ground cover well suited to both shady and sunny locations.

Description: The golden dead nettle produces weak stems from 1 to 2 feet high. The leaves are heart-shaped and attractively mottled with silver. Although the plant is naturally dome-shaped in appearance, it spreads so quickly via runners that it takes on a carpetlike appearance. The hood-shaped flowers are bright yellow and are borne in spring. Although partially hidden under the leaves, the flowers are quite showy.

Ease of care: Easy.

How to grow: This plant does equally well in rich or poor soil, full sun or deep shade. It requires watering during periods of drought but will not grow well in constantly wet soil. Space plants 1 to 2 feet apart for a quick and easy ground cover.

Propagation: By division or cuttings.

Uses: Golden dead nettle is an ideal ground cover for all uses, especially where its rather invasive growth is contained by a barrier of some sort. It can also be used in borders and makes an excellent hanging basket plant for both indoor and outdoor use.

Related genus: 'Dead nettle' (*Lamium* sp.) is similar in all ways to the golden dead nettle, but it has pink to white flowers instead of yellow ones.

American Maidenhair Fern

Adiantum pedatum
Zone: USDA 3

Ferns are probably the first plants that come to mind when you think of a shade garden. With their lacy, airy foliage and their capacity to grow with practically no sun at all, they are ideal candidates. The maidenhair fern is typical among ferns and is certainly a plant to recommend for shade gardens everywhere.

Description: The maidenhair fern bears finger-like fronds, which is the source of its second common name: 'five-finger maidenhair.' The 1- to 2½-foot deciduous fronds are supported by thin, wiry, black to deep brown stems borne on creeping rhizomes that form just beneath the surface of the soil. Each leaflet is wedge-shaped. The overall effect is of a delicate plant. But the plant is inherently tough: It is a common woodland resident in forests from Louisiana to Maine and Alaska.

Ease of care: Moderately easy.

How to grow: The maidenhair fern is ideally suited to moist, but not wet, soil, especially soil rich in humus. It prefers some protection from strong winds. Most ferns prefer acid soils, but the maidenhair fern grows best in neutral or even alkaline ones.

Propagation: By division. It can also be grown from spores, a technique beyond the scope of most amateur gardeners.

Uses: Naturalized in a forested area, maidenhair ferns help create a fresh, airy, "wild woods" look. Placed in the context of a more controlled garden, their fine-textured appearance helps impart an almost tropical feeling.

Related species: 'Southern maidenhair' (*Adiantum Capillus-Veneris*), a native of southeastern North America, is similar but less hardy (USDA zone 7), with twice-divided fronds.

Japanese Painted Fern

Athyrium Goeringianum 'Pictum'
Zone: USDA 4

Everyone knows ferns have green fronds, but obviously no one told the Japanese painted fern. This plant, also listed as *A. nipponicum* 'Pictum,' is unusual in that it has multicolored foliage. That attribute alone would be enough to ensure its popularity, but it is also an easy-to-grow fern that would be attractive even if it were all green.

Description: The deeply cut fronds grow to 1½ feet long and about 1 foot high. Each leaflet is a spectacular combination of purple, lavender, and silver on a green base. The fronds are deciduous, dying back when touched by hard frost.

Ease of care: Easy.

How to grow: Plant in rich, damp soil in partial to full shade. The Japanese painted fern is slow growing, forming clusters that gradually increase in size over a number of years.

Propagation: By division or spores.

Uses: An attractive fern for border and foundation plantings and also along pathways in shaded areas. It can also be grown indoors in pots.

Related species: 'Lady fern' (*Athyrium Felix-femina*), native to both the Old and New Worlds, reaches 3 to 4 feet in height with lacy, yellow-green fronds on red or light green stalks. It has a general vase-shaped growth habit: narrow at the base, broad at the top. It spreads quite abundantly when happy.

Allegheny Foamflower

Tiarella cordifolia
Zone: USDA 3

This eastern North American wildflower is native to rich moist woodlands. It does equally well in similar conditions in culture.

Description: Allegheny foamflower is a spreading, 6- to 12-inch high perennial with broad, heart-shaped leaves that are lobed and toothed along the edges. The leaves are a bright green and are clothed in soft hairs. The unbranching flower stems are fingerlike and covered with a hazy cloud of white (rarely pink) flowers for about six weeks in the spring. It is deciduous in colder climates but partly to entirely evergreen in warmer zones. The foliage develops burgundy markings in the fall and often turns a beautiful bronze. The plant spreads by stolons, forming a dense carpet.

Ease of care: Easy.

How to grow: This plant does well in rich, moist, slightly acidic soils, thriving in light shade. It will grow well in deep shade but not as thickly.

Propagation: By division or seed.

Uses: Allegheny foamflower is a perfect choice for planting in deciduous woods because it competes well with shallow-rooted trees as long as the soil remains slightly moist. It is a good choice for borders and makes an excellent, thick ground cover.

Related Species: *Tiarella Wherryi* (formerly called *T. cordifolia collina*) is similar but has pinkish flowers and does not form runners. *T. unifoliata* has simple, palmately-lobed leaves. *T. laciniata* produces deeply cut and irregularly toothed leaves. *T. trifoliata* has compound leaves with three distinct leaflets.

European Wild Ginger

Asarum europaeum
Zone: USDA 4

This is an attractive yet little-known ground cover that is perfectly adapted to shady spots in the garden. Although this particular species is native to Europe, there are several interesting North American wild gingers. The name "wild ginger" comes from the fact that the rhizomes of its eastern North American cousin, *A. canadense,* were once harvested as a ginger substitute.

Description: European wild ginger produces glossy, evergreen leaves about 3 inches in diameter on 5-inch stalks. They are rounded and kidney-shaped in form. The brown flowers are almost unnoticeable, being formed at the base of the plant, under the leaves.

Ease of care: Easy.

How to grow: Plant in partial to full shade. It does well in average soil but spreads faster in rich humus.

Propagation: By division in spring.

Uses: An excellent ground cover for shaded spots. In fact, some experts consider it the single best choice for such locations.

Related species: 'Canada wild ginger' (*Asarum canadense*), native to northeast North America, has leaves that are larger than the European species (up to 7 inches) but not glossy. This species is hardy (USDA zone 3). 'British Columbia wild ginger' (*A. caudatum*), USDA zone 4, is semievergreen. 'Mottled wild ginger' (*A. Shuttleworthii*), USDA zone 6, has mottled, deciduous leaves. 'Virginia wild ginger' (*A. virginicum*), USDA zone 5, is similar to Canadian wild ginger but with evergreen leaves.

Tree Ivy

x Fatshedera lizei
Zone: USDA 7

This plant is a botanical curiosity: a natural hybrid occurring not between two species of the same genus, which is a relatively frequent occurrence, but between two different genera. It is, in other words, the horticultural equivalent of a mule. The plant resulted from a cross between Japanese fatsia (*Fatsia japonica*), a large-leaved evergreen shrub, and English ivy (*Hedera Helix*), a small-leaved climbing plant.

Description: The tree ivy bears large, deeply cut evergreen leaves, shaped rather like a giant ivy leaf. Its growth habit is intermediate between its two parents: It tries to climb like an ivy but with stiff, thick branches. Unable to fix itself satisfactorily to a support on its own, it generally ends up taking on a shrubby appearance.

Ease of care: Easy.

How to grow: Avoid full sun; tree ivy is subject to sunburn during the winter months. It grows well, however, in light to heavy shade, particularly on the north and east sides of buildings. It should be protected from drying winds at all seasons.

Propagation: By cuttings.

Uses: Tree ivy can be pruned into a shrubby form or allowed to trail along the ground as an evergreen ground cover. It will also climb well as long as it is attached manually to its support. It makes an excellent indoor plant.

Related variety: x *Fatshedera lizei* 'Variegata,' with white-margined leaves, seems to grow better as a houseplant than as an outdoor specimen.

Related genus: 'Japanese fatsia' (*Fatsia japonica*), an evergreen shrub suitable for USDA zone 7 and above, produces large, leathery, evergreen leaves up to 12 inches across and large clusters of yellow flowers followed by blue berries that last all winter.

Jack-in-the-Pulpit

Arisaema triphyllum
Zone: USDA 4

This intriguing wildflower is native to eastern and midwestern North America, but it can easily be grown in shade gardens elsewhere. It gets its common name from its odd flower: a pouch-shaped spathe ("pulpit") with an overhanging hood that surrounds a fingerlike central spadix ("Jack").

Description: Jack-in-the-pulpit produces one to two 3-lobed leaves 12 to 18 inches high. The leaves appear in early spring as does the flower, which is composed of a green-and-purple striped spathe bent over at its tip to partly hide the green clublike spadix. After the flower fades, a cluster of bright red berries appears and lasts for much of the summer. The leaves fade away in midsummer if the plant is not watered regularly but grow back in spring from an underground tuber.

Ease of care: Easy.

How to grow: This plant naturally grows on rich, moist forest floors and so is perfectly suited to shady gardens. Add plenty of compost or peat moss at planting time.

Propagation: By offsets or seed sown ½ inch deep. Seed sown in fall germinates the following spring.

Uses: Plant near a path or the front of the garden where its surprising flowers will be noticed. Jack-in-the-pulpit is an ideal choice for shady spots in the wild flower garden.

Related species: 'Dragonroot' (*Arisaema dracontium*), a native of North America, has a green flower like that of its cousin but with a long, pointed hiplike spadix and a small spathe. Its deeply divided leaves and red berries make it attractive for long periods.

Solomon's Seal

Polygonatum odoratum 'Thunbergii'
Zone: USDA 3

There is considerable confusion as to the exact identity of this Solomon's seal, an old-fashioned garden flower that is often found in great numbers in abandoned gardens surrounding houses of the late 1800s and early 1900s. Most catalogs list it as *Polygonatum odoratum* var. *Thunbergii* or *P. multiflorum,* which are both Asiatic species. However, it is also similar to the wild Solomon's seals of North America. Whatever its true name, the dainty appearance of this simple yet striking plant is a major plus in any garden.

Description: This plant produces individual 3- to 4-foot stems that rise straight up from the ground only to arch gracefully outward when they reach about 1 foot in height. They sprout in early spring from a branching underground rhizome. The oval 3- to 6-inch leaves form two distinct rows on opposite sides of the stem. In spring, 1-inch tubular white flowers with green tips hang down in pairs from the underside of the stem just below the leaves.

Ease of care: Easy.

How to grow: Solomon's seal adapts well to all light conditions, from full sun to full shade, and seems equally tolerant of dry or moist soil. It prefers soil rich in humus.

Propagation: By division.

Uses: This flower is a classic for both old-fashioned gardens and wildflower gardens. Its thick roots compete well with tree roots, making it a good choice for planting under shallow-rooted trees. It also makes a good background plant.

Related species: A variegated Solomon's seal, also of doubtful origin, is listed in most catalogs as *Polygonatum odoratum* var. *Thunbergii* 'Variegata.' Its leaves are striped lengthwise in creamy white. It is smaller than the common garden Solomon's seal: about 2 to 3 feet in height.

Wake-Robin

Trillium grandiflorum
Zone: USDA 4

Trilliums of various sorts can be found in forests throughout North America except in the extreme South. The wake-robin is probably the showiest one. It is certainly the most widely cultivated. Wake-robin blooms for several weeks in midspring.

Description: With the wake-robin, almost everything comes in threes. Each plant produces a single stem bearing a whorl of three deep green, pointed leaves. The leaves are topped by three green sepals that open to reveal a pure white flower with three broad, pointed petals. The long-lasting flower turns pink as it ages. The plant sprouts in early spring, quickly reaches 8 to 18 inches in height, and then blooms. In dry conditions, it dies back to a tuberous root by midsummer.

Ease of care: Easy.

How to grow: Plant in rich, moist, well-drained soil. Apply a thick mulch to imitate the deep leaf litter of the plant's native habitat. If conditions suit it, the wake-robin spreads abundantly but never aggressively.

Propagation: By division or seed. Plants take five to seven years to bloom from seed.

Uses: In forests, the wake-robin can become so numerous that the forest floor seems covered with snow during the plant's blooming season. It can also be grown in beds and borders. Although it would seem to be an attractive cut flower, harvesting it means cutting its leaves as well. This deprives the root of its nourishment, leading to the plant's demise.

Related variety: *Trillium grandiflorum* 'Flore Pleno,' also listed as 'Multiplex,' is a double-flowered form.

Related species: 'Dwarf white trillium' (*T. nivale*), an extremely early bloomer, bears small white flowers on a 4- to 6-inch stem. Purple trillium (*Trillium erectum*) has deep red-purple flowers with narrower petals.

Wintercreeper

Euonymus Fortunei
Zone: USDA 5

The wintercreeper can't seem to make up its mind. Depending on the situation, it can be a glossy-leaved ground cover, an evergreen climber, or a dense shrub. Seed-grown wintercreepers begin by creeping along the ground. When they find a suitable support, such as a tree trunk or wall, they begin to climb it. When they reach full sun at the top of the support, they change to their mature phase, with shrubby branches and larger leaves. Only the mature phase bears flowers and fruit. Interestingly, cuttings taken from the mature form will not revert to the creeping or climbing phases, but instead will produce shrublike plants.

Description: In culture, this plant is highly variable, with many different leaf sizes, growth forms, and foliage colors. Juvenile forms have small, scallop-edged, dark green leaves with lighter veins. At maturity, the leaves become much larger. Mature forms bear insignificant flowers followed by attractive and durable light pink to orange-red berries.

Ease of care: Easy.

How to grow: Plant in full sun or moderate shade in ordinary soil.

Propagation: By cuttings or layering.

Uses: This plant's variability provides a wide variety of uses. It can be a small shrub (up to 4 feet), a low-growing ground cover (excellent for erosion control), or a tall climber that scales trees or walls via clinging aerial roots. It is the hardiest of all evergreen climbers.

Related varieties: The leaves of *Euonymus Fortunei* 'Colorata' turn dark purple in fall and winter. The common wintercreeper (*E. F. radicans*) is all green and is used both as a ground cover and as a climbing shrub. 'Sarcoxie' is an all-green shrubby form, ideal for hedges and as a specimen plant. 'Emerald 'n' Gold,' gold-edged leaves, and 'Emerald Gaiety,' white-edged leaves, are typical of the numerous variegated wintercreepers.

Japanese Yew

Taxus cuspidata
Zone: USDA 4

Most conifers are not shade tolerant, but yews are a major exception. Their dark green needles add a bit of color to the otherwise barren shade garden from fall through early spring.

Description: In its original form, the Japanese yew is a single-trunked tree reaching 50 feet in height. The species is rarely grown in cultivation, having been replaced by the numerous dense, slow-growing varieties that may be globular, vase-shaped, pyramidal, or spreading, depending on the selection. Although they are labelled dwarf plants, most eventually become quite high: 20 feet or more. The dark green needles have rounded tips and are not "scratchy" like most other conifers. Female plants bear bright red berries.

Ease of care: Easy.

How to grow: Yews are perfectly tolerant of moderate shade, and even deep shade, as long as they get some spring sunlight. In dense shade, the shrubs need harsher pruning to help fill in the gaps formed by a more open growth pattern. Yews need fertile soil and ample moisture. They will not tolerate root competition from shallow-rooted trees. Protect them from strong, drying winds.

Propagation: By cuttings, usually carried out by professionals, or seed.

Uses: The Japanese yew is widely used as a foundation plant, especially on the north or east sides of the home. It makes an excellent formal or natural hedge, and dwarf varieties—of which there are many in different sizes, shapes, and colors—are popularly used in rock gardens.

Related species: 'English yew' (*Taxus baccata*) and the hybrid yew (*T. x media*) are similar to the Japanese yew, although the English yew is less hardy (USDA zone 6).

Old World Arrowhead

Sagittaria sagittifolia
Zone: USDA 5

The genus *Sagittaria* actually contains several quite different species, some of which are submerged, grasslike plants. Those called arrowheads, of which the old world arrowhead (*S. sagittifolia*) is the most commonly grown, are emergent plants and have arrow-shaped leaves. They bear edible tubers and are grown commercially as food sources in many countries.

Description: The old world arrowhead produces spearhead leaves and spikes of three-petaled white flowers spotted purple. The flowers last most of the summer. The plant grows to 2 feet or more in height.

Ease of care: Moderately easy.

How to grow: Plant in pots since the arrowhead can spread quite aggressively if it is not contained. Give it full sun to partial shade. The plant can grow in a wide variety of conditions, ranging from damp soil to 6 inches of water. If covered with too much water, it will grow as a submerged plant with narrow, ribbonlike leaves.

Propagation: By division, in spring or fall.

Uses: The arrowhead makes an excellent accent plant. Several pots placed together will also make an attractive border.

Related species: There is a double-flowered form, *S. sagittifolia* 'Flore Pleno,' as well as a variegated one. The giant arrowhead (*S. latifolia*) is a similar but taller plant (up to 4 feet) with larger flowers in pure white. It is native to North America.

Common Cattail

Typha latifolia
Zone: USDA 2

What would a water garden be without cattails? Their strikingly vertical foliage and brown flower heads are among the most typical of all bog plants in the wild. They're a must for a natural look.

Description: The flat green swordlike leaves run straight up and down, perpendicular to the water. They can reach 10 feet in height in the wild but remain smaller when grown in pots. Each cluster of leaves bears a dense brown catkin on a tall straight stem in mid to late summer. The flowers last until fall, sometimes even through much of the winter.

Ease of care: Easy.

How to grow: Grow cattails in containers, otherwise they can be quite invasive. They do well in full sun or partial shade and grow in damp soil or up to 12 inches of water.

Propagation: By division or seed.

Uses: The dramatic effect of the cattail's foliage is most noticeable when there is enough open water in front of the plant that its reflection is seen clearly. It also makes a choice background plant. The flower clusters can be dried for indoor arrangements.

Related species: The common cattail (*Typha latifolia*) is found in the wild throughout the Northern Hemisphere. The narrowleaf cattail (*T. angustifolia*) is similar but has very narrow leaves and forms a shorter plant (4 to 6 feet) than the common cattail. The miniature cattail (*T. minima*) is particularly graceful and attains only 12 to 18 inches in height. It is not as tolerant of deep water or cold temperatures as the other cattails, although it is hardy to zone 5.

Eelgrass

Vallisneria americana
Zone: USDA 4

It's unfortunate that eelgrass grows underwater, as it is quite attractive in its own right. In practice, though, this oxygenating plant is grown more for its usefulness, since it is scarcely visible in its pool bottom habitat.

Description: Eelgrass bears ribbonlike, translucent leaves in pale green that rise gracefully upward, but they rarely reach the surface. The small white flowers are scarcely noticeable. It loses its leaves and goes dormant in the winter, even in zone 10.

Ease of care: Easy.

How to grow: Unlike most submerged plants, eelgrass is not sold in the form of clusters of cuttings but rather as a single rooted plant. Sink its pot so it is 6 to 24 inches underwater. It grows equally well in sun, partial shade, or shade.

Propagation: Eelgrass produces runners that root when they touch the soil. The plantlets thus produced can be cut free and grown separately.

Uses: This plant is an excellent oxygenator and a favorite with fish, which use it both for spawning and as a food source.

Related species: Various submerged sagittarias (*Sagittaria*) look much like eelgrass and perform similar functions. *S. graminea* is one of the larger ones, reaching 3 feet in height. *S. natans* is similar but much smaller, only 3 to 6 inches tall.

Fanwort	Floating-heart	Lotus

Cabomba caroliniana
Zone: USDA 6

The feathery fanlike leaves of the fanwort are attractive in their own right, and the plant is grown just for its beauty in aquariums. In the water garden, though, you'll rarely get to admire this plant, as it grows entirely underwater.

Description: The fragile stems of the fanwort are covered with lacy, fanlike foliage in an attractive bright green shade. Tiny white flowers are borne in summer but are scarcely noticed.

Ease of care: Easy.

How to grow: The fanwort is generally sold in the form of unrooted clusters that can be allowed to float freely. It is most successful, however, when rooted in a pot of sand placed at the bottom of the pool. It prefers cool water and therefore does best in deep ponds. The fanwort can grow at various water levels up to 30 inches. It must be brought indoors for the winter in cold climates.

Propagation: By cuttings.

Uses: The fanwort makes an excellent and popular oxygenating plant. Fish use the leaves for spawning and also nibble on its leaves.

Related species: Other submerged plants sold in clumps and requiring similar care include anacharis (*Elodea canadensis*) and ceratophyllum (*Ceratophyllum demersum*). They are generally hardy to USDA zones 4 or 5.

Nymphoides peltata
Zone: USDA 6

Floating-heart forms a veritable floating carpet of foliage and flowers on the surface of the water only, contrasting nicely with other water plants. It also makes a nice substitute for water lilies in small pools and tubs where water lilies would look out of place.

Description: The bright yellow flowers of the floating-heart appear quite early in spring and continue through summer. The rounded, heart-shaped leaves, green mottled maroon, look much like water lily leaves but on a smaller scale, measuring only about 3 inches across. The plant produces a great many offsets, which in turn root and produce further offsets.

Ease of care: Easy.

How to grow: Floating-heart is an accommodating plant and thrives in sun or partial shade. Cover its crown with 4 to 12 inches of water. Don't hesitate to prune it back if it threatens to take over the pool. In colder zones, make sure to sink its pot to the bottom of the pool, as its roots should not be allowed to freeze.

Propagation: By division.

Uses: This plant can be considered a "ground cover" for water gardens, used to set off larger plants marvelously.

Related species: 'Water snowflake' (*Nymphoides indica*) is larger, with 8-inch leaves. It bears attractive white scented flowers with fuzzy petals and yellow centers. 'Yellow snowflake' (*N. geminata*) is similar, but its yellow flowers are even more highly fringed. Neither are as hardy as the floating-heart: They are best grown in USDA zone 7 or above.

Nelumbo nucifera
Zone: USDA 5

The lotus is venerated in the Far East, where it symbolizes attaining nirvana: It begins its life in the mud but eventually rises to the heavens. The plant is spectacular in both foliage and flower and is an ideal addition to larger water gardens.

Description: The round leaves, up to 3 feet across, float on the surface of the water early in the season but subsequent leaves rise on tall stalks to 6 feet in height. They are a beautiful glaucous green and water droplets bead up on their surface for an attractive and intriguing display. The giant flowers (up to 10 inches across) are delightfully perfumed and open in mid to late summer. They range in color from white to yellow to deep pink. When the petals fall, the drying seed pod adds a further point of interest.

Ease of care: Easy.

How to grow: Plant lotus tubers in spring in large containers, covering all but the growing tip. Submerge in 2 to 6 inches of water. Lotus need full sun and regular fertilizer to grow well. Plants often do not bloom until the second year after purchase.

Propagation: By division.

Uses: A lotus makes a dramatic focal point for a larger water garden, although there are dwarf types that adapt to medium-size pools. The cone-shape seed pods are often used in dried flower arrangements.

Related varieties: A wide range of varieties is available with single to double flowers. 'Mrs. Perry Slocum' is a popular double variety whose giant flowers change from deep pink to creamy yellow as they age. 'Shirokunshi,' with tulip-shaped yellow blooms, is one of the better miniature varieties, reaching only 18 to 24 inches in height. The native North American lotus, *Nelumbo lutea*, produces yellow flowers and is a bit hardier (USDA zone 4) than its Asiatic cousin.

467

Pickerel Rush

Pontederia cordata
Zone: USDA 3

The pickerel rush is a native of North America but is widely planted the world over for its decorative effect. Several color variations are available.

Description: The pickerel rush bears shiny olive green spearhead-shape leaves above 2- to 3-foot stems. It quickly forms dense clumps. The spike-shape blue flower clusters begin to bloom in early summer and last until fall.

Ease of care: Easy.

How to grow: Plant two or three clusters together in a large container for the best effect. This plant does equally well in full sun or partial shade. Its roots should be covered with 2 to 12 inches of water. Move it to the deepest part of the pool during the winter.

Propagation: By division.

Uses: Pickerel rush makes a striking specimen plant for medium to large gardens, but it can be a bit overbearing in a small one. The flowers last well when cut.

Related varieties: Blue to mauve or purple varieties are most common, but white-flowered pickerel rushes are also available.

Variegated Sweet Flag

Acorus Calamus 'Variegatus'
Zone: USDA 4

The green-leaved form of the sweet flag grows wild throughout much of the Northern Hemisphere, but it is the variegated version that is the most popular in water gardens. Its striking season-long color more than makes up for its uninteresting flowers.

Description: The variegated sweet flag bears thick swordlike leaves similar to those of an iris. They are strikingly variegated with green and creamy white horizontal stripes and reaching straight upward to a height of 2 or 3 feet. The brownish green flower heads seem to be borne directly from the leaves but are more a curiosity than an attraction. The common name comes from the sweet scent that the leaves give off when crushed.

Ease of care: Easy.

How to grow: Plant in moist soil or in water up to 6 inches deep. It adapts to both sun and partial shade.

Propagation: By division.

Uses: The variegated sweet flag is the perfect vertical accent plant for pond edges or bog gardens. A clump or two rising from the middle of a pool also creates quite a dramatic effect.

Related varieties: The wild form (*Acorus Calamus*) also makes a good accent plant, although it is not quite as dramatic as its variegated cousin. The dwarf sweet flag (*A. gramineus*) is a small grasslike plant with narrow leaves. It reaches 6 to 12 inches in height, depending on the variety chosen. Variegated forms of the dwarf sweet flag are especially popular.

Water Canna

Thalia dealbata
Zone: USDA 6

Not a true canna, *Thalia* nevertheless looks a great deal like one, especially its leaves. Although quite hardy, its exotic form adds a tropical note to the water garden.

Description: The bold, broad, upright leaves are glaucous green in color with a maroon spot at their base and reach up to 4 feet in height. The water canna bears purple flowers in clusters atop thin, graceful stems rising another foot or more above the leaves.

Ease of care: Moderately easy.

How to grow: Grow in full sun or partial shade. It adapts equally well to damp soil or water up to 12 inches deep. For maximum hardiness in the colder parts of its range, grow it with its roots well-covered in water. In zones 5 and above, bring it indoors for the winter.

Propagation: By division.

Uses: Water canna, with its tropical appearance, makes a striking accent or background plant for the water garden. Grow two or three pots of it for best effect.

Related species: True water cannas (*Canna* sp.) look much like tall versions of the common garden canna. They have similar sword-shaped leaves and bear bright pink, red, orange, or yellow flowers. True cannas are subtropical plants and, in zones 8 and below, should be wintered indoors as dormant rhizomes.

Hardy Water Lily

Nymphaea **species**
Zone: USDA 3

Hardy water lilies result from crosses between European and North American species. They are excellent permanent residents of water gardens. Many pools are designed specifically around their culture.

Description: Hardy water lilies produce round, leathery leaves up to 1 foot across. They can be green or splashed with brown. Their multipetaled flowers measure up to 12 inches across and come in white, pink, yellow, and red. Many have flowers that change color as they age, and most are lightly scented. The flowers open in the morning and close at night. Unlike tropical water lilies, the flowers of hardy water lilies float on the surface of the water, and the plants grow from rhizomes, not tubers.

Ease of care: Easy.

How to grow: To bloom well, hardy water lilies require abundant sunlight (at least 6 hours a day). Plant the rhizome in a large container at a 45° angle with only the tip exposed. Set the container in the pool so it is covered with 6 to 18 inches of water (more vigorous varieties can be set in deeper sections of the pool). Fertilize regularly. Remove browned leaves in the fall.

Propagation: By division.

Uses: Hardy water lilies are grown for their attractive leaves and exotic flowers. They also help reduce algae by shading the water in which they grow. Generally, about half the pond's surface area should be covered by water lily leaves.

Related varieties: The selection of hardy water lilies is vast. Some of the better known varieties are 'Rose Arey,' with clear pink flowers starting early in the season; 'Comanche,' with speckled leaves and flowers that change from yellow to coppery bronze as they mature; and 'Hermine,' one of the smallest hardy white lilies—an ideal choice for smaller ponds.

Tropical Water Lily

Nymphaea **species**
Zone: USDA 10

The exotically colorful flowers and season-long bloom of tropical water lilies make them ideal choices for the water garden. They need more care than their hardy cousins.

Description: Tropical water lilies bear round shiny leaves, often with crinkled edges. They can be green or maroon or green mottled with darker shades. The large flowers (up to 13 inches across) are fragrant and are borne on stems rising above the water. They come in just about every shade, from white, pink, and yellow to purple, blue, and red. Night-blooming tropicals have flowers that open from dusk to mid-morning. Day-bloomers have just the opposite schedule: from mid-day to dusk. Tropical water lilies grow from tubers.

Ease of care: Moderately difficult.

How to grow: Tropical water lilies should not be planted out until the water warms up in late spring or early summer. Plant them in the center of a large container with just the crown showing. They need at least 6 hours of full sun to bloom well and require still water 6 to 18 inches deep over their tubers. Fertilize regularly. Tropical water lilies are usually treated as annuals except in USDA zone 10, but they can be overwintered in a greenhouse in colder climates.

Propagation: By division. Some types produce new plantlets from their leaves.

Uses: Tropical water lilies are the stars of the water garden wherever they are grown and should be placed where they are allowed to steal the show. They also make excellent cut flowers.

Related varieties: Some of the most popular varieties include 'Evelyn Randig,' a pink day-bloomer; 'Wood's White Knight,' a white night-bloomer; and 'Yellow Dazzler,' a yellow day-bloomer. *Nymphaea colorata* is a small-growing day-bloomer with blue flowers, ideal for smaller pools.

Yellow Flag

Iris Pseudacorus
Zone: USDA 4

The genus *Iris* is a particularly vast one, including the common bearded iris of the flower garden, rock garden irises, bulbous irises, and marsh irises. Of the many bog-type irises, none is as striking and popular as the yellow flag. Although a European native, it is widely naturalized in North America.

Description: This is a tall-growing plant with sword-shaped leaves. Its leaves alone can reach 4 to 5 feet, and the flower stalks are often a foot or so taller. The blooms are bright golden yellow and appear in late spring and early summer. Variegated varieties also exist.

Ease of care: Easy.

How to grow: Plant in full sun in either boggy soil or in containers set into the pool. The roots can be covered by a few inches of water to more than a foot. It prefers a slightly acid soil. Remove faded flowers to prevent seed formation.

Propagation: The yellow flag spreads rapidly by rhizomes and is easily reproduced by division. It can also be grown from seed.

Uses: Bog or emergent plant. Excellent background plant for larger water gardens.

Related species: The blue flag (*Iris versicolor*) is basically a blue-flowered version of the yellow flag, although a bit shorter (about 2 feet). Other irises for boggy places include the Japanese iris (*I. ensata*, formerly *I. kaempferi*) and the Siberian iris (*I. sibirica*), both of which are covered more thoroughly in the "Perennials" section. All the above are hardy to zone 4.

VEGETABLES & HERBS

The joys of vegetable gardening range from planning in winter to harvesting in the summer or fall. Nothing adds more to your meals than fresh beans, tomatoes, or zucchini. Enjoy a new crop of vegetable delights every week.

A well-planned garden can produce vegetables from early summer to late fall. This garden—bearing tasty lettuce, beets, and beans— had its start with a plan thought out during the winter months.

PLANNING YOUR GARDEN

W hether it's a garden-fresh tomato on a sandwich or corn on the cob direct from the garden to the stove, you know it's true: The tastiest vegetables come from the home garden. Much enjoyment comes from producing your own crisp vegetables, and it's an activity where everyone in the family can contribute—even the very young.

The best gardens come from careful planning. Winter is a good time to plan your garden. Few things are more enjoyable on a cold winter evening than thumbing through seed catalogs while awaiting spring's arrival. But whether you plan to plant a large garden or just a few containers of vegetables on the patio, gardening is more than just planting seeds. There are many elements to consider for a successful harvest.

The first step is deciding which vegetables to grow. Which vegetables do you and your family like? Can those vegetables grow in your climate? Do you want to freeze or can some of your crop? These questions should be considered before you start planting.

We'll give you information about the essentials of planning a successful vegetable garden: site selection, varieties of vegetables and how much to grow, making a layout plan, and gardening tools. Brought together, these elements can provide you with a rewarding gardening experience.

Climate

The growing season is the length of time that your area has the conditions plants need to reach maturity and produce a crop. The growing season is measured in terms of the number of days between the last frost in spring and the first frost in fall. In general terms, these two dates mark the beginning and end of the time in which plants grow from seed to maturity. Some areas never have frost; instead, their dry season serves as "winter." The length of your growing season is totally dependent on your local climate.

The dates a certain area can expect to have the last spring frost and the first fall frost are called the "average date of last frost" and the "average date of first frost" respectively. These dates are used as reference points for planning and planting vegetables, but they're not infallible. The dates do, however, give you a fairly accurate guide as to which vegetables will do the best in your area. For last and first average frost dates in your area, call your county Cooperative Extension office.

The average date of last frost is not the only reference point used to determine when to plant a garden. The small maps found on the back of seed packages are hardiness zone maps, dividing the United States into areas with fairly similar climates. For more information on hardiness zones, see pages 112 and 113.

The term "hardiness" is specifically used to indicate how well a plant tolerates cold. Vegetables grown in a home garden fall into one of four hardiness categories: very hardy, hardy, tender, and very tender. The date on which you can safely plant each vegetable in your garden depends on its hardiness category.

Very hardy vegetables can tolerate cold and frost and can be planted in the garden four to six weeks before the average date of last frost. Hardy vegetables can handle some cold and frost and can be planted two to three weeks before the average date of last frost. Tender vegetables don't like cold weather. They can be planted on the average date of last frost, but you will need to protect them in some way if there's a late frost. Very tender vegetables will not survive any frost and must be planted after the soil has warmed up in the spring. They can be planted two to three weeks after the average date of last frost.

Vegetables have different temperature preferences and tolerances and are usually classified as either cool-season crops or warm-season crops. Cool-season crops, such as cabbages, lettuce, and peas, must have time to mature before the weather gets too warm; otherwise, they will wilt, die, or go to seed prematurely. These vegetables can be started in warm weather only if there will be a long enough stretch of cool weather in the fall to allow the crop to mature before the first freeze. Warm-season crops, such as peppers, cucumbers, and melons, can't tolerate frost. If the weather gets too cool, their yields will be reduced or they may not grow at all.

474

Climatic factors, such as sunlight, affect which vegetables to grow and when to plant them.

A coldframe is an outside glass-enclosed growing area used to get a jump on the growing season. The coldframe shelters the plants from wind and cold and warms easily on summer days. Hardy vegetables, such as radishes and lettuce, can be grown in a coldframe during most of the year if you live in a mild climate.

Whether you sow seeds directly or use the coldframe to harden-off containerized transplants, you'll have to water the plants regularly. Coldframes dry out easily, so they need plenty of water. However, the soil in the coldframe must be amended and well drained to prevent seedlings from rotting. Use gravel or sandy soil; plants must not be in standing water.

Light is another important factor to consider when you plan your garden. Sunlight—or some type of light—provides the energy that plants need to turn water and carbon dioxide into the sugar they use for food. If light is limited, even a plant that looks green and healthy may never produce flowers or fruit. This can be a problem with such vegetables as tomatoes, where you want to eat the fruit. With lettuce, where you're only interested in the leaves, light is not as much an issue.

Vegetables grown for their fruit need a minimum of six to eight hours of direct light each day. Root crops, such as beets, carrots, radishes, and turnips, store up energy before they flower and do rather well in partial shade. Plants that are grown for their leaves, such as lettuce and spinach, are most tolerant of shade; in fact, where the sun is hot and bright, they may need some shade for protection.

Light for Your Garden

If you have a choice of where to grow your vegetable garden, don't put it in the shade of buildings, trees, or shrubs. Also remember that trees and shrubs, as well as shading an area, have roots that may extend well beyond the reach of their branches. These roots will compete with the vegetable plants for water and nutrients.

Extending the Season with a Coldframe

A coldframe uses solar heat. Built of simple materials—scrap lumber and old storm windows—it's easy to construct. Make the back about 12 inches higher than the front and face the window sash south with hinges on the higher side. During sunny days the sash can be propped open with a stick to prevent sunburning the plants. If the sun is bright, temperatures can reach 85 degrees Fahrenheit even when the temperature outside is freezing. Close the frame at night and during cold weather to protect young plants.

Getting Your Garden Started

Several varieties of the same vegetable meet different cultural needs and have different charactristics.

Most vegetables come in many varieties. After giving thought to the vegetables you want to grow, you're ready to decide which varieties to grow. Seed catalogs, for instance, offer a variety of tomatoes that is totally bewildering: big ones, little ones, cherry ones, green ones, canning ones. Some are disease resistant, some are not; some are hybrids, some are not.

It's worth taking the time to consider why there are so many varieties of one vegetable. A variety is simply a botanical change in the original plant. These changes may be as obvious as a change in the color, size, or shape of the fruit. Other changes, such as improved disease resistance, better flavor, or compact growth, may be less obvious. Hybrids are bred for success. A hybrid may be the result of breeding two different pure lines. A pure line is a plant that has been selected and bred for a certain desirable characteristic, such as the size of its fruit or its ability to resist disease.

With so many varieties available, it can be difficult to choose the right one. The vegetable and herb directory (see page 534) describes many individual vegetables and their cultural requirements; this list includes some of the best and most commonly used varieties. Information on varieties may also be obtained from seed catalog descriptions or from your local Cooperative Extension office. Another indication of the most reliable varieties for your area is All America Selections. This nonprofit organization develops and promotes new varieties of vegetables and flowers. If a variety is listed in your seed catalog as an All-America Selection, it has been tested by growers all over the country; you can be sure it's a good bet for your garden.

Each vegetable variety has its "days to maturity" listed in the seed catalog. This number indicates the average number of days needed from germination or transplanting to harvest. Using a calendar, see how the dates fall for the crops you're thinking of growing. Deciding when to plant involves more than just avoiding killing frosts. It also means pacing your planting so you get the maximum yield from a limited space. This takes careful planning. Some crops can be harvested gradually, others mature all at once.

Pace Your Planting

One way to pace your harvest is to plant several varieties of the same vegetable that will mature at different rates. For instance, two or three weeks before the average date of last frost plant three different varieties of carrot. This can extend your production period over two to three months.

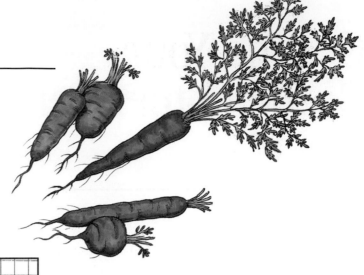

SPRING	SUMMER	FALL
CUCUMBER		BEETS
SUMMER SQUASH		KALE
TOMATO CAGES		
PEPPER EGGPLANT		
IRISH POTATOES		TURNIPS
SPINACH	LIMA BEANS	
BROCCOLI	GREEN BEANS	COVER CROP
LETTUCE ONION	NEW ZEALAND SPINACH	

Succession planting

You can save garden space and get two or more harvests from the same spot through succession planting. After early maturing crops are harvested, replant the space with a new crop. Early cool-season crops can be replaced with warm-season crops. Start off with a fast-growing, cool-season crop that can be planted early: lettuce, spinach, and cabbage are good examples. Warm-weather crops, such as New Zealand spinach, chard, corn, and squash, can then replace the earlier plants. Finally, in the fall make a planting of cole crops (for example, cabbage, broccoli, or cauliflower) or put in root crops such as turnips or beets.

Companion planting

Another way to increase the use of your planting space is through companion planting. This is done by planting short-term crops between plants that will take a longer time to mature. The short-term crops are harvested by the time the long-term crops need the extra room. A good example of this is radishes or lettuce planted between rows of tomatoes or peppers. By the time the tomatoes and peppers need the space, the radishes and lettuce will have been harvested.

Getting Your Garden on Paper

Stakes and raised beds are just two of the items to consider when designing your garden.

You've put a lot of thought into your garden plan. You also know some vital information and dates: The names of the varieties you're going to plant as well as planting and harvest dates. Now comes some substantial paperwork.

The size of your garden depends on your interest in gardening and how much time you'll be able to give to the garden. Some gardeners use every available inch of space; others use a small corner of their property. Some don't have much choice; this may be your case if you have a small garden to begin with or if you're gardening on a patio or balcony. The larger your garden, the more time and work it's going to need. Unless you're already hooked on gardening, it's probably better to start small and let garden size increase as your interest in gardening and confidence in your ability develop.

Before deciding the exact dimensions of your garden, check the list of vegetables you've chosen and the amount you're going to grow for each one. Then calculate if all the vegetables will fit into the allotted space. To determine how much space each plant or row will consume, refer to the chart on pages 504 and 505.

Keep in mind that you'll probably map out successive plantings. Arrange your plantings to make the best use of your available space. Some vegetables (for example, cucumbers) sprawl, taking up much space in the garden. You can make use of vertical space, however, by training vines to grow on a trellis; this will free up usable planting ground.

Drawing the plot plan is the pencil-and-paper stage of planning. If you use graph paper, it will be easier to work to scale. A commonly used scale is one inch of paper to eight feet of garden space, but you can adapt the scale to whatever is easiest for you. Draw up a simple plot plan with your garden's measurements in all directions. Remember, no law requires a garden to be square or rectangular. Your garden can be round, curved, or any shape that fits your landscape.

Sketch circles for individual transplants, and rows for directly sown seeds. Take care in placing the vegetables. Place taller plants in the north or northeast area of the garden so they won't shade other plants as they grow. If you're going to use a rototiller, make sure the rows are wide. In smaller gardens it's more space-efficient to plant in wide rows or in solid blocks four to five feet wide. You must be able to reach the center of a wide row comfortably from either side.

If you're serious about gardening, you should keep records. Planning your records should be part of planning your garden. Build your records the same way you build your garden; profit from past mistakes and incorporate new ideas. Keep a daily record, noting such things as soil preparation, planting, weeding, fertilizing, bloomtime, date crops ripen, and growing results. Also note any problems with weeds, bugs, or rainfall, and whether the harvest of each item was sufficient, too much, or not enough. At the end of the growing season, you'll have a complete record of what you did, and this information will give you the basics for planning next year's garden.

Drawing the Plot Plan

Measure your garden space and plot it on graph paper using a scale that suits the size. Keeping taller vegetables on the north or northeast side, start the plan by sketching in the cool-season varieties. Calculate when those varieties will mature so you can replace them with warm-season crops.

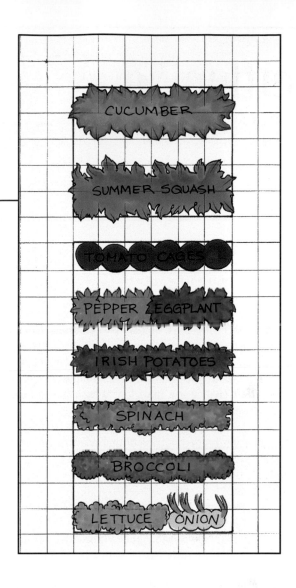

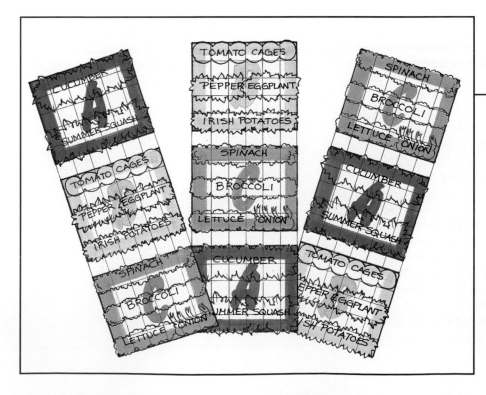

Rotate Your Crops

Do not grow the same plant family in the same spot year after year. Repetition of the same crop gives diseases a chance to build up strength. There are three major vegetable families:

- Cole crops (cabbage family): broccoli, brussels sprouts, cabbage, cauliflower, kohlrabi, rutabaga, and turnip;
- Cucurbits (cucumber family): cucumber, gourd, muskmelon, pumpkin, summer and winter squash, and watermelon;
- Solanaceous plants (tomato and pepper family): eggplant, Irish potato, pepper, and tomato.

After growing a crop from one of these families one year, choose a variety from a different family to plant in the same spot the following season.

Gardening Tools

Gardening tools—such as the watering can shown here—are essential for good vegetable production.

There are a great many garden tools on the market. Some are necessary, while others are helpful but not necessary. Consider the type and amount of gardening you do and choose the implements that best suit your needs. When you decide which tools you need, buy the best you can find and take good care of them. High-quality tools work better and last longer than economy tools that may not have much durability. When you're shopping for a tool, pick it up and see how well it fits in your hands. Determine if the tool is well balanced. Garden tools come in different sizes and weights; you and your equipment should be compatible.

In caring for your tools, follow these basic guidelines:

• Clean your tools before putting them away. If you're storing them for the winter, a thin coat of motor oil will help prevent rusting. Use a file to keep your hoe and spade sharp.

• Have a regular storage area for your tools that is protected from the weather.

• Use each tool the way it was meant to be used. For instance, a rake—even a good quality rake—won't last long if you constantly use it to dig holes or turn soil.

Spade and Shovel—A shovel has a curved scoop and a handle with or without a handgrip. It's used for lifting, turning, and moving soil. A spade is a sturdy tool with a thick handle, a handgrip, and a heavy blade that you press into the ground with your foot. The blade is usually flatter and sharper than a shovel's and usually squared off at the bottom. A spade is for hard digging work; it should be strong but light enough to handle comfortably.

Spading Fork—A spading fork is used for heavy digging. Its prongs make it the best tool for breaking up compacted soil, lifting root vegetables, and digging weeds. The handle is sturdy and has a handgrip; your foot presses the prongs into the ground.

Hoe—The hoe is a tool with a flat blade attached at a right angle to a long handle. It's used for mounding the soil, making rows, cultivating, and cutting off weeds. It is one of the gardener's most necessary tools.

Trowel—This is a hand-held, short-handled tool with a pointed scoop-shaped blade. It's used as a small shovel and is helpful when transplanting young plants into the garden.

Garden Rake—A rake with a long handle and short sturdy metal prongs is used for leveling and grading soil and for removing rocks, soil clods, and shallow-rooted weeds. It's an essential tool for the home gardener.

Basic Tools

To be successful, every gardener needs some basic tools for starting and maintaining the garden. Buy high-quality tools; you'll save money in the end.

Trowel

Spade   **Shovel**   **Spading Fork**   **Hoe**   **Garden Rake**

Wheelbarrow

A wheelbarrow or garden cart is useful for moving tools, soil amendments, fertilizer, plants, and supplies to and from the garden. Available in metal, wood, and plastic, a wheelbarrow or cart can save you a lot of time and backache. It's essential if you have a large garden.

Sprayers

Sprayers are used for applying pesticides evenly to plants or other surfaces. There are two kinds of sprayers for the home garden. A hose-attachment jar sprayer has a container (usually a quart) with a screw-on lid and a nozzle that attaches to the end of your garden hose. It uses the pressure of the hose to mix the concentrated pesticide with water and then spray the pesticide. This type of sprayer is inexpensive but may not dispense an accurate dose. A hand-pump sprayer—either a backpack or a cylinder type—applies the pesticide manually by means of a pump. The backpack can hold anywhere from one to five gallons of pesticide; a cylinder type can hold one pint to one quart. Choose the size that best fits your needs.

Hand Spreader

You can use a hand spreader either to spread dry granule fertilizer or to sow seeds. It's a small box with a handle that you crank; a fan attached to the crank throws out the contents as you walk. It's effective for spreading an even layer of fertilizer or for planting a cover crop in the fall.

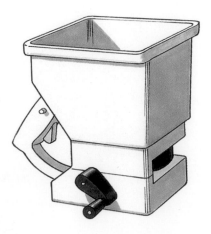

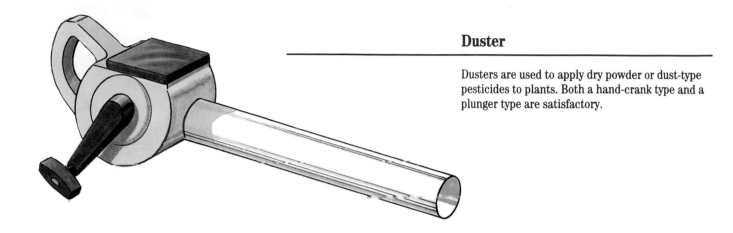

Duster

Dusters are used to apply dry powder or dust-type pesticides to plants. Both a hand-crank type and a plunger type are satisfactory.

Rototiller

A rototiller, usually gas-powered, uses multiple blades to turn soil in preparation for planting or to cultivate between rows. There are rear-type and front-type rototillers. Rear-type tillers are generally larger, more powerful, and easier to operate because they are self-propelled. However, they cost more and are less convenient to move around. Consider renting a rototiller the first year to determine your needs before making the investment.

All vegetables do better in a good, rich, deep soil, making gardening easy and fun. Your vegetable garden will be more productive after adding amendments to improve the pH and organic content.

CHAPTER 2

PREPARING THE SOIL

Count your blessings if you're lucky enough to have a garden with rich fertile loam, which is deep and easy to work. Good garden soil is not easy to find, and most beginning gardeners soon realize they must improve on one or more conditions of their soil.

The function of the soil is fourfold: It must supply water; it must supply nutrients; it must supply air to the roots; and it must be firm enough to support the plant securely. The ideal soil is a middle-of-the-road mixture, holding moisture and nutrients while letting excess water drain away to make room for air.

Vegetables can survive in a wide variety of soil types, but by making some simple preparatory changes, your garden soil can become as easy to use and productive as you'd like. Good soil must be guarded by proper management, involving cultivation, use of organic matter, and maintenance of fertility.

This chapter will take you step-by-step through a soil-improvement program. You'll learn how to test your soil for texture and fertility. Then you will see how to improve soil deficiencies. There's no need to worry if you're not satisfied with the results of your testing. Improving your garden soil is easily accomplished and is a regular part of gardening. Also, the soil-improving process doesn't have to all happen in the first year of gardening. Take time working with your soil, and you'll reap the benefits of many years of fruitful production.

Improving Your Garden Soil

Good soil is a key to healthy vegetable plants.

Good soil is 50 percent solids and 50 percent porous space, which provides room for water, air, and plant roots. The solids are inorganic matter (fine rock particles) and organic matter (decaying plant matter). The inorganic portion of the soil can be divided into three categories based on the size of the particles it contains. Clay has the smallest soil particles; silt has medium-size particles; and sand has the coarsest particles. The amount of clay, silt, and sand in a soil determine its texture. Loam, the ideal garden soil, is a mixture of 20 percent clay, 40 percent silt, and 40 percent sand.

In the interest of harvesting a bigger and better crop of vegetables, you'll want to improve the texture of your soil. This improvement, whether to make the soil drain better or hold more water, can be accomplished quite easily by the addition of organic matter.

Organic matter is material that was once living but is now dead and decaying. You can use such materials as ground corncobs, sawdust, bark chips, straw, hay, peat moss, grass clippings, and cover crops to serve as organic matter. Your own compost pile can supply you with excellent organic matter to enrich the soil.

Each spring, as you prepare the garden for planting, incorporate organic matter into the soil by tilling or turning it under with a spade. If noncomposted materials are used, the microorganisms that break down the materials will use nitrogen from the soil. To compensate for this nitrogen loss, increase the amount of nitrogen fertilizer that you incorporate into the soil.

The next step in your soil-improvement program is to have the soil tested for nutrient levels. The local county Cooperative Extension office can advise you on testing the soil in your area. Your soil sample will be sent to a laboratory to determine any deficiencies of the necessary nutrients needed for successful plant growth. Instructions for taking and preparing soil samples can be found on page 57.

Be sure to tell the laboratory that the samples came from a vegetable garden plot. The test report will recommend the amount and kind of fertilizer needed for a home garden. Follow the laboratory's recommendations as closely as possible during the first growing season. Also see "Fertilizing: How & Why To Do It" on page 488.

The necessary nutrient levels are relative to the soil type and the crop being grown. Although different vegetable plants have varying requirements, the soil test institution calculates an optimum average for fertilizer and lime recommendations.

The results of the soil test will indicate the pH (acid-alkaline balance) of the soil as well as the nitrogen content, phosphorus content, and potassium content. The pH is measured on a scale of 1 (most acid or sour) to 14 (most alkaline or sweet), with 7 representing neutral. Most vegetable plants produce best in a soil that has a pH between 5.5 and 7.5.

The pH number is important because it affects the availability of most of the essential nutrients in the soil. The soil lab will consider the type of soil you have, the pH level, and the crops you intend to produce and make a recommendation for pH adjustment.

Phosphorus (P) and potassium (K) levels will be indicated by a "Low," "Medium," or "High" level. High is the desired level for vegetable gardens for both nutrients. If your test results show other than High, a recommendation of type and amount of fertilizer will be made.

Although nitrogen (N) is also needed in large amounts by plants, the soil nitrates level is not usually routinely tested because rainfall leaches nitrates from the soil, which easily results in low levels. Additional nitrogen through the use of a complete fertilizer is almost always recommended.

Tests for other elements are available on request but are needed only under special circumstances.

SOIL TEST REPORT

Sample No.	NO. OE. AC.	Soil Type	Slope	Soil Prod. Group	Last Crop		Last Crops Fertilization, lb/A			Last Lime Application	
					Name	Yield	N	P₂O₅	K₂O	Mo. Prev.	T/A
Dirty		Clayey			None Applied						1-5 Lb/100

Soil pH	P lb/A	K lb/A	Ca lb/A	Mg lb/A	OM %	SS ppm	NO₃-N ppm	Zn ppm	Mn ppm	Cu ppm	Fe ppm	B ppm
7.5	120 VH	314 VH	2400 VH	240 VH				6.1	16.1	0.7	9.4	1.6

Crop: Vegetable garden

*223. Fertilizer recommendations: Apply 2 lbs of 10-10-10 per square foot. For additional information on fertilization, see note 19 (enclosed).

*619. Lime recommendations: None needed.

Adjusting Soil pH

The soil test results may advise you to raise the pH by adding a recommended amount of lime to the soil. Ground dolomitic limestone is best and can be applied at any time of the year without harm to the plants. You may be advised to lower the pH by adding a recommended amount of a sulfur product. Ammonium sulfate is the sulfur product most commonly used. Spread the lime or sulfur evenly through your garden and incorporate it into the soil by turning or tilling.

Fertilizing: How & Why To Do It

These golden beets need plenty of nutrients in the form of fertilizer.

Many inexperienced gardeners think that since their vegetables have done fine so far without fertilizer, they'll continue to do fine without fertilizer next year. But it's not quite that simple. Although your plants will probably provide you with vegetables without using fertilizer, you won't be getting their best effort. Properly fertilized vegetable plants will be healthier and better able to resist disease and attacks from pests, providing more and higher-quality produce.

There are two types of fertilizers: organic and inorganic. Both contain the same nutrients, but their composition and action differ in several ways. It makes no difference to the plant whether nutrients come from an organic or an inorganic source as long as the nutrients are available. However, the differences between the two types are worth your consideration.

Organic fertilizers come from plants and animals. The nutrients in organic fertilizers must be broken down over a period of time by microorganisms in the soil before they become available to the plants. Therefore, organic fertilizers don't offer instant solutions to nutrient deficiencies in the soil. Dried blood, kelp, and bone meal are types of organic fertilizers.

Manures are also organic. They are bulkier and contain lower percentages of nutrients than other natural fertilizers. However, they offer the advantage of immediately improving the texture of the soil by raising the level of organic matter.

Because organic fertilizers are generally not well-balanced in nutrient content, you'll probably need to use a mixture of them to ensure a balanced nutrient content. The table below, as well as the directions on the package, may be used as a guide to making your own mixture. Incorporate the mixture into the soil while preparing your spring garden. Apply it again as a side-dressing midway through the growing season.

When you fertilize with an inorganic fertilizer, nutrients are immediately available for the plant's use. Any container of fertilizer has three numbers printed on it, such as 5-10-20, to indicate the percentage of major nutrients it contains. Nitrogen is represented by the first number (5 percent in this example); phosphorus is represented by the second number (10 percent); and potassium by the third (20 percent). The remaining 65 percent is a mixture of other nutrients and inert filler. A well-balanced complete fertilizer consists of all three major nutrients in somewhat even proportions. A complete fertilizer is recommended for vegetable garden use as long as the nitrogen content isn't more than 20 percent. A typical complete fertilizer used in vegetable gardens is 10-10-10.

ANALYSIS OF ORGANIC FERTILIZERS

Fertilizer	N-P-K*
Dried Blood	13–1.5–0
Kelp	3–22–0
Cottonseed Meal	6–2.6–2
Cattle Manure	0.5–0.3–0.5
Horse Manure	0.6–0.3–0.5
Chicken Manure	0.9–0.5–0.8

* (N = Nitrogen, P = Phosphorus, K = Potassium)

Fertilizing Your Garden: A Two-Stage Program

1 **Broadcast Fertilizing**—When you're preparing the bed for spring planting, apply a complete fertilizer—such as 10-10-10—evenly to the entire garden according to the soil test recommendations. Do not overfertilize. A hand spreader helps keep the job neat as it distributes the granules. Turn the fertilizer into the soil with a hand spade or tiller and smooth out the surface to prepare for planting. This first fertilizing step will see most of your vegetables through their initial period of growth. Halfway through the growing season, the plants will have used up a lot of the nutrients in the soil, and you'll have to replace these nutrients.

2 **Sidedressing**—As the nutrients are used up by the plants, a second boost of fertilizer will be needed to supply the plants with essential elements through the remainder of the growing season. Use the same complete fertilizer at the same rate as used in the spring, but this time apply it as a sidedressing to the plants.

With a hoe, make a four-inch deep trench along one side of the row, taking care not to disturb the plant's roots. Apply the fertilizer in the trench and then cover the trench with the soil you removed. Rain and irrigation will work the fertilizer into the soil, becoming available to the plants.

Sidedressing Individual Plants

When long-season vegetables such as tomatoes, eggplant, and peppers need a second application of fertilizer, there's no need to trench an entire row. Cut a four-inch-deep collar-trench around the plant 12 to 18 inches from the stem. Spread about ½ cup of the same fertilizer used in the spring around each plant and cover it with soil. Water the garden well after fertilizing.

The Gardener's Recycling Plan

This compost pile will serve many uses in the vegetable garden.

The backyard compost pile is the ideal way to reuse most of your garden and kitchen waste and get benefits galore. Composting is essentially a way of speeding up the natural process of decomposition by which organic materials are broken down and their components returned to the soil. The decaying process happens naturally but slowly. The proximity, moisture, and air circulation of a compost pile encourages this process. Composting converts plant and other organic wastes into a loose, peatlike humus that provides nutrients to growing plants and increases the soil's ability to control water.

Composting can save money you would otherwise spend on soil conditioners and fertilizer. It can save time, too, since it gives you a place to dispose of grass clippings, weeds, and other garden debris.

Garden waste can be turned into good compost in less than a year if the pile is properly managed. When the compost is ready—coarse, dark brown, peatlike material—it can be used for many purposes. Compost can be added to potting soil for starting garden seeds indoors. It can also be used as a mulch to protect a plant's roots from the hot, dry summer sun. Compost is also an excellent material to incorporate into garden soil to help control moisture: either increasing the water-holding capacity in sandy soils or improving drainage in heavy clay soils. The more organic matter you add, the more you improve the texture of the soil. Blend the compost into the soil to a depth of 12 inches, making sure it is evenly dispersed through the entire planting area. When compost is added to the soil, it will absorb some of the soil's nitrogen. To compensate for this, add two handfuls of complete fertilizer (10-10-10) for each bushel of compost, working the fertilizer thoroughly into the soil.

Except for diseased and pest-laden materials or materials that have been treated with herbicides, almost any type of garden waste can be composted. You can also use such kitchen leftovers as vegetable and fruit peels, vegetable tops, coffee grounds, tea leaves, and eggshells. Don't use meat products or greasy foods, which tend to smell bad and attract animals. Composting material should be kept moist but not soggy, and it should be supplied with a nitrogen fertilizer (manure, dried blood, bone meal, or commercial fertilizer) to keep the microorganisms active for faster decay.

Compost forms as organic wastes are broken down by microorganisms in the soil. These microorganisms don't create nutrients; they just break down complex materials into simple ones that the plant can use. Soil microorganisms are most active when soil temperatures are above 60 degrees Fahrenheit, and most of them work best in a moist, slightly alkaline environment. Microorganisms work fastest on small pieces of organic material.

There are two basic types of microorganisms: those that need air to work (aerobic) and those that don't need air (anaerobic). It's possible to compost in an airtight container, thanks to the microorganisms that don't need air. A tightly covered plastic trash can will convert an enormous amount of organic kitchen waste into compost in the course of a winter. The classic outdoor compost pile should be turned regularly (about once every two weeks) with a pitchfork to provide air for the microorganisms that need it.

There are several handy composting devices on the market. Each has its own advantages, but a compost pile need not be fancy to work well. A simple bin made with old cinder blocks, lumber, or fencing material can be used. Tucked aside, but not too far from the garden, the bin can be square, rectangular, or round. It should be four to five feet across and about three feet high.

There are almost as many different methods of composting as there are gardeners. Follow the basic steps of composting on the next page, and your final product is sure to be a success.

How to Start a Compost Pile

1 Start with either a one- to two-foot pile of leaves or 6 to 12 inches or more of compact material, such as grass clippings or sawdust. You can compost hay, straw, hulls, nutshells, and tree trimmings (except walnut). However, unless they're shredded, they'll take a long time to decompose. Use any organic garden or kitchen waste (except meat scraps), as long as it contains no pesticides or diseases.

2 Over this initial pile spread a layer of fertilizer. The nitrogen will help activate the microorganisms, which in turn will speed the decay of the organic materials. Add about ½ cup of ground limestone (most microorganisms like their environment sweet). Then add several shovelfuls of garden soil, which will provide a starter colony of microorganisms. It's handy to have a small pile of soil nearby when you start the compost pile.

3 Water the pile well. The pile should be kept moist, like a squeezed sponge. Keep adding garden waste to the top of the pile as it becomes available. As the layers become thickened and compacted, repeat the layers of fertilizer, lime, and soil.

4 About once every two weeks, turn and mix the pile with a pitch fork or digging fork. This will ensure that all the components of the pile, not just the center, will heat up. As the temperature in the compost pile increases, weed seeds and harmful disease organisms are killed, and the decay process will not be delayed.

1.

2.

3.

4.

Many gardeners enjoy planting time the most of all seasons. Vegetables finally start growing, and other garden adornments, such as this scarecrow, add amusement as well as protection.

CHAPTER 3

PLANTING YOUR GARDEN

Planning and soil preparation both lead to the same purpose—getting the garden planted. Most experienced gardeners will agree: Planting time is their favorite season of the year.

If you're anxious to get your garden started, read on. You'll find useful tips and ideas that will make your garden a success, even if you've never gardened before. It goes without saying that thoughtful planning and carefully prepared soil are essential tasks for successful gardening, but the real fun starts with actually planting. You'll feel a great sense of achievement when you've cared for the tender seedlings through periods of inclement weather: frosty nights, scorching sun, and drought.

There are a number of questions you should consider before you start planting. For one thing, should you be planting seeds or should you be using transplants (seedlings that you have started indoors or have purchased)? Some vegetables are not started from seed at all; new plants can be started from old plants. How should the plants be spaced: single rows, wide rows, or inverted hills? As in every other stage of growing a vegetable garden, planting poses many questions. In the following pages you'll learn which vegetables grow best from seed sown in the garden and which vegetables are best started from transplants.

Starting Transplants Indoors

Plants started indoors may need the protection of a coldframe after being moved outdoors.

Earlier harvest, extended season, and increased varietal choice are some of the reasons you may want to start your own vegetable transplants indoors. Although many vegetable plants are available at garden centers each spring, it is sometimes difficult to find the exact variety that you're looking for. By starting your own transplants, you can plan for a supply of what you want when you want it.

Your first consideration is when to plant. If you plant too early, seedlings will become weak and leggy, which is not much of a start for a productive garden. Use the average date of last frost as a reference point for when to plant each vegetable in the garden. Remember, some vegetables will be planted in the garden several weeks before this date, others near or on this date, and yet others a few weeks after this date. From the planting date, count back six to eight weeks; as a general rule, you can sow seeds indoors on this date. Large-seeded varieties, such as squash and watermelon, should be started only four weeks prior to garden planting.

Although you'll gain confidence with experience, it's best to start with just a few varieties the first year. Taking care of seedlings indoors takes time, the proper conditions, and common sense. It is imperative to provide the plants with the necessary environment for strong, healthy growth. Light, temperature, moisture, and cleanliness are just some of the elements that contribute to the healthy development of your plants.

Light—You'll need a place to start seedlings that gets several hours of light each day. Even close to a window, seedlings often stretch, trying to reach toward the light. If artificial lights are used, the bulbs must not produce too much heat. Fluorescent lights or special plant lights produce plenty of light without excessive heat.

Heat/Temperature—Different varieties of vegetables require different temperatures to germinate. Most seeds will germinate well at 70 to 75 degrees Fahrenheit. Some varieties require cooler temperatures; the seed packet will tell you the precise temperature required. Heating pads are available through garden centers and gardening supply mail-order companies, but a warm spot in the room can often be used.

Water—Since many seeds are small and easily displaced in the soil, it's best to soak the seedling tray in water to absorb water from the bottom drainage holes. Seeds will die if they are allowed to dry out after they have started to germinate.

Planting Medium—The soil you sow seeds and grow young plants in must be light and sterile to prevent a deadly seedling disease called damping-off. It's best to purchase a seed-starter medium from a reputable garden center. Garden soil is too heavy and may contain weed seeds or disease organisms.

Containers—Containers can be store-bought seedling trays or pots or items such as aluminum trays, paper cups, or other kitchen items as long as they can hold the medium and contain adequate drainage holes. Small-seeded varieties may be started in trays and later separated and transplanted to individual containers. Large-seeded varieties should be started in individual containers from the start; their roots do not appreciate being disturbed while being separated. Plantable containers such as peat-pots are handy. These are made of compressed peat, and the pot can be planted in the garden.

VEGETABLES TO START INDOORS

Broccoli	Eggplant
Brussels Sprouts	Lettuce
Cabbage	Onion
Cauliflower	Pepper
Celery	Squash*
Chard	Tomato
Cucumber*	Watermelon*

* Start in individual containers so their root systems are not disturbed.

Starting Seeds Indoors

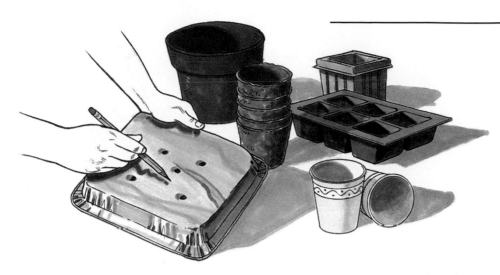

Containers and medium should be selected to suit the needs of the varieties that you will grow. Commercially available flats, seed-starter trays, cell-packs, peat-pots, and flower pots as well as plastic-foam or paper cups and aluminum baking trays are typical containers. Be sure each container has adequate drainage. If containers have been used previously, be sure to clean them with a mild bleach solution to prevent the spread of plant diseases. Choose a light-weight sterile seedling mix to start your seeds. Mix the medium with enough water to moisten the mix well. Fill the container with two to three inches of medium and firm the mix lightly.

Sowing the Seeds

Small vegetable seeds should be sown in rows at a rate of eight to ten seeds per inch. Make row indentations about ¼-inch deep with a label or pencil and sprinkle the seeds evenly in the rows. Cover the seeds with the potting mix and press lightly to ensure contact between the seeds and the medium. If you're using individual containers, sprinkle two to three seeds on the surface. Press them about ¼-inch into the mix and cover. If all three seeds germinate, cut two seedlings off at soil level, leaving the strongest plant.

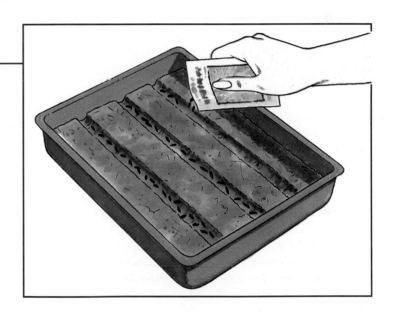

Transplanting to Individual Containers

Seeds grown in flats must be transplanted into individual containers before planting outdoors. Do this after they've developed a couple of "true leaves." The first leaves that appear are seed leaves; the next set of leaves are the true leaves. Gently lift the healthiest looking plants from the seed bed from underneath using a knife or spatula. Hold them by their true leaves and separate them from neighboring plants. Make a hole in the new planting medium deep enough to accept the roots without curling or crowding them. Press the soil firmly around the roots. Water the new plants thoroughly.

495

Caring for Seedlings

A little care and attention to seedlings will go a long way toward healthy, mature plants.

Young seedlings, at this stage of their development, have definite requirements. They need temperatures a little on the cool side. For most vegetables, a nighttime low of 55 degrees Fahrenheit and a daytime high of 70 degrees Fahrenheit is about right. If it's cooler, disease problems may develop; if it's warmer, the plants will become tall and spindly. It's also important that the seedlings get plenty of light: at least six hours of bright light a day. If your indoor space can't provide enough natural light for your seedlings, use artificial light. The best artificial lights are plant growth lights. They emit high levels of blue light, which encourages good, stocky vegetative growth. Ideally, the lights should be about six to eight inches away from the leaves of the plants. Keep the lights on for about 12 hours a day.

New seedlings will need a dose of starter fertilizer to supply them with nutrients for sturdy growth. Seeds don't need fertilizer to germinate; therefore, seedling starter medium is often low in nutrients. A soluble fertilizer is best as a starter solution. Use a complete fertilizer (N-P-K) mixed with water at half strength for new seedlings. An application every two weeks—more often if leaves become pale or reddish—will be adequate to develop strong stems and foliage.

Tender seedlings will die of shock if you take them straight from the protected indoors to the garden. Cold night temperatures, wind, and rain can be detrimental to tender seedlings. You have to prepare them for the change in the environment, a process known in horticultural terms as "hardening off." You do this by taking the plants outside during the day and bringing them back in at night for at least two weeks. Keep them in, though, if there's likely to be a frost. You can also put them outside in a protected place such as a coldframe or a large box that can be covered at night. This treatment will prepare the plants for their final placement in the garden.

You may decide that buying transplants from a nursery or garden center is the easiest way to start your vegetable garden. You'll get high-quality transplants and fewer problems. But it's more expensive to buy transplants, and you'll have fewer varieties to choose from. Apply the same principles in choosing the vegetables you buy as transplants as you would if you were going to grow your own plants from seed. Base your decision on the length of the growing season and the flexibility of the plant variety. Buy your transplants from a reputable nursery or garden center so you'll know the plants have been grown with care.

You'll also be able to ask for advice about choosing the best varieties. Look for plants that have strong stems, dark green leaves, and a healthy root system. You can slip a plant out of its container to make sure the roots are white and healthy. Don't forget to find out if the plants have been hardened off.

Planting Tomato Seedlings

Tomato seedlings often become tall and leggy while sitting in the garden center or on your windowsill. Long-stemmed tomato seedlings can be planted deeply or on their side so they won't become top-heavy. Tomatoes will develop roots along the buried stem that will help support the new growth. Remove the leaves from the part of the stem that will be planted, and dig a hole deep enough for the stem to comfortably support the part of the plant that will remain above ground. Another option is to plant seedlings in a trench on a slant. The tip of the stem will eventually curve upward and grow straight. When you've planted each seedling and firmed the soil, give each plant a boost of starter fertilizer to stimulate root growth.

Moving Transplants into the Garden

When your transplants are ready for planting in the garden, arrange them on the prepared soil bed to judge the correct spacing. Set two stakes with a string to ensure straight rows and use a tape measure if you'd like accurate spacing. Dig a hole for each plant as you're ready to set it in the ground, then gently slip the plant out of its container. If you have to handle the plant, hold it by the leaves so the stem does not become damaged. The top rim of plantable containers should be broken off so it will not stick up out of the garden soil: It will act as a wick and draw moisture out of the root zone. If the roots have become tightly compacted and intertwined, gently pinch off the bottom to initiate new growth. Set each transplant in the soil, and tamp the soil around it firmly with your hands. Don't plant transplants too deep; set them at the same depth they were in the container.

Direct-seeding in the Garden

Direct-seeding is often the beginning of many vegetable gardens.

Seeding directly into the garden is the easiest and least expensive way to grow vegetables. However, you may not have the climate that will let you direct-seed some vegetables: The seedlings may take longer to grow, making them more susceptible to weather conditions than transplants grown indoors. The vegetables to grow from seed are those that will mature within the span of your growing season and those that don't like to be transplanted.

The key to successful planting is proper soil preparation. When the soil is neither too wet nor too dry, turn the soil to a depth of 8 to 12 inches while adding organic matter. You should also apply a complete fertilizer, working it evenly into the soil. As you're preparing the soil, remove all stones, rocks, lumps, and the assorted debris that accumulated over the winter.

The depth you plant your seeds depends on their size. They only need enough soil to cover them and supply moisture for germination. Seeds buried too deep may not be able to struggle through the soil to the surface. The planting guide at the end of this chapter tells you exactly how deep to plant seeds of each type of vegetable. As a rule of thumb, seeds should be covered up to twice their diameter at their largest point. After you've set the seeds at the correct depth, firm the soil by tamping it with your hands or the end of your garden rake. This will improve contact between the seeds and the moist soil.

Seed spacing is also critical: If plants are forced to grow too close together, they may produce little or no yield. If seeds are large enough to handle, such as beans and corn, it's fairly easy to space them correctly. But with tiny seeds, spacing can be tricky. Take your time in spacing while planting, but you'll still probably have to thin seedlings soon after germination. The planting guide at the end of this chapter details the amount of space each plant needs for best growth.

Decide whether you'll sow seeds in a single row or a wide row. Vegetables such as beets, carrots, collards, kale, leaf lettuce, mustard, radishes, and spinach will produce nicely in wide rows while conserving space and water. The rows should be no wider than about 36 inches, making it easy to maintain and harvest vegetables. Prepare the row by loosely raking the soil, leaving the indentations made by the rake. Sprinkle the seeds evenly over the soil, and use the rake to press them into the soil. Cover the row with a thin layer of soil, straw, or loose compost to help keep the soil moist.

Planting in a single row is the most commonly used seeding arrangement. It's the easiest to maintain because you can comfortably cultivate between rows, but it's the least economical. Plants dry out faster, and there is more unused garden space.

Plants such as cucumbers and squash and other trailing vegetables benefit from planting in inverted hills: a shallow depression made by removing an inch of soil from a circle about a foot across and using the soil you've removed to form a rim around the circle. The inverted hill catches and holds extra moisture. During a heavy rain the outer rim of the soil, instead of being washed away, falls in toward the plants, providing extra anchorage for shallow-rooted plants.

Planting Depth for Direct-Seeding

Seeds should be covered up to twice their diameter at their largest point.

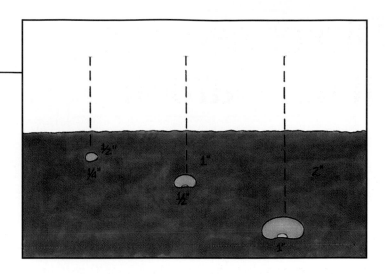

Single-row Planting

Once the soil has been properly prepared and the timing is right, you're ready to plant. Use a planting guide—a string and two stakes—to mark your row. Then with a hoe or the end of a rake handle, follow the string and cut a depression into the soil to a depth twice the seed's diameter. Sprinkle the seeds directly from the package or take a pinch of small seeds from the palm of your hand.

Wide-row Planting

Properly cared for wide-rows will produce higher yields per square foot than single-row planting. Prepare the soil and mark the width of the row with string or a rake depression. If small-seeded varieties are being sown, loosen the soil with the rake and sprinkle seeds on top of the soil. Use the back of the rake to press the seeds into the soil; cover them with a thin layer of soil, straw, or compost. To plant large-seeded varieties, rake one inch of soil from the row to the side and sprinkle the seeds. Cover the seeds with the soil you removed earlier and gently tamp the soil with the rake.

Inverted Hills

Trailing vegetables that sprawl over the garden are well-suited to inverted hills. Use a hoe or rake to pull soil into a mound. Hollow out the hill to form a bowl-like depression. Plant five or six seeds at the correct depth inside the circle. When the seedlings have developed two true leaves, thin them out, leaving the two or three strongest plants.

Thinning Garden Seedlings

Thinning is an essential task in the early stages of a seedling's development. When seeds germinate, seedlings are sometimes close and overplanted. When planting in inverted hills, extra seeds are deliberately planted because not all the seeds will germinate and some seeds will produce weak plants. Thinning must be done early, before plants are weakened by overcrowding. Use a scissors to cut at soil level all seedlings that should be thinned. If you pull seedlings from the soil, you risk damaging the roots of the remaining plants.

Protect Young Plants

Extreme weather conditions pose a threat to tender young plants. If hot sun threatens to dry the topsoil where the roots are developing, shade the plants with a board, a basket, or a layer of burlap. Provide this shade on windy days as well as sunny days until the transplants become established. If there is any risk of frost, cover the seedlings with a type of homemade hot cap: A light covering of straw, bottomless plastic jugs, flower pots, and buckets work well as temporary protection.

Water Seedlings

Don't let seedlings die of thirst. Adequate watering is essential to young plants in their early stages of growth. Water to a depth of six to eight inches to encourage deep rooting and stronger growth. If watering is not deep, shallow roots will develop, making the plant weak and susceptible during dry periods. Using a sprinkler or spray nozzle, apply water long enough to soak the soil but gently enough that seedlings will not be displaced.

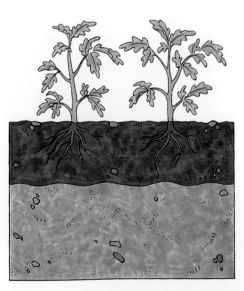

Starting New Plants from Parts

Seeds and transplants, while the forms you'll use most often, are not the only methods to raise new plants. Some vegetables are started from other plant parts: suckers, tubers, slips, crowns, sets, cloves, divisions, or cuttings. In some cases plants can be grown either by seed or from plant parts. Onions, for instance, take a very long time to germinate from seed, so it usually makes more sense to grow them from sets. Other plants grow best from plant parts.

Suckers, or offshoots, are plants that grow or shoot up from the root system of a mature plant. These suckers can be dug up and divided from the mother plant, and then transplanted to mature into new plants. Globe artichoke is usually the only vegetable grown from suckers.

Tubers are specialized swollen underground stems capable of producing roots, stems, and leaves. Irish potatoes and Jerusalem artichokes are usually grown from tubers. When the plants are cut up for planting, as in the case of Irish potatoes, they are called seed pieces.

Slips are young, tender, rooted cuttings or sprouts grown from vegetable roots. Sweet potatoes are the only vegetable commonly grown from slips.

Crowns are compressed stems near the soil surface that are capable of producing leaves and roots. Crowns that are planted with the roots attached are referred to as "roots." Crowns are divided from the mother plant when the plant is dormant. Asparagus is grown from crowns.

Sets are one-year-old onion seedlings that were pulled when the bulbs were young. The bulbs are air-dried, stored for the winter, and planted next spring.

Cloves are the segmented parts of bulbs. Garlic is the only vegetable commonly grown from cloves. Each garlic bulb is made up of a dozen or more cloves, and each clove is planted separately. For the highest yield, separate the cloves as you plant.

Divisions occur naturally in the form of small, rooted plants or bulbs that grow from the mother plant. You separate or divide them off to grow as individual plants. Dig up the mother plant, separate the small new shoots, and replant each new unit. Horseradish and rhubarb are grown from divisions. You can divide plants in the spring or the fall. Fall is preferable because the cool, moist weather helps the plants become well-established.

Rhubarb is an excellent candidate for division.

Cuttings are started by cutting a piece of stem from the plant at the node—the lumpy place on the stem where leaves are attached—and forcing it to develop new roots. This is best done in early summer, when the stems are actively growing. Treat the cut end of the stem with a commercially prepared rooting hormone and stick the cutting in moist soil away from direct sunlight. New roots will form in a few weeks, and the new plant can be placed in the garden. Tomato shoots are often rooted for a late crop.

Dividing Perennial Vegetables

1 You can turn a well-established rhubarb plant into six or eight new plants by simple division. Rhubarb is best divided in the fall or early spring. Choose a specimen with thick, long stalks. Use a spade or digging fork to dig the plant up, keeping intact as much of the root system as possible. After lifting the plant from the hole, shake excess soil from the roots to determine the best natural divisions that can be made.

2 With a sharp knife or spade, slice the fleshy root into as many sections as there are crowns (the part of the plant from which new shoots develop). Each new division should contain a crown and roots. Divisions that have a strong crown and strong roots will easily become established as new plants. Cut off any roots that have become damaged and replant the divisions in their new sites.

PLANTING GUIDE: SPACING

Vegetable	Inches between plants	Inches between rows	Depth of seed (inches)
Artichoke, Globe	36–48	48–60	1–1½
Artichoke, Jerusalem	12–18	24–36	
Asparagus	12–18	36–48	1–1½
Beans, Broad	8–10	36–48	1–2
Beans, Dry	4–6	18–24	1–1½
Beans, Lima			
bush	2–3	18–24	1–1½
pole	4–6	30–36	1–1½
Beans, Snap or Green			
bush	2–3	18–24	1–1½
pole	4–6	30–36	1–1½
Beets	2–3	12–18	1
Broccoli	3	24–36	½
Brussels Sprouts	24	24–36	½
Cabbage	18–24	24–36	½
Cardoon	18–24	36–48	½
Carrot	2–4	12–24	¼
Cauliflower	18–24	24–36	½
Celeriac	6–8	24–30	¼
Celery	8–10	24–30	¼
Chard	9–12	18–24	1
Chayote	24–30	60	
Chick pea	6–8	12–18	½
Chicory	12–18	24–36	1
Chinese Cabbage	8–12	18–30	½
Collards	12	18–24	½
Corn	2–4	12–18	1–1½
Cress	1–2	18–24	¼
Cucumber*†	12	18–72	½
Dandelion	6–8	12–18	¼
Eggplant	18–24	24–36	¼
Endive	9–12	18–24	⅛
Horseradish	24	18–24	¼
Kale	8–12	18–24	½

PLANTING GUIDE: SPACING

Vegetable	Inches between plants	Inches between rows	Depth of seed (inches)
Kohlrabi	5–6	18–24	¼
Leek	6–9	12–18	⅛
Lettuce	6–12	12–18	⅛
Muskmelon*‡	18–24	60–96	1
Mustard	6–12	12–24	½
Okra	12–18	24–36	½–1
Onion			
sets	2–3	12–18	1–2
seeds	1–2	12–18	¼
Parsnip	2–4	18–24	½
Pea, Black–eyed	8–12	12–18	½
Pea, Shelling	1–2	18–24	2
Peanut	6–8	12–18	1
Pepper	18–24	24–36	½
Potato, Irish	12–18	24–36	4
Sweet Potato	12–18	36–48	3–5
Pumpkin*‡	24–48	60–120	1
Radish	1–6	12–18	½
Rhubarb	30–36	36–48	
Rutabaga	6–8	18–24	½
Salsify	2–4	18–24	½
Shallot	6–8	12–18	¼
Sorrel	12–18	18–24	½
Soybean	1½–2	24–30	½–1
Spinach	2–4	12–24	½
Spinach, New Zealand	12	24–36	½
Squash, Summer*§	24–36	18–48	1
Squash, Winter*‡	24–48	60–120	1
Tomato	18–36	24–48	½
Turnip			
greens	2–3	12–24	½
roots	3–4	12–24	½
Watermelon*‡	24–72	60–120	1

*Note: Plants in inverted hills should be thinned to three plants in each hill.
† Hills should be 36 inches apart.
‡ Hills should be 72 inches apart.
§ Hills should be 48 inches apart.

A rich harvest of fresh vegetables awaits those who take the time to care for a garden. These carrots, tomatoes, and zucchini will perk up any meal.

CHAPTER 4

CARING FOR YOUR GARDEN

You can get a great sense of achievement from planting your garden, but keep in mind that your labors are by no means over when the seeds are in the ground. Even a small garden of tomatoes and squash requires a certain amount of time and care.

Besides well-prepared soil and proper planting, plants need water, and since nature is not always cooperative, you may want to devise an easy way to supplement your rainfall through simple irrigation. A watering plan should be designed according to the size of your garden. Your options range from a simple watering can to a sophisticated drip system. You'll even see how low-pressure ooze watering can save you water.

The benefits of a well-maintained, weed-free garden are immeasurable. Vegetables that have to compete with weeds for water and nutrients become frail and sickly; weeds can also harbor diseases and insect pests. We'll show you some time-saving ways to help control these garden invaders, including cover crops that prevent weed growth and the use of mulches to conserve water and inhibit weeds. In addition, end-of-season garden care can save you time. Preparing the soil in winter will save you a great deal of work with wet soil when you plant your early spring crops. These techniques will help you maintain a clean, healthy garden. The end result will be great vegetables as well as a feeling of accomplishment.

Staking & Plant Support

Many plants, as they mature, need support to help them grow. This is especially true of tomato plants and such climbing plants as beans, cucumbers, and winter squash.

As tomato plants mature, they begin to sprawl along the ground because they become heavy with fruit. If left to grow without training, the fruit is exposed to sunscald and inclined to rot. An effective way to prevent these problems is to train the plants to grow vertically by staking the plants. Another simple training method is to build tomato cages. As the vine grows, guide the stems into the cage.

You can use your vertical space by designing a trellis system to support twining and climbing plants like beans, cucumbers, and winter squash. An important consideration is sturdiness. Vines and wind will be tugging on it for several months, so build the trellis well. The stems of bean plants will twine around the trellis for support; with a little bit of guidance, cucurbits will grab the trellis with their tendrils.

Staking helps keep disease and other plant maladies at bay.

Tomato Stakes

Use strong stakes for tomato plants: 2 inches by 2 inches, about eight feet long and driven 24 inches to 30 inches deep will support most tomatoes. Drive in the stake before setting the transplant, so you won't disturb the growing roots. As the vine grows, tie it to the stake with twine or plastic tape.

Tomato Cage

Use 60-inch, 6 × 6-inch welded concrete reinforcement wire to build tomato cages. Regular fence wire won't work because the openings aren't large enough to harvest the fruit. Cut a five- to six-foot section of wire, leaving prongs so the wire can be bent into a cylinder and clamped together with the prongs. Cut off the bottom rim with heavy wire cutters so the bottom spikes can be pushed into the soil around the tomato plant.

Using a Trellis System

Your trellis system will need some kind of support: 4 × 4-inch posts driven into the ground or a tee-pee design that supports itself are typical solutions. From tower to tower, lace heavy twine or wire and pattern string from top to bottom to support the crop.

Weeding: Keep Out Intruders

Weeds, such as this dandelion, should be controlled early in the season.

Cultivating, or weeding, is probably going to be your most demanding task as garden caretaker. Weeds are both resilient and persistent. At times, you'll probably feel that if your vegetables grew as well and as fast as your weeds, gardening would be child's play. It's important to keep down the weeds in your vegetable garden. They steal light, water, and nutrients from the vegetables, and they shelter insects and disease.

To successfully control the weeds in your garden, you have to learn to recognize them when they are young. It helps to understand how and when weeds grow to keep the garden clean and weed free. When weeds are small, regular cultivation will control them easily. If you let them become established, getting rid of weeds will be a struggle.

Annual weeds are like many of the vegetable varieties. There are cool-season annual weeds, and there are warm-season annual weeds. Cool-season weeds, such as chickweed, generally germinate during fall and winter in the garden. They produce flowers and seeds in the spring. Although the weeds disappear, the seeds lie dormant in your soil through the summer. If these weeds are allowed to produce seeds, you'll have the same problem the following season. Warm-season annuals are much the same, but their growing season is spring through fall.

Perennial weeds persist year after year, some with deep taproots, others with a long-spreading network of roots. Some perennial weeds will spread through the garden like wildfire; don't wait for this to happen. A beginning gardener can easily be overwhelmed by such a problem.

Weed seeds will germinate wherever the ground is bare, especially where you have supplied the soil with organic matter, fertilizer, and water. To help prevent weed germination, try to keep the garden covered with mulch or a cover crop. This method isn't always practical when you're waiting for a row of vegetables to germinate, but it will help keep out many weeds.

The best way to control weeds is to chop them off at ground level with a sharp hoe. If a weed is close to your vegetables, don't try to dig out the whole root system of the weed; you may also damage the root systems of neighboring vegetables in the process. Instead, just remove the top of the weed. Persistent weeds, such as dandelions, may have to be cut down several times, but eventually they will die.

Herbicides can be useful in controlling weeds under certain conditions, but these conditions are usually not encountered in the small home garden. In addition, herbicides require such careful handling that the home gardener would be well advised not to use them more than absolutely necessary.

COMMON WEEDS	
Annuals	***Perennials***
Bindweed	Burdock
Chickweed	Canada Thistle
Ground Ivy	Dandelion
Lambs-quarters	Plantain
Pigweed	Poison Ivy
Purslane	Giant Ragweed
	Common Ragweed

Mulches

Mulches are either organic or inorganic material placed on the soil around vegetable plants. Mulches perform a number of useful functions. They protect against soil erosion by breaking the force of heavy rains; they help prevent soil compaction; they discourage the growth of weeds; and they reduce certain disease problems. Mulches are insulators, making it possible to keep the soil warmer during cool weather and cooler during warm weather. Organic mulches also improve the soil texture. Sometimes mulches can improve the appearance of a vegetable garden by giving it a neater, more finished look.

Your plants will need less water if you use a mulch, increasing the time that plants can go between watering. When the soil dries out, plants slow their growth—or stop growing altogether. Swift, steady growth is important for the best-tasting fruits and vegetables. Mulches keep the soil evenly moist.

Mulches do not eliminate weeds. They can, however, help control them if the area has been cleared of weeds to begin with. If the mulch is thick enough, weeds that are already growing won't be able to push through and darkness will frustrate the germination of others. Persistent weeds can push their way through most mulch, but if they're cut off at the soil level a few times, they will die.

Whether you use an organic or an inorganic mulch, take care not to put it down before the soil has warmed up in the spring. If you put it down too soon, mulch will prevent the soil from warming and slow down root development.

Organic mulches are organic materials that, when laid on the soil, decompose to feed soil microorganisms and improve the quality of the soil. If the mulch you've put down is decomposing quickly, add nitrogen to make up for nitrogen consumed by bacteria.

The following are organic materials commonly used as mulches in vegetable gardens.

Compost—Partially decomposed compost looks a little rough, but it makes a great mulch and soil conditioner.

Lawn Clippings—Do not use clippings from a lawn that has been treated with a herbicide or weed killer; these substances can kill the vegetables you're trying to grow. Let untreated clippings dry before putting them around your garden; fresh grass mats down and smells bad while it's decomposing.

Leaf Mold—Leaves are cheap and usually easy to find, but they blow around and are hard to keep in place. They will stay in place better if they're ground up and partially decomposed. Nitrogen should be added to leaf mold. Do not use walnut leaves; they contain iodine, which is toxic to some vegetable plants.

Mulches are a multipurpose item for any garden.

Sawdust—Sawdust is often available for the asking, but it requires added nitrogen to prevent microorganisms from depleting the soil's nitrogen supply. If possible, allow sawdust to decompose for a year before using it as a mulch.

Straw—Straw is messy and hard to apply in small areas, but it is an excellent mulch. Be sure not to use hay, which contains many weed seeds.

Wood Chips or Shavings—Wood chips, like sawdust, decompose slowly and should be allowed to partially decompose for a year before being used as mulch. Additional nitrogen will be needed to supply bacteria during decomposition.

Inorganic mulch, or landscape fabric, is used in small gardens for plants that are grown in a group or a hill, such as cucumbers, squash, or pumpkins. It can also be used for individual plants such as peppers, tomatoes, and eggplants. Fabric should not be used for crops that need a cool growing season—cabbage or cauliflower, for instance—unless it's covered with a thick layer of light-reflecting material, such as sawdust.

There are several advantages to growing with a landscape fabric mulch. Fabric reduces the loss of soil moisture, raises the soil temperature, and speeds up crop maturity. Weeds are discouraged, because the fabric cuts off their light supply. This

511

means you won't have to cultivate as much, reducing the risk of root damage. The fabric also helps keep the plants cleaner. When you're making a new garden in a formerly grassy area—if you've dug up a lawn, for instance—fabric can keep the grass from coming back.

There are some disadvantages to keep in mind as well. You will have to water more frequently, especially well-drained, sandy soils. On the other hand, plants can wilt and rot if the soil moisture is kept at too high a level and there isn't enough air in the soil. Remember too that the fabric is inorganic, and at the end of the season you'll have to remove it from the garden. If the fabric is of high grade, you may be able to reuse it the following season.

Using Organic Mulch

To use an organic mulch, such as straw or compost, spread a layer of the material on the surface of the ground around the plants after the soil has warmed up in the spring. If you're mulching around rows of direct-sown seedlings, wait until the plants are about four inches tall. Otherwise, the mulch will overwhelm the plants. Seedlings will poke through a light layer of organic matter, but several inches of mulch will prevent them from emerging. Avoid using a fluffy material with large particles, like bark chips, because you will have to put down a layer that is too thick. If you're using a denser material, such as straw or grass clippings, a two-inch layer will be enough. Be careful not to suffocate the vegetables while trying to frustrate weeds.

Laying Down Landscape Fabric Mulch

You can buy landscape fabric from many garden centers, hardware stores, and mail-order suppliers. It should be at least three or four feet wide. Put down the fabric before the plants are set out. Try to pick a calm day; a strong wind will whip the fabric around and make laying it down difficult. Prepare the soil with amendments and grade it smoothly with a garden rake. Lay out the row for the mulch with a string. Then, with a hoe, make a three-inch-deep trench along one side of the row for the entire length of the row. Pull some of the soil into the center of the area that will be covered with fabric: You want water to run off the fabric and into the soil rather than pooling on top of the fabric. Lay one edge of the fabric in the trench and cover the edge with soil. Smooth the fabric over the bed and repeat the process on the other side. Be sure the fabric is anchored securely, or the wind will get under it and pull it up.

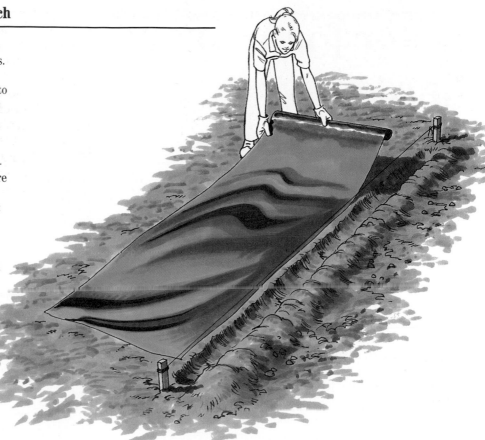

Planting in Landscape Fabric Mulch

When you're ready to plant, cut an "X" about three inches across for each transplant or seed. With a hand trowel, dig through the "X" and plant as usual. Thoroughly water the plants through the holes in the mulch. After a rain, check to see if there are any spots where water is standing. If there are, punch holes through the fabric so the water can run through.

513

Water for Your Garden

Watering, whether for rows of crops or in containers, is often necessary to supplement rainfall.

Some plants are composed of up to 95 percent water. Water is vital from the moment seeds are sown through sprouting to the end of the growing season. Plants need water for cell division, cell enlargement, and even for holding themselves up. If the cells don't have enough water in them, the result is a wilted plant. Water is essential, along with light and carbon dioxide, for producing the sugars that provide the plant with energy for growth. It also dissolves fertilizers and carries nutrients to the different parts of the plant.

Ideally, water for plants comes from rain or other precipitation and from underground sources. In reality, you'll often have to do extra watering by hand or through an irrigation system. How often you should water depends on how often it rains, how long your soil retains moisture, and how fast water evaporates in your climate. Soil type is another important factor. Clay soils hold water very well—sometimes too well. Sandy soils are like a sieve, letting the water run right through. Both kinds of soil can be improved with the addition of organic matter. Organic matter gives clay soils lightness and air; it gives sandy soils something to hold the water.

Other factors may also affect how often you need to water your garden:

- More water evaporates when the temperature is high than when it's low. Plants can rot if they get too much water in cool weather.
- More water evaporates when the relative humidity is low.
- Plants need more water when the days are bright.
- Wind and air movement will increase the loss of water to the atmosphere.
- Water needs vary with the type and maturity of the plant. Some vegetables are tolerant of low soil moisture.
- Sometimes water is not what a wilting plant needs. When plants are growing fast, the leaves sometimes get ahead of the roots' ability to provide them with water. If the day is hot and the plants wilt in the afternoon, don't worry about them; they will regain their balance overnight. But if plants are wilting early in the morning, water them immediately.

So much depends on climate and the ability of different soil types to hold moisture that it's difficult to give specific directions for watering your garden. Generally, however, vegetable plants need about an inch of water a week. The best time to water your garden is in the morning. If you water at night when the day is cooling off, the water is likely to stay on the foliage, increasing the danger of disease. Some people believe that you shouldn't water in the morning because water spots on leaves will cause leaf-burn when the sun gets hot; this isn't the case.

When watering your vegetable garden, there is one rule you should follow: Always soak the soil thoroughly. A light sprinkling can often do more harm than no water at all: It stimulates the roots to come to the surface, where they are killed by exposure to the sun.

Leaky-pipe Irrigation

Overhead watering is most commonly used, but it wastes water because of excessive evaporation and it encourages diseases to settle on the wet foliage. Controlled watering eliminates waste and supplies water to garden plants where they need it—at the base of the plants. Leaky-pipe, or soaker hose, is made of recycled rubber and is as flexible as an ordinary garden hose. Equipped with a female coupling on one end to attach to a water spigot, and a male coupling on the other end to cap off or attach another length of pipe, the soaker hose allows water to slowly permeate the soil. Arrange the soaker hose at the base of the plants in the row; water is then distributed evenly over the roots of the plants.

Trickle Irrigation

Also known as drip irrigation, trickle irrigation saves water. This is a good way to water vegetables that are spaced far apart as well as container gardens on a deck or terrace. Mini-tubes are inserted into holes in the main line at intervals to suit the gardener's needs. Weighted tips at the end of each mini-tube are placed at the base of each plant. Water is dispersed at low pressure wherever the tubes are placed. Kits for trickle systems are available at garden centers and through garden suppliers.

Measuring Precipitation

It's a good idea to keep a rain gauge in the garden to help determine whether plants are receiving enough water. Place a rain gauge or several straight-sided coffee cans in the garden away from plants that may hang over the container. Keep a record of the amount of rain that has fallen and supplement nature with irrigation. Typical garden soil will need about an inch of rain a week. If overhead irrigation is used, time a few waterings to determine how long it takes to supply the garden with one inch of water. By using several measuring cans, you can determine if the garden is being irrigated evenly. To encourage deep rooting, it's better to apply one heavy watering to the garden than several light waterings.

Preparing for Winter

After the final, bountiful harvest in the fall, it's time to prepare the garden for the winter.

The better a cleanup job you do in the fall, the easier it will be to start the new growing season in the spring. You may be tempted to skip some of these last-minute chores, but they're worth doing because they can make a big difference to the success of next year's garden. While these tasks can be put off until the start of the growing season, you can expect to be busy in the garden in the spring. You'll find it useful to have some of the work out of the way ahead of time.

As you finish harvesting crops and rows of garden space become available, it's a good idea to plant a cover crop, or green manure, as part of your preparation for the following year. This is a crop that you don't intend to harvest. It's simply to provide protection for the soil underneath. When you prepare for your spring planting, you dig the whole crop into the soil. A cover crop will keep your precious topsoil from blowing or washing away, and tilling it into the soil in the spring will provide valuable organic matter to enrich the soil. The cover crop will also shade the soil, preventing many cool-season weeds from germinating. It's not necessary to plant the whole cover crop at one time to cover the entire garden; you can plant in each area of the garden as space becomes available. Cover crops are not exclusively used over the winter. If you have a space in the garden that will be vacant for several weeks between plantings, a summer cover of buckwheat makes an ideal green manure. The buckwheat germinates quickly and covers the soil, preventing summer weeds from germinating. It's hollow-stemmed and easy to turn into the soil when you plant your next vegetable.

As an alternative to planting a cover crop, you can prepare the soil ahead of time. Tilling your soil in the fall can save you a great deal of time and help you get an earlier start in the spring because the soil is often too wet in early spring to use a spade or a rototiller. If you do till your soil in the fall, make sure to cover it with mulch to keep it from blowing away and to prevent massive winter weed germination. Consider soil preparation for the area of your garden where you plan to grow next season's cool-season vegetables.

If you're growing perennial vegetables, fall is the time to prepare them for winter survival. Remove old stems and foliage that have been killed back by frost to prevent the spread of disease organisms and insects that winter on old debris. In cold climates, perennial vegetables should be protected with a blanket of mulch to prevent root damage from extreme cold temperatures. In mild climates, a coating of mulch will protect plants from the alternating freeze-and-thaw and prevent plants from heaving from the soil.

COVER CROPS		
Variety	**Season to Grow**	**Amount of Seed/ 1000 Sq. Ft.**
Rye	Winter	1 to 2 lbs.
Crimson Clover	Winter	1 lb.
Soybeans	Summer	3 to 5 lbs.
Hairy Vetch	Winter	¾ to 1½ lbs.
Winter Wheat	Winter	1 to 2 lbs.
Buckwheat	Summer	2 to 3 lbs.
Rape	Winter	2 to 5 oz.
Cowpeas	Summer	3 to 4 lbs.

Preparing Perennial Crops

1 Perennial vegetable varieties grown in cold climates should be prepared and protected against winter temperatures. When frost has killed back the past season's leaves, plants such as asparagus and rhubarb should be cut down to a stubble.

2 Clear the garden of weeds and other debris and apply a mulch over the whole plant after the soil first freezes. If you mulch when the soil is still warm, you'll encourage root rot problems. Remember to remove this mulch as soon as the soil starts to thaw in the spring. The best mulches to use are organic materials, such as straw, hay, leaves, and compost, that will let the plants breathe. Crops you may need to mulch for winter protection include artichokes (in some areas), asparagus, chayotes, and rhubarb.

Planting a Cover Crop

When you close a section of the garden for the winter, use a green manure, or cover crop. Clear the area of weeds and debris and cultivate the soil. Till and grade the soil as you would for spring planting but leave the surface coarse. Choose a cover crop and scatter the seeds over the area you want to plant. If it's a large area, a hand spreader will do the job well. With a garden rake, gently rake the surface to work the seed into the top inch of soil. Turn the rake over and tamp the soil to insure contact between the seed and the soil. A light covering of straw will help keep the soil moist and speed germination. Water the area well to settle the soil. When spring planting time arrives, turn the cover crop into the soil with a spade or rototiller.

To remain healthy, these vegetables need protection from a wide range of pests and diseases. Both chemical and nonchemical means are available to the everyday gardener.

518

CHAPTER 5

GARDEN HEALTH

One of the most challenging—and sometimes frustrating—aspects of being a gardener is the natural forces you have to combat. Even in the unlikely event that you have perfect soil and a marvelous climate, you're still not home free; all sorts of pests are in competition with you for your crop.

In your vegetable garden, you're most likely to encounter insects and the like. Most gardeners have to contend with insect problems at some time during the growing season, but the problems are not always obvious. Just when it looks as though all your hard work is paying off and your plants are progressing toward a fine harvest, it can come as quite a surprise to find that pests are at work.

Your plants are subject to diseases, too. You know you're in trouble when the leaves turn yellow or the plants seem stunted and weak. Fortunately, you can take certain measures to forestall disease problems. Planting varieties that have been bred to be disease-resistant and rotating some crops when possible are just two of many options.

Controlling insect and disease pests can be quite a challenge, but it's not an insurmountable one. First identify the pest or disease. Once you've done this, you'll be able to make a wise choice as to the best means of control. We'll suggest the most effective means of control—both chemical and organic—for the pest and disease problems you're most likely to encounter.

Controlling Insect Pests

Chemical pesticides are effective and safe if used correctly.

For many people, anything in the garden that crawls or flies and is smaller than a chipmunk or a sparrow can be classified as an insect. In fact, many of the creatures that may damage your vegetable plants—mites, slugs, snails, nematodes, and sowbugs among them—are not insects at all. Another popular misconception is that insects and similar creatures are harmful or unnecessary and have no place in a garden. This just isn't true. While some insects are destructive, many are perfectly harmless. These insects are actually important to the healthy development of your garden crop. Some beneficial creatures perform a specific service by keeping down pests that do harm your crop; others pollinate the plants. When you set out to control harmful pests, it's important to realize that indiscriminate controls may destroy useful creatures as well as the harmful ones.

The method you choose for controlling garden pests could be a cause for controversy. Many gardeners rely on chemical insecticides to eliminate the harmful insects competing for their crops. Some, however, object to the use of chemicals. These gardeners prefer to rely on organic, or nonchemical, means of control.

The surest way to control most insects and similar creatures that threaten your vegetable crop is by using a chemical insecticide. A word here about terminology: The terms "pesticide" and "insecticide" are not interchangeable. A pesticide is any form of chemical control used in the garden. An insecticide is a pesticide used specifically to control insects. A herbicide is a pesticide used to control weeds. If you mistakenly use a herbicide to control insects, you'll lose your entire crop for the season because it will kill your vegetable plants.

Insecticides are chemical products that are sprayed or dusted on affected crops. The spray type is bought in concentrated form, diluted with water, and diffused with a hand sprayer or a spray attachment fitted to the end of your garden hose. Dust-on insecticides are powders that you pump onto the plants. Spraying is preferable because it gives more thorough coverage. It's also easier to treat the undersides as well as the tops of leaves and plants with a spray. Another technique is to apply insecticides directly to the soil to kill insects under the surface. This is known as applying a "soil drench."

Used correctly and responsibly, insecticides are not harmful to humans or other animals. However, they are toxic if used incorrectly. It is important to study the label of each pesticide and follow the directions exactly.

Because research is constantly being done to determine the safety of insecticides and improve their effectiveness, it's difficult to give long-term recommendations about their use. Certain basic rules, however, always apply. Read and reread the label and follow all precautions meticulously. Most important, never make the solution stronger than the label says because you think it will work better that way.

If you decide to use a pesticide to control insects in your garden, here are some important points to remember:

- Read the whole label and follow directions exactly.
- Wear rubber gloves, long sleeves and pants, and goggles while handling pesticides.
- Take care not to breathe the spray or dust.
- When the job is completed, wash your clothes separately from the family laundry and wash all exposed parts of your body with soap and water.
- Use equipment that you keep specifically for use with insecticides. Don't use equipment that has been used for herbicides.
- Use insecticides only when the air is still. Wind will carry the chemical away, creating a possible hazard somewhere else. The insecticide must dry on the plants to be effective; rain will wash it off.
- Treat only the affected portions of the plant. Use a light but thorough dose. Don't drench plants unnecessarily.
- Store unused, undiluted material in its original container in a locked area out of the reach of children.
- Dispose of the empty container carefully, according to the label's instructions.
- Wash all treated vegetables carefully before eating them.

Nonchemical Pest Control

Not all insects are harmful to garden plants. This lady bug can actually benefit your vegetables.

For various reasons, some people prefer to use non-chemical means for controlling diseases, insects, and other pests. Allergic reactions to chemicals, a desire to grow purely organic vegetables, or protection for young children are all reasons to use nonchemical controls for pests. If used correctly, nonchemical pest controls can be very effective in keeping your garden healthy.

VFNT Seeds—The easiest way to avoid disease problems is to choose varieties of vegetables that are resistant to disease. Over the years, many disease-resistant vegetable varieties have been developed. You'll notice that seed packages and catalog descriptions of some vegetable varieties include V, F, N, and T in the name. These abbreviations indicate disease resistance that has been bred into the variety. V and F stand for verticillium and fusarium wilts, which are fungi that cause tomato plants to turn yellow, wilt, and die. N indicates nematode tolerance. Nematodes are tiny parasitic worms that cause knots on stems and roots of vegetables. Tobacco mosaic virus, indicated by a T, affects foliage by yellowing and curling; it also causes severe root damage.

Water Early—If you irrigate your garden with a sprinkler from overhead, it's best to water early in the day so plants can dry off before night falls. Foliage that stays wet for long periods of time is susceptible to leaf diseases, fungi that grow on leaves, tender stems, and flower buds. This tends to be a problem when plants stay wet throughout the night: Fungi spread quickly during the cool, moist evening hours. The fungi will cause the plant to be weakened, flowers will fall off, and fruit will begin to spot and become soft.

Crop Rotation—Do not grow the same plant family in the same spot year after year. Repetition of the same crop gives diseases a chance to build up strength. Design your plan so that each family of vegetables—cabbage family, cucumber family, and tomato/pepper family—can be moved to another block of your garden on a three-year rotation.

Paper Collar

You may notice one morning that a couple of healthy young plants have keeled over and died. This is a pretty sure indication that cutworms are present. Feeding at night and hiding during the day, cutworms are most destructive early in the season, cutting off transplants at ground level. To prevent the cutworm from finding your cabbages, peppers, and tomatoes, wrap each stem with a paper or thin cardboard collar as you transplant it into the garden. The collar should reach at least one inch below and one inch above the soil level. In time, the collar will disintegrate; by then the danger of cutworm damage will have passed.

Beer: A Handy Bait

Snails and slugs pose a problem for many garden plants, especially during seasons with plenty of rain and rich, succulent growth. Lettuce and potatoes are especially susceptible to slug damage: Irregular holes will be found in the leaves. Snails and slugs feed mostly at night, hiding from the hot sun.

One way to control these pests is to remove the places where they hide; but if you're using mulch in the garden and supplying plants with the moisture they need, you're still likely to find snails and slugs. Although commercial baits are available, shallow pans of beer placed throughout the garden will attract and drown the pests.

Beneficial Insects

Not all insects in the garden are pests. Some are actually beneficial, providing a means to control insect pests. Insects such as ladybugs, lacewing flies, and praying mantises feed on bugs that are destructive to your crops. You should protect them when you find them in your garden. Harmless to your garden plants, these useful insects gorge on aphids, beetles, caterpillars, grasshoppers, and other bothersome insects.

Pests & Other Problems

A luscious garden is the gardener's reward for keeping pests in check.

The following lists are designed to help you identify the most common vegetable-garden insect and related problems. If you have difficulty identifying your garden's symptoms, take a sample to a garden center or county Cooperative Extension office to have it identified by an expert.

Once you know what your problem is, you can get a recommendation for controlling the pest. If the infestation is light, you may be able to pick the insects off by hand. For a heavy infestation, you'll probably need to turn to chemical insecticides. Disease problems are usually a little more difficult to control. The best method is prevention by choosing resistant varieties and keeping the garden area clear of weeds and infected debris.

INSECTS AND ANIMALS

SYMPTOM	CAUSE	CURE	PLANTS
Cluster of small, soft-bodied insects on buds and growth tips (gray, black, pink, green, red, or yellow in color); sticky secretions may be evident. Leaves are curled.	*Aphids*	Spray with contact poison labeled for aphids on vegetables.	Every garden vegetable
Irregularly shaped holes in the leaves; hard-shelled beetles of many colors and sizes	*Beetles of various kinds*	Pick off by hand or spray with a stomach poison insecticide.	Every vegetable crop can be infested by one or more variety of beetles.

Note: Consult your Cooperative Extension office for approved pesticides for vegetable plants.

INSECTS AND ANIMALS

SYMPTOM	CAUSE	CURE	PLANTS
Growth tips wilted or entire plant wilted; small hole in plant stem at point where wilting begins	*Borers*	Cut out borer, or destroy entire plant if affected at base of plant. Spray base of plant with suitable stomach poison insecticide in late spring and early summer.	Cucumber, Melon, Pumpkin, Squash
Irregular holes in foliage; green caterpillars under and on top of leaves	*Cabbage Worms*	Inspect plants and pick by hand. Spray with Bacillus thuringiensis—an organic insecticide—or a stomach poison insecticide.	Broccoli, Cabbage, Cauliflower, others
Corn kernels eaten within the husk; insides of tomatoes, peppers, and eggplants eaten; yellow-tan worms found inside	*Corn Earworm, Tomato Fruitworm*	Apply insecticide recommended for earworms. Remove infested plant debris at the end of the season.	Corn, Eggplant, Pepper, Tomato
Entire plant wilted or cut off at the base of the plant	*Cutworms*	Use paper collars, one inch above and one inch below ground level, around stems of transplants.	Cabbage, Pepper, Tomato
Slight wilting of the plant; plants growing poorly for no apparent reason; possible root damage	*Grubs*	Control adult beetles with a stomach poison. Apply soil drench of suitable insecticide.	Most vegetables
Foliage turns yellow and begins to curl; small green-patterned, winged insects on undersides of leaves	*Leaf Hoppers*	Spray off light infestations with garden hose. Apply a stomach poison labeled for use on vegetables.	Bean, Carrot, Chayote, Cucumber, Endive, Lettuce, Melon, Potato

INSECTS AND ANIMALS

SYMPTOM	CAUSE	CURE	PLANTS
Whitish trails visible on top sides of leaves; microscopic larvae of tiny flying insects	 *Leaf Miners*	Remove infected leaves by hand. Keep garden weed-free. Remove and destroy infested plants in the fall.	Beet, Cabbage, Chard, Eggplant, Lettuce, Pepper, Squash, Tomato
Wilting of the plant; root inspection indicates yellowish, ¼- to 1¼-inch wormlike creatures.	 *Root Maggots*	Discourage the fly from laying eggs near the seedlings by putting shields of plastic or paper 4 inches square around the seedlings. For heavy infestations, drench soil with insecticide labeled for control of root maggots.	Cabbage, Carrot, Radish, Spinach, Squash, Turnip
A slime trail from plants that have irregular holes in leaves and lower stems	 *Snails and Slugs*	Remove debris where they hide during the day. Shallow pans of beer will attract and drown pests. Commercial baits are available.	Cabbage, Carrot, Lettuce, Tomato, Turnip
Yellowing leaves with speckled look; fine spider webs on backs of leaves and at point where leaves attach to stem; tiny reddish mites on webs and undersides of leaves	 *Spider Mites*	Spray plants with miticide labeled for use on vegetables.	Bean, Cucumber, Eggplant, Tomato
Distorted leaf tips, white irregular marks on leaves	 *Thrips*	Hose off infected areas (insects are nearly invisible to the naked eye). Spray with a contact poison labeled for vegetable garden use.	Bean, Cabbage, Carrot, Celery, Cucumber, Melon, Onion, Pea, Squash, Tomato, Turnip

INSECTS AND ANIMALS

SYMPTOM	CAUSE	CURE	PLANTS
Leaves and fruit of tomatoes and related plants eaten; four-inch green and white caterpillarlike worm found on plants.	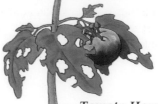 *Tomato Hornworm*	Remove worms by hand as they are discovered. Spray with Bacillus thuringiensis or stomach poison insecticide.	Eggplant, Pepper, Tomato
Tiny white insects fly from plant when disturbed. Large infestations weaken plant by feeding on undersides of foliage.	 *White Flies*	Light infestations can be sprayed off with garden hose. Spray contact poison labeled for white fly on vegetables.	Eggplant, Pepper, Sweet Potato, Tomato
Poorly grown, yellow, wilted plants; hard, one-inch, golden worms feed on seeds, roots, and lower stems.	 *Wireworms*	Drench soil with recommended insecticide. Control adults (click beetles) later in the season.	Carrot, Lettuce, Potato, Tomato, others

DISEASES

SYMPTOM	CAUSE	CURE	PLANTS
Dead areas on leaves and fruits; areas are depressed with slightly raised edge around them. Occurs mostly during wet weather.	 *Anthracnose*	Spray with sulfur fungicide labeled for vegetables.	Bean, Cucumber, Melon, Pepper, Potato, Pumpkin, Squash, Tomato, Watermelon
Water-soaked spots that spread and fuse into irregularly shaped blotches; fruit begins to rot.	 *Blights*	Rotate crops; destroy infected garden debris.	Bean, Eggplant, Pepper, Squash, Tomato
Sunken, black patches on blossom end of fruit	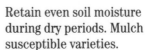 *Calcium Deficiency, Nitrogen Excess*	Retain even soil moisture during dry periods. Mulch susceptible varieties.	Pepper, Squash, Tomato

DISEASES

SYMPTOM	CAUSE	CURE	PLANTS
White, powdery dust appears on leaves. Lower leaves and stem turn grayish.	*Mildews*	Increase air circulation and keep foliage dry. Spray with fungicide labeled for vegetable crops.	Bean, Corn, Cucumber, Melon, Onion, Pea, Pumpkin
Reddish or rusty spots on the leaves; leaves look wilted.	*Rust*	Water early enough for foliage to dry before nightfall. Destroy infected garden debris in fall. Spray with fungicide labeled for vegetables.	Asparagus, Bean, Beet, Chard
Masses of black spores on foliage and growing tips	*Smuts*	Use resistant varieties; rotate crops; destroy infected garden debris.	Corn, Onion
Stunted plants, yellowing of leaves or yellow and green mottled leaves	*Viruses*	Plant resistant varieties; remove infected plants and destroy. Do not smoke when handling plants.	Every garden vegetable variety
Leaves wilt and turn yellow, even when soil is moist.	*Wilt*	Use resistant varieties; rotate crops; remove and destroy affected plants before disease spreads.	Cabbage, Celery, Cucumber, Pea, Sweet Potato, Tomato

An herb garden can be part of your vegetable garden, or you can design a separate, more formal arangement. Herbs are a perfect complement to garden-fresh vegetables.

CHAPTER 6

HERBS IN YOUR GARDEN

Herbs are probably the most popular and intriguing group of plants in existence. Undoubtedly, the explanation for this is that over the centuries herbs have been used in so many different ways. They flavor our foods, perfume our homes and bodies, decorate our gardens, and cure our ills. One way or another, herbs touch each of our lives.

Sooner or later, most of us decide to try our hand at growing a few favorite herbs. It usually starts with a pot of parsley on the kitchen windowsill or a short row of dill in the vegetable patch. Once started, many gardeners find themselves increasing the number of herbs they cultivate simply because so many of them flourish with little care. These rugged, hardy plants survive, and even thrive, in poor soil and wide temperature fluctuations that would prove too difficult for many other cultivated plant varieties. This same vigor makes them admirable choices for use in window boxes and other container situations where they're likely to be subjected to quite a bit of heat and dryness.

Because of their diversity, no group of plants is more difficult to define. How did we decide which plants to include? We simply chose those herbs we judged to be the most foolproof to grow and the most commonly useful to a beginning enthusiast. It should be noted that no attempt has been made to include the medicinal uses of herbs.

Growing Your Own Herbs

A few herb plants grown in a container can spice up a patio with their fragrance.

Herbs fit beautifully into any landscape. Ground-hugging thyme is a perfect choice for planting between the rocks in a flagstone walk. Tall clumps of angelica or rue provide attractive and dramatic accents in flower borders. Nasturtiums and chives add outstanding floral color to a garden, as well as making attractive cut flowers. The purple-leaf variety of basil is an eye-catching accent in any location.

The chart on page 533 will help you quickly identify those plants best suited to your site. It also notes whether plants are annuals, biennials, or perennials, and how large you can expect each herb to be at maturity. Especially attractive landscape varieties are also identified.

Although herbs are often planted in a formal layout separate from the rest of the garden, this is by no means a requirement for success in growing them. Herbs can be mixed into other plantings. The exceptions are those few herbs, such as mint, that will aggressively take over if not curbed. These are best planted in containers or separate beds, where strict control of their spread can be maintained. Most other herbs can be planted along with other row crops in your vegetable garden.

Herbs can be laid out in a very formal or an extremely informal design or anywhere in between. The choice is entirely up to your personal view regarding what will fit best with adjacent garden spaces.

When planning a vegetable garden that includes herbs, the same basic rules of good design apply as when designing any other garden. Tall plants should be located at the rear of side beds, plants of intermediate height in the middle of the bed, and low-growing plants at the front. This way they'll all obtain a maximum share of the available light. In central beds, the tallest plants can be located in the center of the bed, the shortest plants around the outer edge, and the intermediate heights between the two.

The best approach to deciding which herbs to grow is to make a list of herbs you're most likely to use. Write down their soil, light, and water needs; their height and spread; and any special notes such as unusual growth habit. Make a secondary list of plants you might enjoy having if there's any room left.

Sketch the vegetable garden area to scale (for example, 1 inch on the sketch equals 1 foot on the ground), decide on the size and shape of the planting beds, and determine which of the herbs on your list will be located where. Fill in any empty spots with appropriate species from your secondary list.

Harvesting—As a general rule of thumb, herbs have the highest level of flavor in their leaves just before they bloom. Harvesting is best done at this time. In the directory of vegetable and herb plants, you'll find notes regarding the best time to harvest each herb as well as the best methods of preservation.

Harvesting of herbs for fresh use can be done throughout the growing season. Thyme, sage, rosemary, and many other perennials need their active growing shoots snipped in 4- to 6-inch lengths. For annuals collect a few leaves.

When harvesting herbs to preserve for future use, wait until the plant is at its aromatic peak as noted in the directory. Pick it early in the morning when aromatics are at their highest level of the day. Discard any diseased or insect-infested portions. If there is dust present, wash the plant thoroughly and shake off as much of the excess water as possible before processing. If possible, wash the plant a day before harvesting.

Be especially careful when harvesting seeds. The timing must be precise enough to allow the seeds to ripen completely, but they must be caught before they disperse. One way to solve this problem is to keep watch on a daily basis and harvest as soon as the seeds begin to dry. Carefully snip off the heads over a large paper bag, allowing the seeds to fall directly into the bag. Keep

Formal Herb Garden Designs

Formal balanced geometric layouts usually revolve around some sort of special garden feature, such as a fountain, sundial, garden seat, statue, an unusual feature plant, or birdbath. All paths and attention lead to this feature, whether it's in the center of the garden or along one edge.

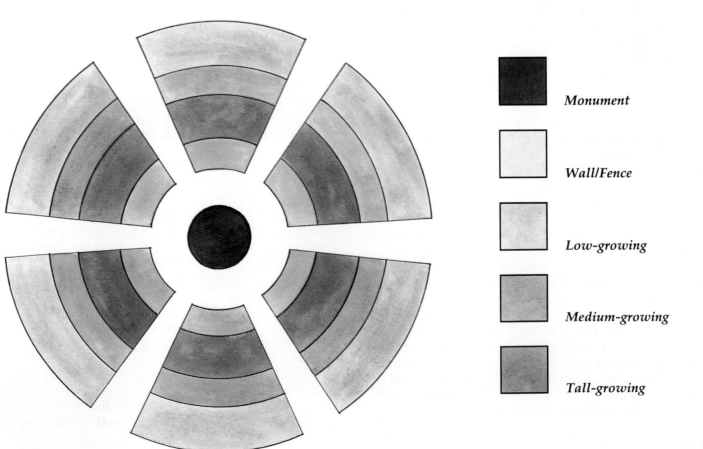

Monument

Wall/Fence

Low-growing

Medium-growing

Tall-growing

them in the bag to complete the drying process. Be careful not to compact the seed heads; air circulation in and around the seed heads is needed to cut down on the possibility of the growth of undesirable molds.

If you cannot keep such close track of the maturation process, another alternative is to enclose each seed head while still on the plant in a small paper bag once all flowering has ended and the green seeds become obvious. Then, when the heads dry, any seeds that fall out will be captured in the bag. Once you notice that seeds are being released, snip off the heads, bag and all, and dry them indoors.

The most common method of herb preservation is by hang drying. Another good way to preserve many herbs is by freezing them. This method is quick and easy, and the flavor is usually closer to fresh than dried. If you have the freezer space available, freezing is probably the most desirable choice for cooking herbs. Some herbs lose flavor when exposed to air, but they will retain it if stored in oil or liquor. Some herbs don't retain as much flavor when preserved by any means—they can only be used fresh. You can, however, extend their season by growing them indoors as pot plants during the winter months.

Informal Herb Garden Layouts

Here are two informal layouts. One backs a wall or fence and the other stands as an island in the middle of a lawn area.

■ *Monument*

□ *Wall/Fence*

□ *Low-growing*

■ *Medium-growing*

■ *Tall-growing*

HERB CHART

Name	Plant	Landscape	Light	Soil	Height*	Spread*	Culture
Angelica	B	•	FS,PS	A,M	60–72	36	E
Anise	A		FS	A,D	18–24	4–8	E
Basil	A	•	FS	R,M	18	10	E
Chervil	A		PS	A,M	18	4–8	A–D
Chives	P	•	FS,PS	A–R,M	8–12	8	E
Coriander	A		FS	R	24–36	6	E
Costmary	P		FS,PS	R	30–36	24	E
Dill	A		FS	A–S,M	24–36	6	E
Fennel	P		FS	R	50–72	18–36	E
Garlic	P		FS	A–P	18	8	E
Geraniums, scented	P	•	FS	A–R	VARIES	VARIES	A
Horehound	P	•	FS	A–P	30	12	E
Marjoram	P,A		FS	R	8–12	12–18	E
Nasturtium	A	•	FS,PS	A–P,M	12–72	18	E
Oregano	P		FS	A–S	18	12	E
Parsley	B	•	FS,PS	R,M	12	8	E
Peppermint	P		FS,PS	R,M	24–30	12	E,R
Rosemary	P	•	FS	S	48–72	18–24	A
Rue	P	•	FS	P,S	24	18	A
Sage	P	•	FS	S	20	24	E
Savory, Summer	A		FS	R–A	18	8	E
Sorrel, French	P		FS,PS	R,M	18	10	E
Southernwood	P	•	FS	ANY	30	24	E
Spearmint	P		FS,PS	R,M	20	12	E,R
Sweet, Woodruff	P	•	S	R,M	6–8	6–8	D
Tansy	P		FS,PS	A–P	40	12–18	E,R
Tarragon, French	P	•	FS,PS	S–R	24	24	A
Thyme	P	•	FS,PS	P–A	1–10	12–18	E,R
Wormwood	P	•	FS	ANY	30–48	15–20	A

*inches
PLANT: A=Annual   B=Biennial   P=Perennial
LIGHT: FS=Full Sun   PS=Partial Shade   S=Shade
SOIL: P=Poor   A=Average   R=Rich   S=Sandy   M=Moist   D=Dry
CULTURE: E=Easy to Grow   A=Average   D=Difficult   R=Rampant Grower/Keep Restricted

Kale is just one of many vegetables you can grow in your backyard. With careful planning, you can reap a plentiful harvest from early spring to late autumn.

ENCYCLOPEDIA OF VEGETABLES & HERBS

The vegetable and herb garden is unlike any other garden on your property. It can be as attractive as a flower border—with many different types of plants: annuals and perennials, warm-season and cool-season plants—as well as productive. Try different types or new varieties of vegetables and herbs. You're not locked into what you planted last year.

Different parts of different plants are considered vegetables: We use carrot roots, asparagus stems, broccoli flower buds, spinach leaves, tomato fruits, and corn seeds all for food. Some varieties, such as turnips, are grown as a dual-purpose plant, where the leaves as well as the roots are edible. Herbs can serve many purposes: culinary, cosmetic, potpourri and sachet, and fresh or dried arrangement material.

There are so many varieties of vegetables and herbs we can't begin to describe them all. Instead, we've chosen a few of the tried and true varieties that will perform best in your garden. You'll find information about what the plant looks like and how to grow it. Use this guide as a handy reference while planning your garden to determine planting dates, soil preferences, and harvesting tips.

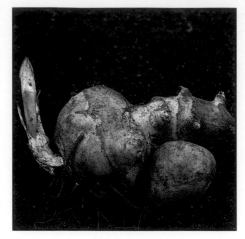

Globe Artichoke

Cynara Scolymus
Tender

Description: This thistlelike tender perennial grows 3 to 4 feet tall and 3 to 4 feet wide. The globe artichoke is grown for its flower buds, which are eaten before they begin to open. Since it is tender and reacts poorly to cold weather, it is not for all gardens.

How to grow: Artichokes have a definite preference for a long frost-free season with damp weather. They will be damaged by heavy frost or snow, and in areas where the temperature goes below freezing, they need special care and mulching. Artichokes are grown from offshoots, suckers, or seed. For best results, start with offshoots or suckers from a reputable nursery or garden center. Plants grown from seed vary tremendously in quality. Artichokes need a position in full sunlight and a rich, well-drained soil that will hold moisture. Too much nitrogen will keep the plant from flowering. Artichokes bear best the second year and should be started from new plants every three to four years. To enable the roots to survive the winter in cooler areas, cut the plant back to about 10 inches, cover it with a bushel basket, and then place mulch around the basket to a thickness of two feet to help maintain an even soil temperature.

Harvest: Timing from planting to harvest is 50 to 100 days for plants grown from suckers. The first buds will take at least a year to form when they are grown from seed. To harvest, cut off the bud with 1 to 1½ inches of stem before the bud begins to open.

Varieties: 'Green Globe' is the best variety; it has 4-inch-large round buds.

Jerusalem Artichoke

Helianthus tuberosus
Hardy

Description: Jerusalem artichoke is a large, upright, hardy perennial. It has small yellow flowers 2 to 3 inches across and rough, hairy leaves 4 to 8 inches long. This plant, which is not related to the globe artichoke, is a type of sunflower and will grow 5 to 10 feet tall. The edible tubers are low in starch and taste a bit like water chestnuts.

How to Grow: Jerusalem artichokes will grow anywhere and in almost any soil, as long as it's warm and well drained. Plant the tubers two to three weeks before the average date of last frost. Plant tubers 2 to 6 inches deep and 12 to 18 inches apart in ordinary soil. Don't fertilize Jerusalem artichokes; rich garden soil will encourage lush leafy growth with a low yield of tubers. Water only during extremely dry periods. The plants themselves can survive long dry periods, but the tubers will not develop without a regular supply of water. As the plants grow, cut off the flower buds as soon as they appear; this will encourage tuber production.

Harvest: The time from planting to harvest is 120 to 150 days. Harvest the tubers when the leaves die back; dig them up with a spading fork. Leave a few in the ground for next year. Plants spread quickly if not harvested.

Varieties: There are no named varieties available. Use tubers found in your grocery.

Asparagus

Asparagus officinalis
Hardy

Description: Asparagus is a long-lived hardy perennial with fleshy roots and fernlike, feathery foliage. The plant grows about 3 feet tall. The part that is eaten is the tender young stem. The popular houseplant asparagus fern is not a fern at all but a diminutive relative of edible asparagus.

How to grow: Asparagus grows well in most areas of the United States, except the Deep South. It thrives in a climate where the winters are cold enough to freeze the top few inches of soil and provide it with the necessary period of dormancy. Although asparagus can be started from seeds, the best-quality plants come from crowns that can be ordered from a nursery. Plant asparagus four to six weeks before the area's average date of last frost. Asparagus needs well-drained soil with a pH above 6. Full sun is best. To plant asparagus crowns, dig a trench or furrow 10 inches wide and 10 to 12 inches deep. Put in 2 to 4 inches of soil mixed with organic matter. Place the crowns on the soil with the roots well spread out. Cover with 2 more inches of soil. As the spears grow, gradually fill in the trench to the top. It's important to give asparagus sufficient water when the spears are forming.

Harvest: Asparagus should not be harvested until it is three years old; the crowns need time to develop fully. During the third season, cut off the spears at or slightly below soil level. Harvest asparagus when the spears are 8 to 10 inches tall; if the stalks have started to feather out, it's too late to eat them. Stop harvesting when the stalks begin coming up pencil-thin.

Varieties: 'Mary Washington' is widely available and resistant to asparagus rust. 'UC 157' was developed for Southern climates. It is resistant to fusarium root.

Green (Snap) Bean, Yellow (Wax) Bean

Phaseolus vulgaris
Tender

The most commonly grown beans are the green, or snap, bean and the yellow, or wax, bean, which is a variety of the green bean. Since 1894, when Burpee introduced the Stringless Green Pod, most beans have been stringless. Beans grow as bushes or vines. Bushes are generally easier to handle; they grow only 1 to 2 feet tall, and they mature earlier. Pole beans grow 6 to 8 feet tall and require a trellis for support. They grow more slowly but produce more beans per plant.

Description: Leaves are usually composed of three leaflets; flowers are pale yellow, lavender, or white. The size and color of the pods and seeds vary.

How to grow: Snap beans require a short growing season—about 60 days of moderate temperatures from seed to first crop. They grow anywhere in the United States and are an encouraging vegetable for the inexperienced gardener. Snap beans require warm soil to germinate and should be planted on the average date of last frost. You can plant bush beans every two weeks to extend the harvest, or you can start with bush beans and follow up with pole beans. Plant seeds an inch deep, directly in the garden. For bush beans, plant the seeds 2 inches apart in single rows or wide rows. Seeds of pole beans should be planted 4 to 6 inches apart in rows 30 to 36 inches apart. Or, plant them in inverted hills, five or six seeds to a hill, with 30 inches of space around each hill. For pole bean varieties, set the trellis at the time of planting to avoid disturbing the roots. Keep the soil evenly moist until the beans have pushed through the ground. When seedlings are growing well, thin the plants to 4 to 6 inches apart. Thin plants by cutting excess seedlings with scissors to avoid disturbing the roots of neighboring seedlings.

Harvest: The immature pod is the part that is eaten. When pods are large enough to eat, harvest by pulling the pods off the plant, taking care not to break the stem. Beans will flower twice and provide a second harvest. Smaller pods are more tender.

Bush varieties: 'Burpee's Tenderpod,' 50 days, has 5-inch-long green pods. 'Blue Lake,' 58 days, has green, 6½-inch pods with white seeds. 'Roma II,' 53 days, has green, flattened pods, 4½ inches long. 'Brittle Wax,' 52 days, has rounded, yellow pods, 7 inches long. 'Royal Burgundy,' 51 days, has 6-inch-long purple pods.

Pole varieties: 'Kentucky Wonder,' 65 days, is a proved standard variety with heavy yields of 9-inch green pods. 'Blue Lake,' 60 days, has pods that are 6 inches long with white seeds. 'Scarlet Runner Bean,' 65 days, is often grown ornamentally for its scarlet flowers; pods are green and up to 12 inches long.

Lima Bean

Phaseolus limensis
Very Tender

This large-seeded annual bean grows as either a bush or a vine. Bush lima beans are generally easier to handle than pole varieties. Bushes grow only 1 or 2 feet tall, and they mature earlier. Pole beans require a trellis for support. They grow more slowly but produce more beans per plant.

How to grow: To germinate properly, lima beans need warmer soil than snap beans. They also need higher temperatures and a longer growing season for a good crop. Lima bean seeds require soil temperatures of at least 65 degrees Fahrenheit for a minimum of five days to germinate. They should be planted two weeks after the average date of the last frost. Plant bush beans every two weeks to extend the harvest, or start with bush beans and follow up with pole varieties. Plant seeds directly in the garden, an inch deep. For bush beans, plant the seeds 2 inches apart in single rows or wide rows. Seeds of pole beans should be planted four to six inches apart in rows 30 to 36 inches apart. Or, plant them in inverted hills, five or six seeds to a hill, with 30 inches of space around each hill. For pole bean varieties, set the trellis at the time of planting to avoid disturbing the roots. The lima bean seed sometimes has trouble pushing through the soil, although this should not happen if the soil is well worked.

Harvest: With this type of bean, the maturing seed is eaten, not the entire pod. Pick pods before the seeds have become tough. Ripe pods usually pop open when you press them along the seams.

Bush varieties: 'Fordhook 242,' 75 days, is a large-seeded lima bean with high yields. 'Henderson Bush,' 65 days, has white beans, three or four to a flattened pod.

Pole varieties: 'Burpee's Best,' 92 days, has 'Fordhook' characteristics: thick, 4½-inch pods with high yield. 'Prizetaker,' 90 days, has 6-inch-long pods with three to five beans.

Beet

Beta vulgaris
Hardy

Description: The beet has a round or tapered swollen root—red, yellow, or white—from which sprouts a rosette of large leaves.

How to grow: Beets tolerate frost and do best in the cooler areas of the country, but they will go to seed without making roots if the plants get too cold when young. Plant them as a winter crop in the southern parts of the country. In a hot climate, pay special attention to watering and mulching to give seedlings a chance to establish themselves. The roots become woody in very hot weather. Plant beets two to three weeks before the average date of last frost. Beets thrive in well-worked, loose soil that is high in organic matter. They do not do well in a very acid soil, and they need a good supply of potassium. Beets are grown from seed clusters that are slightly smaller than a pea and contain several seeds in each. Plant the clusters an inch deep, directly in the garden, an inch apart in rows spaced 12 to 18 inches apart. The seedlings may emerge over a period of time, giving you a group of seedlings of different sizes. Since several seedlings will emerge from each seed cluster, they must be thinned to 2 to 3 inches apart when the seedlings develop true leaves.

Harvest: Both the leaves and the root can be eaten. Eat thinned seedlings like spinach; they do not transplant well. It takes about 60 days for a beet to reach 1½ inches in diameter, a popular size for cooking or pickling. They will quickly grow larger if they have plenty of water. Pull the beets up when they reach your desired size.

Varieties: 'Detroit Dark Red,' 60 days, is a deep red, finely-grained sweet standard beet. 'Golden,' 55 days, has gold-colored skin and flesh. 'Lutz Green Leaf,' 80 days, is often grown as a fall crop; its red flesh has lighter zones.

Broccoli

Brassica oleracea; Botrytis **Group**
Very Hardy

Description: Broccoli is a member of the cabbage, or cole, family. It grows 1½ to 2½ feet tall and looks a bit like cauliflower. Broccoli will grow in most areas of the United States at one season or another, but it is not a suitable crop for very hot climates.

How to grow: The head formation stage of development is essential for the production of the vegetable. Broccoli that's held in check by severe frost, lack of moisture, or too much heat will bolt (go directly to seed without forming a head). Broccoli is frost hardy and can tolerate low 20 degree Fahrenheit temperatures. It's a cool-season crop and does best with day temperatures less than 80 degrees Fahrenheit and night temperatures 20 degrees Fahrenheit lower. Broccoli likes fertile, well-drained soil with a pH within the 6.5 to 7.5 range. Broccoli is usually grown from transplants except where there's a long cool period, in which case you can sow seed directly in the garden in fall for winter harvest. Plant transplants that are four to six weeks old with four or five true leaves. If transplants are leggy with crooked stems, plant them deeply so they won't grow top-heavy. Plant the seedlings 18 to 24 inches apart.

Harvest: Time planting to harvest during cold weather. Transplants can be harvested in 40 to 80 days, depending on the variety. Harvesting can continue over a relatively long period. When it is well developed, cut off the central head with five to six inches of stem. Harvest before the head begins to loosen and separate. If small yellow flowers have started to show, it's past the good eating stage.

Varieties: 'Green Comet Hybrid,' 55 days, is disease resistant and heat resistant and produces 7-inch heads. 'Premium Crop,' 58 days, is an All America Selection.

Brussels Sprouts

Brassica oleracea; Gemmifera **Group**
Very Hardy

Description: Miniature cabbagelike heads, 1 or 2 inches in diameter and nestled in among large green leaves, sprout from a tall main stem. Brussels sprouts belong to the cabbage, or cole, family and are similar to cabbage in their growing habits and requirements. They're hardy—they are the most cold tolerant of the cole family vegetables—and easy to grow in the home garden.

How to grow: Brussels sprouts grow well in fertile soils and are frost-tolerant. They do best in a cool growing season with day temperatures less than 80 degrees Fahrenheit and night temperatures 20 degrees Fahrenheit lower. Weather that's too cold for too long or too warm will make the sprouts taste bitter. If they develop in hot weather, they may not form compact heads but instead will remain loose tufts of leaves. Brussels sprouts are usually grown from transplants. Where there's a long cool period, seeds can be sown directly in the garden in the fall for winter harvest. Plant transplants that are four to six weeks old. If the transplants are leggy or have crooked stems, plant them deeply so they won't grow top-heavy.

Harvest: You can harvest brussels sprouts 75 to 90 days after transplanting. The sprouts mature from the bottom of the stem upward, so start from the bottom and remove leaves and sprouts as the season progresses.

Varieties: 'Jade Cross Hybrid,' 95 days, is resistant to yellow virus. 'Long Island Improved' matures in 90 days.

Cabbage

Brassica oleracea; Capitata **Group**
Very Hardy

Description: Cabbage, a hardy biennial that is grown as an annual, has an enlarged terminal bud made of crowded and expanded overlapping leaves shaped into a head. The leaves are smooth or crinkled in shades of green or purple. The head can be round, flat, or pointed. Cabbage is easy to grow in the home garden.

How to grow: Cabbage is a cool-weather crop that can tolerate frost but not heat. If the plants are cold for too long, or if the weather is too warm, the plants will bolt (go to seed without forming a head). If the head has already formed, it will split in hot weather. Splitting happens when the plant takes up water so fast the excess cannot escape through the tightly overlapped leaves, and the head bursts. Cabbage likes fertile, well-drained soil with a pH in the 6.5 to 7.5 range. Cabbages are usually grown from transplants. Where there's a long cool period, seed can be sown directly in the garden in the fall for winter harvest. Plant transplants that are four to six weeks old; plant two to three weeks before the average date of the last frost.

Harvest: Cabbages mature in 60 to 105 days from transplants. To harvest, cut off the head, leaving the outer leaves on the stem.

Varieties: 'Earliana,' 60 days from transplants, is a small, compact early variety. 'Early Jersey Wakefield,' 63 days, produces heads that are full-sized, pointed, and with a sweet flavor. 'Ruby Ball,' 68 days, produces purple heads that are four to six pounds; it is an All America Selection.

Cardoon

Cynara cardunculus
Tender

Description: Cardoon is a tender perennial grown as an annual for its young leaf-stalks, which are blanched and eaten like celery. A member of the artichoke family, cardoon has the same deeply cut leaves and heavy, bristled flower heads. Cardoon, which will grow anywhere in the United States, can grow to 4 feet tall and 2 feet wide, so it will need plenty of space in your garden.

How to grow: Plant cardoon from transplants in the garden on the date of the last frost in your area. If you're growing your own transplants from seed, start them indoors six to eight weeks before planting in the garden. New plants may also be started from suckers. Cardoon prefers full sun but can tolerate partial shade. It grows quickly in any well-drained, fertile soil. Cardoon stalks can get very tough, so the plant is blanched to improve flavor and make it more tender. Blanch when the plant is about three feet tall, four to six weeks before harvesting. Tie the leaves together in a bunch and wrap paper or burlap around the stems. Or, form a hill of soil around the stem.

Harvest: Harvest the plants four to six weeks after blanching. Cut them off at ground level and trim off the outer leaves.

Varieties: The two most common are 'Large Smooth' and 'Ivory White Smooth.'

Carrot

Daucus Carota sativis
Hardy

Description: Carrots are hardy biennials that are grown as annuals. They have a rosette of finely divided, fernlike leaves growing from a swollen, fleshy taproot. The root, which varies in size and shape, is generally a tapered cylinder that grows up to 10 inches long in different shades of orange.

How to grow: There are all types of carrots—long, short, fat, thin—they differ only in size and shape. Your soil type will influence the variety you choose. Shorter varieties will tolerate heavy soil. Carrots are cool-weather crops and tolerate cold. For a continuous crop, plant carrots every two to three weeks starting two to three weeks before the date of last frost. Sow the seeds directly in the garden. Wide-row planting of carrots gives a good yield from a small area. Carrot seedlings grow slowly when young, so it's important to control weeds during the first few weeks. In areas with high soil temperatures, mulch to regulate soil temperature.

Harvest: The time from planting to harvest is from 55 to 80 days, depending on variety. Pull carrots when the soil is moist: If you try to pull them from hard ground, you'll break the roots. In warmer areas, late season carrots can be kept in the garden throughout most of the winter and harvested as needed.

Varieties: 'Danvers Half Long,' 75 days, is uniform-size at 7½ inches; it is bright orange and sweet. 'Short 'n' Sweet,' 68 days, produces 4-inch roots and is good for heavy soil. 'Thumbelina,' 60 to 70 days, is an All America Selection; bred for heavy soils, it produces 2-inch round carrots. 'Juwarot,' 70 days, is dark orange and grows to 8 inches long.

Cauliflower

Brassica oleracea, Botrytis Group
Very Hardy

Cauliflower is a single-stalked, half-hardy, biennial member of the cole, or cabbage, family. It's grown as an annual, and the edible flower buds form a solid head that may be white, green, or purple. Cauliflower is more restricted by climatic conditions than other cole family members. It's less adaptable to extremes of temperature.

How to grow: Cauliflower needs two cool months to mature and is planted as a spring or fall crop in most areas. Plant for a winter crop if your winters are mild. For a spring crop, plant transplants four to six weeks before the average date of last frost. Start your own transplants from seed indoors about six weeks before garden planting. Plant leggy and crooked transplants deeply in the garden to prevent them from being top-heavy. Unless the buds are supposed to be green or purple, the color should be untinged creamy-white. To protect the head from discoloring, blanch the head when it gets to the size of an egg by gathering three or four leaves and tying them together to cover the head. Self-blanching cauliflower doesn't need to be covered, but it will not blanch in hot weather.

Harvest: Time from planting transplants to harvest is 55 to 100 days. The mature head should be compact and about 6 to 8 inches in diameter. Cut the whole head from the main stem.

Varieties: 'Snow Crown Hybrid,' 52 days, has pure white, 8-inch-diameter heads. 'Super Snowball' is ready to harvest in 55 days. 'Royal Purple,' produces 6- to 7-inch-diameter purple heads.

Celeriac

Apium graveolens rapaceum
Hardy

Description: Celeriac is a form of celery: a member of the same family and similar in growing habits and requirements. The edible root of celeriac is large and swollen and develops at soil level. A rosette of dark green leaves sprouts from the root.

How to grow: Celeriac does best in cool weather and especially enjoys cool nights. To grow celeriac, start in the spring in the North, in late summer in the South. In the North, start from transplants; sow seeds indoors two to three months before your planting date. Plant transplants on the average date of last frost. Celeriac prefers rich soil that is high in organic matter, well able to hold moisture but with good drainage. It needs constant moisture and does well in wet locations. The plant is a heavy feeder and needs plenty of fertilizer to keep it growing quickly. Celeriac cannot compete with weeds. Cultivate conscientiously, but be careful to not disturb the shallow roots. As the root develops, snip off the side roots and hill the soil over the swollen areas for a short time to blanch the tubers. The outer surface will be whitened, but the interior will remain a brownish color.

Harvest: Harvest celeriac when the swollen root is 3 to 4 inches wide. Celeriac increases in flavor after the first frost, but it should be harvested before the first hard freeze.

Varieties: Both 'Alabaster' and 'Prague' mature in 120 days.

Celery

Apium graveolens dulce
Hardy

Description: Celery is a hardy biennial that is grown as an annual. It has a tight rosette of stalks 8 to 18 inches long, topped with divided leaves. It's a versatile vegetable—you can eat the stalks, leaves, and seeds—but it needs a lot of attention. It's not an easy crop for the home gardener.

How to grow: Celery does best in cool weather and especially enjoys cool nights. Grow celery in spring in the North, planting transplants two to three weeks before the average date of last frost; in the South plant in the late summer. Celery prefers rich soil high in organic matter that is well able to hold moisture but with good drainage. It does well in wet locations. Celery is a heavy feeder and needs plenty of fertilizer for quick growth. If you're sowing seeds for transplants, start them two to four months before your estimated planting date: They germinate slowly. Transplant them to trenches 3 to 4 inches deep and two feet apart. Space the seedlings 8 to 10 inches apart. Celery will be bitter if it isn't blanched. Blanching is achieved by covering the plants to protect them from the sun. As the plants grow, pile soil up around them to blanch the stems. Having the plants fairly close together will also help blanching.

Harvest: The time from planting transplants to harvest is 100 to 130 days. Start harvesting before the first hard frost, when the head is about 2 to 3 inches in diameter at the base. Cut off the head at or slightly below soil level.

Varieties: 'Summer Pascal,' 115 days, is medium green in color and is slow-bolting. 'Utah 52-70,' 125 days, is the standard thick-stalked variety.

Swiss Chard

Beta vulgaris, Cicla **Group**
Hardy

Description: Chard is basically a beet without the bottom. It's a biennial that is grown as an annual for its big crinkly leaves. The stalks are red or white with large, dark green leaves.

How to grow: Chard prefers cool temperatures. High temperatures slow down leaf production, but chard tolerates heat better than spinach. In mild regions, you can plant chard from fall to early spring. In the North, plant from spring to midsummer. Plant chard from seed clusters—each cluster contains several seeds—about a week before the average date of last frost. Chard prefers well-worked soil with good drainage and a high organic content; it does not like acid soil. Plant the seeds directly in the garden 2 to 6 inches apart in single or wide rows. Thin seedlings to 12 inches apart when they're large enough to handle. The crop needs enough water to keep the leaves growing quickly, so keep the soil moist at all times.

Harvest: The time from planting to harvest is 55 to 65 days. Start harvesting chard when the outside leaves are three inches long. Don't let the leaves get much longer than 10 inches, or they'll taste earthy. Either take a few leaves off at a time or cut the entire plant down to three inches and let it grow back. If you harvest the leaves as they grow, the plant will go on producing all season.

Varieties: 'Rhubarb Chard,' 60 days, produces red stalks. 'Lucullus,' 50 days, is somewhat like spinach with white stalks and light green leaves. 'Fordhook Giant,' 60 days, produces green leaves and white stalks and is heat tolerant.

Chicory

Cichorium intybus
Hardy

Description: Chicory is a hardy perennial with a long fleshy taproot and a flower stalk that rises from a rosette of ragged lobed leaves. The shoots are known as Belgian endive, which should not be confused with the salad endive, or escarole.

How to grow: Chicory tolerates cold and can be grown for its roots anywhere in the United States. Plant seeds an inch deep in the garden two to three weeks before the average date of last frost. Thin the plants to 12 to 18 inches apart. If chicory is planted in well-cultivated soil rich in organic matter, it should develop large roots. To produce blanched heads, dig the roots out before a hard freeze. Cut off the tops about two inches above the crown, or top, of the root; store the roots in a cool place. In winter, force the roots in a cool, dark room by planting them in moist sand. Keep the emerging shoots covered with seven or eight inches of sawdust and water the plant occasionally. In three to four weeks, when new shoots emerge, cut the heads from the root.

Harvest: Chicory is grown either for its root, which is roasted as a coffee substitute, or for its tender shoots, which are known as Belgian endive. If planting for the roots alone, they'll be ready to harvest in about 120 days.

Varieties: 'Magdeburg,' 100 days, is grown for its root, which is roasted as a coffee substitute. 'Witloof,' 110 days, is also known as Belgian endive; it is grown for its blanched heads, or chicons.

Chinese Cabbage

Brassica Rapa; Pekinensis **Group**
Very Hardy

Description: Chinese cabbage is a hardy biennial that is grown as an annual. It has broad, thick, tender leaves with heavy midribs; it can be either loosely or tightly headed. The plant grows 15 to 18 inches tall. The variety with a large compact heart is called celery cabbage, or Michihli.

How to grow: Chinese cabbage can be grown in cool weather only because it bolts (goes to seed) quickly in hot weather and long days. It's usually grown as a fall crop in the North and as a winter crop in the South. It can be started inside and transplanted outside in the spring. However, Chinese cabbage shocks easily, and transplanting sometimes shocks it into going to seed. Therefore, it's best to sow the seed directly in the garden and thin them to stand 8 to 12 inches apart. Water them frequently to help the young plants grow fast and become tender. They'll probably go to seed if growth slows down.

Harvest: The time from planting to harvest is 50 to 80 days, depending on the variety. Harvest when the heads are compact and firm and before seed stalks form. With a fall crop, harvest before hard-freezing weather. Cut off the whole plant at ground level.

Varieties: 'Pak Choi,' 47 days, produces non-heading, white, celerylike stalks with green leaves. 'Wong Bok,' 85 days, is the standard head-type Chinese cabbage. 'Michihli,' 75 days, has large heads with blanched inside leaves.

Collards

Brassica oleracea; Acephala Group
Very Hardy

Description: A hardy biennial that is grown as an annual, collards grow 2 to 4 feet tall and have tufted rosettes of leaves growing on sturdy stems. Collards are a kind of kale, a primitive member of the cabbage family that does not form a head.

How to grow: Collards are hardy and can tolerate low temperatures. They're also more tolerant of heat than some members of the cabbage family. In the South, get ahead of warm weather by planting collards from fall through March. In the North, you can get two crops by planting in early spring and again in July or August. Collards like fertile, well-drained soil with a pH between 6.5 and 7.5. Collards are usually grown from transplants planted four to six weeks before the average date of last frost. Set transplants deeply if the stems are leggy or crooked to prevent the plants from becoming top heavy. Where there is a long cool period, seeds can be sown directly in the garden in the fall for a winter harvest. Sow seeds an inch deep and thin seedlings to 12 inches apart.

Harvest: The time from planting to harvest is 75 to 85 days for transplants and 85 to 95 days for seeds. Collards become sweeter if harvested after a frost but harvest them before a hard freeze. In warmer areas, harvest the leaves from the bottom up before the leaves get tough.

Varieties: Both 'Georgia' and 'Vates' mature in 75 days.

Corn

Zea mays
Tender

Description: Corn, a tender annual that can grow 4 to 12 feet tall, is a member of the grass family. It produces one to three ears on a stalk. The kernels of sweet corn can be yellow, white, black, red, or a combination of colors. Corn is not the easiest crop to grow in a home vegetable garden, and it doesn't give a lot of return for the space it occupies.

How to grow: Corn can be grown in any region, but the time it will take to mature depends on the amount of heat it gets. Corn doesn't really hit its stride until the weather warms up. Depending on the varieties planted, two crops may be possible. Corn likes well-worked, fertile soil with good drainage, and it must have full sun. Sow the seeds directly in the garden on the average date of last frost. Plant the seeds 2 to 4 inches apart in short rows forming a block rather than a single, long row. Planting in clumps ensures pollination. For a continuous supply, plant early, mid-season, and late varieties at the same time. When the corn is about 6 inches tall, thin short varieties to two feet apart and tall varieties to three feet apart. Although corn can be grown closer together than this, the roots are then more crowded and more watering and feeding are needed. Corn is a heavy user of nitrogen. Fertilize in the spring, again when the corn is 8 inches tall, and again when the plants are 18 inches tall. Side-dress between the rows, using one-third of a pound of complete, well-balanced fertilizer on each side of a 10-foot-long row. Hill soil around the plant roots at this time to help support the stalks. Watering is very important. Keep the soil evenly moist. Corn often grows so fast in hot weather that the leaves wilt because the roots can't keep the leaves supplied with moisture. Although corn requires much water, avoid getting water on the tassels. The pollen from the tassels must fall onto the corn silk to produce kernels, and if pollination does not occur, all that will grow is the cob. Weed early and keep the weeds cut back. Remember that corn has shallow roots, and a vigorous attack on the weeds may destroy the crop.

Harvest: From planting to harvest takes 55 to 95 days, depending on the variety and, to some extent, the weather. Harvest your corn when the kernels are soft and plump and the juice is milky.

Varieties: A large number of varieties are available; just a few of the good varieties available are listed here. 'Early Sunglow,' 63 days, is an early yellow variety that is good for short seasons. 'Butter & Sugar,' 78 days, produces white and yellow kernels. 'Illini Xtra-Sweet,' 85 days, has yellow kernels and is good for freezing. 'Silver Queen,' 92 days, is a very popular white-kernel, sweet, large-ear variety.

Cucumber

Cucumis sativus
Very Tender

Description: Cucumbers are tender annual vines that can sprawl on the ground or be trained to climb. Both the large leaves and the stems are covered with short hairs; the flowers are yellow. Some plants have both male and female flowers on the same vine, and there may be ten male flowers to every female flower. Only the female flowers produce cucumbers. Some hybrid cucumbers have only female flowers but need some male flowers to produce. Seed companies will include seeds—usually indicated by a pink dye on the seed—that will produce male flowers with such hybrid varieties. These hybrids are usually more productive and set earlier than other varieties.

How to grow: The cucumber is a warm-weather vegetable and very sensitive to frost. It will grow anywhere in the United States, however, because it has a very short growing season—only 55 to 65 days from planting to harvest—and most areas can provide it with at least that much sunshine. Cucumbers respond to a rich, well-worked, well-drained soil that is high in organic matter. Sow seeds directly in the garden two to three weeks after the average date of last frost. To grow transplants indoors, sow seeds three to four weeks prior to planting in the garden. Plant cucumbers in inverted hills, leaving the three strongest plants per hill. Cucumbers need plenty of water to keep them growing fast; don't let the soil dry out. In hot weather the leaves may wilt during the day even when soil moisture is high because the plant is using water faster than its roots can supply it. This is normal; just be sure the plant is receiving regular and sufficient water. Mulch to avoid compaction caused by heavy watering.

Harvest: Harvest promptly; mature cucumbers left on the vine suppress the production of more flowers. Pick the cucumbers when they're immature—the size will depend on the variety. When the seeds start to mature, the vines will stop producing.

Varieties: There are many varieties available to the home gardener. The following are just a few of the good varieties. 'Early Pride Hybrid,' 55 days, grows straight, green fruit that is 8½ inches long. 'Cherokee,' 55 days, is smooth-skinned and good for pickling. 'Straight Eight,' 58 days, is an All America Selection. 'Bush Champion,' 55 days, has productive, compact vines producing 11-inch fruit; it's a good variety for containers. 'Sweet Success,' 58 days, is an All America Selection that is thin-skinned and seedless and produces 14-inch fruit. 'Tasty Green Hybrid,' 62 days, produces 10-inch fruit and is a burpless variety.

Dandelion

Taraxacum officinale
Hardy

The dandelion is best known—and feared—by gardeners as a remarkably persistent lawn weed, but its leaves are actually high in vitamin A and four times higher in vitamin C than lettuce. It's also versatile: Dandelion leaves are used raw in salads or boiled like spinach. The roots can be roasted and made into a coffeelike drink.

Description: The dandelion is a hardy perennial that is grown as an annual for its foliage and as a biennial for its roots. The jagged green leaves grow in a short rosette attached by a short stem to a long taproot. Bright yellow flowers 1 to 2 inches wide grow on smooth, hollow stalks.

How to grow: Dandelions are very hardy and can survive the hottest summers and the coldest winters. Plant the seeds in early spring, four to six weeks before the average date of last frost. Dandelions grow best in well-drained, fertile soil but do well in any soil anywhere. If you're growing dandelions for their foliage only, they'll tolerate soil in poorer physical condition. They prefer full sun but will do fine in partial shade. Plant seeds directly in the garden ¼ inch deep in single rows or wide rows. Thin seedlings to 8 inches apart when they have produced their first true leaves.

Harvest: Harvest dandelion greens at your pleasure throughout the growing season. Harvest the roots in the fall of the second year. Pull the whole root from the ground or lift the roots with a fork to avoid breaking them.

Varieties: The two most common varieties are 'Montmagny' and 'Improved Thick-leaved.'

Eggplant

Solanum Melongena
Very Tender

Description: Eggplant is grown as an annual and has large, hairy, grayish-green leaves. The star-shaped flowers are lavender with yellow centers. The long, slender or round, egg-shaped fruit can be creamy white, yellow, brown, or purple, depending on the variety. Eggplants will grow 2 to 6 feet tall, depending on the variety. Typical home garden varieties produce fruit that is rounded with shiny, dark purple skins. The Oriental varieties produce fruit that is slender and elongated with skin that is usually dull purple in color. Eggplant belongs to the tobacco family and is related to tomatoes, potatoes, and peppers.

How to grow: Eggplant is very sensitive to cold and needs a growing season with day temperatures between 80 and 90 degrees Fahrenheit and night temperatures between 70 and 80 degrees Fahrenheit. Although you can grow eggplant from seed, you'll wait 150 days for a harvest. It's easier to grow from transplants started inside about six to eight weeks before your outside planting date, which should be two to three weeks after the danger of frost. Eggplants must have full sun. They'll grow in almost any soil, but they do better in rich soil that is high in organic matter. Excellent drainage is essential. Set the plants 18 to 24 inches apart. Try to maintain an even soil moisture to ensure even growth. In hot climates the soil temperature may become too warm for the roots; in this case, mulch the plants about a month after you set them outside.

Harvest: The time from planting transplants to harvest is 70 to 85 days. Harvest the fruit young, before the flesh becomes pithy. The fruit should be firm and shiny with no brown streaks. The fruit is borne on a sturdy stem that does not break easily from the plant; cut it off with a sharp knife.

Varieties: 'Tycoon,' 54 days, is an Oriental type with slender, purple fruit. 'Bambino,' 60 days, produces small, rounded fruit on compact, 12-inch plants; it is an ideal variety for containers and small spaces. 'Victoria Hybrid,' 61 days, an Italian type with a deep purple skin color, produces fruit that is long and slender and good for slicing. 'Dusky Hybrid,' 62 days from transplants, is good for short seasons, producing slender, oval dark purple fruit. 'Black Beauty,' 80 days from transplants, has rounded, dark purple fruit.

Endive

Cichorium Endivia
Hardy

Description: Endive is a half-hardy biennial that is grown as an annual. It has a large rosette of toothed, curled, or wavy leaves that are used in salads as a substitute for lettuce. Endive is often known as escarole, and the two vegetables are varieties of the same plant. Escarole has broader leaves.

How to grow: Like lettuce, endive is a cool-season crop, although it's more tolerant of heat than lettuce. Grow it from seed planted in your garden four to six weeks before the average date of last frost. Long, hot summers will force the plant to bolt (go to seed). If your region has a short, hot growing season, start endive indoors from seed. Transplant it as soon as possible so the plants mature before the weather gets hot. Starting in midsummer, sow succession crops in well-worked soil with good drainage and water retention. If you're direct-seeding, sow seeds ¼ inch deep in wide rows. Thin the plants to 9 to 12 inches apart; crowded plants may bolt early. Water regularly to keep the plants growing quickly; lack of water will slow growth and cause the leaves to become bitter. Endive tastes better if you blanch it by tying string around the leaves to hold them together. This deprives the plant of sunlight, discouraging the production of chlorophyll.

Harvest: The time from planting to harvest is 90 to 100 days from seed. To harvest, cut the plant off at soil level.

Varieties: 'Green Curled,' 90 days, has fringed leaves that are creamy white in the center. 'Sinco,' 80 days, is a large-headed escarole.

Garlic

Allium sativum
Very Hardy

Description: Garlic is a hardy perennial that looks similar to onion except that the bulb is segmented into cloves. The flower head looks like a tissue paper dunce cap and is filled with small flowers and bulblets.

How to grow: Garlic must have cool temperatures during its early growth period, but it's not affected by heat in the later stages. Plant garlic in the spring in the North; in the South you can get good results with fall planting. You grow garlic from cloves or bulblets, which are planted with the plump side down. The cloves need full sun and well-worked soil that drains well and is high in organic matter. Plant the cloves four to six weeks before the average date of last frost. Plant them 1 to 2 inches deep and 4 to 6 inches apart. Keep garlic slightly dry, especially when the bulbs are near maturity; this will improve flavor. Keep the area cultivated.

Harvest: Harvest the bulbs by digging the entire plant when the tops start to dry: that's the sign the bulbs are mature. Mature plants take 90 days from planting. Use the plumpest cloves for cooking and plant the others.

Varieties: Few varieties are available. Grow plants from cloves purchased from the grocery.

Horseradish

Armoracia rusticana
Very Hardy

Description: Horseradish looks like a giant, 2-foot radish. In fact, it's a hardy perennial member of the cabbage family. Growing up to 30 inches high, the plant has large, coarse leaves. The root of the horseradish has a very strong flavor.

How to grow: Horseradish is a cold-hardy plant that does well in the North and in cool, high-altitude areas in the South. Grow it from crowns or six-inch root cuttings. Plant crowns at soil level. Plant root cuttings with the narrow end downward and the cut end 2 to 3 inches below soil level. Space plants 1 foot apart. Horseradish tolerates partial shade and needs rich, well-drained soil. Turn over the soil to a depth of 10 to 12 inches, and remove stones and lumps that might cause the roots to split. Keep the soil evenly moist so that the roots will be tender and full of flavor; horseradish gets woody in dry soils.

Harvest: Plants grown from roots cannot be harvested until the second year. Horseradish makes its best growth in late summer and fall, so delay harvesting until October or later. Dig the roots as needed, but in areas where the ground freezes hard, dig them in the fall. Leave a little of the root in the ground so you'll have horseradish the following year.

Varieties: 'Maliner Kren' matures in 150 days from root cuttings.

Kale

Brassica oleracea; Acephala **Group**
Very Hardy

Description: Kale, a member of the cabbage family, is a hardy biennial that is grown as an annual. Scotch kale has gray-green leaves that are crumpled and curled. Siberian, or blue, kale is usually less curly.

How to grow: Kale is a cool-weather crop that grows best in fall. It will last through the winter as far north as Maryland and central Indiana. Frost even improves the flavor. Kale doesn't tolerate the heat as well as collards. If your area has cold winters, plant for summer to early fall harvest. In the South, plant for harvest in late fall or winter. Plant kale from transplants early in the spring, and again in the midsummer if your summers aren't too hot. Kale likes fertile, well-drained soil with a pH between 6.5 and 7.5. Plant transplants that are four to six weeks old. If the transplants are leggy or the stems are crooked, plant deeply so they don't become top-heavy. Plant transplants 8 to 12 inches apart. If you're planting seeds, set them ½ inch deep; thin them to 12 inches apart.

Harvest: The time from planting to harvest is 55 days from transplants, 70 to 80 days from seed. Leave kale in the garden until needed, but harvest before it gets old and tough. As the plant matures, take outside leaves, leaving the inner ones to grow. Or, cut off the entire plant.

Varieties: 'Dwarf Blue Curled Vates,' 55 days, produces short-stemmed plants with finely curled, bluish-green leaves. 'Dwarf Siberian Curled,' 65 days, has upright gray-green leaves.

Kohlrabi

Brassica oleracea; Gongylodes Group
Very Hardy

Description: Kohlrabi, a member of the cabbage family, is a hardy biennial that is grown as an annual. It has a swollen stem that makes it look like a turnip growing on a cabbage root. The swollen stem can be white, purple, or green, and is topped with a rosette of blue-green leaves.

How to grow: Although kohlrabi tolerates some heat, planting should be timed for harvesting during cool weather. Kohlrabi has a shorter growing season than cabbage and grows best in cool weather. If your area has cold winters, plant for summer to early fall harvest. In the South, plant for harvest in late fall or early winter. With spring plantings, start kohlrabi early so that most growth will occur before the weather gets too hot. Kohlrabi is usually grown from transplants started indoors, but you can sow seed directly in the garden. Plant the seeds ¼ to ½ inch deep; thin them to 5 to 6 inches when they're large enough to handle. Kohlrabi likes fertile, well-drained soil with a pH between 6.5 and 7.5. The soil should be high in organic matter. Kohlrabi should have even moisture so it doesn't become woody.

Harvest: When the swollen stem enlarges to 2 to 3 inches in diameter, harvest kohlrabi by cutting at ground level.

Varieties: 'Grand Duke,' 45 days, is an All America Selection. 'Early White Vienna,' 55 days, is a commonly grown, light green variety. 'Early Purple Vienna,' 60 days, is a light purple form.

Leek

Allium ampeloprasum; Porrum Group
Very Hardy

Description: The leek is a hardy biennial that is grown as an annual. It's a member of the onion family but has a stalk rather than a bulb. The leaves are flat and straplike instead of hollow.

How to grow: Leeks are a cool-weather crop. They'll tolerate warm temperatures, but the results are better if the days are cool. Temperatures under 75 degrees Fahrenheit produce the best yields. Plant leeks from seed in the spring four to six weeks before the average date of last frost and from transplants in the fall for a late harvest. Plant transplants in spring if you want to speed up the crop to avoid a hot summer. Plant the seeds ⅛ inch deep and thin them to 6 to 9 inches apart. Plant transplants in 6-inch deep holes, in single rows or wide rows. Leeks like a place in full sun and thrive in rich, well-worked soil with good drainage. To grow large, white, succulent leeks, blanch the lower part of the stem by hilling the soil up around the stalk as it develops. Give leeks plenty of water to keep them growing strongly. Around midsummer, start removing the top half of the leaves. This will encourage greater growth of the leek stalk.

Harvest: The time from planting to harvest is about 80 days from transplants and 120 days from seed. Pull the leeks as you need them, but harvest them all before frost.

Varieties: 'Broad London,' 130 days from seed, produces thick mild-flavored stems. 'Titan,' 100 days, is earlier and larger than 'Broad London' and has a broader base.

Lettuce

Lactuca sativa
Very Hardy

Description: Lettuce is a hardy, fast-growing annual with either loose or compact leaves. Leaf color ranges from light green through reddish brown. When it bolts, or goes to seed, the flower stalks are 2 to 3 feet tall, with small, yellowish flowers on the stalk. The lettuce most commonly found in supermarkets (iceberg, or crisphead, lettuce) is the most difficult to grow in the home vegetable garden. Butterhead lettuces, which have loose heads and delicate crunchy leaves, are easier to grow. Cos, or romaine, lettuce forms a loose, long head and is between a butterhead and leaf lettuce in flavor. Leaf lettuce is delightfully easy to grow, grows fast, and provides bulk and color to salads.

How to grow: Lettuce is a cool-season crop, usually grown from seed planted in the garden four to six weeks before the average date of last frost. Long, hot summer days will make the plants bolt. If your area has a short, hot growing season, start head lettuce from seed indoors eight to ten weeks before the average date of last frost; transplant as soon as possible so the plants will mature before the weather gets really hot. Sow succession crops, beginning in midsummer. In climates with mild winters, grow spring, fall, and winter crops. If you are direct-seeding lettuce in the garden, sow seeds ¼ inch deep in wide rows. When the seedlings are large enough to handle, thin leaf lettuce to 8 inches apart and head lettuce to 12 inches apart. Thinning is important: Heading lettuce won't head, and all lettuce may bolt if the plants are crowded. Lettuce needs well-worked soil with good drainage and moisture retention. Always keep the soil evenly moist. Don't let the shallow-rooted lettuce plants dry out.

Harvest: As the lettuce grows, either pick the outer leaves and let the inner leaves develop or harvest the whole plant at once by cutting it off at ground level. Try to harvest when the weather is cool; in the heat of the day the leaves may be limp. Chilling will crisp the leaves again.

Butterhead varieties: 'Bibb,' 75 days, has a delicate-flavored, dark green, open head. 'Buttercrunch,' 75 days, is an All America Selection with compact heads and a buttery texture; it can tolerate some heat.

Cos (Romaine) varieties: 'Little Gem,' 65 days, gives early, compact, and productive plants. 'Paris Island,' 70 days, is the standard romaine type; it has 10-inch heads and resists bolting.

Crisphead varieties: 'Great Lakes,' 90 days, produces a large, full head that will tolerate some heat. 'Iceberg,' 85 days, is compact with a light green color.

Loosehead (Leaf) varieties: 'Green Ice,' 45 days, has crisp, sweet, heavily ruffled green leaves. 'Red Salad Bowl,' 50 days, produces finely divided, dark burgundy leaves. 'Oak Leaf,' 50 days, is a heat-tolerant, deeply lobed, dark green leaf variety.

Muskmelon, Cantaloupe

Cucumis Melo; Reticulatus **Group**
Very Tender

Description: The muskmelon is a long trailing annual vine that belongs to the cucumber family. The netted melon, or muskmelon, is usually called a cantaloupe, but it should not be confused with the real cantaloupe, which is not often grown in home gardens. Honeydew melons have a smoother surface than muskmelons and lack their distinctive odor; they ripen later and require a longer growing season. The following growing information for muskmelons also applies to honeydews.

How to grow: Muskmelon is a warm-weather plant that will not tolerate even the slightest frost. It also has a long growing season, which means you must select a variety suited to your region's climate. In cool areas, grow muskmelons from transplants; use individual, plantable containers so the root system is not disturbed when you transplant. Set the plant in the garden when the ground is warm: two to three weeks after the danger of frost. Muskmelons must have full sun and need a well-drained soil that is high in organic matter. Grow muskmelons in inverted hills spaced 4 to 6 feet apart. If you're planting from seed, plant six to eight seeds per hill and then thin to the strongest two or three seedlings. If you're using transplants, put two or three in each hill. Muskmelons need a lot of water while the vines are growing, but stop watering when the fruit ripens.

Harvest: The time from planting to harvest is 60 to 110 days, depending on the variety. Leave the melons on the vine until they're ripe; mature melons will easily slip off the stem.

Varieties: 'Ambrosia Hybrid,' 86 days, produces thick, firm fruit about 6½ inches in size. 'Sweet 'n' Early Hybrid,' 75 days, is an early variety that is good for short seasons. 'Burpee Hybrid,' 82 days, produces deep orange, firm fruit.

Mustard

Brassica juncea
Tender

Description: Mustard is an annual with a rosette of large light to dark green crinkled leaves that grow up to 3 feet in length.

How to grow: Mustard is a cool-season crop. It's hardy, but the seeds will not germinate well if you sow them too early; plant the seeds in your garden on the average date of last frost. Mustard is grown like lettuce. It is more heat tolerant than lettuce, but long hot summer days will force the plant to bolt (go to seed). Mustard tolerates partial shade. The plant needs well-worked soil that is high in organic matter and with good drainage and moisture retention. Plant the seeds ½ inch deep. Plant a few seeds at intervals rather than as an entire row at one time. When the seedlings are large enough to handle, thin them to 6 to 12 inches apart. As soon as the plants begin to seed, pull them up or they will produce a great number of seeds and sow themselves all over the garden. Plant mustard again when the weather begins to cool off.

Harvest: The leaves and leaf stalks are eaten. The seeds can be ground and used as a condiment. Pick off individual leaves as they grow, or cut the entire plant at ground level. Harvest when the leaves are young and tender; in summer, the texture may become tough and the flavor strong. Harvest the entire crop when some of the plants start to go to seed.

Varieties: 'Southern Giant Curled,' 40 days, has wide, curled leaves on an upright plant. 'Fordhook Fancy,' produces deeply curled, dark green leaves with some heat tolerance.

Okra

Hibiscus esculentus
Very Tender

Description: Okra, a member of the cotton and hibiscus family, is an erect, tender annual with hairy stems and large maplelike leaves. It grows from 3 to 6 feet tall, and has large flowers that look like yellow hibiscus blossoms with red or purplish centers.

How to grow: Okra is very sensitive to cold; the yield decreases with temperatures less than 70 degrees Fahrenheit. However, okra has a short season, which permits it to be grown almost anywhere in the United States. The plant will grow in any warm, well-drained soil and needs a place in full sun. Plant okra from seed in your garden about four weeks after the average date of last frost. Plant the seeds ½ to 1 inch deep. When the seedlings are growing strongly, thin them to stand 12 to 18 inches apart. Keep the plants on the dry side. The stems rot easily in wet or cold conditions. Okra will grow for a year if not killed by frost and if old pods are not left on the plant.

Harvest: The time from planting to harvest is 50 to 65 days. When mature, the pods are 6 to 10 inches long and filled with buckshotlike seeds. When the plants begin to set their pods, harvest them at least every other day. Pods grow quickly, and unless the older ones are cut off, the plant will stop producing new ones. Keep picking the pods when they're quite small; the pods are less gluey when they're only about two inches long.

Varieties: 'Clemson Spineless,' 56 days, an All America Selection, is a compact plant with dark green, straight, spineless pods. 'Annie Oakley,' 52 days, is a compact variety with a short season.

Onion

Allium cepa
Very Hardy

Description: Onions are hardy biennial vegetables that are usually grown as annuals. They have hollow leaves, and the base of the stem enlarges to form a bulb. The bulbs vary in color from white to yellow or red. The flower stalk is also hollow, taller than the leaves, and topped with a cluster of white or lavender flowers.

How to grow: Most onions are sensitive to the length of the day. Bulb-type varieties are classified as either long-day or short-day onions. Long-day onions will produce bulbs when grown in the summer months in the North. Short-day onions produce bulbs in the mild winter climate of the South. American onions and Spanish onions need long days to produce their bulbs; Bermuda onions prefer short days. Onions are also sensitive to temperature. Generally, they require cool weather to produce their tops and warm weather to produce their bulbs. They're frost-hardy, and you can plant four weeks before the average date of last frost. In the South, onions can be planted in the fall or winter, depending on the variety.

Onions are available in three forms: sets, transplants, and seeds. Sets are small bulbs that are dormant. The smaller the sets are, the better. Sets are easiest to plant, but they come in the smallest number of varieties. Transplants are usually more reliable about producing bulbs and are available in more varieties than sets. Seeds are the least expensive and offer the greatest number of varieties, but they take the longest to develop and are most prone to disease and environmental problems.

Onions need a well-prepared bed with all the lumps removed to a depth of at least 6 inches. The soil should be fertile and rich in organic matter. Bulbing onions need full sun, but green onions can be grown in partial shade. Plant transplants or sets 1 or 2 inches deep and 2 to 3 inches apart. If you're planting onions from seed, plant the seeds ¼ inch deep and thin to 1 to 2 inches apart. If you have limited space, you can grow onions between other vegetables, such as cabbages or tomatoes. The soil should not be allowed to dry out until the plants have started to mature, which is marked by the leaves starting to turn yellow and brown and droop over. At this point, let the soil get as dry as possible.

Harvest: All varieties can be eaten as green onions, though some varieties are grown especially for their bulbs. Harvest leaves whenever you need. Harvest green onions when the bulb is not much larger than the leaves. Harvest dry onion bulbs after the leaves have dried. Lift the bulbs completely out of the soil. Dry the bulbs thoroughly before storing.

Green onion (Scallion, Bunching) varieties: 'Evergreen Long White Bunching,' 120 days from seed to maturity, produce long silvery-white stalks in bunches and will not form bulbs. 'Beltsville Bunching,' 120 days, is heat-tolerant and has a mild flavor.

Bulbing onion varieties: 'Southport Red Globe,' 110 days, long-day, has sweet, purple-red flesh. 'Yellow Sweet Spanish,' 110 days, long-day, has large, white flesh. 'Bermuda,' 185 days, short-day, is large and produces white flesh with a mild flavor. 'Yellow Granax,' 120 days, short-day, is large with white flesh.

Parsnip

Pastinaca sativa
Hardy

Description: Parsnips are biennials that are grown as annuals. They belong to the same family as celery, carrots, and parsley. A rosette of celerylike leaves grows from the top of the whitish, fleshy root.

How to grow: Parsnips need a long, cool growing season. They will tolerate cold at the start and the end of the growing season, and they can withstand freezing temperatures. Parsnips prefer full sun but will tolerate partial shade. Plant parsnip seeds two to three weeks before the average date of last frost. Turn the soil completely to a depth of 10 to 12 inches and remove all lumps and rocks. The initial soil preparation is essential for a healthy crop: Soil lumps, rocks, or other obstructions in the soil will cause the roots to split, fork, or become deformed. Since it may also cause forking, don't use manure in the soil bed for root crops unless it is well rotted. Plant seeds ½ inch deep and thin them to 2 to 4 inches apart; parsnips must have adequate space for root development. Thin seedlings with scissors so you don't disturb the tender roots of the remaining plants. Parsnips need plenty of water until they approach maturity. At this point, cut back on watering so the roots don't split.

Harvest: Leave parsnips in the soil as long as possible or until you need them. The roots are not harmed by the ground's freezing, but dig them up before the ground becomes unworkable.

Varieties: 'Hollow Crown,' 105 days, is long and produces mild flavored, white flesh. 'Harris Model,' 110 days, has white flesh with a smooth texture.

California Black-eye Pea

Vigna unguiculata
Very Tender

Description: Black-eyed peas are tender annuals. Depending on the variety, they can be either bushy or climbing plants. The seeds on the dwarf varieties are usually white with a dark spot (the "black eye") where they're attached to the pod; sometimes the spots are brown or purple.

How to grow: Black-eyed peas can tolerate high temperatures but are very sensitive to cold: The slightest frost will harm them. They grow well in the South. Some Northern areas may not have a long enough growing season to accommodate them from seeds; unfortunately, they don't grow well from transplants. If your area has a long enough warm season, plant black-eyed peas from seed four weeks after the average date of last frost. Black-eyed peas will tolerate poor soil. In fact, like other legumes, they're often grown to improve the soil. Well-drained, well-worked soil that's high in organic matter increases their productivity. Sow seeds directly in the garden ½ inch deep and about 2 inches apart. Thin them to 3 to 4 inches apart when they're easy enough to handle.

Harvest: The time from planting to harvest is 70 to 110 days. Pick the pods at whatever stage of maturity you desire—either young and tender or fully matured to use dried.

Varieties: 'California Black-eye,' 75 days, produces 8-inch pods. 'Mississippi Silver,' 65 days, has green pods that are streaked with pink.

Green Pea

Pisum sativum
Very Hardy

Description: Peas are hardy, weak-stemmed climbing annual vines. They have leaflike stipules, leaves with one to three pairs of leaflets, and tendrils for climbing. The flowers are white, streaked, or colored. The fruit is a pod containing 4 to 10 seeds, either smooth or wrinkled depending on the variety.

How to grow: Unlike black-eyed peas, green peas are a cool-season crop that must mature before the weather gets hot. The ideal growing weather is moist with temperatures between 60 and 65 degrees Fahrenheit. Plant peas as soon as the soil can be worked in spring: about six weeks before the average date of last frost. Peas need good drainage in soil that is high in organic material. They produce earlier in sandy soil, but yield a heavier, later crop if grown in clayey soil. Plant peas directly in the garden 2 inches deep and 1 to 2 inches apart. Don't let the soil dry out; peas need ample moisture. Provide a three-foot-high trellis to support the vines.

Harvest: The time from planting to harvest is 55 to 80 days. Pick shelling peas when the pods are full and green, before the peas start to harden. Edible pod peas are grown the same way as sweet peas, but harvest the immature pods before the peas have developed to full size. Pods should be plump, but the individual peas should not be showing through the pod.

Varieties: 'Little Marvel,' 63 days, has compact growth and produces dark green pods. 'Wando,' 68 days, is tolerant of heat. 'Maestro,' 61 days, is prolific, producing 9 to 12 peas per dark green pod. 'Oregon Sugar Pod II,' 68 days, produces a 4½-inch edible snow pea. 'Sugar Snap,' 70 days, an All America Selection, is a 3-inch edible snap pea.

Peanut

Arachis hypogaea
Very Tender

Description: The peanut is a tender annual belonging to the pea family. It grows 6 inches to 2½ feet tall, depending on type. The bunch type grows upright; the runner type spreads out over the ground. Small clusters of yellow, sweet pealike flowers grow on stems called pegs. The pegs grow down and push into the soil, and the nuts develop 1 to 3 inches under ground from the pegs. Peanuts are not grown commercially north of Washington, D.C., but they can be grown farther north for fun.

How to grow: Peanuts need a frost-free growing season four to five months long. If your growing season is short, start peanuts inside two weeks before the average date of last frost then transplant them outside two to three weeks after the average date of last frost. Peanuts like a well-worked sandy soil that is high in organic matter. The pegs have difficulty penetrating soil that has a high clay content. Plant seeds from shelled raw peanuts 1 to 3 inches deep. Space both seeds and transplants 6 to 8 inches apart. Keep soil moisture even until the plants start to flower, then water less. Blind (empty) pods are the result of too much rain or humidity at flowering time. Use a heavy mulch to help the pegs become established.

Harvest: The time from planting to harvest is 120 to 150 days. Start harvesting when frost begins; pull up the whole plant and let the pods dry on the vine.

Varieties: Few varieties are available. You can plant raw peanuts from the grocery. 'Jumbo Virginia,' matures in 120 days.

Pepper, Hot and Sweet

Capsicum annuum
Tender

Peppers come in sweet or hot varieties. Bell peppers are the most familiar; most bell peppers are sweet, but some hot varieties exist. Hot peppers are intensely flavored, and there are more than a hundred varieties.

Description: Peppers are erect perennials that are grown as annuals. One or several flowers grow in the angle between the leaf and stem. America peppers are members of the tobacco family, which includes tomatoes, potatoes, and eggplant. Peppers range in size from the large, sweet bullnose, or mango, pepper to the tiny, fiery bird, or devil, pepper. Peppers grow in many shapes: round, long, flat, and twisted. The large, sweet ones are used raw, cooked, or pickled; the hot ones are used as an unmistakable flavoring relish. Choose peppers carefully when you make a selection to be sure the variety you're growing suits your palate.

How to grow: Peppers prefer a soil temperature above 65 degrees Fahrenheit. They don't produce well when the day temperature gets above 90 degrees Fahrenheit. Hot peppers tolerate hot weather better than sweet peppers. The ideal climate is a daytime temperature around 75 degrees Fahrenheit and a nighttime temperature around 62 degrees Fahrenheit. The easiest way to grow peppers is from transplants. Set transplants in the garden 18 to 24 inches apart two to three weeks after the average date of last frost. You can also grow peppers from seed, starting indoors 7 to 10 weeks before the average date of last frost. If you have a long growing season, you can seed peppers directly in the garden. Peppers do best in a soil that is high in organic matter and that holds water but drains well. Do not overfertilize peppers; too much nitrogen will cause the plants to grow large but produce few peppers. Peppers are shallow-rooted, so cultivate them gently. Use a mulch to keep the soil temperature and moisture even and to suppress weeds.

Harvest: Peppers are usually harvested when green. If you want sweet red peppers, leave the sweet green peppers on the vine until they ripen and turn red. Cut the peppers off the vine; if you pull them off, half the plant may come up with the fruit. Hot peppers can irritate the skin, so wear gloves when you pick them.

Sweet varieties: 'Better Belle,' 65 days, produces peppers that are large, thick-walled, and green. 'Bell Boy,' 70 days, are a large deep green turning to red. 'Golden Bell,' 68 days, is a light green that turns golden yellow. 'Pimento,' 78 days, is heart-shaped and sweet.

Hot varieties: 'Hungarian Yellow Wax,' 65 days, matures to red in color and is medium-hot. 'Red Chili,' 80 days, produces peppers that are 2½ inches long and very hot.

Irish Potato

Solanum tuberosum
Hardy

There are more than 100 varieties of potatoes in the United States. They fall into four basic categories: long whites, round whites, russets, and round reds.

Description: Potatoes are weak-stemmed plants with hairy, dark green compound leaves that look a little like tomato leaves. The plants produce underground stem tubers when mature. It is a member of the tobacco family, related to the tomato, eggplant, and pepper.

How to grow: Potatoes need a frost-free growing season of 90 to 120 days. They're a cool-weather crop, and they grow best in areas with cool summers. Hot weather cuts down on the production of tubers. Grow potatoes in summer in the North, and in fall, winter, and spring in the South. Plant early varieties just before the average date of last frost. Potatoes are grown from whole potatoes or pieces of potatoes, which are called seed pieces. Each piece must have at least one eye. Always plant certified disease-free seed pieces. Don't use supermarket potatoes, which have been chemically treated to prevent sprouting. Potatoes need well-drained, fertile soil that is high in organic matter. The pH level should be between 5.0 and 5.5. Plant potato pieces in full sun, 4 inches deep, and 12 to 18 inches apart. Keep the soil evenly moist and free of weeds.

Harvest: Dig up new potatoes after the plant blooms or when the leaves begin to turn yellow. For mature tubers, use a spading fork to dig up the potatoes two weeks after the vine dies.

Varieties: 'Red Pontiac,' 100 days, are red with thin skin and white flesh. 'Explorer,' 100 days, produces small, white flesh and can be grown from seed. 'White Cobbler,' 90 days, is a baking variety with a short growing season. 'Kennebec,' 105 days, is large and white; it stores well.

Sweet Potato

Ipomoea Batatas
Very Tender

There are two kinds of sweet potato—"dry" and "moist"—which describes the texture of the variety. The moist varieties are often called yams, but the yam is actually a different species that is found in tropical countries.

Description: The sweet potato is a tender vining or semierect perennial plant that is grown as an annual. It has small white, pink, or red-purple flowers. The swollen, fleshy roots range in color from creamy-yellow to deep red-orange.

How to grow: Sweet potatoes are extremely sensitive to frost and need warm, moist weather. They have a long growing season (about 150 days); in areas with a shorter season, the plants tend to produce small potatoes. Plant sweet potatoes four weeks after the average date of last frost or when the soil is thoroughly warm. Sweet potatoes are planted from rooted sprouts, or slips, taken from a mature root. To grow your own slips, place sweet potatoes in a coldframe and cover with two inches of sand or light soil. Keep the bed warm. Add more soil when shoots appear. The shoots will develop roots that can be planted in the garden. You can also buy slips from a reputable garden center or supplier. A light, well-worked soil that is not overly rich produces the best roots. Plant slips 12 inches apart in mounded ridges. Plants do best with even moisture throughout the season until three weeks before harvesting.

Harvest: Dig up the roots before the first frost. The roots are damaged by freezing and cold soils.

Varieties: 'Centennial,' 95 days, has a short growing season and produces orange flesh. 'Bush Porto Rico,' 125 days, has compact growth and produces red-orange flesh.

Pumpkin

Cucurbita species
Very Tender

Description: Pumpkins are tender annuals with large leaves on branching vines that can grow 20 feet long. The male and female flowers grow on the same vine, and the fruit can weigh as much as 100 pounds.

How to grow: Pumpkins need a long growing season. They will grow almost anywhere in the United States, but in cooler areas you'll get better results with a smaller variety. Pumpkins are sensitive to cold soil and frost. Plant them from seed two to three weeks after the average date of last frost, when the soil has warmed up. Bush varieties can be grown if space is limited. Pumpkins prefer well-drained soil that is high in organic matter. Too much fertilizer encourages the growth of vines rather than the production of fruit. Plant seeds directly in the garden in inverted hills six feet apart. Plant several seeds per hill and thin to one plant in each hill. Thin seedlings at soil level to avoid disturbing the roots of the chosen survivor. Pumpkins need plenty of water to keep the fruit growing steadily.

Harvest: The time from planting to harvest is 95 to 120 days. Leave the pumpkins on the vine as long as possible before frost. They become soft after freezing. Cut off the pumpkin with one or two inches of stem.

Varieties: 'Bushkin,' 95 days, produces bright orange, 10-pound fruit; it is good for limited space. 'Jack Be Little,' 95 days, produces 3-inch fruit. 'Jack-O-Lantern,' 110 days, has 10-inch, bright orange fruit. 'Big Max,' 120 days, has reddish pink skin and can weigh up to 100 pounds.

Radish

Raphanus sativus
Hardy

Description: Radishes are hardy biennials that are grown as annuals. They produce rosettes of lobed leaves and white, red, or black roots, depending on the variety.

How to grow: Radishes are cool-season crops that can tolerate temperatures below freezing. They can grow anywhere in the United States. They mature in such a short time that you can get two to three crops in spring alone. Start planting radishes from seed in the garden two to three weeks before the average date of last frost. Radishes germinate quickly and are often used with seeds of slower-growing plants to mark rows. Radishes like well-worked, well-drained soil. Sow seeds directly in the garden ½ inch deep. Thin spring varieties 1 to 3 inches apart; give winter varieties a little more space. Radishes sometimes bolt (go to seed) in the summer, but this is often a question more of day length than of temperature. Cover the plants in midsummer so they get only an 8-hour day; a 12-hour day produces flowers and seeds but no radishes.

Harvest: The time from planting to harvest is 20 to 30 days for spring radishes, 50 to 60 days for winter radishes. Pull up the whole plant when the radishes are the right size.

Varieties: 'Cherry Belle,' 22 days, is an All America Selection producing round, red, ¾-inch roots. 'White Icicle,' 28 days, gives white, icicle-shaped roots that are 5 inches long. 'French Breakfast,' 23 days, is oblong and red with white on the bottom. 'Summer Cross Hybrid,' 45 days, is an Oriental-type, all-season variety that gives white flesh.

Rhubarb

Rheum rhabarbarum
Hardy Perennial

Description: A hardy perennial, rhubarb grows 2 to 4 feet tall, with large, attractive leaves on strong stalks. The leaf stalks are red or green and grow up from a stout rhizome. The flowers are small and grow on top of a dense flower spike.

How to grow: Rhubarb is very hardy and prefers cool weather. In areas where the weather is warm or hot, the leaf stalks become thin and spindly. Although rhubarb can be grown from seed, the plants will not grow 'true,' meaning they won't be the same variety as the parent plant. For a close or exact copy of the parent plant, grow from the divisions separated from the parent stems. Buy divisions or divide your own plants in early spring. Rhubarb likes rich, well-worked soil that is high in organic matter and drains well. Plant the divisions 3 feet apart with the growing tips slightly below the soil surface. Keep the soil evenly moist. Keep weeds away and mulch around the plant, especially in winter. To get earlier and longer leaf stalks, surround the plants with boxes in early spring but do not cover the plant from light. When flower stalks appear, remove them to keep the leaf stalks growing strongly. Divide the plant every three to four years.

Harvest: You'll have to wait two to three years from the time of planting to the first real harvest. To harvest, twist the leaf stalk at the soil line; do not take more than a third of the leaves in any given year. Eat only the stalk, not the leaf.

Varieties: 'MacDonald,' is brilliant red with tender skin. 'Valentine,' has deep red stalks. 'Victoria,' produces green stalks tinged with pink.

Rutabaga

Brassica napus; Napobrassica **Group**
Very Hardy

This plant was created by crossing a cabbage with a turnip.

Description: Rutabaga is a hardy biennial that is grown as an annual. A rosette of smooth, grayish green leaves grows from a swollen stem. The root can be yellow, purple, or white.

How to grow: Rutabagas are very hardy and grow best in cool weather. In hot weather they produce many leaves but only small, stringy roots. Plant rutabagas in late summer in the North, and in the late fall in the South or where the weather gets very hot. For spring plantings sow seed directly in the garden 4 to 6 weeks before the average date of last frost. Rutabagas do best in well-drained soil that is high in organic matter. The plants need well-worked soil with all rocks and soil lumps removed. Plant the seeds ½ inch deep and thin them to 8 inches apart. Thinning is important: Like all root crops, rutabagas must have room to develop. Water often enough to keep the plants growing steadily; if growth slows, the roots will be tough.

Harvest: The time from planting to harvest is 90 to 100 days. To harvest, dig up the whole root when the rutabaga is 3 to 5 inches in diameter. In cold areas, mulch heavily to extend the harvesting period.

Varieties: 'American Purple Top,' 90 days, gives fine-grained, yellow flesh.

Salsify, Oyster Plant

Tragopogon porrifolius
Hardy

Description: Salsify is a hardy biennial that is grown as an annual. It's related to dandelion and chicory, and its flowers look like lavender chicory blossoms. The edible part is the long taproot. Some people claim that salsify has a slight oyster flavor, hence the name "oyster plant."

How to grow: Salsify is hardy and tolerates cold. Like its prolific cousin the dandelion, it's easy to grow anywhere in the United States. Prepare rich soil by removing all stones and lumps. Plant salsify from seed two or three weeks before the average date of last frost. Plant the seeds ½ inch deep. When seedlings are large enough to handle, thin them to stand 2 to 4 inches apart. Don't overfertilize; it will cause the roots to fork and split. Keep the plants evenly moist to prevent the roots from getting stringy.

Harvest: The time from planting to harvest is about 120 days. Salsify roots can tolerate freezing, so leave them in the ground until you want them. The longer they're out of the ground, the less they taste like oysters. To harvest, dig up the whole root.

Varieties: 'Sandwich Island Mammoth,' 120 days, is the most widely available variety.

Shallot

Allium Cepa
Very Hardy

Description: The shallot is a very hardy biennial onion that is grown as an annual. Shallot plants grow 8 inches tall in a clump with narrow green leaves; they look very much like small onions. The roots are very shallow and fibrous, and mature bulbs are about ½ inch in diameter. The small bulbs have a more delicate flavor than regular onions.

How to grow: Shallots are easy to grow. You can grow them anywhere in the United States from cloves planted early in spring. Shallots have shallow roots, and they need little soil preparation. The plants seldom form seed, so they're usually grown from cloves, which should be planted four to six weeks before the average date of last frost. Plant the cloves 6 to 8 inches apart and set them so the tops of the cloves are even with the soil but no deeper. Carefully cultivate when they're small; the shallow root systems don't like to compete with weeds.

Harvest: Cut the green leaves throughout the growing season, but be careful not to cut away any new growth coming from the central stem. Dig up bulbs when the tops wither and fall over.

Varieties: No named varieties are available. Shallots take 90 days to mature from a clove.

Sorrel

Rumex Acetosa
Very Hardy

Description: Garden sorrel grows about 3 feet tall and produces sour-tasting leaves that are good when used fresh in salads. French sorrel grows only 6 to 12 inches tall; its fiddle-shaped leaves make good salad greens. The weed variety is bitter and is not good for eating.

How to grow: Sorrels are very hardy and can be grown in almost every area of the United States. Sorrels require a sunny location with well-drained fertile soil. Plant sorrels from seed two to three weeks before the average date of last frost. Plant the seeds ½ inch deep. When the plants are 6 to 8 weeks old, thin them to 12 to 18 inches apart. Sorrel plants should be kept moist; water them more often than the rest of the garden.

Harvest: Pick the fresh leaves of sorrel throughout the growing season. Pick off flowers before they mature to keep the plant producing new leaves long into the fall.

Varieties: Garden sorrel and French sorrel are sold under their common names. From seed to maturity is about 100 days.

Spinach

Spinacia oleracea
Very Hardy

Description: Spinach is a hardy annual with a rosette of dark green leaves. The leaves may be crinkled (savoy leaf) or flat. Spinach is related to beets and chard.

How to grow: Spinach is very hardy and can tolerate cold; in fact, it thrives in cold weather. Heat and long days make spinach bolt (go to seed) quickly. Spinach grows well in the winter in the South, and in early spring and late summer in the North. Plant spinach about four weeks before the average date of last frost. Spinach tolerates partial shade and requires well-drained soil that's rich in organic matter. Spinach does not like acid soil. The plant is grown from seed clusters that each produce several seedlings. Spinach must be thinned when the seedlings appear. Plant spinach seed clusters ½ inch deep and 2 to 4 inches apart. When the seedlings are large enough to handle, thin them to leave the strongest seedling from each cluster. Spinach does best when the soil is kept uniformly moist. Try not to splash muddy water on the leaves, which will make the spinach difficult to clean after harvesting. Mulch to retain moisture and avoid getting soil on the leaves.

Harvest: The time from planting to harvest is 40 to 45 days. To harvest, either pick the outside leaves periodically or pull up the entire plant.

Varieties: 'Melody Hybrid,' 42 days, is an All America Selection that gives semierect plants with dark green leaves. 'Bloomsdale Long-Standing,' 48 days, produces thick-textured, crinkled, dark green leaves.

New Zealand Spinach

Tetragonia tetragonioides
Hardy

Description: New Zealand spinach is an annual with weak, spreading stems 2 to 4 feet long that are covered with dark green leaves 2 to 4 inches long. New Zealand spinach is not really a spinach at all, but when it's cooked, the two are virtually indistinguishable. The leaves are smaller and fuzzier than those of regular spinach.

How to grow: New Zealand spinach likes long warm days. It grows best at 60 to 75 degrees Fahrenheit. It won't start growing until the soil warms up. The plant has a short season (55 to 65 days), so it can be grown successfully in most areas of the United States. Plant seed directly in the garden on the average date of last frost. When seedlings are large enough to handle, thin the plants to stand 12 to 18 inches apart. New Zealand spinach does not like competition from weeds; cut weeds at ground level to avoid damaging the shallow roots of the crop.

Harvest: The time from planting to harvest is about 60 days. Harvest tender leaves as you need them by cutting them from the tips of the branches. Plants will continue to produce new foliage as leaves are harvested.

Varieties: New Zealand spinach is sold under its common name.

Summer Squash

Cucurbita Pepo
Very Tender

Description: Summer squashes are weak-stemmed, tender annuals. They have large, cucumberlike leaves, and separate male and female flowers appear on the same plant. A summer squash usually grows as a bush, rather than as a vine. The fruits have thin, tender skin and are generally eaten in the immature stage before the skin hardens. Of the many kinds of summer squashes, the most popular are crookneck, straightneck, scallop, and zucchini.

How to grow: Squashes are warm-season crops and are very sensitive to cold and frost. They like night temperatures of at least 60 degrees Fahrenheit. Direct seeding is best for squashes, but if a variety requires a longer growing season than your area has, use transplants from a reputable nursery or garden center or grow your own transplants. To grow transplants, start four to five weeks before the outside planting date. Use individual plantable containers to lessen the risk of shock when the seedlings are transplanted. Squash varieties like well-worked soil with good drainage. They're heavy feeders, so the soil must be well-fertilized. Two to three weeks after the average date of last frost, when the soil is warm, plant squash in inverted hills. The hills should be 3 to 4 feet apart; plant four or five seeds in each hill. When the seedlings are about a week old, thin them to leave the two to three strongest plants. Keep the soil evenly moist: Squashes need a lot of water in hot weather. The vines may wilt on hot days because the plant is using water faster than the roots can supply it. If the vines are getting a regular supply of water, don't worry about the wilting; the plants will liven up as the day cools. If the vines are wilting first thing in the morning, water them immediately.

Winter Squash

Cucurbita maxima
Very Tender

Harvest: The time from planting to harvest, as well as the expected yield, depends on the variety. Harvest summer squashes when they're young: They taste delicious when they're small. If you leave them on the plant too long, they will suppress flowering and reduce your crop. Harvest zucchini and crookneck varieties when they're 6 to 8 inches long. Harvest round types when they're 4 to 8 inches in diameter. Break or cut the fruit from the plant.

Crookneck varieties: 'Early Golden Summer,' 53 days, gives fruit with bright yellow, warted skin. 'Pic-N-Pic,' 50 days, has golden-yellow, smooth skin.

Scallop varieties: 'Peter Pan Hybrid,' 50 days, is an All America Selection that provides meaty, light-green fruit. 'Early White Bush Scallop,' 60 days, produces fruit that has pale green skin and creamy-white flesh.

Straightneck varieties: 'Butterstick,' 50 days, produces bright yellow fruit and has a long harvest period. 'Goldbar,' 53 days, has compact growth and provides fruit with smooth, golden-yellow skin.

Zucchini varieties: 'Burpee Hybrid,' 50 days, has medium-green skin and compact plants. 'Golden Zucchini,' 54 days, gives glossy, bright golden skin.

Description: Winter squashes are weak-stemmed tender annual vines. They have large cucumberlike leaves, and separate male and female flowers grow on the same plant. Most winter squashes grow as vines, but some newer varieties have been bred to have a more compact, bushy habit of growth. Vining types of winter squash can be caged or trained to climb up a fence or trellis to save space. If you're growing a variety that will need support, set the support in place at the time of planting. If you do it later, you risk damaging the plant's roots. Winter squash varieties have hard skins when they're harvested and eaten. Popular types of winter squashes include acorn, banana, buttercup, butternut, cushaw, hubbard, and Turk's turban. Spaghetti squash is technically a small pumpkin and is cared for in the same way as pumpkins.

How to grow: Contrary to what its name suggests, winter squashes are warm-season crops and are very sensitive to cold and frost. Don't plant the seeds until the soil has warmed up in the spring, about two to three weeks after the average date of last frost. Direct-seeding is best. If you're planting a variety that requires a longer growing season than your area has, use transplants from a reputable nursery or garden center, or grow your own transplants. Start four to five weeks before the outdoor planting date, and use individual plantable containers to lessen the risk of shock when the seedlings are transplanted. Squashes like well-worked soil with good drainage. They're heavy feeders so the soil must be well-fertilized. Two to three weeks after the average date of last frost, when the soil is warm, plant squash in inverted hills. Place the hills 3 to 4 feet apart, and plant four or five seeds in each hill. When the seedlings are about a week old, thin them to leave the two to three strongest plants. Keep the soil evenly moist; squashes need a lot of water in hot weather.

Harvest: Leave winter squashes on the vine until the skin is so hard it cannot be dented with your thumbnail. Harvest before the first frost. Break or cut it off the vine. Cure squashes in a dark, humid place for 10 days at 80 to 85 degrees Fahrenheit; then store them at 50 to 60 degrees Fahrenheit in a moderately dry, dark place for five to six months.

Acorn variety: 'Early Acorn,' 75 days, produces fruit with smooth texture and orange flesh on a compact plant. 'Table King,' 75 days, has large fruit and a small seed cavity; it is an All America Selection.

Butternut variety: 'Butter Boy Hybrid,' 80 days, has a sweet, nutty flavor and reddish orange flesh. 'Waltham,' 85 days, is an All America Selection and has orange flesh.

Hubbard variety: 'Blue Hubbard,' 120 days, provides large fruit with blue-gray skin and orange flesh. 'Hubbard Improved Green,' 120 days, has dark green skin and orange flesh.

Spaghetti variety: 'Vegetable Spaghetti,' 100 days, has yellow skin and flesh; it should be stored like winter squash.

Turban variety: 'Buttercup,' 105 days, has dark green skin and orange flesh with a very small seed cavity. 'Turk's Turban,' 105 days, has bright red or orange skin with white and green stripes.

Tomatillo

Physalis ixocarpa
Tender

Description: Tomatillo, a member of the tobacco family, is a tender annual grown for its pulpy fruit, which resembles a small, green tomato. Tomatillo, or ground cherry, grows to 4 feet tall. It has deeply lobed leaves, yellow flowers, and a papery husk that contains a 2½-inch green fruit. The fruit is widely used in making jams and salsa.

How to grow: Tomatillo requires warm soil and a long, warm growing season. They need full sun and prefer a well-drained soil that is rich in organic matter. Plant tomatillo from transplants on the average date of last frost. Start transplants indoors from seed six to eight weeks before the planting date. When transplants are large enough to be planted in the garden, set plants 18 to 24 inches apart. Established plants are drought tolerant.

Harvest: The time from planting to harvest is about 100 days. When the husk begins to turn brown, pick the fruit.

Varieties: Tomatillo is sold under its common name.

Tomato

Lycopersicon lycopersicum
Tender

Description: Tomatoes are tender perennials that are grown as annuals. They have weak stems and lobed and toothed leaves that have a distinctive odor. The yellow flowers grow in clusters. Most tomatoes have vining growth habits and need a fair amount of space. Some tomatoes are described as bush varieties that will save space, but they'll still sprawl if you let them. You may still have to stake or cage the bush types. Depending on the variety, tomatoes vary by the size and shape of the fruit (cherry, plum, pear, etc.), by their color (red, pink, yellow, orange), and by their use (slicing, canning, juicing).

Tomatoes are divided into two main groups according to growth habits: determinate and indeterminate. On the determinate tomato (bush tomato), the plant stops growing when the end buds set fruit, usually at about 3 feet tall. Determinate tomatoes seldom need staking, but a single stake or short cage will help keep them confined. Determinate varieties produce a crop of tomatoes that will all ripen at one time. This type of tomato is used for canning and processing. On the indeterminate tomato (vine tomato), the end buds do not set fruit; the plant continues to grow until it's killed by frost. Indeterminate tomatoes will get quite large, so these varieties should be staked or caged. Staked and caged tomatoes provide cleaner fruit and less loss from rot or problems that occur in warm, humid areas. In addition, they require less room for each plant.

How to grow: Tomatoes grow best when the daytime temperature is between 65 and 85 degrees Fahrenheit. They stop growing above 95 degrees Fahrenheit. If nighttime temperatures are above 85 degrees Fahrenheit, the fruit will not turn red. Tomatoes need full sun and warm, well-drained soil. Start tomatoes either by seed planted in the garden on the average date of last frost or from transplants set in the garden about a week after the average date of last frost. If you use transplants, either purchase them from a reputable nursery or garden center or start your own indoors six to eight weeks before the planting date. Plant transplants 18 to 36 inches apart, depending on whether you will stake or cage the plants or let them sprawl. Set the plants out on a cloudy day or in the late afternoon. If the sun is very hot, protect the plants with a temporary shade of newspapers. Disturb the roots of transplants as little as possible. If the stems are leggy or crooked, set the plants deeply or in a trench. Side roots will develop along the stem, and the top will turn in the right direction. Tomatoes need plenty of water; water before the soil dries out.

Harvest: The time from planting to harvest is 50 to 180 days from transplants, depending on the variety. The color when ripe depends on the variety. Ripe tomatoes should feel firm, neither squashy nor too hard.

Indeterminate varieties: 'Avalanch F,' 77 days, produces medium-size red fruit. 'Beefmaster VFN,' is large and red and resists cracking. 'Better Boy VFN,' 72 days, has large, round, red fruit. 'Better Girl VFN,' 62 days, gives fruit that is early, round, red, and meaty. 'Champion VFNT,' 62 days, produces an early, large beefsteak-type fruit. 'Early Girl V' matures in 54 days. 'Whopper VFNT,' 70 days, provides very large, meaty, red fruit. 'Pink Girl VFT,' 76 days, gives a medium-size fruit with pink skin. 'Golden Boy,' 80 days, has medium-size, round fruit that is bright yellow.

Determinate varieties: 'Celebrity VFNT,' 70 days, produces medium-size, red, round fruit. 'Floramerica VF,' 70 days, is an All America Selection that provides meaty, red, all-purpose fruit. 'The Juice VF,' 65 days, has red, juicy fruit and is good for juice making.

Turnip

Brassica Rapa, Rapifera Group
Hardy

Description: The turnip, a hardy biennial that is grown as an annual, sports a rosette of hairy, bright green leaves growing from a swelling at the base of the stem. The turnip is more commonly grown for use as a root vegetable, but it can also be grown for the leaves, which are used as greens.

How to grow: Turnips are a cool-weather crop. They are grown in the fall, winter, and spring in the South, and in the spring and fall in the North. Turnips need soil that's high in organic matter and well-drained but able to hold moisture. Too much nitrogen in the soil encourages the plant to produce leaves and a seed stalk rather than a good-size root. Turnips don't transplant well, so grow them from seed sown directly in the garden. Sow seeds 1 to 2 inches apart in single or wide rows. When the seedlings are large enough to handle, thin to 3 or 4 inches apart; if you're growing turnips for greens, thin to 2 to 3 inches apart. Water before the soil dries out; water is important to keep turnips growing as fast as possible. If growth is slow, the roots become strong-flavored and woody and the plant will often send up a seed stalk.

Harvest: Harvest turnips when they are 2 to 4 inches in diameter—before they get pithy and bitter. Pull them easily when the soil is moist. Pick greens when they are young and tender; use thinned seedlings for greens.

Varieties: 'Purple Top White Globe' matures in 58 days. 'Tokyo Cross Hybrid,' 35 days, is an All America Selection that produces 2- to 6-inch pure white roots.

Watercress

Nasturtium officinale
Hardy

Description: Watercress is a trailing perennial of European origin with dark green peppery leaves. Plants usually grow in water. If you're fortunate enough to have a stream running through your garden, you can grow watercress on the bank. You can also grow it indoors in pots set in a tray of water. Watercress adds a kick to salads and makes a popular garnish. It's full of vitamin C and minerals.

How to grow: Although watercress is easily grown from seed, it is usually propagated in temperate climates from stem-pieces, which root easily in wet soil. Sow seeds of watercress directly in wet garden soils two to three weeks before the average date of last frost. Cuttings can be taken from the watercress you buy at the grocery. Watercress prefers sun in the North, dappled shade in the South. Sow the seeds thickly ¼ inch deep. Mulch lightly if high water is likely to wash seeds from their bed. As watercress becomes established, the plants will spread and float on the edges of streams, rooting into the soil below.

Harvest: Pick plants when needed for a pungent, peppery flavor.

Varieties: 'Dutch' matures in 53 days.

Watermelon

Citrullus lanatus
Very Tender

Description: The watermelon is a spreading, tender annual vine related to the cucumber. It produces round, oval, or oblong fruits that can weigh anywhere from 5 to 100 pounds. The fruit can have pink, red, yellow, or grayish white flesh. Male and female flowers appear on the same vine. Although smaller varieties are available, watermelons still need a lot of room. They also take a lot of nutrients from the soil.

How to grow: Watermelons require warm soil and warm days. Night temperatures below 50 degrees Fahrenheit will cause the flavor of the fruit to deteriorate. They must have full sun and prefer well-drained soil that holds moisture well. Grow watermelons in inverted hills either by seed or transplants. You can either purchase transplants or start your own indoors three to four weeks before the planting date. Sow seeds or set out transplants two to three weeks after the average date of last frost, when the soil has warmed up. Space the hills 6 feet apart and plant four to five seeds in each hill. When the seedlings have grown large enough, thin to leave the strongest one or two seedlings in each hill. With transplants, set one or two transplants per hill. Watermelons are 95 percent water, so make sure they have enough water to keep them growing well. Don't let the soil dry out and use a mulch to keep the moisture even.

Harvest: A watermelon is ready to harvest when the vine's tendrils begin to turn brown and die off. A ripe watermelon will sound dull and hollow when you tap it with your knuckles.

Varieties: 'Golden Crown Hybrid,' 80 days, is an All America Selection that produces juicy, golden-yellow flesh. 'Sugar Baby,' 75 days, gives round, 12-pound fruits with red flesh and thin rinds. 'Bush Sugar Baby,' 80 days, provides sweet, 12-pound fruit on a compact bush. 'Redball Seedless,' 80 days, gives fruit with red flesh that has a few white seeds.

HERBS

Angelica

Biennial

Angelica archangelica

Height: 60 to 72 inches
Spread: 36 inches
Description: This large, boldly attractive biennial has very lush growth, making it a striking focal point in the garden. It is similar in appearance to celery and parsnip plants. The flowers are white umbels followed by decorative yellow-green seedpods. Its flavor is licoricelike.
Ease of care: Easy
How to grow: Angelica likes a cool, moist location and average to well-drained soil. It will grow in sun or partial shade. Sow seeds in place or transplant them when still very small as they don't like to be moved. One plant is enough to supply the needs of an average family.
Propagation: By seed. Seeds must be no more than a few weeks old to be viable. Sow in late fall or early spring while the ground is still cool. Leave seeds on top of the soil; do not cover them.
Uses: Fresh leaves—soups, stews; Dried leaves—salads, soups, stews, potpourris; Fresh foliage—floral arrangements; Seeds—teas, baked goods; Stems—candy, pork, baked goods; Dried roots—teas, breads; Root oil—baths, lotions
Preservation: Harvest stems during second spring, leaves throughout summer season, roots in fall, and seeds when ripe. Stems can be candied or frozen. Hang-dry or freeze leaves, depending on planned use.

Anise

Annual

Pimpinella anisum

Height: 18 to 24 inches
Spread: 4 to 8 inches
Description: Feathery leaves and a lacy flower umbel are held on a tall and not very strong stem. These annuals look similar to dill and, like that plant, do best when grown closely together either in rows or clumps so that the multiple stems provide support for one another. The flavor is licoricelike.
Ease of care: Easy, but it will take at least 4 frost-free months to grow seeds to maturity. Therefore, in northern areas only the leaves can be obtained from home-grown plants.
How to grow: Plant in full sun and average, light dry soil. Either seed in place where they'll grow or transplant them when they are very small.
Propagation: By seed in early spring.
Uses: Fresh or frozen leaves—salads, cottage cheese, teas, jellies; Seeds—perfumes, soaps, breads, cookies, fish stocks, teas, soups, stews
Preservation: Harvest leaves during late summer for freezing. Harvest seeds when fully ripe, watching carefully to cut plants at ground level when first seeds ripen. Hang-dry the seed heads inside paper bags in a warm, dry place. Store them in tightly sealed containers.

Basil

Annual

Ocimum basilicum

Height: 18 inches
Spread: 10 inches
Description: Basil has a very neat, dense growing habit with attractive, glossy, bright-green, triangular leaves. All varieties of this good-looking annual make effective additions to any garden. They can also be clipped into a neat hedging, if desired. Flowers are not an important feature.
Ease of care: Easy
How to grow: Full sun and rich, moist soil are preferred. Sow seeds when soil is warm, or get a head start by starting them indoors and transplanting seedlings to the garden after danger of frost is past.
Propagation: By seed outdoors in late spring or indoors 8 weeks before the last frost.
Uses: Fresh, dried, and frozen leaves—vinegars, sauces, stews, salads, fish, shellfish, chicken, veal, lamb, tomatoes, potatoes; Dried leaves—potpourris, saches; Fresh branches—floral arrangements; Cosmetic uses—hair rinses, toilet waters, soaps
Preservation: The ideal harvest time, when flavor is at its peak, is when flower buds are about to blossom. Prunings can be used whenever they are taken. Hang-dry and store in airtight containers; better flavor is retained if frozen or stored in oil or vinegar.
Related varieties: Compact dwarf variety, 'Spicy Globe,' makes an outstanding edging or an attractive container plant. 'Purple Ruffles' and 'Dark Opal' are two dramatic, purple-leaved varieties. 'Green Ruffles' has a great lime-green color. Lemon basil has a distinct lemon flavor.

Chervil

Annual

Anthriscus cerefolium

Height: 18 inches
Spread: 4 to 8 inches
Description: Lacy, fernlike, dark green leaves have a coarser texture than carrot foliage, but finer than parsley. Chervil has a very delicate flavor of a licorice/parsley blend. Of the two forms available, the curly variety is more decorative in the garden than the flat variety.
Ease of care: Average to difficult.
How to grow: Chervil likes coolness and does well in partial shade. It likes a moist, well-drained, average or better soil. Do not try to move plants. For a fresh supply throughout the season, plant at 3-week intervals.
Propagation: By seed in the fall or very early spring.
Uses: Fresh or frozen leaves—eggs, salads, soups, fish, stews, veal, add during the last few minutes of cooking; Dried flowers—floral arrangements; Dried leaves—potpourris
Preservation: Pick chervil just before blooming. For culinary use, freeze leaves or store them in a small amount of oil. For potpourri, dry rapidly in an oven and store immediately.

Chives

Perennial

Allium schoenoprasum

Height: 8 to 12 inches
Spread: 8 inches
Description: Chives have very tight clumps of long, skinny, grasslike onion leaves. They produce an abundance of small, rosy purple, globe-shaped flowers in early summer. They can be used as edging plants, grown alone, or with other plants in containers. Chives have a mild onion flavor.
Ease of care: Easy
How to grow: This herb prefers an average to rich, moist soil, but will manage in almost any soil if kept moist. It grows in full sun to partial shade. It can also be grown as a pot plant indoors any time of the year for a source of fresh supply.
Propagation: By seed or division taken at any time during the growing season.
Uses: Fresh, dried, or frozen leaves—cream cheese spreads, cottage cheese, potatoes, salads, eggs, soups, poultry, fish, shellfish, veal. Add during the last few minutes of cooking; Fresh flowers—vinegars, salads, garnishes; Dried flowers—floral arrangements, wreaths
Preservation: Harvest only part of the plant at a time for continuous production through the season. Mince leaves and then freeze them for full flavor; dried leaves are less flavor-filled. Hang-dry the flowers for decorative uses. Pick them before any seeds begin to appear.

Coriander, Cilantro, Chinese Parsley

Annual

Coriandrum sativum

Height: 24 to 36 inches
Spread: 6 inches
Description: The bright green, lacy leaves look very similar to flat-leaved Italian parsley on the lower part of the plant, but become more finely fernlike further up. This large annual has a leaf and root flavor that is a cross between sage and citrus; the seeds, however, are simply citruslike.
Ease of care: Easy
How to grow: Plant in rich, well-drained soil in sun. Coriander plants are best located where they are protected from the wind, since they blow over easily.
Propagation: By seed once the soil is warm in spring.
Uses: Fresh or frozen leaves—potatoes, clams, oysters; Seeds—marinades, cheeses, pickles, mushrooms, stews, curries, chicken, quick breads, potpourris; Fresh roots—salads, relishes
Preservation: Harvest only fresh, young leaves and freeze them promptly. Harvest seeds when they have turned brown, but are not yet released. Cut a whole plant and hang-dry inside paper bags to catch seeds.

Costmary

Perennial

Chrysanthemum balsamita

Height: 30 to 36 inches
Spread: 24 inches
Description: Basal clusters of elongated oval leaves look similar to horseradish growth. This perennial sends up tall flower stems that produce clusters of unremarkable blooms. When the leaves are young and fresh, they're mint scented; the scent changes to balsam when the leaves are dried.
Ease of care: Easy
How to grow: Grow in fertile, well-drained soil, in full sun to partial shade. Divide every few years as the clump becomes too large.
Propagation: By division as needed.
Uses: Fresh leaves—tuna fish, shrimp, eggs, lemonade; Dried leaves—sachets, potpourris, baths, lotions
Preservation: Pick leaves when they are young and tender for immediate fresh use or a few at a time to dry. Costmary retains its scent for a long period when dried.

Dill

Annual

Anethum graveolens

Height: 24 to 36 inches
Spread: 6 inches
Description: Dill has extremely fine-cut, fern-like leaves on tall stems. It is a blue-green annual with attractive yellow flower umbels and yellow-green seed heads.
Ease of care: Easy
How to grow: Dill likes acid, light, moist, and sandy soil in full sun. Since it does not transplant well, sow it in place and thin. Grow it in clumps or rows so stems can give support to one another.
Propagation: By seed in late fall or early spring. Plant at 3-week intervals during spring and early summer for a fresh supply all season.
Uses: Fresh leaves—potatoes, tomatoes, vinegars, pickles, fish, shrimp, stews, cheeses, lamb, pork, poultry; Fresh and dried seed heads—floral arrangements; Seeds—pickles, cheeses
Preservation: Clip fresh leaves as needed. Flavor is best retained for winter use if frozen; pick the leaves just as flowers begin to open. For seeds, harvest entire plants when seed heads are brown but not yet releasing seeds. Hang-dry in paper bags to catch seeds.

Fennel

Perennial

Foeniculum vulgare

Height: 50 to 72 inches
Spread: 18 to 36 inches
Description: Fennel has very fine-cut leaves that look very similar to dill. This half-hardy perennial has a sweetish, licoricelike flavor. The flowers and seed heads are attractive and make appealing additions to floral arrangements.
Ease of care: Easy
How to grow: Fennel likes alkaline soil; add lime if soil is very acid. Grow in full sun in well-drained, rich soil. Locate them where plants are sheltered from heavy winds since they blow over easily.
Propagation: By seed in cold climates, where it will grow as an annual. Sow in late fall or early spring.
Uses: Fresh leaves—sauces, salads, eggs, fish, add during the last few moments of cooking; Dried leaves—cosmetic oils, soaps, facials; Seeds—desserts, cakes, breads, potatoes, spreads
Preservation: Snip individual leaves to use fresh or to freeze. Harvest whole plants just before blooming and hang-dry. To harvest seeds, cut down entire plants when seeds turn brown but before they release. Hang-dry in paper bags to catch the seeds.
Related varieties: Sweet fennel, *Foeniculum vulgare dulce,* is a closely related annual, the base stems of which are eaten as a vegetable in the same manner as celery.

Garlic Chives, Chinese Chives, Chinese Leeks

Perennial
Allium tuberosum

Height: 18 inches
Spread: 8 inches
Description: Garlic chives have compact, grasslike clumps of large, flattened, blue-green leaves that look like a larger version of chives. This perennial has attractive, white, globe-shaped blossoms that last a long time in floral arrangements. It has a definite garlic flavor.
Ease of care: Easy
How to grow: Plant seeds in full sun in average to poor soil.
Propagation: By seed in spring; by division anytime during the growing season.
Uses: Fresh leaves—salads, soups, spreads, vinegars; Dried leaves—soups, cheeses, sauces; Fresh and dried flowers—floral arrangements
Preservation: Harvest only part of the plant at a time for continuous production throughout the season. Mince leaves and then freeze them for full flavor; drying causes some flavor loss. Hang-dry flowers for decorative uses.

Geraniums, Scented

Half-Hardy Perennial
Pelargonium species

Height: Varies with variety
Spread: Varies with variety
Description: These aromatic-leaved perennials come in a variety of scents, including rose, orange, pepper, lemon, lime, mint, and apple. The leaf shapes are also varied, ranging from round to deeply cut, and their color ranges from yellow-green to reddish-purple according to the variety involved. Most make attractive potted plants and several have nice-looking flowers.
Ease of care: Average
How to grow: All prefer full sun and well-drained, rich to average soil. Geraniums overwinter as pot plants in cold climates.
Propagation: By cuttings before flowering.
Uses: Fresh leaves—cakes, cookies, jellies; Dried leaves—potpourris, sachets, baths, facials, teas; Fresh flowers—salads
Preservation: Pick single leaves just as plants begin to develop flower buds and dry them on screens.
Related varieties: Lemon geranium is *P. mellissinum,* lime is *P. nervosum,* apple is *P. odoratissimum,* and peppermint is *P. tomentosum.* These are probably the most common of the many special scented geranium varieties available; choose those you prefer from the selection offered by your local plant supplier.

Horehound

Perennial
Marrubium vulgare

Height: 30 inches
Spread: 12 inches
Description: Horehound has attractive, round, gray, mintlike foliage. The overall look of this perennial is that of a woolly gray bush. It makes an attractive addition to any garden. Flower arrangers will find it an outstanding decorative foliage for fresh or dried use.
Ease of care: Easy
How to grow: Grow in full sun in average to poor, well-drained soil.
Propagation: By seed or division in late spring
Uses: Fresh or dried leaves—candy flavorings, teas; Dried branches—floral arrangements
Preservation: Remove the leaves from the stems at the time of flowering and dry them on screens. Store in airtight containers. Hang-dry whole branches.

Marjoram

Perennial, often grown as Annual
Origanum majorana or
Majorana hortensis

Height: 8 to 12 inches
Spread: 12 to 18 inches
Description: Marjoram is a bushy, spreading, half-hardy perennial that is grown as an annual in climates where it freezes. It has small, oval, gray-green, velvety leaves. This plant is attractive when grown as a pot plant and brought indoors to overwinter.
Ease of care: Easy
How to grow: Marjoram likes rich, well-drained alkaline soil and full sun. Where winters are severe, treat it as an annual or as a pot plant. Locate it in a sheltered spot for best overwinter survival outdoors.
Propagation: By seed early indoors, transplanting seedlings outdoors after danger of frost has passed; by cuttings in spring.
Uses: Fresh or dried leaves—stuffings, soups, stews, meat loaf, pork, poultry, fish, eggs, potatoes, cheeses. Can be used in place of oregano; Dried leaves—baths, potpourris, sachets; Dried flowers—floral arrangements, wreaths
Preservation: Snip fresh when needed. For drying, harvest just before flowering and hang-dry.

Nasturtium

Annual
Tropaeolum majus

Height: 12 inches for bush, 72 inches for vines
Spread: 18 inches for bush
Description: Distinctive, blue-green circular leaves are held up on fleshy stems. These annuals come in a variety of types ranging from compact bushes to long-spreading vines. They make an eye-catching addition to any garden. In addition, they have large attractive blooms that range in color from palest yellows, pinks, and apricots to deep, rich yellows, oranges, and burgundy. The vining types are great in hanging planters, window boxes, or for use on trellises and fences. Aphids love nasturtiums, so be on the lookout for them.
Ease of care: Easy
How to grow: Plant in full sun to partial shade in average to poor, moist soil.
Propagation: By seed in late spring. They're large and can be planted individually where the plants are going to grow.
Uses: Fresh leaves and flowers—salads; Fresh flowers—floral arrangements; Unripe seeds and flower buds—pickled for salads
Preservation: Pickle unripe seeds in vinegar and use them in salads.

Oregano

Perennial
Origanum vulgare

Height: 18 inches
Spread: 12 inches
Description: Oregano is a bushy, spreading perennial with abundant oval leaves and purple blooms. Be careful to get the correct species. To be sure of avoiding disappointment, buy a plant that you've tested by crushing a few leaves and smelling or tasting them beforehand. It should have the distinct aroma of oregano.
Ease of care: Easy
How to grow: Grow in full sun, in average to sandy and preferably alkaline soil (add lime generously if soil is acid).
Propagation: Buy your first plant, then by division, layering, or cuttings to obtain additional ones.
Uses: Fresh or dried leaves—tomatoes, cheeses, eggs, beef, pork, poultry, shellfish, potatoes, sauces; Flowers—floral arrangements; Dried branches—baths
Preservation: Clip fresh as needed. Harvest at the time of bloom and hang-dry or freeze.

Parsley

Biennial grown as Annual
Petroselinum crispum

Height: 12 inches
Spread: 8 inches
Description: Attractive, rich, green, dense leaves form a rosette base. A biennial usually grown as an annual, parsley comes in two cut-leaf forms: ruffled and Italian. The latter has flat leaves and is stronger-flavored than the curly variety. The curly form makes a nice edging plant; both are also easily grown as indoor pot plants.
Ease of care: Easy
How to grow: Plant in place in full sun or partial shade in a moist, rich soil. Presoak seeds between several hours and overnight in warm water to help speed up germination.
Propagation: By seed once the soil is warm.
Uses: Fresh, dried, or frozen leaves—garnishes, potatoes, soups, sauces, pasta, poultry, jellies, baths, shampoos, lotions
Preservation: Snip as needed fresh. Hang-dry the flat variety; snip and freeze the curly variety.

Peppermint

Perennial
Mentha piperita

Height: 24 to 30 inches
Spread: 12 inches
Description: Peppermint has dark green, spear-shaped leaves that come to a point. It has a neat, dense growth habit with tall stems arising from an underground network of spreading stems. Since it can become invasive, plant it in an isolated location or where it can be kept contained. Another alternative is to grow it as a pot plant.
Ease of care: Easy
How to grow: Likes full sun or partial shade and rich, moist soil.
Propagation: By cuttings taken in mid-summer; by division at any time during the growing season.
Uses: Fresh or frozen leaves—garnishes, vinegars, jellies, punches, candy, lamb; Dried leaves—teas.
Preservation: Pick shoots in early to mid-summer. Hang-dry or freeze.
Related varieties: Pineapple mint, apple mint, and lemon mint each have flavors as indicated by their names. (Also refer to the profile on Spearmint.)

Rosemary

Perennial
Rosmarinus officinalis

Height: 48 to 72 inches
Spread: 18 to 24 inches
Description: Rosemary is an attractive, evergreen perennial with a spreading habit of growth. Its gray-green, needle-shaped foliage can be pruned to form a low hedge. Grow rosemary as a pot plant in colder climates, protecting it from winter winds. It makes an attractive addition to any garden. There is a prostrate form that makes a wonderful ground cover where hardy.
Ease of care: Average
How to grow: Likes a sandy, alkaline soil and full sun.
Propagation: By cuttings or by seed in spring, or by layering.
Uses: Fresh or frozen leaves—fish, lamb, potatoes, soups, tomatoes, pork, poultry, cheeses, eggs, breads, fruit salads, jellies; Dried leaves—facials, hair rinses, sachets, potpourris, lotions, toilet waters; Fresh and dried branches—baths
Preservation: Pick rosemary fresh as desired. Hang-dry or freeze the active young 3- to 4-inch growth tips.

Rue

Perennial
Ruta graveolens

Height: 24 inches
Spread: 18 inches
Description: This perennial has blue-green, teardrop-shaped foliage in clusters. Rue is an attractive and unusual plant to use as a focal point in a garden design.
Ease of care: Average
How to grow: Full sun in poor, sandy, alkaline soil. It can also be easily grown as a pot plant.
Propagation: By seed in spring or started ahead of time indoors and transplanted into the garden after the danger of frost has passed; by cuttings in mid-summer.
Uses: Fresh leaves—floral arrangements, tussy mussies; Dried seed heads—floral arrangements
Preservation: Pick just before flowers open and hang-dry. Collect seeds when flower heads ripen.
Related varieties: The variety 'Jackman's Blue' is compact and very blue-leaved. It can also be trimmed to form a lovely low hedge.

Sage

Perennial
Salvia officinalis

Height: 20 inches
Spread: 24 inches
Description: Sage is a perennial with gray-green, pebblelike, textured leaves in a long, oval shape. It has an attractive, compact, spreading growth habit. This plant is also available in variegated and purple-leaved varieties. Sage is a good edging plant and is attractive in any garden.
Ease of care: Easy
How to grow: Grow it in full sun in a well-drained sandy, alkaline soil. Protect it from the wind.
Propagation: By seed, cuttings, or division by layering in the spring.
Uses: Fresh, frozen, or dried leaves—salads, breads, soups, stews, pork, beef, fish, lamb, poultry, stuffings, tomatoes, vegetables, cheeses, teas; Dried branches—baths, lotions, herbal wreaths
Preservation: Use fresh sage as needed. Pick active growth shoots or separate leaves to hang-dry, screen dry, or freeze.
Related varieties: Sage is available in gold and green variegated (*S. officinalis* 'Aurea') and purple-leaved (*S. officinalis* 'Purpurea') varieties.

Savory, Summer

Annual
Satureja hortensis

Height: 18 inches
Spread: 8 inches
Description: This attractive annual has flattened, gray-green, needle-shaped leaves. The leaves are soft rather than stiff and have a slightly peppery flavor. The overall look of the plant is light and airy.
Ease of care: Easy
How to grow: Plant seeds in place in full sun in a light, rich to average soil. They do not transplant well. Summer savory grows well as a container plant with seeds planted directly in a pot.
Propagation: By seed when the soil is warm.
Uses: Fresh, dried, or frozen leaves—tomatoes, pastas, soups, stews, roasts, beans, salads, cheeses, fish, vinegars, vegetables
Preservation: When it begins to flower, dry it on screens or paper.

Sorrel, French

Perennial

Rumex acetosa **or** *R. scutatus*

Height: 18 inches
Spread: 10 inches
Description: Succulent, bright green, spear-shaped leaves in a low rosette send up tall flower stalks that should be removed so that leaf supply will continue. The leaves of this hardy perennial have a pleasant acidity that brightens any salad. Sorrel can also be grown as an indoor pot plant.
Ease of care: Easy
How to grow: Provide full sun or partial shade in a moist, rich acid soil. Shady conditions produce a milder taste.
Propagation: By seed or division in spring.
Uses: Fresh or frozen leaves—soups, lamb, beef, sauces
Preservation: Remove single leaves and use them fresh or freeze them for winter use.

Southernwood

Perennial

Artemisia abrotanum

Height: 30 inches
Spread: 24 inches
Description: Woolly, silver-gray, cut leaves and a dense, branching growth habit make these perennials a very decorative addition to any garden.
Ease of care: Easy
How to grow: Full sun in any kind of soil. Prune southernwood back each spring to encourage new growth and a nice shape.
Propagation: By semi-hardwood cuttings in late summer.
Uses: Fresh branches—floral arrangements, tussy mussies; Dried branches—baths, floral arrangements, wreaths
Preservation: Pick branches just before flowering and hang-dry.

Spearmint

Perennial

Mentha spicata **or** *M. viridis*

Height: 20 inches
Spread: 12 inches
Description: Green, pointed leaves are somewhat hairy compared to peppermint, but the best way to tell them apart is to crush the leaves and taste or smell them. Spearmint has a neat, dense growth with tall stems arising from a network of spreading underground stems. It can become invasive, so plant it in an isolated location or where it can be kept contained. A good solution is to grow it as a pot plant.
Ease of care: Easy
How to grow: Full sun or partial shade in rich, moist soil.
Propagation: By cuttings in mid-summer; by division at any time during the growing season.
Uses: Fresh or frozen leaves—candy, garnishes, jellies, punches, lamb; Dried leaves—teas.
Preservation: Pick shoots in early to mid-summer. Hang-dry or freeze.
Related varieties: Pineapple mint, apple mint and lemon mint each have distinctive flavors as indicated by their name. (Also refer to the profile on Peppermint.)

Sweet Woodruff

Perennial
Galium odoratum or *Asperula odorata*

Height: 6 to 8 inches
Spread: 6 to 8 inches
Description: Single, small, and knife-shaped leaves circle in tiers around the stemlike flattened wheel spokes. This perennial has a rich green color and spreads by means of underground stems to make a lovely ground cover when it has its preferred growing conditions of shade and rich, moist soil.
Ease of care: Difficult unless conditions are exactly to its liking.
How to grow: Grow in rich, moist soil in fairly deep, woodland shade.
Propagation: By seed in fall that will sprout in the spring; by division after flowering.
Uses: Fresh leaves—wine punches; Dried leaves—potpourris, sachets, wreaths
Preservation: Pick fresh sweet woodruff as needed. Cut entire stems when they are in bloom and hang-dry.

Tansy

Perennial
Tanacetum vulgare

Height: 40 inches
Spread: 12 to 18 inches
Description: This hardy perennial has lush, dark green, cut leaves and tall flower stems that produce tight clusters of intense yellow, button-shaped blooms. These are vigorous growers that spread rapidly and can take over; keep them constantly under control or place them where they can be allowed to run wild. The foliage has a strong peppery odor and flavor.
Ease of care: Easy
How to grow: Grow in full sun or partial shade in average to poor soil.
Propagation: By seed in spring; by division in spring or fall; or by layering.
Uses: Fresh or dried flowers—floral arrangements
Preservation: Harvest leaves singly and dry them on screens or harvest entire stems with flowers and hang-dry.

Tarragon

Perennial
Artemisia dracunculus

Height: 24 inches
Spread: 24 inches
Description: This bushy, medium green perennial has long, narrow, pointed leaves and inconspicuous flowers that rarely appear. Be sure to get the French rather than the Russian variety that looks very much the same with somewhat narrower and lighter green leaves. The latter has none of the sweetly aromatic flavor wanted for culinary use. Test it by crushing, smelling, and tasting a few leaves.
Ease of care: Average
How to grow: Likes full sun to partial shade in a sandy to rich alkaline soil that is well drained. It can also be grown successfully as a pot plant. Cut it back in the fall or early spring. Protect it with a mulch during the winter in cold climates.
Propagation: Buy first plant, then by cuttings in summer and fall; by division in early spring; or by layering.
Uses: Fresh, dried, or frozen leaves—fish, vinegars, tomatoes, salads, eggs, chicken, pickles, add during the last few minutes of cooking
Preservation: Pick separate leaves or 3- to 4-inch growth tips at any time for fresh use. Pick just before blooming to freeze or dry. Be careful because the delicate flavor is easily lost if dried too long. Store immediately in an airtight container. The flavor can also be captured in vinegar or oil.
Related varieties: Since it does not produce seeds, if tarragon seeds are offered, they will be those of Russian rather than French tarragon. Buy plants only.

Thyme

Perennial
Thymus vulgaris

Height: 1 to 10 inches depending on variety
Spread: 12 to 18 inches
Description: These tiny-leaved, wide-spreading perennials make a good and inexpensive ground cover. They can be clipped and mowed regularly, if desired. Their profuse blooms are especially attractive to bees; clip off flower heads just before blooming. The lowest-growing varieties are excellent to plant in flagstone walks.
Ease of care: Easy
How to grow: Thyme does well in full sun to partial shade in poor to average, well-drained soil. Trim it back each spring to encourage abundant new growth. It can also be grown as a pot plant.
Propagation: By seed or division in spring or fall; by cuttings in early summer; or by layering.
Uses: Fresh, frozen, or dried leaves—marinades, stuffings, soups, vinegars, poultry, shellfish, fish, cheeses; Dried leaves—sachets, potpourris, floral arrangements, baths, facials, wreaths; Dried flowers—sachets, lotions, baths
Preservation: Harvest anytime for fresh use. Pick before and during flowering to hang-dry.
Related varieties: There are many different thyme species and varieties with self-descriptive names: woolly thyme, silver thyme, lemon thyme, and golden thyme. The variations in their foliage colors, growth habits, and flower colors make them all good candidates for use in garden designs.

Wormwood

Perennial
Artemisia absinthium

Height: 30 to 48 inches
Spread: 15 to 20 inches
Description: A handsome, very fine cut-leaf, silver-green foliage and a spreading growth habit makes this an attractive perennial.
Ease of care: Average
How to grow: Plant in full sun in almost any kind of soil as long as it's alkaline. Add lime if soil is naturally acid.
Propagation: By seed or cuttings in summer; by division in spring or fall.
Uses: Fresh leaves—floral arrangements; Dried leaves—sachets, floral arrangements, wreaths
Preservation: Harvest when in flower and hang-dry.

Index

A

Aaron's rod (*Thermopsis caroliniana*), 280
Abelia, 374
Abelmoschus moschatus, 138
Abies concolor (White fir), 358
Abutilon hybridum (Flowering maple), 380
Acacia longifolia (Sydney golden wattle), 372
Acer
    A. ginnala (Amur maple), 364
    A. saccarum (Sugar maple), 364
Achillea (Yarrow), 295
Acorus Calamus 'Variegatus' (Variegated sweet flag), 468
Actinidia arguta (Bower actinidia), 392
Adiantum pedatum (American maidenhair fern), 462
Aegopodium podagaria 'Variegatum' (Variegated goutweed), 47
Aesculus x carnea 'Briotii' (Ruby horse chestnut), 361
Ageratum houstonianum (Floss flower), 156
Agropyron smithii (Western wheatgrass), 45
Agrostemma githago (Corn cockle), 151
Agrostis
    A. nebulosa (Cloud grass), 162–163
    A. stolonifera palustris (Creeping bentgrass), 43
Ajuga (Bugleweed), 46, 257
Akebia guinata (Five-leaved akebia), 392
Albizia Julibrissin (Silk tree), 369
Alcea rosea (Hollyhock), 164
Alchemilla (Lady's mantle), 276
Alder, common (*Alnus glutinosa*), 354
Allium, 37, 460
    A. ampeloprasum (Leek), 546
    A. cepa (Onion), 548
    A. cepa (Shallot), 553
    A. sativum (Garlic), 545
    A. schoenoprasum (Chives), 559
    A. tuberosum (Chinese chives; Garlic chives), 259
    A. tuberosum (Chinese chives; Garlic chives; Chinese leeks), 561
Almond, flowering (*Prunus triloba multiplex*), 374
Alnus glutinosa (Common alder), 354
Alpine currant (*Ribes alpinum*), 379
Alternanthera, 138
Alumroot (*Heuchera sanguinea*), 263
Amaranthus
    A. caudatus (Love lies bleeding), 165
    A. cruentus (Prince's feather), 165
    A. tricolor (Joseph's coat), 165
Amaryllis, hardy (*Lycoris radiata*), 458
Amelanchier arborea (Juneberry), 362
Amsonia tabernaemontana (Bluestar; Blue-dogbane; Blue-star-of-Texas), 256
Anagallis arvensis (Scarlet pimpernel; Poor-man's weather grass), 182

Anaphalis (Pearly everlasting), 267
Anchusa
    A. azurea (Italian bugloss), 257
    A. capensis (Summer forget-me-not; Cape forget-me-not), 158
Andromeda, Japanese (*Pieris japonica*), 374
Androsace sarmentosa (Rock jasmine), 456
Anemone, 250
Anethum graveolens (Dill), 560
Angelica archangelica (Angelica), 558
Angel's trumpet (*Datura metel*), 139
Anise (*Pimpinella anisum*), 558
Annual ryegrass (*Lolium multiflorum*), 45
Annuals, 52–189
    care and maintenance, 94–117
    colors, 60–62, 65–69
    container, 126–129
    for cutting, 130–131
    for drying, 132–135
    garden plans for, 120–125
    massing, 60–62
    planting, 76–85
    propagation, 86–88
    from seed, 77–81, 84–85, 89–91
    soil, 56–57, 74–75
Antennaria dioica (Pussytoes), 455
Anthracnose, 349, 526
Anthriscus cerefolium (Chervil), 559
Antirrhinum majus (Snapdragon), 183
Aphids, 39, 106, 349, 523
Apium
    A. graveolens dulce (Celery), 540
    A. graveolens rapaceum (Celeriac), 540
Apple, common (*Malus pumila*), 354
Aquilegia (Columbine), 262
Arabis
    A. caucasica (Rock cress), 287
    A. procurrens (Rock cress), 49
Arachis hypogaea (Peanut), 550
Arborvitae, American (*Thuja occidentalis*), 354
Arctotis stoechadifolia (African daisy), 153
Arisaema triphyllum (Jack-in-the-pulpit), 464
Aristolochia durior (Dutchman's-pipe), 394
Armeria maritima (Sea pink; Thrift), 294
Armoracia rusticana (Horseradish), 545
Aronia arbutifolia (Red chokeberry), 378
Arrowhead, old world (*Sagittaria sagittifolia*), 466
Artemisia
    A. abrotanum (Southernwood), 565
    A. absinthium (Wormwood), 295, 567
    A. dracunculus (Tarragon), 566
Artichoke
    globe (*Cynara Scolymus*), 536
    Jerusalem (*Helianthus tuberosus*), 536
Aruncus dioicus (Goat's beard; Wild spirea), 269

Asarum europaeum (European wild ginger), 463
Asclepias tuberosa (Milkweed; Butterfly weed), 258
Ash
    mountain (*Sorbus aucuparia*), 364
    white (*Fraxinus americana*), 355
Asparagus fern (*Asparagus densiflorus*), 139
Asparagus officinalis (Asparagus), 536
Aster
    China (*Callistephus chinensis*), 140
    golden (*Chrysopsis mariana*), 250
    Stoke's (*Stokesia laevis*), 251
Aster (Michaelmas daisy), 264–265
Astilbe (Garden spiraea), 251
Athyrium Goeringianum 'Pictum' (Japanese painted fern), 463
Aubrieta deltoidea (Rockcress), 287
Aurinia saxatilis (Basket-of-gold; Goldentuft; Madwort), 253
Avena sterilis (Wild oats), 162–163
Avens (*Geum*), 252
Azalea (*Rhododendron*), 389

B

Baby blue eyes (*Nemophila menziesii*), 140
Baby's breath (*Gypsophila elegans; G. paniculata; G. repens*), 140, 252
Bachelor's button (*Centaurea cyanus*), 141
Bahia grass (*Paspalum notatum*), 42
Balloon flower (*Platycodon grandiflorus*), 252
Bamboo (*Bambusa glaucescens*), 375
Bambusa glaucescens (Bamboo), 375
Banana shrub (*Michelia Figo*), 375
Baptisia australis (False indigo; Wild indigo), 273
Barberry, Japanese (*Berberis Thunbergii*), 375
Barrenwort (*Epimedium*), 255
Basil (*Ocimum basilicum*), 141, 558
Basket-of-gold (*Aurinia saxatilis*), 253
Bean
    lima (*Phaseolus limensis*), 537
    snap (*Phaseolus vulgarus*), 537
    wax (*Phaseolus vulgarus*), 537
Beard tongue (*Penstemon barbatus; P. heterophyllis*), 253
Bee-balm (*Monarda didyma*), 254
Beech, American (*Fagus grandifolia*), 355
Beefsteak plant (*Perilla frutescens*), 175
Beet (*Beta vulgaris*), 538
Beetles, 106, 350, 523
Begonia
    B. tuberhybrida (Tuberous begonia), 142–143
    B. semperflorens (Fibrous begonia; Wax begonia; Everblooming begonia), 142

Belamcanda chinensis (Leopard lily; Blackberry lily), 278
Bellflower (*Campanula; C. portenschlagiana*), 253–254, 451
Bellis perennis (English daisy), 154
Bells of Ireland (*Molucella laevis*), 143
Belvedere (*Kochia scoparia trichophylla*), 146
Berberis Thunbergii (Japanese barberry), 375
Bergamot (*Monarda didyma*), 254
Bergenia cordifolia (Heartleaf bergenia), 254
Bermudagrass (*Cynodon dactylon*), 42
Beta
    B. vulgaris; Cicla (Swiss chard), 541
    B. vulgaris (Beet), 538
Betula papyrifera (Paper birch), 355
Big blue lily turf (*Liriope Muscari*), 279
Bignonia capreolata (Cross vine), 394
Birch, paper (*Betula papyrifera*), 355
Bishop's hat (*Epimedium*), 255
Bittersweet, American (*Celastrus scandens*), 392
Black cohosh (*Cimicifuga racemosa*), 261
Black-eyed Susan (*Rudbeckia fulgida; R. laciniata*), 263
Black-eyed Susan vine (*Thunbergia alata*), 186
Black medic (*Medicago lupulina*), 35
Black walnut (*Juglans nigra*), 372
Blanket flower (*Gaillardia pulchella; G. x grandiflora*), 144, 255
Blazingstar (*Liatris*), 255
Bleeding heart (*Dicentra*), 256
Blight, 109, 350, 526
Blood leaf (*Iresine herbstii*), 144
Bloodroot (*Sanguinaria canadensis*), 462
Blue-dogbane (*Amsonia tabernaemontana*), 256
Blue lace flower (*Trachymene coerulea*), 145
Blue Marguerite (*Felicia amelloides*), 145
Bluestar (*Amsonia tabernaemontana*), 256
Blue-star-of-Texas (*Amsonia tabernaemontana*), 256
Boltonia asteroides (Boltonia), 256
Borers, 107, 350, 524
Bouncing bet (*Saponaria officinalis*), 29
Bower actinidia (*Actinidia arguta*), 392
Bowman's-root (*Porteranthus trifoliata*), 257
Boxwood, common (*Buxus sempervirens*), 376
Brachycome iberidifolia (Swan River daisy), 154
Brassica
    B. juncea (Mustard), 547
    B. napus (Rutabaga), 552
    B. oleracea (Broccoli; Brussels sprouts), 538
    B. oleracea (Cabbage), 539
    B. oleracea (Cauliflower), 540
    B. oleracea (Collards), 542
    B. oleracea (Kale), 545
    B. oleracea (Kohlrabi), 546
    B. oleracea (Ornamental cabbage), 174
    B. rapa; Pekinensis (Chinese cabbage), 541
    B. rapa (Turnip), 557
Bridal-wreath (*Spiraea x Vanhouttei*), 376

Briza
    B. maxima (Quaking grass), 162–163
    B. media (Quaking grass), 50
Broccoli (*Brassica oleracea; Botrytis*), 538
Broom
    creeping (*Genista pilosa* 'Vancouver Gold'), 451
    Genista tinctoria, 377
Browallia speciosa (Sapphire flower), 181
Brunnera macrophylla (Siberian bugloss), 258
Brussels sprouts (*Brassica oleracea; Gemmifera*), 538
Buchloe dactyloides (Buffalograss), 42
Buddleia alternifolia (Fountain butterfly bush), 377
Buffalograss (*Buchloe dactyloides*), 42
Bugleweed (*Ajuga*), 46, 257
Bugloss
    Italian (*Anchusa azurea*), 257
    Siberian (*Brunnera macrophylla*), 258
Bulbs, 418–425
Burning bush (*Dictamnus albus*), 268
Bush cinquefoil (*Potentilla fruticosa*), 378
Busy Lizzie (*Impatiens wallerana*), 164
Butterfly flower (*Schizanthus x wisetonensis*), 182
Butterfly weed (*Asclepias tuberosa*), 258
Buxus sempervirens (Common boxwood), 376

C

Cabbage
    Brassica oleracea; Capitata, 539
    Chinese (*Brassica Rapa; Pekinensis*), 541
    ornamental (*Brassica oleracea*), 174
Cabbage worms, 524
Cabomba caroliniana (Fanwort), 467
Caladium hortulanum, 146
Calamagrostis acutiflora stricta (Feather reed grass), 51
Calceolaria herbeofruticosa (Pocketbook plant), 176
Calendula officinalis (Field marigold; Pot marigold), 169
California blue bells (*Phacelia campanularia*), 145
Calla lily (*Zantesdeschia aethiopica*), 146
Calliopsis (*Coreopsis tinctoria*), 147
Callistemon citrinus (Crimson bottlebrush), 376
Callistephus chinensis (Aster; China aster), 140
Camellia japonica (Camellia), 378
Campanula
    Bellflower, 253–254
    C. medium (Canterbury bells), 148
    C. portenschlagiana (Dalmatian bellflower), 451
Campsis radicans (Trumpet creeper), 397
Candytuft, annual (*Iberis hybridus*), 147
Candytuft (*Iberis sempervirens*), 259
Canker, 350
Canna, 147
Cantaloupe (*Cucumis Melo*), 547
Canterbury bells (*Campanula medium*), 148
Capsicum (Pepper), 174, 550

Cardinal flower (*Lobelia Cardinalis*), 259
Cardoon (*Cynara cardunculus*), 539
Carnation (*Dianthus*), 285–286
Carolina jessamine (*Gelsemium sempervirens*), 396
Carolina silverbell (*Halesia carolina*), 369
Carpinus betulus (European hornbeam), 361
Carrot (*Daucus Carota sativis*), 539
Carya
    C. illinoinensis (Pecan), 366
    C. ovata (Shagbark hickory), 360
Castor bean (*Ricinus communis*), 148
Catananche caerulea (Cupid's dart), 264
Caterpillars, 107, 350
Catharanthus roseus (Vinca; Madagascar periwinkle), 188
Cathedral bells (*Cobaea scandens*), 151
Cattail, common (*Typha latifolia*), 466
Cauliflower (*Brassica oleracea; Botrytis*), 540
Ceanothus velutinus (Redroot), 000
Cedar
    deodar (*Cedrus deodara*), 356
    eastern red (*Juniperus virginiana*), 368
Cedrus deodara (Deodar cedar), 356
Celastrus scandens (American bittersweet), 392
Celeriac (*Apium graveolens rapaceum*), 540
Celery (*Apium graveolens dulce*), 540
Celosia cristata v. plumosa (Plumed cockscomb), 150
Celtis occidentalis (Common hackberry), 359
Centaurea
    C. cyanus (Bachelor's button; Cornflower), 141
    Knapweed, 275
Centipedegrass (*Eremochloa ophiuroides*), 43
Cerastium tomentosum (Snow-in-summer), 457
Chaenomeles speciosa (Flowering quince), 381
Chamaecyparis
    C. lawsoniana (Lawson cypress), 362
    C. pisifera nana (Dwarf false cypress), 452
Cheiranthus cheiri (English wallflower), 189
Cherry, Sargent (*Prunus sargentii*), 356
Cherry pie (*Heliotrope arborescens*), 163
Chervil (*Anthriscus cerefolium*), 559
Chestnut, ruby horse (*Aesculus x carnea* 'Briotii'), 361
Chickweed, common (*Stellaria media*), 35
Chicory (*Cichorium intybus*), 541
Chilean bell flower (*Nolana paradoxa*), 149
Chinch bugs, 37
Chionodoxa luciliae (Glory-of-the-snow), 459
Chives
    Allium schoenoprasum, 559
    Chinese (*Allium tuberosum*), 259, 561
    garlic (*Allium tuberosum*), 259, 561
Chrysanthemum, 149, 260
    C. balsamita (Costmary), 560
Chrysogonum virginianum (Goldenstar), 270
Chrysopsis mariana (Golden aster), 250
Cichorium
    C. endivia (Endive), 544
    C. intybus (Chicory), 541

Cilantro (*Coriandrum sativum*), 559
Cimicifuga racemosa (Black cohosh), 261
Cinquefoil (*Potentilla thurberi*), 261
Citrullus lanatus (Watermelon), 557
Citrus sinensis (Sweet orange), 366
Cladrastis Kentuckea (Yellowwood), 373
Clarkia amoena (Farewell-to-spring;
    Godetia), 162
Clematis
    C. recta (Clematis, bush; Clematis,
      upright), 261
    C. x Jackmanii (Jackman's clematis), 393
Cleome hasslerana (Cleome; Spider flower),
    150
Clock vine (*Thunbergia alata*), 186
Cloud grass (*Agrostis nebulosa*), 162–163
Cobaea scandens (Cup and saucer vine;
    Cathedral bells), 151
Coffee tree, Kentucky (*Gymnocladus dioica*),
    362
Coix Lacryma-Jobi (Job's tears), 162–163
Colchicum (Meadow saffron; Colchicum), 458
Coleus x hybridus, 150
Collards (*Brassica oleracea; Acephala*), 542
Color
    annuals, 60–62, 65–69
    perennials, 194–195, 200–203
Columbine (*Aquilegia*), 262
Compost, 100, 101, 490–491
Coneflower
    purple (*Echinacea purpurea*), 262
    yellow (*Rudbeckia fulgida*), 263
Consolida ambigua (Larkspur; Annual
    delphinium), 165
Container planting
    annuals, 126–129
    perennials, 246–247
Convallaria majalis (Lily-of-the-valley), 48
Coralbell (*Heuchera sanguinea*), 263
Coreopsis, 263
    C. tinctoria (Calliopsis; Tickseed), 147
Coriander (*Coriandrum sativum*), 559
Coriandrum sativum (Coriander; Cilantro;
    Chinese parsley), 559
Corn, ornamental (*Zea mays*), 173
Corn cockle (*Agrostemma githago*), 151
Cornflower (*Centaurea cyanus*), 141
Cornus
    C. florida (Flowering dogwood), 357
    C. sericea (Red-osier dogwood), 379
Corn (*Zea mays*), 542
Cortaderia selloana (Pampas grass), 50
Cosmos bipinnatus, 151
Costmary (*Chrysantheum balsamita*), 560
Cotinus coggygria (Smoke tree), 389
Cotoneaster apiculatus (Cranberry
    cotoneaster), 46
Crabgrass (*Digitaria*), 36
Crane's-bill (*Geranium*), 264
Crataegus Phaenopyrum (Washington
    hawthorn), 359
Creeping bentgrass (*Agrostis stolonifera
    palustris*), 43
Creeping buttercup (*Ranunculus repens*),
    258
Creeping fig (*Ficus pumila*), 393
Creeping gypsophile/baby's breath
    (*Gypsophila repens*), 452

Creeping juniper (*Juniperus horizontalis*),
    48
Creeping red fescue (*Festuca rubra rubra*),
    43
Crimson bottlebrush (*Callistemon citrinus*),
    376
Crimson glory vine (*Vitis Coignetiae*), 394
Crocus, 458
Cross vine (*Bignonia capreolata*), 394
Cucumber (*Cucumis sativus*), 543
Cucumis
    C. Melo (Muskmelon; Cantaloupe), 547
    C. pepo olifera (Yellow-flowered gourd),
      162
    C. sativus (Cucumber), 543
Cucurbita
    C. maxima (Winter squash), 555
    C. Pepo (Summer squash), 554–555
    Pumpkin, 551
Cup and saucer vine (*Cobaea scandens*),
    151
Cup flower (*Nierembergia hippomanica
    violacae*), 173
Cuphea ignea (Firecracker plant), 156
Cupid's dart (*Catananche caerulea*), 264
Cutting gardens, 130–131
Cutworms, 107, 524
Cynara
    C. cardunculus (Cardoon), 539
    C. Scolymus (Globe artichoke), 536
Cynodon dactylon (Bermudagrass), 42
Cynoglossum
    C. amabile (Chinese forget-me-not;
      Hound's tongue), 157
    C. nervosum (Chinese forget-me-not), 267
Cypress
    bald (*Taxodium distichum*), 357
    dwarf false (*Chamaecyparis pisifera
      nana*), 452
    Lawson (*Chamaecyparis lawsoniana*),
      362

D

Dahlia, 152
Daisy
    African (*Arctotis stoechadifolia;
      Dimorphotheca*), 153
    Barberton (*Gerbera jamesonii*), 155
    Cape (*Venidium fastuosum*), 188
    Dahlberg (*Dyssodia tenuiloba*), 153
    English (*Bellis perennis*), 154
    gloriosa (*Rudbeckia hirta*), 144
    Livingstone (*Dorotheanthus
      bellidiformis*), 154
    Michaelmas (*Aster*), 264–265
    Swan River (*Brachycome iberidifolia*), 154
    Transvaal (*Gerbera jamesonii*), 155
Dalmation Bellflower (*Campanula porten-
    schlagiana*), 451
Damping off, 109
Dandelion (*Taraxacum officinale*), 36, 543
Datura metel (Angel's trumpet; Trumpet
    flower; Horn of Plenty), 139
Daucus Carota sativis (Carrot), 539
Davidia involucrata (Dove tree), 357
Daylily (*Hemerocallis*), 265
Deadheading, 102, 103

Delphinium, annual (*Consolida ambigua*),
    165
Delphinium (Larkspur), 266
Devil in a bush (*Nigella damascena*), 167
Dianthus
    Carnation, 285–286
    D. chinensis (China pink), 149
Dicentra (Bleeding heart), 256
Dichondra micrantha (Dichondra), 46
Dictamnus albus (Burning bush; Gas plant),
    268
Diervilla sessilifolia (Southern bush
    honeysuckle), 377
Digitalis
    D. grandiflora (Yellow foxglove), 268
    D. purpurea (Foxglove), 158
Digitaria (Crabgrass), 36
Dill (*Anethum graveolens*), 560
Dimorphotheca (Cape marigold; African
    daisy; Star-of-the-Veldt), 169
Diospyros virginiana (Common persimmon),
    367
Diseases
    annuals, 109
    vegetable, 526–527
    woody plant, 349–351
Dogwood
    flowering (*Cornus florida*), 357
    red-osier (*Cornus sericea*), 379
Doronicum cordatum (Leopard's-bane), 277
Dorotheanthus bellidiformis (Livingstone
    daisy), 154
Dove tree (*Davidia involucrata*), 357
Draba sibirica (Siberian draba), 456
Dracaena marginata, 157
Drooping leucothoe (*Leucothoe Fonta-
    nesiana*), 385
Dusty miller (*Senecio cineraria*), 155
Dutchman's-pipe (*Aristolochia durior*), 394
Dwarf fothergilla (*Fothergilla Gardenii*), 381
Dyssodia tenuiloba (Dahlberg daisy; Golden
    fleece), 153

E

Echinacea purpurea (Purple coneflower),
    262
Echinops Ritro (Globe thistle), 294
Echium vulgare, 155
Edelweiss (*Leontoposium alpinum*), 266
Eelgrass (*Vallisneria americana*), 466
Eggplant (*Solanum Melongena*), 544
Elaegnus angustifolia (Russian olive), 368
Endive (*Cichorium Endivia*), 544
Epimedium (Bishop's hat; Barrenwort), 255
Eremochloa ophiuroides (Centipedegrass),
    43
Erica carnea (Spring heath), 457
Erigeron hybridus (Fleabane), 267
Eryngium (Sea holly), 271
Escholtzia californica (California poppy), 176
Estoma grandiflorum (Lisianthus; Prairie
    gentian), 166
Euonymus
    E. alata (Winged euonymus), 380
    E. fortunei (Wintercreeper), 465
Eupatorium coelestinum (Hardy ageratum;
    Mist flower), 250

Euphorbia
    E. epithymoides (Cushion spurge), 292
    E. marginata (Snow-in-summer; Ghost weed), 183
Everlasting, pearly (*Anaphalis*), 267
Exacum affine (Persian violet), 189

F

Fagus grandifolia (American beech), 355
False dragonhead (*Physostegia virginiana*), 282
Fanwort (*Cabomba caroliniana*), 467
Farewell-to-spring (*Clarkia amoena*), 162
Fatshedera lizei (Tree ivy), 464
Feather reed grass (*Calamagrostis acutiflora stricta*), 51
Felicia amelloides (Blue Marguerite), 145
Fennel (*Foeniculum vulgare*), 560
Fern
    American maidenhair (*Adiantum pedatum*), 462
    Japanese painted (*Athyrium Goeringianum* 'Pictum'), 463
Fertilizing, 100–101, 220–221, 333–334, 488–489
Festuca
    F. arundinacea (Tall fescue), 44
    F. rubra rubra (Creeping red fescue), 43
Ficus pumila (Creeping fig), 393
Filipendula rubra (Queen-of-the-prairie; Meadowsweet), 281
Fir
    Douglas (*Pseudotsuga Menziesii*), 358
    white (*Abies concolor*), 358
Fireblight, 350
Firecracker plant (*Cuphea ignea*), 156
Fleabane (*Erigeron hybridus*), 267
Floating-heart (*Nymphoides peltata*), 467
Floss flower (*Ageratum houstonianum*), 156
Flowering tobacco (*Nicotiana alata grandiflora*), 172
Foamflower, Allegheny (*Tiarella cordifolia*), 463
Foeniculum vulgare (Fennel), 560
Forget-me-not
    alpine (*Myosotis alpestris*), 452
    cape (*Anchusa capensis*), 158
    Chinese (*Cynoglossum amabile; C. nervosum*), 157
    Myosotis sylvatica, 157
    summer (*Anchusa capensis*), 158
Forsythia ovata (Early forsythia), 381
Fothergilla Gardenii (Dwarf fothergilla), 381
Fountain butterfly bush (*Buddleia alternifolia*), 377
Fountain grass (*Pennisetum alopecuroides*), 50
Four o'clock (*Mirabilit jalapa*), 158
Foxglove
    Digitalis purpurea, 158
    yellow (*Digitalis grandiflora*), 268
Fraxinus americana (White ash), 355
Freckle face (*Hypoestes phyllostachya*), 157
Fried eggs (*Limnanthes douglasii*), 170
Frost, 112–113

Frostweed (*Helianthemum nummularium*), 288
Fungal blight, 350
Fuchsia (Lady's ear drops), 159

G

Gaillardia
    G. pulchella (Blanket flower), 144
    G. x grandiflora (Blanket flower), 255
Galanthus nivalis (Snowdrop), 461
Galium odoratum (Sweet woodruff), 566
Gardenia jasminoides (Gardenia), 382
Garden plans
    annuals, 120–125
    perennials, 238–245
    woody plants, 306–307
Gardens
    annual, 52–189
    bulb, 418–425
    herb, 528–533, 558–567
    perennial, 190–295
    rock, 410–417
    rose, 400–409
    shade, 426–431
    specialty, 398–469
    vegetable, 470–527, 534–557
    water, 432–445
Garden spiraea (*Astilbe*), 251
Garlic (*Allium; A. sativum*), 37
Gas plant (*Dictamnus albus*), 268
Gaura, 268
Gayfeather (*Liatris*), 255
Gazania ringens (Treasure flower), 159
Gelsemium sempervirens (Carolina jessamine), 396
Genista
    G. pilosa 'Vancouver Gold' (Creeping broom), 451
    G. tinctoria (Broom), 377
Geranium
    ivy-leaf (*Pelargonium peltatum*), 160
    Martha Washington (*Pelargonium domesticum*), 160
    regal (*Pelargonium domesticum*), 160
    scented (*Pelargonium*), 561
    zonal (*Pelargonium x hortorum*), 161
Geranium (Crane's-bill), 264
Gerbera jamesonii (Barberton daisy; Transvaal daisy), 155
Geum (Avens), 252
Ghost weed (*Euphorbia marginata*), 183
Ginkgo biloba (Maidenhair tree), 363
Gladiolus hybridus, 161
Glaucium flavum (Horned poppy; Sea poppy), 177
Glechoma hederacea (Ground ivy), 36
Gleditsia triancanthos inermis (Honey locust), 361
Globe amaranth (*Gomphrena globosa*), 139
Globeflower (*Trollius x cultorum*), 269
Glory-of-the-snow (*Chionodoxa luciliae*), 459
Goat's beard (*Aruncus dioicus*), 269
Godetia (*Clarkia amoena*), 162
Golden ageratum (*Lonas inodora*), 153
Golden-chain tree (*Laburnum x Watereri*), 358
Golden fleece (*Dyssodia tenuiloba*), 153

Golden-rain tree (*Koelreuteria paniculata*), 359
Goldenrod (*Solidago*), 269
Goldenstar (*Chrysogonum virginianum*), 270
Golden top (*Lamarkia aurea*), 162–163
Goldentuft (*Aurinia saxatilis*), 253
Gomphrena globosa (Globe amaranth), 139
Gourd
    dishrag (*Luffa aegyptiaca*), 162
    white-flowered (*Lagenaria siceraris*), 162
    yellow-flowered (*Cucumis pepo olifera*), 162
Goutweed, variegated (*Aegopodium podagaria* 'Variegatum'), 47
Gramineae (Ornamental grasses), 30, 31, 270–271
Grasses, 41–45
    ornamental, 50–51
    ornamental (*Gramineae*), 30, 31, 270–271
Ground cover, 35, 37, 39, 46–49
Grubs, 38, 524
Guava, purple (*Psidium littorale longipes*), 382
Gum
    sour (*Nyssa sylvatica*), 370
    sweet (*Liquidambar Styraciflua*), 371
Gymnocladus dioica (Kentucky coffee tree), 362
Gypsophila
    G. elegans (Baby's breath), 140
    G. paniculata (Baby's breath), 252
    G. repens (Creeping baby's breath; Creeping gypsophile), 452

H

Hackberry, common (*Celtis occidentalis*), 359
Halesia carolina (Carolina silverbell), 369
Hamamelis virginiana (Common witch hazel), 391
Hardy ageratum (*Eupatorium coelestinum*), 250
Hawthorn
    Indian (*Raphiolepis indica*), 382
    Washington (*Crataegus Phaenopyrum*), 359
Heartleaf bergenia (*Bergenia cordifolia*), 254
Hedera helix (English ivy), 47, 395
Helenium autumnale (Sneezeweed; Swamp sunflower), 290
Helianthemum nummularium (Rock rose; Sun rose; Frostweed), 288
Helianthus
    H. annuus (Sunflower), 185
    H. tuberosus (Jerusalem artichoke), 536
    H. x multiflorus (Perennial sunflower), 294
Helichrysum bracteatum (Everlasting), 156
Heliopsis helianthoides (False sunflower; Ox-eye), 282
Heliotrope arborescens (Cherry pie), 163
Helleborus (Christmas rose; Lenten rose; Hellebore), 288
Hemerocallis (Daylily), 265
Hemlock, eastern (*Tsuga canadensis*), 360
Hens-and-chicks (*Sempervivum tectorum*), 453

Herbs, 528–533, 558–567
Heuchera sanguinea (Coralbell; Alumroot), 263
Hibiscus
    H. esculentus (Okra), 548
    H. moscheutos (Swamp mallow; Rose mallow), 281
    H. rosa-sinensis (Rose of China; Chinese hibiscus), 163
Hickory, shagbark (*Carya ovata*), 360
Himalaya fleece flower (*Polygonum affine*), 275
Holly
    American (*Ilex opaca*), 360
    Michigan (*Ilex verticillata*), 383
Hollyhock (*Alcea rosea*), 164
Honesty (*Lunaria annua*), 156
Honeysuckle
    southern bush (*Diervilla sessilifolia*), 377
    trumpet (*Lonicera sempervirens*), 395
    winter (*Lonicera fragantissima*), 383
Horehound (*Marrubium vulgare*), 561
Hornbeam, European (*Carpinus betulus*), 361
Horn of Plenty (*Datura metel*), 139
Horseradish (*Armoracia rusticana*), 545
Hosta (Plantain lily), 272
Hound's tongue (*Cynoglossum amabile*), 157
Houttuynia, 273
Hunnemannia fumariaefolia (Mexican tulip poppy), 178
Hyacinthus orientalis (Hyacinth), 459
Hydrangea
    H. paniculata 'Grandiflora' (Peegee hydrangea), 384
    H. quercifolia (Oakleaf hydrangea), 383
Hypoestes phyllostachya (Polka dot plant; Freckle face), 157

I

Iberis
    I. hybridus (Annual candytuft), 147
    I. sempervirens (Candytuft), 259
Ilex
    I. glabra (Inkberry), 384
    I. opaca (American holly), 360
    I. verticillata (Michigan holly), 383
Impatiens wallerana (Busy Lizzie; Patience), 164
Indigo
    false (*Baptisia australis*), 273
    wild (*Baptisia australis*), 273
Inkberry (*Ilex glabra*), 384
Inula, 274
Ipomoea
    I. alba (Moon flower), 171
    I. batatas (Sweet potato), 551
    Morning glory vine, 171
Iresine herbstii (Blood leaf), 144
Iris, 274–275
    I. pseudacorus (Yellow flag), 469
    I. reticulata (Violet-scented iris), 459
Irish moss (*Sagina subulata*), 453
Ivy
    Boston (*Parthenocissus tricuspidata*), 393
    English (*Hedera helix*), 47, 395
    ground (*Glechoma hederacea*), 36
    tree (*Fatshedera lizei*), 464

J

Jacaranda acutifolia (Jacaranda), 384
Jack-in-the-pulpit (*Arisaema triphyllum*), 464
Japanese lawngrass (*Zoysia japonica*), 44
Jasmine
    rock (*Androsace sarmentosa*), 456
    yellow (*Jasminum nudiflorum*), 395
Jasminum nudiflorum (Yellow jasmine), 395
Job's tears (*Coix Lacryma-Jobi*), 162–163
Joseph's coat (*Amaranthus tricolor*), 165
Juglans nigra (Black walnut), 372
Juneberry (*Amelanchier arborea*), 362
Juniperus
    J. horizontalis (Creeping juniper), 48
    J. virginiana (Eastern red cedar), 368

K

Kale (*Brassica oleracea; Acephala*), 545
Kalmia latifolia (Mountain laurel), 385
Kentucky bluegrass (*Poa pratensis*), 44
Knapweed (*Centaurea*), 275
Knotweed (*Polygonum affine; P. aviculare*), 275
Kochia scoparia trichophylla (Burning bush; Summer cypress; Belvedere), 146
Koelreuteria paniculata (Golden-rain tree), 359
Kohlrabi (*Brassica eleracea; Gongylodes*), 546

L

Laburnum x Watereri (Golden-chain tree), 358
Lace bugs, 39
Lactuca sativa, 546–547
Lady's ear drops (*Fuchsia*), 159
Lady's mantle (*Alchemilla*), 276
Lagenaria siceraris (White-flowered gourd), 162
Lagerstroemia indica (Crape myrtle), 356
Lamarkia aurea (Golden top), 162–163
Lamb's-ears (*Stachys byzantina*), 276
Lamb's-tongue (*Stachys byzantina*), 276
Lamiastrum galeobdolon (Golden dead nettle), 462
Lamium maculatum (Dead nettle), 282
Lampranthus spectabilis (Trailing ice plant), 47
Lantana, 165
Larix laricina (Tamarack), 371
Larkspur (*Consolida ambigua; Delphinium*), 165
Lathyrus
    L. latifolius (Sweet pea; Perennial pea), 283
    L. odoratus (Sweet pea), 185
Lavandula angustifolia (Lavender), 276–277
Lavatera trimestris (Rose mallow), 179
Lavender (*Lavandula angustifolia*), 276–277
Lawns, 25–29, 35–37
Layia platyglossa (Tidy tips), 186
Leaf-feeding beetles, 350
Leaf hoppers, 107, 524
Leaf miners, 107, 351, 525

Leaf spot, 109
Leek
    Allium ampeloprasum, 546
    Chinese (*Allium tuberosum*), 561
Leontoposium alpinum (Edelweiss), 266
Leopard's-bane (*Doronicum cordatum*), 277
Lettuce (*Lactuca sativa*), 546–547
Leucothoe Fontanesiana (Drooping leucothoe), 385
Lewisia, 454
Liatris (Blazingstar; Gayfeather), 255
Ligularia, 278
Ligustrum ovalifolium (California privet), 388
Lilac, common (*Syringa vulgaris*), 385
Lilium (Lily), 460
Lily
    blackberry (*Belamcanda chinensis*), 278
    leopard (*Belamcanda chinensis*), 278
    Lilium, 460
    toad (*Tricyrtis hirta*), 278
Lily-of-the-valley (*Convallaria majalis*), 48
Limnanthes douglasii (Fried eggs; Meadow foam), 170
Limonium latifolium (Sea lavender), 277
Linaria maroccana (Toadflax), 187
Linden, American (*Tilia americana*), 363
Linum grandiflorum (Scarlet flax), 181
Liquidambar Styraciflua (Sweet gum), 371
Liriodendron Tulipifera (Tulip tree), 372
Liriope Muscari (Big blue lily turf), 279
Lisianthus (*Estoma grandiflorum*), 166
Lobelia, 166
    L. Cardinalis (Cardinal flower), 259
Lobularia maritima (Sweet alyssum), 138
Locust, honey (*Gleditsia triancanthos inermis*), 361
Lonas inodora (African daisy; Golden ageratum), 153
Lonicera
    L. fragantissima (Winter honeysuckle), 383
    L. sempervirens (Trumpet honeysuckle), 395
Loosestrife
    gooseneck (*Lysimachia clethroides*), 279
    purple (*Lythrum Salicaria*), 279
Lotus
    L. berthelotti (Parrot's beak; Lotus vine), 166
    Nelumbo nucifera, 467
Lotus vine (*Lotus berthelotti*), 166
Love-in-a-mist (*Nigella damascena*), 167
Love lies bleeding (*Amaranthus caudatus*), 165
Luffa aegyptiaca (Dishrag gourd), 162
Lunaria annua (Honesty; Silver dollar plant), 156
Lungwort (*Pulmonaria officinalis*), 280
Lupine
    Carolina (*Thermopsis caroliniana*), 280
    Lupinus, 167
    Lupinus polyphyllus, 280
Lycopersicon lycopersicum (Tomato), 556
Lycoris radiata (Hardy amaryllis), 458
Lysimachia clethroides (Gooseneck loosestrife), 279
Lythrum Salicaria (Purple loosestrife), 279

M

Macleaya cordata (Plume poppy), 286
Madwort (*Aurinia saxatilis*), 253
Magic carpet plant (*Polygonum capitatum*), 168
Magnolia grandiflora (Southern magnolia), 363
Mahonia Aquifolium (Oregon grape), 387
Maidenhair tree (*Ginkgo biloba*), 363
Mallow
   cheese (*Malva sylvestris*), 168
   Malva Alcea, 281
   rose (*Hibiscus Moscheutos*), 179, 281
   swamp (*Hibiscus Moscheutos*), 281
Malus
   M. pumila (Common apple), 354
   M. Sargentii (Sargent crabapple), 379
Malva
   M. alcea (Mallow), 281
   M. sylvestris (Cheese mallow), 168
Maple
   amur (*Acer ginnala*), 364
   flowering (*Abutilon hybridum*), 168, 380
   sugar (*Acer saccarum*), 364
Marigold
   American (*Tagetes erecta*), 169
   Cape (*Dimorphotheca*), 169
   field (*Calendula officinalis*), 169
   French (*Tagetes patula*), 169
   pot (*Calendula officinalis*), 169
Marjoram (*Origanum majorana*), 562
Marrubium vulgare (Horehound), 561
Marvel of Peru (*Mirabilit jalapa*), 158
Matricaria recutita (Sweet false chamomile), 148
Matthiola incana (Stock), 184
Meadow foam (*Limnanthes douglasii*), 170
Meadow saffron (*Colchicum*), 458
Meadowsweet (*Filipendula rubra*), 281
Mealybugs, 107
Medicago lupulina (Black medic), 35
Melampodium, 170
Mentha
   M. piperita (Peppermint), 563
   M. spicata (Spearmint), 564
Mesembryanthemum criniflorum (Livingstone daisy), 154
Michelia Figo (Banana shrub), 375
Mignonette (*Reseda odorata*), 170
Mildew, 527
   downy, 37
   powdery, 39, 109, 351
Milkweed (*Asclepias tuberosa*), 258
Mimulus hybridus (Monkey flower), 171
Mirabilit jalapa (Four o'clock; Marvel of Peru), 158
Miscanthus sinensis 'Zebrinus' (Zebra grass), 51
Mist flower (*Eupatorium coelestinum*), 250
Moles, 38
Molucca balm (*Molucella laevis*), 143
Molucella laevis (Bells of Ireland; Shell flower; Molucca balm), 143
Monarch of the Veldt (*Venidium fastuosum*), 188
Monarda didyma (Bergamot; Bee-balm; Oswego-tea), 254

Monkey flower (*Mimulus hybridus*), 171
Moon flower (*Ipomoea alba*), 171
Morning glory vine (*Ipomoea*), 171
Morus alba 'Striblingii' (Fruitless mulberry), 365
Moses-in-a-boat (*Rhoeo spathacea*), 157
Moses-in-a-cradle (*Rhoeo spathacea*), 157
Moss campion (*Silene acaulis*), 454
Moss rose (*Portulaca grandiflora*), 178
Mountain laurel (*Kalmia latifolia*), 385
Mourning bride (*Scabiosa atropurpurea*), 181
Mulberry, fruitless (*Morus alba* 'Striblingii'), 365
Mulching, 97, 98, 99, 333–334, 511–513
Muskmelon (*Cucumis Melo*), 547
Mustard (*Brassica juncea*), 547
Myosotis
   M. alpestris (Alpine forget-me-not), 452
   M. sylvatica (Forget-me-not), 157
Myrtle
   crape (*Lagerstroemia indica*), 356
   dwarf (*Myrtus communis*), 386
   Vinca minor, 284
Myrtus communis (Dwarf myrtle), 386

N

Narcissus, 460
Nasturtium officinale (Watercress), 557
Nasturtium (*Tropaeolum majus*), 172, 562
Nelumbo nucifera (Lotus), 467
Nemesia, 172
Nemophila menziesii (Baby blue eyes), 140
Nerium Oleander (Oleander), 386
Nettle
   dead (*Lamium maculatum*), 282
   golden dead (*Lamiastrum Galeobdolon*), 462
Nicotiana alata grandiflora (Flowering tobacco), 172
Nigella damascena (Love-in-a-mist; Devil in a bush), 167
Nolana paradoxa (Chilean bell flower), 149
None so pretty (*Silene armeria*), 173
Nymphaea (Water lily), 469
Nymphoides peltata (Floating-heart), 467
Nyssa sylvatica (Sour gum), 370

O

Oak
   white (*Quercus alba*), 365
   willow (*Quercus phellos*), 365
Obedient plant (*Physostegia virginiana*), 282
Ocimum basilicum (Basil), 141, 558
Oenothera
   Evening primrose, 293
   O. biennis (Sundrop), 185
Okra (*Hibiscus esculentus*), 548
Oleander (*Nerium Oleander*), 386
Olive
   Russian (*Elaegnus angustifolia*), 368
   sweet (*Osmanthus fragrans*), 390
Onion
   Allium cepa, 548
   flowering (*Allium*), 460
   wild (*Allium*), 37

Onopordum acathium (Scotch thistle), 183
Orange, sweet (*Citrus sinensis*), 366
Oregano (*Origanum vulgare*), 562
Oregon grape (*Mahonia Aquifolium*), 387
Ornamental grasses (*Gramineae*), 30, 31, 270–271
Origanum
   O. majorana (Marjoram), 562
   O. vulgare (Oregano), 562
Osmanthus fragrans (Sweet olive), 390
Oswego-tea (*Monarda didyma*), 254
Oxalis, 36
Ox-eye (*Heliopsis helianthoides*), 282
Oxydendrum arboreum (Sourwood), 370
Oxypetalum caeruleum (Star of the Argentine; Southern star), 184
Oyster plant (*Tragopogon porrifolius*), 553

P

Pachysandra terminalis (Japanese spurge), 49, 283
Paeonia (Peony), 283–284
Painted tongue (*Salpiglossis sinuata*), 179
Pampas grass (*Cortaderia selloana*), 50
Pansy (*Viola x wittrockiana*), 174
Papaver
   P. nudicaule (Iceland poppy), 177, 453
   P. orientale (Poppy), 286
Parrot's beak (*Lotus berthelotti*), 166
Parsley
   Chinese (*Coriandrum sativum*), 559
   Petroselinum crispum, 563
Parsnip (*Pastinaca sativa*), 549
Parthenocissus tricuspidata (Boston ivy), 393
Paspalum notatum (Bahia grass), 42
Pasqueflower (*Pulsatilla vulgaris*), 454
Passiflora caerulea (Blue passionflower), 396
Passionflower, blue (*Passiflora caerulea*), 396
Pastinaca sativa (Parsnip), 549
Patience (*Impatiens wallerana*), 164
Pea
   California black-eye (*Vigna unguiculata*), 549
   green (*Pisum sativum*), 549
   perennial (*Lathyrus latifolius*), 283
Peanut (*Arachis hypogaea*), 550
Pear, Bradford (*Pyrus Calleryana*), 366
Pecan (*Carya illinoinensis*), 366
Pelargonium
   Geranium, scented, 561
   P. domesticum (Martha Washington geranium; Regal geranium), 160
   P. x hortorum (Zonal geranium), 161
Pennisetum alopecuroides (Fountain grass), 50
Penstemon
   P. barbatus (Beard tongue), 253
   P. heterophyllis (Beard tongue), 141
Peony (*Paeonia*), 283–284
Pepper (*Capsicum*), 174, 550
Peppermint (*Mentha piperita*), 563
Perennials, 190–295
   bloom dates, 204–207
   buying, 215–216
   care of, 217–221

Perennials (*continued*)
  colors, 194–195, 200–203
  container, 246–247
  from cuttings, 227–232
  dividing, 233–235
  garden plans, 238–245
  from seed, 222–226
  transplanting, 210–212
Perilla frutescens (Beefsteak plant), 175
Periwinkle
  Madagascar (*Catharanthus roseus*), 188
  Vinca minor, 48, 284
Perovskia (Russian sage), 289
Persimmon, common (*Diospyros virginiana*), 367
Pests
  annuals, 106–108
  ground cover, 39
  turf, 37–38
  vegetable, 520–527
  woody plant, 349–351
Petroselinum crispum (Parsley), 563
Petunia x hybrida (Petunia), 175
Phacelia campanularia (California blue bells), 145
Phalaris arundinaceae picta (Ribbon grass), 51
Phaseolus
  P. coccineus (Scarlet runner bean), 182
  P. limensis (Lima bean), 537
  P. vulgarus (Snap bean; Wax bean), 537
Philadelphus coronarius (Sweet mock orange), 386
Phlox
  P. drummondii (Annual phlox; Texas pride), 176
  P. paniculata (Garden phlox), 284–285
  P. subulata (Moss pink), 49, 455
Physalis ixocarpa (Tomatillo), 556
Physostegia virginiana (Obedient plant; False dragonhead), 282
Picea abies
  Norway spruce, 370
  P. 'Nidiformis' (Bird's nest spruce), 451
Pickerel rush (*Pontederia cordata*), 468
Pieris japonica (Japanese andromeda), 374
Pimpinella anisum (Anise), 558
Pinching back, 102, 103
Pincushion flower (*Scabiosa atropurpurea; S. caucasica*), 181, 285
Pine
  eastern white (*Pinus strobus*), 367
  southern yellow (*Pinus palustris*), 367
  western yellow (*Pinus ponderosa*), 368
Pink
  China (*Dianthus chinensis*), 149
  Dianthus, 285–286
  moss (*Phlox subulata*), 49, 455
  sea (*Armeria maritima*), 294
Pinus
  P. palustris (Southern yellow pine), 367
  P. ponderosa (Western yellow pine), 368
  P. strobus (Eastern white pine), 367
Pisum sativum (Green pea), 549
Pittosporum Tobira (Pittosporum), 387
Plantago (Plantain), 37
Plantain lily (*Hosta*), 272
Plantain (*Plantago*), 37

Platanus occidentalis (Sycamore), 371
Platycodon grandiflorus (Balloon flower), 252
Plum, American (*Prunus americana*), 387
Plumed cockscomb (*Celosia cristata v. plumosa*), 150
Poa pratensis (Kentucky bluegrass), 44
Pocketbook plant (*Calceolaria herbeofruticosa*), 176
Podocarpus macrophyllus (Japanese podocarpus), 388
Polianthes tuberosa (Tuberose), 187
Polka dot plant (*Hypoestes phyllostachya*), 157
Polygonatum 'Thunbergii' (Solomon's seal), 464
Polygonum
  P. affine (Knotweed; Himalayan fleece flower), 275
  P. aubertii (Silver-lace vine), 396
  P. aviculare (Knotweed), 36
  P. capitatum (Magic carpet plant), 168
Pontederia cordata (Pickerel rush), 468
Poor man's orchid (*Schizanthus x wisetonensis*), 182
Poor-man's weather glass (*Anagallis arvensis*), 182
Poppy
  California (*Escholtzia californica*), 176
  horned (*Glaucium flavum*), 177
  Iceland (*Papaver nudicaule*), 177, 453
  Mexican tulip (*Hunnemannia fumariaefolia*), 178
  Papaver orientale, 286
  plume (*Macleaya cordata*), 286
  sea (*Glaucium flavum*), 177
Porteranthus trifoliata (Bowman's-root), 257
Portulaca
  P. grandiflora (Moss rose; Portulace), 178
  P. oleracea (Purslane), 36
Potato
  Irish (*Solanum tuberosum*), 551
  sweet (*Ipomoea Batatas*), 551
Potentilla
  P. fruticosa (Bush cinquefoil), 378
  P. thurberi (Cinquefoil), 261
Prairie gentian (*Estoma grandiflorum*), 166
Primrose
  evening (*Oenothera*), 293
  Japanese (*Primula Sieboldii*), 287
  polyanthus (*Primula x polyantha*), 455
  Primula, 178, 179
Primula
  P. Sieboldii (Japanese primrose), 287
  P. x polyantha (Polyanthus primrose), 455
  Primrose, 178, 179
Prince's feather (*Amaranthus cruentus*), 165
Privet, California (*Ligustrum ovalifolium*), 388
Propagation
  annuals, 86–88
  cuttings, 86–88, 111, 227–232
  seeds, 77–81, 84–85, 89–91, 111, 222–226
Prunella Webbiana (Self-heal), 290
Pruning, 337–341

Prunus
  P. americana (American plum), 387
  P. sargentii (Sargent cherry), 356
  P. triloba multiplex (Flowering almond), 374
Pseudotsuga Menziesii (Douglas fir), 358
Psidium littorale longipes (Purple guava), 382
Pulmonaria officinalis (Lungwort; Jerusalem sage), 280
Pulsatilla vulgaris (Pasqueflower), 454
Pumpkin (*Cucurbita*), 551
Purple heart (*Setcreasea pallida*), 157
Purslane (*Portulaca oleracea*), 36
Pussytoes (*Antennaria dioica*), 455
Pyracantha coccinea (Scarlet fire thorn), 380
Pyrus Calleryana (Bradford pear), 366

Q

Quaking grass (*Briza maxima; B. media*), 162–163
Queen-of-the-prairie (*Filipendula rubra*), 281
Quercus
  Q. alba (White oak), 365
  Q. phellos (Willow oak), 365
Quince, flowering (*Chaenomeles speciosa*), 381

R

Radish (*Raphanus sativus*), 552
Ranunculus repens (Creeping buttercup), 258
Raphiolepis indica (Indian hawthorn), 382
Red chokeberry (*Aronia arbutifolia*), 378
Redroot (*Ceanothus velutinus*), 388
Reseda odorata (Mignonette), 170
Rheum rhabarbarum (Rhubarb), 552
Rhododendron (Rhododendron; Azalea), 389
Rhoeo spathacea (Moses-in-a-boat; Moses-in-a-cradle), 157
Rhubarb (*Rheum rhabarbarum*), 552
Ribbon grass (*Phalaris arundinaceae picta*), 51
Ribes alpinum (Alpine currant), 379
Ricinus communis (Castor bean), 148
Rock cress (*Arabis caucasica; A. procurrens*), 287
Rockcress (*Aubrieta deltoidea*), 287
Rockfoil (*Saxifraga*), 456
Rock gardens, 410–417
Rodgersia, 288
Root maggots, 525
Rose
  of China (*Hibiscus rosa-sinensis*), 163
  Christmas (*Helleborus*), 288
  Lenten (*Helleborus*), 288
  rock (*Helianthemum nummularium*), 288
  sun (*Helianthemum nummularium*), 288
Rosemary (*Rosmarinus officinalis*), 563
Roses, 400–409
  climbing, 449
  floribunda, 448
  grandiflora, 448
  hybrid tea, 448
  miniature, 449

Roses (*continued*)
polyantha, 449
shrub, 450
species, 450
tree, 450
Rosmarinus officinalis (Rosemary), 563
Rudbeckia
R. fulgida (Black-eyed Susan; Yellow coneflower), 263
R. hirta (Black-eyed Susan; Gloriosa daisy), 144
Rue
meadow (*Thalictrum aquilegifolium*), 289
Ruta graveolens, 564
Rumex
R. acetosa (French sorrel), 553, 565
R. acetosella (Red sorrel), 36
Rust, 109, 527
Rutabaga (*Brassica napus*), 552
Ruta graveolens (Rue), 564

S

Sage
Jerusalem (*Pulmonaria officinalis*), 280
meadow (*Salvia x superba*), 289
Russian (*Perovskia*), 289
Salvia officinalis, 564
scarlet (*Salvia spendens*), 180
Sagina subulata (Irish moss), 453
Sagittaria sagittifolia (Old world arrowhead), 466
St. Augustine decline, 38
St. Augustine grass (*Stenotaphrum secundatum*), 45
Salix
S. alba 'tristis' (Golden weeping willow), 373
S. caprea (Goat willow; Pussy willow), 391
Salpiglossis sinuata (Painted tongue; Salpiglossis), 179
Salsify (*Tragopogon porrifolius*), 553
Salvia
S. officinalis (Sage), 564
S. spendens (Scarlet sage; Salvia), 180
S. x superba (Meadow sage; Salvia), 289
Sanguinaria canadensis (Bloodroot), 462
Sanvitalia procumbens (Creeping zinnia; Sanvitalia), 180
Saponaria officinalis (Soapwort; Bouncing bet), 291
Sapphire flower (*Browallia speciosa*), 181
Sargent crabapple (*Malus Sargentii*), 379
Sassafras albidum (Sassafras), 369
Satureja hortensis (Savory), 564
Savory, summer (*Satureja hortensis*), 564
Saxifraga (Rockfoil), 456
Scabiosa
S. atropurpurea (Pincushion flower; Mourning bride), 181
S. caucasica (Pincushion flower), 285
Scale, 39, 351
Scarlet fire thorn (*Pyracantha coccinea*), 380
Scarlet flax (*Linum grandiflorum*), 181
Scarlet pimpernel (*Anagallis arvensis*), 182
Scarlet runner bean (*Phaseolus coccineus*), 182

Schizanthus x wisetonensis (Butterfly flower; Poor man's orchid), 182
Scilla siberica (Siberian squill), 461
Sea holly (*Eryngium*), 271
Sea lavender (*Limonium latifolium*), 277
Sedum
S. cauticolum (Stonecrop), 457
S. spectabile (Stonecrop), 292–293
Self-heal (*Prunella Webbiana*), 290
Sempervivum tectorum (Hens-and-chicks), 453
Senecio cineraria (Dusty miller), 155
Setcreasea pallida (Purple heart), 157
Shade gardens, 426–431
Shallot (*Allium Cepa*), 553
Shell flower (*Molucella laevis*), 143
Shrubs. *See* Woody plants.
Sidedressing, 100, 101, 220
Silene
S. acaulis (Moss campion), 454
S. armeria (None so pretty), 173
Silk tree (*Albizia Julibrissin*), 369
Silver dollar plant (*Lunaria annua*), 156
Silver-lace vine (*Polygonum aubertii*), 396
Skimmia Reevesiana (Reeves skimmia), 389
Slugs, 39, 108, 522, 525
Smoke tree (*Cotinus coggyrgria*), 389
Smuts, 527
Snails, 39, 108, 522, 525
Snapdragon (*Antirrhinum majus*), 183
Sneezeweed (*Helenium autumnale*), 290
Snowdrop (*Galanthus nivalis*), 461
Snow-in-summer (*Cerastium tomentosum; Euphorbia marginata*), 457
Soapweed (*Yucca glauca*), 291
Soapwort (*Saponaria officinalis*), 291
Soil, 56–57, 74–75, 320–321, 484–487
Solanum
S. melongena (Eggplant), 544
S. tuberosum (Irish potato), 551
Solidago (Goldenrod), 269
Solomon's seal (*Polygonatum odoratum* 'Thunbergii'), 464
Sorbus aucuparia (Mountain ash), 364
Sorrel
French (*Rumex acetosa*), 553, 565
red (*Rumex acetosella*), 36
Sourwood (*Oxydendrum arboreum*), 370
Southern star (*Oxypetalum caeruleum*), 184
Southernwood (*Artemisia abrotanum*), 565
Spearmint (*Mentha spicata*), 565
Speedwell (*Veronica spicata*), 291
Spider flower (*Cleome hasslerana*), 150
Spider mites, 39, 351, 525
Spiderwort (*Tradescantia x Andersoniana*), 292
Spinach, New Zealand (*Tetragonia tetragonioides*), 554
Spinach (*Spinacia oleracea*), 554
Spinacia oleracea (Spinach), 554
Spiraea x Vanhouttei (Bridal-wreath), 376
Spirea, wild (*Aruncus dioicus*), 269
Spittlebugs, 108
Spring heath (*Erica carnea*), 457
Spruce
bird's nest (*Picea abies* 'Nidiformis'), 451
Norway (*Picea Abies*), 370

Spurge
cushion (*Euphorbia epithymoides*), 292
Japanese (*Pachysandra terminalis*), 49, 283
Squash
summer (*Cucurbita Pepo*), 554–555
winter (*Cucurbita maxima*), 555
Squill, Siberian (*Scilla siberica*), 461
Stachys byzantina (Lamb's-ears; Lamb's-tongue), 276
Staking, 104, 105
Star of the Argentine (*Oxypetalum caeruleum*), 184
Star-of-the-Veldt (*Dimorphotheca*), 169
Statice sinuatum, 156
Stellaria media (Common chickweed), 35
Stenotaphrum secundatum (St. Augustine grass), 45
Stock (*Matthiola incana*), 184
Stokesia laevis (Stoke's aster), 251
Stonecrop (*Sedum cauticolum; S. spectabile*), 292, 457
Summer cypress (*Kochia scoparia trichophylla*), 146
Sundrop (*Oenothera biennis*), 185, 293
Sunflower
false (*Heliopsis helianthoides*), 282
Helianthus annuus, 185
Mexican (*Tithonia rotundifolia*), 186
perennial (*Helianthus x multiflorus*), 294
swamp (*Helenium autumnale*), 290
Sweet alyssum (*Lobularia maritima*), 138
Sweet false chamomile (*Matricaria recutita*), 148
Sweet flag, variegated (*Acorus Calamus* 'Variegatus'), 468
Sweet mock orange (*Philadelphus coronarius*), 386
Sweet orange (*Citrus sinensis*), 366
Sweet pea (*Lathyrus latifolius*), 283
Sweet woodruff (*Galium odoratum*), 566
Swiss chard (*Beta vulgaris; Cicla*), 541
Sycamore (*Platanus occidentalis*), 371
Sydney golden wattle (*Acacia longifolia*), 372
Syringa vulgaris (Common lilac), 385

T

Tagetes
T. erecta (American marigold), 169
T. patula (French marigold), 169
Tall fescue (*Festuca arundinacea*), 44
Tamarack (*Larix laricina*), 371
Tanacetum vulgare (Tansy), 566
Tansy (*Tanacetum vulgare*), 566
Taraxacum officinale (Dandelion), 36, 543
Tarragon (*Artemisia dracunculus*), 566
Taxodium distichum (Bald cypress), 357
Taxus
T. canadensis (American yew), 391
T. cuspidata (Japanese yew), 465
Tetragonia tetragonioides (New Zealand spinach), 554
Texas pride (*Phlox drummondii*), 176
Thalia dealbata (Water canna), 468
Thalictrum aquilegifolium (Meadow rue), 289

Thermopsis caroliniana (Aaron's rod; Carolina lupine), 280
Thistle
  globe (*Echinops Ritro*), 294
  Scotch (*Onopordum acathium*), 183
Thrift (*Armeria maritima*), 294
Thrips, 108, 525
Thuja occidentalis (American arborvitae), 354
Thunbergia alata (Black-eyed Susan vine; Clock vine), 186
Thyme (*Thymus vulgaris*), 567
Thymus vulgaris (Thyme), 567
Tiarella cordifolia (Allegheny foamflower), 463
Tickseed (*Coreopsis tinctoria*), 147
Tidy tips (*Layia platyglossa*), 186
Tilia americana (American linden), 363
Tithonia rotundifolia (Mexican sunflower), 186
Toadflax (*Linaria maroccana*), 187
Tomatillo (*Physalis ixocarpa*), 556
Tomato hornworm, 526
Tomato (*Lycopersicon lycopersicum*), 556
Tools, 72–73, 480–483
Torenia Fournieri (Wishbone flower), 187
Trachymene coerulea (Blue lace flower), 145
Tradescantia x Andersoniana (Spiderwort), 292
Tragopogon porrifolius (Oyster plant; Salsify), 553
Trailing ice plant (*Lampranthus spectabilis*), 47
Treasure flower (*Gazania ringens*), 159
Trees. *See* Woody plants.
Tricyrtis hirta (Toad lily), 278
Trillium grandiflorum (Wake-robin), 465
Triticum aestibum (Wheat grass), 162–163
Trollius x cultorum (Globeflower), 269
Tropaeolum majus (Nasturtium), 562
Trumpet creeper (*Campsis radicans*), 397
Trumpet flower (*Datura metel*), 139
Tsuga canadensis (Eastern hemlock), 360
Tuberose (*Polianthes tuberosa*), 187
Tulipa (Tulip), 461
Tulip tree (*Liriodendron Tulipifera*), 372

Turnip (*Brassica Rapa*), 557
Typha latifolia (Common cattail), 466

V

Vallisneria americana (Eelgrass), 466
Vegetables, 470–527, 534–557
  care and maintenance, 506–515
  planting, 492–505
Venidium fastuosum (Monarch of the Veldt; Cape daisy), 188
Verbena, 188
Veronica spicata (Speedwell), 291
Viburnum Carlesii (Korean spice viburnum), 390
Vigna unguiculata (California black-eye pea), 549
Vinca (*Catharanthus roseus*), 188
Vinca minor (Myrtle; Periwinkle), 48, 284
Vines. *See* Woody plants.
Viola x wittrockiana (Pansy), 174
Violet, Persian (*Exacum affine*), 189
Viruses, 109, 351, 527
Vitis Coignetiae (Crimson glory vine), 394
Voles, 38

W

Wake-robin (*Trillium grandiflorum*), 465
Wallflower, English (*Cheiranthus cheiri*), 189
Water canna (*Thalia dealbata*), 468
Watercress (*Nasturtium officinale*), 557
Water gardens, 432–445
Watering, 94–96, 217–219, 514–515
Water lily, hardy/tropical (*Nymphaea*), 469
Watermelon (*Citrullus lanatus*), 557
Webworm, sod, 38
Weeds, 35–37, 97–99
Weigela florida (Old-fashioned weigela), 390
Western wheatgrass (*Agropyron smithii*), 45
Wheat grass (*Triticum aestibum*), 162–163
White flies, 108, 526
Wild ginger, European (*Asarum europaeum*), 463
Wild Oats (*Avena sterilis*), 162–163
Willow
  goat (*Salix caprea*), 391

Willow (*continued*)
  golden weeping (*Salix alba* 'tristis'), 373
  pussy (*Salix caprea*), 391
Wilt, 109, 351, 527
Wintercreeper (*Euonymus Fortunei*), 465
Wireworms, 526
Wishbone flower (*Torenia Fournieri*), 187
Wisteria floribunda (Wisteria), 397
Witch hazel, common (*Hamamelis virginiana*), 391
Woody plants, 296–397
  buying, 317
  care and maintenance, 326–341
  fertilizing and mulching, 333–334
  garden plans, 306–307
  hardiness, 315–316
  injury/damage to, 344–348
  planting, 328–332
  pruning, 337–341
  shapes/sizes, 309–314
  soil, 320–323
Worms, 524
Wormwood (*Artemisia*), 295, 567

X

Xeranthemum annuum, 156

Y

Yarrow (*Achillea*), 295
Yellow flag (*Iris Pseudacorus*), 469
Yellowwood (*Cladrastis Kentuckea*), 373
Yew
  American (*Taxus canadensis*), 391
  Japanese (*Taxus cuspidata*), 465
Yucca glauca (Soapweed), 291

Z

Zantesdeschia aethiopica (Calla lily), 146
Zea mays (Corn; Ornamental corn), 173, 542
Zebra grass (*Miscanthus sinensis* 'Zebrinus'), 51
Zelkova serrata (Japanese zelkova), 373
Zinnia elegans (Zinnia), 189
Zoysia japonica (Japanese lawngrass), 44